The Fourth Genre

The Fourth Genre

Contemporary Writers of/on Creative Nonfiction

THIRD EDITION

Robert L. Root, Jr.
Central Michigan University

Michael Steinberg
Michigan State University

PEARSON
Longman

New York Boston San Francisco
London Toronto Sydney Tokyo Singapore Madrid
Mexico City Munich Paris Cape Town Hong Kong Montreal

Senior Vice President and Publisher: Joseph Opiela
Vice President and Publisher: Eben W. Ludlow
Marketing Manager: Deborah Murphy
Production Manager: Ellen MacElree
Project Coordination, Text Design, and Electronic Page Makeup: Nesbitt Graphics, Inc.
Cover Design Manager: Wendy Ann Fredericks
Cover Designer: Kay Petronio
Cover Photos: © Photodisc
Manufacturing Buyer: Al Dorsey
Printer and Binder: Hamilton Printing Company
Cover Printer: The Lehigh Press

For permission to use copyrighted material, grateful acknowledgement is made to the copyright holders on pp. 484–487, which are hereby made part of this copyright page.

Library of Congress Cataloging-in-Publication Data

The fourth genre : contemporary writers of/on creative nonfiction /
[compiled by] Robert L. Root, Jr., Michael Steinberg.—3rd ed.
    p. cm.
  Includes bibliographical references and index.
  ISBN 0-205-42605-0
  1. Essays. 2. Essays—Authorship.   I. Root, Robert L. II. Steinberg,
Michael, 1940-
PN6142.F68 2004
808.4--dc22   2003028108

Please visit our website at http://www.ablongman.com

ISBN 0-205-42605-0

1 2 3 4 5 6 7 8 9 10—HT—07 06 05 04

The essay is a notoriously flexible and adaptable form. It possesses the freedom to move anywhere, in all directions. It acts as if all objects were equally near the center and as if "all subjects are linked to one another" (Montaigne) by free association. This freedom can be daunting, not only for the novice essayist confronting such latitude but for the critic attempting to pin down its formal properties.

—*Phillip Lopate*

Admirers of nailed-down definitions and tidy categories may not like to hear it, but all writers and readers are full-time imaginers, all prose is imaginative, and fiction and nonfiction are just two anarchic shades of ink swirling around the same mysterious well. Those of us who would tell a story can only dip in our pens. We can never claim full certainty as to which shade of ink we're using.

—*David James Duncan*

The boundaries of creative nonfiction will always be as fluid as water.

—*Mary Clearman Blew*

Don't spread it around, but it's a sweet time to be an essayist.

—*Joseph Epstein*

Contents

PART 2 *Talking about Creative Nonfiction*   273

PART 3 *Composing Creative Nonfiction*   415

Alternative Contents

Subgenres of Creative Nonfiction

Personal Essay

Segmented Essay

Critical Essay

Literary Journalism

PARTS 2 AND 3   *Processes and Criticism of Creative Nonfiction*

Memoir

Writing

Essay

Genre Issues

Academic Writing

Preface

Beginning the Conversation

Rationale and Overview

The Fourth Genre, Third Edition, is an anthology devoted to contemporary works of creative nonfiction. The readings in all three sections encompass the genre's full spectrum: personal essays and memoirs, literary journalism, and academic/cultural criticism. Creative nonfiction is the kind of literary writing that regularly appears in small magazines, reviews, and journals, such as *The Georgia Review, Ascent*, and *The Missouri Review*; in trade magazines, such as *Harper's, Orion*, and *The New Yorker*; in journals focused on creative nonfiction, such as *Fourth Genre, River Teeth, Creative Nonfiction*, and *Under the Sun*; and in book-length essay and memoir collections. One of the hallmarks of this form is that the boundaries between subgenres are quite expansive. That's because its writers often braid narrative telling with fictional and poetic techniques and combine portraiture and self-reflection with reportage and critical analysis. In that regard *The Fourth Genre* highlights the elasticity and versatility of this still-evolving genre.

We also see creative nonfiction as the subject that binds together the three disparate strands in most English departments: literature, creative writing, and composition. Traditionally, the study of literature has been centered on analysis and interpretation in three genres—poetry, fiction, and drama; the study of creative writing has also focused on those genres; and composition has become the domain of nonfiction. We believe that this unnatural separation can be bridged by acknowledging creative nonfiction as the fourth genre. That is, we think of creative nonfiction simultaneously as a form of literature, as a goal of creative writing, and as the aesthetic impulse in composition.

This book then, attempts to present creative nonfiction in a framework that emphasizes its keystone status:

- It is a reader for writers of creative nonfiction, providing a range of samples of the forms and strategies practiced by many contemporary writers.

- It is an anthology for students of nonfiction literature, providing not only examples of its variety but also theoretical and critical responses to the form by critics, teachers, and the writers themselves.
- It is a collection for students of composing practices, providing reflections on the forms and strategies by the essayists, memoirists, literary journalists, cultural critics, poets, and novelists who write creative nonfiction.

These specifications make *The Fourth Genre* most suitable for courses in composition, creative writing, and genre literature. And not coincidentally, these are the courses in which we ourselves used the book in its classroom testing stages.

The fact that each of us was simultaneously asked to develop courses in creative nonfiction at different universities also says something about the emergence of the fourth genre from neglect in the past decade or so. Anthologies and collections of personal essays, nature writing, literary journalism, cultural criticism, travel writing, and memoirs have proliferated in recent years, and literary magazines have begun to include creative nonfiction and the essay among the forms they regularly publish. Workshops in creative nonfiction have also been included for strands of writer's conferences and writer's workshops, and individual conferences have been organized solely around "writing the self," "environmental writing," and "travel writing." *The Fourth Genre*, therefore, represents our attempt to compile a contemporary anthology/reader that approaches creative nonfiction from a number of perspectives, trying not to let our efforts prescribe its boundaries or place limits on its possibilities.

Creative nonfiction encompasses a variety of styles, sensibilities, and forms. Its writers share a common desire to speak in a singular voice as active participants in their own experience. This impulse often overlaps with the writer's need to mediate that experience by serving as a witness/correspondent, thus creating an unique synergy. As a result, creative nonfictionists may write to establish or define an identity, to explore and chronicle personal discoveries and changes, to examine personal conflicts, to interrogate their opinions, and to connect themselves to a larger heritage and community. Given this context, the style, focus, and structure of each work may vary. Any given piece can be lyrical, expository, meditative, informational, reflective, self-interrogative, exploratory, analytical, and/or whimsical. Moreover, a work's structure might be a traditional "linear" narrative or it may create its own disjunctive and segmented form.

To take advantage of the genre's flexibility, as well as of its emphasis on the writer's presence and voice, we have chosen readings that are representative, accessible, and challenging to students in advanced composition and creative writing workshops, as well as to students in genre-specific literature courses. We assume that student readers will be asked to write their own creative nonfiction, and that, at the same time, they will be developing a personal/critical theory that reflects the genre's possibilities.

Perhaps our most vital concern is to initiate a writer-to-reader conversation on and about creative nonfiction. Therefore, we've designed the book to be interactive by dividing it into three separate yet interconnected sections: a representative anthology of personal essays, memoirs, works of literary journalism, and personal/cultural criticism as currently practiced by recognized and emerging writers; a gathering of essays and articles that centers on more general matters of craft, definition, and theory; and a section in which four emergent writers discuss how their accompanying works of creative nonfiction were composed.

This organization encourages student writers to learn their craft the way most successful writers have learned theirs: by reading what other writers have written, by picking up tips and ideas from writers about the way they write, and by applying specific strategies culled from the readings to their own writing.

Selections and Organization

The Fourth Genre's most distinctive features are the range and scope of the readings and the interconnectedness of the three sections. In selecting these particular works, we have tried to maintain a balance between writing that is serious and informal, rigorous and pleasurable. In all instances, our criteria was that the writings be stimulating and that they have literary worth; that they be wide ranging in subject and form, familiar at times and challenging at others; and that they be strong examples of the kind of thought-provoking and authentic writing that is being done in the genre today.

In addition, several other considerations have guided our choices, perhaps the most compelling of which was our desire to counterbalance the recent creative nonfiction anthologies and manuals that identify the genre as equivalent to literary journalism. Such books tend to place little emphasis on the personal, autobiographical, and "literary" impulses (discovery, exploration, reflection) that generate much of the writing that we would call creative nonfiction. While we think of this genre as broad and inclusive, we feel that creative nonfiction's identity is more closely connected to the spirit of Montaigne's work than it is to matters of subject, reportage, and research. That is to say, Montaigne's essays were first and foremost intimate and *personal*, and that he actively cultivated self-exploration and self-discovery. As such, his writings express the digressions, meanderings, meditations, ruminations, and speculations that characterize a singular, idiosyncratic mind at work. As Montaigne himself says, "It is myself I portray."

This point of view is not meant to duck the issue of self-examination as it extends to larger connections and broader subjects; quite the contrary. In fact, we believe along with cultural critic Mariana Torgovnick that "All writing about self and culture is personal in that writers and critics find some of their richest material in experience. . . . Often our search for personal meaning is precisely what generates our passion and curiosity for the subjects we research and write about." It is this kind of curiosity and self-exploration that marks the majority of pieces in this book—be they personal essays, memoirs, reportage, or academic criticism—or a commingling of more than one of those subgenres.

Other concerns that guided our choices were:

- to encourage aspiring writers and curious readers who come to this genre from an assortment of academic disciplines
- to spotlight representative, accessible writers from a variety of fields—literature, science, nature writing, women's studies, journalism, rhetoric and composition, and cultural studies, among them
- to offer readings that remind us of the breadth and possibilities of this continually evolving genre

To these ends, we present the reader with a broad range of examples, as well as essays and articles by writers and teachers about the forms in which they work. Along with pieces by established writers, we've tried to select works that are less frequently taught and anthologized—provocative writing that we think will stimulate fresh and enthusiastic responses from students and teachers. In choosing these particular readings, we're hoping that *The Fourth Genre* will generate numerous alternatives for using creative nonfiction in the classroom.

Part One, Writing Creative Nonfiction, is an anthology/sampler of contemporary creative nonfiction. It is intended to showcase the variety of voices and personas, the flexibility and expansiveness, and the range of subject matter and structures that creative nonfiction is able to embrace. Part One is also a representative mix of thematic explorations, self-portraitures, investigations into subject matter and ideas, and intimate personal discoveries and disclosures. Not only do the specific subjects change as they are taken up by different writers, but the techniques each writer uses to explore his/her subject can vary widely. Some writers use straightforward narrative and reportage; others blend narrative telling with fictional techniques such as scenes, characters, and dialogue; and still others explore their subjects in more lyrical, discursive, or poetic ways.

However diverse these approaches might be, the individual pieces are marked by the distinctiveness of the author's presence, no matter whether he or she is the center of the piece or an observer-reporter. Therefore, in all the writings in this section we witness the mind of the writer as he or she attempts to examine what Mariana Torgovnick describes as "some strongly felt experience, deeply held conviction, long-term interest, or problem that has irritated the mind."

In Part Two, Talking about Creative Nonfiction, we have chosen essays by working writers and teachers who are as passionate about discussing matters of craft as they are articulate in explaining their theories about the nature of creative nonfiction. Because several of these authors have also written pieces that appear in Part One, we invite the reader to pair selections to see what kinds of strategies, theories, and perspectives the writers have developed. In addition, we also suggest that both teachers and students explore how the essays in Part One can serve as examples of the kinds of theoretical stances that the writers and teachers in Part Two advocate.

Another way to approach the writing in Part Two is to view it as a writer's conversation about the possibilities and limits of the genre. Consider for example, the differing views on literal and invented truth in memoir as proposed by Mary

Clearman Blew, Annie Dillard, Patricia Hampl, and Mimi Schwartz; or compare Phillip Lopate's idea of the personal essay as a more "self-interrogative form" with Scott Russell Sanders's notion of the essayist as "the singular first-person"; or examine passionate yet differing approaches by Rebecca Blevins Faery and Mariana Torgovnick to using the personal voice in academic writing.

You can also use this section of the book to probe more deeply into an assortment of composing strategies—that is, the use of differing narrative stances and personas; the employment of disjunctive and segmented mosaics; and the pointedly fictional and poetical techniques that memoirists, personal essayists, literary journalists, and cultural critics adopt in their writings.

All of these perspectives, then, anchor the genre in the notions, theories, and designs of working writers, many of whom are also writing teachers. As such, they give the reader an "inside" and personal look at the various ways the genre is evolving, and at the same time they offer a broader, more inclusive view of how contemporary creative nonfiction is being written and defined.

In Part Three, Composing Creative Nonfiction, four writers add their voices to the conversation in an attempt to help the student (and teacher) bridge the gap between experienced and emergent writers. In addition to the pieces themselves, Maureen Stanton, Simone Poirier-Bures, Mary Elizabeth Pope, and Emily D. Chase discuss their composing processes, sharing decisions on the drafts and revisions that their works-in-progress have undergone. In so doing, they focus our attention on the writing process itself.

We created this section not only to give aspiring student writers an inside look at how these pieces evolved, but also to demonstrate the many possibilities that characterize this genre. We also think that student writers will benefit greatly from paying attention to the disclosures from emerging writers, especially as these writers supplement and reinforce the readings in Parts One and Two. In addition, the cross references between all three sections open up the conversation further by revealing additional aspects of its texts and authors. And finally, by pairing the emerging writers' works with their own comments about their work, we are encouraging and reinforcing the kind of dialogue established in Parts One and Two.

Essentially then, Part One is an anthology *of* creative nonfiction, Part Two is an anthology *on* creative nonfiction, and Part Three is a shorter collection *of and about* the writing of creative nonfiction.

The readings in all three sections and the book's interactive organization, therefore, express why we think that creative nonfiction is the most accessible and personal of all four literary genres, as well as why we believe the time is ripe for extending this dialogue to curious and interested students.

Apparatus

In keeping with the spirit of the genre's flexibility, we have provided a minimum of editorial apparatus. We assume that teachers will mix and match whichever readings suit their inclinations and teaching designs. And rather than impose a thematic, historical, or subgeneric interpretation on its users, or lock the book into a pattern based on our course designs, we prefer to emphasize the genre's multiple dimensions and possibilities. Moreover, in keeping with our intent to acquaint students (and teachers) with the rich body of work that's being produced in creative nonfiction today, we've tried to make this anthology as flexible and user friendly as possible. We want to give students permission to think of themselves as apprentices/fellow writers, to urge them to experience their writing as an inside out activity, and finally to guide them in learning to read in more "writerly" ways.

That said, along with this preface we have provided some guidelines and rationales for using the book. The introduction, for example, offers an expanded discussion of why creative nonfiction is the fourth genre. It also contains a detailed explanation of what we think are the five main elements of creative nonfiction. In the section on Writers, Readers, and the Fourth Genre, we talk about the personal connections between writer and reader while offering specific examples of why we think of creative nonfiction as both a literary and transactional genre. Here we also discuss creative nonfiction as a genre that pushes at boundaries, as well as a genre whose practitioners write primarily to connect themselves in more intimate, expressive, and personal ways with their readers. In the section entitled Joining the Conversation, we expand on the notion of why we designed *The Fourth Genre* as an inclusive, ongoing conversation about the art and craft of writing creative nonfiction. Moreover, in the introductions to all three sections—Part One's anthology, Part Two's readings about the genre, and Part Three's dialogue on composing processes—we offer overviews of each section as well as suggestions for using the book interactively.

Another apparatus is contained in the book's three tables of contents—all of which suggest alternative ways to read and teach *The Fourth Genre*. The table of contents at the front of the book is organized alphabetically to give teachers and students the option of deciding what readings they will match up or pair with one another. Subgenres of Creative Nonfiction, the first alternative contents, cross-references the readings from Parts One and Three according to Forms of Creative Nonfiction, and categorizes the Part Two and Part Three readings under the heading of Processes and Criticism of Creative Nonfiction. Approaches to Writing and Discussing Creative Nonfiction, the second alternative contents, also categorizes the readings according to subgenres. Under each subgenre (memoir, personal essay, etc.) we offer readers three approaches for examining creative nonfiction: Writers on Their Work, Further Examples of the Form, and Further Discussion of the Form. All of these of course, are meant to be suggestive rather than prescriptive. We have also provided Notes on Authors as an aid to further reading.

Instructor's Manual

In addition to the guidelines within the text, we have written a comprehensive and detailed instructor's manual. It gives specific teaching suggestions and explanations for using the book in three different classroom settings. More specifically, it offers an assortment of options for organizing the materials in composition, creative writing, and literary genre courses. In all instances we've included brief discussions of the readings as creative nonfiction, as well as suggestions for pairing or clustering selections according to subgenres, compatible themes, and issues of craft. We've also designed questions that offer different perspectives on the readings and that address matters of composing. Finally, we've provided a variety of writing prompts and suggestions for dealing with students' writing in all three classroom settings.

Acknowledgments

The paths by which the two of us have come to creative nonfiction are familiar ones to many writers and teachers. Writing has played an important role in both of our lives. It has been the subject of college courses and post-college workshops in poetry, fiction, drama, essay, environmental writing, film writing, and professional writing. It has been the preoccupation that has produced both published and unpublished work in a variety of forms—creative nonfiction, of course, but also poetry, fiction, drama, sports journalism, and radio commentary. As it does for so many other writers, the habit of writing colors the way we approach almost everything we do in life.

We also have been teachers for most of our adult lives, particularly of writing courses and courses on the teaching of composition. Happily, the center of our teaching and our scholarship alike has been the study of and immersion in the activity that energizes our nonacademic lives.

In recent years, we have initiated courses in creative nonfiction in Western Michigan University's MFA/Ph.D program, Michigan State University's American Studies graduate program, and in Central Michigan University's Composition and Communication master's program. As we designed these courses and consulted with one another, we agreed to encourage our students to write essays that covered a range of contemporary creative nonfiction and to give them a range of strategies with which to do that. Moreover, we invited them into the genre by asking them to consider not only what contemporary writers were publishing but also what those same writers themselves were saying about the kind of work they do. As an ongoing activity, we continued to share our own work-in-progress with our students and to "publish" anthologies of student writing within the classes.

And so we have come to this book attempting to center creative nonfiction, to keep ourselves centered on it as writers and teachers and students of the fourth genre, and to invite further speculation about it by readers, writers, and teachers interested in how we write, think about, and teach creative nonfiction now.

Along the way we have been aided in our growth as writers and development as teachers of creative nonfiction by an array of colleagues, students, and teachers, as well as by both our partners. In particular we should acknowledge the following:

From Michael Steinberg: The students in English 631 at Western Michigan University and Shirley Clay Scott, former English Chair at Western, who gave me the opportunity to develop the MFA/Ph.D program's first creative nonfiction workshop; the students in American Studies 891 at Michigan State University, and Peter Levine, former program director, and David Cooper, former acting director, for allowing me free rein in designing my course; Donald Murray, whose writing and teaching has inspired my own; Skip Renker, who provided valuable input and advice when I needed it; Doug Noverr, my department chair, and Pat McConeghy, associate dean of Arts and Letters, both of whom granted me release time from teaching to complete this book; Lee Hope, the director of the Stonecoast Writer's Conference, who over the course of three summers gave me the opportunity to develop a creative nonfiction workshop in conjunction with five wonderful colleagues: Phyllis Barber, David Bradley, Stephen Dunn, David Huddle, and Syd Lea. My special thanks to them for showing me how it's done. Thanks as well to Dr. Sam Plyler, who kept the faith throughout this project. And finally to Carole Berk Steinberg, my gratitude, as always, for her unconditional support and unflagging encouragement.

From Robert Root: The students in English 601 and English 593 at Central Michigan University, who first responded to these readings and wrote so many memorable essays themselves, in particular Carol Sanford, Mary Beth Pope, Sandra Smith, Emily D. Chase, and Amy Hough; the clerical staff in the Department of English at CMU, headed by Carol Swan and Carole Pasche, particularly the student assistants who worked on this manuscript, Jennifer Baars, Kelli S. Fedewa, Star Ittu, and Gretchen M. Morley; Becky Wildfong, Tom Root, and Caroline Root, good writers all; and Susan Root, whose understanding and support make all burdens lighter.

We are grateful for the expert guidance of our editor, Eben Ludlow, and for the recommendations and advice of reviewers of previous editions of the anthology, as well as to teachers, students, and readers who have informally shared their responses to readings with us at conferences and workshops and in classrooms and hallways.

Robert L. Root, Jr., and Michael Steinberg

Introduction

Creative Nonfiction, the Fourth Genre

Creative nonfiction is the fourth genre. This assumption, declared in the title of this book, needs a little explaining. Usually literature has been divided into three major genres or types: poetry, drama, and fiction. Poets, dramatists, and novelists might arrange this trio in a different order, but the idea of three literary genres has, until very recently, dominated introductory courses in literature, generic divisions in literature textbooks, and categories of literature in bookstores. Everything that couldn't be classified in one of these genres or some subgenre belonging to them (epic poetry, horror novels) was classified as "nonfiction," even though, as Jocelyn Bartkevicius points out elsewhere in this collection, they could be classified as "nonpoetry" just as well. Unfortunately, this classification system suggests that everything that is nonfiction should also be considered nonliterature, a suggestion that is, well, nonsense.

We refer to creative or literary nonfiction as the fourth genre as a way of reminding readers that literary genres are not limited to three; we certainly do not intend the term to indicate ranking of the genres but rather to indicate their equality. It would be better to have a more succinct, exclusive term for the genre. Writers have been composing literary forms of nonfiction for centuries, even if only recently have they begun to use the terms *creative nonfiction* or *literary nonfiction* to separate it from the nonliterary forms of nonfiction. And, after all, although it is creative or imaginative or literary, its being nonfiction is still what distinguishes it from the other literary genres.

The shape of creative nonfiction is, in Robert Atwan's phrase, "malleable" and, in O. B. Hardison's, "Protean." Perhaps we can picture its throbbing, pulsing, mercurial existence as locations on a series of intersecting lines connecting the poles of the personal and the public, the diary and the report, the informal and the formal, the marginalia and the academic article, the imaginative and the expository. Creative nonfiction essays would be located on these lines somewhere within the boundaries set by neighboring genres, not only "the three creative genres" of fiction, poetry, and drama but also the "expressive" genres of diary, journal, and autobiography and the "objective" genres of traditional (as opposed to literary) journalism, criticism, and polemic and technical writing. It may be fair to say that creative nonfiction centers in the essay but continually strains against the boundaries of other genres, endeavoring to push them back and to expand its own space without altering its own identity.

The Elements of Creative Nonfiction

Yet despite all the elusiveness and malleability of the genre and the variety of its shapes, structures, and attitudes, works of creative nonfiction share a number of common elements, although they may not all be present all the time in uniform proportions. The most pronounced common elements of creative nonfiction are *personal presence, self-discovery and self-exploration, veracity, flexibility of form,* and *literary approaches to nonfiction.*

Personal Presence

Writers of creative nonfiction tend to make their personal presence felt in the writing. Whatever the subject matter may be—and it can be almost anything—most creative nonfiction writing, as Rosellen Brown says of the essay, "presents itself, if not as precisely true, then as an emanation of an identifiable speaking voice making statements for which it takes responsibility" (5). In such writing the reader encounters "a persona through whose unique vision experience or information will be filtered, perhaps distorted, perhaps questioned"; the writer's voice creates an identity that "will cast a shadow as dense and ambiguous as that of an imaginary protagonist. The self is surely a created character" (5).

Throughout the various forms of creative nonfiction, whether the subject is the writer's self (as perhaps in personal essays and memoirs) or an objective, observed reality outside the self (as perhaps in nature essays and personal cultural criticism), the reader is taken on a journey into the mind and personality of the writer. Some writers directly engage in interrogations of the self by unequivocally examining and confronting their own memories, prejudices, fears, even weaknesses. Others are more meditative and speculative, using the occasion of remembered or observed experience to connect to issues that extend beyond the self and to celebrate or question those connections. Still others establish greater distance from their subjects, taking more of an observer's role than a participant's role. Yet even as they stand along the sidelines we are aware of their presence, because their voice is personal, individual, not omniscient.

This sense of the author's presence is a familiar element of essays and memoirs, of course. These center on the author's private reflections and experiences. As essayist Phillip Lopate writes,

> The hallmark of the personal essay is its intimacy. The writer seems to be speaking directly into your ear, confiding everything from gossip to wisdom. Through sharing thoughts, memories, desires, complaints, and whimsies, the personal essayist sets up a relationship with the reader, a dialogue—a

friendship, if you will, based on identification, understanding, testiness, and companionship. (xxiii)

But personal presence can also pull subject-oriented writing (principally journalistic and academic writing) into the realm of creative nonfiction. Arguing a need for "writerly models for writing about culture," Marianna Torgovnick insists, "Writing about culture is personal. Writers find their material in experience as well as books, and they leave a personal imprint on their subjects. They must feel free to explore the autobiographical motivation for their work, for often this motivation is precisely what generates writers' interests in their topics" (3). Including this personal voice in cultural criticism surrenders some of the authority—or the pretense of authority—generally found in academic writing, but substitutes for it the authority of apparent candor or personal honesty. What Rosellen Brown writes of the personal essayist is applicable to all creative nonfiction writers: "the complex delight of the essayist's voice is that it can admit to bewilderment without losing its authority" (7). This sense of personal presence is one of the most forceful elements of creative nonfiction.

Self-Discovery and Self-Exploration

As many writers in this book suggest—either directly or indirectly—this genre encourages self-discovery, self-exploration, and surprise. Often, the writer "is on a journey of discovery, often unasked for and unplanned," Rosellen Brown writes. "The essayist is an explorer, whereas the fiction writer is a landed inhabitant" (7). Phillip Lopate speaks of self-discovery that takes place in essays as writing that "not only monitors the self but helps it gel. The essay is an enactment of the creation of the self" (xliv). This genre grants writers permission to explore without knowing where they will end up, to be tentative, speculative, reflective. Because writing creative nonfiction so often reveals and expresses the writer's mind at work and play, the genre permits us to chart the more whimsical, nonrational twists and turns of our own imaginations and psyches. More frequently than not, the subject matter becomes the catalyst or trigger for some personal journey or inquiry or self-interrogation. Writers who seem most at home with this genre are those who like to delve and to inquire, to question, to explore, probe, meditate, analyze, turn things over, brood, worry—all of which creative nonfiction allows, even encourages.

Such interests may seem at first glance appropriate only to a narrow range of "confessional writing," but in much of the best creative nonfiction, writers use self-disclosure as a way of opening their writing to a more expansive exploration. This genre, then, is a good choice for writers who like to reach for connections that extend beyond the purely personal. As W. Scott Olson writes, "As the world becomes more problematic, it is in the little excursions and small observations that we can discover ourselves, that we can make an honest connection with others, that we can remind each other of what it means to belong to one another" (viii).

Flexibility of Form

One of the most exciting elements of creative nonfiction is the way in which contemporary writers "stretch the limits of the form" and "are developing a [nonfiction] prose that lives along the borders of fiction and poetry" (Atwan x). Contemporary creative nonfiction uses the full range of style and structure available to other literary and nonliterary forms. Most often, readers have noticed the use of fictional devices in creative nonfiction, particularly in what is termed *the nonfiction novel* or in certain examples of literary journalism, which Mark Kramer has defined as "extended digressive narrative nonfiction" (21). Rosellen Brown, who refers to the personal essay as a "nonfiction narrative," believes it is "every bit as much an imaginative construction as a short story" and that "it must use some, if not all, of the techniques of fiction: plot, characterization, physical atmosphere, thematic complexity, stylistic appropriateness, psychological open-endedness" (5).

And yet, while narrative elements may frequently play a part in creative nonfiction, the genre often works with lyrical, dramatic, meditative, expository, and argumentative elements as well. As Annie Dillard says, "The essay can do everything a poem can do, and everything a short story can do—everything but fake it" ("Introduction" xvii). It can also do everything a diary, a journal, a critical article, an editorial, a feature, and a report can do.

Moreover, perhaps more frequently than in other genres, creative nonfiction writers are likely to innovate and experiment with structure. They draw not only on narrative chronology and linear presentation but also on nonlinear, "disjunctive," or associative strategies. They use different angles and perspectives to illuminate a point or explore an idea, drawing on visual and cinematic techniques such as collages, mosaics, montages, and jump cuts. They can leap backward and forward in time, ignoring chronology of event to emphasize nonsequential connections and parallels; they can structure the essay around rooms in a house or cards in a tarot deck; they can interrupt exposition or narrative with passages from journals and letters or scenes from home movies. Part of the excitement of the genre is its openness to creative forms as well as to creative contents, its invitation to experiment and push at boundaries between genres, and its ability to draw on an unlimited range of literary techniques.

Veracity

Because it sometimes draws on the material of autobiography, history, journalism, biology, ecology, travel writing, medicine, and any number of other subjects, creative nonfiction is reliably factual, firmly anchored in real experience, whether the author has lived it or observed and recorded it. As essayist and memoirist Annie Dillard writes, "The elements in any nonfiction should be true not only artistically—the connects must hold at base and must be veracious, for that is the convention and the covenant between the nonfiction writer and his reader" ("Introduction" xvii). Like the rest of us, the nonfiction writer, she says, "thinks about actual things. He can make sense of them analytically or artistically. In either case he renders the real world coherent and meaningful, even if only bits of it, and even if that coherence and meaning reside only inside small texts" (xvii). For critic Barbara Lounsbery, who is principally speaking of literary journalism, factuality is central, by which she means: "Documentable subject matter chosen from the real world as opposed to 'invented' from the writer's mind"; she adds that "anything in the natural world is game for the nonfiction artist's attention" (xiii).

But factuality or veracity is a trickier element than it seems. As David James Duncan observes,

> We see into our memories in much the way that we see across the floor of a sunbaked desert: everything we conjure, every object, creature, or event we perceive in there, is distorted, before it reaches us, by mirages created by subjectivity, time, and distance. . . . The best that a would-be nonfiction writer can do is use imperfect language to invoke imperfectly remembered events based on imperfect perceptions. (55)

Artistry needs some latitude; self-disclosure may be too risky to be total, particularly when it involves disclosure of others. Just as Thoreau compressed two years at Walden Pond into one to get the focus he needed for his great book, creative nonfiction writers sometimes alter the accuracy of events in order to achieve the accuracy of interpretation. Some of this is inadvertent—the great challenge of memoir writing is knowing how much we remember is reliable and accepting the likelihood that we are "inventing the truth." "You can't put together a memoir without cannibalizing your own life for parts," Annie Dillard writes in "To Fashion a Text." "The work battens on your memories. And it replaces them" (70). Memories blur over time and edit themselves into different forms that others who had the same experience might not recognize. Finding the language to describe experience sometimes alters it, and your description of the experience becomes the memory, the way a photograph does. At the least we may feel a need to omit the irrelevant detail or protect the privacy of others not as committed to our self-disclosure as we are. The truth may not necessarily be veracious enough to take into court or into a laboratory; it need only be veracious enough to satisfy the writer's purpose and the art of the writing.

Literary Approaches to Nonfiction

The language of creative nonfiction is as literary, as imaginative, as that of other literary genres and is similarly used for lyrical, narrative, and dramatic effects. What separates creative nonfiction from "noncreative nonfiction" (if we can be forgiven the use of that term for a moment to categorize all nonfiction outside this genre) is not only "the unique and subjective focus, concept, context and point of view in which the information is presented and defined" (Gutkind v–vi) but also the ways in which language serves the subject. This is partly what Chris

Anderson is alluding to when he writes that certain essays and journalism are not literary (x), and what Barbara Lounsbery means by claiming that, no matter how well the other elements of a nonfiction work are achieved, "it may still fail the standards of literary nonfiction if its language is dull or diffuse" (xv). When Annie Dillard turned from writing poetry to writing literary nonfiction, she

> was delighted to find that nonfiction prose can also carry meaning in its structures and, like poetry, can tolerate all sorts of figurative language, as well as alliteration and even rhyme. The range of rhythms in prose is larger and grander than it is in poetry, and it can handle discursive ideas and plain information as well as character and story. It can do everything. I felt as though I had switched from a single reed instrument to a full orchestra. ("To Fashion" 74–75)

When writers of poetry or fiction turn to creative nonfiction, as poet Mary Karr does in her memoir, *The Liar's Club,* or poet Garrett Hongo does in his memoir, *Volcano,* they bring with them the literary language possible in those other genres and are able to use it.

Poets and novelists aren't the only ones drawing on literary techniques in nonfiction. Some journalists have taken so literary an approach to their reportage that they have created a writing form that straddles literature and journalism, and often can be identified as a form of creative nonfiction. In addition, a number of primarily academic writers have sought a more personal perspective in the cultural criticism they write. They have made the language of their academic discourse more expansive, more intimate, more literary, allowing the reader to share their subjective reactions to the ideas and experiences they discuss. Like Thoreau, they retain rather than omit "the *I,* or first person," acknowledging, as he did, that we "commonly do not remember that it is, after all, always the first person that is speaking" (3). By doing so they do not simply present their information or opinions but also extend *themselves* toward the reader and draw the reader closer. In essence, they move the written work beyond presentation into conversation.

The writer in creative nonfiction is often the reader's guide, pointing out the sights along the way, the places of interest where special attention is required. In such writing the reader is treated like a spectator or an audience. But often the writer is the reader's surrogate, inviting her to share the author's space in imagination and to respond to the experience as if she is living it. In such writing the reader is treated like a participant. In creative nonfiction, then, in addition to exploring the information being presented—the ways in which various ideas, events, or scenes connect to one another and relate to some overarching theme or concept or premise—the reader also has to examine the role the writer takes in the work. The writer's role and the structure of the writing are not as predictable in creative nonfiction as they are in other forms, such as the news article or the academic research paper, the sermon or the lecture. The structure of the essay or article may be experimental or unexpected, an attempt to generate literary form out of subject matter instead of trying to wedge subject matter into an all-purpose literary form. When it departs from linear, tightly unified forms to achieve its purpose, contemporary creative nonfiction does not simply meander or ramble like the traditional essay ("My Style and my mind alike go roaming," Montaigne said [761]); instead, it moves in jump cuts, flashbacks, flash-forwards, concentric or parallel or tangential strands. Readers sometimes have to let the works themselves tell them how they should be read.

Writers, Readers, and the Fourth Genre

The interaction between the writer and the genre in which the writer works influences the outcome of the work. Writers of other nonfiction forms such as criticism, journalism, scholarship, or technical and professional writing tend to leave themselves out of the work and to view the work as a means to an end; they want to explain, report, inform, or propose. For them the text they produce is a vehicle, a container or package, to transport information and ideas to someone else, the intended readers. Some people have referred to these forms as *transactional writing*. Writers of other literary forms such as poetry, fiction, and drama tend to put themselves in the work and to view the work as an end in itself; they want to reflect, explore, speculate, imagine, and discover, and the text they create is a structure, an anchored shape like a sculpture or a monument or a building, to which interested readers are drawn. The result is often called *poetic* or *creative writing*. Writers of creative nonfiction by definition share the qualities of both groups of writers, and the work they create reflects varying measures of both kinds of writing.

Many creative nonfiction writers whose works are found in this book joined this conversation from the direction of their writing in other literary genres. Experienced poets or fictionists, they came to the fourth genre by way of personal essays and memoirs, nonfiction forms compatible with the desire for lyric and narrative expression, the desire to give voice to memory and meditation and acts of emotional and intellectual discovery. They came to it not only because of a need to write nonfiction but also because of a desire for creative expression. Similarly, creative nonfiction is also written by critics, journalists, and scholars who approach their writing in the way that essayists and memoirists do—that is, by inhabiting the work and by approaching it from a literary perspective more than (or as much as) from a critical, reportorial, or scholarly perspective.

We do not necessarily see sharply definable boundaries here, whose coordinates we can map precisely—neighboring nonfiction forms often share the same terrain for a long distance on either side of their common border. Yet, just as when you are traveling you don't need precise knowledge of geography or topography to sense that you're not in Kansas (or Vermont or California) anymore, so in reading you can also sense when a text is a work of "literary" nonfiction and not the "transactional" forms usual to journalism, scholarship, or criticism.

Because nonfiction in general has sometimes, mistakenly, been regarded as if it were an arid, barren wasteland of nonliterature surrounding lush, fertile oases of literature, it is important to make this clear: a great deal of nonfiction has always been literary, and it is the contemporary writers of literary or creative forms of nonfiction who are the focus of this book. The nonliterary forms of nonfiction are not our focus, but in some of those forms it is frequently difficult to notice when a writer slips over the border into the literary form. To make it easier to talk about creative nonfiction, then, we urge you to see it centered in the approaches taken by the essayist and memoirist and spiraling outward toward aesthetically oriented critics and literary journalists.

Readers come to creative nonfiction with different expectations from those they bring to the other genres. At the core of those expectations may be, in a sense, the hope of becoming engaged in a conversation. Much fiction, drama, poetry, and film is presented as performance, as entertainment essentially enclosed within itself—we are usually expected to appreciate or admire its creators' artistry whether we are encouraged to acknowledge their intensity or insight. Much nonliterary nonfiction (various forms of journalism and academic writing, for example) is presented as a transaction delivering information, sometimes objective, sometimes argumentative—we are usually expected to receive or accept their creators' knowledge or data the way we would a lecture or a news broadcast. Creative nonfiction, which is simultaneously literary and transactional, integrates these discourse aims: it brings artistry to information and actuality to imagination, and it draws on the expressive aim that lies below the surface in all writing. Expressive writing breaks the surface most notably in personal writing such as journals, diaries, and letters, but it has connected with the reader most prominently in the personal or familiar essay. Other forms of writing have at center the personal impulse, the need for expression, but the essay has traditionally been the outlet by which that impulse finds public voice.

Readers turn to creative nonfiction to find a place to connect to the personal voice, to connect not to art or knowledge alone but to another mind. This means that writers too have a place to connect, a genre that gives them permission to speak in the first person singular, not only about their knowledge and their beliefs but also about their uncertainties and their passions, not only about where they stand but also about the ways they arrived there, not only about the worlds they have either imagined or documented but also about the worlds they have experienced or inhabit now. Creative nonfiction may be the genre in which both reader and writer feel most connected to one another.

Joining the Conversation

We think of *The Fourth Genre* as an inclusive, ongoing conversation about the art and craft of writing creative nonfiction. We want to exemplify and describe this evolving genre, allow it to define itself and preserve its vital elasticity, and avoid arbitrary and imprecise subcategorizing and classifying. Unlike conversations in real life, a conversation in an anthology allows only one speaker at a time to speak and no one is interrupted by anyone else. The reader is the one who has to make the individual speakers connect. We've tried to make the conversation a little easier to follow by putting the speakers in different rooms. The people who simply share their own examples of creative nonfiction have the largest room, at the front of the anthology, where the writing more or less speaks for itself. The people who have ideas and opinions about the nature of this genre, the kinds of writing it contains and the kinds of writers who produce it, have another room, where both those who write creative nonfiction and those who study or examine it have their opportunities to speak. In the final room are those who attempt to explain how they wrote their own specific examples of creative nonfiction—the circumstances of composition and the tribulations of drafting and revising—where the conversation focuses on the composing processes of working writers.

In real life you would not be able to hear all the speakers in this conversation, but in an anthology you can, because the speakers wait until you get to them before they speak. In spite of the layout of the place, you should feel free to wander back and forth among the rooms, following someone else's recommendations or your own inclinations and intuitions. Naturally, we encourage you to join the conversation, provide your own examples, discuss your own ideas of genre, theory, and technique, share your own composing processes.

Read selections in Part One, Writing Creative Nonfiction, to get a sense of the range of contemporary creative nonfiction. The writers here reveal the variety of voices and personas, the flexibility and expansiveness, and the breadth of subject matter and structures creative nonfiction may adopt. It is a representative blend. It includes examples of the personal essay, the memoir, the travel essay, the nature essay, literary journalism, and personal cultural criticism. (See the Alternative Contents: Subgenres of Creative Nonfiction for further subdivisions and categories.) These selections also present a range of forms and structures, from the narrative and the lyrical to the discursive and the reportorial, from the traditional (chronology or argument) to the individual and unconventional (unique arrangements of segments or organization around a pattern of tarot cards).

Many of these works demonstrate the futility of labels, qualifying easily under the genre heading of creative nonfiction for personal presence, literary language, and other defining elements but straddling the boundaries of two or more subgenres, perhaps simultaneously literary journalism and personal essay, travel narrative and environmental reporting, or memoir and cultural criticism. Instead they model the intimate relationship between form and content in creative nonfiction. Perhaps they will also suggest to you ways to invent forms that serve your own ends as a writer.

Read selections in Part Two, Talking about Creative Nonfiction, to get a sense of what writers, critics, and scholars have to say about the nature of creative nonfiction and its various subgenres. Many of the authors in this section have also written selections in Part One. They take the form personally, sometimes discussing their own personal motives and composing strategies, sometimes the elements of the form in which they work. As some of them point out, the tradition of essayist goes back centuries, to the work of Montaigne, Addison and Steele, Lamb and Hazlitt, and as this genre reemerges, it is contemporary practitioners, for the most part—the people who write and teach creative nonfiction—who are setting the terms of this conversation. This section mixes thoughts, opinions, speculations, critiques, theories, and assertions by working writers about the art and craft of their genre.

Many of the Part Two pieces can be paired with essays in Part One. Writing in Part One often serves as examples of the more theoretical positions in Part Two; writing in Part Two often gives new perspective on writing in Part One. So you can compare memoirs with the memoirists' discussion of the form, essays with the essayists' reflections on being essayists, cultural criticism with the critics' justifications for personal academic writing.

Other authors also give us insight into the forms and issues of creative nonfiction—the art of the memoir or of literary journalism, the elements of the disjunctive form or the question of truthfulness in nonfiction texts. Such essays attempt to give a personal perspective to a critical speculation on the forms in which the writers are working. They ground the genre in the behaviors and motives of working writers rather than in disembodied theories of literature or composing. They give the reader the opportunity to step back from the individual readings and take a longer view of process and text.

Read selections in Part Three, Composing Creative Nonfiction, for a sense of the work habits, craft techniques, and serendipity used to create a work of creative nonfiction. Here a group of writers discuss their composing processes for specific works, also reproduced in this section. They share drafts, explain revisions, and map the motives for changes in their works-in-progress. They focus our attention in this conversation on the most fundamental aspect of the work, the composing itself, and bring us to the place where the reader can continue the conversation as a writer. If Part One gives us examples of the variety of creative nonfiction and Part Two gives us a lively discussion of the practices and products of the genre, Part Three gives us a chance to sit at the shoulder of the writer herself and follow her through the twists and turns of creation. These writers reflect in their practices the ways writers in other parts of the book created their own selections. By example they suggest ideas and strategies that we can use in our own composing processes.

We think the fourth genre is the most accessible and urgent genre. It may not be necessary to read all three parts of this book or to read all selections in the parts you do read to get a sense of what creative nonfiction is about. We hope the book is flexible enough that readers can get what they want from it by coming at it from a number of different directions. Yet readers who do read in all three parts will get a fuller understanding of the breadth and power of this genre. And because the time is particularly right for other writers to join this conversation, we hope that wide reading in this book will help spur your writing of creative nonfiction and give you a writer's perspective on the art and craft of the fourth genre.

Robert L. Root, Jr., and Michael Steinberg

Works Cited

Anderson, Chris. "Introduction: Literary Nonfiction and Composition." *Literary Nonfiction: Theory, Criticism, Pedagogy.* Ed. Chris Anderson. Carbondale: Southern Illinois UP, 1989. ix–xxvi.

Atwan, Robert. "Foreword." *The Best American Essays 1988.* Boston: Ticknor and Fields, 1988. ix–xi.

Brown, Rosellen. "Introduction." *Ploughshares* 20:2/3 (Fall 1994): 5–8.

Dillard, Annie. "Introduction." *The Best American Essays 1988.* Boston: Ticknor and Fields, 1988. xiii–xxii.

———. "To Fashion a Text." *Inventing the Truth: The Art and Craft of Memoir.* Ed. William Zinsser. Boston: Houghton-Mifflin, 1987. 53–76.

Duncan, David James. "Nonfiction = Fiction." *Orion* 15:3 (Summer 1996): 55–57.

Gutkind, Lee. "From the Editor." *Creative Nonfiction* 1:1 (1993): v–vi.

Hongo, Garrett. *Volcano: A Memoir of Hawai'i.* New York: Knopf, 1995.

Karr, Mary. *The Liar's Club: A Memoir.* New York: Viking Penguin, 1995.

Kramer, Mark. "Breakable Rules for Literary Journalists." *Literary Journalism.* Ed. Norman Sims and Mark Kramer. New York: Ballantine, 1995. 21–34.

Lopate, Phillip. "Introduction." *The Art of the Personal Essay: An Anthology from the Classical Era to the Present.* New York: Anchor/Doubleday, 1994. xxiii–liv.

Lounsbery, Barbara. *The Art of Fact: Contemporary Artists of Nonfiction.* Contributions to the Study of World Literature, No. 35. New York: Greenwood Press, 1990.

Montaigne, Michel de. *The Complete Works.* Trans. Donald M. Frame. Stanford: Stanford UP, 1957. 761.

Olson, W. Scott. "Introduction." *Old Friends, New Neighbors: A Celebration of the American Essay.* Ed. W. Scott Olson. *American Literary Review* 5:2 (Fall 1994): v–viii.

Thoreau, Henry. *Walden.* Ed. J. Lyndon Shanley. Princeton: Princeton UP, 1973. 3.

Torgovnick, Marianna. "Introduction." *Eloquent Obsessions: Writing Cultural Criticism.* Ed. Marianna Torgovnick. Durham: Duke UP, 1994.

The Fourth Genre

Part 1

Writing Creative Nonfiction

Contemporary creative nonfiction, like any other literary genre, offers a great deal of latitude to writers in terms of what they are able to do in the form. "There are as many kinds of essays as there are human attitudes or poses," the great American essayist E. B. White once observed. "The essayist rises in the morning and, if he has work to do, selects his garb from an unusually extensive wardrobe: he can pull on any sort of shirt, be any sort of person, according to his mood or his subject matter—philosopher, scold, jester, raconteur, confidant, devil's advocate, enthusiast" (vii). In general the observation is appropriate for the whole range of creative nonfiction.

This section of the book samples widely from the range of contemporary creative nonfiction. Its selections reveal the variety of voices and personas, the flexibility and expansiveness, and the range of subject matter and structures creative nonfiction may adopt. It is a representative blend, demonstrating the malleability of the genre. Some pieces are fairly straightforward examples of the traditional personal essay, such as Dagoberto Gilb tracing a random encounter on a train and Phillip Lopate rambling discursively over the subject of his own body. Others center on nature or environmental or ecological topics, but vary their approaches; Linda Hogan centers on a single flower discovered while walking, Annie Dillard makes an intimate experience of an encounter with a weasel, and Gretel Ehrlich gives us a journal-like essay on sheepherding. Some examples of literary journalism center on different approaches to examining place, as Pico Iyer does with Los Angeles International Airport, John McPhee with Atlantic City, and André Aciman with Illiers-Combray. The personal approach to cultural criticism allows Chet Raymo to explore the intersection of science and religion and Jane Tompkins to ponder the significance of a museum commemorating Buffalo Bill Cody.

The range of approaches within a subgrouping suggests the flexibility of the form, the ways writers use creative nonfiction not as a vessel to be filled with meaning but rather as a way of constructing a shape appropriate to the meaning they create by writing. The ways that Mary Clearman Blew, Judith Ortiz Cofer, and Patricia Hampl present their remembrances of parents and of childhood vary

1

as much as their experiences growing up did. The techniques with which other memoirists present the past vary as well. For example, Jo Ann Beard uses a highly fictional technique to record her disturbing encounter on a highway, Frank Conroy presents his memoir of shooting pool almost as an instruction manual, and Naomi Shihab Nye conducts her piece as a lyrical essay rather than as a personal narrative. These readings suggest that the writer's feeling about the subject has more to do with the way the final version reads than any arbitrary set of generic guidelines. Even as we hint at the variety of the pieces in this part of the book, we have to acknowledge the futility of labels. Most of the selections can be classified a number of different ways. For example, Brenda Peterson's "Animal Allies" can be treated as another example of American nature writing and placed alongside the other writing on that subject, but it is set in a classroom with such detail that it can also be regarded simultaneously as a personal essay on child psychology and as an article on teaching. Here, as in so many of these readings, we discover again that it is not a uniform structure or organization that links these selections but the common thread of the writer's personal presence, sometimes at considerable remove in essays not obviously about personal experience yet nevertheless there, examining subject matter in the light of personal inquiry.

A number of these pieces are what we term *segmented essays,* selections that try out nonlinear patterns or structures. Mary Clearman Blew's essay weaves among different family members and different times and events to piece together elements of family history; Nancy Willard builds her essay about friendship around an arrangement of tarot cards; Naomi Shihab Nye collects three miniature memoirs under one collective heading. Such structures let us see how intimately form and content are connected in creative nonfiction, and how they can be invented to serve the ends of the author. Moreover, they help extend our understanding of the range of writing that creative nonfictionists do.

"What happened to the writer is not what matters; what matters is the larger sense that the writer is able to *make* of what happened," Vivian Gornick once observed, writing about the author's presence in memoirs. "The narrator in a memoir is an instrument of illumination, but it's the writing itself that provides revelation" (5). These selections suggest to us the possibilities of form, structure, voice, persona, approach, presentation, ways of describing what happened, ways of making sense of what happened. Reading widely in Part One will not only give you a solid sense of what we write when we write creative nonfiction, but also open up your own possibilities for subject matter and design. Reading other writers triggers our own memories and our own speculations. We don't so much imitate others' subjects and structures as use them as a bridge to our resources and inventions.

Part One, Writing Creative Nonfiction, is in effect a mini-anthology of contemporary writing. As such it is complemented by the other two parts of the book, and we invite you to explore those other sections in connection with your reading in this part. For example, when reading the memoirs by Mary Clearman Blew and Patricia Hampl in Part One, you may want to read their essays about the memoir in Part Two, a section where writers talk about creative nonfiction, and Simone Poirier-Bures's selections about memoir in Part Three, which pairs writers' essays with articles explaining how they wrote them. Or you might follow up Jane Tompkins's essay on the Buffalo Bill Museum in Part One with reading Marianna Torgovnick's article about personal academic writing in Part Two and Emily D. Chase's pair of readings in Part Three, a literary essay and an account of writing the literary essay. There are many possibilities for interaction among these three sections of the book.

Writers always find it helpful to see what other writers are doing, to hear them talk about how they are doing it, and to free-associate with their own memories and reflections from the ideas and stories that others share. Those who read these selections with a writer's eye will discover insights and perspectives that will serve their own writing well.

Works Cited

Gornick, Vivian. "The Memoir Boom." *Women's Review of Books* 13: 10–11 (July 1996): 5.
White, E. B. "Foreword." *Essays of E. B. White*. New York: HarperCollins, 1997.

In Search of Proust

André Aciman

It was by train that I had always imagined arriving in Illiers-Combray—not just any train but one of those drafty, pre–World War, rattling wagons which I like to think still leave Paris early every morning and, after hours of swaying through the countryside, squeak their way into a station that is as old and weather-beaten as all of yesteryear's provincial stops in France. The picture in my mind was always the same: the train would come to a wheezing halt and release a sudden loud chuff of steam; a door would slam open; someone would call out "Illiers-Combray"; and, finally, like the young Marcel Proust arriving for his Easter vacation just over a century ago, I would step down nervously into the small, turn-of-the-century town in Eure-et-Loir which he described so lovingly in *À la Recherche du Temps Perdu*.

Instead, when I finally made my way to Illiers-Combray, late last year, I arrived by car with Anne Borrel, the curator of the Proust Museum there, who had offered to pick me up at my Paris hotel that morning. In my pocket was a cheap and tattered Livre de Poche edition of *Swann's Way*, which I had brought in the hope that I'd find a moment to read some of my favorite passages on holy ground. That was to be my way of closing the loop, of coming home to a book I had first opened more than thirty years before.

I had bought it with my father, when I was fifteen, one summer evening in Paris. We were taking a long walk, and as we passed a small restaurant I told him that the overpowering smell of refried food reminded me of the tanneries along the coast road outside Alexandria, in Egypt, where we had once lived. He said he hadn't thought of it that way, but, yes, I was right, the restaurant did smell like a tannery. And as we began working our way back through strands of shared memories—the tanneries, the beaches, the ruined Roman temple west of Alexandria, our summer beach house—all this suddenly made him think of Proust. Had I read Proust? he asked. No, I hadn't. Well, perhaps I should. My father said this

5

with a sense of urgency, so unlike him that he immediately tempered it, for fear I'd resist the suggestion simply because it was a parent's.

The next day, sitting in the sun on a metal chair in Lamartine Square, I read Proust for the first time. That evening, when my father asked how I had liked what I'd read, I feigned indifference, not really knowing whether I intended to spite a father who wanted me to love the author he loved most or to spite an author who had come uncomfortably close. For in the eighty-odd pages I had read that day I had rediscovered my entire childhood in Alexandria: the impassive cook, my bad-tempered aunts and skittish friends, the buzz of flies on sunny afternoons spent reading indoors when it was too hot outside, dinners in the garden with scant lights to keep mosquitoes away, the "ferruginous, interminable" peal of the garden bell announcing the occasional night guest who, like Charles Swann, came uninvited but whom everyone had nevertheless been expecting.

Every year, thousands of Prousto-tourists come to the former Illiers, which extended its name in honor of Proust's fictional town, Combray, in 1971, on the centennial of his birth. The town knows it, proclaims it, milks it. Today, Illiers-Combray sells around two thousand madeleine pastries a month. The shell-shaped cakes are displayed in the windows of pastry shops like propitiatory offerings to an unseen god and are sold by the dozen—in case one wants to take some home to friends or relatives, the way pilgrims take back holy water from the Jordan or an olive twig from Gethsemane.

For the reader on a Proustian pilgrimage, tasting a madeleine is the supreme tribute to Proust. (As no pâtisserie fails to remind the tourists, it was on tasting a madeleine, now the most famous sponge cake in the history of world literature, that the adult narrator of Proust's novel was transported to his boyhood days in Combray.) It is also a gesture of communion through which readers hope, like Proust, to come home to something bigger, more solid, and ultimately, perhaps, truer than fiction itself. Anne Borrel often tells these Proust groupies that the cult of the madeleine is blasphemous, as are the claims made by one of the *pâtissiers* that members of the *famille* Proust used to purchase their madeleines on his premises. (In earlier drafts of the novel, Proust's madeleines may have been slices of melba toast, which evolved into toasted bread, only later to metamorphose into the sponge cakes.) But no one listens. Besides, going to Illiers-Combray and not tasting a madeleine would be like going to Jerusalem and not seeing the Wailing Wall or to Greenwich and not checking your watch. Luckily, I was able to resist temptation: during my visit, on a Sunday just a few days before Christmas, all the pastry shops were closed.

Before going to the Proust Museum, Anne Borrel and I had lunch at a tiny restaurant called Le Samovar. Plump and middle-aged, Borrel is the author of a cookbook and culinary history titled *Dining with Proust*. She told me that some of the tourists come from so far away and have waited so long to make the trip that as soon as they step into Proust's house they burst into tears. I pictured refugees getting off a ship and kneeling to kiss the beachhead.

I asked about Proust's suddenly increasing popularity. "Proust," Borrel replied, "is a must." (She repeated these four words, like a verdict, several times during the day.) She reminded me that there were currently six French editions of *À la Recherche du Temps Perdu* in print. I told her that a fourth English-language edition was due to appear in 2001. And that wasn't all: trade books on Proust and coffee-table iconographies were everywhere; in Paris, I had seen at least half a dozen new books that bore Proust's name or drew on Proustian characters occupying precious space on the display tables of bookstores and department stores. Even Proust's notes, manuscripts, and publishing history had been deemed complicated enough to warrant a book of their own, called *Remembrance of Publishers Past*. Add to that T-shirts, watches, CDs, concerts, videos, scarves, posters, books on tape, newsletters, and a comic-strip version, entitled "Combray," whose first printing, of twelve thousand copies, sold out in three weeks. Not to mention the 1997–98 convention in Liège celebrating the seventy-fifth anniversary of Proust's death, with sessions on music and Proust, eating and Proust, a writing competition (on the subject of "Time Lost and Time Regained"), and a colloquium on asthma and allergies.

This kaleidoscope of Proustophernalia is matched by as many testimonials and tributes to Proust, in which he takes many forms. There is Proust the élitist and high-society snob; Proust the son of a Jewish mother; Proust the loner; Proust the dandy; Proust the analytical aesthete; Proust the soulful lovelorn boy; Proust the tart, the dissembling coquette; the Belle Époque Proust; the professional whiner; the prankster; the subversive classicist; the eternal procrastinator; and the asthmatic, hypochondriac Proust.

But the figure who lies at the heart of today's Proust revival is the intimate Proust, the Proust who perfected the studied unveiling of spontaneous feelings. Proust invented a language, a style, a rhythm, and a vision that gave memory and introspection an aesthetic scope and magnitude no author had conferred on either before. He allowed intimacy itself to become an art form. This is not to say that the vertiginous spate of memoirs that have appeared recently, with their de-rigueur regimens of child, spouse, and substance abuse, owe their existence, their voice, or their sensibility to Proust—clearly, they owe far more to Freud. But it does help to explain why Proust is more popular today, in the age of the memoir, than he has been at any other time in the century.

Like every great memoirist who has had a dizzying social life and a profoundly lonely one, Proust wrote because writing was his way of both reaching for an ever elusive world and securing his distance from it. He was among the first writers in this century to disapprove of the critics' tendency to seek correspondences between an artist's work and his private life. The slow, solitary metamorphosis of what truly happened into what, after many years, finally emerges in prose is the hallmark of Proust's labor of love.

Proust is at once the most canonical and the most uncanonical author, the most solemnly classical and the most subversive, the author in whom farce and lyricism, arrogance and humility, beauty and revulsion are indissolubly fused, and whose ultimate contradiction reflects an irreducible fact about all of us: we are driven by something as simple and as obvious as the desire to be happy, and, if that fails, by the belief that we once have been.

My conversation with Anne Borrel was interrupted by the arrival of customers outside Le Samovar. "Take a look at those four," Borrel said, pointing to the two couples dawdling at the entrance. "I'll bet you anything they're *proustiens*." She referred to all tourists as *proustiens*—meaning not Proust scholars but individuals whom the French like to call *les amis de Proust*, Proustologues, Proustolaters, Proustocentrics, Proustomaniacs, Proustophiles, Proustophiliacs, Proustoholics . . . or *fidèles* (to use a term dear to Proust's malevolent arch-snob, Mme. Verdurin).

One of the four opened the door of the restaurant and asked in a thick Spanish accent whether lunch was still being served. "*Pintades*"—Guinea hens—"are all that's left," snapped the owner of Le Samovar. Borrel and I exchanged a complicitous glance, because talk of fowl immediately brought to mind a discussion we'd had in the car about Proust's servant, Françoise, who in *Swann's Way* butchers a chicken and then curses it for not dying fast enough.

The four tourists were shown to a table. One asked the proprietor what time the Proust Museum would open that afternoon, and he regretfully informed them that the museum was closed for the holidays. They were crestfallen. "What a pity! And we've come all the way from Argentina."

Anne Borrel had heard every word of the exchange. She reminded me of a teacher who with her back turned to the class while she's writing on the blackboard knows exactly who's whispering what to whom. She leaned over and told one of the Argentines, "You may have come to the right place."

Overjoyed, the Argentine blurted out, "You mean Marcel Proust used to eat here, in this restaurant?"

"No," Borrel answered, smiling indulgently. She told them that an improvised tour of the house could be arranged after coffee, and the Argentines went back to talking softly about Proust, staring every once in a while at our table with the thrilled and wary gaze of people who have been promised a miracle.

By the time our coffee was served, we had also acquired two English and three French *proustiens*, and a warm, festive mood permeated Le Samovar. It was like the gathering of pilgrims in Chaucer's Tabard Inn. Introductions were unnecessary. We knew why we were there, and we all had a tale to tell. By then, some of us would have liked nothing more than a fireplace, a large cognac, and a little prodding to induce us to recount how we had first come to read Proust, to love Proust, how Proust had changed our lives. I was, it dawned on me, among my own.

After dessert, Borrel put on her coat. "*On y va?*" she asked, rattling a giant key chain that bore a bunch of old keys with long shafts and large, hollowed oval heads. She led us down the Rue du Docteur Proust, named after Proust's father, who by the turn of the century had helped to halt the spread of cholera in Europe. The sidewalks and streets were empty. Everyone seemed to be away for the holidays.

Franco-jazz Muzak emanated from loudspeakers, mounted on various lampposts, that were apparently intended to convey a festive yule spirit, but otherwise Illiers-Combray was deserted and gray—a dull, cloying, humdrum, wintry, ashen town, where the soul could easily choke. Small wonder that Marcel developed asthma, or that he had the heebie-jeebies on returning home after long evening walks with his parents, knowing that by the time dinner was served life would hold no surprises—only the inevitable walk up the creepy staircase and that frightful drama called bedtime.

Borrel stopped at one of many nondescript doors along the empty street. She stared at it for a moment, almost as though she were trying to remember whether this was indeed the right address, then took out her keys, inserted one into the lock, and suddenly gave it a vigorous turn, yanking the door open.

"*C'est ici que tout commence,*" she said.

One by one, we filed into Proust's garden. Fortunately, no one cried. Borrel pointed to a little bell at the top of the gate. I couldn't contain myself. "Could this be the ferruginous bell?" I asked. It was a question she'd heard before. She took a breath. "You mean not the large and noisy rattle which deafened with its ferruginous, interminable, frozen sound any member of the household who set it off by coming in 'without ringing,' but the double peal, 'timid, oval, gilded,' of the visitor's bell, whereupon everyone would exclaim, 'A visitor! Who on earth could it be?'" (She was quoting from memory, and every time one of us asked a question after that she would recite the answer.)

Next she led us into the restored, relatively humble middle-class house—by no means the large villa I'd always imagined. The kitchen, where I'd envisaged Françoise cooking the chicken she had viciously butchered, was a sunless alcove. The dining room, with a small round table and dark wood panelling, was a depressing melee of browns. Then we came to Marcel's bedroom, with its tiny Empire-style bed, the magic lantern that kept him company at night when he dreaded sleep, and nearby the George Sand novel bound in red. In another room was the sofa that Proust had given to his maid, Céleste Albaret, and which her daughter had donated to the museum—and which was perhaps the inspiration for the fictional sofa that Marcel inherited from his Tante Léonie, made love on, and eventually passed along to the owner of a brothel.

When Borrel indicated another room, on the second floor, I interrupted her to suggest that it must surely be the room where, under lock and key, Marcel discovered the secret pleasures of onanism. Borrel neither confirmed nor denied my allegation. She said only, "The little room that smelt of orris-root . . . [where] I explored, across the bounds of my own experience, an untrodden path which I thought was deadly." In this way, I was summarily put in my place—for presuming to show off and for implying that I could make obvious what Proust's oblique words had made explicit enough.

Back in the garden, I told her that the way she had opened the main door had reminded me of the moment in the novel when, after a long, moonlit family walk, Marcel's father pretends to be lost. Everyone in our group suddenly remembered the episode, and, excited, one of the Englishmen described it to his friend, explaining that it was only after making everyone else panic in the dark that Marcel's father had finally taken a key out of his pocket and quietly inserted it in what the others until then had failed to see was the back gate to their very own house. According to the Englishman, Marcel's admiring mother, stunned by her husband's ability to save the day, had exclaimed, *"Tu es fantastique!"*

"Tu es extraordinaire!" Borrel corrected him.

I had always liked that scene: the family wandering in the moonlight, the boy and his mother convinced that they're lost, the father teasing them. It reminded me of the way Proust's sentences roam and stray through a labyrinth of words and clauses, only to turn around—just when you are about to give up—and show you something you had always suspected but had never put into words. The sentences tell you that you haven't really drifted far at all, and that real answers may not always be obvious but aren't really hidden, either. Things, he reminds us, are never as scary as we thought they were, nor are we ever as stranded or as helpless as we feared.

Borrel left us for a moment to check on something inside the museum, and we spent some time discussing our favorite Proust passages. We all wondered which gate Swann's prototype would come through in the evenings, and where the aunts had been sitting when they refused to thank him for his gift but finally consented to say something so indirect that Swann failed to realize that they actually were thanking him.

"It all seems so small," said the Englishman, who was visibly disappointed by the house.

My thoughts drifted to a corner of the garden. The weather was growing colder, and yet I was thinking of Marcel's summer days, and of my own summer days as well, and of the garden where, deaf to the world, I had found myself doing what Proust described in his essay "On Reading":

> giving more attention and tenderness to characters in books than to people in real life, not always daring to admit how much I loved them . . . those people, for whom I had panted and sobbed, and whom, at the close of the book, I would never see again, and no longer know anything about. . . . I would have wanted so much for these books to continue, and if that were impossible, to have other information on all those characters, to learn now something about their lives, to devote mine to things that might not be entirely foreign to the love they had inspired in me and whose object I was suddenly missing . . . beings who tomorrow would be but names on a forgotten page, in a book having no connection with life.

The guided tour took more than two hours. It ended, as all guided tours do, in the gift shop. The guests were kindly reminded that, despite the impromptu nature of today's visit, they shouldn't forget to pay for their tickets. Everyone dutifully scrambled to buy Proust memorabilia. I toyed with the idea of buying a Proust watch on whose dial were inscribed the opening words of *À la Recherche du Temps Perdu*: *"Longtemps, je me suis couché de bonne heure."* But I knew I'd never wear it.

The visitors began talking of heading back to Paris. I was almost tempted to hitch a ride with one of them, but Borrel had promised to take me for a night walk through the streets of Illiers-Combray and then accompany me to the train station. The others stood idly about in the evening air, obviously reluctant to put Illiers-Combray behind them. They exchanged addresses and telephone numbers. "Proust is a must," I heard the Argentine say, an infatuated giggle in his voice. When Borrel left the shop to lock the back door, I was suddenly alone.

As I looked out the window at the garden where the Proust family had dined on warm summer evenings, I was seized with a strange premonition of asthma. How could Marcel have ever loved such a place? Or had he never loved it? Had he loved only the act of returning to it on paper, because that was how he lived his life—first by wanting to live it, and later by remembering having wanted to, and ultimately by writing about the two? The part in between—the actual living—was what had been lost.

Proust's garden was little more than a place where he had once yearned to be elsewhere—never the primal scene or the ground zero. Illiers itself was simply a place where the young Proust dreamed of a better life to come. But, because the dream never came true, he had learned to love instead the place where the dream was born. That life did happen, and happened so intensely, to someone who seemed so reluctant to live it is part of the Proustian miracle.

This is the irony that greets all Proust pilgrims: they go in search of things that Proust remembered far better than he had ever really known them, and which he yearned to recover more than he had ever loved them. In the end, like the boy mentioned by Freud who liked to lose things because he enjoyed finding them, Proust realized that he couldn't write about anything unless he thought he had lost it first. Perhaps I, too, had come here in order to lose Combray, if only to rediscover it in the pages I knew I would read on the way home.

My train wasn't due for an hour and a half, and Anne Borrel invited me to have a cup of tea at her house before our walk. We closed the door to the museum and set off down dark and deserted alleys.

"Illiers gets so empty," she said, sighing.

"It must be lonely," I said.

"It has its plusses."

Her house was bigger than Proust's and had a far larger garden and orchard. This seemed odd to me—like finding that the gatekeeper owns a faster car and has better central heating than the owner of the palace.

As we headed back to the train station after our tea, I walked quickly. Borrel tried to stop long enough to show me the spot where the Prousts had returned from their Sunday promenades, but I didn't want to miss my connection to Paris. It seemed a shame that, after so many years, this longed-for moonlit walk, so near at hand, should be the very thing I'd forfeit. But the last thing I needed was to be sentenced to a sleepless night in Proust's boyhood town. I alluded to a possible next time. Borrel mentioned spring, when Proust's favorite flower, the hawthorn, would be in bloom. But I knew, and perhaps she knew, too, that I had no plan to return.

On my way to Paris, I skimmed through the pages of "Combray," the first chapter of *In Search of Lost Time*. As I read about the steeples of Martinville or Tante Léonie, eternally perched in her bedroom, on the first floor, overlooking Rue Saint-Jacques, it occurred to me that I had rushed back to the book not to verify the existence of what I had just seen but to make certain that those places I remembered and loved as though my own childhood had been spent among them had not been altered by the reality of the dull, tile-roofed town shown to me by Anne Borrel.

I wanted to return to my first reading of Proust—the way, after seeing a film based on a novel, we struggle to resurrect our private portrait of its characters and their world, only to find that the images we've treasured for so long have vanished, like ancient frescoes exposed to daylight by a thoughtless archeologist. Would my original image of a stone villa with a spacious dining room and a wide staircase leading to the child's solitary bedroom be able to withstand the newly discovered little house with its squeaky wooden stairwell and drab, sunless rooms? And could this tawdry garden really be the glorious place where Marcel read away entire afternoons on a wicker chair under a chestnut tree, lost to the voices of those calling him inside and to the hourly chime of the church of Saint-Hilaire—whose real name, as I had found out that day, was not Saint-Hilaire but Saint Jacques, which, moreover, was not really the name of the street watched over by Tante Léonie, who, it turned out, was herself more likely to have been an uncle.

Inside the sepia cover of *Swann's Way* I searched also for the sense of wonder I had brought to it that summer evening more than thirty years before, when I'd had the good fortune to be with a man who was the first person to mention Proust to me and who, because he was unable to give me so many things then, had only this to give me, and gave it tentatively, self-consciously, as though he were giving part of himself, as he told me about Proust—how Proust remembered things that everyone else seemed to forget, how he saw through people though they still managed to fool him, and how he did all those things in sentences that were ever so long—and steered me, as we rushed to buy the first volume before the stores closed, to a writer I have since loved above all others, not just because of who he was and what he wrote, or because of who I became the more I read him, but because on that late-summer evening I already knew I had just received, perhaps without my father's knowing it, his dearest, most enduring gift of love.

Dumpling

Angela M. Balcita

My mother is serious. She looks into my eyes demanding my attention. "One cup rice, two cup water, put all in rice cooker, press button." She turns toward the simple, white machine.

"For how long?" I ask her. But I already know; I've watched her make rice a million times. It's done when the big cloud of steam shrinks to just a puff, when the bubbling turns into a gurgle.

"Oh, you know, like twenty minute," she says, "Til is puffy and little sticky. That how we like it, right?" When she says *we,* she's not just talking about me and her, not just talking about our family. *We* means *we Filipinos.* "You know those Americans, they eat potatoes every night. Pasta, even!"

She continues, "Okay, next is—"

But I'm already gone—out the front door and down the street where I will ride bikes, make believe and play tag.

From the porch, my mother yells, "Okay, *anak,* but tomorrow, you cook!" I cringe at the sound of her voice. Her heavy accent bounces off the long line of identical houses, off the corrugated roofs, over the broad green lawns.

The summer is extraordinarily hot, and I'm spending too much time in the sun. My mother can tell by the color of my skin, which has turned a few shades darker than its usual brown. The neighborhood girls are amazed by how dark I get without burning. We sprawl in the wet grass like dogs. They touch my dark arms and my shiny shins, all warm from absorbing the heat of the sun. The blond girl with the braids can't stop looking at me. She's older, lives in the house behind ours. She has kissed, at least, one boy I know of. She asks me, "You mean you don't get sunburned at all?"

"No," I say, not quite sure what *sunburned* means, "I don't think so."

Her soft bubble gum lips swell slightly in a circle when she replies, "Oh." Her straight teeth are as clean as her chalky complexion. She shows me where the sun has made her skin the color of strawberries. "Here, see my shoulders, see the tops of my feet." Grass pokes out between her orange painted toenails. "That's neat that you don't burn. You get so tanned."

My mother, however, does not approve. It's an American thing. "Is low class," she says. "Back home, the field workers are dark." Her skin, lighter than mine, is pale like butter, smooth as cream. "Don't let yourself get *uling, anak.*" *Uling*, the Filipino word for *charcoal*, is the color she's afraid my skin will turn. To prevent this, she has decided that this summer will be spent in the kitchen learning to cook. It is the summer after my Barbie phase, the summer before I start to like boys. I am not at all intrigued by the idea of cooking, and I whine my way through my second lesson.

"Empanadas—you like, right?" she asks, her eyes searching for hope. Yes, I do. The small purses of baked dough filled with meat and raisins are perfect treats for little hands like mine. Of course, I like them. But in protest, I shrug indifferently.

"Okay, you know, we need meat, peas, raisins . . ." she recites the ingredients as half her body sticks out of the fridge. From what I can see, her form is completely different from my skinny, undeveloped frame. She is short and plump. Her body curves in places mine does not: around the hips, down her legs. Her face is wide and pale, her eyes thinner than mine. My boyish legs are slim, my arms awkward. Everyone says I take after my father.

The heat from the skillet makes the kitchen unbeatably warm. I pose in front of the window above the sink. Outside, the sun seems to be heating everything, too. The pavement on the driveway looks sticky and moist, too dangerous to walk on with bare feet. I try to ignore my mother mumbling behind me, and the sweet smell of the onions caramelizing, and the rich, nutty aroma of beef simmering in the pan. I try to ignore the growl in my stomach. "In the fridge, *anak*," she calls to me, "there is some dough. Can you get it?" I turn around to find her with one hand on her hip, the other holding a spatula over the pot on the stove. I think she looks like a professional, like she knows what she's doing, like maybe this could be her job if she had one.

The pasty dough is stiff from resting in the fridge. "How are we going to make anything from this?" I ask her. "It's like a rock."

"I show you," she says. Taking the dough from me, she throws it down on the counter. With the heel of her hand she pushes the center of the clump down, then pulls its sides up with her fingers. "*Ay, anak,* is not too hard." She does this repeatedly and swiftly, talking the whole time. "We make it flat, and we make circles for the *empanadas*. Feel it. Is not so hard, no?" The pastry, now warm and soft, feels like clay in my hands. I grab at its swollen pockets of air. It curls within my fingers with ease and delicacy. It is elastic, like skin, when I pinch it. She tells me to roll it out with the pin, cut out the thin disks with the cookie cutter. "Flat like paper, 'kay?" she says. I use all my effort to push and roll out the dough. So much that my palms stick to the wood of the pin. I use the sharp, metal cookie cutter to press out little circles. They come cleanly away.

She turns to the iron pot cooling over the stove. "Okay, now you like extra raisins, right? The raisins are good but, you make sure the meat has pepper. Or else, is no good." She tastes a small amount of the meat, nodding after she swallows. "Okay, is good." She holds out some for me to try. I bite in, recognizing all the flavors that pass over my tongue: the fruitiness of the raisins, the freshness of the tiny green peas, the pepper on the meat. She's right. The pepper adds enough spice to tingle in my mouth.

She pushes the pot closer to me and puts the spoon in my hand. I try to remember what empanadas look like. Filling a disk with a spoonful of mixture, I fold the center to make a half moon. On the open side, I crimp the dough with a series of little folds to make a seam.

"You know is good when you fit eighteen folds," my mother says. She is watching me. I feel her there, nodding with my every move.

I do eighteen folds on my first try and glance at her for approval. "Good, *anak*," she says. When she smiles, her small eyes disappear into straight black lines and her smooth white checks engulf her entire face.

By August, I start to sense that the season will end soon. The ice cream trucks will be replaced with school buses. My play clothes will dissolve into uniforms. The heart of my summer nights outside will drift from the low-lit, softly humming skies to the smooth, rounded cushions of the living room sofa. But when school finally starts, neither excitement nor anxiety hit me. I do not worry about the homework, or the newness of a classroom on the third floor. I sit in class all day thinking about what I will cook when I get home.

Sio Pao. My last lesson. The dumpling is a symbol of perfection. If it's made right, it will be perfectly round, perfectly white, smooth and shiny.

"The trick is the dough," my mother says. She squints with intensity. "You sift flour good, you knead dough good, you be okay." Gently rocking the flour in a mesh sieve, she blows white powder in the air. She hums while she sifts. She pours water into the bowl of flour, and blending those ingredients together, her bony hands slowly produce an airy ball of dough. She lays that on the counter. She starts to knead it, working her arms low, her shoulders rising and falling with all her weight.

"Now you help," and she pulls me towards her. Both our hands are working intensely into the pillow of white. I can feel the muscles in my forearms stretch and tighten. Before long, our hands are the same, the same skinny fingers, the same longish nails, the same joints and knuckles.

"You pull the dough away like this," she says, grabbing a fistful. She pokes her finger into the center of the small ball to make an indentation. "You put the meat in here," she says, "and one slice of hard-boiled egg. Mmmm, so good with egg, right?"

When all the balls are filled, we set them on the counter to rise. "Now, to steam," she says. My mother takes a tall bamboo steamer from behind the pantry door. It looks ancient. The wooden edges are frayed, and the rim has blackened with heat and use. She places it above a pot of boiling water. Immediately, the vapor rises through the grid inside the steamer.

When the dough balls are ready to be cooked, she leans over the steamer, and places one inside. The vapor rises around her face, through her hair. I want to tell her that she looks like an angel, like she's breaking through a cloud. But, instead, I tell her she looks like a witch making her brew.

She laughs. "If I am, you are, too, right?" She snorts a bit when she laughs. Her nose stretches flatly over her face. I place the rest of the dumplings inside for steaming. After they have all cooked, we take one out, and it is perfect. Its surface is shiny with no blemishes. It smells fresh and moist. I hold it up for her to look at.

"Wow, *anak*, how nice," she says. "You did it." There is a delight in her eyes, something I feel good about seeing. The idea suddenly comes to me that a dumpling this perfect should be shared, or at least shown off.

"I will bring it for lunch tomorrow," I tell her.

"Yes," she says, nodding, happy I am happy.

I wait all day for lunch. In the cafeteria, the long rectangular tables are covered with Ziploc bags and drink boxes. At first, the rustling never seems to stop. But patiently I wait for the perfect moment to unleash my special treat . . . my baby . . . my Sio Pao!

"What's that?" The boy sitting across from me is the first person to notice. His red hair shoots out from the back of his head like a fan.

"It's Sio Pao," I say proudly. "I made it myself." The white dumpling is tightly wrapped in cellophane to display its complete roundness.

"Is it like a Hostess snowball?" another boy asks. "You know, with coconut and stuff."

"No, it's filled with meat and egg."

"Eeeewwwww," small voices cry in unison.

"Where'd you get it?" the redhead asks.

"I told you I made it."

The girl next to me leans over and sniffs. "It smells weird," she says.

A singular, piercing voice calls out, "It's chink food!"

It is silent for a moment. Then, slowly, a chorus of giggles begin. Little ones that ring on and on. I feel the heat under my skin slowly climb up my face. My hands and armpits feel tingly and wet.

"Mike, that's not nice," my best friend's voice cuts through the laughter. I can only focus on her wide green eyes and the tiny freckles sprinkled over her nose. She tries to save me, but it doesn't help. I feel naked, or like I've peed myself and I stink.

I eat my Sio Pao in silence and quickly, not finishing the entire dumpling. The rest of the afternoon is endless.

When I get home, my mother is in the kitchen. Her hair is pulled back showing the gray in her roots. "Well, *anak*, how was your day?" She extends her hand to touch my hair, but I swerve to avoid her.

"Fine," I say, and walk past her to the living room.

"What we make tonight, huh?" she asks, smiling. Her voice is soft and comforting, but all I hear is her accent, her broken sentences, her unfinished words.

"Nothing," I say.

"*Anak*, what wrong?"

"Nothing," I snap back, "I don't want any of your chink food. I don't want anything." My voice is unbelievably loud, louder than I mean it to be. It vibrates against the hallway walls and in my ears. "Why can't you cook normal food?"

And with that, I have the strength to look into her face. The skin between her eyebrows is wrinkled; she's trying to understand. Her small eyes are open, glassy and unclear. It would be easy to look away now, but I try to stand my ground, to stay strong, to keep looking at her.

"Why, *anak*?" It's all she can say. She searches my face for some sign. But I don't want to talk about it.

"Forget it." I turn around, defiantly. Walking away, I leave her standing there stunned and alone.

Upstairs in my room, silence crawls around me. The bed feels larger than I remember, even though I'm sure I've grown an inch taller this year. I think she'll probably come and save me. I think if I wait long enough she'll come up here with something to eat or she'll persuade me down to dinner. I wait forever. Eventually, I fall asleep.

The windows are dark when I wake. My room has grown cooler, and other than that, the only thing I can feel is hunger.

Downstairs, dinner has been eaten without me. In the living room, my mother does not turn away from the TV show she is watching. She does not stir at my arrival. From behind, I stare into her black curtain of hair. If I stare long enough, she'll feel me there. Maybe she didn't hear me come in. I clear my throat, and cough pathetically. But she never turns around.

There are Japanese eggplants on the kitchen table, rice and fish. My older brother is the only one left finishing his plate. "Mom says if you don't want to eat what we eat, then you can get food somewhere else," he says, with no hint of sympathy.

I go outside, and listen to the sounds of our street. There are lightning bugs dotting the air in front of the house. They are green and sparkling. I think maybe I can stay out here and look at them forever, but then I remember that they'll be gone in a week.

Out of the Garden

Jocelyn Bartkevicius

1

My grandmother crouches in the garden, dress flecked with mud and grass stains, pulling weeds and telling stories. I am seven and frightened; I can't always decipher her accent and my father has disappeared. "Tomatoes," she says, and she means "tomatoes." She looks up toward the house. "Where father go?" she says, meaning "Where did your father go?" I am alone with her. "What?" I am always asking, "What?"

Suddenly she is talking of soldiers, waves of armies. "Farm in Europe," she says, meaning Eastern Europe, Lithuania, her uncle's farm. "Prussians then Russians," she says, "stomp through fields, take food, take animals, take garden." I picture men in green fatigues marching over hills—scenes from the World War II movies my stepfather watches on TV. "Then must make bread," my grandmother says, "put in jar."

She is on her knees now in the straw-covered row between the tomato plants, intent on her weeding. The plants rise up to my waist. I snap a small shoot, lift it to my nose, and smell. Pungent, like the tomatoes picked fresh from her garden, but with bitter undertones. I drop the shoot so she won't see that I've broken a plant, and raise my fingers to my nose to catch the lingering fragrance.

"In night," my grandmother says, "run through fields to forest, bury jar in bushes." I picture the forest. It is dark, primeval, like the forests in the illustrated *Grimm's Fairy Tales* my mother reads to me at night. "Then cook in dark," she says. She stands up and wipes her hands on her apron. She wears a dress, always a dress, small floral print this time, tiny pink flowers against a cream background. "Hard to cook in dark," she says, "but soldiers don't see smoke." I move closer to her, the way I edge over to my mother when she is reading, when Puss in Boots almost gets caught, when the giant spies Jack's beanstalk. My grandmother looks at me hard. She lifts her glasses, closes her eyes, pinches and rubs the bridge of her nose. We are nearly eye-to-eye, for she is stooped from years of gardening, and even at full height she is barely five feet tall. She sighs. "But you are an American," she says, "you don't understand." Her words stun me. Silently, she returns to her weeding.

But I do understand, I think, following along so closely when she tells me stories, imagining myself there in the woods, hiding from soldiers. And because of her stories, I frown every time we drive past the intersection where men from Eastern Europe have parked a flatbed truck full of mock gravestones, one etched with the name "Lithuania." But now I stand accused of being an outsider to all that pain. And I had thought that she was the stranger. People who know—my father, my mother, my other grandmother—call her an immigrant, alien, even peasant. Although they speak in praise of her hard work, stamina, and all that she has endured, it's clear that my grandmother is the one who doesn't belong.

I'm confused. In my first grade classroom I rise each morning to say "The Pledge of Allegiance" and sing "The Star Spangled Banner" with my classmates. Each spring, I go to the Memorial Day parade and watch marching bands, row after row of battered veterans from World War II, all the while anticipating the baton twirlers and the chance to buy a bright balloon, happy for shorts and the arrival of spring. One minute, being an American means being part of a crowd. The next, it means being a stranger, cut off from my grandmother's stories, thrown out of the garden.

Dusk now, and we move inside. My father and grandfather sit at the round kitchen table. The silver rim, the gray and white Formica are scrubbed clean with homemade soap. My grandfather nods, rises silently, and leaves the room. My grandmother makes tea, pours me some milk, and then we sit in awkward silence with my father. "Tell her how we came to America," my father says. Either he hates the silence or knows I like the stories.

My grandmother's hands lie quiet on the table. She looks past me, but she tells it again, the story I have heard in bits and pieces. In it, my grandmother is the young woman in the picture over her couch, dark hair pulled back, mouth pressed in a firm, grim line, holding two frightened children one cold January in 1930, first crossing borders in a train, then descending into a lower berth of the *S.S. George Washington*. Storms brew on the Atlantic, and she heads into the future dizzy, sick, and tied to the bed in that rocking ship. She farms out the daughter to other emigrants and ties her son to the next bed. My father crosses the Atlantic bound and abandoned, seeing his mother but unable to reach her. As for my grandmother, any thoughts she has—when she's not too sick to think—would light upon the husband waiting across the Atlantic, a man she hasn't seen for three years. The ocean rises and falls, the boat pitches, she spins and spins; this is the only passage her husband can afford after three years in a New England rivet factory. She is still Elena Sophia Bartoska Bartkeciene—a name that bespeaks her past—lying between lives in the hold of the ship. She tosses and turns in that wretched cocoon, about to emerge on the far shore as

Helen Bartkevicius—a name that means nothing, a mere replica of her husband's. She is so shaken by the waves and the stench that, poised between a small familiar village in Lithuania and a small industrial city in Connecticut, her only desire is death.

But the ocean liner docks at last. Dry land calms her stomach, restores her practical mind. When my grandfather brings her to Railroad Avenue in Milford, Connecticut, a neighborhood where other women speak Lithuanian and Polish, she quickly learns the ways of her new soil: how much lime to sprinkle from her stocking to keep insects off young plants, how newspaper can substitute for straw in garden rows, what mushrooms grow down behind the railroad tracks near the stream that runs through the woods. Soon, she can go out into a field and come back with dinner. She picks through poisonous mushrooms and fills her apron with edible varieties. She grows potatoes for pancakes. She grows horseradish to grate and mix with vinegar, and serves it with pan-fried eels bargained for at the dock. She scoops seeds out of fresh tomatoes, boils the pulp into juice, and carefully dries the seeds on the windowsill for next year's garden.

She makes soap from fat, pan drippings, and lye. She feeds her family all year on a backyard garden, a few chickens scratching between rows of vegetables, a couple of trips to the small market and docks.

For years she carries on just so. And then World War II breaks out. While the neighbor women do laundry in wringer washers and stir up Betty Crocker cake mix, my grandmother cans bread and runs out into the night to bury it beneath the trees.

We move to her scratchy gray living room couch, and I open the photo album. Faded, gap-toothed people stand before unpainted weather-worn buildings, hungry-looking hounds beside them. An old woman poses with her arm around a gravestone. A handsome young man sits rigidly in a military uniform. "Petras, brother," my grandmother says, noticing my interest in the picture. "Die in war." I ask her to tell me the story, but she tells another: "We sleep in field," she says, "by horses, legs tied, hobbled. They walk, we wake, bring back." Her clipped words and sentences never change. I forget that in the garden she called me an American who would not understand. *She* becomes the stranger, and I sit at the kitchen table saying, "What? What?"

2

In the deepening dusk, in the forest, my father drives too fast down narrow Transylvania Road, winding along the edge of a cliff. It is summer, 1967, and my father is going back to the land and taking me with him.

For an hour, we followed a river the color of his Marine fatigues, heading north out of industrial southern Connecticut. The river's wretched smell permeated the closed-up car. "Tire factories," my father said. I looked outside and saw a thick, oily layer of green along the river, smokestacks in the distance. Soon we left the highway and followed a narrow, winding road west, away from the river, away from the smell. Factories and strip malls tapered off, and we raced past farmhouses and open fields. Now, I look down on treetops as he speeds toward some farm up for sale, talking about living far away from the factory, about putting money to work. At the bottom of a long hill surrounded by tall grass and bushes, he slows down. "The pond must be in there," he says, consulting a hand-drawn map. At the hairpin curve he realizes we've passed the overgrown driveway and backs up fast, transmission whining. He turns in; plants and rocks scrape the floorboards.

We wade through waist-high grass between a bramble of berries and a crumbling stone foundation. "The house burned down," he says. We walk between a dull brown barn and sheds barely visible in the fading light. Bats and swallows swoop in and out of a gaping hole in the top of the barn. I reach for my father's hand. It's spring and crickets chirp, much louder than in Milford. A higher chorusing joins them as we walk, a sound I don't recognize, for the frogs that must once have inhabited the marsh behind my mother's house have been gone for as long as I can remember. My father lets go of my hand to open the barn door. He struggles against the rusty horseshoe-and-wheel contraption until the door slides open. Musty damp smell, the sweet redolence of decay. He steps tentatively into complete darkness, then immediately withdraws. I hear a noise down the hill near where the pond should be: something walking, parting grass. My father walks toward it, hushing me. The remaining sunlight fades to nothing. He holds a flashlight but won't turn it on.

I take his hand again. Tall grass clings to my pants, scratches my naked arms. Stars become visible in a sky I've never seen before. At home, lights come on at dusk—streetlights, house lights, headlights, factory lights, landing lights on low planes descending to the airport across the marsh. But here, in the deep dark of the country, as we walk down the hill toward the pond, I can't see my father even though our hands are touching. I can't tell if my eyes are open or shut.

My father buys that hundred-acre farm and lives there for the rest of my childhood, in a small log cabin built from native hand-hewn logs. He trades in his gold Mustang for a sky blue Chevy pickup and makes a red and white label for the dashboard: Transylvania Farm. "'Transylvania' means 'through the forest,'" he tells me, "'trans' is through, 'sylvania' is like 'sylvan'—forest." But to me, Transylvania means Bella Lugosi, blood-sucking bats, the dark mysteries of Eastern Europe.

At the farm, my father becomes the Marlboro cowboy with an Eastern European twist; he follows a '60s hippie impulse with the flourish of an ex-Marine. He buys cowboy hats and boots for both of us at Dan's Western Supply Company. He scares off copperheads to draw water from a stone well, and when I ask for the bathroom—until he gets the electricity connected and the water pump going—he points to the old oak behind the cabin. He buys a miniature John Deere tractor with a sickle bar and cuts wild grass around the barns and cabin. He buys two hard-mouthed, half-wild, former rental horses from a Connecticut cowboy with a Western drawl. He buys a machete, and I walk behind him picking up the young trees, weeds, tall grass, and bushes he hacks down to clear trails to the pond and through his woods. He buys lumber for split-rail fences and spends a weekend wearing dirty Marine pants and a sweat-drenched undershirt, slamming the posthole digger into the earth. Over and over, around the barns, down the hill to the stone wall at the pond. He measures carefully, then digs, measures then digs, before setting pine posts into the holes. I help him guide the long rails into post notches. At the end of each day, our blistered hands smell of pine.

He gets a cattle farmer with a real tractor to cut and bale hay and takes a quarter of the yield. Prickly hay pierces my skin, and sweat stings the tiny punctures as we stack forty-pound bales into the back of the truck. I ride on top, higher than the pickup's cab, swaying over uneven ground as my father drives to the barn. Afterwards, we jump into a river a few miles down the road, climb the banks to soap ourselves, and jump back in again. We pick blackberries for breakfast and eat them on the cabin's back porch, horses sniffing us through the screen. I run around barefooted with country neighbors who teach me to climb a rope swing and tell ghost stories in their dark shed. I learn to ride horses and to race them. We don't hobble the horses or sleep in the fields beside them, but we do tend them, filling buckets with grain, using long, slender pneumatic pumps to coat their bodies with insecticide. Horseflies subside, but botflies fat as hummingbirds persist, laying yellow eggs in the horses' fetlocks. I swat the flies and comb and pick at the tiny eggs. From the tall roan's back, I nearly swat a hummingbird as we ride through high lilies. My father shoots woodchucks to keep the horses from stepping in their holes. To protect the hay from droppings, he teaches me to shoot bats with a BB gun. I learn to love animals and to kill them. I learn to love the wild woods and to hack it down.

3

My grandparents' house becomes increasingly remote. Our time is filled with long drives out of Milford, the work the farm demands, and rural adventures (riding horses through the woods, searching for fossils, scouting out animals, like the muskrat swimming beneath the ice of the frozen pond, the woodchuck in the oak tree, the bobcat in the field). But when we make time for a visit, I watch my grandmother read through a stack of tissuey letters with foreign stamps, incomprehensible words. I'm mystified by the newspapers and conversations in that strange other language that my father knows too—though he responds in English. I ask for lessons and they teach me a greeting: what sounds like "Kapetowanis" *How are you*. And the appropriate answer, something like "Garrday"—*Fine*. Everything is fine, and they keep the rest to themselves.

Though I don't know the language, I practice the accent, and when my mother overhears the imitation, she urges me to perform for her. "No," I say shyly. "Come on," she says. And so I parody my grandmother's accent and her work ethic too, the way she objects to my small frame (a legacy of my mother's family). "Too teen," I say, instead of "too thin." When my mother laughs, I'm inspired to exaggerate her praise for my bulkier cousins: "Beek, strrronk like bool. Vwerrrk many hours in fielt."

Though they seldom turn to such mocking, even my grandmother's own children, intent on being Americans, shun her ways. They wear store-bought clothes with a vengeance, and refuse to plant gardens, cook potato pancakes, make homemade kielbasa, or bake cookies without sugar. They eat steak and potatoes with salad. "Ma!" they say, and roll their eyes because she's once again saved every scrap of fat trimmings for her homemade soap. They urge her to get a private phone instead of a party line, to get a hot water heater, to buy prepared food at the supermarket, to live an easier life.

Three names on a plaque near my grandparents' doorbell: Bartkevicius, Bartkewicz, Barker. "Barker is for convenience," my father says. "Use it to make reservations, drop off your film, talk to people you don't really know." Bartkewicz is harder to explain. With a serious expression he tells me a story I can't really follow, all borders, politics, betrayals, and allegiances. I ask him to teach me Lithuanian—he went to kindergarten with a neighbor's note pinned to his shirt: *I do not speak English*. But now, while he can understand his parents, he has lost his tongue for it. "Kapetowanis," he says. "Garrday." I beg for more, and he teaches me a little Polish rhyme about a boy who tells his mother about droppings in a chicken coop.

At school, kids tell Polack jokes, and my Polish schoolmates blush silently. I force a smile and worry. I know that Poland borders Lithuania, that of the three names under my grandparents' doorbell, one is Polish. But no one from school goes to my grandparents' house. And I take comfort in my schoolmates' ignorance of geography. "What kind of name is that?" they ask occasionally. "Lithuanian," I answer, and watch them shrug.

All that summer, the Summer of Love, I move between two places: my mother's house in Milford (and the nightclub she helps my stepfather run) and the woods of Transylvania, a place lit by stars, moon, and fireplace or not lit at all, a magical darkness once frightening but now increasingly familiar. At Transylvania Farm, I leave behind what seems to me the essence of Milford: poisoned beaches, factory smoke, trucks, cars, trains, planes. I revel in the difference, playing Joni Mitchell and Neil Young albums, all about getting ourselves back to the garden and country girls. I wear patched jeans and ride into the forest on horseback or race the paint horse through the pasture at night.

On long walks through the woods, my father and I try to name what we see. Silver and white birch. Pine. Frogs and toads. Deer in the woods and fields. Raspberry bushes along the old foundation. Horse chestnuts, inedible. Apples, full of worms. Blackberries, thick and tart, on thorny bushes along the edge of the field. Field mouse in the grain bucket. Copperhead in the well. Black snake sunning itself on the stone wall. Chipmunk disappearing into loose piles of fieldstone. Woodchuck in the field, bat in the barn, both doomed to be shot. Barn swallows sweeping the evening sky.

The next autumn, my grandfather dies in the hospital elevator on the way to have his chest pains examined. I am in a church play that day, and I sense my father's uneasiness, but he waits until the play ends to tell me what's wrong. The funeral is stiff and awkward, everyone sitting quietly in black. Afterwards, I follow my grandmother out to her garden. I want something, but don't know what it is. When she moves around to the side of the house to trim the bushes and trees, I thrust myself into a spectacular yellow rosebush. My eyes fill with yellow and I can almost feel the flowers' roundness. She coaxes me out, and I let her soak the infected foot I've refused to let anyone else touch. I watch quietly as she mixes powders and herbs in a bucket. She rolls a thick needle over the infected bulb of pus, then pierces and drains it. She hands me a little silver piece, a New York subway token from years past. I don't ask what place it holds in her memory, but accept it as some kind of promise, a gift whose value I will some-day understand.

When the sun sets we sit on her front porch, gently rocking together in her green metal glider, watching the cars race by and the street lamps light up, listening to ambulances rush past.

4

In Milford, I stare out the window of my mother's car and dream that underneath beer cans and broken bottles lies a clean white beach, that underneath concrete, asphalt, and block buildings is a vast farm with fragrant black soil. "What do you do at the farm on a Saturday night," my mother and stepfather tease, "throw rocks in the river?" I laugh, but their comment stings. I know how they love their nightclub, how they believe that "civilization"—lights, cocktails, and music—means excitement, while "wilderness" means animals and boredom. The closest they get to nature is driving the Buick to the coal dock on the Housatonic River and parking between the tall cement towers that elevate Interstate 95 and the railroad tracks. Together, we sit on the hood watching power boats and barges. Or we go clamming and stand waist deep in salt water where the sun sets behind POISON signs posted along the shore. When they tease me about the farm, I feel a torn loyalty to my father's place. I miss high school dances and parties when I go to the farm. I miss Saturday nights dressing up to work at the nightclub—live jazz, jokes, dancing, dazzling lights, money to make and people to watch.

Saturday night at Transylvania Farm we read and sit by the fire. In the morning, we ride the horses for miles. We ride into town for ice cream, and on the way back take the horses swimming in the river.

Just after Woodstock, even my father's small town crackles with excitement. The oldest neighbor kids have gone to Woodstock and returned with long hair, leather pouches of pot, and stories the rest of us hang on. Even my father is intrigued, and he considers a proposal from local concert producers to run a similar event on his farm. The small town doesn't want to be a second Woodstock, and it suits my rebellious streak to see our name in the local newspaper.

My father revels in the stir. He plans out the concert; he wants to use a local motorcycle gang as bouncers. We talk it over on horseback, returning from the river. About three miles from the farm, we cross a neighbor's land. The owner comes out, pretends to admire the horses, and gets right to the gossip. "Listen Mr. Barker," he says. "Have you heard about that Polack down the road who wants to run a rock concert?" (These more distant neighbors have never heard our real last name.) My father pauses—for effect, perhaps, or to wrestle with his conscience. "I'm that Polack down the road," he says, turns his appaloosa, and rides away. I smile, half meek, half bold, and turn the roan and follow: Hopalong Bartkevicius and his little sidekick riding off into the sunset.

When our concert doesn't come off—too much opposition, expensive insurance—we distract ourselves by finally planting a garden. My father digs up hard soil with a long spade, and I dig compost from the bottom of the horse manure pile. We plant carrots, onions, and tomatoes. When the tiny green plants appear between rows of hay, instead of spraying insecticide, we shake lime from a stocking as my grandmother does. I carry my organic carrots to school and crunch them theatrically in the lunchroom while the cheerleaders eat tuna sandwiches and make comments about "that girl with the carrots." When it's cold I wear a fringed leather Western jacket. When it's milder I wear my father's Marine jacket with a peace sign sewn on. Transylvania Farm becomes the vehicle for my adolescent rebellion against my Republican hometown. I tell stories of my father and his log cabin, of our brush with rock-concert celebrity. We could have been the second Yasgur's farm.

In my back-to-the-land fervor, I ask my reticent, elegant mother if she breast-fed my half-sister and me. She gasps and looks offended. "That's for animals," she says. Stung, I retreat with the sketchbook I've kept since childhood, and look over old portraits of my mother, sketches of cartoon characters, and a series of drawings of the yard. A birch tree sketch brings to mind a similarly disappointing exchange with my mother. Halfway done with the drawing, I'd noticed wires running from the utility pole through the tree and to our house. I asked her if she would draw the wires. "Of course I would," she'd answered, "they're there." Suddenly my decision was clear. I would not draw them. "You're a Romantic," she'd said, as if it were something bad.

5

In Milford Center, in the fall of 1973, I'm hanging out downtown with my best friend, Joan, talking about high school graduation, wearing faded, patched dungarees and army jackets. In school we've just chosen slogans for our yearbook pictures. Mine is from *Easy Rider:* "Like a true nature's child, we were born to be wild." Stripped of the raucous music and vision of motorcycles racing down the street, it loses much of its appeal; roaring rebellion is reduced to a sentimental rhymed couplet. But I haven't been able to think of anything else. I like the incongruity—flower child with the flourish of a biker gang member—which I don't recognize as a legacy of my father. I like how it will irritate the cheerleaders I'm so bent on opposing.

Suddenly, just ahead, my grandmother appears—the first time I've seen her away from her house or yard. She is tiny, frail, formal, and foreign, a little old woman in a dull cloth overcoat and kerchief tied babushka style. "Grandma," I say. She stops, turns, and looks up at me. Jeans and tie-dye dresses hang in the shop windows behind her. Cars race by. Joan chuckles softly. My grandmother and I stare at each other as if we were strangers, and trade forgettable pleasantries.

As she walks toward home, and Joan and I head the other way, I turn and look at her over my shoulder. She has a short stride, a slight waddle. I watch her disappear. "That was your *grandmother*?" Joan asks.

In all the years my father owns the farm, my grandmother never comes to visit. She likes home and the circle around it: the market, a friend's house, church. She never learns to drive. Nor do I ever see her in a car, although I know she gets rides from the Polish neighbor who, like her, prays daily at St. Mary's Catholic Church several miles away. Long after her neighborhood has turned commercial, she maintains the house she and her husband bought a few years after her arrival. While long-time neighbors sell to doctors—Milford Hospital is just a block away—my grandmother hangs on to home and walks to the Grand Union, to Cumberland Farms, to the post office, to Grants Department Store. As office buildings rise up around it, her small brown house looks like a relic of the 1930s, increasingly frail and diminished.

Before I leave for college, my father and I sit in her spotless kitchen, and I look down at the burnt orange linoleum floor everyone says you could eat from. She serves her specialty: thick, nearly sugarless cookies, something between sweet biscuit and dry cookie. She busies herself making tea, moving from the table to the old-fashioned, deep white sink to refrigerator, to stove. "Tell me about Lithuania," I say. She repeats the familiar stories: sleeping beside the hobbled horses; putting bread in jars, crossing the Atlantic. But she is in a good mood, mischievous. She rummages through her pantry, finds a Mason jar she's saved since World War II and sets it on the kitchen table. I look at the bread inside—not the thick, homemade bread I've imagined, but thin slices of store-bought bread, Wonder Bread, perhaps. "Yes," she says, "I make when war start, like in Europe. I think same. Neighbors laugh. I stop." She laughs and turns the jar. The bread is pure and white, not a trace of mold.

After a silence, she says, "Story about father." He glances up from his newspaper. "Second baby," she says, nodding her chin at him. "Cry, never stop. Old woman with a stick walk from village to village, my baby cry and cry, my husband work in America to send money and she walk and walk many days to farm. Old woman says, 'you miss husband.'" *Hwahsbund*, my grandmother pronounces it. She pauses and looks at her hands. "Old woman says, 'Miss husband, sadness goes into milk. Baby feeds at breast, sadness goes into him. Do not feed from breast when miss husband.'" My father blushes and leaves the room.

She shakes her head. "Another one," she says, and speaks of a distant moment held in memory: A young Prussian soldier rides his horse up to her gate. "I am thirsty," he says, in her language. Young, unmarried, alone that day near the house, she dips into the well to get him a drink. Even though he might come back in the night to pillage and kill, she brings him a pitcher of water. She stands at the gate as he drinks, mounts his horse, and rides away.

More memories rise up; I can tell from her hands, moving slightly on the table. Her eyes shift, she lifts her glasses, strokes the bridge of her nose. The stories lie behind there, just beyond reach. When I ask, she waves her hand, waves me out of her past. Her hands, spotted and old, strong and callused, have ceased tending the garden out back, ceased canning anything, making kielbasa or other fresh foods. The cookies are the last of the old ways, and soon they will stop, too. In years to come, when my grandmother starts to speak of dying and my father and I remind her that her own mother lived to be 104, she shakes her head. "That was Europe," she says, "Difference, all difference."

And her illnesses come on like a prophesy.

6

In a prefab log cabin, in the winter of 1990, I sit across from my grandmother in the mild terror that has gripped me since childhood whenever I'm left alone with her. It has always been the same: my father and I arrive for a visit; he leaves the room; I am alone with her accent and small voice, afraid the words will die between us.

"Did he brinck machine?" she asks.

"What?" I say.

She has moved, and we sit in her special day room at the side of my cousin Donna's new house. Donna is abundance, a big woman, a Madonna in the making, pregnant with her third child, in the kitchen baking Christmas cookies. With the wide bones and round face of my grandmother's early pictures, my cousin looks Lithuanian. My grandmother sits upright on the scratchy gray couch that stung my legs when I was a little girl. Beside it, in the old house, was a polished cherry end table with a green glass ashtray rimmed in silver. But now no one smokes anymore, not in houses, anyway, and there is nothing beside the couch.

Above her hangs a wedding portrait: she and her new husband sitting for a photographer in Lithuania. Stern-faced, they do not touch. The photographer has added peach to cheeks and blue to eyes. My grandparents look bright and ruddy against the steel-gray background that obliterates all sense of place. But even in art they are not happy. And in the photographs in her album, bound by black-cornered triangles to thick, yellowing pages, they are still not happy. In the portrait, as in the snapshots, my grandmother stands upright, stiff, to her full five feet. She is young, has not yet left her home-grown foods, has not rocked and pitched her way across the Atlantic, has not tasted pesticides and herbicides, has not eaten white bread. Now, at ninety-three, when she pushes herself up from the couch, her spine, though still straight, tilts forward fast. Her torso and head fall, and her chest is parallel to the floor unless she catches onto something. She sits back on the couch. Her legs do not reach the floor.

"Did he brinck machine?" she asks again.

"The machine?" I ask. I can decipher more sentences than I could as a child, but now she asks unanswerable questions.

"Father say he get machine so I walk again by myself," she says. I try to imagine what she could mean.

"He did?" I ask.

"Yes, for Christmas." She rolls the *r* softly. She blushes.

"I don't know," I say. "Let's ask him when he comes in." It doesn't sound like she means a walker or even a wheelchair, but I'm afraid to ask, and she's afraid to ask him. I wonder if she is afraid of *him* or of disappointment. Is there some part of her that no longer trusts her own memory? She sits up straight, back propped against the chair. Her glasses are thick; I can't read her eyes, or see them, even. I remember, or imagine, them as blue.

She holds out a Whitman's Sampler because this is America and because, anyway, she can no longer stand up in the kitchen to make her confections. "And you," she says. I think the words are part of the offer, but even after I take one and bite into the dark chocolate, she continues. "And you, you want my bread."

"Your bread?"

"Yes," she says, "you need for stories."

I figure she means the bread from World War II, that one jar she's saved. I don't know if it's an offer or an accusation. But my father comes back in, and we can work on the machine. "Grandma wants to know if you've brought a machine to help her walk," I say. The words are ridiculous once he's in the room. Of course there is no machine. So I pass the blame over to her, make it something between the two of them. "She said you'd promised to bring something."

"No Ma, you dreamed it," he says. "There's no such machine." With her severe osteoporosis, she wants to become a cyborg, a woman with a brand-new back. It should be possible here, in the industrial belt of the Northeast. My father works at the aircraft plant, building engines for military planes. Why should a small portion of a back be any more complicated? But my father settles into his usual strategy with her. Where I evade, he refuses. There is no such thing; you imagined, you dreamed, I've heard him say, crushing her belief, whether in magic (Lithuania) or technology (America). She has a look of disappointed diffidence. Glancing down, child-like, she laughs. "Oh," she says, "dream," with her nicely rolled *r*.

It's not magic she wants, just what was once hers: straight posture, a smooth walk. "I can get you a walker, Ma," he says. "Walker?" she looks hopeful. "You know," he says, "a metal stand you hold yourself up with." She shakes her head. "No, no, no," she says, "for old people."

By the time my grandmother dies, my father has sold Transylvania Farm. High tension wires were slated to run through it. And anyway it was the season—as The Byrds sang, *turn turn turn*—the end of the '70s, the beginning of the '80s, the end of the garden, the beginning of investment property and zero-lot lines.

The horses are gone, our garden dies out, and the cabin stands empty. The barns begin to fall apart, and the grass grows tall again. In Milford, my grandmother's house is gutted by a doctor who builds an office and turns her long back yard into an asphalt parking lot. The downtown council considers turning the town green into a parking lot, too. And at the beach nearby, houses are torn down to erect condominium complexes, and POISON signs line the shore.

Just before my grandmother died, when I asked to see her photo album again, she couldn't find it. Though my cousin says she has never seen it, some of the old photos hang on her walls, valued, it seems, for their sepia color: valued like the Americana she buys at antique stores—old signs, baskets, photographs of people she's never met—things my grandmother called "junks" and spent a lifetime getting rid of. For a while, I imagine that because what I've wanted from my grandmother is stories, my notion of value is somehow superior. But I catch myself romanticizing. In an effort to move closer to the Catholicism that was so much a part of my grandmother's everyday life (but that I was not raised in), I buy a rosary in an antique shop on the premise that it belonged to *somebody's* grandmother. I buy a guidebook on Lithuania, which claims that of all Europeans, Lithuanians held on most tenaciously to a "pagan past," a magical notion of place. It tells the story of Vilnius, a capital founded and named for a dream of a wolf. When I buy the book, I have recently dreamed of a wolf myself, and I imagine it is a prophesy—a magical connection with a land I have never seen.

Over her lifetime, in addition to her stories, my grandmother gave me a plastic biscuit cutter, an old New York subway token, two chiffon scarves, and, in a gesture I never completely understood, when I married, some of her clothes—skirts and sweaters that, given the difference in our sizes, could only have been symbolic of some sad divestment. The meaning of these gifts, like the meaning of her stories, lies somewhere just out of reach.

7

In the Midwest, in the fall of 1982, I learn to backpack and canoe, portage and hike, sleep under the open sky. In the forest, on a remote and narrow trail, I realize that I am a stranger in this world. To compensate, I carry small guidebooks in my increasingly heavy pack: guides to North American trees, wildflowers, mushrooms, animal tracks, birds, mammals, weather, the night sky.

A few years later, on Isle Royale, an "international biosphere" and wilderness area, I sit on a boulder sketching a wildflower from a guidebook. The day before, in a storm, I crossed Lake Superior by ferry, and while the other hikers huddled in the cabin's warmth, I stood alone on the deck in the rain, leaning over the rail to be sick. As the waves rocked the small boat, I became increasingly dizzy and disoriented, and leaned over the side until the spray of the waves hit my face. Rain poured down on my body. I thought of my grandmother on her passage across the Atlantic, and knew for the first time what it means to be so nauseated that you begin to dream of death.

Dry land calmed my stomach, and now ten miles into the island, I am alone. My friends and I hike separately, at our own paces, meeting each evening at designated sites to set up tents and cook. For miles I walk alone, stopping frequently to observe and sketch. I page through my guidebooks and struggle to identify the unfamiliar trees, mushrooms, flowers, and birds. I finish sketching an eastern columbine, pluck a small sample to put between the pages where it appears in the guidebook, put everything in my pack, turn to go, and wonder which direction I've been headed. Even with a compass and a stack of books I am lost in this world.

I hear loons chorusing on an interior lake. At a turn in the trail, I surprise a fox, who immediately jumps into the air like a cat, tries to stare me down, then turns to run. A pair of pileated woodpeckers lands on the tree above me (I recognize them by their call, like Woody Woodpecker's laugh). At dusk, I step out of the tent and walk into the path of a circling bat whose wings lightly brush my ear. Moose stomp around our campsite but run off when they see our shadowy shapes. In the middle of the night we hear a howling that could be loon or wolf. Gray wolves are present, but remain hidden. In the morning, a snowshoe hare darts out before me on the path. I hike past berry bushes that resemble the blackberries on my father's farm. I am weary of the dried fruit I carry, but even with my books, I can't identify the berries with certainty. And so I pass them by. I kneel before a bright orange mushroom, but don't dare even to touch it.

After a week of hiking, we return to the edge of Lake Superior, near the ferry pickup. That night, a ranger leads us to the edge of a clearing, and we stare into the darkening forest at a woodcock. The bird flies straight into the sky and flutters back down in swooping circles, emitting a haunting call. The ranger talks softly as we wait for the woodcock's next flight. "If you ever get lost in the wilderness," he says, "remember that nearly every part of the pine tree is edible." The woodcock flies again, and the ranger is silent. But after a while, he begins pointing out stars and constellations, rattling off Latin names I find vaguely familiar. After another flight of the woodcock, the ranger starts in with new stories and names, drawing lines between different stars, attributing this new cosmology to several Indian tribes. I confess that Orion is the only constellation I can recognize, having seen it on a grade school trip to a planetarium. "Why don't you make up your own?" he says. "Why accept the sky of the ancient Greeks or Romans or even American Indians? Draw your own lines," he says. "Make up your own stories."

Later that night, in my sleeping bag, I think of my grandmother. I envy her ease in the forest. Yet I must remember how that ease came from violence; being tied to the land meant being forced out of your house, beaten back into the forest, desperate for survival. I look up at the night sky. There are no lights for hundreds of miles, and the sky is darker and filled with even more stars than at Transylvania Farm. I locate Orion. But the rest of the sky is an unknown sprinkling of planets and stars. I am lost in it. I can study scientific guidebooks or even stories of the night sky handed down by one or more cultures. Or I can invent a fictional cosmology of my own. But the fact remains: I can negotiate a grocery store, but not a forest.

In the morning, we make breakfast on a portable Coleman stove. We light fuel with a lighter, boil water, and mix in instant oatmeal with raisins. Though we've dipped into the lake for water, we have carried in packaged food. As I eat from a metal bowl, I feel a tug on the back of my shirt. I turn, expecting to see one of my friends. Instead, a red squirrel stands on the rock I am leaning against, begging for scraps. In the island's interior, where few hikers venture, wildlife fled when they heard us coming, but here along the shore, closer to civilization, even the animals aren't quite wild. Like the red fox that stood in the near distance as we cooked the night before, this squirrel would rather share our processed food than scavenge on his own.

I stand up, turn my back to the lake, and look out into the forest. I am hungry, but I don't know what I hunger for. Before me is a forest floor with medallions of mushrooms, but I don't know which ones I can eat.

Out There

Jo Ann Beard

It isn't even eight A.M. and I'm hot. My rear end is welded to the seat just like it was yesterday. I'm fifty miles from the motel and about a thousand and a half from home, in a little white Mazda with 140,000 miles on it and no rust. I'm all alone in Alabama, with only a cooler and a tape deck for company. It's already in the high 80s. Yesterday, coming up from the keys through Florida, I had a day-long anxiety attack that I decided last night was really heat prostration. I was a cinder with a brain; I was actually whimpering. I kept thinking I saw alligators at the edge of the highway.

There were about four hundred exploded armadillos, too, but I got used to them. They were real, and real dead. The alligators weren't real or dead, but they may have been after me. I'm running away from running away from home.

I bolted four weeks ago, leaving my husband to tend the dogs and tool around town on his bicycle. He doesn't love me anymore, it's both trite and true. He does love himself, though. He's begun wearing cologne and staring into the mirror for long minutes, trying out smiles. He's become a politician. After thirteen years he came to realize that the more successful he got, the less he loved me. That's how he put it, late one night. He won that screaming match. He said, gently and sadly, "I feel sort of embarrassed of you."

I said, "Of what? The way I look? The way I act?"

And he said, softly, "Everything, sort of."

And it was true. Well, I decided to take a trip to Florida. I sat on my haunches in Key West for four weeks, writing and seething and striking up conversations with strangers. I had my thirty-fifth birthday there, weeping into a basket of shrimp. I drank beer and had long involved dreams about cigarettes, I wrote nearly fifty pages on my novel. It's in my trunk at this very moment, dead and decomposing. Boy, do I need a cup of coffee.

There's not much happening this early in the morning. The highway looks interminable again. So far, no alligators. I have a box of seashells in my back seat and I reach back and get a fluted one, pale gray with a pearly interior, to put on the dashboard. I can do everything while I'm driving. At the end of this trip I will have driven 3,999 miles all alone, me and the windshield, me and the radio, me and the creepy alligators. Don't ask me why I didn't get that last mile in, driving around the block a few times or getting a tiny bit lost once. I didn't though, and there you have it. Four thousand sounds like a lot more than 3,999 does; I feel sort of embarrassed for myself.

My window is broken, the crank fell off in Tallahassee on the way down. In order to roll it up or down I have to put the crank back on and turn it slowly and carefully, using one hand to push up the glass. So, mostly I leave it down. I baked like a biscuit yesterday, my left arm is so brown it looks like a branch. Today I'm wearing a long-sleeved white shirt to protect myself. I compromised on wearing long sleeves by going naked underneath it. It's actually cooler this way, compared to yesterday when I drove in my swimming suit top with my hair stuck up like a fountain on top of my head. Plus, I'm having a nervous breakdown. I've got that wild-eyed look.

A little four-lane blacktop running through the Alabama countryside, that's what I'm on. It's pretty, too, better than Florida, which was billboards and condos built on old dump sites. This is like driving between rolling emerald carpets. You can't see the two lanes going in the opposite direction because there's a screen of trees. I'm starting to get in a good mood again. The best was Georgia, coming down. Willow trees and red dirt and snakes stretched out alongside the road. I kept thinking, That looks like a *rope*, and then it would be a huge snake. A few miles later I would think, That looks like a *snake*, and it would be some snarl of something dropped off a truck.

Little convenience store, stuck out in the middle of nothing, a stain on the carpet. I'm gassing it up, getting some coffee. My white shirt is gaping open and I have nothing on underneath it, but who cares, I'll never see these people again. What do I care what Alabama thinks about me. This is a new and unusual attitude for me. I'm practicing being snotty, in anticipation of being dumped by my husband when I get back to Iowa.

I swagger from the gas pump to the store, I don't even care if my boobs are roaming around inside my shirt, if my hair is a freaky snarl, if I look defiant and uppity. There's nothing to be embarrassed of. I bring my coffee cup along and fill it at the counter. Various men, oldish and grungy, sit at tables eating eggs with wadded-up toast. They stare at me carefully while they chew. I ignore them and pay the woman at the counter. She's smoking a cigarette so I envy her.

"Great day, huh?" I ask her. She counts out my change.

"It is, honey," she says. She reaches for her cigarette and takes a puff, blows it up above my head. "Wish I wudn't in *here*."

"Well, it's getting hotter by the minute," I tell her. I've adopted an accent in just four weeks, an intermittent drawl that makes me think I'm not who everyone thinks I am.

"Y' all think this's hot?" she says idly. "*This* ain't hot."

When I leave, the men are still staring at me in a sullen way. I get in, rearrange all my junk so I have everything handy that I need, choose a Neil Young tape and pop it in the deck, fasten the belt, and then move back out on the highway. Back to the emerald carpet and the road home. Iowa is creeping toward me like a panther.

All I do is sing when I drive. Sing and drink: coffee, Coke, water, juice, coffee. And think. I sing and drink and think. On the way down I would sing, drink, think, and weep uncontrollably, but I'm past that now. Now I suffer bouts of free-floating hostility, which is much better. I plan to use it when I get home.

A car swings up alongside me so I pause in my singing until it goes past. People who sing in their cars always cheer me up, but I'd rather not be caught doing it. On the road, we're all singing, picking our noses, embarrassing ourselves wildly; it gets tiresome. I pause and hum, but the car sticks alongside me so I glance over. It's a guy. He grins and makes a lewd gesture with his mouth. I don't even want to say what it is, it's that disgusting. Tongue darting in and out, quickly. A python testing its food.

I hate this kind of thing. Who do they think they are, these men? I've had my fill of it. I give him the finger, slowly and deliberately. He picked the wrong day to mess with me, I think to myself. I take a sip of coffee.

He's still there.

I glance over briefly and he's making the gesture with his tongue again. I can't believe this. He's from the convenience store, I realize. He has on a fishing hat with lures stuck in it. I saw him back there, but I can't remember if he was sitting with the other men or by himself. He's big, overweight, and dirty, wearing a thin unbuttoned shirt and the terrible fishing hat. His passenger-side window is down. He begins screaming at me.

He followed me from that convenience store. The road is endless, in front there is nothing, no cars, no anything, behind is the same. Just road and grass and trees. The other two lanes are still invisible behind their screen of trees. I'm all alone out here. With him. He's screaming and screaming at me, reaching out his right arm like he's throttling me. I speed up. He speeds up, too, next to me. We're only a few feet apart, my window won't roll up.

He's got slobber on his face and there's no one in either direction. I slam on my brakes and for an instant he's ahead of me, I can breathe, then he slams on his brakes and we're next to each other again. I can't even repeat what he's screaming at me. He's telling me, amid the hot wind and poor Neil Young, what he wants to do to me. He wants to kill me. He's screaming and screaming, I can't look over.

I stare straight ahead through the windshield, hands at ten and two. The front end of his car is moving into my lane. He's saying he'll cut me with a knife, how he'll do it, all that. I can't listen. The front end of his Impala is about four inches from my white Mazda, my little car. This is really my husband's car, my beloved's. My Volkswagen died a lingering death a few months ago. There is no husband, there is no Volkswagen, there is nothing. There isn't even a Jo Ann right now. Whatever I am is sitting here clenched, hands on the wheel, I've stopped being her, now I'm something else. I'm absolutely terrified. He won't stop screaming it, over and over, what he's going to do.

I refuse to give him an inch. I will not move one inch over. If I do he'll have me off the road in an instant. I will not move. I speed up, he speeds up, I slow down, he slows down, I can see him out of the corner of my eye, driving with one hand, reaching like he's grabbing me with the other. "You whore," he screams at me. "I'll *kill* you, I'll *kill* you, I'll *kill* you . . . "

He'll kill me.

If I give him an inch, he'll shove me off the road and get his hands on me, then the end will begin in some unimaginable, unspeakable style that will be all his. I'll be an actor in his drama. We're going too fast, I've got the pedal pressed up to 80 and it's wobbling, his old Impala can probably go 140 on a straightaway like this. There will be blood, he won't want me to die quickly.

I will not lose control. I will ride it out. I cannot let him push me over onto the gravel. His car noses less than two inches from mine; I'm getting rattled. My God, he can almost reach me through his window, he's moved over in his seat, driving just with the left hand, the right is grabbing the hot air. I move over to the edge of my seat, toward the center of the car, carefully, without swerving.

In the rearview mirror a speck appears. Don't look, watch your front end. I glance up again; it's a truck. He can't get me. It's a trucker. Without looking at him I jerk my thumb backward to show him. He screams and screams and screams. He's not leaving. Suddenly a road appears on the right, a dirty and rutted thing leading off into the trees. He hits the brakes, drops behind, and takes it. In my rearview mirror I see that the license plate on the front of his car is buried in dried mud. That road is where he was hoping to push me. He wanted to push my car off the highway and get me on that road. He was hoping to kill me. He was hoping to do what maniacs, furious men, do to women alongside roads, in woods. I can't stop pressing too hard on the gas pedal. I'm at 85 now, and my leg is shaking uncontrollably, coffee is spilled all over the passenger seat, the atlas is wet, Neil Young is still howling on the tape deck. By force of will, I slow down to 65, eject the tape, and wait for the truck to overtake me. When it does, when it comes up alongside me. I don't look over at all, I keep my eyes straight ahead. As it moves in front of me I speed up enough to stay two car lengths behind it. It says *England* on the back, ornate red letters outlined in black. England.

That guy chased me on purpose, he *hated* me, with more passion than anyone has ever felt for me. Ever. Out there are all those decomposing bodies, all those disappeared daughters, discovered by joggers and hunters, their bodies long abandoned, the memory of final desperate moments lingering on the leaves, the trees, the mindless stumps and mushrooms. Images taped to tollbooth windows, faces pressed into the dirt alongside a path somewhere.

I want out of Alabama, I want to be in England. The air is still a blast furnace. I want to roll my window up, but I'd have to stop and get the crank out and lift it by hand. I'm too scared. He's out there still, waiting behind the screen of trees. I have to follow England until I'm out of Alabama. Green car, old Impala, unreadable license plate, lots of rust. Seat covers made out of that spongy stuff, something standing on the dashboard, a coffee cup or a sad Jesus. The fishing hat with a sweat ring around it right above the brim. Lures with feathers and barbs. I've never been so close to so much hatred in my whole life. *He wanted to kill me.* Think of England, with its white cows and broken-toothed farmers and dark green pastures. Think of the Beatles. I'm hugging the truck so closely now I'm almost under it. Me, of all people, he wanted to kill. Me. Everywhere I go I'm finding out new things about myself. Each way I turn, there it is. It's Jo Ann he wanted to kill.

By noon I want to kill him. I took a right somewhere and got onto the interstate, had the nerve to pee in a rest area, adrenaline running like an engine inside me, my keys threaded through my fingers in case anyone tried anything. I didn't do anything to earn it, I realize. His anger. I didn't do anything. Unless you count giving him the finger, which I don't. *He* earned that.

As it turned out, my husband couldn't bring himself to leave me when I got back to Iowa, so I waited awhile, and watched, then disentangled myself. History: We each got ten photo albums and six trays of slides. We took a lot of pictures in thirteen years. In the early years he looks stoned and contented, distant; in the later years he looks straight and slightly worried. In that last year he only appears by chance, near the edges, a blur of suffering, almost out of frame.

Just before we split, when we were driving somewhere, I told him about the guy in the green car. "Wow," he said. Then he turned up the radio, checked his image in the rearview mirror, and smiled sincerely at the passing landscape.

The Unwanted Child

Mary Clearman Blew

December 1958. I lie on my back on an examination table in a Missoula clinic while the middle-aged doctor whose name I found in the Yellow Pages inserts his speculum and takes a look. He turns to the sink and washes his hands.

"Yes, you're pregnant," he says. "Congratulations, Mommy."

His confirmation settles over me like a fog that won't lift. Myself I can manage for, but for myself and *it?*

After I get dressed, he says, "I'll want to see you again in a month, Mommy."

If he calls me Mommy again, I will break his glasses and grind them in his face, grind them until he has no face. I will kick him right in his obscene fat paunch. I will bury my foot in his disgusting flesh.

I walk through the glass doors and between the shoveled banks of snow to the parking lot where my young husband waits in the car.

"You're not, are you?" he says.

"Yes."

"Yes, you're not?"

"Yes, I am! Jeez!"

His feelings are hurt. But he persists: "I just don't think you are. I just don't see how you could be."

He has a theory on the correct use of condoms, a theory considerably more flexible than the one outlined by the doctor I visited just before our marriage three months ago, and which he has been arguing with increasing anxiety ever since I missed my second period. I stare out the car window at the back of the clinic while he expounds on his theory for the zillionth time. What difference does it make now? Why can't he shut up? If I have to listen to him much longer, I will kill him, too.

At last, even his arguments wear thin against the irrefutable fact. As he turns the key in the ignition his eyes are deep with fear.

"But I'll stand by you," he promises.

Why get married at eighteen?

When you get married, you can move into married student housing. It's a shambles, it's a complex of converted World War II barracks known as the Strips, it's so sorry the wind blows through the cracks around the windows and it lacks hot-water heaters and electric stoves, but at least it's not the dormitory, which is otherwise the required residence of all women at the University of Montana. Although no such regulations apply to male students, single women must be signed in and ready for bed check by ten o'clock on weeknights and one on weekends. No alcohol, no phones in rooms. Women must not be reported on campus in slacks or shorts (unless they can prove they are on their way to a physical education class), and on Sundays they may not appear except in heels, hose, and hat. A curious side effect of marriage, however, is that the responsibility for one's virtue is automatically transferred from the dean of women to one's husband. Miss Maurine Clow never does bed checks or beer checks in the Strips.

When you get married, you can quit making out in the back seat of a parked car and go to bed in a bed. All young women in 1958 like sex. Maybe their mothers had headaches or hang-ups, but *they* are normal, healthy women with normal, healthy desires, and they know the joy they will find in their husbands' arms will—well, be better than making out, which, though none of us will admit it, is getting to be boring. We spend hours shivering with our clothes off in cars parked in Pattee Canyon in subzero weather, groping and being groped and feeling embarrassed when other cars crunch by in the snow, full of onlookers with craning necks, and worrying about the classes we're not attending because making out takes so much time. We are normal, healthy women with normal, healthy desires if we have to die to prove it. Nobody has ever said out loud that she would like to go to bed and *get it over with* and get on with something else.

There's another reason for getting married at eighteen, but it's more complicated.

By getting married I have eluded Dean Maurine Clow only to fall into the hands of in-laws.

"We have to tell the folks," my husband insists. "They'll want to know."

His letter elicits the predictable long-distance phone call from them. I make him answer it. While he talks to them I rattle dishes in the kitchen, knowing exactly how they look, his momma and his daddy in their suffocating Helena living room hung with mounted elk antlers and religious calendars, their heads together over the phone, their faces wreathed in big grins at his news.

"They want to talk to you," he says finally. Then, "Come on!"

I take the phone with fear and hatred. "Hello?"

"Well!!!" My mother-in-law's voice carols over the miles. "I guess this is finally the end of college for you!"

A week after Christmas I lean against the sink in my mother's kitchen at the ranch and watch her wash clothes.

She uses a Maytag washing machine with a wringer and a monotonous, daylong chugging motor which, she often says, is a damn sight better than a washboard. She starts by filling the tub with boiling water and soap flakes. Then she agitates her whites for twenty minutes, fishes them out with her big fork, and feeds them sheet by sheet into the wringer. After she rinses them by hand, she reverses the wringer, and feeds them back through, creased and steaming hot, and carries them out to the clothesline to freeze dry. By this time the water in the tub has cooled off enough for the coloreds. She'll keep running through her loads until she's down to the blue jeans and the water is thick and greasy. My mother has spent twenty-five years of Mondays on the washing.

I know I have to tell her I'm pregnant.

She's talking about college, she's quoting my grandmother, who believes that every woman should be self-sufficient. Even though I'm married now, even though I had finished only one year at the University of Montana before I got married, my grandmother has agreed to go on lending me what I need for tuition and books. Unlike my in-laws, who have not hesitated to tell me I should go to work as a typist or a waitress to support my husband through college (after all, he will be supporting me for the rest of my life), my grandmother believes I should get my own credentials.

My mother and grandmother talk about a teaching certificate as if it were a gold ring which, if I could just grab it, would entitle the two of them to draw a long breath of relief. Normally I hate to listen to their talk. They don't even know you can't get a two-year teaching certificate now, you have to go the full four years.

But beyond the certificate question, college has become something that I never expected and cannot explain: not something to grab and have done with but a door opening, a glimpse of an endless passage and professors who occasionally beckon from far ahead—like lovely, elderly Marguerite Ephron, who lately has been leading four or five of us through the *Aeneid*. Latin class has been my sanctuary for the past few months; Latin has been my solace from conflict that otherwise has left me as steamed and agitated as my mother's whites, now churning away in the Maytag; Latin in part because it is taught by Mrs. Ephron, always serene, endlessly patient, mercilessly thorough, who teaches at the university while Mr. Ephron works at home, in a basement full of typewriters with special keyboards, on the translations of obscure clay tablets.

So I've been accepting my grandmother's money under false pretenses. I'm not going to spend my life teaching around Fergus County the way she did, the way my mother would have if she hadn't married my father. I've married my husband under false pretenses, too; he's a good fly-fishing Helena boy who has no idea in the world of becoming a Mr. Ephron. But, subversive as a foundling in a fairy tale, I have tried to explain none of my new aspirations to my mother or grandmother or, least of all, my husband and his parents, who are mightily distressed as it is by my borrowing money for my own education.

"—and it's all got to be paid back, you'll be starting your lives in *debt!*"

"—the important thing is to get *him* through, *he's* the one who's got to go out and face the world!"

"—what on earth do you think you'll do with your education?"

And now all the argument is pointless, the question of teaching certificate over quest for identity, the importance of my husband's future over mine, the relentless struggle with the in-laws over what is most mine, my self. I'm done for, knocked out of the running by the application of a faulty condom theory.

"Mom," I blurt, "I'm pregnant."

She gasps. And before she can let out that breath, a frame of memory freezes with her in it, poised over her rinse tub, looking at me through the rising steam and the grinding wringer. Right now I'm much too miserable to wonder what she sees when she looks at me: her oldest daughter, her bookish child, the daydreamer, the one she usually can't stand, the one who takes everything too seriously, who will never learn to take no for an answer. Thin and strong and blue-jeaned, bespectacled and crop-haired, this girl could pass for fifteen right now and won't be able to buy beer in grocery stores for years without showing her driver's license. This girl who is too miserable to look her mother in the face, who otherwise might see in her mother's eyes the years of blight and disappointment. She does hear what her mother says:

"Oh, Mary, no!"

My mother was an unwanted child. The fourth daughter of a homesteading family racked by drought and debt, she was only a year old when the sister nearest her in age died of a cancerous tumor. She was only two years old when the fifth and last child, the cherished boy, was born. She was never studious like her older sisters nor, of course, was she a boy, and she was never able to find her own ground to stand on until she married.

Growing up, I heard her version often, for my mother was given to a kind of continuous oral interpretation of herself and her situation. Standing over the sink or stove, hoeing the garden, running her sewing machine with the permanent angry line deepening between her eyes, she talked. Unlike the stories our grandmothers told, which, like fairy tales, narrated the events of the past but avoided psychological speculation ("Great-great-aunt Somebody-or-other was home alone making soap when the Indians came, so she waited until they got close enough, and then she threw a ladle of lye on them . . ."), my mother's dwelt on the motives behind the darkest family impulses.

"Ma never should have had me. It was her own fault. She never should have had me if she didn't want me."

"But then you wouldn't have been born!" I interrupted, horrified at the thought of not being.

"Wouldn't have mattered to me," she said. "I'd never have known the difference."

What I cannot remember today is whom my mother was telling her story to. Our grandmothers told their stories to my little sisters and me, to entertain us, but my mother's bitter words flowed past us like a river current past small, ignored onlookers who eavesdropped from its shores. I remember her words, compulsive, repetitive, spilling out over her work—for she was always working—and I was awed by her courage. What could be less comprehensible than not wanting to be? More fearsome than annihilation?

Nor can I remember enough about the circumstances of my mother's life during the late 1940s and the early 1950s to know why she was so angry, why she was so compelled to deconstruct her childhood. Her lot was not easy. She had married into a close-knit family that kept to itself. She had her husband's mother on her hands all her life, and on top of the normal isolation and hard work of a ranch wife of those years, she had to provide home schooling for her children.

And my father's health was precarious, and the ranch was failing. The reality of that closed life along the river bottom became more and more attenuated by the outward reality of banks and interest rates and the shifting course of agribusiness. She was touchy with money worries. She saw the circumstances of her sisters' lives grow easier as her own grew harder. Perhaps these were reasons enough for rage.

I recall my mother in her middle thirties through the telescoped eye of the child which distorts the intentions of parents and enlarges them to giants. Of course she was larger than life. Unlike my father, with his spectrum of ailments, she was never sick. She was never hospitalized in her life for any reason but childbirth, never came down with anything worse than a cold. She lugged the armloads of wood and buckets of water and slops and ashes that came with cooking and washing and ironing in a kitchen with a wood range and no plumbing; she provided the endless starchy meals of roast meat and potatoes and gravy; she kept salads on her table and fresh or home-canned vegetables at a time when iceberg lettuce was a town affectation.

She was clear-skinned, with large gray eyes that often seemed fixed on some point far beyond our familiar slopes and cutbanks. And even allowing for the child's telescoped eye, she was a tall woman who thought of herself as oversized. She was the tallest of her sisters. "*As big as Doris* is what they used to say about me!"

Bigness to her was a curse. "You big ox!" she would fling at me over some altercation with my little sister. True to the imperative that is handed down through the generations, I in turn bought my clothes two sizes too large for years.

All adult ranch women were fat. I remember hardly a woman out of her teens in those years who was not fat. The few exceptions were the women who had, virtually, become a third sex by taking on men's work in the fields and corrals; they might stay as skinny and tough in their Levis as hired hands.

But women who remained women baked cakes and cream pies and breads and sweet rolls with the eggs from their own chickens and the milk and butter and cream from the cows they milked, and they ate heavily from appetite and from fatigue and from the monotony of their isolation. They wore starched cotton print dresses and starched aprons and walked ponderously beside their whiplash husbands. My mother, unless she was going to be riding or helping in the hayfields, always wore those shapeless, starched dresses she sewed herself, always cut from the same pattern, always layered over with an apron.

What was she so angry about? Why was her forehead kneaded permanently into a frown? It was a revelation for me one afternoon when she answered a knock at the screen door, and she smiled, and her voice lifted to greet an old friend of hers and my father's from their single days. Color rose in her face, and she looked pretty as she told him where he could find my father. Was that how outsiders always saw her?

Other ranch women seemed cheerful enough on the rare occasions when they came in out of the gumbo. Spying on them as they sat on benches in the shade outside the horticulture house at the county fair or visited in the cabs of trucks at rodeos, I wondered if these women, too, were angry when they were alone with only their children to observe them. What secrets lay behind those vast placid, smiling faces, and what stories could their children tell?

My mother believed that her mother had loved her brother best and her older sisters next best. "He was always The Boy and they were The Girls, and Ma was proud of how well they did in school," she explained again and again to the walls, the stove, the floor she was mopping, "and I was just Doris. I was average."

Knowing how my grandmother had misjudged my mother, I felt guilty about how much I longed for her visits. I loved my grandmother and her fresh supply of stories about the children who went to the schools she taught, the games they played, and the books they read. School for me was an emblem of the world outside our creek-bottom meadows and fenced mountain slopes. At eight, I was still being taught at home; our gumbo road was impassable for most of the school months, and my father preferred that we be kept safe from contact with "them damn town kids," as he called them. Subversively I begged my grandmother to repeat her stories again and again, and I tried to imagine what it must be like to see other children every day and to have a real desk and real lessons. Other than my little sister, my playmates were mostly cats. But my grandmother brought with her the breath of elsewhere.

My mother's resentment whitened in intensity during the weeks before a visit from my grandmother, smoldered during the visit itself, and flared up again as soon as my grandmother was safely down the road to her next school. "I wonder if she ever realizes she wouldn't even have any grandchildren if I hadn't got married and had some kids! *The Girls* never had any kids! Some people should never have kids! Some people should never get married!"

With a child's logic, I thought she was talking about me. I thought I was responsible for her anger. I was preoccupied for a long time with a story I had read about a fisherman who was granted three wishes; he had used his wishes badly, but I was sure I could do better, given the chance. I thought a lot about how I would use three wishes, how I would use their potential for lifting me out of the present.

"What would you wish for, if you had three wishes?" I prodded my mother.

She turned her faraway gray eyes on me, as though she had not been ranting about The Girls the moment before. "I'd wish you'd be good," she said.

That was what she always said, no matter how often I asked her. With everything under the sun to wish for, that unfailing answer was a perplexity and a worry.

I was my grandmother's namesake, and I was a bookworm like my mother's older sisters. Nobody could pry my nose out of a book to do my chores, even though I was marked to be the outdoor-working child, even though I was supposed to be my father's boy.

Other signs that I was not a boy arose to trouble us both and account, I thought, for my mother's one wish.

"Mary's getting a butt on her just like a girl," she remarked one night as I climbed out of the tub. Alarmed, I craned my neck to see what had changed about my eight-year-old buttocks.

"Next thing, you'll be mooning in the mirror and wanting to pluck your eyebrows like the rest of 'em," she said.

"I will not," I said doubtfully.

I could find no way through the contradiction. On the one hand, I was a boy (except that I also was a bookworm), and my chores were always in the barns and corrals, never the kitchen. *You don't know how to cook on a wood stove?* my mother-in-law was to cry in disbelief. *And you grew up on a ranch?*

To act like a boy was approved; to cry or show fear was to invite ridicule. *Sissy! Big bellercalf!* On the other hand, I was scolded for hanging around the men, the way ranch boys did. I was not a boy (my buttocks, my vanity). What was I?

"Your dad's boy," my mother answered comfortingly when I asked her. She named a woman I knew. "Just like Hazel. Her dad can't get along without her."

Hazel was a tough, shy woman who rode fences and pulled calves and took no interest in the country dances or the "running around" her sisters did on weekends. Hazel never used lipstick or permed her hair; she wore it cut almost like a man's. Seen at the occasional rodeo or bull sale in her decently pressed pearl-button shirt and new Levis, she stuck close to her dad. Like me, Hazel apparently was not permitted to hang around the men.

What Hazel did not seem interested in was any kind of fun, and a great resolve arose in me that, whatever I was, I was going to have . . . whatever it was. I would get married, even if I wasn't supposed to.

But my mother had another, darker reason to be angry with me, and I knew it. The reason had broken over me suddenly the summer I was seven and had been playing, on warm afternoons, in a rain barrel full of water. Splashing around, elbows and knees knocking against the side of the barrel, I enjoyed the rare sensation of being wet all over. My little sister, four, came and stood on tiptoe to watch. It occurred to me to boost her into the barrel with me.

My mother burst out of the kitchen door and snatched her back.

"What are you trying to do, kill her?" she shouted.

I stared back at her, wet, dumbfounded.

Her eyes blazed over me, her brows knotted at their worst. "And after you'd drowned her, I suppose you'd have slunk off to hide somewhere until it was all over!"

It had never crossed my mind to kill my sister, or that my mother might think I wanted to. (Although I had, once, drowned a setting of baby chicks in a rain barrel.) But that afternoon, dripping in my underpants, goose-bumped and ashamed, I watched her carry my sister into the house and then I did go off to hide until it was, somehow, all over, for she never mentioned it at dinner.

The chicks had been balls of yellow fuzz, and I had been three. I wanted them to swim. I can just remember catching a chick and holding it in the water until it stopped squirming and then laying it down to catch a fresh one. I didn't stop until I had drowned the whole dozen and laid them out in a sodden yellow row.

What the mind refuses to allow to surface is characterized by a suspicious absence. Of detail, of associations. Memories skirt the edge of nothing. There is for me about this incident that suspicious absence. What is being withheld?

Had I, for instance, given my mother cause to believe I might harm my sister? Children have done such harm, and worse. What can be submerged deeper, denied more vehemently, than the murderous impulse? At four, my sister was a tender, trusting little girl with my mother's wide gray eyes and brows. A younger sister of an older sister. A good girl. Mommy's girl.

What do I really know about my mother's feelings toward her own dead sister? Kathryn's dolls had been put away; my mother was never allowed to touch them.

"I'll never, never love one of my kids more than another!" she screamed at my father in one of her afternoons of white rage. The context is missing.

During the good years, when cattle prices were high enough to pay the year's bills and a little extra, my mother bought wallpaper out of a catalog and stuck it to her lumpy walls. She enameled her kitchen white, and she sewed narrow strips of cloth she called "drapes" to hang at the sides of her windows. She bought a stiff tight cylinder of linoleum at Sears, Roebuck in town and hauled it home in the back of the pickup and unrolled it in a shiny flowered oblong in the middle of her splintery front room floor.

Occasionally I would find her sitting in her front room on her "davenport," which she had saved for and bought used, her lap full of sewing and her forehead relaxed out of its knot. For a moment there was her room around her as she wanted it to look: the clutter subdued, the new linoleum mopped and quivering under the chair legs that held down its corners, the tension of the opposing floral patterns of wallpaper, drapes, and slipcovers held in brief, illusory harmony by the force of her vision.

How hard she tried for her daughters! Over the slow thirty miles of gumbo and gravel we drove to town every summer for dentist appointments at a time when pulling teeth was still a more common remedy than filling them, when our own father and his mother wore false teeth before they were forty.

During the good years, we drove the thirty miles for piano lessons. An upright Kimball was purchased and hauled home in the back of the pickup. Its carved oak leaves and ivories dominated the front room, where she found time to "sit with us" every day as we practiced. With a pencil she pointed out the notes she had learned to read during her five scant quarters in normal school, and made us read them aloud. "F sharp!" she would scream over the throb of the Maytag in the kitchen as one of us pounded away.

She carped about bookworms, but she located the dim old Carnegie library in town and got library cards for us even though, as country kids, we weren't strictly entitled to them. After that, trips home from town with sacks of groceries included armloads of library books. Against certain strictures, she could be counted on. When, in my teens, I came home with my account of the new book the librarian kept in her desk drawer and refused to check out to me, my mother straightened her back as I knew she would. "She thinks she can tell one of my kids what she can read and what she can't read?"

On our next visit to the library, she marched up the stone steps and into the mote-filled sanctum with me.

The white-haired librarian glanced up inquiringly.

"You got *From Here to Eternity?*"

The librarian looked at me, then at my mother. Without a word she reached into her drawer and took out a heavy volume. She stamped it and handed it to my mother, who handed it to me.

How did she determine that books and dentistry and piano lessons were necessities for her daughters, and what battles did she fight for them as slipping cattle prices put even a gallon of white enamel paint or a sheet of new linoleum beyond her reach?

Disaster followed disaster on the ranch. An entire season's hay crop lost to a combination of ancient machinery that would not hold together and heavy rains that would not let up. A whole year's calf crop lost because the cows had been pastured in timber that had been logged, and when they ate the pine needles from the downed tops, they spontaneously aborted. As my father grew less and less able to face the reality of the downward spiral, what could she hope to hold together with her pathetic floral drapes and floral slipcovers?

Bundled in coats and overshoes in the premature February dark, our white breaths as one, my mother and I huddle in the shadow of the chicken house. By moonlight we watch the white-tailed deer that have slipped down out of the timber to feed from the haystack a scant fifty yards away. Cautiously I raise my father's rifle to my shoulder. I'm not all that good a marksman, I hate the inevitable explosive crack, but I brace myself on the corner of the chicken house and sight carefully and remember to squeeze. Ka-crack!

Eight taupe shapes shoot up their heads and spring for cover. A single mound remains in the snow near the haystack. By the time my mother and I have climbed through the fence and trudged up to the haystack, all movement from the doe is reflexive. "Nice and fat," says my mother.

Working together with our butcher knives, we lop off her scent glands and slit her and gut her and save the heart and liver in a bucket for breakfast. Then, each taking a leg, we drag her down the field, under the fence, around the chicken house and into the kitchen, where we will skin her out and butcher her.

We are two mid-twentieth-century women putting meat on the table for the next few weeks. Neither of us has ever had a hunting license, and if we did, hunting season is long closed, but we're serene about what we're doing. "Eating our hay, aren't they?" says my mother. "We're entitled to a little venison. The main thing is not to tell anybody what we're doing."

And the pregnant eighteen-year-old? What about her?

In June of 1959 she sits up in the hospital bed, holding in her arms a small warm scrap whose temples are deeply dented from the forceps. She cannot remember birthing him, only the long hours alone before the anesthetic took over. She feels little this morning, only a dull worry about the money, money, money for college in the fall.

The in-laws are a steady, insistent, increasingly frantic chorus of disapproval over her plans. *But, Mary! Tiny babies have to be kept warm!* her mother-in-law keeps repeating, pathetically, ever since she was told about Mary's plans for fall quarter.

But, Mary! How can you expect to go to college and take good care of a husband and a baby?

Finally, *We're going to put our foot down!*

She knows that somehow she has got to extricate herself from these sappy folks. About the baby, she feels only a mild curiosity. Life where there was none before. The rise and fall of his tiny chest. She has him on her hands now. She must take care of him.

Why not an abortion?

Because the thought never crossed her mind. Another suspicious absence, another void for memory to skirt. What she knew about abortion was passed around the midnight parties in the girls' dormitory: *You drink one part turpentine with two parts sugar. Or was it the other way around? . . . two parts turpentine to one part sugar. You drink gin in a hot bath . . .*

She has always hated the smell of gin. It reminds her of the pine needles her father's cattle ate, and how their calves were born shallow-breathed and shriveled, and how they died. She knows a young married woman who begged her husband to hit her in the stomach and abort their fourth child.

Once, in her eighth month, the doctor had shot her a look across his table. "If you don't want this baby," he said, "I know plenty of people who do."

"I want it," she lied.

No, but really. What is to become of this eighteen-year-old and her baby?

Well, she's read all the sentimental literature they shove on the high school girls. She knows how the plot is supposed to turn out.

Basically, she has two choices.

One, she can invest all her hopes for her own future in this sleeping scrap. *Son, it was always my dream to climb to the stars. Now the tears of joy spring at the sight of you with your college diploma . . .*

Even at eighteen, this lilylicking is enough to make her sick.

Or two, she can abandon the baby and the husband and become really successful and really evil. This is the more attractive version of the plot, but she doesn't really believe in it. Nobody she knows has tried it. It seems as out of reach from ordinary daylight Montana as Joan Crawford or the Duchess of Windsor or the moon. As she lies propped up in bed with the sleeping scrap in her arms, looking out over the dusty downtown rooftops settling into noon in the waning

Eisenhower years, she knows very well that Joan Crawford will never play the story of her life.

What, then? What choice is left to her?

What outcome could possibly be worth all this uproar? Her husband is on the verge of tears these days; he's only twenty himself, and he had no idea what trouble he was marrying into, his parents pleading and arguing and threatening, even his brothers and their wives chiming in with their opinions, even the minister getting into it, even the neighbors; and meanwhile his wife's grandmother firing off red-hot letters from her side, meanwhile his wife's mother refusing to budge an inch—united, those two women are as formidable as a pair of rhinoceroses, though of course he has no idea in the world what it took to unite them.

All this widening emotional vortex over whether or not one Montana girl will finish college. What kind of genius would she have to be to justify it all? Will it be enough that, thirty years later, she will have read approximately 16,250 freshman English essays out of an estimated lifetime total of 32,000?

Will it be enough, over the years, that she remembers the frozen frame of her mother's face over the rinse tub that day after Christmas in 1958 and wonders whether she can do as much for her son as was done for her? Or that she often wonders whether she really lied when she said, *I want it?*

Will it be enough? What else is there?

Independence Day, Manley Hot Springs, Alaska

Lisa D. Chavez

Independence Day, 1975. I was twelve. A little more than a month before, my mother had withdrawn me from school early, loaded up our car—a flashy but impractical Camaro with dual side-pipes—and headed north for Alaska. She brought with her everything she thought essential: daughter; dog; photos of the family she was leaving behind; a haphazard scattering of household goods; and two army surplus sleeping bags, purchased especially for the trip. What she was traveling toward was uncertain but full of promise—a mysterious box, beguilingly wrapped.

What she was leaving behind was certain; perhaps that is why she was so eager to go. A narrow rented house in southern California; a steady, if boring, secretarial job; a marriage proposal from a man she didn't love. What she was leaving behind were her everyday fears: her route to work through Watts, a place blighted and dangerous even then. The muggings in the company parking lot. The fear of being a young woman alone with her child in a decaying neighborhood, a derelict factory looming across the street. The fear, perhaps, of succumbing to a loveless marriage for the security it offered.

I was too young to really understand my mother's concerns, but I felt her tension. My mother and her women friends wore their fears like perfume, like the lingering scent of smoke from the erupting fires of those violent days. I remember the things my mother's friends talked about: the Manson murders; the serial killer who left body parts scattered on the freeway in trash bags; the man in our own town who killed five people in a movie theater. And the more personal terrors, the ones they alluded to less directly: fear of the arm slipping around the neck from behind, fear of the window breaking in the house in the middle of the night.

Fear for their children in a place gone crazy. Or just the fear of being alone. And while my world was a child's world, full of long imaginative games in the park near our house, or afternoons watching Disney movies at the mall, I also heard my mother and her friends talking about getting out, moving to someplace safe. My mother was looking for sanctuary, and for a new start. She picked Alaska, as far north as she could drive.

Independence Day, 1975. We've been in Alaska less than a month and are still exploring. Now we have driven as far north as the road will take us, landed here, on the banks of the Tanana River. Manley Hot Springs. A town with no function really, except for the raw springs: two pools of hot water bubbling up out of the ground. There's a lodge with a few desultory cabins ringing it. A combination gas station/store. That is all. Down the river a half a dozen miles lies Minto, an Athabascan Indian village. Fairbanks, the biggest city in the interior, swollen to a population of 60,000 by pipeline construction, lies less than a hundred miles south, far enough away—along these rough gravel roads—to be totally insignificant.

And I am twelve. Everything new astounds me, and everything is new. My mother parks near the river and goes to find a place to stay. Instantly I am occupied, walking our dog, wetting the toes of my canvas tennis shoes in the silty current, kicking sprays of gravel into the air. Under my breath a constant stream of conversation. I narrate the scene to myself, add it to the elaborate and constant story I whisper of my adventures in Alaska. Drunk on the stories of Jack London, the poems of Robert Service, I imagine myself a lone adventurer, a sled dog driver, a saloon girl. I do not see what is in front of me: a shabby small town where people stare openly at that frivolous car—bright orange and marked by its out-of-state plates—and the young woman in white, high-heeled sandals and her daughter that have emerged from it. I do not see the men swigging out of a bottle at the picnic table by the river. I do not see the people getting out of a banged up riverboat, or the beer cans they toss in the current. No. I am in my own Alaska, and it is beautiful. I erase the people, and I am alone in my fantasy of wilderness, only graceful paper birch and the sun turning the river to tinfoil. Even when two men pull a rifle out of the boat, aim it at the sky and shoot, I am unsurprised. Only when my mother hurries me into the car do I understand I should be afraid.

There is only one place to stay, in the hulking log building that serves as a lodge. And there is only one room left, above the bar. We take it, noting the sagging double bed and rust-stained sink. The bathroom is down the hall.

Manley holds few attractions. The hot springs itself—housed in another log structure, this one with steamy windows that gaze at the road like rheumy eyes—is booked out by the hour, and we discover it is rented for the entire evening. We go for a walk with our German shepherd, but we quickly run out of road to walk on. We circle the gas station yet again.

"When does it get dark?" I ask my mother; even though I already know that it does not get dark at night in Fairbanks, I cannot be sure the rules are not different here.

"In August," my mother replies, an answer she has learned from the locals. She looks nervous, walks fast. Finally, I manage to really see around me, to note the people drinking at picnic tables, the hairy-faced men entering the store with guns in holsters. She hustles us back to our little room.

And I continue to ponder the light. If it never gets dark, I wonder, when do kids get to shoot off their fireworks? This year I have no fireworks, no magical cones of cardboard with their heady black smell of powder, cones with names like "Showers of Falling Stars" and "Golden Peacock" that spray the summer night with shivering sparks of sheer delight. Fireworks are illegal here, my mother tells me, and I feel sorely cheated.

All through the sunlit night we hear voices shout and slur from the bar, and outside gunfire and laughter. Years later I will discover that Alaska is not the only place where people discharge guns on holidays, but then I knew only my mother's fear which passed to me like a virus. I lay still on the double bed beside her, pretending to sleep. At 5:00 A.M. a shot in the bar and a shuddering silence. From the car, distant and insistent, our dog's furious barking.

Time passes. I pretend to sleep. The dog barks. My mother nudges me. "Someone needs to walk the dog." That someone is me.

Years later I recount the story. People question me. Why did she send you, a child? What they are asking, what they are telling me, is that my mother was a bad mother. Perhaps. But maybe she thought it was safe; how could she know? And she was tired, and scared herself, and perhaps she thought my childishness would protect me in a way her youth and gender might not protect her.

Perhaps it was a mark of my mother's blind innocence. I like to think that she had some of the indomitable optimism of those who made the same trek before: the stampeders to the gold rush of '98, or the others that came, like we did, lured north by the pipeline boom of '74 and '75. She wanted to believe—like so many did—that Alaska was a land of golden opportunity. Think of what she had done: left a good-paying job and man who wanted to marry her to journey to a place where she knew no one, where she had no prospects at all. For her, I think Alaska represented the possibility of the undiscovered, while California was a territory already mapped with freeways and shopping malls, mile upon mile of housing developments, and the barbed wire threat of barrio and ghetto.

That summer, we were still caught up in the romance of Alaska. We sang Johnny Horton songs on the Alcan Highway: "North to Alaska," and "When It's Springtime in Alaska It's Forty Below." I wrote "Alaska or Bust" with my finger in the dust that caked the car, and my mother smiled and let it stay. She told me that we would have our own house in the country, and I believed her, even though when we got to Fairbanks we lived in a campground next to the fairgrounds, and I stayed there all day exploring muskeg woods behind the camp while my mother worked at Dairy Queen. There were none of the expected high-paying jobs, none of the dream houses that we could afford. We knew no one. But my mother, like me, was lost in her own dream of Alaska, and she refused to be discouraged. So now, when I think back to that time, I try not to judge her too harshly. Alaska was her sanctuary, and she could not imagine, then, that anything could go wrong.

I am a child; I do what she asks. Put on my worn jean jacket. Push my straight dark hair behind my ears, then tie it back with a blue bandana. This is the look I have adopted since I arrived, Indian chic. I do not know what it means, exactly, to dress like this, but I have seen young men and women outfitted in this way—people my mother told me were Indian—and I decide I will dress that way too, because Indians are cool, aren't they? And as I am a bit Indian—a mixture of Chicana and Southwestern Indian and Norwegian that I will much later learn to call Mestiza—I am determined to dress appropriately. My attire adjusted, I move toward the door. Look pleadingly at my mother's blanketed back. I really don't want to go out. Then, in imitation of my mother, I sigh loudly, pick up the keys. Step out into the hall.

Creep down the narrow stairs. Afraid, in my childish way, of strangers, of being where I think I am not supposed to be, up late in a room above a bar. And I see a man on the landing. His back to me. And he whips around and raises a shotgun and aims it at my face. "I told all you goddamn Indians to get the fuck out of my bar."

I am twelve, and I have never seen a gun before. I am twelve, and I come from California, where night follows day in an orderly fashion, where on the Fourth of July I whirl like a comet with sparklers clutched tight in two hands. Where I place black pellets on the pavement to watch them transform into sooty snakes. I am twelve, and I am frozen on the landing of a strange staircase, with a shotgun staring in my face with its one, unblinking eye.

I am usually a silent child, but my fear makes me speak. My mouth opens and out rush words, tumbling over one another like frightened animals. My mother. California. The dog in the car, maybe already peeing on the seat. The dog is like a ship I swim to, desperately. He lowers the gun and I skitter past, fly to the door. Which I cannot open; it is locked. The man raises the latch, shoves me outside.

I stand outside on the cool grass, the early morning bright and exotic around me. I close my eyes for a moment and wish hard for home. Then open them to see revelers sway aimlessly by, laughing, cursing, swigging from bottles. I move toward the safety of the car.

And I am twelve, and I don't know what to do, can't think about what happened to me in any coherent fashion. I do not understand. I know racism exists—though I do not know what it is called—but not like this. I thought it was something else, people who called black people bad names, people who snickered when they heard my last name. Mexican, they'd sneer. I knew that. Knew shame, about my last name, which I claimed was Spanish, not Mexican, knowing that to be less shameful, although I didn't know why. But nothing more. Not then. And Indian, what was that to me? An exotic people with feathers, that had some slight relation to my father, to me. But I was not Indian. Nor Mexican. Nor Norwegian. Not really. I am just myself, a quiet girl who liked to read, to write, a girl who had always loved the Fourth of July, the night's rich promise broken by the sizzle and spark of fire.

And now I have been shaken into a world I don't understand, a cold, foreign world, where men I don't know can hate me for the way I look. I don't know what to do, so I take the dog for a walk. She sniffs desultorily, squats on the lawn to pee. I look at the new grass stains on my jeans, souvenirs from the fall I took from the man's push. Two young men pass by, say hello. They have witnessed my ejection from the lodge.

"Did he hurt you?" one asks. They are both Indian; their glossy black hair is tied back with bandanas. They wear T-shirts, jean jackets.

I am afraid to answer, but I shake my head.

"He's an asshole," the other young man says. His words are slow and strangely accented; I will soon learn to recognize this as a village accent. "Fucking white man." He shakes a fist at the lodge.

I try to smile to show my gratefulness, and watch them with head bowed as they walk away. They are drunk; I know that even then, but their words redeem me nonetheless. Later I will understand those words as my introduction into a place I will dwell for all my time in Alaska, those words which delineate me as one of them, as a Native person. For in Alaska, as I would learn, the complexity of my ethnicity was irrelevant; I looked Native, therefore I was.

For a long time I crouch beside the car with my arms around the dog's neck. What will I do? I could sleep in the car, but my mother will be mad. But can I go back in? What if the man won't let me? What if he . . . my thoughts veer away from certain subjects. The dog pulls away, shakes herself. I must go back.

I stand at the door. Through the window I can see the man watching, see the slim shadow of the gun. I am afraid. My legs shake; my hand is weak, but I push the door open.

And the man grabs my shoulder hard. Twists me toward him. Peers down into my face. He is bearded and the hair on his face makes him as frightening as a fierce animal. "All right," he says, though I have no idea what he means. For me, nothing is right. He pushes me toward the stairs and I run up them, breathless, heart somersaulting. I imagine too clearly a sudden crack, a searing pain in my spine. In our room I collapse on the bed as if shot. Tears first, then the story.

My mother waits until the next morning to confront the lodge owner. She gets the story while I mop a pancake around my plate, too scared and shamed to eat. The bearded man is the man who owns the lodge, and he tells his side calmly, reasonably, as if there is nothing unusual about pointing shotguns at twelve-year-olds. Some Indians from Minto were partying in the bar, he tells us, and wouldn't leave at closing time. So he fired a shot of tear gas, cleared the place out. As for me, "she looks like a goddamn Native," he says, and shrugs. And the other guests eating breakfast look at me, nod. There is nothing more to say, no apologies necessary. And my mother's angry words are just irritations, like BBs fired at a grizzly bear.

We left soon after that, and my mother drove as fast as she dared on that gravel road, gripping the steering wheel tight, her hands like fists clenched. I was quiet.

I didn't know I should be angry. Didn't know, really, why I felt so ashamed. Even my mother's anger couldn't take that shame away, for under her anger I sensed her own fear of this place she'd brought me to, of these people. Her confusion. She repeated that the man had thought I was Indian, as if somehow that should explain it. But that confused me. Because I *was* Indian, though not Alaskan Indian, and not all Indian. Did that make what the man did excusable? My mother did not explain.

What did it mean to be Indian? Did I put it on with the clothes I wore? Why was my appearance read one way in California and another way in Alaska? In California, where everyone aimed for a tan, my skin color was something to be envied, when it could be separated from the stigma of my Mexican last name. I had grown vain of it, in a childish way. Proud that I often had the best "tan." I secretly looked down on lighter-skinned children, was sure their pink and white skin was ugly, undesirable. Otherwise why would my mother and so many others spend hours roasting themselves brown on the beach? I got it naturally; I must be superior. In Alaska, far from beaches, where the long dark winters bleached skin as pale as the long months of snow, brown skin did not mean beach and health, but it meant something else, something I would understand some people thought shameful. Native. That's what it meant, and I would discover how that word could be spit out with as much disgust as any racial slur.

Manley Hot Springs was a defining moment of my life in Alaska. It was the first time someone mistook me for an Alaskan Native—and one of the most frightening—but it would not be the last. My entire life in Alaska has been shaped by the fact that people—both white and Native—think I am Athabascan or Yupik, Tlingit or Inupiat. I reaped the benefits of that: smiles and conversation from old Yupik women on the bus, an unquestioned acceptance in villages and at Native cultural events. When I taught at the university, I connected easily with Native students. But I also reaped the pain.

When I tell this story to people, there is a coda I usually include. A few years after our trip up to Manley, a similar thing happened; again the lodge owner tried to throw some people out of the bar; again he waved a shotgun. But this time it was not at a child who looked Native. It was at a man—and while I don't know if he was white or Native, I do know he was armed, and he shot first and killed the lodge owner. As vengeful as it sounds, my mother and I were pleased by this, and when I retell it as the logical end to my own story, I smile. He infected me with his hatred, and I was—am—glad he is dead. I like this end because it is satisfying; it gives the story a sort of rough justice. It gives life—so messy and vague—an aesthetically pleasing shape, as neat as fiction. I also like the way I appear in this version: invulnerable, a tough person who can speak of death coolly. Perhaps my liking for this end is left over from my turbulent adolescence, a time so fraught with pain that my only tool of survival was the tough facade I adopted and my insistence that nothing could hurt me. Perhaps the story, ended this way, is proof of that.

The real end of the story is more complicated. Because of course I was not untouched. I learned to be afraid, learned that Alaska—as beloved as it would become—was not the sanctuary my mother had hoped for. My mother was able to close her eyes and keep hoping. For me, any possibility of sanctuary was shattered. On the drive back to Fairbanks, I had asked my mother if we could go home. She knew I didn't mean the campground. We live here now, was what she told me, and I remember crying when she said that. I think even then I wondered how I would survive.

In a few years, my mother would have what she dreamed of—the high-paying construction job, her own house. In a few years she would also slam into prejudice and violence on the job, but by then, Alaska was home, so she never seriously considered leaving.

In a few years, I would hear things and learn more: hear the smug tone of the high-school counselor as he tried to steer me into the vocational track—despite my good grades; hear, more than once, the anxiety in a white boyfriend's voice as he asked for assurance that I wasn't really Native; hear the nervous laughter at a party when a white man told how he raped "a squaw" in the back of a truck. Hear the silence that followed that laughter. I was spit at in small towns, refused service in bars. In just a few years, I could recite the litany of insults so many people of color know. But I would also learn to put a name to what was happening to me, and learn to be angry. I would learn that what happened to me was not my fault, nor was it unique to Alaska. Even later, I would learn to mold my anger into something I could use.

But I didn't know any of that then. I only knew fear, and shame.

I never wore the bandana or jean jacket again.

Silent Dancing

Judith Ortiz Cofer

We have a home movie of this party. Several times my mother and I have watched it together, and I have asked questions about the silent revelers coming in and out of focus. It is grainy and of short duration, but it's a great visual aid to my memory of life at that time. And it is in color—the only complete scene in color I can recall from those years.

We lived in Puerto Rico until my brother was born in 1954. Soon after, because of economic pressures on our growing family, my father joined the United States Navy. He was assigned to duty on a ship in Brooklyn Yard—a place of cement and steel that was to be his home base in the States until his retirement more than twenty years later. He left the Island first, alone, going to New York City and tracking down his uncle who lived with his family across the Hudson River in Paterson, New Jersey. There my father found a tiny apartment in a huge tenement that had once housed Jewish families but was just being taken over and transformed by Puerto Ricans, overflowing from New York City. In 1955 he sent for us. My mother was only twenty years old, I was not quite three, and my brother was a toddler when we arrived at El Building, as the place had been christened by its newest residents.

My memories of life in Paterson during those first few years are all in shades of gray. Maybe I was too young to absorb vivid colors and details, or to discriminate between the slate blue of the winter sky and the darker hues of the snow-bearing clouds, but that single color washes over the whole period. The building we lived in was gray, as were the streets, filled with slush the first few months of my life there. The coat my father had bought for me was similar in color and too big; it sat heavily on my thin frame.

I do remember the way the heater pipes banged and rattled, startling all of us out of sleep until we got so used to the sound that we automatically shut it out or raised our voices above the racket. The hiss from the valve punctuated my sleep (which has always been fitful) like a nonhuman presence in the room—a

55

dragon sleeping at the entrance of my childhood. But the pipes were also a con-nection to all the other lives being lived around us. Having come from a house de-signed for a single family back in Puerto Rico—my mother's extended-family home—it was curious to know that strangers lived under our floor and above our heads, and that the heater pipe went through everyone's apartment. (My first spanking in Paterson came as a result of playing tunes on the pipes in my room to see if there would be an answer.) My mother was as new to this concept of bee-hive life as I was, but she had been given strict orders by my father to keep the doors locked, the noise down, ourselves to ourselves.

It seems that Father had learned some painful lessons about prejudice while searching for an apartment in Paterson. Not until years later did I hear how much resistance he had encountered with landlords who were panicking at the influx of Latinos into a neighborhood that had been Jewish for a couple of generations. It made no difference that it was the American phenomenon of ethnic turnover which was changing the urban core of Paterson, and that the human flood could not be held back with an accusing finger.

"You Cuban?" one man had asked my father, pointing at his name tag on the navy uniform—even though my father had the fair skin and light brown hair of his northern Spanish background, and the name Ortiz is as common in Puerto Rico as Johnson is in the United States.

"No," my father had answered, looking past the finger into his adversary's angry eyes. "I'm Puerto Rican."

"Same shit." And the door closed.

My father could have passed as European, but we couldn't. My brother and I both have our mother's black hair and olive skin, and so we lived in El Building and visited our great-uncle and his fair children on the next block. It was their pri-vate joke that they were the German branch of the family. Not many years later that area too would be mainly Puerto Rican. It was as if the heart of the city map were being gradually colored brown—*café con leche* brown. Our color.

The movie opens with a sweep of the living room. It is "typical" immigrant Puerto Rican decor for the time: the sofa and chairs are square and hard-looking, upholstered in bright colors (blue and yellow in this instance) and covered with the transparent plastic that fur-niture salesmen then were so adept at convincing women to buy. The linoleum on the floor is light blue; where it had been subjected to spike heels, as it was in most places, there were dime-size indentations all over it that cannot be seen in this movie. The room is full of peo-ple dressed up: dark suits for the men, red dresses for the women. When I have asked my mother why most of the women are in red that night, she has shrugged and said, "I don't remember. Just a coincidence." She doesn't have my obsession for assigning symbolism to everything.

The three women in red sitting on the couch are my mother, my eighteen-year-old cousin, and her brother's girlfriend. The novia *is just up from the Island, which is appar-ent in her body language. She sits up formally, her dress pulled over her knees. She is a pretty girl, but her posture makes her look insecure, lost in her full-skirted dress, which she has carefully tucked around her to make room for my gorgeous cousin, her future sister-in-law. My cousin has grown up in Paterson and is in her last year of high school. She doesn't have a trace of what Puerto Ricans call* la mancha *(literally, the stain: the mark of the new immigrant—something about the posture, the voice, or the humble demeanor that makes it obvious to everyone the person has just arrived on the mainland). My cousin is wearing a light, sequined, cocktail dress. Her brown hair has been lightened with peroxide around the bangs, and she is holding a cigarette expertly between her fingers, bringing it up to her mouth in a sensuous arc of her arm as she talks animatedly. My mother, who has come up to sit between the two women, both only a few years younger than herself, is somewhere between the poles they represent in our culture.*

It became my father's obsession to get out of the barrio, and thus we were never permitted to form bonds with the place or with the people who lived there. Yet El Building was a comfort to my mother, who never got over yearning for *la isla.* She felt surrounded by her language: the walls were thin, and voices speaking and arguing in Spanish could be heard all day. *Salsas* blasted out of radios, turned on early in the morning and left on for company. Women seemed to cook rice and beans perpetually—the strong aroma of boiling red kidney beans permeated the hallways.

Though Father preferred that we do our grocery shopping at the supermarket when he came home on weekend leaves, my mother insisted that she could cook only with products whose labels she could read. Consequently, during the week I accompanied her and my little brother to La Bodega—a hole-in-the-wall grocery store across the street from El Building. There we squeezed down three narrow aisles jammed with various products. Goya and Libby's—those were the trademarks that were trusted by her *mamá,* so my mother bought many cans of Goya beans, soups, and condiments, as well as little cans of Libby's fruit juices for us. And she also bought Colgate toothpaste and Palmolive soap. (The final *e* is pronounced in both these products in Spanish, so for many years I believed that they were manufactured on the Island. I remember my surprise at first hearing a commercial on television in which "Colgate" rhymed with "ate.") We always lingered at La Bodega, for it was there that Mother breathed best, taking in the familiar aromas of the foods she knew from Mamá's kitchen. It was also there that she got to speak to the other women of El Building without violating outright Father's dictates against fraternizing with our neighbors.

Yet Father did his best to make our "assimilation" painless. I can still see him carrying a real Christmas tree up several flights of stairs to our apartment, leaving a trail of aromatic pine. He carried it formally, as if it were a flag in a parade. We were the only ones in El Building that I knew of who got presents on both Christmas and *día de Reyes,* the day when the Three Kings brought gifts to Christ and to Hispanic children.

Our supreme luxury in El Building was having our own television set. It must have been a result of Father's guilt feelings over the isolation he had imposed on us, but we were among the first in the barrio to have one. My brother quickly became an avid watcher of Captain Kangaroo and Jungle Jim, while I loved all the series showing families. By the time I started first grade, I could have drawn a map of Middle America as exemplified by the lives of characters in *Father Knows Best, The Donna Reed Show, Leave It to Beaver, My Three Sons,* and (my favorite) *Bachelor Father,* where John Forsythe treated his adopted teenage daughter like a princess because he was rich and had a Chinese houseboy to do everything for him. In truth, compared to our neighbors in El Building, we were rich. My father's navy check provided us with financial security and a standard of living that the factory workers envied. The only thing his money could not buy us was a place to live away from the barrio—his greatest wish, Mother's greatest fear.

In the home movie the men are shown next, sitting around a card table set up in one corner of the living room, playing dominoes. The clack of the ivory pieces was a familiar sound. I heard it in many houses on the Island and in many apartments in Paterson. In Leave It to Beaver, *the Cleavers played bridge in every other episode; in my childhood, the men started every social occasion with a hotly debated round of dominoes. The women would sit around and watch, but they never participated in the games.*

    Here and there you can see a small child. Children were always brought to parties and, whenever they got sleepy, were put to bed in the host's bedroom. Babysitting was a concept unrecognized by the Puerto Rican women I knew: a responsible mother did not leave her children with any stranger. And in a culture where children are not considered intrusive, there was no need to leave the children at home. We went where our mother went.

Of my preschool years I have only impressions: the sharp bite of the wind in December as we walked with our parents toward the brightly lit stores downtown; how I felt like a stuffed doll in my heavy coat, boots, and mittens; how good it was to walk into the five-and-dime and sit at the counter drinking hot chocolate. On Saturdays our whole family would walk downtown to shop at the big department stores on Broadway. Mother bought all our clothes at Penney's and Sears, and she liked to buy her dresses at the women's specialty shops like Lerner's and Diana's. At some point we'd go into Woolworth's and sit at the soda fountain to eat.

    We never ran into other Latinos at these stores or when eating out, and it became clear to me only years later that the women from El Building shopped mainly in other places—stores owned by other Puerto Ricans or by Jewish merchants who had philosophically accepted our presence in the city and decided to make us their good customers, if not real neighbors and friends. These establishments were located not downtown but in the blocks around our street, and they were referred to generically as La Tienda, El Bazar, La Bodega, La Botánica. Everyone knew what was meant. These were the stores where your face did not turn a clerk to stone, where your money was as green as anyone else's.

One New Year's Eve we were dressed up like child models in the Sears catalogue: my brother in a miniature man's suit and bow tie, and I in black patent-leather shoes and a frilly dress with several layers of crinoline underneath. My mother wore a bright red dress that night, I remember, and spike heels; her long black hair hung to her waist. Father, who usually wore his navy uniform during his short visits home, had put on a dark civilian suit for the occasion: we had been invited to his uncle's house for a big celebration. Everyone was excited because my mother's brother Hernan—a bachelor who could indulge himself with luxuries— had bought a home movie camera, which he would be trying out that night.

Even the home movie cannot fill in the sensory details such a gathering left imprinted in a child's brain. The thick sweetness of women's perfumes mixing with the ever-present smells of food cooking in the kitchen: meat and plantain *pasteles,* as well as the ubiquitous rice dish made special with pigeon peas—*gandules*—and seasoned with precious *sofrito* sent up from the Island by somebody's mother or smuggled in by a recent traveler. *Sofrito* was one of the items that women hoarded, since it was hardly ever in stock at La Bodega. It was the flavor of Puerto Rico.

The men drank Palo Viejo rum, and some of the younger ones got weepy. The first time I saw a grown man cry was at a New Year's Eve party: he had been reminded of his mother by the smells in the kitchen. But what I remember most were the boiled *pasteles,* plantain or yucca rectangles stuffed with corned beef or other meats, olives, and many other savory ingredients, all wrapped in banana leaves. Everybody had to fish one out with a fork. There was always a "trick" *pastel*—one without stuffing—and whoever got that one was the "New Year's Fool."

There was also the music. Long-playing albums were treated like precious china in these homes. Mexican recordings were popular, but the songs that brought tears to my mother's eyes were sung by the melancholy Daniel Santos, whose life as a drug addict was the stuff of legend. Felipe Rodríguez was a particular favorite of couples, since he sang about faithless women and brokenhearted men. There is a snatch of one lyric that has stuck in my mind like a needle on a worn groove: *De piedra ha de ser mi cama, de piedra la cabezera . . . la mujer que a mi me quiera . . . ha de quererme de veras. Ay, Ay, Ay, corazón, porque no amas . . .* I must have heard it a thousand times since the idea of a bed made of stone, and its connection to love, first troubled me with its disturbing images.

The five-minute home movie ends with people dancing in a circle—the creative filmmaker must have set it up, so that all of them could file past him. It is both comical and sad to watch silent dancing. Since there is no justification for the absurd movements that music provides for some of us, people appear frantic, their faces embarrassingly intense. It's as if you were watching sex. Yet for years, I've had dreams in the form of this home movie. In a recurring scene, familiar faces push themselves forward into my mind's eye, plastering their features into distorted close-ups. And I'm asking them: "Who is *she?* Who is the old woman I don't recognize? Is she an aunt? Somebody's wife? Tell me who she is."

"See the beauty mark on her cheek as big as a hill on the lunar landscape of her face—well, that runs in the family. The women on your father's side of the family wrinkle early; it's the price they pay for that fair skin. The young girl with the green stain on her wedding dress is *la novia*—just up from the Island. See, she lowers her eyes when she approaches the camera, as she's supposed to. Decent girls never look at you directly in the face. *Humilde,* humble, a girl should express humility in all her actions. She will make a good wife for your cousin. He should consider himself lucky to have met her only weeks after she arrived here. If he marries her quickly, she will make him a good Puerto Rican–style wife; but if he waits too long, she will be corrupted by the city, just like your cousin there."

"She means me. I do what I want. This is not some primitive island I live on. Do they expect me to wear a black mantilla on my head and go to mass every day? Not me. I'm an American woman, and I will do as I please. I can type faster than anyone in my senior class at Central High, and I'm going to be a secretary to a lawyer when I graduate. I can pass for an American girl anywhere—I've tried it. At least for Italian, anyway—I never speak Spanish in public. I hate these parties, but I wanted the dress. I look better than any of these *humildes* here. *My* life is going to be different. I have an American boyfriend. He is older and has a car. My parents don't know it, but I sneak out of the house late at night sometimes to be with him. If I marry him, even my name will be American. I hate rice and beans—that's what makes these women fat."

"Your *prima* is pregnant by that man she's been sneaking around with. Would I lie to you? I'm your *tía política*, your great-uncle's common-law wife—the one he abandoned on the Island to go marry your cousin's mother. *I* was not invited to this party, of course, but I came anyway. I came to tell you that story about your cousin that you've always wanted to hear. Do you remember the comment your mother made to a neighbor that has always haunted you? The only thing you heard was your cousin's name, and then you saw your mother pick up your doll from the couch and say: 'It was as big as this doll when they flushed it down the toilet.' This image has bothered you for years, hasn't it? You had nightmares about babies being flushed down the toilet, and you wondered why anyone would do such a horrible thing. You didn't dare ask your mother about it. She would only tell you that you had not heard her right, and yell at you for listening to adult conversations. But later, when you were old enough to know about abortions, you suspected.

"I am here to tell you that you were right. Your cousin was growing an *americanito* in her belly when this movie was made. Soon after, she put something long and pointy into her pretty self, thinking maybe she could get rid of the problem before breakfast and still make it to her first class at the high school. Well, *niña,* her screams could be heard downtown. Your aunt, her *mamá,* who had been a midwife on the Island, managed to pull the little thing out. Yes, they probably flushed it down the toilet. What else could they do with it—give it a Christian burial in a little white casket with blue bows and ribbons? Nobody wanted that baby—least of all the father, a teacher at her school with a house in West Paterson that he was filling with real children, and a wife who was a natural blonde.

"Girl, the scandal sent your uncle back to the bottle. And guess where your cousin ended up? Irony of ironies. She was sent to a village in Puerto Rico to live with a relative on her mother's side: a place so far away from civilization that you have to ride a mule to reach it. A real change in scenery. She found a man there—women like that cannot live without male company—but believe me, the men in Puerto Rico know how to put a saddle on a woman like her. *La gringa,* they call her. Ha, ha, ha. *La gringa* is what she always wanted to be. . . ."

The old woman's mouth becomes a cavernous black hole I fall into. And as I fall, I can feel the reverberations of her laughter. I hear the echoes of her last mocking words: *la gringa, la gringa!* And the conga line keeps moving silently past me. There is no music in my dream for the dancers.

When Odysseus visits Hades to see the spirit of his mother, he makes an offering of sacrificial blood, but since all the souls crave an audience with the living, he has to listen to many of them before he can ask questions. I, too, have to hear the dead and the forgotten speak in my dream. Those who are still part of my life remain silent, going around and around in their dance. The others keep pressing their faces forward to say things about the past.

My father's uncle is last in line. He is dying of alcoholism, shrunken and shriveled like a monkey, his face a mass of wrinkles and broken arteries. As he comes closer I realize that in his features I can see my whole family. If you were to stretch that rubbery flesh, you could find my father's face, and deep within *that* face—my own. I don't want to look into those eyes ringed in purple. In a few years he will retreat into silence, and take a long, long time to die. *Move back, Tío, I tell him. I don't want to hear what you have to say. Give the dancers room to move. Soon it will be midnight. Who is the New Year's Fool this time?*

Running the Table

Frank Conroy

When I was fifteen and living in New York City, I was supposed to be going to Stuyvesant High School and in fact I did actually show up three or four times a week, full of gloom, anger and adolescent narcissism. The world was a dark place for me in those days. I lived in a kind of tunnel of melancholy, constantly in trouble at home, in school and occasionally with the police. (Pitching pennies, sneaking into movies, jumping the turnstile in the subway, stealing paperback books—fairly serious stuff in that earlier, more innocent time.) I was haunted by a sense of chaos, chaos within and chaos without. Which is perhaps why the orderliness of pool, the Euclidean cleanness of it, so appealed to me. The formality of pool struck me as soothing and reassuring, a sort of oasis of coolness, utterly rational and yet not without its elegant little mysteries. But I'm getting ahead of myself.

One day, meandering around 14th Street, I stepped through the open doors on an impulse and mounted the long, broad stairway. Halfway up I heard the click of the balls. What a marvelous sound! Precise, sharp, crisp, and yet somehow mellow. There was an intimacy to the sound that thrilled me. At the top of the stairs I pushed through saloon-style swinging doors and entered a vast, hushed, dim hall. Rows of pool tables stretched away in every direction, almost all of them empty at this early hour, but here and there in the distance, a pool of light, figures in silhouette circling, bending, taking shots. Nearby, two old men were playing a game I would later learn to be billiards on a large table without pockets. The click of the three balls, two white, one red, was what I had heard on the stairs. The men played unhurriedly, pausing now and then with their cues held like walking sticks to stare down at the street below. Cigar smoke swirled in the air.

I had walked into Julian's, little knowing that it was one of the most important pool halls on the East Coast. I was impressed by the stark functionality of the place—the absence of decoration of any kind. It seemed almost institutional in its atmosphere, right down to the large poster hung on the cashier's cage setting out the rules and regulations. No drinking, no eating, no sitting on the edges of the tables, no spitting except in the cuspidors, no massé shots, etc. Tables were twenty-five cents an hour. Cue sticks were to be found on racks against the walls. Balls available from the cashier as he clocked you in.

"How do you play?" I asked.

The cashier was bald and overweight. He wore, for some reason, a green eyeshade. "You from Stuyvesant?"

I nodded, and he grunted, reached down to some hidden shelf and gave me a small paper pamphlet, pushing it forward across the worn wooden counter. I scanned it quickly. Basic information about straight pool, eight ball, nine ball, billiards, snooker, and a few other games. "Start with straight pool," he said. "Go over there and watch those guys on twenty-two for a while. Sit still, don't talk, and don't move around."

I did as I was told, sitting on a kind of mini-bleachers against the wall, my chin in my hands. The two men playing were in their twenties, an Abbott-and-Costello duo, thin Bud wearing a vest and smoking constantly, pudgy Lou moving delicately around the table, using the bridge now and then because of his short arms. They paid no attention to me and played with concentration, silent except for calling combinations.

"Six off the thirteen," Lou said.

Bud nodded. They only called combinations. All straight shots, no matter how difficult, were presumably obvious. After a while, with a few discreet glances at my pamphlet, I began to get the hang of it. All the balls, striped and solid, were fair game. You simply kept shooting until you missed, and then it was the other guy's turn. After each run, you moved some beads on a wire overhead with the tip of your cue, marking up the number of balls you'd sunk. So much for the rules. What was amazing was the shooting.

Object balls clipped so fine they moved sideways. Bank shots off the cushion into a pocket. Long combinations. Breakout shots in which a whole cluster of balls would explode in all directions while one from the middle would limp into a nearby pocket. And it didn't take long to realize that making a given shot was only part of what was going on. Controlling the position of the cue ball after the shot was equally important, so as to have a makable next shot. I could see that strategy was involved, although how they made the cue ball behave so differently in similar situations seemed nothing short of magical. Lou completed a run of nine or ten balls and reached fifty on the wire overhead. He had won, apparently.

"Double or nothing?"

Bud shook his head. Money changed hands. Lou put the balls in a tray, turned out the light over the table, and both men checked out at the cashier's. I sat for a while, thinking over what I had seen, reading the pamphlet again. I didn't have enough money to play that day, but I knew I was coming back.

Sometime in the late sixties, as an adult, I went to the Botanic Garden in Brooklyn to visit the recently completed Zen rock garden. It was a meticulous re-creation of a particular installation from a particular Japanese monastery. No one else was there. I sat on the bench gazing at the spiral patterns in the sand, looking at the black rocks set like volcanic islands in a white sea. Peace. Tranquility. As absurd as it may sound, I was reminded of my childhood experience of Julian's on a quiet afternoon—a sense of harmony, of an entirely disinterested material world entirely unaffected by one's perception of it.

For me, at fifteen, Julian's was a sort of retreat, a withdrawal from the world. I would shoot for hours at a time, racking up, breaking, shooting, racking up, breaking, shooting, in a solitary trance. Or I would surrender to the ritual of practice—setting up long shots over the length of the table again and again, trying to sink a shot with the same configuration ten times in a row, and then twenty, and then a more difficult configuration to a different pocket three times in a row, and then five, etc. I did not get bored with the repetition. Every time a ball went in the pocket I felt satisfaction. When I missed I simply ignored the fact, reset the shot and tried again. This went on for several weeks at a remote table in a far corner of the hall—table nineteen—which nobody else ever seemed to want. Once in a while I'd play with another kid, usually also from Stuyvesant, and split the time. After a couple of months I would sometimes play for the time—loser pays—against opponents who looked even weaker than myself. But most of the time I played alone.

Late one afternoon, racking up on table nineteen for perhaps the tenth time, I noticed a man sitting in the gloom up against the wall. He was extremely thin, with a narrow face and a protruding brow. He wore a double-breasted suit and two-tone shoes, one leg dangling languidly over the other. He gave me an almost imperceptible nod. I chalked the tip of my cue, went to the head of the table and stroked a clean break. Aware that I was being watched, I studied the lie of the balls for a moment and proceeded to sink seven in a row, everything going according to plan, until I scratched. I pulled up the cue ball and the object ball, recreated the shot and scratched again.

"Why don't you use English?" he asked quietly.

I stared at the table. "What's English?"

A moment's pause. "Set it up again," he said.

I did so.

"Aim, but don't hit. Pretend you're going to shoot."

I made a bridge with my left hand, aimed at the object ball and held the tip of my stick right behind the center of the cue ball.

"All right. All lined up?"

"Yes," I said, almost flat on the table.

"Do not change the line. Are you aiming at the center of the cue ball?"

"Yes."

"Aim a quarter of an inch higher."

"You mean I should. . . ." For some reason what he was suggesting seemed almost sacrilegious.

"Yes, yes. Don't hit the cue ball in the center. Strike a quarter of an inch above. Now go ahead. Shoot."

I made my stroke, watched the object ball go in, and watched the cue ball take a different path after impact than it had before. It didn't scratch this time, but missed the pocket, bounced smartly off the cushion and rolled to a stop near the center of the table for an easy next shot.

"Hey. That's terrific!" I said.

"That's English." He unfolded his legs and stood up. He came over and took the pool cue from my hands. "If a person pays attention," he said, "a person can learn about ninety-five percent of what he needs to know in about ten minutes. Ten minutes for the principles, then who knows how many years for the practice." His dark, deep-set eyes gave his face a vaguely ominous cast. "You want to learn?"

"Absolutely," I said without hesitation. "Yes."

As it turned out, it took about half an hour. The man teaching me was called Smilin' Jack, after the comic-strip character and presumably because of his glum demeanor. He was a Julian's regular, and it was my good luck to have caught him when somebody had stood him up for what was to have been a money game. I could sense that he enjoyed going through the drill—articulate, methodical, explicating on cause and effect with quiet relish, moving the balls around the table with no wasted motion whatsoever, executing the demo shots with a stroke as smooth as powdered silk—it was an elegant dance, with commentary. A sort of offering to the gods of pool.

I cannot possibly recount here what I learned. Follow, draw, left and right English and how they affect the movement of the cue ball after impact. The object ball picking up opposite English from the cue ball. The effectiveness of different kinds of English as a function of distance (between cue ball and object ball) and of speed. *Sliding* the cue ball. Playing the diamond points. Shooting a ball frozen on the cushion. How to read combinations, and on and on. I paid very close attention and jotted down what notes I could. (*Over*shoot bank shots to the side pockets. *Under*shoot bank shots to the corner pockets.) At the end of the half hour my head ached. In addition to trying to grasp the principles, I'd been trying to film the whole thing, to superimpose an eidetic memory on the cells of my brain, so I could retrieve what I'd seen at will. I was exhausted.

He handed me the stick, shot his cuffs and adjusted the front of his jacket with a slight forward movement of his shoulders. "That should keep you busy for a while." Then he simply walked away.

"Thanks," I called after him.

Without looking back, he raised his hand and gave a laconic little wave.

Practice, practice. Months of practice. It was a delicate business, English, affected by things like the relative roughness of the cue tip and its ability to hold chalk, or the condition of the felt, or infinitesimal degrees of table lean. But it worked. There was no doubt about it, when you got the feel of it you greatly increased your power over the all-important position of the cue ball. There was a word for it—the "leave," as in "good shot, but a tough leave." And of course the more you could control the leave, the more deeply involved was the strategy—planning out how to sink twelve balls in a row, rather than just five or six. Progress was slow, but it was tangible, and very, very satisfying. I began to beat people. I moved off table nineteen up toward the middle of the hall and began to beat almost everybody from Stuyvesant.

The most important hurdle for a straight-pool player involves being able to run into the second rack. You have to sink fourteen balls and leave the fifteenth ball and the cue ball positioned in such a way as to be able to sink the last ball (breaking open the new rack at the same time) and have a good enough leave to start all over again. I achieved this shortly before my sixteenth birthday, with a run of twenty-three.

The owners of Julian's recognized the accomplishment as a significant rite of passage and awarded certain privileges to those who had achieved it. During my last year of high school a cue of my own selection, with my name taped to the handle, was kept in a special rack behind the cashier's cage. No one else could use that particular cue stick. It was reserved, along with thirty or forty others for young players who had distinguished themselves.

I was a nonentity at school, but I could walk up to the cage at Julian's and the cashier would reach back for my stick and say, "Hey, Frank. How's it going?"

What a splendid place it was.

There's a lot to feel in pool, a physical aspect to the game, which means you have to play all the time to stay good. I've lost most of my chops (to borrow a word from jazz), but I still drop down to my local bar, the Foxhead, every now and then to play on the undersize table. It's a challenge arrangement. Put your name on the chalkboard, slip two quarters in the slot when it's your turn, and try to win.

There's a good deal more chance in eight ball, your basic bar game, than in straight pool, but it's fun. We've got some regulars. Jerry, a middle-aged man with a gorgeous stroke (a nationally ranked player in his youth), can beat any-body who walks into the place if he isn't furious at having to play doubles, at kids slopping beer onto the felt, or some other infraction of civilized behavior. There's Doug, a graduate student who always looks as if he'd spent the previous night in a cardboard box in an alley and who hits every shot as hard as he can, leaving the question of where the cue ball is going to end up more or less to the gods, in the hope that they will thus tangibly express the favor in which they hold him. (He is a poet.) We have George, an engineer, who exhausts our patience by approaching each situation with extreme care, circling the table several times, leaning over to stare down at a cluster of balls in what appears to be a hypnotic trance, chalking up with the care of Vermeer at the easel and running through a complicated series of various facial and physical tics before committing himself. There's Henry, who programs the jukebox to play "Brown Sugar" ten times in a row before he racks up. We've got students, working people, teachers, nurses (Yes. Women! Smilin' Jack would be scandalized) and barflies. We've got every-body at the Foxhead.

There are nights when I can hold the table for a couple of hours, but not very often. My touch is mostly gone, and bifocals make things difficult. Still, a bit of Julian's is still with me and, at the very least, I talk a good game.

On the Fringes of the Physical World

Meghan Daum

It started in cold weather; fall was drifting away into an intolerable chill. I was on the tail end of twenty-six, living in New York City, and trying to support myself as a writer. One morning I logged on to my America Online account to find a message under the heading "is this the real meghan daum?" It came from someone with the screen name PFSlider. The body of the message consisted of five sentences, written entirely in lowercase letters, of perfectly turned flattery, something about PFSlider's admiration of some newspaper and magazine articles I had published over the last year and a half, something else about his resulting infatuation with me, and something about his being a sportswriter in California.

I was charmed for a moment or so, engaged for the thirty seconds that it took me to read the message and fashion a reply. Though it felt strange to be in the position of confirming that I was indeed "the real meghan daum," I managed to say, "Yes, it's me. Thank you for writing." I clicked the "Send Now" icon and shot my words into the void, where I forgot about PFSlider until the next day when I received another message, this one entitled "eureka." "wow, it is you," he wrote, still in lowercase. He chronicled the various conditions under which he'd read my few and far between articles: a boardwalk in Laguna Beach, the spring training pressroom for the baseball team he covered for a Los Angeles newspaper. He confessed to having a "crazy crush" on me. He referred to me as "princess daum." He said he wanted to propose marriage or at least have lunch with me during one of his two annual trips to New York. He managed to do all of this without sounding like a schmuck. As I read the note, I smiled the kind of smile one tries to suppress, the kind of smile that arises during a sappy movie one never even admits to seeing. The letter was outrageous and endearingly pathetic, possibly the practical joke of a friend trying to rouse me out of a temporary writer's block.

But the kindness pouring forth from my computer screen was unprecedented and bizarrely exhilarating. I logged off and thought about it for a few hours before writing back to express how flattered and touched—this was probably the first time I had ever used the word "touched" in earnest—I was by his message.

I had received e-mail messages from strangers before, most of them kind and friendly and courteous—all of those qualities that generally get checked with the coats at the cocktail parties that comprise what the information age has now forced us to call the "three-dimensional world." I am always warmed by an unsolicited gesture of admiration or encouragement, amazed that anyone would bother, shocked that communication from a stranger could be fueled by anything other than an attempt to get a job or make what the professional world has come to call "a connection."

I am not what most people would call a "computer person." I have utterly no interest in chat rooms, news groups, or most Web sites. I derive a palpable thrill from sticking an actual letter in the U.S. mail. But e-mail, though at that time I generally only sent and received a few messages a week, proves a useful forum for my particular communication anxieties. I have a constant, low-grade fear of the telephone. I often call people with the intention of getting their answering machines. There is something about the live voice that has become startling, unnervingly organic, as volatile as incendiary talk radio. PFSlider and I tossed a few innocuous, smart-assed notes back and forth over the week following his first message. His name was Pete. He was twenty-nine and single. I revealed very little about myself, relying instead on the ironic commentary and forced witticisms that are the conceit of most e-mail messages. But I quickly developed an oblique affection for PFSlider. I was excited when there was a message from him, mildly depressed when there wasn't. After a few weeks, he gave me his phone number. I did not give him mine but he looked me up anyway and called me one Friday night. I was home. I picked up the phone. His voice was jarring yet not unpleasant. He held up more than his end of the conversation for an hour and when he asked permission to call me again, I accepted as though we were in a previous century.

Pete, as I was forced to call him on the phone—I never could wrap my mind around his actual name, privately referring to him as PFSlider, "e-mail guy," or even "baseball boy"—began calling me two or three times a week. He asked if he could meet me in person and I said that would be okay. Christmas was a few weeks away and he would be returning east to see his family. From there, he would take the short flight to New York and have lunch with me. "It is my off-season mission to meet you," he said. "There will probably be a snowstorm," I said. "I'll take a team of sled dogs," he answered. We talked about our work and our families, about baseball and Bill Clinton and Howard Stern and sex, about his hatred for Los Angeles and how much he wanted a new job. Other times we would find each other logged on to America Online at the same time and type back and forth for hours. For me, this was far superior to the phone. Through typos and misspellings, he flirted maniacally. "I have an absurd crush on you," he said. "If I like you in person you must promise to marry me." I was coy and conceited, telling him to get a life, baiting him into complimenting me further, teasing him in a way I would never have dared in the real world or even on the phone. I would stay up until 3 A.M. typing with him, smiling at the screen, getting so giddy that I couldn't fall asleep. I was having difficulty recalling what I used to do at night. My phone was tied up for hours at a time. No one in the real world could reach me, and I didn't really care.

In off moments, I heard echoes of things I'd said just weeks earlier: "The Internet is destroying the world. Human communication will be rendered obsolete. We will all develop carpal tunnel syndrome and die." But curiously, the Internet, at least in the limited form in which I was using it, was having the opposite effect. My interaction with PFSlider was more human than much of what I experienced in the daylight realm of live beings. I was certainly putting more energy into the relationship than I had put into any before, giving him attention that was by definition undivided, relishing the safety of the distance by opting to be truthful rather than doling out the white lies that have become the staple of real life. The outside world—the place where I walked around on the concrete, avoiding people I didn't want to deal with, peppering the ground with half-truths, and applying my motto of "let the machine take it" to almost any scenario—was sliding into the periphery of my mind. I was a better person with PFSlider. I was someone I could live with.

This borrowed identity is, of course, the primary convention of Internet relationships. The false comfort of the cyberspace persona has been identified as one of the maladies of our time, another avenue for the remoteness that so famously plagues contemporary life. But the better person that I was to PFSlider was not a result of being a different person to him. It was simply that I was a desired person, the object of a blind man's gaze. I may not have known my suitor, but for the first time in my life, I knew the deal. I knew when I'd hear from him and how I'd hear from him. I knew he wanted me because he said he wanted me, because the distance and facelessness and lack of gravity of it all allowed him to be sweeter to me than most real-life people had ever managed. For the first time in my life, I was involved in a ritualized courtship. Never before had I realized how much that kind of structure was missing from my everyday life.

And so PFSlider became my everyday life. All the tangible stuff—the trees outside, my friends, the weather—fell away. I could physically feel my brain. My body did not exist. I had no skin, no hair, no bones; all desire had converted itself into a cerebral current that reached nothing but my frontal lobe. Lust was something not felt but thought. My brain was devouring all of my other organs and gaining speed with each swallow. There was no outdoors, the sky and wind were irrelevant. There was only the computer screen and the phone, my chair and maybe a glass of water. Pete stared calling every day, sometimes twice, even three times. Most mornings I would wake up to find a message from PFSlider, composed in Pacific time while I slept in the wee hours. "I had a date last night," he wrote, "and I am not ashamed to say it was doomed from the start because I couldn't stop thinking about you." Then , a few days later, "If you stood before me now, I would plant the warmest kiss on your check that I could muster."

I fired back a message slapping this hand. "We must be careful where we tread," I said. This was true but not sincere. I wanted it, all of it. I wanted the deepest bow down before me. I wanted my ego not merely massaged but kneaded. I wanted unfettered affection, soul mating, true romance. In the weeks that had elapsed since I picked up "is this the real meghan daum?" the real me underwent some kind of meltdown, a systemic rejection of all the savvy and independence I had worn for years like a grown-up Girl Scout badge. Since graduating from college, I had spent three years in a serious relationship and two years in a state of neither looking for a boyfriend nor particularly avoiding one. I had had the requisite number of false starts and five-night stands, dates that I wasn't sure were dates, emphatically casual affairs that buckled under their own inertia even before dawn broke through the iron-guarded windows of stale, one-room city apartments. Even though I was heading into my late twenties, I was still a child, ignorant of dance steps or health insurance, a prisoner of credit-card debt and student loans and the nagging feeling that I didn't want anyone to find me until I had pulled myself into some semblance of an adult. I was true believer in the urban dream—in years of struggle succumbing to brilliant success, in getting a break, in making it. Like most of my friends, I was selfish by design. To want was more virtuous than to need. I wanted someone to love me but I certainly didn't need it. I didn't want to be alone, but as long as I was, I had no choice but to wear my solitude as though it were haute couture. The worst sin imaginable was not cruelty or bitchiness or even professional failure but vulnerability. To admit to loneliness was to slap the face of progress. It was to betray the times in which we lived.

But PFSlider derailed me. He gave me all of what I'd never realized I wanted. He called not only when he said he would, but unexpectedly, just to say hello. His guard was not merely down but nonexistent. He let his phone bill grow to towering proportions. He thought about me all the time and admitted it. He talked about me with his friends and admitted it. He arranged his holiday schedule around our impending date. He managed to charm me with sports analogies. He courted and wooed and romanced me. He didn't hesitate. He was unblinking and unapologetic, all nerviness and balls to the wall. He wasn't cheap. He went out of his way. I'd never seen anything like it.

Of all the troubling details of this story, the one that bothers me the most is the way I slurped up his attention like some kind of dying animal. My addiction to PFSlider's messages indicated a monstrous narcissism. But it also revealed a subtler desire that I didn't fully understand at the time. My need to experience an old-fashioned kind of courtship was stronger than I had ever imagined. The epistolary quality of our relationship put our communication closer to the eighteenth century than the uncertain millennium. For the first time in my life, I was not involved in a protracted "hang out" that would lead to a quasi-romance. I was involved in a well-defined structure, a neat little space in which we were both safe to express the panic and intrigue of our mutual affection. Our interaction was refreshingly orderly, noble in its vigor, dignified despite its shamelessness. It was far removed from the randomness of real-life relationships. We had an intimacy that seemed custom-made for our strange, lonely times. It seemed custom-made for me.

The day of our date was frigid and sunny. Pete was sitting at the bar of the restaurant when I arrived. We shook hands. For a split second he leaned toward me with his chin as if to kiss me. He was shorter than I had imagined, though he was not short. He registered to me as neither handsome nor un-handsome. He had very nice hands. He wore a very nice shirt. We were seated at a very nice table. I scanned the restaurant for people I knew, saw no one and couldn't decide how I felt about that.

He talked and I heard nothing he said. He talked and talked and talked. I stared at his profile and tried to figure out if I liked him. He seemed to be saying nothing in particular, though it went on forever. Later we went to the Museum of Natural History and watched a science film about the physics of storms. We walked around looking for the dinosaurs and he talked so much that I wanted to cry. Outside, walking along Central Park West at dusk, through the leaves, past the horse-drawn carriages and yellow cabs and splendid lights of Manhattan at Christmas, he grabbed my hand to kiss me and I didn't let him. I felt as if my brain had been stuffed with cotton. Then, for some reason, I invited him back to my apartment, gave him a few beers, and finally let him kiss me on the lumpy futon in my bedroom. The radiator clanked. The phone rang and the machine picked up. A car alarm blared outside. A key turned in the door as one of my roommates came home. I had no sensation at all, only the dull déjà vu of being back in some college dorm room, making out in a generic fashion on an Indian throw rug while Cat Stevens' *Greatest Hits* played on the portable stereo. I wanted Pete out of my apartment. I wanted to hand him his coat, close the door behind him, and fight the ensuing emptiness by turning on the computer and taking comfort in PFSlider.

When Pete finally did leave, I sulked. The ax had fallen. He'd talked way too much. He was hyper. He hadn't let me talk, although I hadn't tried very hard. I berated myself from every angle, for not kissing him on Central Park West, for letting him kiss me at all, for not liking him, for wanting to like him more than I had wanted anything in such a long time. I was horrified by the realization that I had invested so heavily in a made-up character, a character in whose creation I'd had a greater hand than even Pete himself. How could I, a person so self-congratulatingly reasonable, have gotten sucked into a scenario that was more akin to a television talk show than the relatively full and sophisticated life I was so convinced I led? How could I have received a fan letter and allowed it to go this far? Then a huge bouquet of FTD flowers arrived from him. No one had ever sent me flowers before. I was sick with sadness. I hated either the world or myself, and probably both.

No one had ever forced me to forgive them before. But for some reason, I forgave Pete. I cut him more slack than I ever had anyone. I granted him an official pardon, excused his failure for not living up to PFSlider. Instead of blaming him, I blamed the Earth itself, the invasion of tangible things into the immaculate communication PFSlider and I had created. With its roommates and ringing phones and subzero temperatures, the physical world came barreling in with all the obstreperousness of a major weather system, and I ignored it. As human beings with actual flesh and hand gestures and Gap clothing, Pete and I were utterly incompatible, but I pretended otherwise. In the weeks that followed I pictured him and saw the image of a plane lifting off over an overcast city. PFSlider was otherworldly, more a concept than a person. His romance lay in the notion of flight, the physics of gravity defiance. So when he offered to send me a plane ticket to spend the weekend with him in Los Angeles, I took it as an extension of our blissful remoteness, a three-dimensional e-mail message lasting an entire weekend. I pretended it was a good idea.

The temperature on the runway at JFK was seven degrees Fahrenheit. We sat for three hours waiting for de-icing. Finally we took off over the frozen city, the DC-10 hurling itself against the wind. The ground below shrank into a drawing of itself. Laptop computers were plopped onto tray tables. The air recirculated and dried out my contact lenses. I watched movies without the sound and thought to myself that they were probably better that way. Something about the plastic interior of the fuselage and the plastic forks and the din of the air and the engines was soothing and strangely sexy, as fabricated and seductive as PFSlider. I thought about Pete and wondered if I could ever turn him into an actual human being, if I could ever even want to. I knew so many people in real life, people to whom I spoke face-to-face, people who made me laugh or made me frustrated or happy or bored. But I'd never given any of them as much as I'd given PFSlider. I'd never forgiven their spasms and their speeches, never tied up my phone for hours in order to talk to them. I'd never bestowed such senseless tenderness on anyone.

We descended into LAX. We hit the tarmac and the seat belt signs blinked off. I hadn't moved my body in eight hours, and now, I was walking through the tunnel to the gate, my clothes wrinkled, my hair matted, my hands shaking. When I saw Pete in the terminal, his face registered to me as blank and impossible to process as the first time I'd met him. He kissed me chastely. On the way out to the parking lot, he told me that he was being seriously considered for a job in New York. He was flying back there next week. If he got the job he'd be moving within the month. I looked at him in astonishment. Something silent and invisible seemed to fall on us. Outside, the wind was warm and the Avis and Hertz buses ambled alongside the curb of Terminal 5. The palm trees shook and the air seemed as heavy and earthly as Pete's hand, which held mine for a few seconds before dropping it to get his car keys out of his pocket. The leaves on the trees were unmanageably real. He stood before me, all flesh and preoccupation. The physical world had invaded our space. For this I could not forgive him.

Everything now was for the touching. Everything was buildings and bushes, parking meters and screen doors and sofas. Gone was the computer; the erotic darkness of the telephone; the clean, single dimension of Pete's voice at 1 A.M. It was nighttime, yet the combination of sight and sound was blinding. We went to a restaurant and ate outside on the sidewalk. We were strained for conversation. I tried not to care. We drove to his apartment and stood under the ceiling light not really looking at each other. Something was happening that we needed to snap out of. Any moment now, I thought. Any moment and we'll be all right. These moments were crowded with elements, with carpet fibers and direct light and the smells of everything that had a smell. They left marks as they passed. It was all wrong. Gravity was all there was.

For three days, we crawled along the ground and tried to pull ourselves up. We talked about things that I can no longer remember. We read the *Los Angeles Times* over breakfast. We drove north past Santa Barbara to tour the wine country. I stomped around in my clunky shoes and black leather jacket, a killer of ants and earthworms and any hope in our abilities to speak and be understood. Not until studying myself in the bathroom mirror of a highway rest stop did I fully realize the preposterousness of my uniform. I felt like the shot in a human shot put, an object that could not be lifted, something that secretly weighed more than the world itself. We ate an expensive dinner. We checked into a hotel and watched television. Pete talked at me and through me and past me. I tried to listen. I tried to talk. But I bored myself and irritated him. Our conversation was a needle that could not be threaded. Still, we played nice. We tried to care and pretended to keep trying long after we had given up. In the car on the way home, he told me I was cynical, and I didn't have the presence of mind to ask him just how many cynics he had met who would travel three thousand miles to see someone they barely knew. Just for a chance. Just because the depths of my hope exceeded the thickness of my leather jacket and the thickness of my skin. And at that moment, I released myself into the sharp knowledge that communication had once again eliminated itself as a possibility.

Pete drove me to the airport at 7 A.M. so I could make my eight o'clock flight home. He kissed me goodbye, another chaste peck I recognized from countless dinner parties and dud dates from real life. He said he'd call me in a few days when he got to New York for his job interview, which he had discussed only in passing and with no reference to the fact that New York was where I happened to live. I returned home to the frozen January. A few days later, he came to New York and we didn't see each other. He called me from the plane back to Los Angeles to tell me, through the static, that he had gotten the job. He was moving to my city.

PFSlider was dead. Pete had killed him. I had killed him. I'd killed my own persona too, the girl on the phone and online, the character created by some writer who'd captured him one morning long ago as he read the newspaper. There would be no meeting him in distant hotel lobbies during the baseball season. There would be no more phone calls or e-mail messages. In a single moment, Pete had completed his journey out of our mating dance and officially stepped into the regular world, the world that gnawed at me daily, the world that fed those five-night stands, the world where romance could not be sustained because we simply did not know how to do it. Here, we were all chitchat and leather jackets, bold proclaimers of all that we did not need. But what struck me most about this affair was the unpredictable nature of our demise. Unlike most cyber romances, which seem to come fully equipped with the inevitable set of misrepresentations and false expectations, PFSlider and I had played it fairly straight. Neither of us had lied. We'd done the best we could. We were dead from natural causes rather than virtual ones.

Within a two-week period after I returned from Los Angeles, at least seven people confessed to me the vagaries of their own e-mail affairs. This topic arose, unprompted, over the course of normal conversation. Four of these people had gotten on planes and met their correspondents, traveling from New Haven to Baltimore, New York to Montana, Texas to Virginia, and New York to Johannesburg. These were normal people, writers and lawyers and scientists, whom I knew from the real world. They were all smart, attractive, and more than a little sheepish about admitting just how deep they had been sucked in. Very few had met in chat rooms. Instead, the messages had started after chance meetings at parties and on planes; some, like me, had received notes in response to things they'd written online or elsewhere. Two of these people had fallen in love, the others chalked it up to a strange, uniquely postmodern experience. They all did things they would never do in the real world: they sent flowers, they took chances, they forgave. I heard most of these stories in the close confines of smoky bars and crowded restaurants, and we would all shake our heads in bewilderment as we told our tales, our eyes focused on some distant point that could never be reigned in to the surface of the Earth. Mostly it was the courtship ritual that had drawn us in. We had finally wooed and been wooed, given an old-fashioned structure through which to attempt the process of romance. E-mail had become an electronic epistle, a yearned-for rule book. The black and white of the type, the welcome respite from the distractions of smells and weather and other people, had, in effect, allowed us to be vulnerable and passionate enough to actually care about something. It allowed us to do what was necessary to experience love. It was not the Internet that contributed to our remote, fragmented lives. The problem was life itself.

The story of PFSlider still makes me sad. Not so much because we no longer have anything to do with one another, but because it forces me to grapple with all three dimensions of daily life with greater awareness than I used to. After it became clear that our relationship would never transcend the screen and the phone, after the painful realization that our face-to-face knowledge of each other had in fact permanently contaminated the screen and the phone, I hit the pavement again, went through the motions of real life, said "hello" and "goodbye" to people in the regular way. In darker moments, I remain mortified by everything that happened with PFSlider. It terrifies me to admit to a firsthand understanding of the way the heart and the ego are entwined. Like diseased trees that have folded in on one another, our need to worship fuses with our need to be worshipped. Love eventually becomes only about how much mystique can be maintained. It upsets me even more to see how this entanglement is made so much more intense, so unhampered and intoxicating, by way of a remote access like e-mail. But I'm also thankful that I was forced to unpack the raw truth of my need and stare at it for a while. This was a dare I wouldn't have taken in three dimensions.

The last time I saw Pete he was in New York, thousands of miles away from what had been his home and a million miles away from PFSlider. In a final gesture of decency, in what I later realized was the most ordinary kind of closure, he took me out to dinner. We talked about nothing. He paid the bill.

He drove me home in his rental car, the smell and sound of which was as arbitrary and impersonal as what we now were to each other. Then he disappeared forever. He became part of the muddy earth, as unmysterious as anything located next door. I stood on my stoop and felt that familiar rush of indifference. Pete had joined the angry and exhausted living. He drifted into my chaos, and joined me down in reality where, even if we met on the street, we'd never see each other again, our faces obscured by the branches and bodies and falling debris that make up the ether of the physical world.

Living Like Weasels

Annie Dillard

A weasel is wild. Who knows what he thinks? He sleeps in his underground den, his tail draped over his nose. Sometimes he lives in his den for two days without leaving. Outside, he stalks rabbits, mice, muskrats, and birds, killing more bodies than he can eat warm, and often dragging the carcasses home. Obedient to instinct, he bites his prey at the neck, either splitting the jugular vein at the throat or crunching the brain at the base of the skull, and he does not let go. One naturalist refused to kill a weasel who was socketed into his hand deeply as a rattlesnake. The man could in no way pry the tiny weasel off, and he had to walk half a mile to water, the weasel dangling from his palm, and soak him off like a stubborn label.

And once, says Ernest Thompson Seton—once, a man shot an eagle out of the sky. He examined the eagle and found the dry skull of a weasel fixed by the jaws to his throat. The supposition is that the eagle had pounced on the weasel and the weasel swiveled and bit as instinct taught him, tooth to neck, and nearly won. I would like to have seen that eagle from the air a few weeks or months before he was shot: was the whole weasel still attached to his feathered throat, a fur pendant? Or did the eagle eat what he could reach, gutting the living weasel with his talons before his breast, bending his beak, cleaning the beautiful airborne bones?

I have been reading about weasels because I saw one last week. I startled a weasel who startled me, and we exchanged a long glance.

Twenty minutes from my house, through the woods by the quarry and across the highway, is Hollins Pond, a remarkable piece of shallowness, where I like to go at sunset and sit on a tree trunk. Hollins Pond is also called Murray's Pond; it covers two acres of bottomland near Tinker Creek with six inches of water and six thousand lily pads. In winter, brown-and-white steers stand in the middle of it, merely dampening their hooves; from the distant shore they look like miracle itself, complete with miracle's nonchalance. Now, in summer, the steers are gone. The water lilies have blossomed and spread to a green horizontal plane that is terra firma to plodding blackbirds, and tremulous ceiling to black leeches, crayfish, and carp.

This is, mind you, suburbia. It is a five-minute walk in three directions to rows of houses, though none is visible here. There's a 55 mph highway at one end of the pond, and a nesting pair of wood ducks at the other. Under every bush is a muskrat hole or a beer can. The far end is an alternating series of fields and woods, fields and woods, threaded everywhere with motorcycle tracks—in whose bare clay wild turtles lay eggs.

So. I had crossed the highway, stepped over two low barbed-wire fences, and traced the motorcycle path in all gratitude through the wild rose and poison ivy of the pond's shoreline up into high grassy fields. Then I cut down through the woods to the mossy fallen tree where I sit. This tree is excellent. It makes a dry, upholstered bench at the upper, marshy end of the pond, a plush jetty raised from the thorny shore between a shallow blue body of water and a deep blue body of sky. The sun had just set. I was relaxed on the tree trunk, ensconced in the lap of lichen, watching the lily pads at my feet tremble and part dreamily over the thrusting path of a carp. A yellow bird appeared to my right and flew behind me. It caught my eye; I swiveled around—and the next instant, inexplicably, I was looking down at a weasel, who was looking up at me.

Weasel! I'd never seen one wild before. He was ten inches long, thin as a curve, a muscled ribbon, brown as fruitwood, soft-furred, alert. His face was fierce, small and pointed as a lizard's; he would have made a good arrowhead. There was just a dot of chin, maybe two brown hairs' worth, and then the pure white fur began that spread down his underside. He had two black eyes I didn't see, any more than you see a window.

The weasel was stunned into stillness as he was emerging from beneath an enormous shaggy wild rose bush four feet away. I was stunned into stillness twisted backward on the tree trunk. Our eyes locked, and someone threw away the key.

Our look was as if two lovers, or deadly enemies, met unexpectedly on an overgrown path when each had been thinking of something else: a clearing blow to the gut. It was also a bright blow to the brain, or a sudden beating of brains, with all the charge and intimate grate of rubbed balloons. It emptied our lungs. It felled the forest, moved the fields, and drained the pond; the world dismantled and tumbled into that black hole of eyes. If you and I looked at each other that way, our skulls would split and drop to our shoulders. But we don't. We keep our skulls. So.

He disappeared. This was only last week, and already I don't remember what shattered the enchantment. I think I blinked, I think I retrieved my brain from the weasel's brain, and tried to memorize what I was seeing, and the weasel felt the yank of separation, the careening splashdown into real life and the urgent current of instinct. He vanished under the wild rose. I waited motionless, my mind suddenly full of data and my spirit with pleadings, but he didn't return.

Please do not tell me about "approach-avoidance conflicts." I tell you I've been in that weasel's brain for sixty seconds, and he was in mine. Brains are private places, muttering through unique and secret tapes—but the weasel and I both plugged into another tape simultaneously, for a sweet and shocking time. Can I help it if it was a blank?

What goes on in his brain the rest of the time? What does a weasel think about? He won't say. His journal is tracks in clay, a spray of feathers, mouse blood and bone: uncollected, unconnected, loose-leaf, and blown.

I would like to learn, or remember, how to live. I come to Hollins Pond not so much to learn how to live as, frankly, to forget about it. That is, I don't think I can learn from a wild animal how to live in particular—shall I suck warm blood, hold my tail high, walk with my footprints precisely over the prints of my hands?—but I might learn something of mindlessness, something of the purity of living in the physical senses and the dignity of living without bias or motive. The weasel lives in necessity and we live in choice, hating necessity and dying at the last ignobly in its talons. I would like to live as I should, as the weasel lives as he should. And I suspect that for me the way is like the weasel's: open to time and death painlessly, noticing everything, remembering nothing, choosing the given with a fierce and pointed will.

I missed my chance. I should have gone for the throat. I should have lunged for that streak of white under the weasel's chin and held on, held on through mud and into the wild rose, held on for a dearer life. We could live under the wild rose wild as weasels, mute and uncomprehending. I could very calmly go wild. I could live two days in the den, curled, leaning on mouse fur, sniffing bird bones, blinking, licking, breathing musk, my hair tangled in the roots of grasses. Down is a good place to go, where the mind is single. Down is out, out of your ever-loving mind and back to your careless senses. I remember muteness as a prolonged and giddy fast, where every moment is a feast of utterance received. Time and events are merely poured, unremarked, and ingested directly, like blood pulsed into my gut through a jugular vein. Could two live that way? Could two live under the wild rose, and explore by the pond, so that the smooth mind of each is as everywhere present to the other, and as received and as unchallenged, as falling snow?

We could, you know. We can live any way we want. People take vows of poverty, chastity, and obedience—even of silence—by choice. The thing is to stalk your calling in a certain skilled and supple way, to locate the most tender and live spot and plug into that pulse. This is yielding, not fighting. A weasel doesn't "attack" anything; a weasel lives as he's meant to, yielding at every moment to the perfect freedom of single necessity.

I think it would be well, and proper, and obedient, and pure, to grasp your one necessity and not let it go, to dangle from it limp wherever it takes you. Then even death, where you're going no matter how you live, cannot you part. Seize it and let it seize you up aloft even, till your eyes burn out and drop; let your musky flesh fall off in shreds, and let your very bones unhinge and scatter, loosened over fields, over fields and woods, lightly, thoughtless, from any height at all, from as high as eagles.

From a Sheepherder's Notebook: Three Days

Gretel Ehrlich

When the phone rang, it was John: "Maurice just upped and quit and there ain't nobody else around, so you better get packed. I'm taking you out to herd sheep." I walked to his trailerhouse. He smoked impatiently while I gathered my belongings. "Do you know *anything* about herding sheep after all this time?" he asked playfully. "No, not really." I was serious. "Well, it's too late now. You'll just have to figure it out. And there ain't no phones up there either!"

He left me off on a ridge at five in the morning with a mare and a border collie. "Last I saw the sheep, they was headed for them hills," he said, pointing up toward a dry ruffle of badlands. "I'll pull your wagon up ahead about two miles. You'll see it. Just go up that ridge, turn left at the pink rock, then keep agoing. And don't forget to bring the damned sheep."

Morning. Sagesmell, sunsquint, birdsong, cool wind. I have no idea where I am, how to get to the nearest paved road, or how to find the sheep. There are tracks going everywhere so I follow what appear to be the most definite ones. The horse picks a path through sagebrush. I watch the dog. We walk for several miles. Nothing. Then both sets of ears prick up. The dog looks at me imploringly. The sheep are in the draw ahead.

Move them slow or fast? Which crossing at the river? Which pink rock? It's like being a first-time mother, but mother now to two thousand sheep who give me the kind of disdainful look a teenager would his parent and, with my back turned, can get into as much trouble. I control the urge to keep them neatly arranged, bunched up by the dog, and, instead, let them spread out and fill up. Grass being scarce on spring range, they scatter.

Up the valley, I encounter a slalom course of oil rigs and fenced spills I hadn't been warned about. The lambs, predictably mischievous, emerge dripping black. Freed from those obstacles, I ride ahead to find the wagon which, I admit, I'm afraid I'll never see, leaving the sheep on the good faith that they'll stay on their uphill drift toward me.

"Where are my boundaries?" I'd asked John.

"Boundaries?" He looked puzzled for a minute. "Hell, Gretel, it's all the outfit's land, thirty or forty miles in any direction. Take them anywhere they want to go."

On the next ridge I find my wagon. It's a traditional sheepherder's wagon, rounded top, tiny wood cookstove, bed across the back, built-in benches and drawers. The rubber wheels and long tongue make it portable. The camp tender pulls it (now with a pickup, earlier with teams) from camp to camp as the feed is consumed, every two weeks or so. Sheep begin appearing and graze toward me. I picket my horse. The dog runs for shade to lick his sore feet. The view from the dutch doors of the wagon is to the southeast, down the long slit of a valley. If I rode north, I'd be in Montana within the day, and next week I'll begin the fifty-mile trail cast to the Big Horns.

Three days before summer solstice; except to cook and sleep I spend every waking hour outside. Tides of weather bring the days and take them away. Every night a bobcat visits, perched at a discreet distance on a rock, facing me. A full moon, helium-filled, cruises through clouds and is lost behind rimrock. No paper cutout, this moon, but ripe and splendid. Then Venus, then the North Star. Time for bed. Are the sheep bedded down? Should I ride back to check them?

Morning. Blue air comes ringed with coyotes. The ewes wake clearing their communal throats like old men. Lambs shake their flop-eared heads at leaves of grass, negotiating the blade. People have asked in the past, "What do you do out there? Don't you get bored?" The problem seems to be something else. There's too much of everything here. I can't pace myself to it.

Down the valley the sheep move in a frontline phalanx, then turn suddenly in a card-stacked sequential falling, as though they had turned themselves inside out, and resume feeding again in whimsical processions. I think of town, of John's trailerhouse, the clean-bitten lawn, his fanatical obsession with neatness and work, his small talk with hired hands, my eyesore stacks of books and notes covering an empty bed, John smoking in the dark of early morning, drinking coffee, waiting for daylight to stream in.

After eating I return to the sheep, full of queasy fears that they will have vanished and I'll be pulled off the range to face those firing-squad looks of John's as he says, "I knew you'd screw up. Just like you screw up everything." But the sheep are there. I can't stop looking at them. They're there, paralyzing the hillside with thousands of mincing feet, their bodies pressed together as they move, saucerlike, scanning the earth for a landing.

Thunderstorm. Sheep feed far up a ridge I don't want them to go over, so the dog, horse, and I hotfoot it to the top and ambush them, yelling and hooting them back down. Cleverly, the horse uses me as a windbreak when the front moves in. Lightning fades and blooms. As we descend quickly, my rein-holding arm looks to me like a blank stick. I feel numb. Numb in all this vividness. I don't seem to occupy my life fully.

Down in the valley again I send the dog "way around" to turn the sheep, but he takes the law into his own hands and chases a lamb off a cliff. She's wedged upside down in a draw on the other side of the creek. It will take twenty minutes to reach her, and the rest of the sheep have already trailed ahead. This numbness is a wrist twisting inside my throat. A lone pine tree whistles, its needles are novocaine. "In nature there are neither rewards nor punishments; there are only consequences." I can't remember who said that. I ride on.

One dead. Will she be reborn? And as what? The dog that nips lambs' heels into butchering chutes? I look back. The "dead" lamb convulses into action and scrambles up the ledge to find his mother.

Twin terrors: to be awake; to be asleep.

All day clouds hang over the Beartooth Mountains. Looking for a place out of the wind, I follow a dry streambed to a sheltered inlet. In front of me, there's something sticking straight up. It's the shell of a dead frog propped up against a rock with its legs crossed at the ankles. A cartoonist's idea of a frog relaxing, but this one's skin is paper-thin, mouth opened as if to scream. I lean close. "It's too late, you're already dead!"

Because I forgot to bring hand cream or a hat, sun targets in on me like frostbite. The dog, horse, and I move through sagebrush in unison, a fortress against wind. Sheep ticks ride my peeling skin. The dog pees, then baptizes himself at the water hole—full immersion—lapping at spitting rain. Afterward, he rolls in dust and reappears with sage twigs and rabbit brush strung up in his coat, as though in disguise—a Shakespearian dog. Above me, oil wells are ridge-top jewelry adorning the skyline with ludicrous sexual pumps. Hump, hump go the wells. Hump, hump go the drones who gather that black soup, insatiable.

We walk the fuselage of the valley. A rattlesnake passes going the other way; plenty of warning but so close to my feet I hop the rest of the day. I come upon the tin-bright litter of a former sheep camp: Spam cans flattened to the ground, their keys sticking up as if ready to open my grave.

Sun is in and out after the storm. In a long gully, the lambs gambol, charging in small brigades up one side, then the other. Ewes look on bored. When the lamb-fun peters out, the whole band comes apart in a generous spread the way sheep ranchers like them. Here and there lambs, almost as big as their mothers, kneel with a contagiously enthusiastic wiggle, bumping the bag with a goatlike butt to take a long draw of milk.

Night. Nighthawks whir. Meadowlarks throw their heads back in one ecstatic song after another. In the wagon I find a piece of broken mirror big enough to see my face: blood drizzles from cracked lips, gnats have eaten away at my ears.

To herd sheep is to discover a new human gear somewhere between second and reverse—a slow, steady trot of keenness with no speed. There is no flab in these days. But the constant movement of sheep from water hole to water hole, from camp to camp, becomes a form of longing. But for what?

The ten other herders who work for this ranch begin to trail their sheep toward summer range in the Big Horns. They're ahead of me, though I can't see them for the curve of the earth. One-armed Red, Grady, and Ed; Bob, who always bakes a pie when he sees me riding toward his camp; Fred, wearer of rags; "Amorous Albert"; Rudy, Bertha, and Ed; and, finally, Doug, who travels circus-like with a menagerie of goats, roosters, colts, and dogs and keeps warm in the winter by sleeping with one of the nannies. A peaceful army, of which I am the tail end, moving in ragtag unison across the prairie.

A day goes by. Every shiver of grass counts. The shallows and dapples in air that give grass life are like water. The bobcat returns nightly. During easy jags of sleep the dog's dreampaws chase coyotes. I ride to the sheep. Empty sky, an absolute blue. Empty heart. Sunburned face blotches brown. Another layer of skin to peel, to meet myself again in the mirror. A plane passes overhead—probably the government trapper. I'm waving hello, but he speeds away.

Now it's tomorrow. I can hear John's truck, the stock racks speak before I can actually see him, and it's a long time shortening the distance between us.

"Hello."

"Hello."

He turns away because something tender he doesn't want me to see registers in his face.

"I'm moving you up on the bench. Take the sheep right out the tail end of this valley, then take them to water. It's where the tree is. I'll set your wagon by that road."

"What road?" I ask timidly.

Then he does look at me. He's trying to suppress a smile but speaks impatiently.

"You can see to hell and back up there, Gretel."

I ride to the sheep, but the heat of the day has already come on sizzling. It's too late to get them moving; they shade up defiantly, their heads knitted together into a wool umbrella. From the ridge there's whooping and yelling and rocks being thrown. It's John trying to get the sheep moving again. In a dust blizzard we squeeze them up the road, over a sharp lip onto the bench.

Here, there's wide-open country. A view. Sheep string out excitedly. I can see a hundred miles in every direction. When I catch up with John I get off my horse. We stand facing each other, then embrace quickly. He holds me close, then pulls away briskly and scuffles the sandy dirt with his boot.

"I've got to get back to town. Need anything?"

"Naw . . . I'm fine. Maybe a hat. . . ."

He turns and walks his long-legged walk across the benchland. In the distance, at the pickup, an empty beer can falls on the ground when he gets in. I can hear his radio as he bumps toward town. Dust rises like an evening gown behind his truck. It flies free for a moment, then returns, leisurely, to the habitual road—that bruised string which leads to and from my heart.

Northeast Direct

Dagoberto Gilb

I'm on board Amtrak's number 175 to Penn Station. I've traveled by train a couple of times in the past year, but last time I discovered that each car had one electrical outlet. Besides lots of room, besides that comforting, rolling motion, it's what I think about now when I think about the train. My Powerbook has a weak battery, and I can plug in and type as long as I want.

The car is empty. Maybe three of us new passengers, two previously seated. So I do feel a little awkward taking the seat right behind this guy who I saw hustle on several minutes before I did. He'd already reclined his aisle seat, thrown his day bag and warm coat on the one by the window. He was settled. I'm sure he was more than wondering why, with so many empty seats all around, I had to go and sit directly behind him. But I felt something too. Why did *he* have to pick a seat a row in front of the electrical outlet? And if he grumbled when I bumped the back of his seat to get by, I grumbled because I had to squeeze past to get over to the window seat behind him.

I'm over it quickly because I've got my machine on and I'm working. And he seems to be into his world too. He's taken a daily planner out, and he's checking a few things. I see this because, his seat reclined, I'm given a wedge view of his face looking forward and to the side. I see his left eye and the profile of his nose when he turns toward his window. When the conductor comes by for our tickets, he asks if there's a phone, then gets up to use it. I get immersed and barely notice him return.

I pause, and my eyes float up. He's holding a thick new book. I'm sort of looking it over with him. The way the cover feels, the way the chapters are set out. It seems like an attractively produced history book, and I bet he just bought it. He puts it down, then reaches over to the seat in front of me and brings up another.

The other book is the paperback of my novel! I *cannot* believe it! He stares at the cover for a moment, then he opens it. He's reading the acknowledgments page! When he's done he turns back to the title page for a moment, then puts the book down. He gets up and goes to a forward car, where the conductor said he'd find a phone.

How improbable is this? I mean, mine is definitely not a Danielle Steel, not a John Grisham. If it is this much shy of miraculous that I would be on a train with someone who had heard of my books at all, how much more miraculous that, because of an electrical outlet on a train, I'd be sitting inches from a person who just purchased the book and is opening it before my eyes? And look at it this way: of the possible combinations of seating arrangements in the train car, how many could give me this angle? And what if he hadn't put his seat back?

I know what you're thinking. That I should lean over and say, Hey man, you will *never* guess who's sitting behind you! No, that's not me. I don't want to do that. I won't. I want him to be my anonymous reader. How many opportunities does a writer have to learn a truthful reaction, really truthful, to his writing? How absorbed will he be? Will he smile at parts, groan at others? How about his facial expressions? Will his eyes light up or go dull?

As he's walking back, he's staring at me a little too strongly—but he can't know who I am. I'm feeling, naturally enough, self-conscious. He can't possibly know he's in the eyes of the author himself—to think it would be even *more* ridiculous than that it's true. It could be the bright yellow shirt I have on, which is a banner really, a United Farm Workers T-shirt celebrating Cesar Chávez. It reads *Cada trajabador es un organizador*. People are always looking at it and I practically can't wear it because they do. But he's not paying attention to my shirt. It's that I'm the dude sitting behind him, typing into his ear, breathing on his neck while we're on this empty train, with so much room, so many seats, with so much possible spacing. I think he probably doesn't like me. He's probably got names for me.

He sits down. He's picked up the book! He's gone to page one and he's *reading!* Somehow I just can't believe it, and I'm typing frantically about him and this phenomenon. He's a big guy, six-two. Wire glasses, blue, unplayful eyes. Grayish hair, indicating he's most likely not an undergrad, and beneath a Brown University cap, which, because he's wearing the cap, indicates he's probably not a professor. Grad student in English? Or he's into reading about the Southwest? Or maybe the cover has drawn him to the purchase. He's turned to page two! He's going! I have this huge smile as I'm typing. Bottom page two, and yes, his eyes shift to page three!

Suddenly he stops there. He gets up again. The phone is my bet. I'm taking the opportunity. I'm dying to know the name of the bookstore he's gone to, and I kind of arch upwards, over the back of the seat in front of me, to see a glossy store bag, when just as suddenly he's on his way back and he's eyeing me again. I squirm under the psychic weight of these circumstances, though now also from the guilty fact that I'm being so nosy. I pretend I am stretching, looking this way and that, rotating my neck—such uncomfortable seats, wouldn't you say?

He's reading the novel *again*. Page four, page five, page six! A woman walks by and he doesn't even glance up, isn't even curious whether she is attractive or not. He's so engrossed! He's *totally* reading now. No, wait. He stops, eyes to the window where it's New England, beautifully composed and framed by this snowy winter. Those tall, boxy two- and three-story board-and-batten houses painted colonial gray and colonial blue, two windows per floor, hip and gable roof, nubs of chimney poking up. Oh no, he's putting the book down. Closes it, mixes it into his other belongings on the seat next to him. It's because he's moving. He must hear my manic typing and he feels crowded and so he's picking up his stuff and going up an aisle. What an astute, serious, intelligent reader I have to feel so cramped! My reader wants to read in silence, be alone with his book and the thoughts generated by it and his reaction to it and he doesn't like some dude behind him jamming up his reading time and space with this muttering keyboard sound—it just makes me *smile* thinking how keen my reader's psychic synapses are to be responding to what his conscious mind cannot know is occurring. It must be a raging psychic heat, a dizzying psychic pheromone. When he has settled comfortably into his new seat, he pulls the novel back up. He's reading again! Reading and reading! When that young woman passes through on her return, no, again, he does not look up. He's dedicated, fully concentrating. He's really reading, one page after another.

New England: white snow, silver water, leafless branches and limbs. Lumber and boat and junk yards. The bare behind of industry, its dirty underwear, so beautifully disguised by winter.

My reader has fallen asleep. We haven't been on the train an hour and my writing has made him succumb to a nap? Nah, I don't find it a bad thing. Not in the slightest. It's really a compliment. How many books do you fall asleep with? The conductor wakes him up, though. He's sorry but he found that daily planner on the seat behind him and wanted to make sure it belonged to him. But my reader goes right back to sleep. He's dead asleep now. A goner. I pass him on my way to buy myself a drink, and he's got his left thumb locked inside the book, his index finger caressing the spine, pinching. You see, my reader does not want to lose his place.

We both wake up at New Haven. Probably getting a little carried away. I thought he might get off here—walking the book into Yale. He reopens it. He's at the beginning of chapter two. He does read slowly. He's lazy? I say he's thoughtful, a careful, considerate reader, complementing precisely the manner in which I wrote the novel. It's not meant to be read quickly. He's absolutely correct to read it the way he does.

Forty-five minutes outside Penn Station, many passengers have boarded, cutting my reader and me off. He is still up there reading, but with the passage of time, and our physical distance blunted more by a clutter of other minds sitting between and around us, the shock and mystery have lessened in me. I have adjusted, accepted it. By now I am behaving as though it were ordinary that a stranger two aisles above is reading my work. Like every other miracle that happens in life, I am taking the event for granted already, letting it fade into the everyday of people filling trains, going home from work, going. He is reading the novel, and I am certain, by the steady force and duration of his commitment, that he fully intends to read unto the end. He and I both can look around, inside the car and out the window, and then we go back, him to the book, me to the computer keyboard, no longer writing about this.

So when the moment comes, ask what, how? Tap him on the shoulder, say excuse me, but you know I couldn't help but notice that book you're reading, and it's such an amazing coincidence, it *really* is *so* amazing how this can happen, but I was just talking with a friend about that very novel this morning—change that—I was talking to two friends, and one thought it was just great, while the other—change that—and one thought it was just great, and I wondered what you felt about it, and how did you hear of it anyway?

After the conductor announces Penn Station, we stand and get our coats on, and, the train still swaying, move down the aisle and toward the door with our bags. I'm waiting right behind him. Can easily tap him on the shoulder. But nobody else is talking. No one, not a word. So I can't either, especially when I'd be making fake conversation. Train stops, door opens, people in front of him move forward, and a woman in an aisle steps in between me and him with her large, too-heavy-for-her suitcase. He's shot out quickly ahead of me now, up an escalator, several more people between us. When I reach the main floor of the station, get beneath the flapping electronic board that posts trains and times and departure tracks, I have caught up with him. He has stopped to get his bearings. Just as I am at his shoulder, he takes off in the same direction I'm going.

So we're walking briskly side by side in cold Penn Station. You know what? He doesn't want to talk. I am sure he has no desire to speak with me. Would definitely not want to have that conversation I'd planned. No time for me to fumble around and, maybe, eventually, tell him how I am the writer. This is New York City, no less. He's in a hurry. He'd grimace and shake his head, brush me off. He already thinks I am one of those irritating people you encounter on a trip, the one always at the edge of your sight, the one you can never seem to shake. And so as I begin a ride up the escalator toward the taxi lines, I watch him go straight ahead, both of us covered with anonymity like New England snow.

The People on the Bus

Adam Gopnik

Lately, I like to ride the bus. I don't mean the double-decker tourist buses that, half empty, warily circle the city, like dazed displaced troop carriers, or the long-distance buses that come sighing into the Port Authority Terminal, where it is eternally 3 A.M. and everyone looks exhausted before the journey starts, or even the yellow-and-blacks that still delicately deliver children from downtown to uptown at eight in the morning. I mean the ordinary city buses, those vaguely purposeless-looking, bulbous-faced, blue-and-bone M2s and 3s and 4s and 5s that chug up and down the avenues and along the cross streets, wheezing and whining, all day and night.

For twenty-odd years in New York, I never rode the bus at all—not, at least, after a single, traumatic bus experience. On the very first day I visited Manhattan, in the anxious (though, looking back, mostly unfrightened) summer of 1978—the summer when Jimmy Carter turned down the air-conditioning all over town—I got on a bus outside the Metropolitan Museum, saw that the fare was fifty cents, and, with the unquenchable cheerfulness of the visiting Canadian, proudly pulled out a dollar bill—an American dollar bill—folded it up neatly, stuffed the dollar in the fare box, two fares, and looked up, expecting the driver to beam at my efficiency. I will never forget his look of disbelief and disgust, mingled, I think, with a certain renewed awe at the enormities that out-of-towners were capable of.

From that day on, I don't think I ever rode another bus. I suppose I must have; transportational logic says that I must have—there must be a crosstown M86 or an uptown limited in there somewhere—but, if I did, I don't know when. Even if I had been on a bus, I don't think I would recall it. Bus-blindness is a standard New York illness; of all the regularities of life here, the bus is the least celebrated, the least inclined to tug at the heart, or be made into a symbol of our condition. The taxi has its checkered lore, the subway its legend, the limo a certain Michael Douglas-in-"Wall Street" icon quality—but if there is a memorable bus scene in literature, or an unforgettable moment in a movie that takes place on a

New York City bus, I have not found it. (If you Google New York buses in movie scenes, you end up with a bus-enthusiasts' site and a shot of a New York City bus from a Sylvester Stallone movie called "Driven," and this bus turns out to be dressed up like a Chicago city bus, and filmed on location in Toronto.) There is nothing about buses that makes them intrinsically symbol-repellent: the London bus has a poetry as rich as the Tube's—there is Mary Poppins, there is Mrs. Dalloway. In Paris, Pascal rides the bus, Zazie rides the Métro, and that is, evenly, that. But as a symbolic repository the New York City bus does not exist. The only significant symbolic figure that the New York bus has had in Ralph Kramden, and what he symbolizes about the bus is that being stuck in one is in itself one more form of comic frustration and disappointment; the New York City bus might best be described by saying that it is exactly the kind of institution that would have Ralph Kramden as its significant symbolic figure.

If you had asked me why I avoided the bus, I suppose I would have said that the bus was for old people—or that taking the bus was one step short of not actually living in New York at all, and that if you stayed on the bus long enough it would take you right out of town. Riding the bus was one of those activities, like going to Radio City, that was in New York but not really of it. My mother-in-law rode the bus when she came to New York to visit, and that, I thought, said whom the bus was made for: elegant older women who didn't mind traveling forty-five minutes every morning to visit their grandchildren.

And then I didn't ride the bus because I loved the subway so. Compared with the vivid and evil and lurid subway, the bus seemed a drab bourgeois necessity—Shirley Booth to the subway's Tallulah Bankhead. When I began to ride the subway, particularly in the late seventies and early eighties, it was both grander and stranger than a newcomer can imagine now. The graffiti, for one thing, were both more sordid inside—all those "tags"—and more beautiful outside. When the wild-style cars came roaring into a station, they were as exciting and shimmering as Frank Stella birds. The air-conditioning was a lot spottier, too, and sometimes the windows were open, driving the stale and fetid air around in an illusion of cooling. When the air-conditioning worked, it was worse. You walked from steam bath to refrigerator, a change like a change of continents, and your perspiration seemed to freeze within your shirt, a phenomenon previously known only to Antarctic explorers.

Feral thugs and killer nerds rode the subway together, looking warily at one another. And yet there was something sublime about the subway. Although it was incidentally frightening, it was also systematically reassuring: it shouldn't have worked; it had stopped working; and yet it worked—vandalized, brutalized, a canvas and a pissoir, it reliably took you wherever you wanted to go. It was a rumbling, sleepless, snorting animal presence underfoot, more a god to be appeased and admired than a thing that had been mastered by its owners. If the stations seemed, as people said, Dantesque, that was not simply because the subway was belowground, and a punishment, but also because it offered an architectural order that seemed to be free from any interfering human hand, running by itself in its own grim circles. It was religious in the narrow sense as well: terror and transportation were joined together, fear propelled you to a higher plane. (The taxis, an alternative if you had the money, were alarming then, too—a silent or determined driver in a T-shirt resting on a mat of beads and demanding, fifty blocks before your destination, which side of the street you wanted—without being at all sublime.)

Coming home in 2000 after five years abroad, I took it for granted that I would return to the subway and the taxi, only to be stunned by the transformation in them both. The subway, now graffiti free, with dully gleaming metal cars (though obviously made to be as resistant to vandalism as a prison), had recorded announcements, and for a while a picture of the station manager at every stop. It seemed obviously improved but somehow degraded, grimly utilitarian, intended to suggest the receding future vision of "RoboCop": automatic voices encased in armor. The chaos was gone from inside the cabs, and held on only around them. After five years in Paris, where one phones for a cab or lines up in an orderly manner at a station, logically and fairly, I nearly wept tears of frustration at the anarchy of the street system—you waited for fifteen minutes and someone waltzed out into the middle of the block and stepped in front of you as a cab approached. (There is, of course, an implicit system of fair dealing in this—one block away is legitimate; the same corner is not—but I could no longer remember the rules, much less find the patience to practice them.)

And so the bus. Almost every day for the past year and a half, I've found myself taking a limited bus down an East Side avenue, and then, a few hours and frustrations later, taking it back uptown on the adjoining avenue. I stand or, in good hours, sit among the usual bus riders. The bus I find humane, in several ways. There is, first of all, the non-confrontational and yet collaborative nature of the seating. You look over people's shoulders, closely, and yet only rarely look directly at them, face to face, as you must on the subway. There is a hierarchy of seating on the bus, far more articulate than that of the subway. There are seats you must give up to handicapped people, seats you ought to give up to handicapped people if you have any decency at all, and seats—the bumpy, exhaust-scented row in the very back—that you never have to give up to anyone, if you're willing to sit there. (The reason for all those designated spaces is that law and propriety dictate that when someone in a wheelchair rolls up to a bus stop, the bus has to stop and let him on.) There is also on almost every New York bus a little single seat tucked in near the back door, which has the air of a dunce chair in a classroom. You can sit there, but you wouldn't want to. Late at night, there is even a policy of optional stops. You ask the driver to stop the bus where you're going and, if he can, he will.

The bus also has order, order as we know it from the fading patriarchal family, visible order kept by an irritable chief. The driver has not only control over his world but the delight of the exercise of arbitrary authority, like that of a French bureaucrat. Bus riders learn that, if your MetroCard turns out to be short fifty cents, the driver will look at you with distaste, tell you to find change from fellow-passengers (surprisingly, to a subway rider, people dig into their purses cheerfully), and, if this doesn't work, will wearily wave you on back.

You are included, fool though you are, and this often at the moment when the driver is ignoring the pounded fists and half-audible pleas for admission of the last few people who, running for the bus, arrived a second too late. The driver's control of the back door is just as imperious. A red zone of acceptability exists around the bus stop, known only to the driver, who opens and closes the door as he senses the zone appearing and receding.

It is uniquely possible to overhear conversations on the bus. The other morning, for instance—a beautiful morning of our time, the sky blue, the alert orange, and the *Times* sports pages ominously upside down—a man behind me was trying to remember the names of popular Drake's snacks from his childhood.

"What are those things? There were Ring-Dings and Drake's cakes."

"You mean Twinkies," the man he was with said, with assurance. I couldn't see either face, but their voices had the peaceable quarrelsomeness of those who have just passed from middle-aged to elderly.

"No, I don't mean Twinkies," he said angrily. "I mean them other things."

Long pause. We couldn't resist. "Devil Dogs," someone said, "Devil Dogs."

"Yes, thanks, Devil Dogs. How come you don't ever see Devil Dogs these days?"

This is a typical bit of bus talk. (In a taxi you would stew on the issue all by yourself. The millionaire in his limo could ask the driver, I suppose, but he would be too embarrassed to answer. On the subway, no one would hear, in the first place; and if the words "Devil Dog" were said with enough emphasis to be heard, it would cause a panicked mass exodus.) On another morning, a man and a woman were riding together down Fifth Avenue and saw the new, comically twinned, comically misnamed AOL Time Warner Center—the Delusional States Building, as it will doubtless someday be known—come into view. (And those two towers rising, however plainly, have become a source of pride: *something's* rising.) "That Trump," the man said, chuckling. "He always does things in twos. Have you ever noticed how he always does things in twos?"

"I've noticed that. That's his thing, his signature, doing two of everything."

"Well, there he does it again. Two towers again."

Sage nods. The fact that, as it occurred to me later, the towers are not by Trump, and that, in any case, Trump, in his long career, has never done two of anything, should not diminish the glory of this exchange. If you were on the subway, there would be nothing to look at; if you were in a limo, you would actually be Trump, building things, gloriously, in nonexistent pairs.

When I first started riding the bus, I mentioned it to people sheepishly, almost apologetically, as one might mention having had a new dental plate put in, or the advantages of low-fat yogurt—as one might mention something that, though not downright shameful, might still seem mildly embarrassing. But, to my surprise, almost everyone I talked to (and women, I think, in particular) turned out to feel the same way I do about the bus. "The bus lets you feel that you're in control, or that someone's in control," one woman said to me, and another friend said flatly, "You can see what's coming." The bus feels safe. Of course, there is no reason for the bus to feel safe. (A friend from Jerusalem got on the bus with understandable watchfulness.) Yet we have decided to create in the city a kind of imaginary geography of fear and safety that will somehow make us safer from It—from the next attack, of course, from the Other Shoe, the Dreadful Thing that we all await.

I have thought about it a lot while I am riding the bus, and I have come to the conclusion that, while anxiety seeks out the company of excitement, fear seeks out the illusion of certainty. People tend to write these days about anxiety and fear as though they were equal, or anyway continuous, emotions, one blending into the other, but anyone who has felt them—and anyone who hasn't felt them, at least a little, hasn't been living in New York in the past year—knows that they are as distinct as a bus from a subway, as a Devil Dog from a Ring-Ding. Anxiety is the ordinary New York emotion. It is a form of energy, and clings, like ivy to a garden wall, to whatever is around to cling to, whether the object is nationalism or the Knicks or Lizzie Grubman, as readers of the New York *Post* recognize. At the height of the bubble, anxiety was all around us: the anxiety of keeping up, of not falling behind, of holding one's place.

Fear, well earned or not, is a different thing. People who live with the higher kinds of fear—the ill, soldiers—live with it mostly by making structures of delusional domesticity. They try to create an illusion of safety, and of home. At Waterloo, soldiers welcomed the little signs of farm-keeping evident around them; in the dugouts of the Somme, every rat-ridden alley had a designation and every rat itself a pet name. The last time New Yorkers were genuinely afraid, as opposed to merely anxious, during the great crime wave of the sixties and mid-seventies, they responded in the same way: by constructing an elaborate, learn-it-by-heart geography of safe and unsafe enclaves, a map of safe rooms. The knowledge that the map could not truly protect you from what you feared then, any more than riding the bus can save you from it now, did not alter the need to have a map. People say that twentysomethings have sex out of fear—it is called terror sex—but twentysomethings have sex out of sex, and the adjective of the decade is always attached to it. In the eighties, they had safe sex, and in the nineties boom sex, and they will have sex-among-the-ruins, if it comes to that.

What we have out of fear is not sex, or any other anxiety-energized activity, but stillness. It's said that people in the city are nicer now, or more cooperative, and I suppose this is true. But it is true for reasons that are not themselves entirely nice. The motivation of this niceness is less rectitude and reform than just plain old-fashioned fright. There are no atheists in foxholes, but there are no religious arguments in foxholes, either. The fear we feel isn't as immediate or as real as the fear soldiers feel. But our response is the same. These structures of delusional domesticity are the mainstay of the lives of many of us in New York now. The bus, a permanently running dinner party among friends, a fiction of family for a dollar-fifty, a Starbucks on wheels, is the rolling image of the thing we dream of now as much as we wanted the Broadband Pipe to wash away our sins three years ago, and that is the Safe Room. For the first time, the bus has something to symbolize.

On the bus the other morning, the worst regularly scheduled thing that can happen on the bus happened. A guy in a wheelchair held things up for three minutes—no time at all, really, but an eternity on television, or in the subway, or, usually, in the city. As bus riders know, buses are equipped to stop and, by lowering a clever elevator device, let a wheelchair-bound rider board the bus. This, though a civic mitzvah, involves a sequence where the driver locks the front door, works the elevator at the rear door, hoists up the wheelchair on the lift, and then folds up the designated seats to give the wheelchair man room (it is nearly always a man). There is something artisanal, handmade about it—the lock, the voyage, working the elevator—in which a municipal employee is reduced, or raised, to a valet.

"It's the lame and the halt on the bus," one woman said.

"What's the difference between the lame and the halt?"

"The lame are, like, lame, and the halt, halt."

"You mean the halt don't walk."

"I mean they halt. But they halt because they're lame."

It is the kind of conversation—discursive, word-sensitive—that is possible on the bus right now, and nowhere else. I keep meaning to look up the difference.

Parish Streets

Patricia Hampl

Lexington, Oxford, Chatsworth, continuing down Grand Avenue to Milton and Avon, as far as St. Albans—the streets of our neighborhood had an English, even an Anglican, ring to them. But we were Catholic, and the parishes of the diocese, unmarked and ghostly as they were, posted borders more decisive than the street signs we passed on our way to St. Luke's grade school or, later, walking in the other direction to the girls-only convent high school.

We were like people with dual citizenship. I *lived* on Linwood Avenue, but I *belonged* to St. Luke's. That was the lingo. Mothers spoke of daughters who were going to the junior-senior prom with boys "from Nativity" or "from St. Mark's" as if from fiefdoms across the sea.

"Where you from?" a boy livid with acne asked when we startled each other lurking behind a pillar in the St. Thomas Academy gym at a Friday night freshman mixer.

"Ladies' choice!" one of the mothers cried from a dim corner where a portable hi-fi was set up. She rasped the needle over the vinyl, and Fats Domino came on, insinuating a heavier pleasure than I yet knew: *I found my thrill . . . .*

"I'm from Holy Spirit," the boy said, as if he'd been beamed in to stand by the tepid Cokes and tuna sandwiches and the bowls of sweating potato chips on the refreshments table. Parish members did not blush to describe themselves as being "from Immaculate Conception." Somewhere north, near the city line, there was even a parish frankly named Maternity of Mary. But then, in those years, the 1950s and early 1960s, breeding was a low-grade fever pulsing amongst us unmentioned, like a buzz or hum you get used to and cease to hear. The white noise of matrimonial sex.

On Sundays the gray stone nave of St. Luke's church, big as a warehouse, was packed with families of eight or ten sitting in the honey-colored pews. The fathers wore brown suits. In memory they appear spectrally thin, wraithlike and spent, like trees hollowed of their pulp. The wives were petite and cheerful, with

94

helmet-like haircuts. Perkiness was their main trait. But what did they say, these small women, how did they talk? Mrs. Healy, mother of fourteen ("They can afford them," my mother said, as if to excuse her paltry two, "he's a doctor."), never uttered a word, as far as I remember. Even pregnant, she was somehow wiry, as if poised for a tennis match. Maybe these women only wore a *look* of perkiness, and like their lean husbands, they were sapped of personal strength. Maybe they were simply tense.

Not everyone around us was Catholic. Mr. Kirby, a widower who was our next door neighbor, was Methodist—whatever that was. The Nugents across the street, behind their cement retaining wall and double row of giant salvia, were Lutheran, more or less. The Williams family, who subscribed to the *New Yorker* and had a living room outfitted with spare Danish furniture, were Episcopalian. They referred to their minister as a priest—a plagiarism that embarrassed me for them, because I liked them and their light, airy ways.

As for the Bertrams, our nearest neighbors to the west, it could only be said that Mrs. Bertram, dressed in a narrow suit with a peplum jacket and a hat made of the same heathery wool, went *somewhere* via taxi on Sunday mornings. Mr. Bertram went nowhere—on Sunday or on any other day. He was understood, during my entire girlhood, to be indoors, resting.

Weekdays, Mrs. Bertram took the bus to her job downtown. Mr. Bertram stayed home behind their birchwood Venetian blinds in an aquarium half-light, not an invalid (we never thought of him that way), but a man whose occupation it was to rest. Sometimes in the summer he ventured forth with a large wrench-like gadget to root out the masses of dandelions that gave the Bertrams' lawn a temporary brilliance in June. I associated him with the Wizard of Oz. He was small and mild-looking, going bald. He gave the impression of extreme pallor except for small, very dark eyes.

It was a solid neighborhood rumor that Mr. Bertram had been a screenwriter in Hollywood. Yes, that pallor was a writer's pallor; those small dark eyes were a writer's eyes. They saw, they noted.

He allowed me to assist him in the rooting-out of his dandelions. I wanted to ask him about Hollywood—had he met Audrey Hepburn? I couldn't bring myself to maneuver for information on such an elevated subject. But I did feel something serious was called for here. I introduced religion while he plunged the dandelion gadget deep into the lawn.

No, he said, he did not go to church. "But you do believe in God?" I asked, hardly daring to hope he did not. I longed for novelty. He paused for a moment and looked up at the sky where big, spreading clouds streamed by. "God isn't the problem," he said.

Some ancient fissure split open, a fine crack in reality: so there *was* a problem. Just as I'd always felt. Beneath the family solidity, the claustrophobia of mother-father-brother-me, past the emphatic certainties of St. Luke's catechism class, there was a problem that would never go away. Mr. Bertram stood amid his dandelions, a resigned Buddha, looking up at the sky, which gave back nothing but drifting white shapes on the blue.

What alarmed me was my feeling of recognition. Of course there was a problem. It wasn't God. Life itself was a problem. Something was not right, would never be right. I'd sensed it all along, some kind of fishy vestigial quiver in the spine. It was bred in the bone, way past thought. Life, deep down, lacked the substantiality that it *seemed* to display. The physical world, full of detail and interest, was a parched topsoil that could be blown away.

This lack, this blankness akin to chronic disappointment, was everywhere, under the perkiness, lurking even within my own happiness. "What are you going to do today?" my father said when he saw me digging in the backyard on his way to work at the greenhouse.

"I'm digging to China," I said.

"Well, I'll see you at lunch," he said, "if you're still here."

I wouldn't bite. I frowned and went back to work with the bent tablespoon my mother had given me. It wasn't a game. I wanted out. I was on a desperate journey that only looked like play.

The blank disappointment, masked as weariness, played on the faces of people on the St. Clair bus. They looked out the windows, coming home from downtown, unseeing: clearly nothing interested them. What were they thinking of? The passing scene was not beautiful enough—was that it?—to catch their eye. Like the empty clouds Mr. Bertram turned to, their blank looks gave back nothing. There was an unshivered shiver in each of us, a shudder we managed to hold back.

We got off the bus at Oxford where, one spring, in the lime green house behind the catalpa tree on the corner, Mr. Lenart (whom we didn't know well) had slung a pair of tire chains over a rafter in the basement and hanged himself. Such things happened. Only the tight clutch of family life ("The family that prays together stays together.") could keep things rolling along. Step out of the tight, bright circle, and you might find yourself dragging your chains down to the basement.

The perverse insubstantiality of the material world was the problem: reality refused to be real enough. Nothing could keep you steadfastly happy. That was clear. Some people blamed God. But I sensed that Mr. Bertram was right not to take that tack. *God isn't the problem.* The clouds passing in the big sky kept dissipating, changing form. That was the problem—but so what? Such worries resolved nothing, and were best left unworried—the unshivered shiver.

There was no one to blame. You could only retire, like Mr. Bertram, stay indoors behind your birchwood blinds, and contemplate the impossibility of things, allowing the Hollywood glitter of reality to fade away and become a vague local rumor.

There were other ways of coping. Mrs. Krueger, several houses down with a big garden rolling with hydrangea bushes, held as her faith a passionate belief in knowledge. She sold *World Book* encyclopedias. After trying Christian Science and a stint with the Unitarians, she had settled down as an agnostic. There seemed to be a lot of reading involved with being an agnostic, pamphlets and books, long citations on cultural anthropology in the *World Book*. It was an abstruse religion, and Mrs. Krueger seemed to belong to some ladies' auxiliary of disbelief.

But it didn't really matter what Mrs. Krueger decided about "the deity-idea," as she called God. No matter what they believed, our neighbors lived not just on Linwood Avenue; they were in St. Luke's parish too, whether they knew it or not. We claimed the territory. And we claimed them—even as we dismissed them. They were all non-Catholics, the term that disposed nicely of all spiritual otherness.

Let the Protestants go their schismatic ways; the Lutherans could splice themselves into synods any which way. Believers, non-believers, even Jews (the Kroners on the corner) or a breed as rare as the Greek Orthodox whose church was across the street from St. Luke's—they were all non-Catholics, just so much extraneous spiritual matter orbiting the nethersphere.

Or maybe it was more intimate than that, and we dismissed the rest of the world as we would our own serfs. We saw the Lutherans and Presbyterians, even those snobbish Episcopalians, as rude colonials, non-Catholics all, doing the best they could out there in the bush to imitate the ways of the homeland. *We* were the homeland.

Jimmy Guiliani was a bully. He pulled my hair when he ran by me on Oxford as we all walked home from St. Luke's, the girls like a midget army in navy jumpers and white blouses, the boys with the greater authority of free civilians without uniforms. They all wore pretty much the same thing anyway: corduroy pants worn smooth at the knees and flannel shirts, usually plaid.

I wasn't the only one Jimmy picked on. He pulled Moira Murphy's hair, he punched Tommy Hague. He struck without reason, indiscriminately, so full of violence it may have been pent-up enthusiasm released at random after the long day leashed in school. Catholic kids were alleged, by public school kids, to be mean fighters, dirty fighters. Jimmy Guiliani was the worst, a terror, hated and feared by Sister Julia's entire third grade class.

So, it came as a surprise when, after many weeks of his tyranny, I managed to land a sure kick to his groin and he collapsed in a heap and cried real tears. "You shouldn't *do* that to a boy," he said, whimpering. He was almost primly admonishing. "Do you know how that feels?"

It's not correct to say that it was a sure kick. I just kicked. I took no aim and had no idea I'd hit paydirt—or why. Even when the tears started to his eyes and he doubled over clutching himself, I didn't understand.

But I liked it when he asked if I knew how it felt. For a brief, hopeful moment I thought he would tell me, that he would explain. Yes, tell me: how *does* it feel? And what's *there,* anyway? It was the first time the male body imposed itself.

I felt an odd satisfaction. I'd made contact. I wasn't glad I had hurt him, I wasn't even pleased to have taken the group's revenge on the class bully. I hadn't planned to kick him. It all just *happened*—as most physical encounters do. I was more astonished than he that I had succeeded in wounding him, I think. In a simple way, I wanted to say I was sorry. But I liked being taken seriously, and could not forfeit that rare pleasure by making an apology.

For a few weeks after I kicked him, I had a crush on Jimmy Guiliani. Not because I'd hurt him. But because he had paused, looked right at me, and implored me to see things from his point of view. *Do you know how that feels?*

I didn't know—and yet I did. As soon as he asked, I realized obscurely that I did know how it felt. I knew what was there between his legs where he hurt. I ceased to be quite so ignorant. And sex began—with a blow.

The surprise of knowing what I hadn't realized I knew seemed beautifully private, but also illicit. That was a problem. I had no desire to be an outlaw. The way I saw it, you were supposed to know what you had been *taught*. This involved being given segments of knowledge by someone (usually a nun) designated to dole out information in measured drams, like strong medicine. Children were clean slates others were meant to write on.

But here was evidence I was not a blank slate at all. I was scribbled all over with intuitions, premonitions, vague resonances clamoring to give their signals. I had caught Mr. Bertram's skyward look and its implicit promise: Life will be tough. There was no point in blaming God—the Catholic habit. Or even more Catholic, blaming the nuns, which allowed you to blame Mother and God all in one package.

And now, here was Jimmy Guiliani drawing out of me this other knowledge, bred of empathy and a swift kick to his balls. *Yes, I know how it feels.*

The hierarchy we lived in, a great linked chain of religious being, seemed set to control every entrance and exit to and from the mind and heart. The sky-blue Baltimore Catechism, small and square, read like an owner's manual for a very complicated vehicle. There was something pleasant, lulling and rhythmic, like heavily rhymed poetry, about the sing song Q-and-A format. Who would not give over heart, if not mind, to the brisk nannyish assurance of the Baltimore prose:

> Who made you?
> *God made me.*

> Why did God make you?
> *God made me to know, love and serve Him in this world, in order to*
> *be happy with Him forever in the next.*

And how harmless our Jesuitical discussions about what, exactly, constituted a meatless spaghetti sauce on Friday. Strict constructionists said no meat of any kind should ever, at any time, have made its way into the tomato sauce; easy liberals held with the notion that meatballs could be lurking around in the sauce, as long as you didn't eat them. My brother lobbied valiantly for the meatball *intactus* but present. My mother said nothing doing. They raged for years.

Father Flannery, who owned his own airplane and drove a sports car, had given Peter some ammunition when he'd been asked to rule on the meatball question in the confessional. My mother would hear none of it. "I don't want to know what goes on between you and your confessor," she said, taking the high road.

"A priest, Ma, a *priest*," my brother cried. "This is an ordained priest saying right there in the sanctity of the confessional that meatballs are OK."

But we were going to heaven my mother's way.

Life was like that—crazy. Full of hair-splitting, and odd rituals. We got our throats blessed on St. Blaise's day in February, with the priest holding oversized beeswax candles in an X around our necks, to ward off death by choking on fish-bones, a problem no one thought of the rest of the year. There were smudged foreheads on Ash Wednesday, and home May altars with plaster statuettes of the Virgin festooned with lilacs. Advent wreaths and nightly family rosary vigils during October (Rosary Month), all of us on our knees in the living room in front of the blank Magnavox.

The atmosphere swirled with the beatific visions and heroic martyrdoms of the long dead and the apocryphal. In grade school we were taken to daily Mass during Lent, and we read the bio notes of the saints that preceded the readings in the Daily Missal, learning that St. Agatha had had her breasts cut off by the Romans. We thrilled at the word *breast,* pointing to it and giggling, as if it were a neon lingerie ad flashing from the prayerbook.

Most of the women saints in the Missal had under their names the designation *Virgin and Martyr,* as if the two categories were somehow a matched set. Occasionally a great female figure canonized for her piety and charitable works received the label *Queen and Widow*. The men were usually *Confessor* or, sometimes, *Martyr*, but none of them was ever *Virgin*.

The lives of the saints were not only edifying stories but cautionary tales. Chief here was St. Maria Goretti, early-twentieth-century *Virgin and Martyr*, who had been stabbed to death by a sex-crazed farmworker. She preserved her honor to the end. Her murderer, "alive to this day," we were told, had gone to her canonization in St. Peter's Square on his knees.

More troubling still was the story of Thomas à Kempis, the great author of *The Imitation of Christ*, one of the treasures of medieval scholasticism. Why, asked someone in Sister Hilaria's fifth-grade class, was Thomas à Kempis not *St. Thomas?*

Ah, Sister Hilaria said, pausing, looking at us to see if we were ready for this truth. We were ready.

Naturally, Sister said, there had been a canonization effort. All the usual procedures had been followed. Thomas was coming down the homestretch of the investigation when "very disturbing evidence was discovered." She paused again.

"The body of Thomas à Kempis was exhumed, children, as all such persons must be," Sister said reasonably. We nodded, we followed the macabre corporate ladder of sainthood without dismay. "When they opened that casket, boys and girls, Thomas à Kempis was lost." For upon opening the moldy box, there he was, the would-be saint, a ghastly look of horror on his wormy face, his hand clawing upward toward the air, madly. "You see, children, he did not die in the peace of the Lord." They shut him up and put him back. "A good man still," Sister said, "and a good writer." But not, we understood, a saint.

There were, as well, snatches of stories about nuns who beat kids with rulers in the coat room; the priest who had a twenty-year affair with a member of the Altar and Rosary Society; the other priest in love with an altar boy—they'd had to send him away. Not St. Luke's stories—oh no, certainly not—but stories, floating, as stories do, from inner ear to inner ear, respecting no parish boundaries. Part of the ether.

And with it all, a relentless xenophobia about other religions. "It's going to be a mixed marriage, I understand," one of my aunts murmured about a friend's daughter who was marrying an Episcopalian. So what if he called himself High Church? What did that change? He was a non-Catholic.

And now, educated out of it all, well climbed into the professions, the Catholics find each other at cocktail parties and get going. The nun stories, the first confession traumas—and a tone of rage and dismay that seems to bewilder even the tellers of these tales.

Nobody says, when asked, "I'm Catholic." It's always, "Yes, I was brought up Catholic." Anything to put it at a distance, to diminish the presence of that heritage that is not racial but acts as if it were. "You never get over it, you know," a fortyish lawyer told me a while ago at a party where we found ourselves huddled by the chips and dip, as if at a St. Thomas mixer once again.

He seemed to feel he was speaking to someone with the same hopeless congenital condition. "It's different now, of course," he said. "But when we were growing up back there. . . ." There it was again: the past isn't a time. It's a place. A permanent destination: *back there*.

He had a very Jimmy Guiliani look to him. A chastened rascal. "I'm divorced," he said. We both smiled: there's no going to hell anymore. "Do they still have mortal sin?" he asked wistfully.

The love-hate lurch of a Catholic upbringing, like having an extra set of parents to contend with. Or an added national allegiance—not to the Vatican, as we were warned that the Baptists thought during John Kennedy's campaign for president. To a different realm. It was the implacable loyalty of faith, that flawless relation between self and existence into which we were born. A strange country where people prayed and believed impossible things.

The nuns who taught us, rigged up in their bold black habits with the big round wimples stiff as frisbees, walked our parish streets, moving from convent to church in twos or threes, dipping in the side door of the huge church "for a little adoration," as they would say. The roly-poly Irish-born monsignor told us to stand straight and proud when he met us slouching toward class along Summit. Fashionable Father Flannery took a companionable walk with the old pastor every night. The two of them took out white handkerchiefs and waved them for safety as they crossed the busy avenue on the way home in the dark, swallowed in their black suits and cassocks, lost in the growing gloom.

But the one I would like to summon up most and to have pass me on Oxford as I head off to St. Luke's in the early morning mist, one of those mid-May weekdays, the lilacs just starting to spill, the one I want most to materialize from "back there"—I don't know her name, where, exactly, she lived, or who she was. We never spoke, in fact. We just passed each other, she coming home from six o'clock daily Mass, I going early to school to practice the piano for an hour before class began.

She was a "parish lady," part of the anonymous population that thickened our world, people who were always there, who were solidly part of us, part of what we were, but who never emerged beyond the bounds of being parishioners to become full-fledged persons.

We met every morning, just past the Healys' low brick wall. She wore a librarian's cardigan sweater. She must have been about forty-five, and I sensed she was not married. Unlike Dr. and Mrs. Harrigan, who walked smartly along Summit holding hands, their bright Irish setter accompanying them as far as the church door, where he waited till Mass was over, the lady in the cardigan was always alone.

I saw her coming all the way from Grand where she had to pause for the traffic. She never rushed across the street, zipping past a truck, but waited until the coast was completely clear, and passed across keeping her floating pace. A peaceful gait, no rush to it.

When finally we were close enough to make eye contact, she looked up, straight into my face, and smiled. It was such a *complete* smile, so entire, that it startled me every time, as if I'd heard my name called out on the street of a foreign city.

She was a homely woman, plain and pale, unnoticeable. But I felt—how to put it— that she shed light. The mornings were often frail with mist, the light uncertain and tender. The smile was a brief flood of light. She loved me, I felt.

I knew what it was about. She was praying. Her hand, stuck in her cardigan pocket, held one of the crystal beads of her rosary. I knew this. I'd once seen her take it out of the left pocket and quickly replace it after she had found the handkerchief she needed.

If I had seen a nun mumbling the rosary along Summit (and this did happen), it would not have meant much to me. But here on Oxford, the side street we used as a sleepy corridor to St. Luke's, it was a different thing. The parish lady was not a nun. She was a person who prayed, who prayed alone, for no reason that I understood. But there was no question that she prayed without ceasing, as the strange scriptural line instructed.

She didn't look up to the blank clouds for a response, as Mr. Bertram did in his stoic way. Her head was bowed, quite unconsciously. And when she raised it, keeping her hand in her pocket where the clear beads were, she looked straight into the eyes of the person passing by. It was not an invasive look, but it latched. She had me. Not an intensive gaze, but one brimming with a secret which, if only she had the words, it was clear she'd want to tell.

Walking

Linda Hogan

It began in dark and underground weather, a slow hunger moving toward light. It grew in a dry gulley beside the road where I live, a place where entire hillsides are sometimes yellow, windblown tides of sunflower plants. But this plant was different. It was alone, and larger than the countless others that had established their lives farther up the hill. This one was a traveler, a settler, and like a dream beginning in conflict, it grew where the land had been disturbed.

I saw it first in early summer. It was a green and sleeping bud, raising itself toward the sun. Ants worked around the unopened bloom, gathering aphids and sap. A few days later, it was a tender young flower, soft and new, with a pale green center and a troop of silver-gray insects climbing up and down the stalk. Over the summer this sunflower grew into a plant of incredible beauty, turning its face daily toward the sun in the most subtle of ways, the black center of it dark and alive with a deep blue light, as if flint had sparked an elemental fire there, in community with rain, mineral, mountain air, and sand.

As summer changed from green to yellow there were new visitors daily, the lace-winged insects, the bees whose legs were fat with pollen, and grasshoppers with their clattering wings and desperate hunger. There were other lives I missed, those too small or hidden to see. It was as if this plant with its host of lives was a society, one in which moment by moment, depending on light and moisture, there was great and diverse change.

There were changes in the next larger world around the plant as well. One day I rounded a bend in the road to find the disturbing sight of a dead horse, black and still against a hillside, eyes rolled back. Another day I was nearly lifted by a wind and sandstorm so fierce and hot that I had to wait for it to pass before I could return home. On this day the faded dry petals of the sunflower were swept across the land. That was when the birds arrived to carry the new seeds to another future.

In this one plant, in one summer season, a drama of need and survival took place. Hungers were filled. Insects coupled. There was escape, exhaustion, and death. Lives touched down a moment and were gone.

I was an outsider. I only watched. I never learned the sunflower's golden language or the tongues of its citizens. I had a small understanding, nothing more than a shallow observation of the flower, insects, and birds. But they knew what to do, how to live. An old voice from somewhere, gene or cell, told the plant how to evade the pull of gravity and find its way upward, how to open. It was instinct, intuition, necessity. A certain knowing directed the seed-bearing birds on paths to ancestral homelands they had never seen. They believed it. They followed.

There are other summons and calls, some even more mysterious than those commandments to birds or those survival journeys of insects. In bamboo plants, for instance, with their thin green canopy of light and golden stalks that creak in the wind. Once a century, all of a certain kind of bamboo flower on the same day. Neither the plants' location, in Malaysia or in a greenhouse in Minnesota, nor their age or size make a difference. They flower. Some current of an inner language passes among them, through space and separation, in ways we cannot explain in our language. They are all, somehow, one plant, each with a share of communal knowledge.

John Hay, in *The Immortal Wilderness*, has written: "There are occasions when you can hear the mysterious language of the Earth, in water, or coming through the trees, emanating from the mosses, seeping through the undercurrents of the soil, but you have to be willing to wait and receive."

Sometimes I hear it talking. The light of the sunflower was one language, but there are others, more audible. Once, in the redwood forest, I heard a beat, something like a drum or heart coming from the ground and trees and wind. That underground current stirred a kind of knowing inside me, a kinship and longing, a dream barely remembered that disappeared back to the body. Another time, there was the booming voice of an ocean storm thundering from far out at sea, telling about what lived in the distance, about the rough water that would arrive, wave after wave revealing the disturbance at center.

Tonight I walk. I am watching the sky. I think of the people who came before me and how they knew the placement of stars in the sky, watched the moving sun long and hard enough to witness how a certain angle of light touched a stone only once a year. Without written records, they knew the gods of every night, the small, fine details of the world around them and of immensity above them.

Walking, I can almost hear the redwoods beating. And the oceans are above me here, rolling clouds, heavy and dark, considering snow. On the dry, red road, I pass the place of the sunflower, that dark and secret location where creation took place. I wonder if it will return this summer, if it will multiply and move up to the other stand of flowers in a territorial struggle.

It's winter and there is smoke from the fires. The square, lighted windows of houses are fogging over. It is a world of elemental attention, of all things working together, listening to what speaks in the blood. Whichever road I follow, I walk in the land of many gods, and they love and eat one another. Walking, I am listening to a deeper way. Suddenly all my ancestors are behind me. Be still, they say. Watch and listen. You are the result of the love of thousands.

Where Worlds Collide

Pico Iyer

They come out, blinking, into the bleached, forgetful sunshine, in Dodgers caps and Rodeo Drive T-shirts, with the maps their cousins have drawn for them and the images they've brought over from *Cops* and *Terminator 2;* they come out, dazed, disoriented, heads still partly in the clouds, bodies still several time zones—or centuries—away, and they step into the Promised Land.

In front of them is a Van Stop, a Bus Stop, a Courtesy Tram Stop, and a Shuttle Bus Stop (the shuttles themselves tracing circuits A, B, and C). At the Shuttle Bus Stop, they see the All American Shuttle, the Apollo Shuttle, Celebrity Airport Livery, the Great American Stageline, the Movie Shuttle, the Transport, Ride-4-You, and forty-two other magic buses waiting to whisk them everywhere from Bakersfield to Disneyland. They see Koreans piling into the Taeguk Airport Shuttle and the Seoul Shuttle, which will take them to Koreatown without their ever feeling they've left home; they see newcomers from the Middle East disappearing under the Arabic script of the Sahara Shuttle. They see fast-talking, finger-snapping, palm-slapping jive artists straight from their TV screens shouting incomprehensible slogans about deals, destinations, and drugs. Over there is a block-long white limo, a Lincoln Continental, and, over there, a black Chevy Blazer with Mexican stickers all over its windows, being towed. They have arrived in the Land of Opportunity, and the opportunities are swirling dizzily, promiscuously, around them.

They have already braved the ranks of Asian officials, the criminal-looking security men in jackets that say "Elsinore Airport Services," the men shaking tins that say "Helping America's Hopeless." They have already seen the tilting mugs that say "California: a new slant on life" and the portable fruit machines in the gift shop. They have already, perhaps, visited the rest room where someone has written, "Yes on Proposition 187. Mexicans go home," the snack bar where a slice of pizza costs $3.19 (18 quetzals, they think in horror, or 35,000 dong), and the sign that urges them to try the Cockatoo Inn Grand Hotel. The latest arrivals at Los Angeles International Airport are ready now to claim their new lives.

Above them in the terminal, voices are repeating, over and over, in Japanese, Spanish, and unintelligible English, "Maintain visual contact with your personal property at all times." Out on the sidewalk, a man's voice and a woman's voice are alternating an unending refrain: "The white zone is for loading and unloading of passengers only. No parking." There are "Do Not Cross" yellow lines cordoning off parts of the sidewalk and "Wells Fargo Alarm Services" stickers on the windows; there are "Aviation Safeguard" signs on the baggage carts and "Beware of Solicitors" signs on the columns; there are even special phones "To Report Trouble." More male and female voices are intoning, continuously, "Do not leave your car unattended" and "Unattended cars are subject to immediate towaway." There are no military planes on the tarmac here, the newcomers notice, no khaki soldiers in fatigues, no instructions not to take photographs, as at home; but there are civilian restrictions every bit as strict as in many a police state.

"This Terminal Is in a Medfly Quarantine Area," says the sign between the terminals. "Stop the Spread of Medfly!" If, by chance, the new Americans have to enter a parking lot on their way out, they will be faced with "Cars left over 30 days may be impounded at Owner's Expense" and "Do not enter without a ticket." It will cost them $16 if they lose their parking ticket, they read, and $56 if they park in the wrong zone. Around them is an unending cacophony of antitheft devices, sirens, beepers, and car-door openers; lights are flashing everywhere, and the man who fines them $16 for losing their parking ticket has the tribal scars of Tigre across his forehead.

The blue skies and palm trees they saw on TV are scarcely visible from here: just an undifferentiated smoggy haze, billboards advertising Nissan and Panasonic and Canon, and beyond those an endlessly receding mess of gray streets. Overhead, they can see the all-too-familiar signs of Hilton and Hyatt and Holiday Inn; in the distance, a sea of tract houses, mini-malls, and high-rises. The City of Angels awaits them.

It is a commonplace nowadays to say that cities look more and more like airports, cross-cultural spaces that are a gathering of tribes and races and variegated tongues; and it has always been true that airports are in many ways like miniature cities, whole, self-sufficient communities, with their own chapels and museums and gymnasiums. Not only have airports colored our speech (teaching us about being upgraded, bumped, and put on standby, coaching us in the ways of fly-by-night operations, holding patterns, and the Mile High Club); they have also taught us their own rules, their own codes, their own customs. We eat and sleep and shower in airports; we pray and weep and kiss there. Some people stay for days at a time in these perfectly convenient, hermetically sealed, climate-controlled duty-free zones, which offer a kind of caesura from the obligations of daily life.

Airports are also, of course, the new epicenters and paradigms of our dawning post-national age—not just the bus terminals of the global village but the prototypes, in some sense, for our polyglot, multicolored, user-friendly future. And in their very universality—like the mall, the motel, or the McDonald's outlet—they advance the notion of a future in which all the world's a multiculture. If you believe that more and more of the world is a kind of mongrel hybrid in which many cities (Sydney, Toronto, Singapore) are simply suburbs of a single universal order, then Los Angeles's LAX, London's Heathrow, and Hong Kong's Kai Tak are merely stages on some great global Circle Line, shuttling variations on a common global theme. Mass travel has made L.A. contiguous to Seoul and adjacent to São Paulo, and has made all of them now feel a little like bedroom communities for Tokyo.

And as with most social trends, especially the ones involving tomorrow, what is true of the world is doubly true of America, and what is doubly true of America is quadruply true of Los Angeles. L.A., legendarily, has more Thais than any city but Bangkok, more Koreans than any city but Seoul, more El Salvadorans than any city outside of San Salvador, more Druze than anywhere but Beirut; it is, at the very least, the easternmost outpost of Asia and the northernmost province of Mexico. When I stopped at a Traveler's Aid desk at LAX recently, I was told I could request help in Khamu, Mien, Tigrinya, Tajiki, Pashto, Dari, Pangasinan, Pampangan, Waray-Waray, Bambara, Twi, and Bicolano (as well, of course, as French, German, and eleven languages from India). LAX is as clear an image as exists today of the world we are about to enter, and of the world that's entering us.

For me, though, LAX has always had a more personal resonance: it was in LAX that I arrived myself as a new immigrant, in 1966; and from the time I was in the fourth grade, it was to LAX that I would go three times a year, as an "unaccompanied minor," to fly to school in London—and to LAX that I returned three times a year for my holidays. Sometimes it seems as if I have spent half my life in LAX. For me, it is the site of my liberation (from school, from the Old World, from home) and the place where I came to design my own new future.

Often when I have set off from L.A. to some distant place—Havana, say, or Hanoi, or Pyongyang—I have felt that the multicultural drama on display in LAX, the interaction of exoticism and familiarity, was just as bizarre as anything I would find when I arrived at my foreign destination. The airport is an Amy Tan novel, a short story by Bharati Mukherjee, a Henry James sketch set to an MTV beat; it is a cross-generational saga about Chang Hsieng meeting his daughter Cindy and finding that she's wearing a nose ring now and is shacked up with a surfer from Berlin. The very best kind of airport reading to be found in LAX these days is the triple-decker melodrama being played out all around one—a complex tragicomedy of love and war and exile, about people fleeing centuries-old rivalries and thirteenth-century mullahs and stepping out into a fresh, forgetful, born-again city that is rewriting its script every moment.

Not long ago I went to spend a week in LAX. I haunted the airport by day and by night, I joined the gloomy drinkers listening to air-control-tower instructions on earphones at the Proud Bird bar. I listened each morning to Airport Radio (530 AM), and I slept each night at the Airport Sheraton or the Airport Hilton. I lived off cellophaned crackers and Styrofoam cups of tea, browsed for hours among Best Actor statuettes and Beverly Hills magnets, and tried to see what kinds of America the city presents to the new Americans, who are remaking America each day.

It is almost too easy to say that LAX is a perfect metaphor for L.A., a flat, spaced-out desert kind of place, highly automotive, not deeply hospitable, with little reading matter and no organizing principle. (There are eight satellites without a center here, many international arrivals are shunted out into the bleak basement of Terminal 2, and there is no airline that serves to dominate LAX as Pan Am once did JFK.) Whereas "SIN" is a famously ironical airline code for Singapore, cathedral of puritanical rectitude, "LAX" has always seemed perilously well chosen for a city whose main industries were traditionally thought to be laxity and relaxation. LAX is at once a vacuum waiting to be colonized and a joyless theme park—Tomorrowland, Adventureland, and Fantasyland all at once.

The postcards on sale here (made in Korea) dutifully call the airport "one of the busiest and most beautiful air facilities in the world," and it is certainly true that LAX, with thirty thousand international arrivals each day—roughly the same number of tourists that have visited the Himalayan country of Bhutan in its entire history—is not uncrowded. But bigger is less and less related to better: in a recent survey of travel facilities, *Business Traveller* placed LAX among the five worst airports in the world for customs, luggage retrieval, and passport processing.

LAX is, in fact, a surprisingly shabby and hollowed-out kind of place, certainly not adorned with the amenities one might expect of the world's strongest and richest power. When you come out into the Arrivals area in the International Terminal, you will find exactly one tiny snack bar, which serves nine items; of them, five are identified as Cheese Dog, Chili Dog, Chili Cheese Dog, Nachos with Cheese, and Chili Cheese Nachos. There is a large panel on the wall offering rental-car services and hotels, and the newly deplaned American dreamer can choose between the Cadillac Hotel, the Banana Bungalow (which offers a Basketball Court, "Free Toast," "Free Bed Sheets," and "Free Movies and Parties"), and the Backpacker's Paradise (with "Free Afternoon Tea and Crumpets" and "Free Evening Party Including Food and Champagne").

Around one in the terminal is a swirl of priests rattling cans, Iranians in suits brandishing pictures of torture victims, and Japanese girls in Goofy hats. "I'm looking for something called Clearasil," a distinguished-looking Indian man diffidently tells a cashier. "Clearasil?" shouts the girl. "For your face?"

Upstairs, in the Terrace Restaurant, passengers are gulping down "Dutch Chocolate" and "Japanese Coffee" while students translate back and forth between English and American, explaining that "soliciting" loses something of its cachet when you go across the Atlantic. A fat man is nuzzling the neck of his outrageously pretty Filipina companion, and a few Brits are staring doubtfully at the sign that assures them that seafood is "cheerfully served at your table!" Only in America, they are doubtless thinking. A man goes from table to table, plunking down on each one a key chain attached to a globe. As soon as an unsuspecting customer picks one up, touched by the largesse of the New World and convinced now that there is such a thing as a free lunch in America, the man appears again, flashes a sign that says "I Am a Deaf," and requests a dollar for the gift.

At a bank of phones, a saffron-robed monk gingerly inserts a credit card, while schoolkids page Jesse Jackson at the nearest "white courtesy telephone." One notable feature of the modern airport is that it is wired, with a vengeance: even in a tiny, two-urinal men's room, I found two telephones on offer; LAX bars rent out cellular phones; and in the Arrivals area, as you come out into the land of plenty, you face a bank of forty-six phones of every kind, with screens and buttons and translations, from which newcomers are calling direct to Bangalore or Baghdad. Airports are places for connections of all kinds and *loci classici*, perhaps, for a world ruled by IDD and MCI, DOS and JAL.

Yet for all these grounding reminders of the world outside, everywhere I went in the airport I felt myself in an odd kind of twilight zone of consciousness, that weightless limbo of a world in which people are between lives and between selves, almost sleepwalking, not really sure of who or where they are. Light-headed from the trips they've taken, ears popping and eyes about to do so, under a potent foreign influence, people are at the far edge of themselves in airports, ready to break down or through. You see strangers pouring out their life stories to strangers here, or making new life stories with other strangers. Everything is at once intensified and slightly unreal. One L.A. psychiatrist advises shy women to practice their flirting here, and religious groups circle in the hope of catching unattached souls.

Airports, which often have a kind of perpetual morning-after feeling (the end of the holiday, the end of the affair), are places where everyone is ruled by the clock, but all the clocks show different times. These days, after all, we fly not only into yesterday or this morning when we go across the world but into different decades, often, of the world's life and our own: in ten or fifteen hours, we are taken back into the twelfth century or into worlds we haven't seen since childhood. And in the process we are subjected to transitions more jolting than any imagined by Oscar Wilde or Sigmund Freud: if the average individual today sees as many images in a day as a Victorian saw in a lifetime, the average person today also has to negotiate switches between continents inconceivable only fifty years ago. Frequent fliers like Ted Turner have actually become ill from touching down and taking off so often; but, in less diagnosable ways, all of us are being asked to handle difficult suspensions of the laws of Nature and Society when moving between competing worlds.

This helps to compound the strange statelessness of airports, where all bets are off and all laws are annulled—modern equivalents, perhaps, to the hundred yards of no-man's-land between two frontier crossings. In airports we are often in dreamy, floating, out-of-body states, as ready to be claimed as that suitcase on Carousel C. Even I, not traveling, didn't know sometimes if I was awake or asleep in LAX, as I heard an announcer intone, "John Cheever, John Cheever, please contact a Northwest representative in the Baggage Claim area. John Cheever, please contact a service representative at the Northwest Baggage Claim area."

As I started to sink into this odd, amphibious, bipolar state, I could begin to see why a place like LAX is a particular zone of fear, more terrifying to many people than anywhere but the dentist's office. Though dying in a plane is, notoriously, twenty times less likely than dying in a car, every single airline crash is front-page news and so dramatic—not a single death but three hundred—that airports are for many people killing grounds. Their runways are associated in the mind's (televisual) eye with hostages and hijackings; with bodies on the tarmac or anti-terrorist squads storming the plane.

That general sense of unsettledness is doubtless intensified by all the people in uniform in LAX. There are ten different security agencies working the Tom Bradley Terminal alone, and the streets outside are jam-packed with Airport Police cars, FBI men, and black-clad airport policemen on bicycles. All of them do as much, I suspect, to instill fear as to still it. "People are scared here," a gloomy Pakistani security guard told me, "because undercover are working. Police are working. You could be undercover, I could be undercover. Who knows?"

And just as L.A. is a province of the future in part because so many people take it to be the future, so it is a danger zone precisely because it is imagined to be dangerous. In Osaka's new $16 billion airport recently, I cross-examined the Skynet computer (in the Departures area) about what to expect when arriving at LAX or any other foreign airport. "Guard against theft in the arrival hall," it told me (and, presumably, even warier Japanese). "A thief is waiting for a chance to take advantage of you." Elsewhere it added, "Do not dress too touristy," and, "Be on your guard when approached by a group of suspicious-looking children, such as girls wearing bright-colored shirts and scarves." True to such dark prognostications, the side doors of the Airport Sheraton at LAX are locked every day from 8:00 P.M. to 6:00 A.M., and you cannot even activate the elevators without a room key. "Be extra careful in parking garages and stairwells," the hotel advises visitors. "Always try to use the main entrance to your hotel, particularly late in the evening. Never answer your hotel room door without verifying who is there."

One reason airports enjoy such central status in our imaginations is that they play such a large part in forming our first (which is sometimes our last) impression of a place; this is the reason that poor countries often throw all their resources into making their airports sleek, with beautifully landscaped roads leading out of them into town. L.A., by contrast, has the bareness of arrogance, or simple inhospitality. Usually what you see as you approach the city is a grim penitential haze through which is visible nothing but rows of gray buildings, a few dun-hued warehouses, and ribbons of dirty freeway: a no-colored blur without even the comforting lapis ornaments of the swimming pools that dot New York or Johannesburg. (Ideally, in fact, one should enter L.A. by night, when the whole city pulses like an electric grid of lights—or the back of a transistor radio, in Thomas Pynchon's inspired metaphor. While I was staying in LAX, Jackie Collins actually told *Los Angeles* magazine that "Flying in [to LAX] at night is just an orgasmic thrill.") You land, with a bump, on a mess of gray runways with no signs of welcome, a hangar that says "T ans W rld Airlines," another broken sign that announces "Tom Bradl y International Ai port," and an air-control tower under scaffolding.

The first thing that greeted me on a recent arrival was a row of Asians sitting on the floor of the terminal, under a sign that told them of a $25,000 fine for bringing in the wrong kinds of food. As I passed through endless corridors, I was faced with almost nothing except long escalators (a surprisingly high percentage of the accidents recorded at airports comes from escalators, bewildering to new-comers) and bare hallways. The other surprise, for many of my fellow travelers, no doubt, was that almost no one we saw looked like Robert Redford or Julia Roberts or, indeed, like anyone belonging to the race we'd been celebrating in our in-flight movies. As we passed into the huge, bare assembly hall that is the Customs and Immigration Center here, I was directed into one of the chaotic lines by a Noriko and formally admitted to the country by a C. Chen. The man waiting to transfer my baggage (as a beagle sniffed around us in a coat that said "Agriculture's Beagle Brigade" on one side and "Protecting American Agriculture" on the other) was named Yoji Yosaka. And the first sign I saw, when I stepped into America, was a big board being waved by the "Executive Sedan Service" for one "Mr. T. Ego."

For many immigrants, in fact, LAX is quietly offering them a view of their own near futures: the woman at the Host Coffee Shop is themselves, in a sense, two years from now, and the man sweeping up the refuse is the American dream in practice. The staff at the airport seems to be made up almost entirely of recent immigrants: on my very first afternoon there, I was served by a Hoa, an Ephraim, and a Glinda; the waitpeople at a coffee shop in Terminal 5 were called Ignacio, Ever, Aura, and Erick. Even at the Airport Sheraton (where the employees all wear nameplates), I was checked in by Viera (from "Bratislavia") and ran into Hasmik and Yovik (from Ethiopia), Faye (from Vietnam), Ingrid (from Guatemala City), Khrystyne (from Long Beach, by way of Phnom Penh, I think), and Moe (from West L.A., she said). Many of the bright-eyed dreamers who arrive at LAX so full of hope never actually leave the place.

The deeper drama of any airport is that it features a kind of interaction almost unique in our lives, wherein many of us do not know whom we are going to meet or whom others are going to meet in us. You see people standing at the barriers outside the Customs area looking into their pasts, while wide-open newcomers drift out, searching for their futures. Lovers do not know if they will see the same person who kissed them good-bye a month ago; grandparents wonder what the baby they last saw twenty years ago will look like now.

In L.A. all of this has an added charge, because unlike many cities, it is not a hub but a terminus: a place where people come to arrive. Thus many of the meet-ings you witness are between the haves and the hope-to-haves, between those who are affecting a new ease in their new home and those who are here in search of that ease. Both parties, especially if they are un-American by birth, are eager to stress their Americanness or their fitness for America; and both, as they look at each other's made-up self, see themselves either before or after a stay in L.A.'s theater of transformation. And so they stream in, wearing running shoes or cow-boy hats or 49ers jackets, anxious to make a good first impression; and the people who wait for them, under a halfhearted mural of Desertland, are often American enough not to try to look the part. Juan and Esperanza both have ponytails now, and Kimmie is wearing a Harley-Davidson cap backward and necking with a

Japanese guy; the uncle from Delhi arrives to find that Rajiv not only has grown darker but has lost weight, so that he looks more like a peasant from back home than ever.

And the newcomers pour in in astonishing numbers. A typical Sunday evening, in a single hour, sees flights arriving from England, Taiwan, the Philippines, Indonesia, Mexico, Austria, Germany, Spain, Costa Rica, and Guatemala; and each new group colors and transforms the airport: an explosion of tropical shades from Hawaiian Air, a rash of blue blazers and white shirts around the early flight from Tokyo. Red-haired Thais bearing pirated Schwarzenegger videos, lonely Africans in Aerial Assault sneakers, farmers from changeless Confucian cultures peering into the smiles of a Prozac city, children whose parents can't pronounce their names. Many of them are returning, like Odysseus, with the spoils of war: young brides from Luzon, business cards from Shanghai, boxes of macadamia nuts from Oahu. And for many of them the whole wild carnival will feature sights they have never seen before: Japanese look anxiously at the first El Salvadorans they've ever seen, and El Salvadorans ogle sleek girls from Bangkok in thigh-high boots. All of them, moreover, may not be pleased to realize that the America they've dreamed of is, in fact, a land of tacos and pita and pad thai—full, indeed, of the very Third World cultures that other Third Worlders look down upon.

One day over lunch I asked my Ethiopian waitress about her life here. She liked it well enough, she said, but still she missed her home. And yet, she added, she couldn't go back. "Why not?" I asked, still smiling. "Because they killed my family," she said. "Two years back. They killed my father. They killed my brother." "They," I realized, referred to the Tigreans—many of them working just down the corridor in other parts of the hotel. So, too, Tibetans who have finally managed to flee their Chinese-occupied homeland arrive at LAX to find Chinese faces everywhere; those who fled the Sandinistas find themselves standing next to Sandinistas fleeing their successors. And all these people from ancient cultures find themselves in a country as amnesiac as the morning, where World War II is just a rumor and the Gulf War a distant memory. Their pasts are escaped, yes, but by the same token they are unlikely to be honored.

It is dangerously tempting to start formulating socioeconomic principles in the midst of LAX: people from rich countries (Germany and Japan, say) travel light, if only because they are sure that they can return any time; those from poor countries come with their whole lives in cardboard boxes imperfectly tied with string. People from poor countries are often met by huge crowds—for them each arrival is a special occasion—and stagger through customs with string bags and Gold Digger apple crates, their addresses handwritten on them in pencil; the Okinawan honeymooners, by contrast, in the color-coordinated outfits they will change every day, somehow have packed all their needs into a tiny case.

If airports have some of the excitement of bars, because so many people are composing (and decomposing) selves there, they also have some of the sadness of bars, the poignancy of people sitting unclaimed while everyone around them has paired off. A pretty girl dressed in next to nothing sits alone in an empty Baggage

Claim area, waiting for a date who never comes; a Vietnamese man, lost, tells an official that he has friends in Orange County who can help him, but when the friends are contacted, they say they know no one from Vietnam. I hear of a woman who got off and asked for "San Mateo," only to learn that she was meant to disembark in San Francisco; and a woman from Nigeria who came out expecting to see her husband in Monroe, Louisiana, only to learn that someone in Lagos had mistaken "La." on her itinerary for "L.A."

The greetings I saw in the Arrivals area were much more tentative than I had expected, less passionate—as ritualized in their way as the kisses placed on Bob Barker's cheek—and much of that may be because so many people are meeting strangers, even if they are meeting people they once knew. Places like LAX—places like L.A.—perpetuate the sense that everyone is a stranger in our new floating world. I spent one afternoon in the airport with a Californian blonde, and I saw her complimented on her English by a sweet Korean woman and asked by an Iranian if she was Indian. Airports have some of the unsteady brashness of singles bars, where no one knows quite what is expected of them. "Mike, is that you?" "Oh, I didn't recognize you." "I'd have known you anywhere." "It's so kind of you to come and pick me up." And already at a loss, a young Japanese girl and a broad, lonely-looking man head off toward the parking lot, not knowing, in any sense, who is going to be in the driver's seat.

The driving takes place, of course, in what many of the newcomers, primed by video screenings of *L.A. Law* and *Speed*, regard as the ultimate heart of darkness, a place at least as forbidding and dangerous as Africa must have seemed to the Victorians. They have heard about how America is the murder capital of the world; they have seen Rodney King get pummeled by L.A.'s finest; they know of the city as the site of drive-by shootings and freeway snipers, of riots and celebrity murders. The "homeless" and the "tempest-tost" that the Statue of Liberty invites are arriving, increasingly, in a city that is itself famous for its homeless population and its fires, floods, and earthquakes.

In that context, the ideal symbol of LAX is, perhaps, the great object that for thirty years has been the distinctive image of the place: the ugly white quadruped that sits in the middle of the airport like a beached white whale or a jet-age beetle, featuring a 360-degree circular restaurant that does not revolve and an observation deck from which the main view is of twenty-three thousand parking places. The Theme Building, at 201 World Way, is a sad image of a future that never arrived, a monument to Kennedy-era idealism and the thrusting modernity of the American empire when it was in its prime; it now has the poignancy of an abandoned present with its price tag stuck to it. When you go there (and almost nobody does) you are greeted by photos of Saturn's rings and Jupiter and its moons, by a plaque laid down by L.B.J. and a whole set of symbols from the time when NASA was shooting for the heavens. Now the "landmark" building, with its "gourmet-type restaurant," looks like a relic from a time long past, when it must have looked like the face of the future.

Upstairs, a few desperately merry waiters are serving nonalcoholic drinks and cheeseburgers to sallow diners who look as if they've arrived at the end of the world; on the tarmac outside, speedbirds inch ahead like cars in a traffic jam. "Hello All the New People of LAX—Welcome," says the graffiti on the elevator.

The Theme Restaurant comes to us from an era when L.A. was leading the world. Nowadays, of course, L.A. is being formed and reformed and led by the world around it. And as I got ready to leave LAX, I could not help but feel that the Theme Building stands, more and more, for a city left behind by our accelerating planet. LAX, I was coming to realize, was a good deal scruffier than the airports even of Bangkok or Jakarta, more chaotic, more suggestive of Third World lawlessness. And the city around it is no more golden than Seoul, no more sunny than Taipei, and no more laid-back than Moscow. Beverly Hills, after all, is largely speaking Farsi now. Hollywood Boulevard is sleazier than 42nd Street. And Malibu is falling into the sea.

Yet just as I was about to give up on L.A. as yesterday's piece of modernity, I got on the shuttle bus that moves between the terminals in a never-ending loop. The seats next to me were taken by two tough-looking dudes from nearby South Central, who were riding the free buses and helping people on and off with their cases (acting, I presumed, on the safe assumption that the Japanese, say, new to the country and bewildered, had been warned beforehand to tip often and handsomely for every service they received). In between terminals, as a terrified-looking Miss Kudo and her friend guarded their luggage, en route from Nagoya to Las Vegas, the two gold-plated sharks talked about the Raiders' last game and the Lakers' next season. Then one of them, without warning, announced, "The bottom line is the spirit is with you. When you work out, you chill out and, like, you meditate in your spirit. You know what I mean? Meditation is recreation. Learn math, follow your path. That's all I do, man, that's all I live for: learnin' about God, learnin' about Jesus. I am *possessed* by that spirit. You know, I used to have all these problems, with the flute and all, but when I heard about God, I learned about the body, the mind, and the flesh. People forget, they don't know, that the Bible isn't talkin' about the flesh, it's talkin' about the spirit. And I was reborn again in the spirit."

His friend nodded. "When you recreate, you meditate. Recreation is a spiritually uplifting experience."

"Yeah. When you do that, you allow the spirit to breathe."

"Because you're gettin' into the physical world. You're lettin' the spirit flow. You're helpin' the secretion of the endorphins in the brain."

Nearby, the Soldiers of the Cross of Christ Church stood by the escalators, taking donations, and a man in a dog collar approached another stranger.

I watched the hustlers allowing the spirit to breathe, I heard the Hare Krishna devotees plying their wares, I spotted some Farrakhan flunkies collecting a dollar for a copy of their newspaper, *The Final Call*—redemption and corruption all around us in the air—and I thought: welcome to America, Miss Kudo, welcome to L.A.

Life in Motion

Nicole Lamy

1

Three years ago I took pictures of all the houses I've lived in. The houses impress not in beauty but in number—twelve houses before I turned thirteen. For me the moves had always resisted coherent explanation—no military reassignments or evasion of the law. I wanted to gather the photos as charms against fallible memory, like the list of lost things I used to keep: a plastic purse filled with silver dollars, a mole-colored beret, a strip of negatives from my brother's first day of kindergarten. I planned to bind the photos in an album and give them to my mother. Maybe then, I thought, we could read our lives like straightforward narratives. Wise readers know that all stories follow one of two paths: The Stranger Comes to Town or The Journey. My life in motion suggested both.

2

When idea turned to plan, I asked my father for a list of the addresses I couldn't remember. Instead, as I had hoped, he offered to drive me through Maine, New Hampshire, and Massachusetts himself. My father, too, took photographs, and I wanted to draw him into my life a little, remind him of the times during car trips when, as dusk deepened, he would switch on the light inside the car, without prompting, so that I could continue to read.

3

I photographed the houses and the apartments and the surprising number of duplexes (so often did we live in the left half of a house that I wonder if I've developed a right-hemisphere problem—I imagine the right side of my brain paler and more shriveled than its better half, as atrophied and bleached as an arm that has been in a cast all summer), though I never asked to be let inside. I remembered the flow of rooms in most houses and I could imagine walking through them in a sort of Ciceronian memory system for childhood.

4

The photographs pretend no artistic merit. I centered most of the houses in my viewfinder as I stood on opposite sidewalks. Occasionally a branch or a piece of the neighboring house appears at the edge of the frame. Otherwise the book is a collection of residential mug shots. I wasn't accustomed to snapping pictures of whole buildings without people cluttering the frames, and as I focused before each shot I thought of the pictures my father had taken during his early twenties: ducks and snowdrifts and weathered cottages. Looking through my father's pictures, my mother would squint with mock earnestness at yet another image of a dilapidated barn and ask, "Where were we, behind the barn?"

5

At the first house—125 Wood Street, a gray three-family at the edge of the campus where my father had been a sophomore—I toyed with perspective. I held my camera at my hip; I crouched by the mailboxes, trying to imagine a toddler's vantage point. No pre-school impressions came flooding back; I gained nothing but stares from the neighbors. I thought of the family lore about the short time we lived on Wood Street. By 1972, the sixties still hadn't retreated from Lewiston, Maine. The perennial students who shared our building kept the house reeking pleasantly of weed, and our downstairs neighbor wandered up to our apartment now and again to shower, since her bathtub was occupied by her pet duck. Her thesis, my mother insisted, had something to do with roller skates, and she decorated her apartment with black lights and mini-marshmallows, dipped in fluorescent paint, which she stuck to branches that hung from her ceiling. At night, when the lights came on, visitors were treated to an electrifying set of unlikely constellations.

6

From Maine we moved south to New Hampshire. Rooting out the apartments in the freshly overdeveloped landscape of New Hampshire was a trickier prospect; some of the photos of these houses show unfamiliar additions, self-installed skylights. Some had new, paved-over driveways, others aluminum siding. One apartment complex in southern New Hampshire remained intact, though the surrounding woods had been leveled to receive three new strip malls. When we wandered closer to the Massachusetts border, images reversed themselves and I found myself remembering the houses' odd absences: an oval of yellowed grass showed where an above-ground pool had sat; a chimney stopped abruptly with no fireplace attached.

During each move, after the boxes had been unpacked, my father would turn their openings to the ground and use a pocketknife to cut windows and doors. The refrigerator boxes were best, skyscrapers with grass floors. In my cardboard house I would read cross-legged into the evening, ignoring my parents' invitations to take-out dinners in our new yard until my father lifted the box off me and walked away, bearing my cardboard home, leaving me blinking in the dusk.

7

Now when I leave my apartment for vacation, no matter how anticipated the trip, I experience numbing panic—will I ever see home again? I'm sympathetic to Rilke's Eurydice: What did she care about Orpheus and his willpower? Sure, she had her reasons: hell living had filled her with death and isolated her from human touch. No doubt she could have grown accustomed to the rocks and rivers of Hades. Who among us can get our mind around a move that drastic? From one side of the eternal duplex to the other. Each time I return home from vacation, rooms don't appear the same as I left them. Walls seem to meet floors at subtly altered angles. Careful inspections—heel-toe, heel-toe around each of the rooms—reveal no evidence of the perceived.

8

After my parents split, I kept most of my assorted five-year-old's treasures at the white three-family where I lived with my mother, watched over by a grim, disapproving landlady. My father's wall-to-wall-carpeted bachelor apartment always smelled faintly of hops; he and his two roommates all owned water beds and motorcycles. My personal inventory at my father's new home was limited to a Holly Hobbie nightgown, *The Little Princess*, and Milton Bradley's Sorry!, a game that requires players to apologize without sincerity after forcing their competitors to start again.

9

I found the post-divorce houses on my own. At one address, the brown-stained house I had known in early grade school wasn't there at all. Developers had knocked it down, then paved over the spot to provide parking for the neighboring convenience store and candy shop. On the winter afternoon when I visited, I snapped a photo of a stray shopping cart that had rolled away from the convenience store to the spot where the kitchen had been. The shot, of the lonely shopping cart illuminated by a hazy beam of light, has a Hallmark devotional-card quality. I have no sentimental feelings about the house, though. I even felt satisfaction when I saw the smoothly paved parking lot; it was as though I had willed the destruction of the site of many childhood disappointments (new stepfather! mid-first-grade school switch! dog runs away from home!).

The edges of the photograph give more away. At the top of the frame I can spot a sliver of the foundation of the house that backed up to ours. My friend Annette lived there, an only child whose mother cut women's hair in the pink room adjacent to their dining room and whose father cured meat, hung in strips—dark and pale, meat and fat—in their cellar.

At the left edge of the frame, the tail of an *a* is visible, part of a glowing sign advertising "Gina—Psychic," the fortune-teller who set up shop next door.

10

In a decorative gesture, I planned to hand-color the photographs as if they were pre-Kodachrome portraits of children with blossom-pink cheeks and lips. Armed with the oils and pencils, however, I only touched up a piece of every home—a chimney, a storm door, a front gate. If stacked, they'd make a flip-book composite of a home.

Red shutters and verdant bushes decorate the house after the last fold in the book. There, the three of us—mother, sister, and new brother, aged three—began living alone together for the first time. The stepfather had come and gone, leaving the three of us to find balance in our uneasy triumvirate. Neighbors and shopkeepers looked at us, curious. I could tell that the age gaps perplexed them—too few years between a mother and daughter who chatted like girlfriends and too many between a sister and brother who looked almost like mother and son. Their confusion was compounded by my mother's youth and beauty and by the way at age thirteen I seemed to have passed directly to thirty-five.

The red-shuttered house was home the longest, and it is the only house my brother remembers. When I handed the coloring pencils over to him to spruce up the image of the old house, he colored the whole thing. He and my mother still live in that duplex, formerly the parish house for the Congregational church across the street. We haven't been the only ones comfortable there. Pets and pests flourish: a dog, rabbits, guinea pigs, escaped reptiles, moths and silverfish, hollow shells of worms in macaroni boxes, squirrels in the attic.

The parish house has walls that slant toward the middle and floorboards that creak too frequently and too loudly to be creepy. During the first year, while discovering the rules and limits of our new family, we cleared the dining room table each night after dinner and began to play.

The three of us played games from my mother's childhood—tiddledywinks, pick-up-sticks, PIT. And after my brother fell asleep, my mother and I drank tea and played Password, Boggle, and Scrabble, stopping only when the board was almost filled and our wooden racks held two or three impossible consonants. A few years ago, chasing a marble that had slipped through a wrought iron heating grate, my brother lifted the panel by one of its iron curls and found, caught in the black cloth, game pieces of all kinds: dice, tiddledywinks, cribbage pegs, smooth wooden squares with black letters—pieces we had barely missed from games we had continued to play.

11

When the photo project was complete, I felt a historian's satisfaction. I had gathered the proof of my life and given it a shape. To create the album I cut a long strip of black paper and folded and flipped it as if to cut paper dolls. I printed the images small and pasted them in the accordion book. Held from the top, the book tumbles open to reveal twelve homes logically connected.

My mother saw the book as evidence of a life hastily lived. When she unknotted the ribbon around the tidy package and allowed it to unfold, I watched her face seize up.

"Ha, ha," she pushed the sounds out with effort. "All my failures," she said as she held the book away from her in an exaggerated gesture. I had tried to piece a story out of a life that I saw as largely unplanned. For my mother, this life led by reaction had eventually settled into a kind of choice. I was ashamed I thought it was mine to figure out.

12

One night, a few weeks before I moved out of the parish house duplex into my own apartment, I returned home and wheeled my bike around to the back of the house. Glancing up at the brightly lit windows, I was afforded an unusual glimpse of the daily theater of my family. From my spot in the yard I saw a woman in the kitchen chopping vegetables and talking on the phone, while a couple of rooms over, a gangly teenage boy sat in a chair by the television. Startled to be given a chance to see the house as a stranger might, I watched for a few moments and tried to imagine the lives of those inside.

Portrait of My Body

Phillip Lopate

I am a man who tilts. When I am sitting, my head slants to the right; when walking, the upper part of my body reaches forward to catch a sneak preview of the street. One way or another, I seem to be off-center—or "uncentered," to use the jargon of holism. My lousy posture, a tendency to slump or put myself into lazy, contorted misalignments, undoubtedly contributes to lower back pain. For a while I correct my bad habits, do morning exercises, sit straight, breathe deeply, but always an inner demon that insists on approaching the world askew resists perpendicularity.

I think if I had broader shoulders I would be more squarely anchored. But my shoulders are narrow, barely wider than my hips. This has always made shopping for suits an embarrassing business. (Françoise Gilot's *Life with Picasso* tells how Picasso was so touchy about his disproportionate body—in his case all shoulders, no legs—that he insisted the tailor fit him at home.)

When I was growing up in Brooklyn, my hero was Sandy Koufax, the Dodgers' Jewish pitcher. In the doldrums of Hebrew choir practice at Feigenbaum's Mansion & Catering Hall, I would fantasize striking out the side, even whiffing twenty-seven batters in a row. Lack of shoulder development put an end to this identification; I became a writer instead of a Koufax.

It occurs to me that the restless angling of my head is an attempt to distract viewers' attention from its paltry base. I want people to look at my head, partly because I live in my head most of the time. My sister, a trained masseuse, often warns me of the penalties, like neck tension, that may arise from failing to integrate body and mind. Once, about ten years ago, she and I were at the beach and she was scrutinizing my body with a sister's critical eye. "You're getting flabby," she said. "You should exercise every day. I do—look at me, not an ounce of fat." She pulled at her midriff, celebrating (as is her wont) her physical attributes with the third-person enthusiasm of a carnival barker.

"But"—she threw me a bone—"you do have a powerful head. There's an intensity. . . ." A graduate student of mine (who was slightly loony) told someone that she regularly saw an aura around my head in class. One reason I like to teach is that it focuses fifteen or so dependent gazes on me with such paranoiac intensity as cannot help but generate an aura in my behalf.

I also have a commanding stare, large sad brown eyes that can be read as either gentle or severe. Once I watched several hours of myself on videotape. I discovered to my horror that my face moved at different rates: sometimes my mouth would be laughing, eyebrows circumflexed in mirth, while my eyes coolly gauged the interviewer to see what effect I was making. I am something of an actor. And, as with many performers, the mood I sense most in myself is that of energy-conserving watchfulness; but this expression is often mistaken (perhaps because of the way brown eyes are read in our culture) for sympathy. I see myself as determined to the point of stubbornness, selfish, even a bit cruel—in any case, I am all too aware of the limits of my compassion, so that it puzzles me when people report a first impression of me as gentle, kind, solicitous. In my youth I felt obliged to come across as dynamic, arrogant, intimidating, the life of the party; now, surer of myself, I hold back some energy, thereby winning time to gather information and make better judgments. This results sometimes in a misimpression of my being mildly depressed. Of course, the simple truth is that I have less energy than I once did, and that accumulated experiences have made me, almost against my will, kinder and sadder.

Sometimes I can feel my mouth arching downward in an ironic smile, which, at its best, reassures others that we need not take everything so seriously—because we are all in the same comedy together—and, at its worst, expresses a superior skepticism. This smile, which can be charming when not supercilious, has elements of the bashful that mesh with the worldly—the shyness, let us say, of a cultivated man who is often embarrassed for others by their willful shallowness or self-deception. Many times, however, my ironic smile is nothing more than a neutral stall among people who do not seem to appreciate my "contribution." I hate that pain-in-the-ass half-smile of mine; I want to jump in, participate, be loud, thoughtless, vulgar.

Often I give off a sort of psychic stench to myself, I do not like myself at all, but out of stubborn pride I act like a man who does. I appear for all the world poised, contented, sanguine when inside I may be feeling self-revulsion bordering on the suicidal. What a wonder to be so misread! Of course, if in the beginning I had thought I was coming across accurately, I never would have bothered to become a writer. And the truth is I am not misread, because another part of me is never less than fully contented with myself.

I am vain about these parts of my body: my eyes, my fingers, my legs. It is true that my legs are long and not unshapely, but my vanity about them has less to do with their comeliness than with their contribution to my height. Montaigne, a man who was himself on the short side, wrote that "the beauty of stature is the only beauty of men." But even if Montaigne had never said it, I would continue to attribute a good deal of my self-worth and benevolent liberalism to being tall. When I go out into the street, I feel well-disposed toward the (mostly shorter) swarms of humanity; crowds not only do not dismay, they enliven me; and I am tempted to think that my passion for urbanism is linked to my height. By no means am I suggesting that only tall people love cities; merely that, in my case, part of the pleasure I derive from walking in crowded streets issues from a confidence that I can see above the heads of others, and cut a fairly impressive, elevated figure as I saunter along the sidewalk.

Some of my best friends have been—short. Brilliant men, brimming with poetic and worldly ideas, they deserved all of my and the world's respect. Yet at times I have had to master an impulse to rumple their heads; and I suspect they have developed manners of a more formal, *noli me tangere* nature, largely in response to this petting impulse of taller others.

The accident of my tallness has inclined me to both a seemingly egalitarian informality and a desire to lead. Had I not been a writer, I would surely have become a politician; I was even headed in that direction in my teens. Ever since I shot up to a little over six feet, I have had at my command what feels like a natural, Gregory Peck authority when addressing an audience. Far from experiencing stage fright, I have actually sought out situations in which I could make speeches, give readings, sit on panel discussions, and generally tower over everyone else onstage. To be tall is to look down on the world and meet its eyes on your terms. But this topic, the noblesse oblige of tall men, is a dangerously provoking one, and so let us say no more about it.

The mental image of one's body changes slower than one's body. Mine was for a long while arrested in my early twenties, when I was tall and thin (165 pounds) and gobbled down whatever I felt like. I ate food that was cheap and filling, cheeseburgers, pizza, without any thought to putting on weight. But a young person's metabolism is more dietetically forgiving. To compound the problem, the older you get, the more cultivated your palate grows—and the more life's setbacks make you inclined to fill the hollowness of disappointment with the pleasures of the table.

Between the age of thirty and forty I put on ten pounds, mostly around the midsection. Since then my gut has suffered another expansion, and I tip the scales at over 180. That I took a while to notice the change may be shown by my continuing to purchase clothes at my primordial adult size (33 waist, 15 ½ collar), until a girlfriend started pointing out that all my clothes were too tight. I rationalized this circumstance as the result of changing fashions (thinking myself still subconsciously loyal to the sixties' penchant for skintight fits) and laundry shrinkage rather than anything to do with my own body. She began buying me larger replacements for birthdays or holidays, and I found I enjoyed this "baggier" style, which allowed me to button my trousers comfortably, or to wear a tie and, for the first time in years, close my top shirt button. But it took even longer before I was able to enter a clothing store myself and give the salesman realistically enlarged size numbers.

Clothes can disguise the defects of one's body, up to a point. I get dressed with great optimism, adding one color to another, mixing my favorite Japanese and Italian designers, matching the patterns and textures, selecting ties, then proceed to the bathroom mirror to judge the result. There is an ideal in my mind of the effect I am essaying by wearing a particular choice of garments, based, no doubt, on male models in fashion ads—and I fall so far short of this insouciant gigolo handsomeness that I cannot help but be a little disappointed when I turn up so depressingly myself, narrow-shouldered, Talmudic, that grim, set mouth, that long, narrow face, those appraising eyes, the Semitic hooked nose, all of which express both the strain of intellectual overachieving and the tabula rasa of immaturity . . . for it is still, underneath, a boy in the mirror. A boy with a rapidly receding hairline.

How is it that I've remained a boy all this time, into my late forties? I remember, at seventeen, drawing a self-portrait of myself as I looked in the mirror. I was so appalled at the weak chin and pleading eyes that I ended up focusing on the neckline of the cotton T-shirt. Ever since then I have tried to toughen myself up, but I still encounter in the glass that haunted uncertainty—shielded by a bluffing shell of cynicism, perhaps, but untouched by wisdom. So I approach the mirror warily, without lighting up as much as I would for the least of my acquaintances; I go one-on-one with that frowning schmuck.

And yet, it would be insulting to those who labor under the burden of true ugliness to palm myself off as an unattractive man. I'm at times almost handsome, if you squinted your eyes and rounded me off to the nearest *beau idéal.* I lack even a shred of cowboy virility, true, but I believe I fall into a category of adorable nerd or absentminded professor that awakens the amorous curiosity of some women. "Cute" is a word often applied to me by those I've been fortunate enough to attract. Then again, I attract only women of a certain lopsided prettiness: the head-turning, professional beauties never fall for me. They seem to look right through me, in fact. Their utter lack of interest in my appeal has always fascinated me. Can it be so simple an explanation as that beauty calls to beauty, as wealth to wealth?

I think of poor (though not in his writing gifts) Cesare Pavese, who kept chasing after starlets, models, and ballerinas—exquisite lovelies who couldn't appreciate his morose coffeehouse charm. Before he killed himself, he wrote a poem addressed to one of them, "Death Will Come Bearing Your Eyes"—thereby unfairly promoting her from rejecting lover to unwitting executioner. Perhaps he believed that only beautiful women (not literary critics, who kept awarding him prestigious prizes) saw him clearly, with twenty-twenty vision, and had the right to judge him. Had I been more headstrong, if masochistic, I might have followed his path and chased some beauty until she was forced to tell me, like an oracle, what it was about me, physically, that so failed to excite her. Then I might know something crucial about my body, before I passed into my next reincarnation.

Jung says somewhere that we pay dearly over many years to learn about ourselves what a stranger can see at a glance. This is the way I feel about my back. Fitting rooms aside, we none of us know what we look like from the back. It is the area of ourselves whose presentation we can least control, and which therefore may be the most honest part of us.

I divide backs into two kinds: my own and everyone else's. The others' backs are often mysterious, exquisite, and uncannily sympathetic. I have always loved backs. To walk behind a pretty woman in a backless dress and savor how a good pair of shoulder blades, heightened by shadow, has the same power to pierce the heart as chiseled cheekbones! . . . I wonder what it says about me that I worship a part of the body that signals a turning away. Does it mean I'm a glutton for being abandoned, or a timid voyeur who prefers a surreptitious gaze that will not be met and challenged? I only know I have often felt the deepest love at just that moment when the beloved turns her back to me to get some sleep.

I have no autoerotic feelings about my own back. I cannot even picture it; visually it is a stranger to me. I know it only as an annoyance, which came into my consciousness twenty years ago, when I started getting lower back pain. Yes, we all know that homo sapiens is constructed incorrectly; our erect posture puts too much pressure on the base of the spine; more workdays are lost because of lower back pain than any other cause. Being a writer, I sit all day, compounding the problem. My back is the enemy of my writing life: if I don't do exercises daily, I immediately ache; and if I do, I am still not spared. I could say more, but there is nothing duller than lower back pain. So common, mundane an ailment brings no credit to the sufferer. One has to dramatize it somehow, as in the phrase "I threw my back out."

Here is a gossip column about my body: My eyebrows grow quite bushy across my forehead, and whenever I get my hair cut, the barber asks me diplomatically if I want them trimmed or not. (I generally say no, associating bushy eyebrows with Balzackian virility, *élan vital;* but sometimes I acquiesce, to soothe his fastidiousness.) . . . My belly button is a modest, embedded slit, not a jaunty swirl like my father's. Still, I like to sniff the odor that comes from jabbing my finger in it: a very at ripe, underground smell, impossible to describe, but let us say a combination of old gym socks and stuffed derma (the Yiddish word for this oniony dish of ground intestines is, fittingly, *kish-kas*). . . . I have a scar on my tongue from childhood, which I can only surmise I received by landing it on a sharp object, somehow. Or perhaps I bit it hard. I have the habit of sticking my tongue out like a dog when exerting myself physically, as though to urge my muscles on; and maybe I accidentally chomped into it at such a moment. . . . I gnash my teeth, sleeping or waking. Awake, the sensation makes me feel alert and in contact with the world when I start to drift off in a daydream. Another way of grounding myself is to pinch my cheek—drawing a pocket of flesh downward and squeezing it—as I once saw JFK do in a filmed motorcade. I do this cheek-pinching especially when I am trying to keep mentally focused during teaching or other public situations. I also scratch the nape of my neck under public stress, so much so that I raise welts or sores which then eventually grow scabs; and I take great delight in secretly picking the scabs off. . . . My nose itches whenever I think about it, and I scratch it often, especially lying in bed trying to fall asleep (maybe because I am conscious of my breathing then). I also pick my nose with formidable thoroughness when no one, I hope, is looking. . . . There is a white scar about the size of a quarter on the juicy part of my knee; I got it as a boy running into a car fender, and I can still remember staring with detached calm at the blood that gushed from it like a pretty, half-eaten peach. Otherwise, the sight of my own blood makes me awfully nervous. I used to faint dead away when a blood sample was taken, and now I can control the impulse to do so only by biting the insides of my cheeks while steadfastly looking away from the needle's action. . . . I like to clean out my ear wax as often as possible (the smell is curiously sulfurous; I associate it with the bodies of dead insects). I refuse to listen to warnings that it is dangerous to stick cleaning objects into your ears. I love Q-Tips immoderately; I buy them in huge quantities and store them the way a former refugee will stock canned foodstuffs. . . . My toes are long and apelike; I have very little fellow feeling for them; they are so far away, they may as well belong to someone else. . . . My flattish buttocks are not offensively large, but neither do they have the "dream" configuration one sees in jeans ads. Perhaps for this reason, it disturbed me puritanically when asses started to be treated by Madison Avenue, around the seventies, as crucial sexual equipment, and I began to receive compositions from teenage girl students declaring that they liked some boy because he had "a cute butt." It confused me; I had thought the action was elsewhere.

About my penis there is nothing, I think, unusual. It has a brown stem, and a pink mushroom head where the foreskin is pulled back. Like most heterosexual males, I have little comparative knowledge to go by, so that I always feel like an outsider when I am around women or gay men who talk zestfully about differences in penises. I am afraid that they might judge me harshly, ridicule me like the boys who stripped me of my bathing suit in summer camp when I was ten. But perhaps they would simply declare it an ordinary penis, which changes size with the stimulus or weather or time of day. Actually, my penis does have a peculiarity: it has two peeing holes. They are very close to each other, so that usually only one stream of urine issues, but sometimes a hair gets caught across them, or some such contretemps, and they squirt out in two directions at once.

This part of me, which is so synecdochically identified with the male body (as the term "male member" indicates), has given me both too little, and too much, information about what it means to be a man. It has a personality like a cat's. I have prayed to it to behave better, to be less frisky, or more; I have followed its nose in matters of love, ignoring good sense, and paid the price; but I have also come to appreciate that it has its own specialized form of intelligence which must be listened to, or another price will be extracted.

Even to say the word "impotence" aloud makes me nervous. I used to tremble when I saw it in print, and its close relation, "importance," if hastily scanned, had the same effect, as if they were publishing a secret about me. But why should it be *my* secret, when my penis has regularly given me erections lo these many years—except for about a dozen times, mostly when I was younger? Because, even if it has not been that big a problem for me, it has dominated my thinking as an adult male. I've no sooner to go to bed with a woman than I'm in suspense. The power of the flaccid penis's statement, "I don't want you," is so stark, so cruelly direct, that it continues to exert a fascination out of all proportion to its actual incidence. Those few times when I was unable to function were like a wall forcing me to take another path—just as, after I tried to kill myself at seventeen, I was obliged to give up pessimism for a time. Each had instructed me by its too painful manner that I could not handle the world as I had previously construed it, that my confusion and rage were being found out. I would have to get more wily or else grow up.

Yet for the very reason that I was compelled to leave them behind, these two options of my youth, impotence and suicide, continue to command an underground loyalty, as though they were more "honest" than the devious strategies of potency and survival which I adopted. Put it this way: sometimes we encounter a person who has had a nervous breakdown years before and who seems cemented over sloppily, his vulnerability ruthlessly guarded against as dangerous; we sense he left a crucial part of himself back in the chaos of breakdown, and has since grown rigidly jovial. So suicide and impotence became for me "the roads not taken," the paths I had repressed.

Whenever I hear an anecdote about impotence—a woman who successfully coaxed an ex-priest who had been celibate and unable to make love, first by lying next to him for six months without any touching, then by cuddling for six more months, then by easing him slowly into a sexual embrace—I think they are talking about me. I identify completely: this, in spite of the fact, which I promise not to repeat again, that I have generally been able to do it whenever called upon. Believe it or not, I am not boasting when I say that: a part of me is contemptuous of this virility, as though it were merely a mechanical trick that violated my true nature, that of an impotent man absolutely frightened of women, absolutely secluded, cut off.

I now see the way I have idealized impotence: I've connected it with pushing the world away, as a kind of integrity, as in Molière's *The Misanthrope*—connected it with that part of me which, gregarious socializer that I am, continues to insist that I am a recluse, too good for this life. Of course, it is not true that I am terrified of women. I exaggerate my terror of them for dramatic effect, or for the purposes of a good scare.

My final word about impotence: Once, in a period when I was going out with many women, as though purposely trying to ignore my hypersensitive side and force it to grow callous by thrusting myself into foreign situations (not only sexual) and seeing if I was able to "rise to the occasion," I dated a woman who was attractive, tall and blond, named Susan. She had something to do with the pop music business, was a follower of the visionary religious futurist Teilhard de Chardin, and considered herself a religious pacifist. In fact, she told me her telephone number in the form of the anagram, N-O-T-O-W-A-R. I thought she was joking and laughed aloud, but she gave me a solemn look. In passing, I should say that all the women with whom I was impotent or close to it had solemn natures. The sex act has always seemed to me in many ways ridiculous, and I am most comfortable when a woman who enters the sheets with me shares that sense of the comic pomposity behind such a grandiloquently rhetorical use of the flesh. It is as though the prose of the body were being drastically squeezed into metrical verse. I would not have known how to stop guffawing had I been D.H. Lawrence's lover, and I am sure he would have been pretty annoyed at me. But a smile saying "All this will pass" has an erotic effect on me like nothing else.

They claim that men who have long, long fingers also have lengthy penises. I can tell you with a surety that my fingers are long and sensitive, the most perfect, elegant, handsome part of my anatomy. They are not entirely perfect—the last knuckle of my right middle finger is twisted permanently, broken in a softball game when I was trying to block the plate—but even this slight disfigurement, harbinger of mortality, adds to the pleasure I take in my hands' rugged beauty. My penis does not excite in me nearly the same contemplative delight when I look at it as do my fingers. Pianists' hands, I have been told often; and though I do not play the piano, I derive an aesthetic satisfaction from them that is as pure and Apollonian as any I am capable of. I can stare at my fingers for hours. No wonder I have them so often in my mouth, biting my fingernails to bring them closer. When I write, I almost feel that they, and not my intellect, are the clever progenitors of the text. Whatever narcissism, fetishism, and proud sense of masculinity I possess about my body must begin and end with my fingers.

Brothers

Bret Lott

This much is fact: There is a home movie of the two of us sitting on the edge of the swimming pool at our grandma and grandpa's old apartment building in Culver City. The movie, taken sometime in early 1960, is in color, though the color has faded, leaving my brother Brad and me milk white and harmless children, me a year and a half old, Brad almost four, our brown hair faded to only the thought of brown hair. Our mother, impossibly young, sits next to me on the right of the screen. Her hair, for all the fading of the film, is coal black, shoulder length, and parted in the middle, curled up on the sides. She has on a bathing suit covered in purple and blue flowers, the color in them nearly gone. Next to me on the left of the screen is Brad, in his white swimming trunks. I am in the center, my fat arms up, bent at the elbows, fingers curled into fists, my legs kicking away at the water, splashing and splashing. I am smiling, the baby of the family, the center of the world at that very instant, though my little brother, Tim, is only some six or seven months off, and my little sister, Leslie, the last child, just three years distant. The pool water before us is only a thin sky blue, the bushes behind us a dull and lifeless light green. There is no sound.

My mother speaks to me, points at the water, then looks up. She lifts a hand to block the sun, says something to the camera. Her skin is the same white as ours, but her lips are red, a sharp cut of lipstick moving as she speaks. I am still kicking. Brad is looking to his right, off the screen, his feet in the water, too, but moving slowly. His hands are on the edge of the pool, and he leans forward a little, looks down into the water. My mother still speaks to the camera, and I give an extra-hard kick, splash up shards of white water.

Brad flinches at the water, squints his eyes, while my mother laughs, puts a hand to her face. She looks back to the camera, keeps talking, a hand low to the water to keep more from hitting her. I still kick hard, still send up bits of water, and I am laughing a baby's laugh, mouth open and eyes nearly closed, arms still up, fingers still curled into fists.

More water splashes at Brad, who leans over to me, says something. Nothing about me changes: I only kick, laugh. He says something again, his face leans a little closer to mine. Still I kick.

This is when he lifts his left hand from the edge of the pool, places it on my right thigh, and pinches hard. It's not a simple pinch, not two fingers on a fraction of skin, but his whole hand, all his fingers grabbing the flesh just above my knee and squeezing down hard. He grimaces, his eyes on his hand, on my leg.

My expression changes, of course: In an instant I go from a laughing baby to a shocked one, my mouth a perfect O, my body shivering so that my legs kick even harder, even quicker, but just this one last time. They stop, and I cry, my mouth open even more, my eyes all the way closed. My hands are still in fists.

Then Brad's hand is away, and my mother turns from speaking to the camera to me. She leans in close, asking, I am certain, what's wrong. The movie cuts then to my grandma, white skin and silver hair, seated on a patio chair by the pool, above her a green-and-white-striped umbrella. She has a cigarette in one hand, waves off the camera with the other. Though she died eight years ago, and though she, too, loses color with each viewing, she is still alive up there, still waves, annoyed, at my grandpa and his camera, the moment my brother pinched hell out of me already gone.

This much is fact, too: Thumbtacked to the wall of my office is a photograph of Brad and me taken by my wife in November 1980, the date printed on the border. In it we stand together, me a good six inches taller than him, my arm around his shoulder. The photograph is black and white, as though the home movie and its sinking colors were a prophecy pointing to this day twenty years later: We are at the tidepools at Portuguese Bend, out on the Palos Verdes Peninsula; in the background are the stone-gray bluffs, to the left of us the beginning of the black rocks of the pools, above us the perfect white of an overcast sky.

Brad has on a white Panama hat, a collarless shirt beneath a gray hooded sweatshirt. His face is smooth shaven, and he is grinning, lips together, eyes squinted nearly shut beneath the brim of the hat. It is a goofy smile, but a real one.

I have on a cardigan with an alpine design around the shoulders, the rest of it white, the shawl collar on it black here, though I know it to have been navy blue. I have on a buttondown Oxford shirt, sideburns almost to my earlobes. I have a mustache, a pair of glasses too large for my face; and I am smiling, my mouth open to reveal my big teeth. It isn't my goofy smile, but it's a real one too.

These are the facts of my brother: the four-year-old pinching me, the twenty-four-year-old leaning into me, grinning.

But between the fact of these two images lie twenty years of the play of memory, the dark and bright pictures my mind has retained, embroidered upon, made into things they are and things they are not. There are twenty years of things that happened between my brother and me, from the fistfight we had in high school over who got the honey bun for breakfast, to his phone call to me from a tattoo parlor in Hong Kong where he'd just gotten a Chinese junk stitched beneath the skin of his right shoulder blade; from his showing me one summer day how to do a death drop from the jungle gym at Elizabeth Dickerson Elementary, to him watching while his best friend and our next-door neighbor, Lynn Tinton, beat me up on the driveway of our home in a fight over whether I'd fouled Lynn or not at basketball. I remember—no true picture, necessarily, but what I have made the truth by holding tight to it, playing it back in my head at will and in the direction I wish it to go—I remember lying on my back, Lynn's knees pinning my shoulders to the driveway while he hit my chest, and looking up at Brad, the basketball there at his hip, him watching.

I have two children now. Both boys, born two and a half years apart. I showed the older one, Zeb—almost eight—the photograph, asked him who those two people were. He held it in his hands a long while.

We were in the kitchen. The bus comes at seven-twenty each morning, and I have to have lunches made and breakfasts set out—all before that bus comes and before Melanie takes off for work, Jacob in tow, to be dropped off at the Montessori school on her way in to her office.

I waited, and waited, finally turned from him to get going on his lunch.

"It's you," he said. "You have a lot of hair," he said.

"Who's the other guy?" I said. I looked back at him, saw the concentration on his face, the way he brought the photograph close, my son's eyes taking in his uncle as best he could.

He said, "I don't know."

"That's your uncle Brad," I said. "Your mom took that picture ten years ago, long before you were ever born."

He still looked at the picture. He said, "He has a beard now."

I turned from him, finished with the peanut butter, and spread jelly on the other piece of bread. This is the only kind of sandwich he will eat at school. He said from behind me, "Only three years before I was born. That's not a long time." I stopped, turned again to him. He touched the picture with a finger. He said, "Three years isn't a long time, Dad."

But I was thinking of my question: *Who's the other guy?* and of the truth of his answer: *I don't know.*

Zeb and Jake fight. Melanie and I were upstairs wrapping Christmas presents in my office, a room kept locked the entire month of December for the gifts piled up in there. We heard Jake wailing, dropped the bucket of Legos and the red-and-green HO! HO! HO! paper, ran for the hall and down the stairs.

There in the kitchen stood my two sons, Jacob's eyes wet, him whimpering now, a hand to his bottom lip. I made it first, yelled, "What happened?"

"I didn't do it," Zeb said, and backed away from me, there with my hand to Jacob's jaw.

Melanie stroked Jacob's hair, whispered, "What's wrong?"

Jacob opened his mouth then, showed us the thick wash of blood between his bottom lip and his tongue, a single tooth, horribly white, swimming up from it. "We were playing Karate Kid," Zeb said, and now he was crying. "I didn't do it," he said, and backed away even farther.

One late afternoon a month or so ago, Melanie backed the van into the driveway to make it easier to unload all the plastic bags of groceries. When we'd finished we let the boys play outside, glad for them to be out of the kitchen while we sorted through the bags heaped on the counter, put everything away. Melanie's last words to the two of them, her leaning out the front door into the near-dark: "Don't play in the van!"

Not ten minutes later Jacob came into the house, slammed shut the front door like he always does. He walked into the kitchen, his hands behind him. He said, "Zeb's locked in the van." His face takes on the cast of the guilty when he knows he's done something wrong: His mouth gets pursed, his eyebrows go up, his eyes look right into mine. He doesn't know enough yet to look away. "He told me to come get you." He turned, headed for the door, and I followed him out onto the porch, where, before I could even see the van in the dark, I heard Zeb screaming.

I went to the van, tried one of the doors. It was locked, and Zeb was still screaming.

"Get the keys!" he was saying. "Get the keys!" I pressed my face to the glass of the back window, saw Zeb inside jumping up and down. "My hand's caught," he cried.

I ran into the house, got the keys from the hook beneath the cupboard, only enough time for me to say to Melanie, "Zeb's hand's closed in the back door," and turn, run back out. I made it to the van, unlocked the big back door, and pushed it up as quick as I could, Melanie already beside me.

Zeb stood holding the hand that'd been closed in the door. Melanie and I both took his hand, gently examined the skin, wiggled the fingers, and in the dull glow of the dome light we saw that nothing'd been broken, no skin torn. The black foam lining the door had cushioned his fingers, so that they'd only been smashed a little, but a little enough to scare him, and to make blue bruises there the next day. Beneath the dome light there was the sound of his weeping, then the choked words, "Jacob pulled the door down on me."

From the darkness just past the line of light from inside the van came my second son's voice: "I didn't do it."

I have no memory of the pinch Brad gave me on the edge of that apartment-complex pool, no memory of my mother's black hair—now it's a sort of brown—nor even any memory of the pool itself. There is only that bit of film.

But I can remember putting my arm around his shoulder in 1980, leaning into him, the awkward and alien comfort of that touch. In the photograph we are both smiling, me a newlywed with a full head of hair, him only a month or so back from working a drilling platform in the Gulf of Mexico. He'd missed my wedding six months before, stranded on the rig, he'd told us, because of a storm.

What I believe is this: That pinch was entry into our childhood; my arm around him, our smiling, is the proof of us two surfacing, alive but not unscathed.

And here are my own two boys, already embarked.

Goodbye to All This

Rebecca McClanahan

"It's a lot like dying," Donald has begun telling our friends. "Except you get to see where all your stuff goes." He's referring to the state of our rapidly emptying home. Each week another room is decluttered, swept free of its past, its stories. I box up books, dishes, paintings, photos that house our history. Then, with a black marker, I make my selections, dividing the goats from the lambs: *NYC Urgent. Goodwill. Garage Sale. Store. No Rush. Attic, keep dry. Breakable.* The emptying is partly for our benefit, an attempt to sweep the path clean for the journey ahead. We'll be leaving in a few months, perhaps sooner if the sale goes quickly.

The emptying is also for prospective buyers, the strangers who will soon walk through these rooms. "It's time to start wearing buyers' glasses," our agent has advised. "To see your house through their eyes. Your house should look occupied by someone—just not a *particular* someone. Do you understand?"

Yes, I understand perfectly. We want to give the impression that somebody still lives here—no desperation sale, we're in no rush, we won't take just any offer. On the other hand, if we continue to fully inhabit this place, we will leave no room for the buyer's dream. A buyer must be able to imagine himself as the inhabitant—sitting at the dining room table, filling the bird feeder, stoking the fire. Our home is a stage to be set, everything polished and gleaming, all the props arranged for the upcoming show, or *showing*, as the realtor calls it. "Your house shows well," he says as he walks through the rooms carrying a clipboard. "Except for. And maybe. And you might consider. Nothing drastic, you understand. Just."

"Certainly," we say. "We'll get right on it." Since the money from the sale of the house must support us for the next year or two, we can't afford sentimentality. First we remove all that might offend: incense burners, the photograph of two nude men embracing, the sculpture of bare-breasted crones dancing in a circle, the Buddhist quotes over my writing desk. Then, item by item, we hide traces of ourselves, anything that might keep a prospective buyer from inhabiting his own dream: the cat's bowl, my grandmother's moth-nibbled afghan, my husband's pipe and brandy snifter.

What is left is tasteful, the way chicken cutlets are tasteful. Or fish that you buy because it tastes like chicken. A house prepared for the eyes of others allows only what is tasteful. A home, on the other hand, is like a family member or a trusted friend, the kind you don't dress up for. A home has seen you at your worst: morning breath, worn corduroy robe, feverish head hanging over the toilet bowl. As you've seen it: cluttered, dust-bunnied, bare-mattressed, smudged. Why then this sadness, this longing to stay? A week before the showing, I cry, I scream, I rant, I kick boxes, I sink down onto the floor of the tasteful, gleaming room and cry.

Donald knows better than to try to console me. "I wish I could do that," he says, "let it all out, say goodbye. Months from now it will ambush me, I'm sure of it. I'll be walking in midtown, maybe getting into a taxi or standing in line"—"on line," I correct him, translating the phrase to its New York equivalent. "And it will hit me," he says. "What have we done, what were we thinking. And it will be too late to go back."

To leave a place you love, you must be willing to go the distance. Once our home is listed, the contract signed, there will be no going back. Our leaving, for the past few months a mere hum on rumor's vine, will be public knowledge. Strangers will call, real estate rubberneckers will slow to stare, voyeurs will walk through our garden and peek into our windows which, the realtor is advising, should glisten, every room ablaze with light.

"You know you're ready," the agent is telling us, "when you can call it a *house*, not a *home*. Are you sure you're ready?" He doesn't want us backing out at the last moment, after he's taken the photos, printed the brochures, registered the property with Multiple Listing Service, planted the "For Sale" sign in my azalea garden. *The* garden, I mean. The garden that borders the street. "You're lucky," the realtor says. "It's a well-traveled street. Lots of eye traffic."

This is not our first house, but it is the first one we've called home. In the other house, where my husband and I lived for 13 years, our feeling of tenancy went beyond the fact that we didn't own the property. More to the point, we didn't inhabit it. *Inhabit*, rooted in the Germanic *ghabh*, implies both giving and receiving; it is attached to the Old English *forgiefan*, meaning to give up, leave off, forgive. To inhabit a place, you must move in fully—body and spirit, heart and hand. You must give yourself to it.

When I first met Donald, he was living alone in that first house, paying rent to his parents, who owned the property. He had shared the house with his wife and young son, and though he and his wife had been separated nearly a year, some of her clothes still hung in the closet. That was fine with me. I was barely a year out of a disastrous first marriage, one in which I had given everything and received, or so it seemed at the time, almost nothing. To inhabit another marriage was the last thing I wanted. I was content where I was, subletting an apartment one hundred miles away in the university town where I was pursuing graduate studies. One hundred miles seemed just the right amount of distance.

We dated for over a year, spent weekends together at his house, and cautiously began to consolidate our possessions. (A strange word, *possessions*. Shades of demonic powers, exorcisms. Do we own our possessions, or do they possess us?) Then, out of the blue of a bright November Friday, we drove separate cars to a justice of the peace halfway between our towns, quickly drew up an agreement promising as little as possible, and signed a marriage contract. We did not have a honeymoon, we had a weekend. Monday morning, very early, I left to drive back to the city where I would live from Monday through Friday for the next few years. When my graduate studies were completed, I moved into Donald's house, and for the next several years we substituted a safe psychic distance—separate checkbooks, separate lives—for the physical distance that had once sustained us.

A stranger looking on might not have been surprised that such a partnership would eventually coax its partners, fearful of *habitation* yet needful of it, farther and farther apart. Now, nearly ten years later, we mark the time-line of our marriage at the point of its breaking. "Before the separation," we say. Or, "After we got back together." Our home, the one we are about to leave, marks the place where our separate pasts collided and our life together began. Also the azalea garden, the diamond ring (my first), the cat, and the neighborhood restaurant, Carpe Diem, which we've come to think of as ours.

Home is a space you inhabit fully, a place where body and spirit dwell. For some people, *home* denotes—even requires—ownership. My father is one of those people. A Marine officer, during the course of his career he moved with his wife and children 19 times, but the only places he called home were the five or six houses he owned. As a child of tenant farmers, he'd been aware that the cramped farmhouses he shared with his parents and siblings did not belong to them, nor did the fields they worked from dawn to dusk.

Which may be why he reacts so personally to the news that Donald and I are selling our home in Charlotte, North Carolina, and moving to, of all places, New York City. Home, to my father, is a place where you put down roots. You do not pull up those roots unless you are forced to. Or unless a larger, more beautiful place awaits you. An apartment in Manhattan (any apartment, whatever we can find, even if it belongs to someone else, we've decided) is not what my father would consider home.

Now that the listing contract is signed and the stakes of the "For Sale" sign securely planted, the phone is ringing off the hook, the mail box is full, and people keep dropping by—friends, family, neighbors, colleagues, each with his own take on the news of our upcoming move. Each person seems to react to the news based on his or her own relationship to leaving, or to change in general, or to heartbreaks that are currently mending, or those that will never mend. A former writing student, a man just shy of middle-age, sends a letter with a red stop sign centered on the page and DON'T GO emblazoned in huge block letters. (I learn, a few days later, that he and his wife have separated and that he is now living alone.) My best friend, who has known her share of endings, leaves tears on my answering machine. "Life is change," says my sister Lana, cheerfully offering a dream catcher to hang in my window. "Follow your heart."

My mother's reaction to the news is calm, accepting, exactly the reaction I'd expected. "Moving isn't easy," she says, "but you'll make a home wherever you go." To my mother, home is the people in it and the life lived within its walls: *That was the kitchen I painted Chinese red after Uncle Dale died.* Or, *That was where all the kids had the mumps at the same time. That was the year I made matching Easter dresses for the girls. That was the house where Tommy jumped off the garage roof.* My parents' first home was in Jacksonville, Florida, where she'd joined my father at the base where he was training as a fighter pilot. They lived there two months, in a single room in a boarding house. They weren't supposed to cook in the room, but my mother, intent on serving warm meals to her new husband, used a hot plate, warming canned soup and frying eggs. Since they had no table, they knelt on the floor beside the hot plate to eat their meals. "The food always tasted so good," she recalls. "Those were two wonderful months."

Because, to my mother, home is where the stories are; the 19 houses are remembered not as addresses but as serial installments in our family's domestic drama. She moves into each new story fully, heart and hand, and when the time is up, she leaves as fully as she once entered. Never regretful—"the past is the past," she says—and never fearful of the next move.

Every move I've ever made has begun the same way. I wake in the night, my flesh goose-bumped with sweat, my chest thumping as if a small bird were trapped there. This isn't the way I want to be, aligned with the nay-sayers, the friends and family members who keep calling with advice and warnings. They can't believe, after twenty-five years in this town, that we're going to pack it all in. "Sell your house?" they say. "Leave your business?" they ask Donald. "But what if?" I'd prefer to side with the cheerleaders, the small band of coaches standing on the sidelines, urging us on. "What courage," they say. "At this time in your lives, to make such a change. Most people move to New York when they're young. How brave of you."

The thumping in my chest continues, a rhythmic *What if, What if, What if.* What if we can't find an apartment we can afford? What if we find the apartment, put money down on it, but can't sell the house? What if we sell the house but can't find an apartment? What if we can't find a home for the cat? What if we can't find work? What if we hate New York?

Donald's night sweats began years ago, but they had nothing to do with moving. And though he didn't voice his feelings of anxiety and sadness, I sensed them. Finally, when I insisted, he spoke them aloud. He couldn't keep on doing what he was doing. He couldn't see himself, ten or fifteen or twenty years down the line, still driving hundreds of miles a week, hauling lighting and sound equipment, setting up stages, pulling the same puppets out of the same trunks, lifting his arms to perform for the hundredth, or thousandth time, the kinds of shows local audiences would pay to see, the shows he would have to perform to keep his company afloat and pay the mortgage on our home. He'd long ago disengaged himself from his work. During shows, he felt as though he were lifting above the stage, above himself, watching his hands perform movements that no longer held any surprise. In the meantime, all the shows he wanted to build—experimental shadow plays, quirky table top shows, toy theatre, object theatre—stayed locked in his head. And he wasn't sure how long they'd hang around.

"Plus," he said. He hesitated, them looked up at me with that half dreamy/half guilty expression in his eyes, the one he always gets when he's visiting the home he carries in his head, his childhood dreamscape. Ever since he was a boy visiting his grandparents in Washington Heights, he has been trying to go back.

"I love our home, you know that," he said, his eyes scanning the lofted ceiling, the crown molding, the oak mantle and the gold-leaf mirror.

"I know," I said.

"There's just one thing wrong with it."

"I know," I said. "It's not in New York."

Do all people carry inside them, like a dream wallet snapshot, the image of a place that feels more like home than any place they've ever lived? Why else do we draw dream houses, design blueprints of a space that doesn't yet exist, walk the rooms of model homes, our heads brimming with plans. Let's see, this wall here will be coral, and we'll put a round table in the corner, with a satin tablecloth and stained glass lamp. We can almost see ourselves in the small rocker by the window, a leather-bound book in our hands. No matter that we've never owned a leather-bound book, that our daylight self prefers the casual intimacy of a dog-eared paperback. In our dream house, things will be different. We will be different. Those unused parts of ourselves, the places we've as yet barely touched, will come forth—our pasts, our memories, our future selves. All the lives begun years ago but never nurtured, will find their way into this home.

Even if the home is a studio apartment, a room so small that your bed pulls out from the wall, and your dining table folds down each night to make room for that bed, then opens in the morning to become the desk where you write your as yet unwritten stories, your poems. In a dream room, everything fits. In mine, there is room for my farmhouse past, for Grandma Sylvie's and Grandma Goldie's wicker baskets filled with "makings," the strips and squares of cloth they will weave into rugs and stitch into quilts. Room, too, for Aunt Bessie's magazines and books and seed catalogs and Grandpa Arthur's hammer and milk bucket and rubber hip boots and Grandpa Clarence's big black Chevrolet and rusting tractor and wire-rimmed glasses and the ashtray that was always within reach, the metal tray weighted with sand and covered in plaid corduroy.

And because I now fully inhabit a marriage, the dream home allows for my husband's past as well. It is a crowded room, half midwestern farmhouse/half Washington Heights one-bedroom flat, Sylvie and Goldie and Clarence and Arthur and Bessie sharing a table with Donald's Uncle Alex, on leave from his travels, and with Boris, Donald's Marxist grandfather, and Boris's Russian-speaking wife Ria.

Donald's young parents are at the table, too, having made their twice-yearly journey with their son and newborn daughter. Like his brother Alex, Dave could not wait to get out of New York. When they were old enough to leave home, each signed away his Russian surname and adopted an Americanized version, setting off on his respective dream—Alex to the Merchant Marines, sailing around the world eight times, and Dave to a ranger's station in Oklahoma. *What were they running from?* Donald wonders aloud to this day. *Why did my uncle go to sea and my father to the woods?* Maybe, I'm thinking, home is the place where we begin. The center of the compass, the fulcrum that spins us out.

The dream room is swirling with smoke—my grandfather's Camels, Boris's unfiltered hand rolled cigarettes. Someone has ordered take-out from the local deli. "Probably my aunt," Donald remembers. "Always the most expensive foods, a real feast, more than anyone could afford, but they ordered it anyway," and Boris is getting ready to leave, to pick up the order. But first he must get into his shoes. "It was a big production," Donald says. "Because of the bunions. He had to use a shoe horn, and it took forever."

Later, when young Donald is tucked away on the Army cot between Grandma Ria's bed, where his parents will sleep, and the portable crib they've borrowed for his sister, he will lie awake and listen to the grownups laughing, arguing, clinking vodka glasses, talking politics. At this point, I imagine my ancestors, Protestant teetotalers for whom *blacklisted* and *communism* are but dark smudges in their local newspaper, excusing themselves, having picked their way through the unrecognizable smoked meats, pickled oysters, thick black bread dipped in olive oil from Lebanon, and bowls of purple borscht dolloped with sour cream.

Lying on the cot with the whole of New York blaring outside the small window, Donald is smug with plans. Tomorrow he will put on his best suit and his parents will take him on the subway downtown for lunch—to the automat, he hopes, where his mother will retrieve from her pocketbook a handful of coins and let him choose from the array of sandwiches and fried chicken platters and slices of fruit pies behind the glass doors. Afterwards they will go to Gimbel's or Macy's, then to FAO Schwartz. Donald doesn't yet know that his father will surprise him by buying a small wooden boat with a battery powered propeller, and that the day will end more perfectly than any day in his life has yet ended—at Central Park, on the bank of Conservatory Lake, where he will wind the propeller as tightly as it will go, then kneel to place the boat in the water and watch as it makes its way through the miniature armada of sailboats and battleships and canoes, each boat followed by a pair of eyes belonging to a child whose dreams follow the boat across the blue water.

In Thornton Wilder's *Our Town*, Emily, newly dead, asks the other dead ones how long it takes before you stop feeling a part of the other world. A while, they tell her. It takes a while. But that's not what you should think about, they say. You must focus on what is ahead. Besides, one of them says, it wasn't so great to be part of the living anyway. Be grateful it's over.

To leave a home, you must find ways to fall out of love with it. Those minor irritations which have come to seem, at times, almost endearing—the rusty gate, the roaring heat pump, the perpetually leaky faucet, the tiles that don't quite match—must be allowed to grow to major proportions. *Thank God we won't have to worry about* that *anymore*, you bluster to friends and family. *When we get to New York. . . .*

And if you must not only leave but also sell the home you love, as we are doing, you must steel yourself against criticisms that might once have cut deeply or roused you to battle. You must dismiss the comments, the offhand remarks from realtors, buyers, well-meaning neighbors. When you need to fall out of love with your home, there are dozens of people ready to help. Workmen are perhaps the most effective dream busters. *No*, you tell them, *you'd never really noticed that water stain above the chimney. And no, you haven't been up on the roof in years—not since that tree limb cracked during the ice storm. Really,* you say. *That bad?* And the painter, eyeing your faux Tuscan kitchen wall and the plum colored entry hall, is more than happy to announce how many coats of eggshell white it will take to cover such indiscretions and to provide prospective buyers with a clean canvas.

So by the time King of Steam arrives, you welcome his big cloud-colored truck, the compressor he wedges into your garage between stacks of packing boxes, the thick-as-an-elephant's-trunk hose he unwinds from his truck. You know what's coming. The judgmental eye, the lectures on carpet maintenance and six-month check-ups, the Scotchgard recommendations. He's just what you need on this miserable August afternoon in the jungle heat of Charlotte—92 degrees, 95 percent humidity, a host of mosquitoes swarming around the bird bath. *Come in*, you say. *What's a little more steam on a day like today?*

But King of Steam has a more intimate relationship with humidity. Although he is already dripping with sweat—the king is virtually *glistening*—he refuses the glass of iced tea you offer. He's at least six feet two, and dressed in a checkered shirt and khaki shorts with complicated pockets and snaps, he resembles an overgrown Boy Scout or one of those lederhosened men from cough drop commercials. His calves bulge with thick muscles.

"I see I've got my work cut out for me," he says with a sigh, looking down at the beige plush carpet, which was new when we moved in nine years ago but is not new now. Life happens, what can I say? Now he's warning me that his hose, which he's preparing to wrestle the two flights up to our bedroom, could possibly, just possibly, scratch the wood stairs. "It's my duty to warn you," he says solemnly. When I hesitate, he is quick to point out that it's all my decision, of course, but if this were his house ("And I have a *big* house," he says, "twenty-six hundred square feet, a *nice* house") he wouldn't hesitate to give permission. "Besides," he says, kneeling on the stairway, "there are more scratches here than these hoses could ever leave. Now, with finely varnished floors, well, it might make a difference."

"Fine," I say. "Be my guest." I sign the release form.

"Scotchgard?" he asks, and when I shake my head, he's off, tripping the light Steamatic up the stairs, his hose thumping, step by step, behind him. He flips a switch, and the compressor in the garage, two flights down, rumbles into action. In an hour or two he will be gone, taking with him the dirt and grime, the stains, our whole ground-in history—the ink I've dribbled, my nephews' crayon smudges, the Carolina clay tracked in from the garden, stray ashes from Donald's pipe, sloshes of red wine from last month's dinner party, the dander and gray fur from the cat I must soon find a home for.

When you empty a home, you start with what you need least, those items you've either outlived or put away toward some future life you've dreamed of inhabiting but probably never will: the hand-tatted placemats, the satin smoking jacket, doll size espresso cups, the bamboo vegetable steamer. I once went through a period of believing I would actually wear all the hats I'd bought on rainy afternoons while wandering the aisles of musty antique stores. Hats from the forties, the thirties, the twenties. Hats with feathers and black veils. Then there was my natural-fiber year, when I allowed only silk, cotton, wool, and perpetually wrinkled linen into my closet. If you look deeper into that closet, you will find remnants of the six-month period Donald and I were separated. Skinny from grief and dazed with newfound freedom, I bought short leather skirts, Spandex capri pants, midriff blouses, and slinky dresses with peek-a-boo backs.

Next to go are those things that simply won't fit into the life you are about to inhabit. For us, this means practically everything. Though we've succeeded in finding a New York apartment we can actually afford—a miracle in itself—the apartment is a furnished sublet belonging to friends of friends, a couple who are leaving their possessions behind ("down to the plates and spoons," the wife tells us as she leads us from room to room) to pursue the Hollywood dream they've carried in their heads for years. She opens a closet, its shelves stacked with boxes marked Xmas, Winter Clothes, Memories, DO NOT CRUSH. I tell her not to worry, that we'll be careful with her things. "Especially the china," she says, her eyes clouding over. "It means a lot to me."

Our tenancy might last a few months or it might stretch to years, depending on how the gold of their Hollywood dream pans out. This uncertainty as to the length of our stay, coupled with uncertainty about where we will end up—I started to write *permanently*, but how can you ever be sure—compounds the already nerve-splitting stress of the packing process. What to take with us, what to give away, what to store, what to loan? If our New York dream pans out, we won't be returning to Charlotte or to any space large enough to house all our belongings. I like calling them belongings rather than possessions. They are belongings because they belong where they are, in the life we inhabit in this place.

But if I'm ever going to finish packing, I've got to stop calling everything a belonging. *The past is the past*: my mother's voice in my ear. What belongs in a three-level townhouse with a garden and two decks owned by a long-married couple with a steady income is not what belongs in a prewar furnished midtown Manhattan sublet rented month-by-month by a couple of terrified middle-aged freelancers. Something's got to give. Almost everything. The garden tools, wheelbarrow, wrought iron bench, patio umbrella, birdhouses, planters, stereo cabinet, television console, twin love seats, end tables, coffee table, bookcases, bedroom chairs, bureaus, lamps, paintings, mirrors, shelf after shelf of books, the dining room hutch and everything on it, the Stickley table that belonged to my parents, along with the seven Stickley chairs ("Somehow, in one of the moves," my mother recalls, "the eighth one disappeared, how could that have happened?"), the dark cherry bed we recently re-slatted to support the queen-size mattress we graduated to on our twenty-second anniversary.

And the piano, my first acquisition as a young bride preparing to leave my parents' home. A piano was the one thing I knew I could not live without. Music was my solace, my companion, the keyboard on which I wrote my first wordless poems. Though I could not remember when my parents had bought their shiny black spinet, the one I'd played throughout childhood and adolescence, I couldn't remember it *not* being there. What is a home without a piano?

So I cashed in my savings account and bought what I could not live without, a used spinet with a Swedish walnut veneer. My father and brothers hoisted it into a U-Haul and unloaded it at the shag-carpeted patio apartment where my new husband and I would spend out first six months ("Are all first years this hard?" I asked my mother) before moving to another patio apartment where we dodged the landlord who kept asking for rent money we didn't have. Despite my husband's protests, the piano went with us to the second apartment, then to his father's house where we lived rent-free for a few months, then to my father's house where I waited out my husband's boot camp months, then to the military base 400 miles north where he was stationed, then 3,000 miles east to the next base, and the next. After the divorce, the piano went with me to the southern university town where I shared a duplex apartment with a stranger, then to a rent-subsidized apartment I sublet from a single mother, then to a garage apartment, then to the house where Donald had lived with his ex-wife, and finally here, to our home.

The piano is the only possession—the only *belonging*—that has survived all the moves, all the lives I've inhabited since I first left my parent's home. And three mornings after we sign the real estate contract, I wake up knowing the piano has to go. More precisely, I have to go, and the piano cannot go with me. I briefly consider storing the piano in my brother's basement, alongside the other furniture that we hope, one day, to retrieve. But knowing what moisture can do to a piano, I decide against this. My sister Claudia has always wanted a piano, and I consider loaning it to her, then retrieving it when we can afford an apartment of our own, although instinct warns me we'll never be able to afford a New York apartment large enough to house a piano.

Besides, I've never had much luck loaning things out to people. After a while, they start believing that the ottoman, or the fur coat, or the mirror belongs to them, and when I return months later to ransom it, their eyes widen in surprise. "My ottoman?" they say. "But I thought. . . ."

Or worse, they take no possession at all, and the object I care for so deeply gets thrown into the back of a closet or tool shed or barn where it rusts or rots or mildews or sprouts weeds or otherwise languishes. Bessie, my grandmother's older, childless sister, once possessed many beautiful things—chests with inlaid wood, solid wood tables and headboards, a hand-carved Victrola, and a mahogany upright with ivory keys. After her husband died, she sold their home to move into a smaller house, then a yet smaller house, and in the process most of her possessions were either sold or stolen; the remaining items were loaned out to friends and family members. On returning from an extended cross-country visit where she had been caring for an aging cousin, Bessie found that the prized piano she had entrusted to a nephew for safe-keeping had been abandoned on his farmhouse porch, exposed not only to the elements but to the caprices of the family cats, dogs, goats, and chickens.

I pick up the phone and dial Claudia's number. It will be a gift, free and clear. No loan, no retrieval. Oh well, I tell myself. The piano would have eventually ended up at her house anyway; it's been written into my will for a long time now.

"Have I got a deal for you," I begin, and within minutes my sister has re-designed her living and dining rooms.

"I can see it now," she says. "It will be the center of our home."

While she's talking, I walk into my living room, stretching the phone cord as far as it will go. The piano is still where it's always been, topped with a dresser scarf that my friend Carolyn, dead now a year, gave me during my last visit to her home. She knew she was dying, knew it would be our last time together. "Take anything you want," she said, gesturing dramatically with one hand as if to include everything—the clothes, the jewelry, the books and the stories in them, her life.

"Oh, I'm so excited," Claudia says. "Remember how it was at Mom's? How we all gathered around it?"

"I remember," I say. "What's a home without a piano?"

Or without a cat. My neighbor two doors down has agreed to take our deck-leaping, mouse-chasing, tree-climbing Mr. Dibbs. It would be cruel, we've decided, to cage him in a New York apartment. Better to leave him to wander his old haunts, to come and go as he pleases. The transition shouldn't be too difficult, we figure, since the floor plan of my neighbor's townhouse is identical to ours. I pack up his bowl, his litter box, his grooming brush, his toys, the igloo-shaped bed he has yet to use—he prefers the pillow where I lay my head—and carry him to my neighbor's door, where she is waiting with cat treats. Dibbs accepts her open arms too easily, and I begin to think maybe this isn't such a good idea after all. We form a pact: in exchange for her generosity, I promise not to allow Dibbs back into our house. "You're right," I say. "He has to get used to his new home. We don't want to confuse him."

The next morning when I open the front door, he is there waiting, curled beside the newspaper. How many of his lives have already passed, pages in a cat's calendar? How many did he pass with us? On habit, I reach to pick him up and take him inside, then, remembering my promise, I carry him down the porch steps and set him down beside the gate.

"Stay," I say.

I hurry up the steps, but Dibbs scurries behind me, close at my heels. I pick him up again, carry him down the steps, out the gate, down the sidewalk to my neighbor's house. My hands want to pet him—fur hunger—but I won't let them. How long will it take until he no longer comes to call? Until he knows we are gone, and lifts his tail and walks toward his other life? I lean down and place him, like a package, on her welcome mat. "Stay," I say.

This evening, sitting on the sofa, I study the footprints of the couple who, according to the realtor, will probably buy our house. They must have come again today, during the hours I disappeared. It's what I do now, my new job. Prospective buyers need time alone with the house, the realtor tells us. They want to look into closets and cabinets. They want to turn on faucets and flush toilets. Some bring their tape measures. Some bring their contractors. How much will it cost to tear out this wall, refinish these floors, repaint these faux Tuscan walls? Where will we hang Mother's antique mirror?

Each time the realtor calls, I make a clean sweep of the house—wiping down counters, smoothing the bed, emptying the trash cans, spraying something sweet into the air. Then I walk through the rooms, turning on every light. Finally, I step out of my shoes and vacuum the carpet thoroughly, backing myself out of each room.

Then I disappear. Sometimes I visit a friend. Sometimes I go to the library or to the gym. Mostly I just drive around, slowly circling the neighborhood, viewing my home from a respectful distance, wondering how it looks to those who drive by. When the allotted time is up, I cautiously make my approach to the house. If someone is still there, standing on the porch or walking through the garden, I keep driving. When the realtor calls with his nightly report, I tell him I don't want to know the details—their names, their occupations, how much money they have in the bank.

Footprints provide enough information for me. It's a kind of rudimentary archaeology. Since King of Steam's visit, the carpet is so clean and fluffy that the imprints are clearly visible, down to the smallest detail. I am able to guess not only the size and personality of the ghost guests (spike heels, sandals, tennis shoes) but also the route of their travels. Did they walk to the kitchen twice, three times? Did they avoid the wet bar?

I sit on the sofa and study the prints of the couple, imagining their lives. The larger prints are short for a man's, but very wide, with a substantial heel print, an expensive logo visible in each heel. He has left several trails, round-trip tracks from the door to the fireplace, the door to the balcony, the door to the window, the door to the phone. Was he measuring for new carpet? Was he phoning his bank? The smaller print—the wife's, I presume—was made by a waffle-heeled no-nonsense shoe. The shoe of a waitress, perhaps, or a school teacher. Someone who spends a lot of time on her feet. That's good, I think. The stairs won't be a problem for her. I slip one foot, then the other, into her prints and stand there a minute. When I step away I can see, centered in her tracks, the fossils of my bare feet.

To fully leave a place you love, you must view it from afar, from across a wide expanse of time, space or feeling. After a while, the wise ones tell you, you will begin to align yourself not with the old place and those who inhabit it, but to the clean white canvas that awaits your marking. In this way, Joan Didion, having fully aligned herself with California, was able to write, without a hint of remorse or homesickness, of her years in New York City. The title of her essay, "Goodbye to All That," demonstrates the distance she had traveled between then and now, old and new. *Goodbye* denotes an ending, as opposed to *farewell*, the word my best friend insists on using for the party she is hosting for me. The word *that* suggests a separation; *that* is a place you've already left.

This morning on my customary walk, one of the last I will take in this place, I am thinking about Didion's essay, and as I round the corner by the neighborhood pub, Didion's phrase is in my head. I try saying it to the air but it doesn't feel right. *That* is already far removed—the ice frozen over, the wound healed. *That* is to *this* as *there* is to *here*. I pass the dry cleaner's, the fish market, the stylish brick apartment house where my friend lives, a novelist with whom I've shared tea, lemon-flavored cookies, and hour after hour of talk. He lived in New York when he was young and believes everyone should live there at least once. Then why was he so sad the last time we were together, why was I sad? I wind down the path that leads through the city park near the pink-gabled Victorian house and my neighbor's townhouse, where the cat I gave up now lives quite contentedly, it seems, at least he looks content there, sunning himself on her deck with a full bowl of food within paw's reach.

Last week, the footprints in our carpet grew bodies and names. The contract is signed and the earnest money is in the bank. According to the realtor, the couple is already making big plans to tear out walls, put in new floors, new tile. The closing is scheduled for tomorrow. I've cried my last tears, I'm sure of it. A few nights ago, while Donald and I sat at the dining room table eating Chinest take-out on paper plates, I began to weep. "I'm going to miss our home," I said, "Aren't you going to miss our home? How can you just sit there, eating?"

He stood up, pushed his chair away from the table, and walked over to me. He reached out with both hands as if inviting me to dance. I stood up and, still crying, leaned against his chest. When I tried to break away, he held me tighter, and when I finally quieted, he stepped back a little, making a circle with his arms, enclosing me, leaving only a small column of air between us. "See this?" he said, meaning the circle in which our bodies floated. "*This* is our home."

Now the floors of the house are empty except for a broom, a dustpan, a few packing boxes, a roll of bubble wrap, and a portable radio whose voices keep me company while I work. The NPR host is interviewing the author of a self-help book that combines ancient Buddhist teachings with tips for coping with modern-day stress. One of the best coping skills, he believes, is humor, so he's telling jokes: What did the Zen Buddhist say to the hot dog vendor? (Make me one with everything.) How can you recognize a Buddhist vacuum cleaner? (It has no attachments.)

I've saved the hall closet for last. It's filled with boxes, folders, bags, old suit-cases stuffed with mementos. Most people mispronounce the word. I used to, too, until my high school English teacher corrected me. It's easy to see why we call them *momentos*. We link them with *moment, momentous,* perhaps even *momentum,* the force of motion propelling us forward. The boxes in our closets—filled with love letters, family photographs, old report cards, school records, awards, cita-tions, obituary clippings—mark the moments of our lives, those brief occasions from which our pasts set sail. "A voyage of great moment," one writer called the journey, and it is indeed a momentous journey, weighted with grave implications.

"No," the English teacher said. "It's memento, as in remember. A memento is a relic, a reminder of the past. Related to the Latin *memento mori:* Remember that you will die." When it became clear that Aunt Bessie would die, my parents moved her from the log cabin she'd lived in as a child and to which she'd re-turned after the last of her cross-country journeys, into a spare bedroom in their home. They packed all her remaining possessions into a mahogany chest that stood at the foot of her bed.

After she died, my parents cleared out the room to make space for my mother's parents, Sylvie and Arthur. The accumulated belongings of their sixty-year marriage had been culled to fit into the space of one small bedroom. My par-ents filled the bureau top with framed photos, and over the double bed they hung the monogrammed gate latch—*Double S Ranch*—that had once marked the entrance to Sylvie and Arthur's hundred-acre farm. Set adrift from their pasts, cut free from the duties and chores that had defined their lives, my grandparents' marriage shrank back to the size of their original union. They had nothing left to do but keep each other company. Which they did quite well, sitting side by side on my parents' sofa like a young couple who are just now beginning to court each other.

It's a mistake, the dead ones tell Emily, to go back. Emily doesn't listen, of course. Had she listened to their advice, there would be no play, no rising and falling ac-tion, no final act. She is certain that they are wrong, that if she picks a happy mo-ment to return to, a sunny day to relive—she chooses her twelfth birthday—she will not be saddened by what was. As it turns out, her decision only sharpens the sadness. It hurts as much, perhaps more, to return to a place where we were happy. Especially when we look back on that place, as we must, with new eyes. We hadn't meant to change, we'd thought we could hold things as they were. "Don't worry," I tell my brother, my neighbor, my best friend. "I'll be back for visits, lots of them," and I pull out the calendar to show proof.

"Sure," my brother says. "You know you're welcome any time."

"Dibbs will be glad to see you," my neighbor says.

"It won't be the same," says my friend. Darkness, like a sudden cloud cover, sweeps across her eyes, and I sense that already things are changing, have changed, that a door in her is closing, as it must. In six months, a year, two years, I might revisit the scene, but that's all it will be, a visit.

Home is the place where, once you have left, you cannot return. I used to think you could. I mean, why not? There's the road to the schoolhouse, there's the fencepost where you sat, there's the garage apartment where you typed your dissertation, why not go back?

"It's never the same," my mother said.

I pointed to the small white house with the peeling shutters, the house where I was born. My mother sat behind the steering wheel. At my request, she had driven me out into the Indiana countryside, forty-five years into my past.

"That's not the place it was," she said.

But the photograph was in my hand. It looked the same to me.

My mother shook her head and turned away, and in her eyes I saw the home she had left, the one we'd never get back. It was larger and brighter and sadder and sweeter, swelled up with context: the morning light across the rain barrel, my brother circling the driveway on his tricycle with the metal wheels, the rich compost smells of hay and dust and washing powder and sun-starched sheets, a baby (that would be me) crawling toward the porch steps, and—in the center of it all—a beautiful black-haired woman holding the sheets close to her breast, her eyes fixed on the scene at hand.

The Search for Marvin Gardens

John McPhee

Go. I roll the dice—a six and a two. Through the air I move my token, the flatiron, to Vermont Avenue, where dog packs range.

The dogs are moving (some are limping) through ruins, rubble, fire damage, open garbage. Doorways are gone. Lath is visible in the crumbling walls of the buildings. The street sparkles with shattered glass. I have never seen, anywhere, so many broken windows. A sign—"Slow, Children at Play"—has been bent backward by an automobile. At the lighthouse, the dogs turn up Pacific and disappear. George Meade, Army engineer, built the lighthouse—brick upon brick, six hundred thousand bricks, to reach up high enough to throw a beam twenty miles over the sea. Meade, seven years later, saved the Union at Gettysburg.

I buy Vermont Avenue for $100. My opponent is a tall, shadowy figure, across from me, but I know him well, and I know his game like a favorite tune. If he can, he will always go for the quick kill. And when it is foolish to go for the quick kill he will be foolish. On the whole, though, he is a master assessor of percentages. It is a mistake to underestimate him. His eleven carries his top hat to St. Charles Place, which he buys for $140.

The sidewalks of St. Charles Place have been cracked to shards by through-growing weeds. There are no buildings. Mansions, hotels once stood here. A few street lamps now drop cones of light on broken glass and vacant space behind a chain-link fence that some great machine has in places bent to the ground. Five plane trees—in full summer leaf, flecking the light—are all that live on St. Charles Place.

Block upon block, gradually, we are cancelling each other out—in the blues, the lavenders, the oranges, the greens. My opponent follows a plan of his own devising. I use the Hornblower & Weeks opening and the Zuricher defense. The first game draws tight, will soon finish. In 1971, a group of people in Racine, Wisconsin, played for seven hundred and sixty-eight hours. A game begun a month later in Danville, California, lasted eight hundred and twenty hours. These are official records, and they stun us. We have been playing for eight minutes. It amazes us that Monopoly is thought of as a long game. It is possible to play to a complete, absolute, and final conclusion in less than fifteen minutes, all within the rules as written. My opponent and I have done so thousands of times. No wonder we are sitting across from each other now in this best-of-seven series for the international singles championship of the world.

On Illinois Avenue, three men lean out from second-story windows. A girl is coming down the street. She wears dungarees and a bright-red shirt, has ample breasts and a Hadendoan Afro, a black halo, two feet in diameter. Ice rattles in the glasses in the hands of the men.

"Hey, sister!"

"Come on up!"

She looks up, looks from one to another to the other, looks them flat in the eye.

"What for?" she says, and she walks on.

I buy Illinois for $240. It solidifies my chances, for I already own Kentucky and Indiana. My opponent pales. If he had landed first on Illinois, the game would have been over then and there, for he has houses built on Boardwalk and Park Place, we share the railroads equally, and we have cancelled each other everywhere else. We never trade.

In 1852, R. B. Osborne, an immigrant Englishman, civil engineer, surveyed the route of a railroad line that would run from Camden to Absecon Island, in New Jersey, traversing the state from the Delaware River to the barrier beaches of the sea. He then sketched in the plan of a "bathing village" that would surround the eastern terminus of the line. His pen flew glibly, framing and naming spacious avenues parallel to the shore—Mediterranean, Baltic, Oriental, Ventnor—and narrower transsecting avenues: North Carolina, Pennsylvania, Vermont, Connecticut, States, Virginia, Tennessee, New York, Kentucky, Indiana, Illinois. The place as a whole had no name, so when he had completed the plan Osborne wrote in large letters over the ocean, "Atlantic City." No one ever challenged the name, or the names of Osborne's streets. Monopoly was invented in the early nineteen-thirties by Charles B. Darrow, but Darrow was only transliterating what Osborne had created. The railroads, crucial to any player, were the making of Atlantic City. After the rails were down, houses and hotels burgeoned from Mediterranean and Baltic to New York and Kentucky. Properties—building lots—sold for as little as six dollars apiece and as much as a thousand dollars. The original investors in the railroads and the real estate called themselves the Camden & Atlantic Land Company. Reverently, I repeat their names: Dwight Bell, William Coffin, John DaCosta, Daniel Deal, William Fleming, Andrew Hay, Joseph Porter, Jonathan Pitney, Samuel Richards—founders, fathers, forerunners, archetypical masters of the quick kill.

My opponent and I are now in a deep situation of classical Monopoly. The torsion is almost perfect—Boardwalk and Park Place versus the brilliant reds. His cash position is weak, though, and if I escape him now he may fade. I land on Luxury Tax, contiguous to but in sanctuary from his power. I have four houses on Indiana. He lands there. He concedes.

Indiana Avenue was the address of the Brighton Hotel, gone now. The Brighton was exclusive—a word that no longer has retail value in the city. If you arrived by automobile and tried to register at the Brighton, you were sent away. Brighton-class people came in private railroad cars. Brighton-class people had other private railroad cars for their horses—dawn rides on the firm sand at water's edge, skirts flying. Colonel Anthony J. Drexel Biddle—the sort of name that would constrict throats in Philadelphia—lived, much of the year, in the Brighton.

Colonel Sanders' fried chicken is on Kentucky Avenue. So is Clifton's Club Harlem, with the Sepia Revue and the Sepia Follies, featuring the Honey Bees, the Fashions, and the Lords.

My opponent and I, many years ago, played 2,428 games of Monopoly in a single season. He was then a recent graduate of the Harvard Law School, and he was working for a downtown firm, looking up law. Two people we knew—one from Chase Manhattan, the other from Morgan, Stanley—tried to get into the game, but after a few rounds we found that they were not in the conversation and we sent them home. Monopoly should always be *mano a mano* anyway. My opponent won 1,199 games, and so did I. Thirty were ties. He was called into the Army, and we stopped just there. Now, in Game 2 of the series, I go immediately to jail, and again to jail while my opponent seines property. He is dumbfoundingly lucky. He wins in twelve minutes.

Visiting hours are daily, eleven to two; Sunday, eleven to one; evenings, six to nine. "NO MINORS, NO FOOD, Immediate Family Only Allowed in Jail." All this above a blue steel door in a blue cement wall in the windowless interior of the basement of the city hall. The desk sergeant sits opposite the door to the jail. In a cigar box in front of him are pills in every color, a banquet of fruit salad an inch and a half deep—leapers, co-pilots, footballs, truck drivers, peanuts, blue angels, yellow jackets, redbirds, rainbows. Near the desk are two soldiers, waiting to go through the blue door. They are about eighteen years old. One of them is trying hard to light a cigarette. His wrists are in steel cuffs. A military policeman waits, too. He is a year or so older than the soldiers, taller, studious in appearance, gentle, fat. On a bench against a wall sits a good-looking girl in slacks. The blue door rattles, swings heavily open. A turnkey stands in the doorway. "Don't you guys kill yourselves back there now," says the sergeant to the soldiers.

"One kid, he overdosed himself about ten and a half hours ago," says the M.P.

The M.P., the soldiers, the turnkey, and the girl on the bench are white. The sergeant is black. "If you take off the handcuffs, take off the belts," says the sergeant to the M.P. "I don't want them hanging themselves back there." The door shuts and its tumblers move. When it opens again, five minutes later, a young white man in sandals and dungarees and a blue polo shirt emerges. His hair is in a ponytail. He has no beard. He grins at the good-looking girl. She rises, joins him. The sergeant hands him a manila envelope. From it he removes his belt and a small notebook. He borrows a pencil, makes an entry in the notebook. He is out of jail, free. What did he do? He offended Atlantic City in some way. He spent a night in the jail. In the nineteen-thirties, men visiting Atlantic City went to jail, directly to jail, did not pass Go, for appearing in topless bathing suits on the beach. A city statute requiring all men to wear full-length bathing suits was not seriously challenged until 1937, and the first year in which a man could legally go bare-chested on the beach was 1940.

Game 3. After seventeen minutes, I am ready to begin construction on overpriced and sluggish Pacific, North Carolina, and Pennsylvania. Nothing else being open, opponent concedes.

The physical profile of streets perpendicular to the shore is something like a playground slide. It begins in the high skyline of Boardwalk hotels, plummets into warrens of "side-avenue" motels, crosses Pacific, slopes through church missions, convalescent homes, burlesque houses, rooming houses, and liquor stores, crosses Atlantic, and runs level through the bombed-out ghetto as far—Baltic, Mediterranean—as the eye can see. North Carolina Avenue, for example, is flanked at its beach end by the Chalfonte and the Haddon Hall (908 rooms, air-conditioned), where, according to one biographer, John Philip Sousa (1854–1932) first played when he was twenty-two, insisting, even then, that everyone call him by his entire name. Behind these big hotels, motels—Barbizon, Catalina—crouch. Between Pacific and Atlantic is an occasional house from 1910—wooden porch, wooden mullions, old yellow paint—and two churches, a package store, a strip show, a dealer in fruits and vegetables. Then, beyond Atlantic Avenue, North Carolina moves on into the vast ghetto, the bulk of the city, and it looks like Metz in 1919, Cologne in 1944. Nothing has actually exploded. It is not bomb damage. It is deep and complex decay. Roofs are off. Bricks are scattered in the street. People sit on porches, six deep, at nine on a Monday morning. When they go off to wait in unemployment lines, they wait sometimes two hours. Between Mediterranean and Baltic runs a chain-link fence, enclosing rubble. A patrol car sits idling by the curb. In the back seat is a German shepherd. A sign on the fence says, "Beware of Bad Dogs."

Mediterranean and Baltic are the principal avenues of the ghetto. Dogs are everywhere. A pack of seven passes me. Block after block, there are three-story brick row houses. Whole segments of them are abandoned, a thousand broken windows. Some parts are intact, occupied. A mattress lies in the street, soaking in a pool of water. Wet stuffing is coming out of the mattress. A postman is having a rye and a beer in the Plantation Bar at nine-fifteen in the morning. I ask him idly if he knows where Marvin Gardens is. He does not. "HOOKED AND NEED HELP? CONTACT N.A.R.C.O." "REVIVAL NOW GOING ON, CONDUCTED BY REVEREND H. HENDERSON OF TEXAS." These are signboards on Mediterranean and Baltic. The second one is upside down and leans against a boarded-up window of the Faith Temple Church of God in Christ. There is an old peeling poster on a warehouse wall showing a figure in an electric chair. "The Black Panther Manifesto" is the title of the poster, and its message is, or was, that "the fascists have already decided in advance to murder Chairman Bobby Seale in the electric chair." I pass an old woman who carries a bucket. She wears blue sneakers, worn through. Her feet spill out. She wears red socks, rolled at the knees. A white handkerchief, spread over her head, is knotted at the corners. Does she know where Marvin Gardens is? "I sure don't know," she says, setting down the bucket. "I sure don't know. I've heard of it somewhere, but I just can't say where." I walk on, through a block of shattered glass. The glass crunches underfoot like coarse sand. I remember when I first came here—a long train ride from Trenton, long ago, games of poker in the train—to play basketball against Atlantic City. We were half black, they were all black. We scored forty points, they scored eighty, or something like it. What I remember most is that they had glass backboards—glittering, pendent, expensive glass backboards, a rarity then in high schools, even in colleges, the only ones we played on all year.

I turn on Pennsylvania, and start back toward the sea. The windows of the Hotel Astoria, on Pennsylvania near Baltic, are boarded up. A sheet of unpainted plywood is the door, and in it is a triangular peephole that now frames an eye. The plywood door opens. A man answers my question. Rooms there are six, seven, and ten dollars a week. I thank him for the information and move on, emerging from the ghetto at the Catholic Daughters of America Women's Guest House, between Atlantic and Pacific. Between Pacific and the Boardwalk are the blinking vacancy signs of the Aristocrat and Colton Manor motels. Pennsylvania terminates at the Sheraton-Seaside—thirty-two dollars a day, ocean corner. I take a walk on the Boardwalk and into the Holiday Inn (twenty-three stories). A guest is registering. "You reserved for Wednesday, and this is Monday," the clerk tells him. "But that's all right. We have *plenty* of rooms." The clerk is very young, female, and has soft brown hair that hangs below her waist. Her superior kicks her.

He is a middle-aged man with red spiderwebs in his face. He is jacketed and tied. He takes her aside. "Don't say 'plenty,'" he says. "Say 'You are fortunate, sir. We have rooms available.'"

The face of the young woman turns sour. "We have all the rooms you need," she says to the customer, and, to her superior, "How's that?"

Game 4. My opponent's luck has become abrasive. He has Boardwalk and Park Place, and has sealed the board.

Darrow was a plumber. He was, specifically, a radiator repairman who lived in Germantown, Pennsylvania. His first Monopoly board was a sheet of linoleum. On it he placed houses and hotels that he had carved from blocks of wood. The game he thus invented was brilliantly conceived, for it was an uncannily exact reflection of the business milieu at large. In its depth, range, and subtlety, in its luck-skill ratio, in its sense of infrastructure and socio-economic parameters, in its philosophical characteristics, it reached to the profundity of the financial community. It was as scientific as the stock market. It suggested the manner and means through which an underdeveloped world had been developed. It was chess at Wall Street level. "Advance token to the nearest Railroad and pay owner twice the rental to which he is otherwise entitled. If Railroad is unowned, you may buy it from the Bank. Get out of Jail, free. Advance token to nearest Utility. If unowned, you may buy it from Bank. If owned, throw dice and pay owner a total ten times the amount thrown. You are assessed for street repairs: $40 per house, $115 per hotel. Pay poor tax of $15. Go to Jail. Go directly to Jail. Do not pass Go. Do not collect $200."

The turnkey opens the blue door. The turnkey is known to the inmates as Sidney K. Above his desk are ten closed-circuit-TV screens—assorted viewpoints of the jail. There are three cellblocks—men, women, juvenile boys. Six days is the average stay. Showers twice a week. The steel doors and the equipment that operates them were made in San Antonio. The prisoners sleep on bunks of butcher block. There are no mattresses. There are three prisoners to a cell. In winter, it is cold in here. Prisoners burn newspapers to keep warm. Cell corners are black with smudge. The jail is three years old. The men's block echoes with chatter. The man in the cell nearest Sidney K. is pacing. His shirt is covered with broad stains of blood. The block for juvenile boys is, by contrast, utterly silent—empty corridor, empty cells. There is only one prisoner. He is small and black and appears to be thirteen. He says he is sixteen and that he has been alone in here for three days.
 "Why are you here? What did you do?"
 "I hit a jitney driver."

The series stands at three all. We have split the fifth and sixth games. We are scrambling for property. Around the board we fairly fly. We move so fast because we do our own banking and search our own deeds. My opponent grows tense.

Ventnor Avenue, a street of delicatessens and doctors' offices, is leafy with plane trees and hydrangeas, the city flower. Water Works is on the mainland. The water comes over in submarine pipes. Electric Company gets power from across the state, on the Delaware River, in Deepwater. States Avenue, now a wasteland like St. Charles, once had gardens running down the middle of the street, a horse-drawn trolley, private homes. States Avenue was as exclusive as the Brighton. Only an apartment house, a small motel, and the All Wars Memorial Building—monadnocks spaced widely apart—stand along States Avenue now. Pawnshops, convalescent homes, and the Paradise Soul Saving Station are on Virginia Avenue. The soul-saving station is pink, orange, and yellow. In the windows flanking the door of the Virginia Money Loan Office are Nikons, Polaroids, Yashicas, Sony TVs, Underwood typewriters, Singer sewing machines, and pictures of Christ. On the far side of town, beside a single track and locked up most of the time, is the new railroad station, a small hut made of glazed firebrick, all that is left of the lines that built the city. An authentic phrenologist works on New York Avenue close to Frank's Extra Dry Bar and a church where the sermon today is "Death in the Pot." The church is of pink brick, has blue and amber windows and two red doors. St. James Place, narrow and twisting, is lined with boarding houses that have wooden porches on each of three stories, suggesting a New Orleans made of salt-bleached pine. In a vacant lot on Tennessee is a white Ford station wagon stripped to the chassis. The windows are smashed. A plastic Clorox bottle sits on the driver's seat. The wind has pressed newspaper against the chain-link fence around the lot. Atlantic Avenue, the city's principal thoroughfare, could be seventeen American Main Streets placed end to end—discount vitamins and Vienna Corset shops, movie theatres, shoe stores, and funeral homes. The Boardwalk is made of yellow pine and Douglas fir, soaked in pentachlorophenol. Downbeach, it reaches far beyond the city. Signs everywhere—on windows, lampposts, trash baskets—proclaim "Bienvenue Canadiens!" The salt air is full of Canadian French. In the Claridge Hotel, on Park Place, I ask a clerk if she knows where Marvin Gardens is. She says, "Is it a floral shop?" I ask a cabdriver, parked outside. He says, "Never heard of it." Park Place is one block long, Pacific to Boardwalk. On the roof of the Claridge is the Solarium, the highest point in town—panoramic view of the ocean, the bay, the salt-water ghetto. I look down at the rooftops of the side-avenue motels and into swimming pools. There are hundreds of people around the rooftop pools, sunbathing, reading—many more people than are on the beach. Walls, windows, and a block of sky are all that is visible from these pools—no sand, no sea. The pools are craters, and with the people around them they are countersunk into the motels.

The seventh, and final, game is ten minutes old and I have hotels on Oriental, Vermont, and Connecticut. I have Tennessee and St. James. I have North Carolina and Pacific. I have Boardwalk, Atlantic, Ventnor, Illinois, Indiana. My fingers are forming a "V." I have mortgaged most of these properties in order to pay for others, and I have mortgaged the others to pay for the hotels. I have seven dollars. I will pay off the mortgages and build my reserves with income from the three hotels. My cash position may be low, but I feel like a rocket in an underground silo. Meanwhile, if I could just go to jail for a time I could pause there, wait there, until my opponent, in his inescapable rounds, pays the rates of my hotels. Jail, at times, is the strategic place to be. I roll boxcars from the Reading and move the flatiron to Community Chest. "Go to Jail. Go directly to Jail."

The prisoners, of course, have no pens and no pencils. They take paper napkins, roll them tight as crayons, char the ends with matches, and write on the walls. The things they write are not entirely idiomatic; for example, "In God We Trust." All is in carbon. Time is required in the writing. "Only humanity could know of such pain." "God So Loved the World." "There is no greater pain than life itself." In the women's block now, there are six blacks, giggling, and a white asleep in red shoes. She is drunk. The others are pushers, prostitutes, an auto thief, a burglar caught with pistol in purse. A sixteen-year-old accused of murder was in here last week. These words are written on the wall of a now empty cell: "Laying here I see two bunks about six inches thick, not counting the one I'm laying on, which is hard as brick. No cushion for my back. No pillow for my head. Just a couple scratchy blankets which is best to use it's said. I wake up in the morning so shivery and cold, waiting and waiting till I am told the food is coming. It's on its way. It's not worth waiting for, but I eat it anyway. I know one thing when they set me free I'm gonna be good if it kills me."

How many years must a game be played to produce an Anthony J. Drexel Biddle and chestnut geldings on the beach? About half a century was the original answer, from the first railroad to Biddle at his peak. Biddle, at his peak, hit an Atlantic City streetcar conductor with his fist, laid him out with one punch. This increased Biddle's legend. He did not go to jail. While John Philip Sousa led his band along the Boardwalk playing "The Stars and Stripes Forever" and Jack Dempsey ran up and down in training for his fight with Gene Tunney, the city crossed the high curve of its parabola. Al Capone held conventions here—upstairs with his sleeves rolled, apportioning among his lieutenant governors the states of the Eastern seaboard. The natural history of an American resort proceeds from Indians to French Canadians via Biddles and Capones. French Canadians, whatever they may be at home, are Visigoths here. Bienvenue Visigoths!

My opponent plods along incredibly well. He has got his fourth railroad, and patiently, unbelievably, he has picked up my potential winners until he has blocked me everywhere but Marvin Gardens. He has avoided, in the fifty-dollar zoning, my increasingly petty hotels. His cash flow swells. His railroads are costing me two hundred dollars a minute. He is building hotels on States, Virginia, and St. Charles. He has temporarily reversed the current. With the yellow monopolies and my blue monopolies, I could probably defeat his lavenders and his railroads. I have Atlantic and Ventnor. I need Marvin Gardens. My only hope is Marvin Gardens.

There is a plaque at Boardwalk and Park Place, and on it in relief is the leonine profile of a man who looks like an officer in a metropolitan bank—"Charles B. Darrow, 1889–1967, inventor of the game of Monopoly." "Darrow," I address him, aloud. "Where is Marvin Gardens?" There is, of course, no answer. Bronze, impassive, Darrow looks south down the Boardwalk. "Mr. Darrow, please, where is Marvin Gardens?" Nothing. Not a sign. He just looks south down the Boardwalk.

My opponent accepts the trophy with his natural ease, and I make, from notes, remarks that are even less graceful than his.

Marvin Gardens is the one color-block Monopoly property that is not in Atlantic City. It is a suburb within a suburb, secluded. It is a planned compound of seventy-two handsome houses set on curvilinear private streets under yews and cedars, poplars and willows. The compound was built around 1920, in Margate, New Jersey, and consists of solid buildings of stucco, brick, and wood, with slate roofs, tile roofs, multimullioned porches, Giraldic towers, and Spanish grilles. Marvin Gardens, the ultimate outwash of Monopoly, is a citadel and sanctuary of the middle class. "We're heavily patrolled by police here. We don't take no chances. Me? I'm living here nine years. I paid seventeen thousand dollars and I've been offered thirty. Number one, I don't want to move. Number two, I don't need the money. I have four bedrooms, two and a half baths, front den, back den. No basement. The Atlantic is down there. Six feet down and you float. A lot of people have a hard time finding this place. People that lived in Atlantic City all their life don't know how to find it. They don't know where the hell they're going. They just know it's south, down the Boardwalk."

The Queimada

Michele Morano

And later, after the mussels, after the pulpo a la gallega, the swirling bits of octopus flesh in a sauce of garlic and tomatoes, after the glasses of wine and loaves of bread broken and passed hand to hand, after the strong local blue cheese spread thick on thin crackers and the apples drizzled with honey, after we have all eaten as much as we can and then picked the remains from one another's plates, tucking into our mouths one more bite, one more spoonful, one more tangy or sweet or salty fingertip, then we turn, lights dimmed and candles aflame, to the Queimada.

In the kitchen Chus shows me the brown ceramic bottle, the label handwritten: Aguardiente. I say it aloud. The other words I cannot pronounce because they are in the dialect of Galicia, the province where Chus was born. He is the only Gallego among us, the only person with roots in the land of magic and spirits, of incantations. Chus opens the bottle, holds it out for me to smell, explains that this is liquor made from the skins of grapes, not quite wine, not quite whiskey, and stronger than either. May I taste it, I ask, and Chus smiles, not yet, not until we tame it with fire.

His smile is full, expectant. In this apartment, which is not where he lives but where he spends his extra time with a dozen other artists, painting, sculpting, developing photographs, Chus is more himself than anywhere else. I have seen him in bars, at the homes of mutual friends, on the street as he heads off to work, and nowhere else does he look quite so full, quite so content. And above all tonight, a night on which he has brought this group together—his coworkers from the newspaper, their partners and friends—to share food and drink and the experience of calling spirits to us.

Around the table there is silence and arms resting on stomachs. Rays of moonlight outline the window shades, outline Chus positioning the large clay bowl in the middle of the table. I say that the moon is full on the winter solstice, imagine, and the others sigh yes, how amazing. I arrived with a full moon, I do not

155

say, and I will see six more, perhaps seven, and then I will leave. I am already nostalgic, already sad for the day I arrived here, so impressionable and with so much faith. And sad for this night, too, which I am already imagining as memory, the night of my first Queimada in a cold apartment on Calle Independencia, Oviedo, Spain.

And then we begin. Chus says to me, the foreigner, the person for whom every ritual is new: Pretend we're on a beach. The waves are rolling into the shore, the sand is moving under our feet. We can feel the spirits rushing on the wind to listen to our pleas. His eyes move around the table, to Lola, to Begoña and Pascual, to Isabel and her eight-year-old daughter Virginia, to Alberto, to Pilar, to me. He waits until we are all focused intently on him. And then he smiles and shrugs and begins.

The wooden ladle brims at the level of our eyes. Pilar lights a match, and we inhale as the fire erupts, pulsing over the ladle, dripping down and across the surface of the sugared Aguardiente in the bowl. Chus stirs carefully before scooping again, lifting and holding and releasing a long blue stream of liquid fire. Over and over, the motion in his wrist hypnotic, he stirs and lifts and spills, finding a rhythm that the words begin to ride.

Three months ago, I did not understand the language here. I listened to the words and sometimes understood them but not the language, not at all. Spanish. Castellano. And then early one morning in a lighted bar when I was tired from a long day, a day of taking Spanish classes and teaching English classes and making my way through the unfamiliar streets, Lola and Pilar talked and I listened to the sounds like short, lapping waves. The table was round, I remember, and small. They smoked Ducados, lighting and exhaling, waving their hands, and I drifted off as in a dream. In this dream I could hear their words and the words came not singly but in pairs or triangles and then in long lines that slipped by inseparable. The lines floated around me, background noises circling closer and closer, until words draped themselves in sentences upon and around and within my mind and there, in a lighted bar at 5:00 A.M. with Lola and Pilar laughing, the dialogue sprang alive and I understood.

Now I listen and the words float through me in phrases that will never make sense. Now I look around at the faces, the slight smiles, closed eyes, the full-stomached belief in the power of rituals even though not one of us understands what is happening here. Even Chus does not understand, or remember, all of what he says. This is a poem, a prayer to the dark spirits, a rhyme he tries to call back from the depths of memory. In place of certain lines, he hums, the rhythm held deep within his throat, within the motion of his arm and shoulder. Our faces are beginning to glisten, and I am memorizing the movements, listening to the almost familiar sounds, like Castellano but not quite, like the language of my sleeping dreams, on the verge always of being remembered. The sounds swirl and lift and pour and burn, and I am so open, so thankful for the warmth and the transport back into the part of my mind where language rises and falls like fire dancing on liquid, that I don't notice Chus is humming and humming, dissolving with the last line, the final word, into laughter.

And later, after the fire has calmed itself, after our faces have turned red and we have dabbed them with napkins, after we have pushed back our chairs and Isabel's eight-year-old daughter Virginia has come to stand beside me, beside the only other person as amazed as she is, Chus covers the bowl with a white cloth and in a moment there is only the liquid, warm and sweet.

And familiar. I drink from a ceramic cup with no handle, and nod to Chus. Yes, I like it. Yes, it's strong. I rub my stomach, where the heat pools. Alberto puts his hand on my shoulder, jostling me in the rough way he jostles everyone. You'll be a Spaniard soon, his mustache smiles, and everyone smiles, at me, at each other, at the middle of the table. And yes, it seems possible that I may become a Spaniard. That I may be transformed so entirely by this place and these people, whose goal one Friday night each month is to gather together, to eat and drink and introduce the American roommate of Lola to some specialty of this land. Last month it was cheese, ten kinds of cheese from the region of Asturias, and sidra, hard cider poured from a bottle held over the head into a glass held below the hip. Everyone marveled at how much I love sidra, and I couldn't tell them that it wasn't the taste at all, that the taste was neither here nor there, something one gets accustomed to, but rather it was the feeling. Drinking sidra, every time, my body turns into a sponge. Even before the alcohol can take hold, my shoulders broaden, my hips relax, I expand.

Or the month before, paella. Gazpacho. Red wines from Andalucia. Hard green olives stuffed with anchovies, fried sardines. And in months to come, Spanish tortillas, Spanish crepes, sangria. Deep-fried onions which Lola and I will spend an entire day stuffing with tuna fish. We will skip the month of January because Chus and Begoña and Pascual will be skiing in France, but as the spring moves on we will rearrange our schedules, plan and cajole and set aside the time because the time will be moving more quickly and this will be our way of marking it. Our way of making sure it doesn't get ahead of us, of measuring the months by the stacks of dishes in the sink, by the number of people we squeeze around the dining room table.

As the liquid cools, it thickens. I sip and kiss, drawing my lips together and slowly apart. Syrup builds on the rim of my cup, on all the cups and on all the mouths glistening in the candlelight. Begoña rests an arm on Pascual's knees, Lola strokes Virginia's hair, Chus leans back, legs extended beneath the table, hands clasped across his chest. We are full.

My thoughts rise and fall, bobbing through months and moments, coming to rest finally at the darkening end of a cold day last week. I was walking the northern edge of the Parque de San Francisco where the kiosks selling Christmas wares made me homesick for something I couldn't identify, something I've never even had. The bag on my shoulder was heavy, my coat was heavy as well, though not particularly warm, and I felt small within my skin, aware that with each step I took things rattled loose inside me. And then, miraculously, a new kiosk appeared up ahead, on the corner of the park. An older woman dressed in a blue coat gestured toward the setting sun, toward the mountains where she'd collected the chestnuts, and I nodded as she rolled a piece of newspaper into a cone, filled it, took the 150 pesetas I handed her. Chestnuts! I nearly burst out laughing, walking slowly and then more quickly, with no destination in mind. One by one I extracted them, pulled away the hulls, held the warm flesh on my tongue. I walked for a long time, delighting in the texture and the taste, in the practicality of the newspaper and my good fortune.

Now, as I settle into the fullness, I think it is for this that I travel, for this that I sold all my belongings and took off for a place I didn't know. These moments, walking through a park eating chestnuts, sitting at this table where by now no one is speaking, are why I have liked myself in Spain more than I have ever liked myself before. I am less encumbered here, more receptive to experience. And more appreciative of the texture of daily life. Which includes these people. My God, look how beautiful they are, how generous and happy. And this room, with the artwork, the photographs and paintings made by Chus and all of his artist friends. And the table itself. Look at this table! Plates and glasses and cups and candles and crumbs and rings of wine, the stains of consummation. My eyes close. I see my own blood, pressing against my skin, pulsing.

And later, after the second cupful, after the flush has receded, after Virginia has become bored with watching and begun to draw pictures of Papa Noël on a sketch pad belonging to Chus, after Pilar and Alberto have located the full moon over the city from the windows of the front room and described it to the rest of us who cannot move, I turn to Lola.

Years later, when I have not heard from Lola for a long, long time, I will have periodic dreams about her, wild, grief-stricken dreams from which I will wake sobbing. In my subconscious she will become an emblem of loss, of what we give up when we travel, what we leave behind. But now, half-way through my year of living in her apartment, Lola simply *is*, every day.

She is thirty-three. She is beautiful. She is quiet, graceful, present. When something delights her she smiles with her whole body, and when something makes her angry or sad she speaks more quickly than I can follow. She is the connective tissue here, the person most responsible for this particular group of people coming together. From the day I moved in, after answering Lola's advertisement for a bedroom to rent—to a foreign graduate student, preferably—she has shared her friends with me.

We are shy with each other sometimes, polite and careful about the intertwining of our lives in such a small space. But at other times, after an evening with friends, Lola's friends from the newspaper or my friends from the English department, after some beer and then whiskey and then cognac, we walk along the cobbled streets of the old section of town, past the lighted cathedral, through the empty fish market, arm in arm the way Spanish women do.

Lola's best friend is also named Lola, so that I've taken to distinguishing them as "my Lola" and "the other Lola." When I see Pilar or Begoña on the street they sometimes say, Lola was here just minutes ago—*your* Lola.

One day months ago I came home and found my Lola sitting on the couch, pale. This was before the language got inside me, before I stopped wrestling with individual words, and although I knew that what she was telling me was very serious, I didn't understand exactly what it was. She said, someone called you today, a man with a very unusual name. She said, placing her hand in the middle of her chest: *hearing that name affected me.*

Now, her eyes are focused on the table, but she is listening to Isabel, nodding in agreement about the problem of Papa Noël, the increasing commercialization of Christmas in this country. She sees me watching, smiles and flushes. What I understand now, now that I understand, is this: four years ago, the love of Lola's life, a man with a very unusual name, died in a helicopter crash in the mountains east of Oviedo. He was a rescue worker, searching for a young boy who had wandered off a trail on a very cold day. I have heard the story in bits and pieces, from various people on various occasions, and mostly I force myself not to think about it because when I think about it I can't breathe.

I have seen photographs, heard details. They were magic together. The first time he saw her, in the psychology department office where she was a student worker, he walked right up and kissed her full on the lips, then left without saying a word. A week later he came back and a week after that he showed up at her apartment with a pan of chicken he had baked. He was married, and by then Lola knew it and refused to let him in. So he walked across the street to a pay phone, called her up and said, "You don't have to become involved with me, but you do have to eat this chicken because I made it for you. And you will love it." And she did. And shortly after, he left his wife and moved in with Lola in the kind of move that rarely happens in these situations, and for four years they were magic until he fell out of the sky and died.

I want to ask Chus to light the fire again, to stir the names and repeat the incantation. I want to drink again from the first cup and feel its magic, its hope, its eternal buoyancy eternally veering toward loss.

And later, after Isabel leaves with the sleepy Virginia, after the circle shrinks and we have each put on a sweater or wrapped a blanket around our shoulders in this ancient, heatless building, after the conversation has turned to work and the clock moves toward two, Chus ladles out a third helping to each of us. We clutch our cups, lukewarm now, in both hands and raise them toward we know not what. May the evil spirits be banished, says Chus, humming again to mock his priestly self.

It is December 21, the beginning of winter, the night of a full moon. I know that in seven days I will ride a bus to Madrid to meet the man I love, the man who is coming to visit me from New York. I know that in seven days I will hold my breath waiting to see him, and that when he leaves two weeks later I will hold my breath again, against the riskiness of this long separation. But I do not know that months later, after a series of angry phone calls and pleading letters, I will sit heartbroken in a crowded movie theater with Lola by my side. When a man on screen dies in a car accident, Lola will begin to cry and will lean over to whisper harshly that at least the man I love is alive, at least I can see him again if I choose to. And she will be right about the simplicity of things, and also wrong, and I will hold her hand until the lights come on.

In the spring that is yet to come, on a night that will be hotter than it should be, Lola and I will ride down Calle Argüelles and see Chus leaning against a dark building, pleading with a small blond woman who sobs and slaps her palms against the stone wall. Lola will slow the car until Chus looks toward us and then she will speed up and say, "Poor Chus. Life is hard," and we will never mention it again. I will think then and always after of his face tonight, of the smile and the secrets and the way his throat moves as he hums, begging in the wordless way we all must for the spirits to be kind.

Three Pokes of a Thistle

Naomi Shihab Nye

Hiding Inside the Good Girl

"She has the devil inside her," said my first report card from first grade. I walked home slowly, holding it out from my body, a thistle, a thorn, to my mother, who read the inside, then the note on the back. She cried mightily, heaves of underground rivers, we stood looking deep into the earth as water rushed by.

I didn't know who he was.

One day I'd smashed John's nose on the pencil sharpener and broken it. Stood in the cloakroom smelling the rust of coats. I said No. No thank you. I already read that and it's not a very good story. Jane doesn't do much. I want the spider who talks. The family of little women and their thousand days. No. What I had for breakfast is a secret. I didn't want to tell them I ate dried apricots. I listened to their lineage of eggs. I listened to the bacon crackle in everyone else's pail. Thank you.

What shall we do, what shall we do? Please, I beg you. Our pajamas were flying from the line, waists pinned, their legs fat with fabulous air. My mother peeled beets, her fingers stained deep red. She was bleeding dinner for us. She was getting up and lying down.

Once I came home from school in the middle of the day in a taxi. School gave me a stomachache. I rode in the front passenger seat. It would be expensive. My mother stood at the screen door peering out, my baby brother perched on her hip. She wore an apron. The taxi pulled up in front of the blue mailbox I viewed as an animal across from our house—his opening mouth. Right before I climbed out, another car hit the taxi hard from behind so my mother saw me fly from the front seat to the back. Her mouth wide open, the baby dangling from her like fringe. She came toward us running. I climbed up onto the ledge inside the back window to examine the wreckage. The taxi driver's visored cap had blown out the window. He was shaking his head side to side as if he had water in his ears.

You, you, look what a stomachache gets you. Whiplash.
The doctor felt my neck.

Later I sat on the front steps staring at the spot where it had happened. What about that other driver? He cried when the policeman arrived. He was an old man coming to mail a letter. I was incidental to the scene, but it couldn't have happened without me. *If you had just stayed where you belonged....* My classmates sealed into their desks laboring over pages of subtraction, while out in the world, cars were banging together. Yellow roses opened slowly on a bush beside my step. I was thinking how everything looked from far away.

Then I was old. A hundred years before I found it, Mark Twain inscribed the front of his first-edition leatherbound book, "BE GOOD—AND YOU WILL BE LONE-SOME." In black ink, with a flourish. He signed his name. My friend had the book in a box in her attic and did not know. It was from her mother's collection. I carried it down the stairs, trembling. My friend said, "Do you think it is valuable?"

Language Barrier

Basically our father spoke English perfectly, though he still got his *b*s and *p*s mixed up. He had a gentle, deliberate way of choosing words. I could feel him reaching up into the air to find them. At night, he told us whimsical, curling "Joha" stories which hypnotized us to sleep. I especially liked the big cooking pan that gave birth to the little pan. My friend Marcia's father who grew up in the United States hardly talked. He built airplanes. I didn't think I would want to fly in anything he made. When Marcia asked him a question, he grunted a kind of pig sound. He sank his face into the paper. My father spilled out musical lines, a horizon of graceful buildings standing beside one another in a distant city. You could imagine people living inside one of my father's words.

He said a few things to us in Arabic—fragrant syllables after we ate, blessings when he hugged us. He hugged us all the time. He said, "I love you" all the time. But I didn't learn how to say "Thank you" in Arabic till I was fourteen, which struck me, even then, as a preposterous omission.

Marcia's father seemed tired. He had seven children because he was a Catholic, Marcia said. I didn't get it. Marcia's mother threw away the leftovers from their table after dinner. My mother carefully wrapped the last little mound of mashed potato inside waxed paper. We'd eat it later.

I felt comfortable in the world of so many different people. Their voices floated around the neighborhood like pollen. On the next block, French-Canadians made blueberry pie. I wanted a slice. It is true that a girl knocked on our door one day and asked to "see the Arab," but I was not insulted. I was mystified. Who?

Sometimes Marcia and I slept together on our screened-in back porch, or in a big green tent in her yard. She was easy to scare. I said the giant harvest moon was coming to eat her and she hid under her pillow. She told me spider stories. We had fun trading little terrors.

When I was almost ready to move away, Marcia and I stood in Dade Park together one last time. I said good-bye to the swings and benches and wooden seesaws with chipped red paint. Two bigger boys rode up on bicycles and circled us. We'd never seen them before. One of them asked if we knew how to do the F-word. I had no idea what they were talking about. Marcia said she knew, but wouldn't tell me. The boys circled the basketball courts, eyeing us strangely. Walking home with Marcia, I felt almost glad to be moving away from her. She stuck her chest out. She said, "Did you ever wish someone would touch you in a private place?"

I looked in the big dictionary at home. Hundreds of F-words I didn't know reached their hands out so it took a long time. And I asked my mother, whose face was so smooth and beautiful and filled with sadness because nothing was quite as good as it could be.

She didn't know either.

Bra Strap

It felt like a taunt, the elastic strap of Karen's bra visible beneath her white blouse in front of me in fifth grade. I saw it even before Douglas snapped it. Who did she think she was, growing older without me?

I spent the night with her one Saturday. In the bathtub together, we splashed and soaped, jingling our talk of teachers, boys, and holidays. But my eyes were on her chest, the great pale fruits growing there. Already they mounded toward stems.

She caught me looking and said, "So?" Sighing, as if she were already tired. Said, "In my family they grow early." Downstairs her bosomy mother stacked cups in a high old cabinet that smelled of grandmother's hair. I could hear her clinking. In my family they barely grew at all. I had been proud of my mother's boyishness, her lithe trunk and straight legs.

Now I couldn't stop thinking about it: what was there, what wasn't there. The mounds on the fronts of certain dolls with candy-coated names. One by one, watching the backs of my friends' blouses, I saw them all fall under the spell. I begged my mother, who said, "For what? Just to be like everybody else?"

Pausing near the underwear displays at Famous and Barr, I asked to be measured, sizing up boxes. "Training Bra"—what were we in training for?

When Louise fell off her front porch and a stake went all the way through her, I heard teachers whispering, "Hope this doesn't ruin her for the future." We discussed the word "impaled." What future? The mysteries of ovaries had not yet been explained. Little factories for eggs. Little secret nests. On the day we saw the film, I didn't like it. If that was what the future meant, I didn't want it anymore. As I was staring out the window afterwards, my mouth tasted like pennies, my throat closed up. The leaves on the trees blurred together so they could carry me.

I sat on a swivel chair practicing handwritings. The backwards slant, the loopy up-and-down. Who would I ever be? My mother was inside the lawyer's office signing papers about the business. That waiting room, with its dull wooden side tables and gloomy magazines, had absolutely nothing to do with me. Never for a second was I drawn toward the world of the dreary professional. I would be a violinist with the Zurich symphony. I would play percussion in a traveling band. I would bake zucchini muffins in Yarmouth, Nova Scotia.

In the car traveling slowly home under a thick gray sky, I worked up courage. Rain, rain, the intimacy of cars. At a stoplight, staring hard at my mother, I asked, "What really happens between men and women to make babies?"

She jumped as if I'd thrown ice at her.

"Not *that!* Not *now!*" From red to green, the light, the light. "There is *oh so much you do not know.*"

It was all she ever told me. The weight of my ignorance pressed upon us both.

Later she slipped me a book, *Little Me, Big Me.* One of the more incomprehensible documents of any childhood: "When a man and a woman love one another enough, he puts his arms around her and part of him goes into part of her and the greatness of their love for one another causes this to feel pleasurable."

On my twelfth birthday, my father came home with our first tape recorder. My mother produced a bouquet of shiny boxes, including a long, slim one. My Lutheran grandparents sat neatly on the couch as the heavy reels wound up our words. "Do you like it? Is it just what you've been waiting for?"

They wanted me to hold it up to my body, the way I would when I put it on. My mother shushing, "Oh, I guess it's private!"

Later the tape would play someone's giggles in the background. My brother? Or the gangs of little girl angels that congregate around our heads, chanting, "Don't grow up, don't grow up!"

I never liked wearing it as much as I did thinking about it.

The Best Cake Made Both of Us Sad

Chris Offutt

Last night's rain has drained the air of all but blue. I am outside listening to the singing of birds. The Daniel Boone National Forest begins at the tip of my fingertips, while civilization spreads the opposite way. My sons are in the house playing a board game, one I played with my brother as a child, but one of the boys gets mad and the laughter stops. As the sun rises high, the heat douses the singing of the birds.

I am left soundless—feeling as if I should enter the house and settle the kids or enter the woods and revive the birds. Instead, I remain marooned in the shade. Today is that rare day when I'm content to sit in the sun and straddle the boundaries of my life.

Earlier this morning, I watched my children sleep. Their bodies lay in such abandon, sprawled across the sheet, a testament to the safety they feel at home. I kiss their cheeks, knowing that they will never remember it, but hoping that the ghost of my kiss will carry throughout their days. The children cheer me up and give me light. Sometimes I lie beside their warmth and worry about my future life after they leave home. Where will I find moments of joy? Who will make me smile and hug me tight? How will I live in a house with no laughter? Perhaps it will be like the woods in winter—occasional visits from the birds who sing briefly and alone.

Last night I talked to Arthur on the phone. He tells me he is lonely. His friends are dead; he's outlived them all. He is back-up man at his temple in order to make a quorum for a minyan, and he sees some people then. They are all retired. They look at their lives and examine what they've done with them. One man says, I've made a million dollars. Another says, I've made two. Someone else has a yacht and a place in Florida. Arthur claims none of these. He says that he is shrinking.

The cabinet doors of his kitchen no longer bang the top of his head. He spent years walking into the doors from his blind side, then getting angry at his wife for leaving them open. At last, he says, old age has made him safe from himself in the kitchen. His body is drawing up, shriveling in advance of death. As he becomes smaller, so does his world, the places he goes—a deli, his backyard, a bakery.

Yesterday at the bakery, a woman cut line in front of him, but he let it go. Another woman did the same thing, and he said that he was there first, and the clerk apologized. She hadn't seen him standing there. Good thing, Arthur says to me, that she didn't say I was short.

I laugh because this is a reference to his having once knocked a young man to the floor of a bank for calling him short. It occurred 10 years ago, the day before a visit to Rita and me in Iowa. He was running late. He was nervous about the flight. He told the story with shame and humility, but secret pride. At age 70, he could still take care of himself. Now, at 80, he cannot. The last time he tried to kneel, he was unable to rise. He cannot run and he cannot punch. His bowels treat him unfairly. Waw, he says, it's no fun, this getting old. No fun at all.

The key to understanding Arthur is knowing something of myself. I can never be truly happy because I mourn everything in advance—the wilting of flowers before they bloom, children leaving home, the end of each season while still at its apex. I enjoy the sunniest of days while bemoaning that there are not more of them. The same is true of food and sex. Every meal is the finest, which means there will never be another. The last time I made love was the best ever. All further sex will be downhill.

Arthur never thinks something is the best, but that it might be a little better. If he brings home the finest cake from the bakery, he worries that there was one more tasty that he didn't get. I, on the other hand, worry that there will never be a cake as good. The best cake in the house always makes us sad.

Quite simply, Arthur is adept at surviving rather than living. He knows how to get through a situation. He knows how to circumvent, to tolerate, to withstand, to compromise, to accept. He knows how to hope. He knows how to suffer. He knows how to try. It's the living that he has trouble with, the same as me.

He and I both live in the moment, but Arthur looks at the future and I at the past. Perhaps this is why we enjoy each other's company—an unlikely match surely—an 80-year-old Polish Jew and a 40-year-old Kentucky hillbilly. We recognize in each other what we crave for ourselves. My exuberance for the best is quickly replaced by a sense of loss. What he has lost makes him always on the lookout for what will be better.

On the phone last night, he was lonely and tired. He is becoming one of the last survivors of his community of Holocaust survivors. One by one his extended family died. After 60 years, he still misses his brother. Irene's condition requires his constant care. She cannot stand from a chair or roll over in bed without help. He has not made a million dollars, designed great buildings, and doesn't own a yacht. He's not sure what he's done with his life.

I get pissed—we are always getting pissed at each other—and I shout into the phone. You have a successful marriage to one woman all your life. You have two daughters who love you. Your sons-in-law work hard. You have three grand-sons who adore you. That is the definition of success, Arthur. Most people don't have any of that. You have it all.

There is a silence on the other end of the phone. He is sitting in his chair in a dim room in Queens, a man who never in his life expected such an outcome— alive at 80 across the sea from home, listening to a gentile son-in-law shout praise in a foreign language. Before the war, he was both a boxer and a pianist. His hands are enormous, and he dreamed of being an architect.

Into the silence, I say, to hell with the yacht.

What's wrong with a yacht, he says immediately. You don't want a yacht? Take your family on the ocean. Hire a captain and a cook and lady to massage your back.

Look, I say, if I were you, I'd look back on your life with satisfaction. You've done a lot. You're an ethical man and your family loves you. All except one thing—you're short.

You had to say it! He yells. You son of a bitch, you had to say it.

But he is laughing, the first time in days, and I know that is partly why he called. I have done my duty. He now wants to hang up the phone, still chuckling. I have restored his dignity with a grave insult. He's still alive, one of the gang, able to take a good joke. Goodbye, sonny, he says. Goodbye.

The conversation has saddened me. I walk through the house to find my own family. My boys grin expectantly when I enter the room. I look at each face and wait for them to make me laugh.

Animal Allies

Brenda Peterson

"My imaginary friend really lived once," the teenage girl began, head bent, her fingers twisting her long red hair. She stood in the circle of other adolescents gathered in my Seattle Arts and Lectures storytelling class at the summer Seattle Academy. Here were kids from all over the city—every color and class, all strangers one to another. Over the next two weeks we would become a fierce tribe, telling our own and our tribe's story. Our first assignment was to introduce our imaginary friends from childhood. This shy fourteen-year-old girl, Sarah, had struck me on the first day because she always sat next to me, as if under my wing, and though her freckles and stylish clothes suggested she was a popular girl, her demeanor showed the detachment of someone deeply preoccupied. She never met my eye, nor did she join in the first few days of storytelling when the ten boys and four girls were regaling one another with futuristic characters called Shiva and Darshon, Masters of the Universe. So far the story lines we'd imagined were more Pac-Man than drama. After the first two days I counted a legion of characters killed off in intergalactic battle. The settings for all these stories portrayed the earth as an environmental wasteland, a ruined shell hardly shelter to anything animal or human. One of the girls called herself Nero the White Wolf and wandered the blackened tundra howling her powerful despair; another girl was a unicorn whose horn always told the truth. All the stories were full of plagues and nuclear wars—even though this is the generation that has witnessed the fall of the Berlin Wall, the end of the Cold War. Their imaginations have been shaped by a childhood story line that anticipates the end of this world.

After three days of stories set on an earth besieged by disease and barren of nature, I made a rule: No more characters or animals could die this first week. I asked if someone might imagine a living world, one that survives even our species.

It was on this third day of group storytelling that Sarah jumped into the circle and told her story:

"My imaginary friend is called Angel now because she's in heaven, but her real name was Katie," Sarah began. "She was my best friend from fourth to tenth grade. She had freckles like me and brown hair and more boyfriends—sometimes five at a time—because Katie said, 'I *like* to be confused!' She was a real sister too and we used to say we'd be friends for life. . . ." Sarah stopped, gave me a furtive glance and then gulped in a great breath of air like someone drowning, about to go down. Her eyes fixed inward, her voice dropped to a monotone. "Then one day last year, Katie and I were walking home from school and a red sports car came up behind us. Someone yelled, 'Hey, Katie!' She turned . . . and he blew her head off. A bullet grazed my skull, too, and I blacked out. When I woke up, Katie was gone, dead forever." Sarah stopped, stared down at her feet and murmured in that same terrible monotone, "Cops never found her murderer, case is closed."

All the kids shifted and took a deep breath, although Sarah herself was barely breathing at all. "Let's take some time to write," I told the kids and put on a cello concerto for them to listen to while they wrote. As they did their assignment, the kids glanced over surreptitiously at Sarah, who sat staring at her hands in her lap.

I did not know what to do with her story; she had offered it to a group of kids she had known but three days. It explained her self-imposed exile during lunch hours and while waiting for the bus. All I knew was that she'd brought this most important story of her life into the circle of storytellers and it could not be ignored as if *she* were a case to be closed. This story lived in her, would define and shape her young life. Because she had given it to us, we needed to witness and receive—and perhaps tell it back to her in the ancient tradition of tribal call and response.

"Listen," I told the group as the cello faded and they looked up from their work. "We're going to talk story the way they used to long ago when people sat around at night in circles just like this one. That was a time when we still listened to animals and trees and didn't think ourselves so alone in this world. Now we're going to carry out jungle justice and find Katie's killer. We'll call him before our tribe. All right? Who wants to begin the story?"

All the Shivas and Darshons and Masters of the Universe volunteered to be heroes on this quest. Nero the White Wolf asked to be a scout. Unicorn, with her truth-saving horn, was declared judge. Another character joined the hunt: Fish, whose translucent belly was a shining "soul mirror" that could reveal one's true nature to anyone who looked into it.

A fierce commander of this hunt was Rat, whose army of computerized comrades could read brain waves and call down lightning lasers as weapons. Rat began the questioning and performed the early detective work. Katie, speaking from beyond the earth, as Sarah put it, gave us other facts. We learned that two weeks before Katie's murder, one of her boyfriends was shot outside a restaurant by a man in the same red car—another drive-by death. So Sarah had not only seen her best friend killed at her side, but she had also walked out into a parking lot to find Katie leaning over her boyfriend's body. For Sarah, it had been two murders by age thirteen.

With the help of our myriad computer-character legions we determined that the murderer was a man named Carlos, a drug lord who used local gangs to deal cocaine. At a party Carlos has misinterpreted Katie's videotaping her friends dancing as witnessing a big drug deal. For that, Rat said, "This dude decides Katie's got to go down. So yo, man, he offs her without a second thought."

Bad dude, indeed, this Carlos. And who was going to play Carlos now that all the tribe knew his crime? I took on the role, and as I told my story I felt my face hardening into a contempt that carried me far away from these young pursuers, deep into the Amazon jungle where Rat and his own computer armies couldn't follow, where all their space-age equipment had to be shed until there was only hand-to-hand simple fate.

In the Amazon, the kids changed without effort, in an easy shape-shifting to their animal selves. Suddenly there were no more Masters of the Universe with intergalactic weapons—there was instead Jaguar and Snake, Fish and Pink Dolphin. There was powerful claw and all-knowing serpent, there was Fish who could grow big and small, and a dolphin whose sonar saw past the skin. We were now a tribe of animals, pawing, running, invisible in our jungle, eyes shining in the night, seeing Carlos as he canoed the mighty river, laughing because he did not know he had animals tracking him.

All through the story I'd kept my eye on Sarah who played the role of her dead friend. The detachment I'd first seen in her was in fact the deadness Sarah carried, the violence that had hollowed her out inside, the friend who haunted her imagination. But now her face was alive, responding to each animal's report of tracking Carlos. She hung on the words, looking suddenly very young, like a small girl eagerly awaiting her turn to enter the circling jump rope.

"I'm getting away from you," I said, snarling as I'd imagined Carlos would. I paddled my canoe and gave a harsh laugh, "I'll escape, easy!"

"No!" Sarah shouted. "Let *me* tell it!"

"Tell it!" her tribe shouted.

"Well, Carlos only thinks he's escaping," Sarah smiled, waving her hands. "He's escaped from so many he's harmed before. But I call out 'FISH!' And Fish comes. He swims alongside the canoe and grows bigger, bigger until at last Carlos turns and sees this HUGE river monster swimming right alongside him and that man is afraid because suddenly Fish turns his belly up to Carlos's face. Fish forces him to look into that soul mirror. Carlos sees everyone he's ever killed and all the people who loved them and got left behind. And Carlos sees Katie and me and what he's done to us. He sees everything and he knows his soul is black. And he really doesn't want to die now because he knows then he'll stare into his soul mirror forever. But Fish makes him keep looking until Carlos starts screaming he's sorry, he's so sorry. Then . . . Fish *eats* him!"

The animals roared and cawed and congratulated Sarah for calling Fish to mirror a murderer's soul before taking jungle justice. Class had ended, but no one wanted to leave. We wanted to stay in our jungle, stay within our animals—and so we did. I asked them to close their eyes and call their animals to accompany them home. I told them that some South American tribes believe that when you are born, an animal is born with you. This animal protects and lives alongside you even if it's far away in an Amazon jungle—it came into the world at the same time you did. And, I told them, it dies with you to guide you back into the spirit world.

The kids decided to go home and make animal masks, returning the next day wearing the faces of their chosen animal. When they came into class the next day it was as if we never left the Amazon. Someone dimmed the lights, there were drawings everywhere of jaguars and chimps and snakes. Elaborate masks had replaced the Masters of the Universe who began this tribal journey. We sat behind our masks in a circle with the lights low and there was an acute, alert energy running between us, as eyes met behind animal faces.

I realize that I, who grew up in the forest wild, who first memorized the earth with my hands, have every reason to feel this familiar animal resonance. But many of these teenagers have barely been in the woods; in fact, many inner-city kids are *afraid* of nature. They would not willingly sign up for an Outward Bound program or backpacking trek; they don't think about recycling in a world they believe already ruined and in their imaginations abandoned for intergalactic nomad futures. These kids are not environmentalists who worry about saving nature. And yet, when imagining an Amazon forest too thick for weapons to penetrate, too primitive for their futuristic Pac-Man battles, they return instinctively to their animal selves. These are animals they have only seen in zoos or on television, yet there is a profound identification, an ease of inhabiting another species that portends great hope for our own species's survival. Not because nature is "out there" to be saved or sanctioned, but because nature is *in* them. The ancient, green world has never left us though we have long ago left the forest.

What happens when we call upon our inner landscape to connect with the living rainforests still left in the natural world? I believe our imagination can be as mutually nurturing as an umbilical cord between our bodies and the planet. As we told our Amazon stories over the next week of class, gathered in a circle of animal masks, we could feel the rainforest growing in that sterile classroom. Lights low, surrounded by serpents, the jaguar clan, the elephants, I'd as often hear growls, hisses, and howls as words. Between this little classroom and the vast Amazon rainforest stretched a fine thread of story that grew thicker each day, capable of carrying our jungle meditations.

When Elephant stood in the circle and said simply, "My kind are dying out," there was outrage from the other animals.

"We'll stop those poachers!" cried Rat and Chimp. "We'll call Jaguar clan to protect you." And they did.

This protection is of a kind that reaches the other side of the world. Children's imagination is a primal force, just as strong as lobbying efforts and boycotts and endangered species acts. When children claim another species as not only their imaginary friend, but also as the animal within them—their ally—doesn't that change the outer world?

This class believes it to be so. They may be young, but their memories and alliances with the animals are very old. By telling their own animal stories they are practicing ecology at its most profound and healing level. Story as ecology—it's so simple, something we've forgotten. In our environmental wars the emphasis has been on saving species, not *becoming* them. We've fallen into an environmental fundamentalism that calls down hellfire and brimstone on the evil polluters and self-righteously struts about protecting other species as if we are gods who can save their souls.

But the animals' souls are not in our hands. Only our own souls are within our ken. It is our own spiritual relationship to animals that must evolve. Any change begins with imagining ourselves in a new way. And who has preserved their imaginations as a natural resource most deeply? Not adults, who so often have strip-mined their dreams and imagination for material dross. Those who sit behind the wheel of a Jaguar have probably forgotten the wild, black cat that first ran with them as children. Imagination is relegated to nighttime dreams, which are then dismissed in favor of "the real world." But children, like some adults, know that the real world stretches farther than what we can see—that's why they shift easily between visions of our tribal past and our future worlds. The limits of the adult world are there for these teenagers, but they still have a foot in the vast inner magic of childhood. It is this magical connection I called upon when I asked the kids to do the Dance of the Animals.

The day of the big dance I awoke with a sharp pain at my right eye. Seems my Siamese, who has always slept draped around my head, had stretched and his claw caught the corner of my eye. In the mirror I saw a two-inch scratch streaking from my eye like jungle make-up or a primitive face-painting. "The mark of the wildcat," the kids pronounced it when I walked into the dimly lit room to be met by a circle of familiar creatures. Never in ten years had my Siamese scratched my face. I took it as a sign that the dance began in his animal dream.

I put on my cobra mask and hissed a greeting to Chimp, Rat, Jaguar, and Unicorn. Keen eyes tracked me from behind colorful masks. I held up my rain stick which was also our talking stick and called the creatures one by one into the circle. "Sister Snake!" I called. "Begin the dance!"

Slowly, in rhythm to the deep, bell-like beat of my Northwest Native drum, each animal entered the circle and soon the dance sounded like this: Boom, step, twirl, and slither and stalk and snarl and chirp and caw, caw. Glide, glow, growl, and whistle and howl and shriek and trill and hiss, hiss. Each dance was distinct—from the undulating serpent on his belly, to the dainty high hoofing of Unicorn, from the syncopated stomps of Chimp on all-fours to Rat's covert jitterbug behind the stalking half-dark Jaguar. We danced, and the humid, lush jungle filled this room.

In that story line stretching between us and the Amazon, we connected with those animals and their spirits. And in return, we were complete—with animals as soul mirrors. We remembered who we were, by allowing the animals inside us to survive.

The dance is not over as long as we have our animal partners. When the kids left our last class, they still wore their masks fiercely. I was told that even on the bus they stayed deep in their animal character. I like to imagine those strong, young animals out there now in this wider jungle. I believe that Rat will survive the inner-city gangs; that Chimp will find his characteristic comedy even as his parents deal with divorce; I hope that Unicorn will always remember her mystical truth-telling horn. And as for Sarah who joined the Jaguar clan, elected as the first girl-leader over much mutinous boy-growling—Sarah knows the darkness she stalks and the nightmares that stalk her. She has animal eyes to see, to find even a murderer. Taking her catlike, graceful leave, she handed me a poem she'd written; it said "Now I can see in the dark" and was signed "Jaguar—Future Poet."

Virtually Romance
A Discourse on Love in the Information Age

Wendy Rawlings

> *In the* Atharvaveda *time is regarded as the generator of all things, including Brahman, and will be the source of their destruction.*
>
> —Dictionary of Philosophy and Religion

> *The key points of Netiquette serve a useful purpose: they keep the information flow efficient, civil, and comprehensible.*
>
> —Navigating the Internet with your Macintosh

> *Women take a haptic, holistic view of men.*
>
> —John Updike

In a computer store, out-of-season greeting cards tilting in their rickety racks, in a depressed Utah town east of Salt Lake City, I observe my companion, a writer visiting the university here for a week. I know him about as well as I know this depressed town. And yet already to look at him is as unbearable as it is to look away. The hands jammed in jeans pockets. Quizzical tilt of the head, this almost constant, the way dogs' heads cock when receiving sounds far out of human range. Listening, lips pressed together, a smile barely suppressed. Not "good features." Not "handsome." Only gesture, a premonition of touch.

It's no longer bearable. I look up at the ceiling. I can still hear him gently barraging the man behind the counter: "What's the economy like in this place?" "How do Anglos and Native Americans get along?" "What do people around here do for work?"

The ceiling. Quite unexpectedly in a shop so rundown that generations of black flies are living and dying in the front window, the ceiling is magnificent, ornate as an antebellum ballroom's. There should be a chandelier hanging from it. "Look," I tell him. Up his head tilts.

At Marion's Five and Dime Luncheonette we both order grilled cheese on white as everything else on the menu starts with Spam. Spam and beans. Spam and mashed potatoes. Spam on toast. It is at once understood that neither of us trusts meat byproduct shaped like the can it's packaged in, though as a child of a dual-career couple Spam and Mary Kitchen Hash were my dual-career dinner, a marriage made in aluminum. Looking elsewhere so as to observe something other than my companion sitting across the Formica-topped table from me, my eyes catch Elvis clocks, hips swinging with each tick: spam-spam-spam.

At the Protestant church on the Indian Reservation more generations of black flies live by stained glass and die on the carpet. "This time of day is the worst, with the sun," says the pastor, a man with denim shorts and braids to his waist. Cheapie pictures on the walls depict Jesus lugging the cross all over the place.

My companion, head cocked, is pointing out the window. "What's with that little model of the church?"

Out behind the church is a child-size facsimile of a church, ramshackle and littered with trash. The pastor shrugs. "We built that a few years ago for the kids. I keep meaning to repair it." Later, in the Indian burying ground, my companion tells me, "That's how they are about time." I find an unexpired state identification card on the ground. He shows me relics left at the gravestones: a Budweiser can, dirty one-eared porcelain bunnies, a tiny pile of fading green M&M's, a hank of hair tied to a stick.

"You looked up. That's great. I never look up," he says.

I've knocked him a little sideways. I too am out of my groove. Bad had been brewing between my live-in boyfriend and me, but now I've upped the ante. We are driving back from the Reservation to the city and I'm two hours later than I told my boyfriend I would be.

"When you're forty I'll be sixty. When you're fifty I'll be seventy. When you're seventy-five I'll be ninety-five." All this math and we haven't even touched each other yet. He of the gloomy algebra and moss growing on his antlers thinks he knows the kind of woman I am. The kind of woman he thinks I am: observant. Indeed I am observant; in fact, I am a deeply distracted and by the standards of late-twentieth-century capitalism shamefully unproductive woman. I have no husband or children to take care of, no yard to weed; I'm a dismal cook whose culinary forays are restricted to boiling freeze-dried Indian meals. By my own shaky algebra I spend sixty-five to seventy percent of an average day observing. And yet I looked up not because I was particularly curious about the ceiling but because I was worried he might catch me in an act of naked observation: staring. At what? At him.

He loves my hair, he confesses. My hair? He has been looking at me all day. I punctuate our kisses with little sighs out of range of human hearing. When I take off my glasses I don't hear as acutely. "I'm glad you can't see without your glasses," he says. He feels he's fat. Oh, Jesus. Vanity the cross we all lug. He might be fat but what would I care? I only care if I'm fat. This is the way women's lust works. On the counter in his hotel room sit two bags, up close I see without my glasses are Doritos and Twizzlers. "When you're seventy I'll be in an urn," he says. I think of Jack Nicholson and Helen Hunt, Warren Beatty and Annette Bening, Anthony Hopkins and any number of starlets. "I don't even think about your age," I say. The sort of thing young women are supposed to tell men worried about moss and math.

He's is town a week, and then he has to go back where he came from.

Cyberspace

From: Tully@aol.com
To: Wendy@aol.com
Subject: Re: Romance

In a message dated XX/XX/XX 02:18:31 EST, you write:
<< I knew I never should have allowed you to take off my underwear. . .>>

Sweetie, I don't mean to be critical, but you DO seem to have a slightly irrational attachment to your underwear, and a slightly exaggerated sense of your underwear's magical ability to ward off evil (or me). We'll have to work on this, perhaps get you a therapist . . .

Tempus Fugit

Virtual romance is a freeze-dried package of Saag Paneer. It is Saag Paneer, yes: by American standards an adventurous meal. It is not, say, chicken-flavored ramen noodles. It is not a can of Spam. And yet, when you slit the silver package open and pour its contents on a bed of basmati rice, there is the infinitely disappointing trace odor of whatever chemicals are used to preserve this food in freeze-dried form. A food facsimile. You feel you are eating a meal poured out of a Mylar balloon. If you keep a jar of chutney in the refrigerator you have, nonetheless, in a hundred and twenty shifts of Elvis's hips, a virtual Indian meal.

Cyberspace

From: Tully@aol.com
To: Wendy@aol.com
Subject: Re: Romance

It's amazing that we'll see each other so soon (given the distance) and it'll be nice to be together around Christmas. And then it won't be so long before it's your birthday. Shit—I really have to get off and get to work. But I wanted to tell you that everything's okay for December, that I am incredibly in love with you, that you will have to use a crowbar to get my arms off you when I see you (do you REALLY have to pee alone? do you really like being apart from me that much?).

Mostly Incommunicado, Tortola, British Virgin Islands

"Tortola" is a word that feels like food. "Tor-tolla!" my father exhorts in a bad Italian accent. My father, he of the moss rapidly accumulating on at least one antler, is recovering from an earlier fiasco alfresco with a cocktail at the Moorings boat charter clubhouse. He and my sister compete to see who will be the first to tie a maraschino cherry stem with their tongues. At four-thirty that morning, he warned my sister and me about not forgetting things, then misplaced the plane tickets and made us miss the flight. The tickets were in the car trunk the whole time, so we can make jokes about senility. *You'll be in an urn.* We are chartering a sailboat for five days, a Christmas trip my father has talked about for years.

At the dock he examines the boat's steering mechanism and finds a penny going green as the Statue of Liberty. "The wire's snapped," he says, spinning the steering wheel in futile circles. "They don't maintain these." *A marriage made in aluminum.* He and my mother have been divorced just over a year, my mother in menopause too high maintenance. Maraschino cherries prick in me a bright nostalgia for before divorce, the four of us at restaurants for seafood, "Shirley Temples for the girls."

My sister's popping Bonine to ward off even the idea of sickness. I keep thinking *home* instead of *sea*. It's my computer I miss out here. Black women have provisioned our boat, named *Karen Anne* as if it's a girlfriend you climb on. Over Triscuits and Cheez Wiz I feel guilty. I'm white and sailing, they're not and not. "Is there any Spam down there?" I call to my sister in the galley. No, she says, but nine cans of Coco Lopez. It takes three sips of a Painkiller before I taste it's rancid and spit.

At the topmost island, The Bitter End, as I am lovesick and hungerless, I can't abide the all-you-can-eat buffet ($32.50 per person). Instead I order drinks, three Painkillers at $6.25 each.

We return to our boat in the dinghy, me holding the hurricane lamp out in front. Up fish jump in the path the light casts. I shout for my father and sister to look.

Tully calls on our ship-to-shore phone from a blizzard in New York: Subzero. Ice storms. Power lines down. And me? Snorkeling. Rancid Coco Lopez. Too many Painkillers. My guide to Caribbean marine life says the brown fish I saw today, with prominent lips and what look like thick eyebrows, are called Jewfish. Racial slur? Trying to describe snorkeling to someone who has never snorkeled is like trying to describe making love to someone who has never loved.

Underneath the boat a barracuda spooks my sister, transfixed by swarms of white fish. "That's some sick rush hour," she says as she climbs up *Karen Anne*'s ladder. For dinner the next night we have the special, trigger fish.

Synchronous, Manhattan

Tully is vexed at the sight of my suntanned torso. At fifty, his flesh next to mine makes him think of death. At the hotel he unpacks not Doritos and Twizzlers but economy-sized bottles of Listerine and conditioner. Will we co-gargle? We'll only be here for two days, never mind that he of the mossy antlers might have more in the way of moss than hair. Why condition?

He gives me a Maxfield Parrish pop-up book, a naked nymphette bending on the cover. Can he imagine me at thirty an old Lolita? "You're not supposed to *read* it," he says. Chastened, I look and pull the pop-up tabs.

In bed he talks about the 1850s in England and the concept of the individual. As he speaks I'm already counting the hours until I'll have to be back on the plane to Utah: 32.5. *That's how they are about time.* I like the middle of the night because I can't guess the hour. "You're not supposed to *laugh* during sex," he says, chagrined beneath me. But always in the middle of it I think of a word like "spatula."

My sister works in pharmaceuticals. For Monday lunch we take a subway to meet her. I show Tully my T-shirt declared *The Zoloft Smile*. "You have to get me one of those," he says. A shirt or a smile? It is the late twentieth century; it is America. Maybe even a smile can be purchased. At the pharmaceutical company the wall in the reception area has water running down it, like nature. I say it's like nature the way smiling on Zoloft is like being happy. We are clearly out of place here. Water on a wall. He in a wool hat pulled to his eyebrows like a terrorist, me in a thrift store plaid man's winter jacket. All around us swirl people done up in suits and hair gel, including my sister. "Everyone says it's very feng-shui," she says of the water-on-wall.

At a sushi place we talk divorce. No very feng-shui. He's been divorced a year and thinks in the end the ones who might be worse fucked up than him are his kids. My gelled sister of divorced parents soothes him, trades some of her California rolls for his kappa maki. The Zoloft Smile. Maybe he will fall for her and dump ungelled me, Spam in jeans. *I too am out of groove.*

Naked, I am peeing in the hotel bathroom. Two and a half hours before I have to catch a shuttle to La Guardia. In my stomach is the start of a little sickness, not home not sea. I might cry. *Spatula. Spatula.* In the bedroom he's combing through newspaper advertisements for computers, as his hard drive is growing moss. *When you're forty I'll be sixty.* I'm on the toilet and in he walks with the newspaper, slips one hand between my legs and tastes his wet palm. Later, in a deli near Grand Central: "Did that shock you?" I admit it did. Across the table he is blinking at me, his eyes sea. *Up fish jump.*

And then I have to go back where I came from.

Tempus Fugit

Virtual romance is the runway at La Guardia airport. Planes more often than they should during takeoff career into the water surrounding the airport: the runway is too short. In the beginning you have every intention of taking off. Back in Utah, I think not of him but of his e-mails: *You will have to use a crowbar to get my arms off you when I see you again. Right now, any part of you I touched would burn me.*

Interim, Utah

I return to the apartment where my boyfriend and I still live with each other. *Spins the steering wheel in futile circles.* We'll get through Christmas together and I'll move out New Year's Day. We're splitting for good in a social season, everyone decking halls and coming all ye faithful except me, he the cuckolded. Will I go with him to his company Christmas party anyway? All around us swirl people done up in hair gel and holiday attire. "Are they all Mormon?" I ask, already woozy on wine. Of four conversations I have, two concern fertility issues. Of two men in couples concerned with fertility issues two are named Bryce, one with an "I." I want to say, "We have futility issues."

My boyfriend gets an award for on-time delivery: fifty bucks and a toy FedEx truck as big as my leg. He's on time, I'm thinking about moss and math. Several people comment on what a great couple we make. Does no one else see our futility issues? After the party we sit in our holiday attire on the kitchen floor and drink Painkillers made with rum I got from Cane Garden Bay. Grating the nutmeg I cut my finger.

"So you and grandpa really dig each other?" he asks. Is it possible for a heart to go rancid? "Do me a favor and don't go running in to check your e-mail in your underwear," he says. We walk together with our drinks from one end of the apartment to another. Feeble box elder bugs, refugees from summer, make cameo appearances on the windowsills. He smears them with his hand.

"I waited eight years to live together, then two more after you moved in. You never talked," I say. He shrugs, nonplussed by my calculations. "Irish people don't talk." We're standing on the balcony, me shivering in velvet, him with his ubiquitous pack of smokes. It's my computer I miss.

Cyberspace

From: Tully@aol.com
To: Wendy@aol.com
Subject: Re: Romance

In a message dated XX/XX/XX 13:53:44 EST, you write:
<<You know, to me it's just an organ that for the most part all I do is WIPE.>>

You know, sweetie, there are ways of writing about this that can imbue it with epic romance—and you choose these words? For example, I prefer to think of it/you as the humid scabbard into which I will thrust my fiery sword! :)

Tempus Fugit

In what ways does a romance in cyberspace collapse the opposition between silence and speech? Between being there in person and not being there at all? Between saying and feeling? Online, we send and receive messages so quickly and so often that my typing (hurried, harried) and reading (hurried, harried) of messages feels like feeling itself, like ink spreading on cloth.

Cyberspace

From: Tully@aol.com
To: Wendy@aol.com
Subject: Re: Romance

You know I'm kidding, right? About the scabbard and the fiery sword?

Remote, Utah

Our landlord has promised me an apartment four blocks from our apartment. It's New Year's Eve, two hours until the year is new, eleven until I make my move. The two of us, each on our own sections of the sectional sofa, are watching Dick Clark's Rockin' Eve and drinking Painkillers. In between the bands people have volunteered to do what the host calls "the world's most dangerous stunts." *You will have to use a crowbar.* The evening's pièce de résistance will be a man in a truck dropped from a crane an absurd yet calculated number of feet. He's going to escape the truck before impact.

"A cat lives in the boiler room of that apartment," my landlord calls to tell me. (It's 10:37 P.M. on New Year's Eve.) "It's forced heat. Are you that allergic to cats?"

I'm that allergic. Cats give me a necklace of hives, just for starters. The landlord has an apartment I can rent in the building next door.

"Next door?"

My ex says he'll help me move my things across the courtyard. *The runway is too short.* On e-mail, Tully will want to know how far from the ex-boyfriend's door to mine. How far can I stretch sixty feet?

Cyberspace

From: Tully@aol.com
To: Wendy@aol.com
Subject: Re: pining

Anyway I am writing this in haste so you have something to read when you get up in the morning.

Adjacent, Utah

My ex has overnight guests. I have my computer. In my underwear I trip straight from sleep each morning, a beeline to online. *This time of day is the worst.* Sometimes there are no messages; sometimes the modem buzzes and halts like a dying fly. Sometimes in my underwear I hit my computer with the heel of my hand: virtual domestic violence.

The overnight guest's name is LaHoma. "What fucking kind of name is that?" I ask. He says Indian. "Indian Indian or Indian Native American?" "American Indian." I think of the pastor with braids to his waist. "So where did you meet this person?" "On my pick-up route." Pick-up route! "How old is she?" She's twenty-three.

Cyberspace

From: Tully@aol.com
To: Wendy@aol.com
Subject: Re: pining

In a message dated XX/XX/XX 14:50:02 EST, you write:
<< It's okay that you've abandoned me; I have a call in to my therapist and she says the Zoloft prescription will be ready this afternoon. Meanwhile, I'm testing my shower rod to see if it can hold a 120 lb. woman >>

Okay okay I am trying to race out of here but I got all your messages just now finally and want to let you know I haven't abandoned you . . .

Tempus Fugit

Virtual romance, the heart's bulimia. You fill and fill and fill on words, and yet it is the necessary silences that absent themselves. "When I look down, I miss all the good stuff," a woman on the radio sings, "when I look up, I just trip over things." *The ceiling is magnificent.*

Cyberspace

From: Tully@aol.com
To: Wendy@aol.com
Subject: Re: lonely online

Sweetheart:
What was I doing? I was trying to catch up with my life. I was going to write you last night but I couldn't get online (AOL is sometimes packed). I think of you about every three minutes.

Abiding, Utah

"What if we get married?" my ex says. We are sitting on his kitchen floor with an almost empty magnum of cheapie Chardonnay. "Is that a proposal?" I ask. *A marriage made.* "What if it is?" On his bulletin board, postcards depicting the British Virgin Islands and Palm Springs. "Who went to Palm Springs?" I ask. "LaHoma." "Why are you asking me to get married?" I ask. "I'm not asking you to get married, I'm saying what if we get married." *The Irish don't talk.* Drunk, I climb back into our old bed with him and go to sleep. In the middle of the night we wake together, groggy and hellbent for water. "That whole proposal thing probably wasn't a good idea," he says. We're in the dark kitchen, trading swigs out of his bottled water. *A virtual proposal.* "No," I say. "Even though you still love me in some sad and belated way," he says. *Me pricked bright.* I recognize his words. "That's from my e-mails."

"I know," he says. "I read them all."

Retreat, Utah

In my economy-sized box of Q-Tips, I find a plastic calling card worth ten free minutes of long distance phone conversation: an excuse to call Tully midday, a break with protocol. But bending the rules isn't always welcome: "He *read* them all?" (Emphasis on *read*.) "He read them *all*?" (Emphasis on *all*.). He's been violated, he says.

Cyberspace

From: Tully@aol.com
To: Wendy@aol.com
Subject: Re: hello (again)

For whatever reason I've been drifting farther and farther out of that zone of passion that drove us at first.

How to Purchase a Personal Computer

Midtown, Computerland—Used computers are cheap, but also a risk. They have the marks of other people's labor: a faded shift key, scuffmarks, some other small but intolerable shoddiness. We wandered through the store in our frayed wool coats, him in his terrorist hat, our noses cold, neither of us able to pay proper attention. *I just trip over things.* He, the potential computer buyer, was making an attempt to put aside our romance for a moment so he could make his purchase. The sales clerks, all men, seemed to have the same disinterested and elite-sounding accent. *Indian Indian or Indian Native American?* Tully got one man to set up some laptops so he could try them. THIS IS A NICE LITTLE MACHINE. I CAN TYPE VERY QUICKLY, he typed very quickly. I stood beside him, hands jammed in my pockets. Secretly I was watching his face. I LOVE YOU WENDY, he typed. Secretly I was watching his face.

A Guide to Snorkeling in the British Virgin Islands

Common sense will serve you as well in the Caribbean as it does on Nantucket or Catalina. The classic rule around water remains: Don't go alone. Diving with someone of equal ability makes it more fun.

—Adventuring in the Caribbean

Snorkelers are advised to wear long-sleeved shirts and drawstring pants while in the water in order to protect their skin from sunburn and coral scrapes: "Remember that if you get hurt on coral, you have also injured the coral's own delicate protoplasm." And yet I cannot bring myself to empty my mailbox of the one hundred and sixty-seven messages he sent. *There is the infinitely disappointing trace odor.* If they were letters at least I could build a fire and, as lovers have for centuries, burn them. *I'll be in an urn.* The messages scroll up each time I log onto my account. *Right now, any part of you I touched would burn me.*

Would I like them better if they were a thousand white fish? A thousand bits of shredded paper? I see myself drifting still in bright water, my arms loose and weightless, surrounded by white swarms. Thousands of them. We never touch.

reflective

Celebrating Creation

Chet Raymo

Even the sparrow finds a home, and the swallow a nest, where she rears her brood beside thy altars.

Psalm 84:3

Late last summer, in the west of Ireland, I spent a night in the Gallarus Oratory, a tiny seventh-century church of unmortared stone. It is the oldest intact building in Ireland, and one of the oldest in Europe. The oratory is about the size of a one-car garage, in the shape of an overturned boat. It has a narrow entrance at the front and a single tiny window at the rear, both open to the elements. Even during the day one needs a flashlight to explore the interior.

I can't say exactly why I was there, or why I intended to sit up all night, sleeplessly, in that dark space. I had been thinking about skepticism and prayer, and I wanted to experience something of whatever it was that inspired Irish monks to seek out these rough hermitages perched on the edge of Europe, or—as they imagined—the edge of eternity. They were pilgrims of the Absolute, seeking their God in a raw, ecstatic encounter with stone, wind, sea, and sky.

The Gallarus Oratory is something of a tourist mecca, but at night the place is isolated and dark, far from human habitation. From the door of the oratory, one looks down a sloping mile of fields to the twinkling lights of the village of Ballydavid on Smerwick Harbor.

The sun had long set when I arrived, although at that latitude in summer the twilight never quite fades from the northern horizon. It was a moonless night, ablaze with stars, Jupiter brightest of all. Meteors occasionally streaked the sky, and satellites cruised more stately orbits. Inside, I snuggled into a back corner of the oratory, tucked my knees under my chin, and waited. I could see nothing but the starlit outline of the door, not even my hand in front of my face. The silence was broken only by the low swish of my own breath.

As the hours passed, I began to feel a presence, a powerful sensation of something or someone sharing that empty darkness. I am not a mystical person, but I knew that I was not alone, and I could imagine those hermit monks of the seventh century sharing the same intense conviction of "someone in the room." At last, I was spooked to the point that I abandoned my interior corner and went outside.

A night of exceptional clarity! Stars spilling into the sea. And in the north, as if as a reward for my lonely vigil, the aurora borealis danced toward the zenith. How can I describe what I saw? Rays of silver light streaming up from the sea, as if from some enchanted Oz just over the horizon, shimmering columns of fairy radiance. As I watched from the doorway of oratory, I remembered something the nineteenth-century explorer Charles Francis Hall wrote about watching the aurora from the Arctic: "My first thought was, 'Among the gods there is none like unto Thee, O Lord; neither are there any works like unto thy works!' . . . We looked, we SAW, we TREMBLED."

Hall knew he was watching a natural physical phenomenon, not a miracle, but his reaction suggests the power of the aurora even on a mind trained in the methods of science. What then did the monks of Gallarus think of the aurora, 1,300 years ago, at a time when the supernatural was the explanation of choice for exceptional phenomena? Stepping out from the inky darkness of their stone chapel, they must surely have felt that the shimmering columns of light were somehow meant for them alone, a sign or a revelation, an answer to their prayers.

We have left the age of miracles behind, but not, I trust, our sense of wonder. Our quest for encounter with the Absolute goes arm in arm with our search for answers. We are pilgrim scientists, perched on the edge of eternity, curious and attentive. The Gallarus Oratory was built for prayer, at a time when the world was universally thought to be charged with the active spirit of a personal God: Every stone might be moved by incantation, every zephyr blew good or ill; springs flowed or dried up at the deity's whim; lights danced in a predawn sky as a blessing or portent. Today, we know the lights are caused by electrons crashing down from the sun, igniting luminescence. But our response to the lights might still be one of prayerful attention, and they lead us, if we let them, into encounter with the Absolute.

Traditional religious faiths have three components: a shared cosmology (a story of the universe and our place in it), spirituality (personal response to the numinous), and liturgy (public expressions of celebration and gratitude, including rites of passage). The apparent antagonism of science and religion centers almost entirely on cosmology: What is the universe? Where did it come from? How does it work? What is the human self? What is our fate? Humans have always had answers to these questions. The answers have been embodied in stories—tribal myths, scriptures, church traditions. All of these stories derived from a raw experience of the creation, such as my experiences inside and outside of the Gallarus Oratory. All of them contain enduring wisdom. But as a reliable cosmological component of religious faith they have been superseded by what cultural historian and Roman Catholic priest Thomas Berry calls the New Story—the scientific story of the world.

The New Story is the product of thousands of years of human curiosity, observation, experimentation, and creativity. It is an evolving story, not yet finished. Perhaps it will never be finished. It is a story that begins with an explosion from a seed of infinite energy. The seed expands and cools. Particles form, then atoms of hydrogen and helium. Stars and galaxies coalesce from swirling gas. Stars burn and explode, forging heavy elements—carbon, nitrogen, oxygen—and hurl them into space. New stars are born, with planets made of heavy elements. On one planet near a typical star in a typical galaxy life appears in the form of microscopic self-replicating ensembles of atoms. Life evolves, over billions of years, resulting in ever more complex organisms. Continents move. Seas rise and fall. The atmosphere changes. Millions of species of life appear and become extinct. Others adapt, survive, and spill out progeny. At last, human consciousness appears. One species experiences the ineffable and wonders what it means, and makes up stories—of invisible spirits who harbor in darkness, of gods who light up the sky in answer to our prayers—eventually making up the New Story.

The New Story has important advantages over all the stories that have gone before:

It works. It works so well that it has become the irreplaceable basis of technological civilization. We test the New Story in every way we can, in its particulars and in its totality. We build giant particle accelerating machines to see what happened in the first hot moments of the Big Bang. We put telescopes into space to look for the radiation of the primeval explosion. With spectroscopes and radiation detectors we analyze the composition of stars and galaxies and compare them to our theories for the origin of the world. Always and in every way we try to prove the story wrong. When the story fails, we change it.

It is a universal story. Although originally a product of Western culture, it has become the story of all educated peoples throughout the world; scientists of all cultures, religions, and political persuasions exchange ideas freely and apply the same criteria of verification and falsification. Like most children, I was taught that my story—Adam and Eve, angels, miracles, incarnation, heaven, hell, and all the rest—was the "true story," and that all others were false. Sometimes our so-called "true" stories gave us permission to hurt those who lived by other stories. The New Story, by its universality, helps put the old animosities behind us.

It is a story that emphasizes the connectedness of all people and all things. Some of the old stories, such as the one I was taught as a child, placed humankind outside of space and time, gifted us with unworldly spirit, and gave us dominion over the millions of Earth's other creatures. The New Story places us squarely in a cosmic unfolding of space and time, and teaches our biological affinity to all humanity. We are ephemeral beings, inextricably related to all of life, to the planet itself, and even to the lives of stars.

It is a story that asserts our responsibility for our own lives and the future of the planet. In the New Story, no omniscient deity intervenes at will in the creation, answers prayers, or leads all things to a predetermined end. We are on our own, in the immensity of creation, with an awesome responsibility to use our talents wisely.

It is a story that reveals a universe of unanticipated complexity, beauty, and dimension. The God revealed by the New Story is not the paltry personal projection of ourselves who attracted and bedeviled our ancestors. It is, in the words of the Jesuit theologian David Toolan, "the Unnamable One/Ancient of the Days of the mystics, of whom we can only speak negatively (not this, not that), a 'wholly other' hidden God of Glory," or in the felicitous phrase of novelist Nikos Kazantzakis, "the dread essence beyond logic."

We should treasure the ancient stories for the wisdom and values they contain. We should celebrate the creation in whatever poetic languages and rituals our traditional cultures have taught us. But only the New Story has the global authority to help us navigate the future. It is not the "true" story, but it is certainly the truest. Of all the stories that might provide the cosmological basis of contemporary religious feeling, it is the only one that has had its feet held to the fire of exacting experience.

The New Story informed my response to the dancing lights in the night sky at Gallarus. What I saw was not a portent or miracle, but rather nature's exquisite signature of the magnetic and material entanglement of Earth and sun.

As the sun brightened the eastern horizon and the last shreds of aurora faded, I was suddenly startled by a pair of swallows that began to dart in and out of the Gallarus Oratory, hunting insects on the wing. I followed them inside and discovered a nest with three chicks perched on a protruding stone just above the place I had been sitting. The mysterious presence I had felt so strongly in the darkness was not a god, nor spirit, nor succubus, nor demon, but the respirations and featherings of swallows.

Knowing Where You've Been

Robert L. Root, Jr.

The first afternoon. We head for the Blodgett Creek Trail. Our environmental writing workshop at the Teller Refuge takes up the mornings but leaves us the afternoons free, and the three of us are eager to get out into the Montana wilderness. We are midwestern flatlanders, all raised not far inland from the shores of the Great Lakes, though Ron has been a Montanan for nine years now. Waiting after lunch for someone who never shows up, we start out an hour later than we hoped. I drive the Refuge minivan and Linda navigates, directing me from Corvallis across the valley floor to Hamilton and into the foothills of the Bitterroot Mountains. Dirt roads take us gradually up out of pasture land into steep forest. We round a bend, cross Blodgett Creek, and park at the trailhead.

Blodgett Creek is swollen and foaming, a roar and blur of tumbling white water just beyond the trees along the trail. In mid-May western Montana is just beginning its second week of summer-like temperatures, and rapid snow melt generates swift, turbulent run-off. Farmers and ranchers in the Bitterroot Valley worry whether the supply of water will last the growing season.

We strangers, however, eagerly immerse ourselves in new terrain. We set off briskly from the trailhead and, in very little time, see canyon walls, sheer granite facing with jagged rims, emerge above the trees. The trail roughly parallels the creek, passing through narrow bands of ponderosa pine and larch that line its banks. Here the forest is hemmed in by the canyon's narrowness, its inhospitable granite walls, and thick layers of talus piled on the sides of the canyon floor. At a couple of places on the trail we skirt the limits of talus, looking up a forty-five degree angle across a vast slope of dark boulders that ends a third of the way up toward a sheer precipice. The canyon wall here is so solid and impervious that a channel-less white stream of snow melt merely slides down the stone face like hose water down a sidewalk.

We dawdle along the trail. Linda identifies the birds, Ron the flowers, trees, and shrubs; I can only nod appreciatively at each of their pronouncements, finding no rhetorical forms to point out in return. We stroll rather than hike, looking around us as we move. We pause to search for a winter wren or a varied thrush singing in the trees, to examine a ring of blue clematis or some alum root saxifrage rising from the mossy ground, to gaze at a bend in the creek where the overflow has created a calm backwater and the dark shape of a trout drifts through dapples of sunlight. At times we dance up the trail, straddling runoff, leaping from stone to stone, dry spot to damp spot, following the worn path of horses and hikers.

An hour into the walk conversation ebbs and we begin to hike more rapidly. The canyon floor widens and the trail veers away from the creek bed, still tracing the talus wall. Where the forest opens temporarily at a recent burn, Linda drops behind to write in her journal and return more slowly down the slope; Ron and I quicken our pace through the charred trees and flourishing ground cover. The rocky terrain demands more of our attention as we move. Ahead of us, some three miles up from the trailhead, a packbridge crosses the creek, and we set that milestone as our destination. We hike with uncertain urgency, knowing that soon we will have to start back to the workshop for evening events.

Sunday hikers coming down the trail greet us. We overtake a slow-moving family who tell us they have seen a moose three hundred yards back, close to the trail. The pack bridge is still perhaps half a mile ahead, but we turn back, searching the brush for the moose we had overlooked in our rush upward. When we find her, she is lying down behind a log, her long dark head raised just into our view, her large ears scanning the sounds around her. The trail is still on rocky ground, but the moose is twenty yards away amidst a floor of rich green grass spreading among widely-spaced Douglas firs from the slope to the creek. For a few minutes we stand silently, watching her ostentatiously ignore us. Turning back to find her has inadvertently been decisive. By unspoken agreement we hurry back down the trail.

Returning toward the trailhead, I see only the forest ahead of me and occasionally the craggy rim of the canyon emerging on either side. Soon we are in the trees again. I wonder how close we came to the pack bridge, what we might have seen of Blodgett Canyon as we looked back at the Bitterroot Valley crossing the creek, and I find my appetite for the mountains sharpened, not sated, by the hike.

"When you look back at where you have been," Norman Maclean writes, "it often seems as if you have never been there or even as if there were no such place." In his story "USFS 1919: The Logger, the Cook, and the Hole in the Sky," the narrator has paused at the top of a divide, reflecting on where he has been and where he is going. Where he has been is Idaho, at a U.S. Forest Service camp, and more particularly at a lookout tower on Grave Peak; where he is going is Hamilton, in Montana, on the other side of the Bitterroot Mountains, his summer job ended. The distance is thirty-four miles, "fourteen miles up and fourteen miles down with five or six miles still left to go." He intends to walk it in a single day.

Beginning in a mountain meadow he climbs toward gray cliffs that eventually will place him higher than the mountain goats he spots in the distance; along the way he spooks a bull moose on the trail. On the divide, after marking his own version of the state line in urine, he locates Grave Peak. "From the divide the mountain I had lived on was bronze sculpture. It was all shape with nothing on it, just nothing. It was just color and shape and sky." He muses, "So perhaps at a certain perspective what we leave behind is often wonderland, always different from what it was and generally more beautiful."

From the top of the divide, looking into Blodgett Canyon, he recognizes its glacial orgins. "Coming at me from almost straight below was a Jacob's ladder of switchbacks, rising out of what I later discovered geologists call a cirque but what to me looked like the original nest of a green coiled glacier." He plunges down the Montana side of the divide, cutting straight across the switchbacks, little avalanches following his path. From the bottom of the basin he follows Blodgett Creek to the mouth of the canyon and trudges the remaining five or six miles to Hamilton.

When I told a friend from Montana that I would be spending a week in the Bitterroot Valley, he referred me immediately to Maclean's story and urged me to hike in the canyon. On the flight west I read the story. Disappointed in its lack of detail about the canyon (it really isn't a hiking story, after all) and immediately aware that I wouldn't have time to trek the fourteen miles to Blodgett Pass, I nonetheless checked the trail in a Bitterroots guide and, before the plane had reached Montanan airspace, set myself that goal of reaching the pack bridge.

Now, as I came away from the canyon, pleased with my companions and energized by the experience of the trail, I realized that I was disappointed, and I struggled to figure out why. Perhaps it had to do with not reaching the pack bridge,—with failing to achieve a relatively simple destination—but I wasn't certain why that mattered. Perhaps I hoped to have looked around me and somehow recognized the canyon, discovered the distant switchbacks and the rim of the pass. Perhaps I had hoped that standing on the pack bridge would have placed me so I could see where I had been, where I could be going. While Linda and Ron talked in the van, I tried to remember the words to the children's song about the bear going over the mountain, "to see what he could see." I identified with that bear. As far as I had gone, I still hadn't come away with a sense of knowing where I had been.

The second afternoon. We mill around after the morning workshop, plans shifting, destinations uncertain, finally resolving to go back into the mountains, to another trail. Though eight of us are going, we are all "environmental writers" (by official designation of the Institute) and tend to go to wilderness for solitude, not companionship. At the trailhead, people plan to drop out or stay behind, and the progress up the Mill Creek Trail spreads us out and separates us. Some start out slowly and fall to the rear; others keep on far enough to separate themselves from those behind, then slow down to let those ahead go on without them.

Mill Creek is only a few miles north of Blodgett Creek, descending at the easternmost point of the promontory between Blodgett Canyon and the next canyon north. After a short stretch in open forest, the terrain is often rocky. The forest is dense and broad on either side of the stream, unrestrained by canyon walls. A mile or so along the trail we cross to the north side of the creek on a solid double-log bridge and find ourselves moving parallel to the creek but often away from its banks, intermittently but persistently climbing. Not far beyond the bridge the group is reduced to Ron, Jeff, and me. We begin to push ourselves to reach the falls a couple more miles ahead, making it harder on ourselves by talking about writing most of the way without slackening our pace.

For a little while we parallel sheer canyon walls but soon we are deep into the forest. The walking is easier than in Blodgett Canyon, the terrain more varied, the forest seemingly older, denser. Within a couple miles of the log bridge, past a large boulder and a big wooden sign, we enter the Selway-Bitterroot National Wilderness. Soon the trail steepens and repeatedly winds away from the creek until a final loop brings it closer again. The creek's continuous rumble becomes a roar. Through the trees we can see the foaming waters of the falls and follow the trail up to an opening in the forest near the top.

Beyond the clearing the ground rises sharply again and ahead of us the trail disappears back into forest, but this rounded hump of basalt is covered shallowly with only lichens, wildflowers, and low grasses. Near the creek nothing grows except for a few stunted pines; most of the rock is naked and exposed, shaved clean by plummeting snow melt. Upstream the forest closes in tightly on the creek bed; below the falls the creek is all foamy billows of whitewater slicing through towering forests of ponderosa pine and Douglas fir; across the stream, on the south bank, the trees are thick, impenetrable. Only on the north bank of the falls is the rock swept clean and the surface open to the sun.

We take our time surveying the falls, moving slowly up and down its rock face to consider it from above and below, all the while inundated by the sound of mountain water. As falls go this one is neither majestic nor exceptional, angling down sixty to eighty feet or so rather than plunging vertically from the lip of a precipice. Swollen with snow melt, its foam as white as the snowpack that feeds it, the creek plummets over rugged terraces and outcroppings. We feel its wild power and stand smiling in the spray and the sound, respectful of its reckless turbulence.

The roar makes conversation difficult but Jeff and Ron survey the plant life away from the brink and we each independently declare a desire to camp on the level ground across the clearing. Someone wonders where the trail goes, and I look longingly at the point where it reenters the forest and disappears. The wall of trees prevents us from knowing where we might have gone and, aware that we have overstayed, we turn back toward where we have been to head down the mountainside toward the trailhead and the rest of our party. Our retreat is so swift that I don't notice when I can no longer hear the thunder of the falls and our pace allows me no time to look back.

When I asked my friend from Montana about places to hike in the Bitterroot Valley, he looked thoughtful for a moment, shook his head, and said, "Well, as early as you're going, there'll be too much snow to bag a peak." I laughed and assured him that "bagging a peak" wasn't a priority with me. But the term tended to stay with me on the trip, especially as I trudged along the flat farm roads of the Teller Refuge where the snow-capped peaks of the Bitterroot Range punctuated the horizon. After our return from the Mill Creek Trail, when someone asked me later in the day if I had been "one of the *men* who had gone for distance" on the trail, I thought again about the concept of bagging a peak.

We'd come back to the Mill Creek Trailhead to find the van gone and a note promising that someone would return for us. No doubt we'd delayed people eager to get back to the Refuge, and those who'd stopped along the way had returned to the trailhead with a sense of accomplishment and completion far sooner than we had. If they had been waiting for us, we owed them apologies. But I really couldn't accept the implicit gender explanation for our approach to the hike—after all, I knew from reading their essays that some of the women in the Environmental Writing Institute had had far more arduous adventures than I was ever likely to attempt. The only peaks I've "bagged" not only have not been hard to reach but also were ascended for the view rather than for distance or height.

But the Mill Creek Falls hadn't been a peak, after all, and its distance had only been a few miles. Though I knew what *hadn't* moved me to reach the falls, I wasn't certain what *had,* or why it felt so good to have been there.

The final afternoon. The morning workshop over, the group disperses for various tours and activities. Ron, Valerie, and I meet Janine Benyus and her father, Doug, who both live in the Bitterroot Valley. Janine, whose *Northwoods Wildlife Guide* I value, has volunteered to take workshoppers hiking. Somehow I expect a leisurely excursion and don't bother to change out of sneakers. Although her plan had been to take us to either Blodgett or Mill Creek, when she learns that Ron and I have been to both, she opts for the Bear Creek Overlook Trail instead, a change from creek-bed habitat, a promise of a vista.

Janine drives the minivan to the trailhead, pointing out from the highway the shoulder of the mountain where the Bear Creek Overlook is located. We climb the foothills on back roads threading through pasture lands, then swing onto a twisting, narrow, shoulderless dirt road, an eighty-degree grade sloping away from it. In the front passenger seat my attention is divided between Janine's conversation and the slope we lean toward with every other lurch of the vehicle. Doug Benyus recounts hitting a patch of ice on otherwise dry road a few weeks earlier and plunging over the edge in a Toyota Four-Runner; luckily he had hit a tree a little ways past the edge and was able to back up the slope and continue down the road. Father and daughter tell of other switchback terrors as we ride, but Janine doesn't slow down. I tell myself she knows how to drive these roads better than I, and remind myself to sit in the back on the way down.

The trailhead is an open area on the side of the mountain, with the valley floor a couple thousand feet below, spread out in a gray haze not thick enough to obscure the distant outline of the Sapphire Mountains across the valley. We set out hiking easily through open forest. Lodgepole pines tower above us; the forest floor is carpeted with needles. The wide trail follows a series of switchbacks that take us rapidly up the mountainside with little need for the attentive footing that the creek trails demanded. The day is warm, the mountain breezes refreshing, and our progress consistent. We pause from time to time when Janine draws our attention to some element of the habitat—dwarf mistletoe sprouting from a limb of lodgepole pine, its seeds released by an inner "spring" that fires it fifty feet into the forest, to stick to another tree or be transported on the feathers of the bird that triggered its release; the activity of pitch beetles that bore into pines and, through a symbiotic relationship with bacteria in their mouths and their own excavating, girdle a tree and plug its channels of sap until the tree dies; a blue grouse spooked by Doug Benyus's hound, Barney, fluttering out of reach into a spruce and perching, immobile, waiting for us to lose sight of her. The Benyuses instruct us through a genial symbiosis, feeding each other questions, volunteering each other's information.

Less than halfway up the trail we discover patches of snow across the path. The trees change to spruce and Douglas fir. We look for blazed tree trunks more frequently now, as the trail disappears beneath the snow for longer and longer stretches. Finally, an hour or so into the trail, we reach a turn of a switchback and see an unbroken field of snow stretching through the trees. Janine tells us that it will be mostly snow the rest of the way, and gives us the option of struggling up the slope or turning back and looking for a creekbed. Valerie votes for turning back. Ron and I make noises about not caring either way until the possibility of turning back becomes too real; then we admit to wanting to continue to the overlook. We have seen creek beds, we say, and Valerie urges us to go on while she meanders back.

We are all in tee-shirts, Janine and Ron in shorts, but are kept warm by exertion as we cross the snow. We slip with every step as it gives way beneath us. Often we find ourselves postholing across the snow, sinking in past our ankles, sometimes up to our knees. On separate occasions Janine and I each strike a pocket of air beneath the snow, where it has covered a fallen tree, and plunge in up to our crotches with one leg while the other slips across firmer footing. The icy granules of snow soak through my sneakers and socks and I grumble to myself about my lack of planning until I realize that my hiking boots too would have eventually succumbed to wetness.

It takes us longer than we hoped to reach the crest. The terrain opens up, the trees more stunted and sparse than at lower levels, the snow ranging in ever larger fields. Suddenly we emerge onto the base of a rocky ridge. The timbers of a collapsed line cabin or watch tower poke through a deep covering of empacked snow. Rising above the ridge is a barren crag with contorted shapes of scrub around its base; through the trees on the top of the ridge I look across at a snowy peak dotted with scruffy trees, extending another thousand feet or more above us. The way to the top of the crag is rough and tricky, along precipices and across barren, lichen-free basalt. The west side of our mountain is almost vertical, nearly devoid of plant life except for occasional pioneers jutting from scanty toe-holds in the cliff face. But from that exposed peninsula of rock the three valleys of Bear Creek open out to us.

Directly to the west the South Fork of Bear Creek runs down the center of the valley, lush and green and thickly carpeted with conifers. From where we stand we can see the mountains beyond the valley, the distant sources of Bear Creek's water. To the northwest is another valley, another fork of the creek, that we can trace glinting through the trees until it divides into two more streams, the Middle and North Forks, each descending its own valley. The trees thin out along the slopes of these valleys, turn darker the higher up they go, until they are only random silhouettes against ever-broadening snowfields. All the peaks around us are snow-covered, as must be the peak of the mountain upon whose shoulder we stand.

We are viewing classic glacial terrain. Empty white basins of snow identify cirques, the glacial bowls that will become Bryan Lake and Bear Lake by the end of summer. Above and around them are weathered horns and aretes, the peaks that formed them and the ridges that hold them in place; the valleys extending from the cirques take the wide U-shape of the glaciers that carved them. Directly below us the merged forks of Bear Creek produce a wide foaming cataract rushing snow melt and glacial debris toward the outwash plains that form part of the foothills.

Janine tells us that, when the Pacific plate pushed under the North American plate, it raised the mountains of the Idaho Batholith to a point where the mountaintops became unstable and slid off to the east, creating the broad level plain that would become the Bitterroot Valley (itself later scoured by glaciers) and ending up as the Sapphire Mountains. From this crag we can see beyond the Sapphires to spires of the Garnet Range and the Continental Divide near Anaconda. We can also see a long way toward the beginning of time.

I slowly scan it all with my binoculars. I know that I could sit for hours minutely surveying those valleys and still not feel I had taken them in. Nonetheless I feel myself smiling all the while, feel myself stirred and moved by everything around me. It isn't just the beauty, though it is transcendently beautiful, and it certainly isn't the distance, because everything around us reminds us of how much further we could go. It isn't how far at all but how deep.

That's it. That's the epiphany that dispells my uncertainty about my motives on these hikes. That's what I've been pursuing after all. I simply need to go as deeply into wilderness as it takes before the wilderness comes into me. Sometimes you need to go as deeply as possible where you've never been to reach a place you recognize at once, recognize entirely. That's where I find myself in the Bitterroots.

We stand there a while longer, reveling in arrival. When we finally, reluctantly, turn to descend, I don't need to look back to know where I've been.

How to Play

Arthur Saltzman

SORRY

Invented by Parker Brothers in 1934, Sorry has kept its tenure because it speaks to something fundamental in modern consciousness. Because of the several treacheries and disappointments we suffer during adulthood—indeed, because adulthood is itself a treachery and a disappointment—we feel that some compensation is due us. No compensation arrives, though we keep the phone clear and check the mail daily, so we decide to settle for an explanation. No explanation is forthcoming, though we keep strict accounts and submit to physical exams, so we hold out for an apology. It is our line in the sand, which we constantly patrol. Behind our sundry, sundered psychic parapets, we scan the city's sad expanses, the office horizon, and the weathered driveway for signs of its approach. For life owes us that much, of that much we are certain at least, at the very least, our ration of regret. Our Sorry.

Try it out on your spouse some day. Statistics dictate that, greeted first thing in the morning by an apology, most people will respond with "That's okay" or "Forget it" or "Just don't let it happen again." Even if you have no idea what wrong you're lamenting, more likely than not, your significant other has been waiting to have *something* righted. Some hide their gripes better than others, but you'd be hard-pressed to find someone who isn't steaming over *some* slight or another. If you listen closely in the middle of the night, if you pry beneath your wife's sighs or your husband's snores, you will hear a faint sound as if an aerosol can were leaking beneath the sheets. Deep within, we are all bottled hiss. Yeats famously bemoaned that the ceremony of innocence is lost in this decadent century, but do not underestimate the importance of the ceremony of *guilt* for getting a loving couple through the day. The ad line for *Love Story*—"Love means never having to say you're sorry"—does not hold up under duress. On the contrary, love requires that we swaddle one another in apologies, not necessarily because we did the bruising, but because we know how much it hurts.

The rules of Sorry are clearer to someone who has been weaned on the competition from Milton Bradley, Chutes and Ladders, a game which demands no capacity whatsoever from its players apart from a passing familiarity with counting to six. ("An exciting game of ups and downs for little people," Chutes and Ladders gently grazes the gross realities of Sorry, but it is no more edifying than when elementary school kids, visiting their fathers at work, are shunted off to the outer office to play with the adding machine while the dads deal behind closed doors.) From another perspective, because strategy is positively irrelevant to Chutes and Ladders—a plastic spinner, when it does not stick, is the sole arbiter of Fate—it is perhaps a less purely existential experience than Sorry, which by virtue of its more complicated set of choices and forking paths better sustains the illusion that one participates in the formation of his destiny.

In Sorry, each player is parsed into four pawns, whose goal, like the climax of a Thanksgiving television special, is to reassemble at Home. (This is a subtle but welcome dose of wholesomeness for kids who, all too often these days when both parents tend to hold jobs, must fend for themselves when they return from school.) The pawns are launched upon the board's squared streets, a marvel of exacting regulation and civil engineering. A pawn may clamber over an opponent on its way to finishing its turn; if the number of spaces prescribed by the turn of the card lands the pawn on an opponent's square, the opponent must return to Start. How many corporate advancements and misfortunes afford such equilibrium and statistical sanity? A given business may grow lousy with vice presidents, but in Sorry no gain is achieved without a countervailing loss, and any promotion directed by the board necessitates a demotion somewhere else along the line. When a player is bumped, the bumper offers his "Sorry." Indeed, when a run of contrapuntal "sorrys" occurs, the game takes on the atmosphere of a vaudeville routine or rush hour on the subway, where, more reflexive than sincere, the "sorrys" likewise compound.

The bumper may choose among several tones of delivery to alert and assuage the bumped. Chief among these: the sheepish, the teasing, the confidential, the ironic, the humiliating, the vindicated. Players should also be alert to the Sorry Cards that turn up during the course of play. These are the most flagrant, and thus the most delicious, of trumps because they allow the fortunate recipient to select any one of his pawns which still nests in the Start Circle to take the place of any enemy pawn at whatever stage of its career, thereby returning the supplanted pawn to its own point of origin. The tactic recalls how the brash and unforgivably young executive whose ascent threatens the summit is exiled to the branch office in Terre Haute or how a screw-up son-in-law is sent back down to Sales. Only one brand of "Sorry" will suffice in this case: it should be brayed just inches behind the ear and rolled down its octave like Sisyphus's rock to drive home for the opponent his plummet. Oh, possibly he had navigated the subterranean Slide spaces and patiently, uncomplainingly abided by the game's geometry until his reward was but a brief corner away. Now, discharged to his humble beginnings, he must slink to the circle's edge, trying to avoid attention at the re-union, which unavoidably falls at the time he falls, and in sober isolation relive his moves and imagine no alternative at all.

The logic of Sorry is sudden and ruthless. It is a game of primary colors and first principles, in which successes and reversals strike like hawks. Paradoxically, then, the winner will be the player who has been most obsessively apologetic, for, like Shakespeare's Claudius, he agonizes over dozens of distressed lines, but he never relinquishes his hoard. The throne is its own justification, and he whose offense is rank may equivocate, disclaim, or confess, but he does not atone or relax his grip.

MONOPOLY

The choice of playing piece is crucial. The cannon and the race car are the most desirable of the motley options, and the makers recommend calling dibs the moment you agree to play. The cannon's fortitude (thin-barreled but undeniably phallic) and the race car's brisk resolve are clearly in keeping with the pursuit of capital. If those pieces have already been wrested, consider the ship or the cowboy on horseback. The ship's insinuations of opulence and class distinction are impressive enough to make up for its connotation of indolence, a trait against which the true monopolist must forever guard. The anachronistic cowboy is woefully out of his depths in the burgeoning metropolis, as his horse, stymied by modern traffic, bucks amongst the gleaming utilities and bunched hotels; however, as a longstanding embodiment of the American myth of intrepidness and self-reliance, the cowboy retains sufficient, viable charm. (The fact is not lost on the many corporations that employ cowboys in their advertising.) But it would be better to surrender the chance to be the Banker than have to identify oneself as a thimble when trying to collect rent. The thimble, the boot, the hat, the wheelbarrow, and the iron are all such humble commodities—made things, not their makers—and their objectification of subservience, their representation of the lower end of labor, indicates that the struggle has already been lost. As for the Scottie, its cuteness may enchant the youngest players, but it is hardly built for the dagger-and-claw rise to prominence. Perhaps a Horatio Alger could climb the ladder of success without putting down his dog, but for serious getting and spending, you will need undivided interests and both hands free.

One advantage of the disparate and seemingly unprincipled nature of the playing pieces is that as they are lost over time, markers from other games or, for that matter, any nearby bits of household jetsam may replace them without disturbing the contest. Should the cat abscond with the race car or baby brother gulp the boot, a rook may be recruited from a chess game or a piece of evidence from Clue—the stamped plastic coil of rope; the revolver, surprisingly substantial, like an ingot rolled between the fingers, the seductively supple lead pipe—and the game can continue without interruption. In contrast, come up a checker short, and whatever scab you attempt to press into service, be it a borrowed quarter, a slick backgammon disk, or an antacid tablet, will throw off the balanced arrays of red platoons versus black, scuttling your plans; similarly, once army soldiers are called in to cover for missing Uncle Wigglies or to shore up devastated forces in chess, you might as well junk the remains altogether. But Monopoly cannot be compromised, it can survive any work stoppage, epidemic, or on-site disaster.

The sole authenticating law of Monopoly is acquisition. If the Zen Buddhist, believing that everything is God, becomes more endowed by divinity with every molecule he absorbs, experiences, and consumes, the savvy Monopolist takes on the properties of the properties he obtains: weight, stature, prominence, the smug gravity of a Sidney Greenstreet. The secret of greed is that you amass to master. Practice buying farther, buying faster. Neither the regimental Euclidean traffic of play nor the enforced courtesy of waiting one's turn should distract the player from the only real goal of the game.

Nevertheless, you will encounter players who take other approaches to Monopoly, who abide by different rationales. A given player may cling to designs impenetrable to the rest. For instance, one may forsake all enterprises other than the railroads. He may fall desperately in love with Boardwalk and Park Place, to the extent that he makes ill-advised, even outrageous offers to add that pretentious pair to his portfolio. He may crave a satisfying color scheme at the expense of sound business dealings. In the rebellious spirit of the OuLiPo Group, he may sell off any avenue containing the letter "e." But such eccentric motives need not be understood to be defeated. In Monopoly, aesthetics cannot save you. While the superstitious player dithers and the sentimentalist strums guitar, to the ransacker go the spoils.

Although the conclusion of Monopoly is rather quickly determined—as in Restoration comedy, true quality quickly emerges in Monopoly; as in Restoration comedy, it is rewarded with purchasing power—the game may go on indefinitely, inevitable ends teased out to epic duration by the eventual winner. He may, like the purring villain of melodrama, toy with his prey, offering to take a few mortgaged properties off his hands or to loan a few stray bills to encourage him not to resign. Wealth can go stale apart from the manipulations that earned it, so, in the manner of grinning Errol Flynn flipping the dropped foil back to Basil Rathbone, one may urge a destitute opponent into persevering until he has spent himself entirely. In this way, one can be both the predator and the scavenger after the bleached remains, the gourmet who claims the virgin taste and the kid in the kitchen who steals back later to lick the bowl. The very imagination that established an empire is capable of figuring and financing entertainments that those hopelessly piling up debts to him may never appreciate.

Note: It is theoretically possible to cling to the bars of the prison that Milton Bradley based at the end of the lower-rent district. Rolling doubles will get a player out, of course, but the vicissitudes of the dice may never grant him a reprieve. Worse, after several turns of denied parole, he may come to depend on that cramped space for definition, and indeed, fear that he will no longer be able to recognize himself out on the streets. Such a player may disdain the offer of a GET OUT OF JAIL FREE card no matter how meager the price. It is an object lesson against hubris: even the budding entrepreneur may be stalemated by a

Bartleby. Rockefeller may be the guiding spirit of the game, but the potential for a parable from Kafka looms only a block beyond the cheerful blue sky above Connecticut Avenue, where loiterers may lose the thread of purpose and waste away, unredeemed.

CAREERS

Your first task is the most important one; in truth, it is the essential burden of the game. You must propose and chart your fate. It is like buying off the astrologer or transacting with a genie. You register for outcomes like a still unravish'd bride for china patterns. You parcel out your potential in stars, hearts, and dollar signs.

It is a complicated business, authoring your prospects before they bud. For example, you can plot to become rich, famous, and happy in equal measures. You can contract to be happier than you are rich and remain utterly anonymous in the bargain. You can stipulate your wish to be showered with renown and barely pay the bills. You can be completely yet unaccountably content. Thus Careers provides not only an introduction to the uncertainties of the job market but also a philosophical debate. Just how rigid are the divisions between wealth and fame? Can you realistically live on romance apart from financial support? Is pure happiness possible? Novices tend to shy away from this sort of rigorous self-evaluation and more or less equitably distribute their desires. The experienced player, however, recognizes that there are more opportunities to earn happiness points on the board and in the cards, whereas fame is fleeting and money is tight; so he optimistically relies on a steady stream of hearts and wagers on euphoria to come.

The number of available career tracks is necessarily limited, but they have been cunningly devised to furnish players as much variety, personal fulfillment, and upward mobility as might reasonably be expected. Certainly, the breadth of opportunity on display at least matches, if it does not actually exceed, what awaits the players beyond the boundaries of the board in postindustrial America. One may quibble about the absence of one or more careers that currently dominate the classifieds, such as computer programming, hotel and restaurant management, crime prevention, trucking, telephones sales, or inner-city social work; however, second guessing so fluid and unpredictable an economy as faces us today would force the manufacturers to produce a new version of the game every five years or so, and the extra expense would undoubtedly descend upon the consumer. To the game's credit, Careers emphasizes prudent investment and obliges every player to go through College, for a degree is a prerequisite for accomplishment in all of the job tracks on the board save Sports and Hollywood. Admittedly, this sometimes encourages impatient, starry-eyed players to bypass College and go directly after these chancier disciplines. (Still, Careers is infinitely more responsible to young players than Life, in which the whole point is to marry as quickly as possible, then to propagate until the car is full. Indeed, Life bestows cars upon its participants at the outset, so they never learn what it takes to earn them, much less to pay for insurance. Parents should be cautioned that their children should engage in Life only under their supervision, if at all.)

Depending on how you have defined your dreams, you may circulate endlessly within a given career, dutifully accumulating dividends—a dependable, if rather tedious, method—or, like a rich dilettante or a Kerouac devotee, you may see what doors the dice deliver you to, emboldened by the belief put forth by novelist John Barth that roads should be laid where people walk.

The game ends when one player achieves the aspirations he outlined for himself. One admonition: Careers is an exceptionally long game. Typically it is reserved for rainy Sundays when there is nothing but televised golf to compete with it. Nowadays, it is usually the youngest child who, denied access to the Internet, campaigns for Careers as a way of extending the length of time his siblings will have to tolerate him. So although it is possible in theory for the remaining players to continue to play, in practice they will not persist after the inferiority of their futures has been assured. In Edwin Arlington Robinson's poem "Richard Cory," the poor masses strove and sacrificed in the hope of someday imitating his excellence—"So on we worked, and waited for the light, / And went without the meat, and cursed the bread"—but the poem ends abruptly once news of Cory's suicide spreads. It can only be assumed that they have no reason and no way to go on. One can only speculate as to what acids burned beneath Richard Cory's elegant tailoring or upon what awful precipice success abandoned him. Was he never able to fill his heart flush? Or was he destroyed by a fatal allotment of stars?

Scrabble

It is merciless. It reveals too much. No other game is so charged with implication and prospects for shame. If your errant thumb topples the Jenga tower or fuddles the clump of Pick Up Sticks, nothing other than your dexterity is doubted; if you cannot make your Rube Goldberg variation operate in Mousetrap or maintain your fleet in Battleship, no negative resonance or scent of failure follows you. But Scrabble always indicts someone in the room. It masquerades as play, but don't be fooled: it is another test.

Let's say that rain washes out the concert in the park, or you forgot to reserve the theater tickets, or the one sensitive film showing at the local cineplex has suddenly been shown the gate. Consider miniature golf to salvage the date. There, all you need do is demonstrate that you recognize the irrelevance of the score to prove your maturity, which, in the effort to impress a partner, is an underrated trait. Beware of announcing strokes as they're taken, resist becoming arthritic about the rules, and grant mulligans with casual largesse. (You may have seen doomed couples wrangle at the water hazard or, worse, a woman deliberately duff her putt on the seventeenth, throwing the match to soothe her man's ego, which it took him six errant jabs to extract from the alligator's jaws on fifteen. Take heed.) But do not try to placate your date with a round of Scrabble. Imagine her enjoying a regular diet of natural morphemes and ready blends, snaring the x early and pinching q and u at once, while you get stuck with a line of uninterrupted, nearly pointless vowels, which reads like the howl of a comic book character. No attachment can prosper in the wake of a double-digit trouncing. Better to go childless, she'll realize, than connect with someone who answers her formidable *quake* with a pipsqueak *tin*, who responds to her exotic *exotic* with stuttered *its* and stubbed *toes*; or who, after she plays *banjo* with flair, can only pick *nits*. She lays her tiles intricately, articulately down like a Byzantine mosaicist, while you can't even make a *name* for yourself. Any complaint about bad luck will sound like a whine. And it goes without saying that the belle lettered competitor will not endear herself either. Vanquishment never did lead to healthy, mutually sustaining passions.

For those who brave the game nonetheless, there is another issue to be faced. If victory is what you're after, the most effective strategy is to play defensively. If you've earned any lead at all, you must try to block up the board, providing no outlet whatsoever for your opponent's tiles. Crush any possible linkage like a cigarette on the sidewalk. Make the other player swallow his consonants. Practice the gag rule, and shove the utterances back down his throat. If you know he holds a *u*-less *q*, tuck away any *u* you have or jam it into a useless corner of the board so no *q* can queue up behind it. Force him like a bee trapped in a jar to buzz over his fruitless *z*. After a painfully protracted game—in this predicament, your opponent will pore over the dictionary like a Dominican prowling for grace in the hope of finding some archaism or slang to release him—it's a good idea to have something to occupy you in the widening intervals between your turns. Looming or scowling only makes the game go on forever, and you might be moved to surrender despite your insurmountable lead just to bring these stalled revels to an end. Instead, you might trim the nails you never get to or reconcile your checkbook.

There is an alternative approach worth considering. It is collaborative. As a team you can try to build as monumental a score as possible. Agree to be Beaumont to his Fletcher, Watson to his Crick. Agree to share the glory whose glow you nurse together. Build each word so it trails as invitingly as a stripper's boa. Mount rich upon richer syllable like some extravagant dessert. Open up double- and triple-word spaces like mini-Bastilles for one another's joyful assault. There are more ways to win than to win, you know? This life is too short to be cramped and miserable. And too long.

Cloud Crossing

Scott Russell Sanders

Clouds are temporary creatures. So is the Milky Way, for that matter, if you take the long entropic view of things. I awake on a Saturday in mid-October with the ache of nightmares in my brain, as if I have strained a muscle in my head. Just a week before I turn thirty-three, just a month before my son turns one, I do not need physics or nightmares to remind me that we also are temporary creatures.

Baby Jesse is changing cloud-fast before my eyes. His perky voice begins pinning labels on dogs and bathtubs and sun. When I say, "Want to go for a walk?" on this morning that began with nightmares of entropy, he does not crawl towards me as he would have done only a few days ago. He tugs himself upright with the help of a chair, then staggers toward me like a refugee crossing the border, arms outstretched, crowing, "Wa! Wa!"

So I pack baby and water and graham crackers into the car, and drive thirty miles southeast of Eugene, Oregon, to a trailhead on Hardesty Mountain. There are several hiking paths to the top, ranging in length from one mile to six. I choose the shortest, because I will be carrying Jesse's twenty-two pounds on my back. I have not come here to labor, to be reminded of my hustling heart. I have come to watch clouds.

Markers on the logging road tell us when we drive up past 2,500 feet, then 2,750 and 3,000. Around 3,250 the Fiat noses through the first vapors, great wrinkled slabs of clouds that thicken on the windshield. In the back seat Jesse strains against his safety harness, his hands fisted on the window, hungry to get out there into that white stuff. I drive the last few hundred yards to the trailhead with lights on, in case we meet a car groping its way down the mountain.

Beside a wooden sign carved to announce HARDESTY MOUNTAIN TRAIL, I park the Fiat with its muzzle downhill, so we can coast back to the highway after our walk in case the weary machine refuses to start. I lean the backpack against the bumper and guide Jesse's excited feet through the leg-holes, one of his calves in each of my hands. "Wa! Wa!" he cries, and almost tips the pack over into the sorrel dust of the logging road. Shouldering the pack requires acrobatic balancing, to keep him from tumbling out while I snake my arms through the straps. Once safely aloft, assured of a ride, he jounces so hard in the seat that I stagger a few paces with the same drunken uncertainty he shows in his own walking.

Clouds embrace us. Far overhead, between the fretted crowns of the Douglas fir, I see hints of blue. Down here among the roots and matted needles, the air is mist. My beard soon grows damp; beads glisten on my eyelashes. A few yards along the trail a Forest Service board, with miniature roof to protect its messages, informs us we are at 3,600 feet and must hike to 4,237 in order to reach the top of Hardesty. Since I came to see the clouds, not to swim in them, I hope we are able to climb above them into that tantalizing blue.

On my back Jesse carries on a fierce indecipherable oration concerning the wonders of this ghostly forest. Giddy with being outside and aloft, he drums on my head, yanks fistfuls of my hair. Every trunk we pass tempts him more strongly than the apple tree could ever have tempted Eve and Adam. He lurches from side to side, outstretched fingers desperate to feel the bark. I pause at a mammoth stump to let him touch. Viewed up close, the bark looks like a contour map of the Badlands, an eroded landscape where you might expect to uncover fossils. While Jesse traces the awesome ridges and fissures, I squint to read another Forest Service sign. No motorized vehicles, it warns, and no pack animals.

I surely qualify as a pack animal. For long spells in my adult life, while moving house or humping rucksacks onto trains or hauling firewood, I have felt more like a donkey than anything else. I have felt most like a beast of burden when hauling my two children, first Eva and now Jesse. My neck and shoulders never forget their weight from one portage to another. And I realize that carrying Jesse up the mountain to see clouds is a penance as well as a pleasure—penance for the hours I have sat glaring at my typewriter while he scrabbled mewing outside my door, penance for the thousands of things my wife has not been able to do on account of my word mania, penance for all the countless times I have told daughter Eva "no, I can't; I am writing." I know the rangers did not have human beasts in mind when they posted their sign, yet I am content to be a pack animal, saddled with my crowing son.

As I resume walking, I feel a tug. Jesse snaps a chunk of bark from the stump and carries it with him, to examine at leisure. Beneath one of the rare cottonwoods I pick up a leathery golden leaf, which I hand over my shoulder to the baby, who clutches it by the stem and turns it slowly around, tickling his nose with the starpoints. The leaf is a wonder to him, and therefore also to me. Everything he notices, every pebble, every layered slab of bark, is renewed for me. Once I carried Eva outside, in the first spring of her life, and a gust of wind caught her full in the face. She blinked, and then gazed at the invisible breath as if it were a flight of angels streaming past. Holding her in the crook of my arm that day, I rediscovered wind.

Fascinated by his leaf, Jesse snuggles down in the pack and rides quietly. My heart begins to dance faster as the trail zigzags up the mountain through a series of switchbacks. Autumn has been dry in Oregon, so the dirt underfoot is powdery.

Someone has been along here inspecting mushrooms. The discarded ones litter the trail like blackening pancakes. Except for the path, worn raw by deer and hikers, the floor of the woods is covered with moss. Fallen wood is soon hidden by the creeping emerald carpet, the land burying its own dead. Limegreen moss clings fuzzily to the upright trunks and dangles in fluffy hanks from limbs, like freshly dyed wool hung out to dry. A wad of it caught in the fist squeezes down to nothing.

A lurch from the backpack tells me that Jesse has spied some new temptation in the forest. Craning around, I see his spidery little hands reaching for the sky. Then I also look up, and notice the shafts of light slanting down through the treetops. The light seems substantial, as if made of glass, like the rays of searchlights that carve up the night sky to celebrate a store's opening or a war's end. "Light," I say to Jesse. "Sunlight. We're almost above the clouds." Wherever the beams strike, they turn cobwebs into jeweled diagrams, bracelet limbs with rhinestones of dew. Cloud vapors turn to smoke.

The blue glimpsed between trees gradually thickens, turns solid, and we emerge onto a treeless stony ridge. Clear sky above, flotillas of clouds below, mountains humping their dark green backs as far as I can see. The sight of so many slick backs arching above the clouds reminds me of watching porpoises from a ship in the Gulf of Mexico. Vapors spiral up and down between cloud layers as if on escalators. Entire continents and hemispheres and galaxies of mist drift by. I sit on the trail with backpack propped against a stone ledge, to watch this migration.

No peace for meditation with an eleven-month-old on your back. An ache in my shoulders signals that Jesse, so near the ground, is leaning out of the pack to capture something. A pebble or beetle to swallow? A stick to gnaw? Moss, it turns out, an emerald hunk of it ripped from the rockface. "Moss," I tell him, as he rotates this treasure about three inches in front of his eyes. "Here, feel," and I stroke one of his palms across the velvety clump. He tugs the hand free and resumes his private exploration. This independence grows on him these days faster than his hair.

"Clouds," I tell him, pointing out into the gulf of air. Jesse glances up, sees only vagueness where I see a ballet of shapes, and so he resumes his scrutiny of the moss. "Not to eat," I warn him. When I check on him again half a minute later, the moss is half its former size and his lips are powdered with green. Nothing to do but hoist him out of the pack, dig what I can from his mouth, then plop him back in, meanwhile risking spilling both of us down the mountainside. A glance down the dizzying slope reminds me of my wife's warning, that I have no business climbing this mountain alone with a baby. She's right, of course. But guilt, like the grace of God, works in strange ways, and guilt drives me up here among the skittery rocks to watch clouds with my son.

"Let Daddy have it," I say, teasing the hunk of moss from his hand. "Have a stick, pretty stick." While he imprints the stick with the marks of his teeth, four above and two below, I spit on the underside of the moss and glue it back down to the rock. Grow, I urge it. Looking more closely at the rockface, I see that it is crumbling beneath roots and weather, sloughing away like old skin. The entire mountain is migrating, not so swiftly as the clouds, but just as surely, heading grain by grain to the sea.

Jesse seems to have acquired some of the mountain's mass as I stand upright again and hoist his full weight. With the stick he idly swats me on the ear.

The trail carries us through woods again, then up along a ridge to the clearing at the top of Hardesty Mountain. There is no dramatic feeling of expansiveness, as there is on some peaks, because here the view is divvied up into modest sweeps by Douglas firs, cottonwoods, great gangling heaps of briars. The forest has laid siege to the rocky crest, and will abolish the view altogether before Jesse is old enough to carry his own baby up here. For now, by moving from spot to spot on the summit, I can see in all directions. What I see mostly are a few thousand square miles of humpbacked mountains looming through the clouds. Once in Ohio I lived in a valley which the Army Corps of Engineers thought would make a convenient bed for a reservoir. So the Mahoning River was dammed, and as the waters backed up in that valley, covering everything but the highest ridges, drowning my childhood, they looked very much like these clouds poured among the mountains.

"Ba! Ba!" Jesse suddenly bellows, leaping in his saddle like a bronco rider.

Bath, I wonder? Bed? Bottle? Ball? He has been prolific of B-words lately, and their tail-ends are hard to tell apart. Ball, I finally decide, for there at the end of the arrow made by his arm is the moon, a chalky peachpit hanging down near the horizon. "Moon," I say.

"Ba! Ba!" he insists.

Let it stay a ball for a while, something to play catch with, roll across the linoleum. His sister's first sentence was, "There's the moon." Her second was, "Want it, Daddy." So began her astronomical yearnings, my astronomical failures. She has the itch for space flight in her, my daughter does. Jesse is still too much of a pup for me to say whether he has caught it.

We explore the mountaintop while the ocean of cloud gradually rises. There are charred rings from old campfires. In a sandy patch, red-painted bricks are laid in the shape of a letter A. Not large enough to be visible from airplanes. If Hardesty Mountain were in a story by Hawthorne, of course, I could use the scarlet A to accuse it of some vast geological harlotry. If this were a folklore mountain, I could explain the letter as an alphabetical inscription left by giants. But since this is no literary landscape, I decide that the bricks formed the foundation for some telescope or radio transmitter or other gizmo back in the days when this summit had a lookout tower.

Nearby is another remnant from those days, a square plank cover for a cistern. The boards are weathered to a silvery sheen, with rows of rustblackened nailheads marking the joints. Through a square opening at the center of the planks I catch a glint. Water? Still gathering here after all these years? Leaning over the hole, one boot on the brittle planks, I see that the glint is from a tin can. The cistern is choked with trash.

At the very peak, amid a jumble of rocks, we find nine concrete piers that once supported the fire tower. By squatting down beside one of those piers I can rest Jesse's weight on the concrete, and relieve the throb in my neck. I imagine the effort of hauling enough materials up this mountain to build a tower. Surely they used horses, or mules. Not men with backpacks. So what became of the tower when the Forest Service, graduated to spotter planes, no longer needed it? Did they pry out every nail and carry the boards back down again? A glance at the ground between my feet supplies the answer. Wedged among the rocks, where rains cannot wash them away, are chunks of glass, some of them an inch thick. I pick up one that resembles a tongue, about the size for a cocker spaniel. Another one, a wad of convolutions, might be a crystalline brain. Peering up through it at the sun, I see fracture lines and tiny bubbles. Frozen in the seams where one molten layer lapped onto another there are ashes. Of course they didn't dismantle the tower and lug its skeleton down the mountain. They waited for a windless day after a drenching rain and they burned it.

The spectacle fills me: the mountain peak like a great torch, a volcano, the tower heaving on its nine legs, the windows bursting from the heat, tumbling among the rocks, fusing into molten blobs, the glass taking on whatever shape it cooled against.

There should be nails. Looking closer I find them among the shards of glass, sixteen-penny nails mostly, what we called spikes when I was building houses. Each one is somber with rust, but perfectly straight, never having been pried from wood. I think of the men who drove those nails—the way sweat stung in their eyes, the way their forearms clenched with every stroke of the hammer—and I wonder if any of them were still around when the tower burned. The Geological Survey marker, a round lead disk driven into a rock beside one of the piers, is dated 1916. Most likely the tower already stood atop the mountain in that year. Most likely the builders are all dead by now.

So on its last day the Hardesty fire tower became a fire tower in earnest. Yesterday I read that two American physicists shared the Nobel Prize for discovering the background radiation left over from the Big Bang, which set our universe in motion some fifteen billion years ago. Some things last—not forever, of course, but for a long time—things like radiation, like bits of glass. I gather a few of the nails, some lumps of glass, a screw. Stuffing these shreds of evidence in my pocket, I discover the graham cracker in its wrapping of cellophane, and I realize I have not thought of Jesse for some minutes, have forgotten that he is riding me. That can mean only one thing. Sure enough, he is asleep, head scrunched down into the pack. Even while I peek at him over my shoulder he is changing, neurons hooking up secret connections in his brain, calcium swelling his bones as mud gathers in river deltas.

Smell warns me that the clouds have reached us. Looking out, the only peaks I can see are the Three Sisters, each of them a shade over 10,000 feet. Except for those peaks and the rocks where I stand, everything is cotton. There are no more clouds to watch, only Cloud, unanimous whiteness, an utter absence of shape. A panic seizes me—the same panic I used to feel as a child crossing the street when approaching cars seemed to have my name written on their grills.

Suddenly the morning's nightmare comes back to me: everything I know is chalked upon a blackboard, and, while I watch, a hand erases every last mark.

Terror drives me down the Hardesty trail, down through vapors that leach color from the ferns, past trees that are dissolving. Stumps and downed logs lose their shape, merge into the clouds. The last hundred yards of the trail I jog. Yet Jesse never wakes until I haul him out of the pack and wrestle him into the car harness. His bellowing defies the clouds, the creeping emptiness. I bribe him with sips of water, a graham cracker, a song. But nothing comforts him, or comforts me, as we drive down the seven graveled miles of logging road to the highway. There we sink into open space again. The clouds are a featureless gray overhead.

As soon as the wheels are ringing beneath us on the blacktop, Jesse's internal weather shifts, and he begins one of his calm babbling orations, contentedly munching his cracker. The thread of his voice slowly draws me out of the annihilating ocean of whiteness. "Moon," he is piping from the back seat, "moon, moon!"

Pliny and the Mountain Mouse

Reg Saner

Dim though his brain may be, the marmot feels winter will come soon. And long. Longer than any of his previous twelve. From each of these, gaunt after seven or more months of hibernation in a rocky burrow, he has wakened; to at once waddle forth, to rummage spring snow for juicy alpine tundra plants, to mate, to sun, now and then to frolic with others in his chummy colony, and—properly fattened—to reenter the burrow: again to sleep away winter.

His "language" of gesture and squeaks is enormously older than words; but no European language names even the continent this particular marmot lives on. His region of high rocks hasn't yet been discovered by Old World tongues, though one day it will be called "colorado" by men speaking a version of Latin. That his home among granite chunks sits twelve thousand feet in the air, with superb mountain views on three sides, the marmot-brain translates to *always,* and *always* to *is.*

Even for this marmot, whose sense of history isn't wider than body fat and the sun's present height, today's rise and set of sky is numbered: August 24, A.D. 79.

You and I aren't here yet. At such altitude, nobody is. In A.D. 79, "nobody" is still only Indians. "Somebody" is only a marmot. Cool wind, blowing lightly out of late summer, licks his pelt. Opulent tufts of cinnamon fur lift along the plump back, slur a moment, subside. Because in the warmish afternoon, his ridgeline is only just dappled by the fast blue shadows of cloud-faces that mythologies copy, this marmot suns. He lies full-stretch on a rock slab. To stir himself overmuch would burn off precious fat his busy incisors have nibbled all the brief tundra summer to acquire, so he moves only his head, in those quick, darting glances small animals learn from their instructors the foxes, the coyotes, the eagles.

Close cousin to groundhogs and woodchucks, the high-country *Marmota fla-viventris,* or yellow-bellied kind, often relies on talus-piles of granite to provide fortresslike burrows only a bear or wolverine could dilapidate. Such hideaways protect the numerous offspring, five or six to a litter, which by summer's end are full grown.

Does the marmot breed to defeat predators, or do they prey on his colony to defeat his fast breeding? The answer is part of that circle whose opposites create each other; the molecular keys in the blood, the living shapes taken by time. A ravenous hawk; a slightly ludicrous bag of fat fur. Appetites that have learned how to repeat themselves. To what end? None that any living creature—now or to come—ever will know. To be. Each to do its kind.

Seven thousand miles to the east, in the Roman resort town of Herculaneum, guests leaving a dinner party find their way home through moonlit, sultry, sea-level air; air that thickens to an indigo blur across the Neapolitan bay toward the naval base at Misenum. There, sweating out the dog days of August—even at night—sits Pliny the Elder, a science writer whose tireless goose quill nibbles away at the creamy blankness on a fresh vellum. Pliny is himself fat as butter, and sweats as if he were melting, but he is as usual hard at it well before dawn, an omnivore of other men's books, which—he frankly admits—his own writing feeds on, just as his compulsive quill-nib feeds on blank vellum like a tiny animal storing up fame.

Among stones of a continent Pliny never heard of, the marmot has eaten back his lost bulk hardly a day too soon, and has almost finished lining his burrow with tundra grasses gathered for stuffing into the sleeping chamber as insulation and nest. Food will be body fat, however much his summer's nibbling has managed to accrue. And high-country autumn comes early. He knows it not as a name but a time when his world begins entering more into shadow. *If* the oncoming winter is neither too deep nor too long, his body fat will suffice.

During hard winters, however, dormancy proves a risky survival device. One marmot in five either freezes outright or starves. Among the small mercies of nature, on this twenty-fourth day of Augustus, is this particular marmot's blindness to his future. Breeze tousling his glossy pelt doesn't tell what it hears: that the oncoming season is coming to kill him, turn him to stone. And to quench the others sharing the family burrow.

Heat haze of southern Italy, moon-silvered. Pliny sweats, dips his quill into an inkhorn, and shares the same ignorance.

Just now, however, his scientific compulsion spurs him to update earlier pages of his already voluminous *Natural History.* Pliny is inserting some new facts about marmots, which he calls Alpine mice; "Some people say they form a chain and let themselves down into their cave that way, male and female alternately holding the next creature's tail by the teeth. One, lying on its back, hugs a bundle of grass and is hauled in by the others. Consequently at this season their backs show marks of rubbing."

Pliny's view of human life is rather gloomy; mankind as he knows it staggers along from misery to fresh misery, ruin to ruin. But the natural world! As inexhaustible as fascinating. "Some people say" may sound, he is fully aware, hardly better than gossip; yet nature is so prodigal of oddities that one's wildest guess may prove too tame. Like the haymaking marmot his pen has just described, Pliny's habit of reaping truth from old books and storing it up in his own year-upon-year scribbling, book after book, rules his waking hours so compulsively he hardly spares time to bathe, much less to ask himself, "Why?" Nor will he ever.

He never will, because what neither Pliny-the-nature-writer nor his friends across the bay in Herculaneum and Stabiae foresee is, simply, "Nature": in a few hours the trim, vineyarded summit of Vesuvius will blow sky high. In a few hours, Pliny's concern for those friends and his scientific curiosity will combine to strangle him. Soon, on the undiscovered continent of which Pliny knows nothing, a particular "Alpine mouse" will waddle into his burrow, plug the entrance with small stones and hay, then begin a winter trance no summer can waken.

The same incurable yen that draws Pliny unaware toward his suffocation saves his nephew. Before setting sail across the Bay of Naples for his fatal lesson in volcanology, the uncle invites Pliny the Younger—an eighteen-year-old—to come along if he wants. In aftertimes, by then an author himself, the nephew will recall, "To this invitation I answered that I'd rather continue studying. Besides, as it happened, my uncle had assigned me an essay to write." Writer's itch runs in the family.

At twelve thousand feet along an unknown continental divide, the night of twenty-fourth Augustus opens with snow crystals flying past; ice migrations of white flies that sting like salt. Meanwhile, along the Vesuvian shores it is finally morning. All night a hailstorm of pumice has scorched the roofs of Stabiae, piling up, drifting. A cinder snow that smokes. Roof beams crack and collapse, house walls totter.

By the seashore Pliny the Elder gulps at the air, supported between two slaves who lay him down on a scrap of sailcloth. He calls for cold water, drinks it, flops back. By now volcanic ash has begun its steady, floating fall. It descends soundlessly. Panicked Romans scatter the stuff as they run, stumble, collapse. Lightly, the ash begins to clothe each fallen body. In a few days it will smother the town. Years hence, in a reminiscent mood Pliny the Younger will sit—obese as his uncle—pushing a quill across vellum: "Three mornings later his body was found on the spot, intact . . . more like a man asleep than dead."

Three mornings later it is evening in another country, whose mountain sun has just set. Lofty ridgelines looking down into their own lakes see that sunset dismantled. Summer-plump, backside ruddied by alpenglow, the marmot stands hindlegged atop his rock, forepaws snugged against chest-fur, nose whiskers twitching, brown eyes staring east. He gives a reedy squeak. Answered by another . . . then another. A marmot "harem" and colony, a dozen in all, talking to themselves. They've harvested tundra plants, almost enough. How hard they've worked their worn pelts show: the narrow squeeze to and fro since midsummer, carrying cut grasses past snug entrance rocks and deep into the burrow, has scraped their back-fur haggard.

A trained and patient ear, or a marmot's, could identify as many as six distinctive variants on the shrill calls that led ancient Alpine people to nickname these animals "whistlers": Calls of "Eaglehawk!" Calls of "My rock, not yours!" Calls of "Fox!" Calls of "Love *me*! Love *me*! Love *me*!" Calls of "Wingflown! Fox-gone!" No wonder their silly, piping squeaks this evening are almost musical. After a gestation of about a month, the summer's young have reached full size of six to ten pounds in just weeks. Only the last of the haymaking remains. Abruptly the east-squinting marmot, boss male of the harem, falls silent. Up out of the distant, alluvial, proto-Coloradan plain floats a great fullness, a moon pale as winter; pale as a sun made of snow.

We can be here now. It's our turn . . . to be, and be curious. We know all about Pompeii, Stabiae; know Herculaneum too was buried. Oh yes, volcanic detritus enclosed many of the dead so perfectly that—in modern times, once Pliny's contemporaries had, as it were, evaporated—plaster casts could be made of their living absences. Lime-white, like snowmen. Startlingly "us," therefore touching. Theoretically. Anyhow, we ourselves avoid erupting volcanoes.

And, yes, it is poignant—in theory—to think of a marmot family in its burrow, like a banked fire; each furry curl asleep, nose between hind paws, like so many embers ashed over. Winter sets in: the marmot body temperature dips to about ten degrees above freezing. From pulsing twice every second the hibernating heart slows to half that. Then slower. Finally, as much as a full quarter-minute or more goes by . . . between beats.

During hibernation marmots rouse, stir somewhat, then sleep again—unless their body fat runs out, or winter cold runs too long too deep, and the tiny heart ceases. As when a lit match, held upright, weakens till its shrunken flame seeps back into the matchhead; a glow, a red cinder—suddenly black.

But the small, distant deaths of animals common as wind don't sadden anyone. No more than we're saddened by all the once-upon-a-time crickets and dormice ashed over at Pompeii. Besides, those life-like but plaster agonies recovered from Pompeiian dailyness are of folks who would have died ages ago, even if Vesuvius's summit hadn't smithereened. Centuries *are* distance, aren't they?

Of his unswerving industry, how much did Pliny expect would survive? Apart from his considerable military service, he wrote a work twenty "books" long on Rome's wars with Germany, wrote an eight-book text on rhetoric, penned a lengthy chronicle of his own times in thirty-one books, and crowned his literary achievement with that eccentric museum, his *Natural History,* gleaned from authors and treatises innumerable. Time, which called Pliny out of the dust into sunlight, and which lent him his encyclopaedic curiosity, has ground nearly all that to powder. He knew well how "Nature" begets and devours us, just as Chronos ate his own children. Of Pliny's written mind, only the *Natural History* has made it all the way to now.

As for his year upon year of curious labor, might some lost remnants exist as an undetectable nuance in what the European mind has become? Surely so.

However, such consolation feels cheerless as a cubic meter of interstellar medium: one or two floating atoms, the rest a black vacuum.

Which makes Pliny's compulsive curiosity, despite his patchwork and pack-rat science, all the more touching. Laborious days and nights belied his own glum estimate of the human situation. We survive by not believing what we know. Is that because our unconscious knows something truer than fact? Maybe it knows that what we most admire can't die, including the best of ourselves—which we don't invent, merely inherit or borrow. And which, like the world, is nobody's possession. Is wave-lengths, passing through us.

And passing through those wilderness creatures that cold will freeze solid this winter? A gnat is the weight of astonishing centuries, surely as a finch wing has been shaped by however old the sky is. But our emotions require of objects a certain size to help bridge the gap between them and ourselves. Where's the line to be drawn? At bugs on a windshield? By no means even then. So says reason. Reason says the line must be a circle wide as our minds.

So when it comes to the spark in all animal hardihood—meaning ours—I often see an outcrop on Colorado's continental divide. To think mountains "majestic" we mustn't inhale overlong their bone-barren summits and crazed smash-ups of rock. A few hours, or days; then clear out. Nothing has been here since the beginning, but great crags pretend they have. They pretend we living things aren't here at all; or if so, mere passing fancies of the sun. Even in midsummer their petrified light can chill, so winter near their summits can be—in the root sense of the word—terrific. To look at ice cliffs long, and in storm, and alone . . . kills the heart. Nonetheless, atop one uppermost slab near the Corona trail suns a lone marmot; sluggish, dim-witted, inconsiderable, heroic.

Straight overhead the sky is an ultraviolet blue so intense it verges on purple. Late August sun drills down. Light breeze pours over the divide, ruffling the marmot's pelt, glossy as a chestnut. Moment to moment his head winks north, winks west in quick, circumspicuous caution. The sunning torso, plump as a loaf, doesn't stir. He sees me, and sees me keeping my distance. He has no idea.

He knows nothing, really, of the success of his own species, doesn't know that his ancestors reached North America from Asia, across the land bridge spanning what is now the Bering Strait, and were at home here, just like this, when Pliny the Elder wrote and Vesuvius erupted. Now found all over the globe, he has gone where not even the map can go, hearing rivers that had never been heard. He has been snared, trapped, poisoned, and shot: for his fur in Mongolia, for his oil in lands diverse as Switzerland and Siberia. Under the guise of woodchuck he is thought a mere varmint and thus—in much of the United States—an appropriate focus for gunsights. His avatars waddled about and snoozed beneath Pleistocene skies of the Ice Age. He is content to live where little else can. He endures.

How could he know that I, the biped who under a backpack leans slightly forward and stares, admire his stamina entirely? How could either of us foresee that his serio-comic, jawless profile, his buck teeth, twitchy nose whiskers and sluff of a tail, his wide-eyed blinkings and lookouts for predators will combine with the twelve thousand foot altitude to make his silly bump of a figure not only wholeheartedly dear to me but—long as I live—half immortal?

When did humans first find the marmot amusing? Pliny's account seems to have been written with a smile. Certainly the mountain mouse—as the French tongue still names him—once delighted Europeans visiting the fairs and markets where animal trainers entertained; among the camels and tame bears, spectators could see many a humble marmot "dancing" to flute notes played by its keeper, often a child from the Tyrol.

Amusement, however, did not prevent Alpine dwellers in modern times from hunting the slow creature almost to extinction, both for its fat—reputed to cure rheumatism, among other ills—and for its pelt. As late as 1944 an estimated sixteen thousand marmots were killed in Switzerland alone, till naturalists persuaded pharmaceutical dealers that marmot-annihilation would benefit no one. Though belief in the curative powers of marmot fat still persists among folk of the European Alps, the animals have dodged the threat of extinction. In contrast, Mongolia's Bobac marmot breeds so fast no such threat exists—despite the millions of furs annually harvested there, and the many hundreds of tons of marmot fat. And despite the fact that Mongolian marmots often carry plague.

As for me, before and since, I've seen marmots by the hundreds, seen their low profiles flow over or peer out of rock piles from here to the end of the world. In Alaska's Brooks Range I made my first acquaintance with his species by way of a raided food cache the critters gnawed into. In Switzerland's sole national park I've watched marmot youngsters wrestle each other repeatedly, as we did when kids, for the sheer fun of it, toppling, flopping, grappling each other and rolling together downhill. That Swiss pair didn't behave *like* human kids. Their play-wrestling seemed *identical*.

On a frosty mid-July night high in Colorado's Gore Range the weird roar that woke me was marmot incisors munching a hole in my empty Nalgene water-bottle. One twilight evening just below the 14,200-foot summit of Longs Peak, bright marmot-whistles seemed to match the first few stars like question and answer. A mile from the crest of Arapahoe Pass there's a particularly untimid marmot who, as I approach, rises hindlegged to his full height of some eighteen inches and, in exactly the same spot, tries to stare me down. Amid that shattered labyrinth of stone chaos, his world and home, what a bold fellow he is! Since marmots live but a dozen years or thereabouts, his annual defiance feels huge. We gaze at each other. In our silence much seems possible, though nothing much happens: two creatures, looking a little farther than themselves.

But that *other* marmot surviving miles away on the Corona Trail—why should he, a dozen years after my glimpse of him, continue to seem so special? There where the left hand slopes away as alpine tundra, half meadow, and the right hand is sheer fall, hundreds of feet down to rockscapes ugly as slag, down toward acres of grit-littered, permanent snow, my emblematic marmot at first seemed no different from hundreds. It's just that, to remember what sheer courage looks like, my mind's eye often invokes him.

There, under a sky barely fly-specked with ravens, and atop a jut of flat granite, he suns. Wind ruffles his fur. He blinks, peers around him at nothing. At what there is. His instincts and eyes, his nut-brown pelt, his nose and paws, all seem shapes taken by a design whose true name I don't know—any more than that dim creature knew his. Which I see, now, given his Old World origins, might as well have been Pliny.

My Father Always Said

Mimi Schwartz

For years I heard the same line: "In Rindheim,[1] you didn't do such things!" It was repeated whenever the American world of his daughters took my father by surprise. Sometimes it came out softly, in amusement, as when I was a Pilgrim turkey in the P.S. 3 Thanksgiving play. But usually, it was a red-faced, high-blood-pressure shout—especially when my sister, Ruth, became "pinned" to Mel from Brooklyn or I wanted to go with friends whose families he didn't know.

"But they're Jewish," I'd say, since much of our side of Forest Hills was. The eight lanes of Queens Boulevard divided the Jews, Irish, and Italians pushing out of Brooklyn, the Bronx, and Manhattan from the old guard WASPs of Forest Hills Gardens. No Jews or Catholics over there—except for a few blocks near the Forest Hills Tennis Stadium where, from fifth grade on, we kids all went to watch what is now the U.S. Tennis Open, our end-of-summer ritual before school.

"You're not going," my father would announce before all such rituals.

"But everybody's going."

It was the wrong argument to make to a man who fled Hitler's Germany because of everybody. But I couldn't know that because he rarely talked about *that* Germany, only about his idyllic Rindheim where everybody (as opposed to the everybody I knew) did everything right. If my friends didn't have an aunt, grandmother, or great grandfather originally from Rindheim or vicinity, they were suspect. They could be anybody, which is exactly why I liked them—not like the Weil kids whose mother was "a born Tannhauser," as if that were a plus.

"I don't care about everybody!" my father would shout (that was his second favorite line); but it was a losing battle for him. My sister smoked at fifteen, I wore lipstick at twelve; we hung out at Penn Drug after Friday night basketball games

---

[1] I've changed the name, but all else is true.

with friends who were third-generation Brooklyn and Rumania—and didn't give a hoot that "In Rindheim, you didn't do such things!"

The irony of those words was inchoate—even to him, I realize now—until we went back to his village to visit the family graves. I was thirteen; it was eight years after World War II ended, and my father wanted to show me where his family had lived for generations, trading cattle. He wanted me, the first American-born in the family, to understand that "Forest Hills, Queens is not the world" (his third favorite line). A hard task to tackle, but my father was tough, a survivor who had led his whole clan, like Moses, out of Nazi Germany and into Queens, New York. He was ready for an American teen-age me.

"So Mimi-a-la, this is Rindheim!" my father boomed as the forest opened upon a cluster of fifty or so red-peaked houses set into the hillside of a tiny, green valley. We had driven for hours through what looked like Hansel and Gretel country, filled with foreboding evergreens that leaned over the narrow, winding roads of the *Schwarzwald*. Even the name, *Schwarzwald*, which meant Black Forest, gave me the creeps after being weaned on Nazi movies at the Midway Theater on 71st Avenue; but I was optimistic. Life here did look prettier than in Queens.

We drove up a rutted main street and stopped before a crumbling stone house with cow dung in the yard. "This was *our* house!" my father announced, as I watched horse flies attacking the dung, not just in *our* yard but in every yard on Eelinger Weg. And there were cows and chickens walking in front of our rented car. What a bust! My mother at least came from a place with sidewalks (we had driven by her old house in Stuttgart, sixty kilometers north, before coming here). My father, I decided at once, was a hick. All his country hero adventures about herding cows with a book hidden in one pocket and his mother's home-baked raspberry *linzertorte* in the other were discounted by two cows chewing away in stalls where I expected a car to be.

A stooped, old man with thick jowls and a feathered leather cap came out of the house with a big smile and a vigorous handshake for my dad who, looking squeezed in his pin-striped suit, nodded now and then and looked polite, but did not smile back.

"Sind Sie nicht ein Loewengart, vielleicht Julius oder Artur?" The man jabbered on, and my mother translated. He was Herr Schmidt, the blacksmith, and recognized my dad at once. "Aren't you a Loewengart, maybe Julius or Arthur?" This man had bought the family house in 1935 from Uncle Julius, the last of my family to leave Rindheim, and was remembering how my father and his brothers, Sol and Julius, used to play in his shop—with all his tools. *"Eine nette Familie, sehr nette,"* ("A fine family, very fine") he kept saying.

I understood nothing because I had learned no German in our house in Queens. When my father reached Ellis Island, he announced that our family would not speak the language of those who drove them out of Germany. Which was fine with me. It was embarrassing enough in those days to have parents who, for all my coaching, couldn't stop saying *'fader'* and *'moder'* to my American-born friends.

The man beckoned us towards my dad's old house, but my father shook his head, *"Nein, Danke!"* and backed us quickly away. I wanted to go in and see his old room; but my father did not. It would be forty years before I'd follow Frau Hummel, the blacksmith's daughter, up the narrow, dark stairs to a loft with two windows like cannon holes and search the heavy low beams for my dad's initials—A. L.—carved in the worn, smooth wood.

"And here's my downtown! No Penn Drugstore to hang around here!" my Dad said cheerfully, as we drove past four buildings leaning together like town drunks. "And here's where Grunwald had his kosher butcher shop and Zundorfer, his dry goods. And here's the *Gasthaus Kaiser*! We Jews had wonderful *Purim* and *Shuvuott* dances here—with green branches and ferns and pink flowers, like marbles in the candlelight. . . ." I could picture Mr. Grundwald—he sold sausages in Queens—but I couldn't picture my big-bellied, bald-headed Dad dancing, a kid like me.

We turned into an alley and stopped next to a gray building with stone columns in the doorway and corners decorated with what looked like railroad ties set into stone. I wouldn't have noticed it tucked among the houses.

"Here's where we spent every Friday night," my father said, getting us out of the car to look at the old synagogue. He pointed to a Hebrew inscription carved onto a stone plaque above the doorway: "How great is God's house and the doorway to Heaven," he translated haltingly in his rusty Hebrew. Right below the stone plaque was a wooden beam with another inscription, this one in German. It said the same thing, my father said, but it was new. He'd never seen it before.

I found out later that the German inscription had been added in 1952, the year before we came. That's when the Jewish synagogue was converted into the Protestant Evangelical Church to accommodate Eastern Germans who, fleeing the Russian troops late in World War II, resettled into the empty Jewish houses of this Catholics/Jewish village. Keeping the same words on the doorway inscription was meant as a tribute of respect: that this building was still God's house. But the 250 Rindheim Jews who had fled to America and Israel were never grateful. Their beautiful synagogue was no more; that's what counted.

"Well, at least it didn't become a gymnasium or a horse stable, like in other villages," the mayor's wife told me huffily in 1993 when I returned to Rindheim on my own. Two other villagers nodded vigorously, but a lively woman, who said she used to live next door to my great uncle, said, *"Na Ja*, I wouldn't be so happy if our Catholic church became a mosque—and believe me, we have plenty of Turks here . . ."

" . . . They are our new Jews," someone interjected.

" . . . *Na Ja*," the lively woman shrugged and continued, "and I wouldn't feel good just because the Moslems said our church was still God's house."

They pointed out "the Moslems," four men squatting around a table and sipping Turkish coffee in a terraced yard below the synagogue. Many came, according to the lively woman, in the the 1960s as guest workers from Turkey and Afghanistan and now made up twenty percent of Rindheim. These men lived in the old *Gasthaus Kaiser*, where my father danced at *Purim* Festivals and where my Aunt

Hilda and family once lived above the restaurant. This village is more like Forest Hills than you thought, Dad, I told myself, wishing he were around to discuss these ironies of migration. (The Forest Hills Gardens of my childhood is now owned by wealthy Asians and our block on 110th Street is now filled with Iranians.)

My father loosened his tie and wiped beads of sweat from his forehead with a checkered handkerchief. "And if you weren't in your synagogue by sundown on Friday, and not a minute later, *and* all day on Saturday, you were fined, a disgrace to your family. Three stars had to shine in the evening sky before *Shabbat* (the Sabbath) was over and you could go home."

I thought of his fury whenever I wanted to go bowling on Saturday at Foxy's Alley where all the boys hung out. Not that my father went to synagogue in Queens. The most religious he got, as far as I could see, was to play his record of Jan Pierce singing the *Kol Nidre* on *Yom Kippur*, the day of repentance. And he fasted—which I tried once or twice but got hungry when my mother ate a bagel. She never fasted.

The sun was high, the car seat sticky on my thighs, so I happily sat in the shade of four tall, arched windows which someone had been fixing. But my mother was heading for the car, saying she didn't like standing in the open where everyone could see us. We should go. In fact, she would have skipped Germany altogether and stayed in Belgium with my sister who had married a Belgian Jew (instead of Mel from Brooklyn); but my father insisted that we make this pilgrimage.

"Aren't we going inside?" I asked when my father started to follow my mother. He was usually the leader on everything, the man who, in 1933, as soon as Hitler came to power, convinced his brothers, sister, cousins, and parents-in-law, forty people in all, to leave Germany as quickly as possible; the man who figured out schemes for smuggling money taped to toilets on night trains to Switzerland—it took two years—so that they'd have enough cash for America to let them in. (Jews without a bank account or sponsor had no country willing to take them from Hitler's Germany.)

"No reason to go in. The building is just a shell. Everything was gutted by fire during *Kristallnacht*."

"What's that?"

I imagined some Jewish festival with candles out of control. In 1953 there was no *Schindler's List*, no Holocaust Museum, so I never heard about one night in 1938, when the Nazis systematically burned all the synagogues in Germany to destroy the Jewish life. All I knew was good Americans, who looked like Jimmy Stewart and Gregory Peck, fighting mean-looking men in black uniforms who clicked their heels a lot and shouted, "Heil Hitler." And we won.

"*Kristallnacht* was when the Jews finally realized they had to leave—and fast—even from Rindheim where it wasn't so bad. Jews felt safe here, too safe—until the synagogue was torched, everything in flames."

He stopped talking. "Go on!" I urged, but he held back, tentative. Not at all like him.

"My cousin Fritz . . . Do you remember him?" I shook my head, no. "He lived over there once," my father pointed down the alley, "and when he smelled smoke, he raced over. He was part of the Fire Brigade and began shouting to others in the Brigade, 'Why don't we do something? Get the hoses!' Men he knew all his life were standing around, silent. 'Against orders!' snapped a Nazi brownshirt, a stranger. 'Except if Christian houses start to burn!' He pointed his rifle at Fritz. So everything inside was lost—the Torah, the Ark. . . ."

I thought about the old blacksmith who lived in our house. Was he there? Was he one of those firemen? Why was he so friendly if he hated the Jews?

"But these people weren't from Rindheim," my father said quickly. "They were thugs from outside, brought in trucks by the Nazis to do their dirty work."

My father, already in America by then, had heard this from many Rindheim Jews who, like Fritz, left as soon after *Kristallnacht* as they could get exit visas. "The Rindheimers we grew up with didn't take part. They wouldn't do such a thing!" my father had been assured by those who resettled in America.

He opened the car door. "In fact many Non-Jews helped the Jews fix the store and house windows that were also smashed that night. But for that the Non-Jews got in trouble. Everyone who helped was sent to the Front as cannon fodder."

"What's that?" I asked.

"It's what you feed into big guns so they will shoot."

I imagined a young man being stuffed into a cannon, like at the circus, and aimed at American guns, his mother in the red doorway of the house we just passed, getting a telegram, crying like in the movies. But I wasn't going to feel sorry, not when they let the synagogue burn.

Later I would hear this term, cannon fodder, used again and again by Rindheim Jews—and always with the same "broken window" story. It was as if they had decided collectively on this tale and how it illustrated that their Non-Jewish neighbors meant well. "It wasn't their fault. They were afraid, too," they'd say with more sympathy than anger. But, like my parents, the Jews who returned to Rindheim to visit the family graves did so quickly, never wanting to stand and talk in the open or re-enter old rooms of memory.

I was hungry, but my father stopped again, this time in front of a shabby building with three tiers of windows. This was his school, he said, and it looked like mine, but P.S. 3 had a paved playground and good swings. This just had dirt.

"We Jews had the first floor and one teacher, Herr Spatz, who taught everybody, in all eight grades, everything. The Christians had the other two floors."

"How come?" I asked, for I'd never heard of dividing kids by anything but age.

My father looked surprised. "That's how it was done. We learned Torah and they didn't. They went to school on Saturdays and we didn't. But to high school, we went together, six kilometers to Horb, those who went."

"And did you talk to each other—and play games?" I thought of Tommy Molloy in the schoolyard, saying that I killed Christ, but then he asked me to play stickball on his team, and I said okay.

"Of course. We all got along. Rindheim was not so big."

I wouldn't argue about that! The schoolyard was deserted and, looking for movement in a meadow on the far hill, I saw a giant white cross ringed by menacing forest that kept its distance, like dark green bodyguards. The cross was also new, my father said. It wasn't even there when he was a child or even when he came home for a *Shabbat*, after moving to the city of Frankfurt in 1921 to work and later to marry.

"Remember how we had to park the car two kilometers away and walk to my father's?" He nudged my mother. "No Jew dared to drive here on *Shabbat*! Am I right?"

"Absolutely not. You'd be run out of town." My mother laughed for the first time all day and turned to tell me about how she, a big city girl from Stuttgart, first came to this village for her cousin Max's wedding. She wore a red, lace dress. "Very shocking!" she said with delight. "Everyone was whispering but your father. He came up and asked for every dance!" Her shoulders eased with nostalgia, wisps of black hair loosened from her chignon, and I leaned forward, close to her neck that always smelled of almond soap, to hear more about my parents having fun.

My father made a sharp left turn up a dirt road that zigzagged up a hill and stopped in front of a run-down stone farmhouse with half a roof. We needed a key for the Jewish cemetery and it was hanging on the peg "where it has always been," my father said. This was the Brenner family house; they were the gravediggers, who had been burying the Rindheim Jews for generations. Before Hitler, of course. A quarter of a mile farther, a giant stone portal emerged from nowhere—the kind that led to castles—and the fat key opened the heavy gate that led us deep into woods.

I still remember the sunlight on that day, how it streamed on the gravestones, a thousand of them tipped but all standing, in an enchanted forest light. It was a place to whisper and walk on tiptoe, even if you were an American thirteen. I remember the softness of the ground, a carpet of moss and leaves, and the stillness, as if the trees were holding their breath until we found everyone: my grandmother, Anna, born Tannhauser (1872–1915), and my grandfather, Rubin (1866–1925), both marked by sleek, dark marble gravestones that looked new despite the underbrush. And Rubin's father, Raphael (1821–1889), and his father, Rubin Feit (1787–1861), their pale sandstone gravestones carved with elaborate vines and scrolls eroded by time.

I tried to imagine faces: a grandfather who enforced strict rules about work, manners, and Torah; a grandmother who, in the faded photo over my parents' bed, laughed with my father's twinkle, when life pleased him. She had died when my father was not much older than I was, of infection, not Hitler, my father said. So had his dad, who refused to go to the hospital two hours away.

But all I could picture were the grandparents I knew: the *Omi* and *Opa* who lived three blocks away in Queens and "babysat," against my loudest objections that I was too old for that. This grandfather walked my dog so I didn't have to and wove yards of intricately patterned shawls and slipcovers on his loom in our attic. This grandmother made delicious, heart-shaped butter cookies and told stories of how they escaped in a little boat from Denmark to Sweden, and then to a chicken farm on Long Island where she, a city woman from Stuttgart, sang to her hens every morning—until my grandfather's heart attack made them move three blocks from us.

"Do you want to put down stones?" my father asked, placing small ones on his father's grave, his lips moving as in prayer, and then on his mother's grave—and on the others. He had found the stones under the wet leaves, and my mother, wobbling in high heels, was searching for more, enough for both of us.

"What for?" I asked, not wanting to take what she was offering. I would find my own.

"It's how you pay tribute to the dead," my father said, looking strangely gaunt despite his bulk. "The dead souls need the weight of remembrance, and then they rise up to God more easily . . . If we lived nearby, there'd be many stones," he said softly to his father's grave.

In later years, there would be more stones, as more Rindheim Jews came to visit the graves of their ancestors, but eight years after the war there were no others. I placed a smooth, speckled white with mica on Anna's grave and rougher grey ones on the men's. My father nodded. Some connection had been made, he knew, the one he had run from and returned to, the one I resisted even as I lay stones.

There were Loewengarts all over the place, mixed in with Pressburgers and Froehlichs and Grunwalds and Landauers, the same names again and again for they all married each other—or someone Jewish from a nearby village. There were four or five with Jews. My father said he had been daring to marry a woman from so far away—sixty kilometers! But when my mother found a gravestone that might be her second cousin on her mother's side, I thought: not *so* daring!

We were next to a wire fence in the far end of the cemetery where the weeds were high. My mother had disappeared, so it was just my father and I among rows of tiny graves no higher than my kneecaps, their writing almost rubbed off.

We were among the children's graves, my father said, slipping on wet leaves, but catching himself as I reached for his hand. I wanted him standing, especially with my mother gone. Above me, I heard the warble of a single bird and shivered. My father pointed out a headstone carved like a tree trunk but with its limbs cut off. It meant the person died young, in the prime of life, he said, and I thought of my sister Hannah who died soon after they arrived in America—before I was born. I didn't know the details then—how their doctor, also a German refugee, didn't know about the new antibiotics on the market—only that the sweet face with green eyes who hung over my parents' bed was buried in New Jersey somewhere.

I was glad to move back among the larger stones, worn and substantial like adults. I saw one dated 1703. You could tell the older stones, my father said, because all the writing—what little was left—was in Hebrew. The newer gravestones were mostly in German because by 1900, Jews no longer had to pay extra taxes as Jews, so they had started to feel very German, as if they really belonged.

"Did all the Rindheim Jews move to New York?" I was thinking about how many came to our house in Queens and pinched my cheeks over the years.

"Many, yes," he lectured, "but some moved to Palestine as a group. Others went to Chicago, Paris, even Buenos Aires . . ." We were now before a headstone carved with a broken flower, its stem snapped in two. He touched it. "And some stayed," he said quietly. "There were many, especially old people, who were like my *Tante* Rosa and thought no one would bother her. 'I'll be fine,' she kept saying. Later . . . we tried to send her money, but then . . ." His voice trailed off.

"Is she buried here?"

He shook his head. "She was deported." I asked no more, for I knew what deported meant, had seen the pictures of Auschwitz in *Life* magazine. I'd always been relieved that my Dad was smart and had gotten the whole family out in time—except for this *Tante* Rosa. I imagined a handful of old people getting into a wagon, but no one I knew, so it didn't seem so bad.

The sun rays had faded, the forest turned gray and dank, and we were near the entrance again, standing before a large monument in black stone, with the inscription, "Erected to honor the victims of the persecution of the Jews—1933–1945." No individual names were listed, so I kept imagining only a handful of old people and walked on, stopping at a memorial that had a face: Joseph Zundorfer, his features carved in bronze above his name. He had been a Jewish fighter pilot in World War I with many medals. "Shot down," my father said, placing a stone on the grave, and I pictured a hero like Gregory Peck.

Eighty-seven Jews, not a handful, were deported from my father's village during 1941 and 1942, I found out forty years later. They died in the concentration camps of Lublin, Riga, Theresienstadt; but with no names engraved in stone and no faces to admire, they remained anonymous to me that day. What registered to an American teenager who lost no one she really knew was the sunlight on my family's graves, and how a thousand Jews, related to me, were buried, safe and secure for centuries in these high woods.

"In Rindheim, we didn't do such things!" suddenly carried more weight, giving me a history and legitimacy that would have made me not mind, as much, if my father continued to say that line. But he didn't. When we came home from that trip, he took up golf and played every weekend with American friends who never heard of Rindheim. Their world of congeniality became ours and I was expected to enter its promise. "Smile, smile! You are a lucky girl to be here!" is what I remember after that as my father's favorite line. His magical village of memory had disappeared among the graves that weren't there and the weightless souls with no stones of remembrance.

Chin Music

Michael Steinberg

I was wrapping up a discussion of *Huck Finn,* and as I began to recite the assignments, my students were already shuffling their feet, packing up books, and grabbing for their coats—the usual cues that it's time for the teacher to quit talking. In the past, I'd often take the hint and end the hour quickly. But lately, I noticed, I'd become less and less patient.

I paused for a second to look at my notes. That's when I spotted Drew—a student I'd already targeted as a trouble maker—moving toward the door. Just as he was about to open it, I said in a tone that was sharper than intended. "Excuse me, but class isn't over yet."

"I thought you were done," he said. Then he murmured under his breath, "You've been lecturing at us for over an hour." Whether it was deliberate or not, he said it loud enough for everyone to hear.

I knew I should let it go, or make light of it somehow. But before I could catch myself, it slipped out. "Drew, you're a fucking piss ant" I said. "Sit your god damned ass down 'til I dismiss the class."

Everyone, including me, was stunned. His eyes blazing, Drew shuffled back to his seat, deliberately kicking the trash can on his way. "Keep it up, pal," I whispered to myself. His coat buttoned to the throat, Drew sat down very slowly and turned his head toward the window.

This wasn't the first time we'd done this little dance. In the first week of the semester, Drew had written an exercise that I liked so much I read it to the class. When I praised the authenticity of the writing, he intervened. "None of that crap was true," he said. "I made the whole thing up."

Students had challenged me before, but never quite this aggressively, and certainly not without some provocation. So, I approached this kid a little more cautiously than I normally do.

"Why did you make it up?" I asked, making certain to keep my tone as neutral as possible.

"Because it was such a Mickey Mouse assignment," he said. So much for being tactful, I thought.

There were some "oohs," followed by a round of nervous giggles. I wanted to lash back, say something nasty or sarcastic. But instead, I took the high ground again. "Fiction or nonfiction," I said, "it's still a good piece of writing." And I left it at that.

Not so tonight, though. Visibly flustered, I stumbled through the litany of assignments. And when the class had filed out, I called Drew up to my desk.

"Look, Drew," I began. "I think you should know why I said wha . . ."

He cut me off in mid-sentence. "You showed me up in front of the whole class," he said. "You owe me an apology."

Then he waited a few seconds while I searched for a reply. Did this kid really believe that he'd done nothing wrong? Just as I was about to respond, he pivoted and headed for the door.

By the time I got home, I was furious—at him, of course—and at myself, for taking the bait. I took a walk around the block to try and calm down. But all I could think about was the anger and resentment that had been building inside me for such a long time.

Even before the eye surgeries, my patience with freshmen was wearing thin. When students said goofy things like "This sucks. Why can't we read happier books?" my comments were becoming more defensive. I even tossed a few guys out of class when they showed up unprepared or without books. Also a first for me.

The eye surgeries had given me a chance to step back from teaching for almost two years. Sometimes an enforced absence is just what you need to reinvigorate yourself. But when I got back in the classroom, I could see right away that things had changed.

Or maybe it was it me who'd changed. By mid-semester, I felt like a space invader in my own classroom. Some of my freshmen glided mindlessly into class on skateboards or roller blades. Some wore headphones and others ate snacks and drank soda while I talked. A few even had the chutzpah to take calls on their cell phones.

Conditions outside of class had also changed. For one, I was receiving frequent reports from the counseling center, bureaucratic memos informing me about students who were in alcohol or drug rehab, or who had eating disorders and histories of family abuse. And then there was the student who sent me an email apologizing for not doing her essay on time. She said, without a trace of irony, that she missed the deadline because she'd attempted suicide that weekend. She hoped I'd understand and that I'd give her an extension. Coupled with the effects of over two decades of student papers, mind-numbing faculty meetings, and obligatory committee work, this latest confrontation left me wondering if maybe it wasn't time to move on.

The next day, I was having lunch with a colleague from the Physiology department—someone who I meet with regularly to talk about teaching. She was telling me about two of her colleagues, one of whom she referred to as "an educator," and the other whom she called "a coach."

The word "coach" hit a nerve, and for a moment I drifted away from the conversation. In a sudden flashback, I saw myself at fifteen, standing next to Tom Sullivan, my old V.F.W. baseball coach. My God, I hadn't thought about this guy in almost forty years. Why now?

Just before I fell asleep that night, it all came rushing back. In my second year on Sullivan's team, I'd had a run-in with him, a skirmish that made me think seriously about quitting the game. A game I loved more than anything else in my adolescent world.

The episode came about on a bone-chilling Saturday morning in early March. It was the last day of tryouts and we were down to the final cut. I was on the mound and my best friend, Mike Rubin, was at bat. Last year we'd both made it to the final tryouts. But for some reason, Sullivan cut Rubin and kept me.

I only got to pitch in a few games that summer, so I was apprehensive when right before this year's tryouts began, Sullivan called me into his office. The room was a steam-heated cubbyhole above the St. Francis De Sales gym. Amidst the banging and hissing of the old pipes he told me in no uncertain terms that if I wanted to pitch this season I'd have to convince him that a Belle Harbor "sugar baby" had what it took to play ball for him.

And now, here I was on the mound of the church field staring down at Mike Rubin, who stood sixty feet six inches away nervously taking his practice cuts. Last year's team almost made it to the state finals at Cooperstown. We got eliminated in Westchester County—the final game of the regionals. I'd been thinking about it all winter, and I didn't want to blow my shot at playing summer league ball. But what about Mike? Since we were eight years old, we'd played on every team from Little League through P.A.L. This was his last chance to make the V.F.W. team. Next year we'd move up to American Legion, a tougher, more competitive league.

I knew Rubin couldn't hit the curve ball. If I threw him low breaking balls, my stock-in-trade, he was finished. Kaput. But if I pitched him too fat, Big Tom would know it. Then I'd be history too. While I was trying to figure out what to throw, Sullivan yelled, "Game situation," and ordered Andy Ortiz to be the runner at third. This was not a good sign. Ortiz was a football player from the Arverne projects. And he could hurt you. That's when Sullivan called for a suicide squeeze. It's a risky play, and it's meant to work like this: as soon as I go into my wind-up, Ortiz will head for home and Rubin will square around to bunt. My job is to make certain he doesn't bunt the ball in fair territory.

Instead of tossing me the ball, Sullivan swaggered out to the mound. As he slapped the grass-stained baseball into my glove, he deliberately sprayed black, bitter tobacco juice across the bridge of my nose. Then he motioned Danny Whalen, another football goon, to the mound.

Sullivan and I were inches apart. I could feel his breath on my right cheek. His nose was red and swollen, and slanted to the right. Broken three times in his college football days. Just as Whalen arrived, Coach rasped, "Steinberg, when Ortiz breaks from third, throw it at his head."

He meant the batter, Rubin. Why would I want to throw a baseball at my best friend's head? It wasn't the right strategy. It was another one of Big Tom's stupid tests of courage. I knew that sooner or later he'd be testing me. I just hadn't expected it to happen now.

"At his head, Coach?" I said, stalling for time.

Sullivan gave me his "that's-the-way-it's-done-around-here" look. It wasn't like I didn't know what he was doing. Everyone on the team understood that if you wanted to play ball for Big Tom you did what you were told and you kept your mouth shut. Why was I being such a smart-ass? It wasn't like me. Why was I so willing to risk it all here?

I tried to calm myself down, remind myself what the costs were. I kept telling myself to cool it. Just try and think it through. Pretend to go along with Big Tom's program. The whole time, though, I could feel the knot in my stomach twist and tighten.

Sullivan glared at the third base bleachers where the final eight guys fidgeted nervously, waiting for their chance to bat. Then he looked back at me. With his cap pulled low, the coach's steel-blue pig eyes seemed all the more penetrating. He smiled, but because part of his mouth was distorted from taking too many football hits without a face mask, it came off looking like a mocking leer. The gesture unnerved me even more. I could feel my palms getting clammy and my armpits were drenched with perspiration.

He said loudly for everyone to hear, "Steinberg, you've been with me for two years; let's show this wet-nosed bunch of rookies how we play this game."

Then he grabbed his crotch with his left hand. It was the old comrade routine. He was giving his second-year pitcher a chance to look like a leader by pretending we were buddies. But we weren't. Big Tom and I didn't operate in the same universe. He was a bull-yock Irishman from Hell's Kitchen, a high school stud who learned to fight in the streets. His platoon had fought in the Pacific, and the pride still showed in his eyes. To him, guys like Rubin and me were too privileged. And he resented us for it.

I turned to glance at Rubin. He looked like a Thanksgiving turkey on the block. I was embarrassed for him. Maybe the wind was just blowing at his sweatpants, the stiff ocean breeze we get on the Long Island south shore in early spring. Then again, maybe his knees really were shaking.

"Let's get the god-damned show on the road," Sullivan muttered. I thought about quitting, but our team was good. I had visions of Linda Foreman, our head cheerleader, walking around school wearing my V.F.W. jacket. And there was another incentive. We all knew that our high school coach, Jack Kerchman, scouted his players in the summer—looking to see who was getting better and who was dogging it.

Whalen trotted back behind the plate and Sullivan turned to leave. To him this kind of stuff was routine. I wanted to refuse, but this was my only chance to make it to Cooperstown, to see my dad sitting in the stands watching me pitch at Doubleday Field. I was red-in-the-face pissed, hoping it looked like windburn.

I tried to buy some time, hoping I could reason with Sullivan. Convince him there was another way to do this.

"You want me to stop the bunt, right?" I said meekly.

He turned. What the hell was I saying? Nobody second-guesses the Coach. Sullivan walked back to the mound and spat another wad of chew on the ground, making sure to splatter some on my new spikes. He looked at Whalen, then at Ortiz. Then he turned to me and shook his head from side to side.

"That's right, Steinberg. You stop the bunt. Now, let's please execute the fucking play, shall we?" He muttered to himself through clenched teeth as he trotted back toward the dugout.

It was out of my mouth before I knew it. "Suppose I hit him in the head?" Sullivan's own head swung around like a tetherball making the last tight twist at the top of the pole.

"Don't worry, it's not a vital organ. Pitch."

I think Big Tom knew that he was undermining his credibility by arguing with a piss-ant kid. So he turned and silenced everyone's murmurs with a long glare. As if rehearsed, the eight guys behind me started to grumble, distancing themselves from me and Sullivan's wrath.

"Pitch the fuckin' ball," yelled Whalen from behind the plate.

"Do what Coach tell you, man," spat Ortiz from third.

To those guys, Sullivan was George God. If he told them to take a dump at home plate, they'd get diarrhea. But me? I'm Gary Cooper in *High Noon.* Everyone's watching, no one's volunteering to help.

Then I noticed Mike Rubin, still frozen in his batter's crouch. He looked like a mannequin with bulging eyes. Poor Mike didn't have a prayer. But before I could think, the words slipped out.

"It's the wrong play, Coach."

It was my voice, all right, but it couldn't have been me who said it. I'd never have the guts to say anything like that to Sullivan's face.

Dead silence. You could hear the breeze whistling through the wire mesh of the backstop. At first, Sullivan was too surprised to even curse me out. But after a long moment, he turned and strode up to Rubin, who was still frozen in the box.

It was a considered ploy. I'd seen it before, in the streets. Coach was going to punish me by humiliating my best friend. Like all of us, Rubin was jack-rabbit scared of Sullivan. And just like a rabbit about to be prey, he stood riveted to the ground.

"God damn it," Sullivan ripped off his cap, exposing a jet black crewcut and sunburned forehead. He spoke like rolling thunder, enunciating every word.

"WHAT DID HE SAY, RUBIN?"

My stomach turned over watching Sullivan humiliate my best friend just for the amusement of the guys in the bleachers. And Big Tom knew it. Knew it oh so well.

Rubin managed weakly; "Uh, wrong—wrong play, Coach?"

Louder then, like a Marine D.I.: "NOBODY IN THE STANDS CAN HEAR YOU, RUBIN."

"WRONG PLAY, COACH."

Still advancing, Sullivan took it to the grandstand.

"ALL YOU LADIES, SAY IT!"

The accusing chorus rained down.

"WRONG PLAY, COACH."

"AGAIN."

"WRONG PLAY, COACH."

Then he ran out to the mound yelling, "YOU TOO, STEINBERG, YOU SAY IT."

He was hopping up and down like someone had pranked him with a hot foot. Adrenaline overcame me then, and before Sullivan could order another round, I let the words tumble out in a single breath. "If I throw a pitch-out chest high in the left hand batter's box, all Danny has to do is take two steps to his right and he has a clear shot at Ortiz." I was parroting what Joe Bleutrich, my P.A.L. coach, had taught me two years ago.

By now, my stomach was in knots, Rubin's eyes looked like marbles, and the whole team was hungry to see what would happen next. Sullivan squared himself and casually put his cap back on. He was trying to regain his composure. He'd let a snot-nosed high school kid get to him and now he had to regain control.

Softly now: "That's enough, Steinberg."

Then to Rubin: "Get back in the box. Let's do the play."

And to be sure there was no misunderstanding, he took it right back to me: "My play," he said deliberately. "My play, my way."

He was giving me a second chance. Why didn't I just fake it? I had good control. I'd brushed off plenty of hitters before. Maybe deep down I believed that Sullivan was right about me. Maybe I didn't have what it took to play for him.

I wanted to give in, get it over with. So I said, "I can't do it."

Sullivan slammed his cap to the ground, and in one honest, reckless moment, it came out:

"You Belle Harbor Jews are all alike. No god-damn guts. You're a disgrace to your own people."

Nobody moved. The wind whipped a funnel of dust through the hard clay infield.

So that's what this was all about. Some of the guys, I'm sure, had thought the same thing. But we were teammates and they'd never say it to my face. We all knew that Big Tom didn't favor Jews. But even in my worst moments I believed that this stuff was for the anti-Semites from the sticks, the ones who say "Jew York."

There was no chance Sullivan would apologize. He'd used tactics like this before—to get us mad, to fire us up. If I wanted to be a real putz, I could report him to the league's advisory board. My dad knew most of the officers. But I knew I wouldn't do it. Because if I turned him in, it would confirm what he already thought of me. And I didn't want to give him the satisfaction. Besides, I needed him. And in some odd way, I must have sensed that he needed me. Why else would he be testing me like this? For the moment we were yoked to each other, like Sidney Poitier and Tony Curtis in that movie *The Defiant Ones.*

I think Sullivan believed that somehow I had made him say what he said. He was angry at me for making him look bad. So to cover himself he had to make it seem like it was my fault.

"Get out of my sight, Steinberg," he snapped. "You make me wanna puke."

He motioned toward the bullpen. "Levy, get your butt in here and pitch."

Why Levy? Bert was also a Belle Harbor Jew. And to my mind, he was more timid than anyone else in the neighborhood. On second thought, maybe that was part of Big Tom's design.

Sullivan grunted, the cords of his muscular neck wound tight. He reached to take the ball. Just as he grabbed for it, something snapped inside me; I snatched the baseball back. Then an eerie calm began to wash over me. My stomach stopped churning, my chest didn't feel as if it was about to burst, and my neck wasn't burning. I could tell that Sullivan sensed something was going on, but he wasn't sure what it was. Neither was I. Not yet, anyway.

"I'm not leaving, Coach," I said.

Yeah, he sensed it all right. But he misread it. He waved Levy away. Maybe this was Sullivan's obtuse way of atoning for the Jew remark, by allowing me to stay on *his* pitcher's mound.

"Get back in the box, Rubin," he snapped.

"No, Coach," I said.

"What?"

"You grab a bat, Coach."

A frozen moment. Was I really doing this? I recalled the day at football practice when Stuie Scheneider had knocked Coach Kerchman right on his ass. Kerchman goaded him into it, and Stuie took the bait. Is this what was happening here?

Sullivan looked at me, then he looked at the guys in the bleachers and laughed out loud. We all knew he was going to do it. He ripped off his windbreaker and took a couple of practice cuts, biceps rippling. Sullivan didn't seem to mind when muffled cheers rose up from the third base side. He was wearing that crooked-ass grin of his. The players in the bleachers spilled into foul territory, inching closer to the backstop.

"Okay, Coach," I'm thinking. "You're gonna get just what you asked for."

I was ready to play me some chin music. Chin music, where the ball whistles as it passes under the batter's throat. Before I went into my windup, Whalen took two steps up the first base line. He was sure I was going to throw the pitch-out. Can't blame him. It's what he would have done. It's what anyone in his right mind would have done. Sullivan must have thought so too, that's why he was grinning.

It was the smirk that did it. "Screw chin music, I'll take his goddamn head off."

Then I saw Ortiz streaking from third toward home. In that split second I realized, maybe for the first time, that this really was happening. As Big Tom squared to bunt, I zeroed in on the black line that runs along the inside corner of the plate. "Calm down," I told myself. "Brush him back. Just let him know you're here."

That's what my head was saying, but when I started my motion I lifted my eyes away from the plate and locked them on the bill of Sullivan's cap. Then I pushed hard off the rubber and cut loose. I watched the ball tailing in, in, in, right toward Sullivan's head. But he didn't back off, not even an inch. That shit-eating grin was still on his face. I yelled, "HEADS UP," tucked my chin into my chest and shut my eyes. Then I heard a dull thud. I opened my eyes and watched his cap fly off his head. And as I saw him crumble, feet splayed in the dirt, I felt nauseous.

Stunned players surrounded the fallen Sullivan, not knowing what to do. With leaden strides, I joined them, growing a little more lucid. Rubin shot me a "Man, you are dead meat" look, and I thought about suspension from school. Jail even. But the coach sat up. Jesus, was he lucky. Was I lucky. I must have clipped him right on the bill of the cap. Why was I so surprised? It was the target I was aiming at.

Sighs escaped as one breath. Legs and arms unraveled. Players backed away. Slowly, Big Tom lifted himself up and brushed the dirt off the seat of his pants. He shook his head like a wet cocker spaniel who'd just taken a dip in the ocean. Then he wobbled to the bleachers, looking like a young girl testing out her mother's high-heeled shoes.

Before I could collect my thoughts, Sullivan's voice boomed out: "All right, here we go again. Ortiz, hustle back to third, Rubin, up to bat, Steinberg, get your butt back on the hill. Suicide squeeze, same play as before. This time I know we will get it right, won't we, ladies?"

He'd caught me by surprise again. I should have known that he'd have the last word. But this time I couldn't—wouldn't—jump through his hoops again. So, I took a deep breath, bowed my head, and slowly walked toward the mound—all the time knowing exactly where I was headed. When I got to the rubber, I kept going. At second base, I pushed off the bag with my right foot and began to sprint. I began unbuttoning my shirt, and as I passed our center fielder, Ducky Warshauer, I tossed my cap and uniform jersey right at him. Ducky stared at me like I'd just gone Section Eight. When I stepped onto the walkway outside the locker room, I heard the metallic clack, clack, clack of my spikes on the concrete floor. I opened the door and inhaled the familiar perfume of chlorine, Oil of Wintergreen, and stale sweat socks. For a moment I thought about going back out there; instead I headed straight for the shower and pushed the lever as far to the right as it would go. As the needle spray bit into my shoulders, I watched the steam rise up to surround me.

On the bus ride home, I was thinking about what I'd just done. I did it, I told myself, because he provoked me. It wasn't a conscious decision; it was a knee-jerk response.

All weekend, I thought about the incident. Should I take what was left of my uniform to his office right before the next practice? Nope, all that would do is let him know he'd won. Ok, I'll wait for him to ask for it. But what if he doesn't? Will I lose my nerve and give in?

Sunday night, seven-thirty, he called me at home. Ten minutes later I was back in that stifling office, the steam pipes hissing and banging away. Sullivan was sitting at his desk, head down, shuffling papers. He made me wait for about two minutes. Didn't even look up. When he knew I couldn't take the tension any longer, he said matter-of-factly—as if nothing had ever happened—"I'll see you at practice on Saturday."

Without taking his eyes off his papers, he handed me my cap and jersey and said, "Get your butt out of here, kid. I got work to do."

Of course I went back. That's what you do when you're fifteen and your identity is wrapped up in playing baseball. I had a pretty good season too. And though we didn't win the state title, we did make it to Cooperstown.

While I was on the mound that summer I'd hear Sullivan razzing us from the bench. I always listened closely, curious to see how far he'd push me. But whatever else he yelled, I never heard him shout "sugar baby." And I later found out that Sullivan did indeed invite Coach Kerchman to scout me. He just never took the trouble to tell me about it.

The "incident" happened over four decades ago, and I still couldn't decide whether I won or lost that confrontation. Sometimes I think I got the best of him, and sometimes I think I misread him—that he deliberately goaded me into throwing the ball at his head.

But wondering who won or lost, I told myself, is really to miss the point. Like me, Sullivan was in his early fifties when this happened. Could it be that now in my fifties, I was turning into a version of my old coach?

In the past few years, I noticed that many of my colleagues had turned cynical in the latter stages of their careers. But they stayed on anyway—out of a kind of inertia or fear, perhaps. Or because they needed to put more time in before they could take their benefits or pensions. It was certainly not the way I wanted to end my teaching career.

When I first began to teach, I promised myself I'd never use fear or intimidation to motivate or punish my students. And for the most part, I'd kept that promise. But in the past decade, I'd noticed that there were more and more students like Drew, who, for one reason or another, could push my hot buttons. They could provoke me in the same way that Sullivan had done four decades ago. And the impulsive severity of my retaliation surprised me as much now as it did then. Having crossed that line with Drew, I wanted to make sure it didn't happen again.

The first order of business was to talk privately with him. Yes, he was a mean-spirited kid. But he was also one of the best writers in the class. And despite our run-in, or maybe even because of it, I knew he would expect a high grade—probably a 4.0. I also knew that if he didn't get it, it was within his rights to file a grievance against me.

You walk a fine line with students like that. You don't want to let their insolence pass. Nor do you want to reward them for it. I thought again about the incident with Sullivan. As bigoted as Big Tom was, and as much as I hold him responsible for the Jew remark, I was still the one that hit him in the head with a baseball. And he was the one that put me back on the team. In his own misguided way then, Sullivan had allowed us both to save face and move on. It wasn't pretty, but it was precisely the outcome I wanted to affect with my belligerent student.

Three days later, I called Drew into my office and calmly explained my side of the story—including the earlier scenario that had triggered my outburst. I waited for him to respond, and when it was clear that he was going to hold his ground, I simply apologized.

Naturally, I was disappointed. But, there were two more issues left to resolve. The next night, I apologized to the class for what I'd said to Drew. But I made it clear that I didn't condone or approve of what either of us had done.

For the final month of the semester, Drew and I did not bait one another again. Nor did I single his work out for praise or censure. As if nothing had ever happened, he continued to write with the same insight and imagination—and defiance—as he had before. And when it came time to give the final grade, it was a 3.5, not the 4.0 I knew he was expecting.

Two weeks after the spring semester ended, I applied for early retirement.

At the Buffalo Bill Museum, June 1988

Jane Tompkins

The video at the entrance to the Buffalo Bill Historical Center says that Buffalo Bill was the most famous American of his time, that by 1900 more than a billion words had been written about him, and that he had a progressive vision of the West. Buffalo Bill had worked as a cattle driver, a wagoneer, a Pony Express rider, a buffalo hunter for the railroad, a hunting guide, an army scout and sometime Indian fighter; he wrote dime novels about himself and an autobiography by the age of thirty-four, by which time he was already famous; and then he began another set of careers, first as an actor, performing on the urban stage in wintertime melodramatic representations of what he actually earned a living at in the summer (scouting and leading hunting expeditions), and finally becoming the impresario of his great Wild West show, a form of entertainment he invented and carried on as actor, director, and all-around idea man for thirty years. Toward the end of his life he founded the town of Cody, Wyoming, to which he gave, among other things, two hundred thousand dollars. Strangely enough, it was as a progressive civic leader that Bill Cody wanted to be remembered. "I don't want to die," the video at the entrance quotes him as saying, "and have people say—oh, there goes another old showman. . . . I would like people to say—this is the man who opened Wyoming to the best of civilization."

"The best of civilization." This was the phrase that rang in my head as I moved through the museum, which is one of the most disturbing places I have ever visited. It is also a wonderful place. It is four museums in one: the Whitney Gallery of Western Art, which houses artworks on Western subjects; the Buffalo Bill Museum proper, which memorializes Cody's life; the Plains Indian Museum, which exhibits artifacts of American Indian civilization; and the Winchester Arms Museum, a collection of firearms historically considered.

The whole operation is extremely well designed and well run, from the video program at the entrance that gives an overview of all four museums, to the fresh-faced young attendants wearing badges that say "Ask Me," to the museum shop stacked with books on Western Americana, to the ladies room—a haven of satiny marble, shining mirrors, and flattering light. Among other things, the museum is admirable for its effort to combat prevailing stereotypes about the "winning of the West," a phrase it self-consciously places in quotation marks. There are placards declaring that all history is a matter of interpretation, and that the American West is a source of myth. Everywhere, except perhaps in the Winchester Arms Museum, where the rhetoric is different, you feel the effort of the museum staff to reach out to the public, to be clear, to be accurate, to be fair, not to condescend—in short, to educate in the best sense of the term.

On the day I went, the museum was featuring an exhibition of Frederic Remington's works. Two facts about Remington make his work different from that of artists usually encountered in museums. The first is that Remington's paintings and statues function as a historical record. Their chief attraction has always been that they transcribe scenes and events that have vanished from the earth. The second fact, related to this, is the brutality of their subject matter. Remington's work makes you pay attention to what is happening in the painting or the piece of statuary. When you look at his work you cannot escape from the subject.

Consequently, as I moved through the exhibit, the wild contortions of the bucking broncos, the sinister expression invariably worn by the Indians, and the killing of animals and men made the placards discussing Remington's use of the "lost wax" process seem strangely disconnected. In the face of unusual violence, or implied violence, their message was: what is important here is technique. Except in the case of paintings showing the battle of San Juan Hill, where white Americans were being killed, the material accompanying Remington's works did not refer to the subject matter of the paintings and statues themselves. Nevertheless, an undertone of disquiet ran beneath the explanations; at least I thought I detected one. Someone had taken the trouble to ferret out Remington's statement of horror at the slaughter on San Juan Hill; someone had also excerpted the judgment of art critics commending Remington for the lyricism, interiority, and mystery of his later canvases—pointing obliquely to the fascination with bloodshed that preoccupied his earlier work.

The uneasiness of the commentary, and my uneasiness with it, were nothing compared to the blatant contradictions in the paintings themselves. A pastel palette, a sunlit stop-action haze, murderous movement arrested under a lazy sky, flattened onto canvas and fixed in azure and ochre—two opposed impulses nestle here momentarily. The tension that keeps them from splitting apart is what holds the viewer's gaze.

The most excruciating example of what I mean occurs in the first painting in the exhibit. Entitled *His First Lesson,* it shows a horse standing saddled but riderless, the white of the horse's eye signaling his fear. A man using an instrument to tighten the horse's girth, at arm's length, backs away from the reaction he clearly anticipates, while the man who holds the horse's halter is doing the same. But what can they be afraid of? For the horse's right rear leg is tied a foot off the ground by a rope that is also tied around his neck. He can't move. That is the whole point.

His First Lesson. Whose? And what lesson, exactly? How to stand still when terrified? How not to break away when they come at you with strange instruments? How to be obedient? How to behave? It is impossible not to imagine that Remington's obsession with physical cruelty had roots somewhere in his own experience. Why else, in statue after statue, is the horse rebelling? The bucking bronco, symbol of the state of Wyoming, on every licence plate, on every sign for every bar, on every belt buckle, mug, and decal—this image Remington cast in bronze over and over again. There is a wild diabolism in the bronzes; the horse and rider seem one thing, not so much rider and ridden as a single bolt of energy gone crazy and caught somehow, complicatedly, in a piece of metal.

In the paintings, it is different—more subtle and bizarre. The cavalry on its way to a massacre, sweetly limned, softly tinted, poetically seized in mid-career, and gently laid on the two-dimensional surface. There is about these paintings of military men in the course of performing their deadly duty an almost maternal tenderness. The idealization of the cavalrymen in their dusty uniforms on their gallant horses has nothing to do with patriotism; it is pure love.

Remington's paintings and statues, as shown in this exhibition, embody everything that was objectionable about his era in American history. They are imperialist and racist; they glorify war and the torture and killing of animals; there are no women in them anywhere. Never the West as garden, never as pastoral, never as home. But in their aestheticization of violent life, Remington's pictures speak (to me, at least) of some other desire. The maternal tenderness is not an accident, nor is the beauty of the afternoons or the warmth of the desert sun. In them Remington plays the part of the preserver, as if by catching the figures in color and line he could save their lives and absorb some of that life into himself.

In one painting that particularly repulsed and drew me, a moose is outlined against the evening sky at the brink of a lake. He looks expectantly into the distance. Behind him and to one side, hidden from his view and only just revealed to ours, for it is dark there, is a hunter poised in the back of a canoe, rifle perfectly aimed. We look closer; the title of the picture is *Coming to the Call.* Ah, now we see. This is a sadistic scene. The hunter has lured the moose to his death. But wait a moment. Isn't the sadism really directed at us? First we see the glory of the animal; Remington has made it as noble as he knows how. Then we see what is going to happen. The hunter is one up on the moose, but Remington is one up on us. He makes us feel the pain of the anticipated killing, and makes us want to hold it off, to preserve the moose, just as he has done. Which way does the painting cut? Does it go against the hunter—who represents us, after all—or does it go against the moose who came to the call? Who came, to what call? Did Remington come to the West in response to it—to whatever the moose represents or to whatever the desire to kill the moose represents? But he hasn't killed it; he has only preserved an image of a white man about to kill it. And what call do we answer when we look at this painting? Who is calling whom? What is being preserved here?

That last question is the one that for me hung over the whole museum.

The Whitney Gallery is an art museum proper. Its allegiance is to art as academic tradition has defined it. In this tradition, we come to understand a painting by having in our possession various bits of information. Something about the technical process used to produce it (pastels, watercolors, woodblock prints, etc.); something about the elements of composition (line and color and movement); something about the artist's life (where born, how educated, by whom influenced, which school belonged to or revolted against); something about the artist's relation to this particular subject, such as how many times the artist painted it or whether it contains a favorite model. Occasionally there will be some philosophizing about the themes or ideas the paintings are said to represent.

The problem is, when you're faced with a painter like Remington, these bits of information, while nice to have, don't explain what is there in front of you. They don't begin to give you an account of why a person should have depicted such things. The experience of a lack of fit between the explanatory material and what is there on the wall is one I've had before in museums, when, standing in front of a painting or a piece of statuary, I've felt a huge gap between the information on the little placard and what it is I'm seeing. I realize that works of art, so-called, all have a subject matter, are all engaged with life, with some piece of life no less significant, no less compelling than Remington's subjects are, if we could only see its force. The idea that art is somehow separate from history, that it somehow occupies a space that is not the same as the space of life, seems out of whack here.

I wandered through the gallery thinking these things because right next to it, indeed all around it, in the Buffalo Bill Museum proper and in the Plains Indian Museum, are artifacts that stand not for someone's expertise or skill in manipulating the elements of an artistic medium, but for life itself, they are the residue of life.

The Buffalo Bill Museum is a wonderful array of textures, colors, shapes, sizes, forms. The fuzzy brown bulk of a buffalo's hump, the sparkling diamonds in a stickpin, the brilliant colors of the posters—the mixture makes you want to walk in and be surrounded by it, as if you were going into a child's adventure story. For a moment you can pretend you're a cowboy too; it's a museum where fantasy can take over. For a while.

As I moved through the exhibition, with the phrase "the best of civilization" ringing in my head, I came upon certain objects displayed in a section that recreates rooms from Cody's house. Ostrich feather fans, peacock feather fans, antler furniture—a chair and a table made entirely of antlers—a bearskin rug. And then I saw the heads on the wall: Alaska Yukon Moose, Wapiti American Elk, Muskox (the "Whitney," the "DeRham"), Mountain Caribou (the "Hyland"), Quebec Labrador Caribou (the "Elbow"), Rocky Mountain Goat (the "Haase," the "Kilto"), Woodland Caribou (world's record, "DeRham"), the "Rogers" freak Wapiti, the "Whitney" bison, the "Lord Rundlesham" bison. The names that appear after the animals are the names of the men who killed them. Each of the animals is scored according to measurements devised by the Boone and Crockett Club, a big-game hunters' organization. The Lord Rundlesham bison, for example, scores 124%, making it number 25 in the world for bison trophies. The "Reed" Alaska Yukon Moose scores 247. The "Witherbee" Canada moose holds the world's record.

Next to the wall of trophies is a small enclosure where jewelry is displayed. A buffalo head stickpin and two buffalo head rings, the heads made entirely of diamonds, with ruby eyes, the gifts of the Russian crown prince. A gold and diamond stickpin from Edward VII; a gold, diamond, and garnet locket from Queen Victoria. The two kinds of trophies—animals and jewels—form an incongruous set; the relationship between them compelling but obscure.

If the rest of the items in the museum—the dime novels with their outrageous covers, the marvelous posters, the furniture, his wife's dress, his daughter's oil painting—have faded from my mind it is because I cannot forget the heads of the animals as they stared down, each with an individual expression on its face. When I think about it I realize that I don't know why these animal heads are there. Buffalo Bill didn't kill them; perhaps they were gifts from the famous people he took on hunts. A different kind of jewelry.

After the heads, I began to notice something about the whole exhibition. In one display, doghide chaps, calfskin chaps, angora goathide chaps, and horsehide chaps. Next to these a rawhide lariat and a horsehair quirt. Behind me, boots and saddles, all of leather. Everywhere I looked there was tooth or bone, skin or fur, hide or hair, or the animal itself entire—two full-size buffalo (a main feature of the exhibition) and a magnificent stone sheep (a mountain sheep with beautiful curving horns). This one was another world's record. The best of civilization.

In the literature about Buffalo Bill you read that he was a conservationist, that if it were not for the buffalo in his Wild West shows the species would probably have become extinct. (In the seventeenth century 40 million buffalo roamed North America; by 1900 all the wild buffalo had been killed except for one herd in northern Alberta.) That the man who gained fame first as a buffalo hunter should have been an advocate for conservation of the buffalo is not an anomaly but typical of the period. The men who did the most to preserve America's natural wilderness and its wildlife were big-game hunters. The Boone and Crockett Club, founded by Theodore Roosevelt, George Bird Grinnell, and Owen Wister, turns out to have been one of the earliest organizations to devote itself to environmental protection in the United States. *The Reader's Encyclopedia of the American West* says that the club "supported the national park and forest reserve movement, helped create a system of national wildlife refuges, and lobbied for the protection of threatened species, such as the buffalo and antelope." At the same time, the prerequisites for membership in the club were "the highest caliber of sportsmanship and the achievement of killing 'in fair chase' trophy specimens [which had to be adult males] from several species of North American big game."

The combination big-game hunter and conservationist suggests that these men had no interest in preserving the animals for the animals' sake but simply wanted to ensure the chance to exercise their sporting pleasure. But I think this view is too simple; something further is involved here. The men who hunted game animals had a kind of love for them and a kind of love for nature that led them to want to preserve the animals they also desired to kill. That is, the desire to kill the animals was in some way related to a desire to see them live. It is not an accident, in this connection, that Roosevelt, Wister, and Remington all went west originally for their health. Their devotion to the West, their connection to it, their love for it are rooted in their need to reanimate their own lives. The preservation of nature, in other words, becomes for them symbolic of their own survival.

In a sense, then, there is a relationship between the Remington exhibition in the Whitney Gallery and the animal memorabilia in the Buffalo Bill Museum. The moose in *Coming to the Call* and the mooseheads on the wall are not so different as they might appear. The heads on the wall serve an aesthetic purpose; they are decorative objects, pleasing to the eye, which call forth certain associations. In this sense they are like visual works of art. The painting, on the other hand, has something of the trophy about it. The moose as Remington painted it is about to become a trophy, yet in another sense it already is one. Remington has simply captured the moose in another form. In both cases the subject matter, the life of a wild animal, symbolizes the life of the observer. It is the preservation of that life that both the painting and the taxidermy serve.

What are museums keeping safe for us, after all? What is it that we wish so much to preserve? The things we put in safekeeping, in our safe-deposit boxes under lock and key, are always in some way intended finally as safeguards of our own existence. The money and jewelry and stock certificates are meant for a time when we can no longer earn a living by the sweat of our brows. Similarly, the objects in museums preserve for us a source of life from which we need to nourish ourselves when the resources that would normally supply us have run dry.

The Buffalo Bill Historical Center, full as it is of dead bones, lets us see more clearly than we normally can what it is that museums are for. It is a kind of charnel house that houses images of living things that have passed away but whose life force still lingers around their remains and so passes itself on to us. We go and look at the objects in the glass cases and at the paintings on the wall, as if by standing there we could absorb into ourselves some of the energy that flowed once through the bodies of the live things represented. A museum, rather than being, as we normally think of it, the most civilized of places, a place most distant from our savage selves, actually caters to the urge to absorb the life of another into one's own life.

If we see the Buffalo Bill Museum in this way, it is no longer possible to separate ourselves from the hunters responsible for the trophies with their wondering eyes or from the curators who put them there. We are not, in essence, different from Roosevelt or Remington or Buffalo Bill, who killed animals when they were abundant in the Wild West of the 1880s. If in doing so those men were practicing the ancient art of absorbing the life of an animal into their own through the act of killing it, realizing themselves through the destruction of another life, then we are not so different from them as visitors to the museum. We stand beside the bones and skins and nails of beings that were once alive, or stare fixedly at their painted images. Indeed our visit is only a safer form of the same enterprise as theirs.

So I did not get out of the Buffalo Bill Museum unscathed, unimplicated in the acts of rapine and carnage that these remains represent. And I did not get out without having had a good time, either, because however many dire thoughts I may have had, the exhibits were interesting and fun to see. I was even able to touch a piece of buffalo hide displayed especially for that purpose (it was coarse and springy). Everyone else had touched it too. The hair was worn down, where people's hands had been, to a fraction of its original length.

After this, the Plains Indian Museum was a terrible letdown. I went from one exhibit to another expecting to become absorbed, but nothing worked. What was the matter? I was interested in Indians, had read about them, taught some Indian literature, felt drawn by accounts of native religions. I had been prepared to enter this museum as if I were going into another children's story, only this time I would be an Indian instead of a cowboy or a cowgirl. But the objects on display, most of them behind glass, seemed paltry and insignificant. They lacked visual presence. The bits of leather and sticks of wood triggered no fantasies in me.

At the same time, I noticed with some discomfort that almost everything in those glass cases was made of feathers and claws and hide, just like the men's chaps and ladies' fans in the Buffalo Bill Museum, only there was no luxury here. Plains Indian culture, it seemed, was made entirely from animals. Their mode of life had been even more completely dedicated to carnage than Buffalo Bill's, dependent as it was on animals for food, clothing, shelter, equipment, everything. In the Buffalo Bill Museum I was able to say to myself, well, if these men had been more sensitive, if they had had a right relation to their environment and to life itself, the atrocities that produced these trophies would never have occurred. They never would have exterminated the Indians and killed off the buffalo. But the spectacle before me made it impossible to say that. I had expected that the Plains Indian Museum would show me how life in nature ought to be lived: not the mindless destruction of nineteenth-century America but an ideal form of communion with animals and the land. What the museum seemed to say instead was that cannibalism was universal. Both colonizer and colonized had had their hands imbrued with blood. The Indians had lived off animals and had made war against one another. Violence was simply a necessary and inevitable part of life. And a person who, like me, was horrified at the extent of the destruction was just the kind of romantic idealist my husband sometimes accused me of being. There was no such thing as the life lived in harmony with nature. It was all bloodshed and killing, an unending cycle, over and over again, and no one could escape.

But perhaps there was a way to understand the violence that made it less terrible. Perhaps if violence was necessary, a part of nature, intended by the universe, then it could be seen as sacramental. Perhaps it was true, what Calvin Martin had said in *Keepers of the Game:* that the Indians had a sacred contract with the animals they killed, that they respected them as equals and treated their remains with honor and punctilio. If so, the remains of animals in the Plains Indian Museum weren't the same as those left by Buffalo Bill and his friends. They certainly didn't look the same. Perhaps. All I knew for certain was that these artifacts, lifeless and shrunken, spoke to me of nothing I could understand. No more did the life-size models of Indians, with strange featureless faces, draped in costumes that didn't look like clothing. The figures, posed awkwardly in front of tepees too white to seem real, carried no sense of a life actually lived, any more than the objects in the glass cases had.

The more I read the placards on the wall, the more disaffected I became. Plains Indian life apparently had been not only bloody but exceedingly tedious. All those porcupine quills painstakingly softened, flattened, dyed, then appliqued through even more laborious methods of stitching or weaving. Four methods of attaching porcupine quills, six design groups, population statistics, patterns of migration. There wasn't any glamour here at all. No glamour in the lives the placards told about, no glamour in the objects themselves, no glamour in the experience of looking at them. Just a lot of shriveled things accompanied by some even drier information.

Could it be, then, that the problem with the exhibitions was that Plains Indian culture, if representable at all, was simply not readable by someone like me? Their stick figures and abstract designs could convey very little to an untrained Euro-American eye. One display in particular illustrated this. It was a piece of cloth, behind glass, depicting a buffalo skin with some marks on it. The placard read: "Winter Count, Sioux ca. 1910, after Lone Dog's, Fort Peck, Montana, 1877." The hide with its markings had been a calendar, each year represented by one image, which showed the most significant event in the life of the tribe. A thick pamphlet to one side of the glass case explained each image year by year: 1800–1801, the attack of the Uncapoo on a Crow Indian Fort; 1802–1803, a total eclipse of the sun. The images, once you knew what they represented, made sense, and seemed poetic interpretations of the experiences they stood for. But without explanation they were incomprehensible.

The Plains Indian Museum stopped me in my tracks. It was written in a language I had never learned. I didn't have the key. Maybe someone did, but I wasn't too sure. For it may not have been just cultural difference that made the text unreadable. I began to suspect that the text itself was corrupt, that the architects of this museum were going through motions whose purpose was, even to themselves, obscure. Knowing what event a figure stands for in the calendar doesn't mean you understand an Indian year. The deeper purpose of the museum began to puzzle me. Wasn't there an air of bad faith about preserving the vestiges of a culture one had effectively extinguished? Did the museum exist to assuage our guilt and not for any real educational reason? I do not have an answer to these questions. All I know is that I felt I was in the presence of something pious and a little insincere. It had the aura of a failed attempt at virtue, as though the curators were trying to present as interesting objects whose purpose and meaning even they could not fully imagine.

In a last-ditch attempt to salvage something, I went up to one of the guards and asked where the movie was showing which the video had advertised, the movie about Plains Indian life. "Oh, the slide show, you mean," he said. "It's been discontinued." When I asked why, he said he didn't know. It occurred to me then that that was the message the museum was sending, if I could read it, that that was the bottom line. Discontinued, no reason given.

The movie in the Winchester Arms Museum, *Lock, Stock, and Barrel,* was going strong. The film began with the introduction of cannon into European warfare in the Middle Ages, and was working its way slowly toward the nineteenth century when I left. I was in a hurry. Soon my husband would be waiting for me in the lobby. I went from room to room, trying to get a quick sense impression of the objects on display. They were all the same: guns. Some large drawings and photographs on the walls tried to give a sense of the context in which the arms had been used, but the effect was nil. It was case after case of rifles and pistols, repeating themselves over and over, and even when some slight variation caught my eye the differences meant nothing to me.

But the statistics did. In a large case of commemorative rifles, I saw the Antlered Game Commemorative Carbine. Date of manufacture: 1978. Number produced: 19,999. I wondered how many antlered animals each carbine had killed. I saw the Canadian Centennial (1962): 90,000; the Legendary Lawman (1978): 19,999; the John Wayne (1980–81): 51,600. Like the titles of the various sections of the museum, these names had a message. The message was: guns are patriotic. Associated with national celebrations, law enforcement, and cultural heroes. The idea that firearms were inseparable from the march of American history came through even more strongly in the titles given to the various exhibits: Firearms in Colonial America; Born in America: The Kentucky Rifle; The Era of Expansion and Invention; The Civil War: Firearms of the Conflict; The Golden Age of Hunting; Winning the West. The guns embodied phases of the history they had helped to make. There were no quotation marks here to indicate that expansion and conquest might not have been all they were cracked up to be. The fact that firearms had had a history seemed to consecrate them; the fact that they had existed at the time when certain famous events had occurred seemed to make them not only worth preserving but worth studying and revering. In addition to the exhibition rooms, the museum housed three "study galleries": one for hand arms, one for shoulder arms, one for U.S. military firearms.

As I think back on the rows and rows of guns, I wonder if I should have looked at them more closely, tried harder to appreciate the workmanship that went into them, the ingenuity, the attention. Awe and admiration are the attitudes the museum invites. You hear the ghostly march of military music in the background; you imagine flags waving and sense the implicit reference to feats of courage in battle and glorious death. The place had the air of an expensive and well-kept reliquary, or of the room off the transept of a cathedral where the vestments are stored. These guns were not there merely to be seen or even studied; they were there to be venerated.

But I did not try to appreciate the guns. They were too technical, too foreign. I didn't have their language, and, besides, I didn't want to learn. I rejoined my husband in the lobby. The Plains Indian Museum had been incomprehensible, but in the Winchester Arms Museum I could hardly see the objects at all, for I did not see the point. Or, rather, I did see it and rejected it. Here in the basement the instruments that had turned live animals into hides and horns, had massacred the Indians and the buffalo, were being lovingly displayed. And we were still making them: 51,600 John Waynes in 1980–81. Arms were going strong.

As I bought my books and postcards in the gift shop, I noticed a sign that read "Rodeo Tickets Sold Here," and something clicked into place. So that was it. *Everything* was still going strong. The whole museum was just another rodeo, only with the riders and their props stuffed, painted, sculpted, immobilized and put under glass. Like the rodeo, the entire museum witnessed a desire to bring back the United States of the 1880s and 1890s. The American people did not want to let go of the winning of the West. They wanted to win it all over again, in imagination. It was the ecstasy of the kill, as much as the life of the hunted, that we fed off here. The Buffalo Bill Historical Center did not repudiate the carnage that had taken place in the nineteenth century. It celebrated it. With its gleaming rest rooms, cute snack bar, opulent museum shop, wooden Indians, thousand rifles, and scores of animal trophies, it helped us all reenact the dream of excitement, adventure, and conquest that was what the Wild West meant to most people in this country.

This is where my visit ended, but it had a sequel. When I left the Buffalo Bill Historical Center, I was full of moral outrage, an indignation so intense it made me almost sick, though it was pleasurable too, as such emotions usually are. But the outrage was undermined by the knowledge that I knew nothing about Buffalo Bill, nothing of his life, nothing of the circumstances that led him to be involved in such violent events. And I began to wonder if my reaction wasn't in some way an image, however small, of the violence I had been objecting to. So when I got home I began to read about Buffalo Bill, and a whole new world opened up. I came to love Buffalo Bill.

"I have seen him the very personification of grace and beauty . . . dashing over the free wild prairie and riding his horse as though he and the noble animal were bounding with one life and one motion." That is the sort of thing people wrote about Buffalo Bill. They said "he was the handsomest man I ever saw." They said "there was never another man lived as popular as he was." They said "there wasn't a man, woman or child that he knew or ever met that he didn't speak to." They said "he was handsome as a god, a good rider and a crack shot." They said "he gave lots of money away. Nobody ever went hungry around him." They said "he was way above the average, physically and every other way."

These are quotes from people who knew Cody, collected by one of his two most responsible biographers, Nellie Snyder Yost. She puts them in the last chapter, and by the time you get there they all ring true. Buffalo Bill was incredibly handsome. He was extremely brave and did things no other scout would do. He would carry messages over rugged territory swarming with hostile Indians, riding all night in bad weather and get through, and then take off again the next day to ride sixty miles through a blizzard. He was not a proud man. He didn't boast of his exploits. But he did do incredible things, not just once in a while but on a fairly regular basis. He had a great deal of courage; he believed in himself, in his abilities, in his strength and endurance and knowledge. He was very skilled at what he did—hunting and scouting—but he wasn't afraid to try other things. He wrote some dime novels, he wrote his autobiography by age thirty-four, without very much schooling; he wasn't afraid to try acting, even though the stage terrified him and he knew so little about it that, according to his wife, he didn't even know you had to memorize lines.

Maybe it was because he grew up on the frontier, maybe it was just the kind of person he was, but he was constantly finding himself in situations that required resourcefulness and courage, quick decisions and decisive action and rising to the occasion. He wasn't afraid to improvise.

He liked people, drank a lot, gave big parties, gave lots of presents, and is reputed to have been a womanizer.[1] When people came to see him in his office tent on the show grounds, to shake his hand or have their pictures taken with him, he never turned anyone away. "He kept a uniformed doorman at the tent opening to announce visitors," writes a biographer. "No matter who was outside, from a mayor to a shabby woman with a baby, the Colonel would smooth his mustache, stand tall and straight, and tell the doorman to 'show 'em in.' He greeted everyone the same."[2]

As a showman, he was a genius. People don't say much about *why* he was so successful; mostly they describe the wonderful goings-on. But I get the feeling that Cody was one of those people who was connected to his time in an uncanny way. He knew what people wanted, he knew how to entertain them, because he *liked* them, was open to them, felt his kinship with them, or was so much in touch with himself at some level that he was thereby in touch with almost everybody else.

He liked to dress up and had a great sense of costume (of humor, too, they say). Once he came to a fancy dress ball, his first, in New York, wearing white tie and tails and a large Stetson. He knew what people wanted. He let his hair grow long and wore a mustache and beard, because, he said, he wouldn't be believable as a scout otherwise. Hence his Indian name, Pahaska, meaning "long hair," which people loved to use. Another kind of costume. He invented the ten-gallon hat, which the Stetson company made to his specifications. Afterward, they made a fortune from it. In the scores of pictures reproduced in the many books about him, he most often wears scout's clothes—usually generously fringed buckskin, sometimes a modified cavalryman's outfit—though often he's impeccably turned out in a natty-looking three-piece business suit (sometimes with overcoat, sometimes not). The photographs show him in a tuxedo, in something called a "Mexican suit" which looks like a cowboy outfit, and once he appears in Indian dress. In almost every case he is wearing some kind of hat, usually the Stetson, at exactly the right angle. He poses deliberately, and with dignity, for the picture. Cody didn't take himself so seriously that he had to pretend to be less than he was.

What made Buffalo Bill so irresistible? Why is he still so appealing, even now, when we've lost, supposedly, all the illusions that once supported his popularity? There's a poster for one of his shows when he was traveling in France that gives a clue to what it is that makes him so profoundly attractive a figure. The poster consists of a huge buffalo galloping across the plains, and against the buffalo's hump, in the center of his hump, is a cutout circle that shows the head of Buffalo Bill, white-mustachioed and bearded now, in his famous hat, and beneath, in large red letters, are the words "Je viens."

Je viens ("I am coming") are the words of a savior. The announcement is an annunciation. Buffalo Bill is a religious figure of a kind who makes sense within a specifically Christian tradition. That is, he comes in the guise of a redeemer, of someone who will save us, who will through his own actions do something for us that we ourselves cannot do. He will lift us above our lives, out of the daily grind, into something larger than we are.

His appeal on the surface is to childish desires, the desire for glamour, fame, bigness, adventure, romance. But these desires are also the sign of something more profound, and it is to something more profound in us that he also appeals. Buffalo Bill comes to the child in us, understood not as that part of ourselves that we have outgrown but as the part that got left behind, of necessity, a long time ago, having been starved, bound, punished, disciplined out of existence. He promises that that part of the self can live again. He has the power to promise these things because he represents the West, that geographical space of the globe that was still the realm of exploration and discovery, that was still open, that had not yet quite been tamed, when he began to play himself on the stage. He not only represented it, he *was* it. He brought the West itself with him when he came. The very Indians, the very buffalo, the very cowboys, the very cattle, the very stage-coach itself which had been memorialized in story. He performed in front of the audience the feats that had made him famous. He shot glass balls and clay pigeons out of the air with amazing rapidity. He rode his watersmooth silver stallion at full gallop. "Jesus he was a handsome man," wrote e. e. cummings in "Buffalo Bill's Defunct."

"I am coming." This appearance of Buffalo Bill, in the flesh, was akin to the apparition of a saint or of the Virgin Mary to believers. He was the incarnation of an ideal. He came to show people that what they had only imagined was really true. The West really did exist. There really were heroes who rode white horses and performed amazing feats. e. e. cummings was right to invoke the name of Jesus in his poem. Buffalo Bill was a secular messiah.

He was a messiah because people believed in him. When he died, he is reputed to have said, "Let my show go on." But he had no show at the time, so he probably didn't say that. Still, the words are prophetic because the desire for what Buffalo Bill had done had not only not died but would call forth the countless reenactments of the Wild West, from the rodeo—a direct descendant of his show—to the thousands of Western novels, movies, and television programs that comprise the Western genre in the twentieth century, a genre that came into existence as a separate category right about the time that Cody died. Don Russell maintains that the way the West exists in our minds today is largely the result of the way Cody presented it in his show. That was where people got their ideas of what the characters looked like. Though many Indian tribes wore no feathers and fought on foot, you will never see a featherless, horseless Indian warrior in the movies, because Bill employed only Sioux and other Plains tribes which had horses and traditionally wore feathered headdresses. "Similarly," he adds, "cowboys wear ten-gallon Stetsons, not because such a hat was worn in early range days, but because it was part of the costume adopted by Buffalo Bill for his show."[3]

But the deeper legacy is elsewhere. Buffalo Bill was a person who inspired other people. What they saw in him was an aspect of themselves. It really doesn't matter whether Cody was as great as people thought him or not, because what they were responding to when he rode into the arena, erect and resplendent on his charger, was something intangible, not the man himself, but a possible way of being. William F. Cody and the Wild West triggered the emotions that had fueled the imaginative lives of people who flocked to see him, especially men and boys, who made up the larger portion of the audience. He and his cowboys played to an inward territory; a Wild West of the psyche that hungered for exercise sprang into activity when the show appeared. *Je viens* was a promise to redeem that territory, momentarily at least, from exile and oblivion. The lost parts of the self symbolized by buffalo and horses and wild men would live again for an hour while the show went on.

People adored it. Queen Victoria, who broke her custom by going to see it at all (she never went to the theater, and on the rare occasions when she wanted to see a play she had it brought to her), is supposed to have been lifted out of a twenty-five-year depression caused by the death of her husband after she saw Buffalo Bill. She liked the show so much that she saw it again, arranging for a command performance to be given at Windsor Castle the day before her Diamond Jubilee. This was the occasion when four kings rode in the Deadwood stagecoach with the Prince of Wales on top next to Buffalo Bill, who drove. No one was proof against the appeal. Ralph Blumenfeld, the London correspondent for the New York *Herald*, wrote in his diary while the show was in London that he'd had two boyhood heroes, Robin Hood and Buffalo Bill, and had delighted in Cody's stories of the Pony Express and Yellow Hand:

> Everything was done to make Cody conceited and unbearable, but he remained the simple, unassuming child of the plains who thought lords and ladies belonged in the picture books and that the story of Little Red Riding Hood was true. I rode in the Deadwood coach. It was a great evening in which I realized a good many of my boyhood dreams, for there was Buffalo Bill on his white rocking horse charger, and Annie Oakley behind him.[4]

Victor Weybright and Henry Blackman Sell, from whose book on the Wild West some of the foregoing information has come, dedicated their book to Buffalo Bill. It was published in 1955. Nellie Snyder Yost, whose 1979 biography is one of the two scholarly accounts of Cody's life, dedicates her book "to all those good people, living or dead, who knew and liked Buffalo Bill." Don Russell's *The Lives and Legends of Buffalo Bill* (1960), the most fact-filled scholarly biography, does not have a dedication, but in the final chapter, where he steps back to assess Cody and his influence, Russell ends by exclaiming, "What more could possibly be asked of a hero? If he was not one, who was?"[5]

Let me now pose a few questions of my own. Must we throw out all the wonderful qualities that Cody had, the spirit of hope and emulation that he aroused in millions of people, because of the terrible judgment history has passed on the epoch of which he was part? The kinds of things he stands for—courage, daring, strength, endurance, generosity, openness to other people, love of drama, love of life, the possibility of living a life that does not deny the body and the desires of

the body—are these to be declared dangerous and delusional although he manifested some of them while fighting Indians and others while representing his vic-
tories to the world? And the feelings he aroused in his audiences, the idealism, the
enthusiasm, the excitement, the belief that dreams could become real—must these
be declared misguided or a sham because they are associated with the imperialis-
tic conquest of a continent, with the wholesale extermination of animals and men?

It is not so much that we cannot learn from history as that we cannot teach
history how things should have been. When I set out to discover how Cody had
become involved in the killing of Indians and the slaughter of buffalo, I found
myself unable to sustain the outrage I had felt on leaving the museum. From his
first job as an eleven-year-old herder for an army supply outfit, sole wage earner
for his ailing widowed mother who had a new baby and other children to support, to his death in Colorado at the age of seventy-one, there was never a time
when it was possible to say, there, there you went wrong, Buffalo Bill, you should
not have killed that Indian. You should have held your fire and made your living
some other way and quit the army and gone to work in the nineteenth-century
equivalent of the Peace Corps. You should have known how it would end. My
reading made me see that you cannot prescribe for someone in Buffalo Bill's position what he should have done, and it made me reflect on how eager I had been to
get off on being angry at the museum. The thirst for moral outrage, for self-vindi-
cation, lay pretty close to the surface.

I cannot resolve the contradiction between my experience at the Buffalo Bill
Historical Center with its celebration of violent conquest and my response to the
shining figure of Buffalo Bill as it emerged from the pages of books—on the one
hand, a history of shame; on the other, an image of the heart's desire. But I have
reached one conclusion that for a while will have to serve.

Major historical events like genocide and major acts of destruction are not
simply produced by impersonal historical processes or economic imperatives or
ecological blunders; human intentionality is involved and human knowledge of
the self. Therefore, if you're really, truly interested in not having any more genocide or killing of animals, no matter what else you might do, if you don't first, or
also, come to recognize the violence in yourself and your own anger and your
own destructiveness, whatever else you do won't work. It isn't that genocide
doesn't matter. Genocide matters, and it starts at home.

Notes

1. Iron Eyes Cody, as told to Collin Perry, *Iron Eyes: My Life as a Hollywood Indian* (New York, 1982), 16.

2. Nellie Irene Snyder Yost, *Buffalo Bill: His Family, Friends, Fame, Failures, and Fortunes* (Chicago, 1979), 436.

3. Don Russell, *The Lives and Legends of Buffalo Bill* (Norman, Okla., 1960), 470.

4. Victor Weybright and Henry Blackman Sell, *Buffalo Bill and the Wild West* (New York, 1955), 172.

5. Russell, 480.

Going to the Movies

Susan Allen Toth

I

Aaron takes me only to art films. That's what I call them, anyway: strange movies with vague poetic images I don't understand, long dreamy movies about a distant Technicolor past, even longer black-and-white movies about the general meaninglessness of life. We do not go unless at least one reputable critic has found the cinematography superb. We went to *The Devil's Eye*, and Aaron turned to me in the middle and said, "My God, this is *funny*." I do not think he was pleased.

When Aaron and I go to the movies, we drive our cars separately and meet by the box office. Inside the theater he sits tentatively in his seat, ready to move if he can't see well, poised to leave if the film is disappointing. He leans away from me, careful not to touch the bare flesh of his arm against the bare flesh of mine. Sometimes he leans so far I am afraid he may be touching the woman on his other side instead. If the movie is very good, he leans forward too, peering between the heads of the couple in front of us. The light from the screen bounces off his glasses; he gleams with intensity, sitting there on the edge of his seat, watching the screen. Once I tapped him on the arm so I could whisper a comment in his ear. He jumped.

After *Belle de Jour*, Aaron said he wanted to ask me if he could stay overnight. "But I can't," he shook his head mournfully before I had a chance to answer, "because I know I never sleep well in strange beds." Then he apologized for asking. "It's just that after a film like that," he said, "I feel the need to assert myself."

II

Bob takes me only to movies that he thinks have a redeeming social conscience. He doesn't call them films. They tend to be about poverty, war, injustice, political corruption, struggling unions in the 1930s, and the military-industrial complex.

247

Bob doesn't like propaganda movies, though, and he doesn't like to be too depressed either. We stayed away from *The Sorrow and the Pity;* it would be, he said, too much. Besides, he assured me, things are never that hopeless. So most of the movies we see are made in Hollywood. Because they are always very topical, these movies offer what Bob calls "food for thought." When we saw *Coming Home,* Bob's jaw set so firmly with the first half that I knew we would end up at Poppin' Fresh Pies afterward.

When Bob and I go to the movies, we take turns driving so no one owes anyone else anything. We park far away from the theater so we don't have to pay for a space. If it's raining or snowing, Bob offers to let me off at the door, but I can tell he'll feel better if I go with him while he parks, so we share the walk too. Inside the theater Bob will hold my hand when I get scared if I ask him. He puts my hand firmly on his knee and covers it completely with his own hand. His knee never twitches. After a while, when the scary part is past, he loosens his hand slightly and I know that is a signal to take mine away. He sits companionably close, letting his jacket just touch my sweater, but he does not infringe. He thinks I ought to know he is there if I need him.

One night after *The China Syndrome* I asked Bob if he wouldn't like to stay for a second drink, even though it was past midnight. He thought awhile about that, considering my offer from all possible angles, but finally he said no. Relationships today, he said, have a tendency to move too quickly.

III

Sam likes movies that are entertaining. By that he means movies that Will Jones of the *Minneapolis Tribune* loved and either *Time* or *Newsweek* rather liked; also movies that do not have sappy love stories, are not musicals, do not have subtitles, and will not force him to think. He does not go to movies to think. He liked *California Suite* and *The Seduction of Joe Tynan,* though the plots, he said, could have been zippier. He saw it all coming too far in advance, and that took the fun out. He doesn't like to know what is going to happen. "I just want my brain to be tickled," he says. It is very hard for me to pick out movies for Sam.

When Sam takes me to the movies, he pays for everything. He thinks that's what a man ought to do. But I buy my own popcorn, because he doesn't approve of it; the grease might smear his flannel slacks. Inside the theater, Sam makes himself comfortable. He takes off his jacket, puts one arm around me, and all during the movie he plays with my hand, stroking my palm, beating a small tattoo on my wrist. Although he watches the movie intently, his body operates on instinct. Once I inclined my head and kissed him lightly just behind his ear. He beat a faster tattoo on my wrist, quick and musical, but he didn't look away from the screen.

When Sam takes me home from the movies, he stands outside my door and kisses me long and hard. He would like to come in, he says regretfully, but his steady girlfriend in Duluth wouldn't like it. When the *Tribune* gives a movie four stars, he has to save it to see with her. Otherwise her feelings might be hurt.

IV

I go to some movies by myself. On rainy Sunday afternoons I often sneak into a revival house or a college auditorium for old Technicolor musicals, *Kiss Me Kate, Seven Brides for Seven Brothers, Calamity Jane,* even, once, *The Sound of Music.* Wearing saggy jeans so I can prop my feet on the seat in front, I sit toward the rear where no one will see me. I eat large handfuls of popcorn with double butter. Once the movie starts, I feel completely at home. Howard Keel and I are old friends; I grin back at him on the screen, admiring all his teeth. I know the sound tracks by heart. Sometimes when I get really carried away I hum along with Kathryn Grayson, remembering how I once thought I would fill out a formal like that. Skirts whirl, feet tap, acrobatic young men perform impossible feats, and then the camera dissolves into a dream sequence I know I can comfortably follow. It is not, thank God, Bergman.

If I can't find an old musical, I settle for Hepburn and Tracy, vintage Grant or Gable, on adventurous days Claudette Colbert or James Stewart. Before I buy my ticket I make sure it will all end happily. If necessary, I ask the girl at the box office. I have never seen *Stella Dallas* or *Intermezzo.* Over the years I have developed other peccadilloes: I will, for example, see anything that is redeemed by Thelma Ritter. At the end of *Daddy Long Legs* I wait happily for the scene where Fred Clark, no longer angry, at last pours Thelma a convivial drink. They smile at each other, I smile at them, I feel they are smiling at me. In the movies I go to by myself, the men and women always like each other.

Reflection Rag: Uncle Joe, Roberto Clemente, and I

Christine White

So much happened so quickly after Uncle Joe died. The tempo changed. This new rhythm blew aside the curtain and there it was, this other order of things that lies beneath or beyond: a hidden stage where we play out our lives and strange bedfellows mingle and the orchestra plays ragtime and spirits stand in the wings, feeding us our lines, leading us home.

Exit Uncle Joe

The year is 1999. the month is July. The day is 9. Uncle Joe dies after just a few days in the hospital. The obituary tells part of his story.

. . . born July 23, 1917, in Pittsburgh, Penn. . . . He lived nearly all his life in the Pittsburgh area before moving to Estes Park two years ago after Dorothy, his wife of fifty-three years, died. He received a degree in Petroleum Engineering. . . . Joe served as a Lt. Commander in the navy during World War II on Midway Island . . . Most of his career was spent as a white hat foreman for U.S. Steel. Joe enjoyed piloting his Cessna 150. . . . He was twice decorated and a recognized elite member of the Transcendental Explorers Club International. He is survived by his son Jimmy and his wife, with whom Joe lived in Estes Park, and four grandchildren.

At the top of the obituary is an old picture of Uncle Joe in his cowboy hat, white beard, and plaid shirt. Uncle Joe dressed that way a lot after his son Michael died. He looks like Gabby Hayes, like a real cowboy. He once was asked to be an extra in a Western movie. He looks like the real thing, Uncle Joe in that hat.

I know about Joe's years in the navy and his work with U.S. Steel, know how he loved to fly. But I don't know about the Transcendental Explorers Club

International and the decorations. I thought I knew Joe pretty well but I don't know about that.

I think about Uncle Joe a lot after he dies. I wonder where he is. Just a few months before his death, Uncle Joe was with me in Illinois, and just two weeks before he died, he had driven his van back to Pittsburgh. Eighty-one years old and still driving from Colorado to Pittsburgh all by himself. Even Joe said it was probably the last time. When he couldn't drive back home any more, I guess Uncle Joe decided it was time to die.

Cousin Jimmy was sitting on the bed next to Uncle Joe when my daughter Gia walked into Joe's room at the hospice in Estes Park. Jimmy looked tired and scraggly. "Pappy has passed. Just a couple minutes ago," Jimmy told her.

Gia sat down in a chair at the foot of the bed. Jimmy left to give the undertaker information for Joe's obituary, so Gia remained alone in the room with her dead great uncle. She watched as an attendant removed an IV tube from Joe's limp arm. Then Gia called me.

"Mom," came her little voice, calling Illinois all the way from Colorado. "Uncle Joe died, right before I got here."

I didn't realize at first that she was still in the room with Uncle Joe's body. "Where is Uncle Joe now?" I asked.

"Right here. I'm with him now," she said.

I suggested she wait someplace else but Gia said being in the room with Joe was a good feeling, that the late-afternoon light coming in the window made the room seem warm and soft, and that Joe, lying alone on the bed with the white sheet drawn up to his white chin, his white hair and white beard and mustache in place, looked peaceful. "Like all the sadness has seeped away," she said. "It's not bad to be where Uncle Joe is."

"When is the funeral?" I asked. Ever since Jimmy had called me two days ago, saying that Joe was dying, I had planned to go to the funeral.

"There is no funeral," Gia said. "Jimmy's having a memorial barbecue and then he's going to scatter Joe's ashes."

The thought of a barbecue in lieu of a funeral didn't strike her as odd.

ENTER ROBERTO CLEMENTE

The year is 1999. The month is July. The day is 16. I am inside the Unity Church in Boulder, Colorado. Uncle Joe, or at least his ashes, will be scattered tomorrow in Estes Park. I am at a performance of the Rocky Mountain Ragtime Festival. Gia and a friend have brought me here. The friend's uncle is a ragtime pianist who will perform as part of the concert this evening. The uncle gave us free tickets.

A pianist named Scott Kirby walks onto the small church stage. Kirby is handsome, dark and bearded. He bows, elegant in a flowing white silk shirt and dark trousers.

"I am going to play 'Roberto Clemente.'" That's all he says as he settles himself on the piano bench. "I am going to play 'Roberto Clemente.'"

This juxtaposition of baseball icon and piano rag jars me. I hear Clemente's name and I am back in Pittsburgh all over again. Back where I spent the first twenty years of my life. Back where Uncle Joe came from until he left Pittsburgh two years ago to live with Jimmy. Moving didn't change anything for Uncle Joe. Until he died last week, but maybe even still, Uncle Joe is always from Pittsburgh.

Kirby plays "Roberto Clemente." The music comes in gently syncopated waves, lapping at my consciousness. Lovely, happy waves. Waves that cut to my heart and steal my breath. Haunting and laughing at the same time. Joyful, really. Joyful and never taking itself too seriously. "I am going to play 'Roberto Clemente,'" he said. Not flamboyant and racing like some ragtime, but thoughtful and elegant, this Roberto Clemente. The repeats bring new waves, each telling the same story, but reinvented. The melodies keep returning, first soft, then strutting, now brassy, now defiant, now poignant. And still joyful.

Oh, I wish you could hear it!

I am entranced, mesmerized by "Roberto Clemente." At intermission, I buy a CD with the piece on it. The next day, as I drive to Estes Park to scatter Uncle Joe, I play "Roberto Clemente." Over and over in my car, driving U.S. 36, climbing into the Rocky Mountains, I listen and, as if for the first time, I introduce myself to Clemente just as he had made his presence known to me, last night, at a ragtime festival in Colorado. The notes flow in my mind, run through my blood, the way the Fall River rushes downhill alongside my car.

Ever since that night in Boulder when I heard the piece called "Roberto Clemente," I've been governed by this music. Music I hear and music I sense. It's become a pulse inside me. I'm not sure why I feel this bond to Roberto Clemente but I know better than to ignore the pull of this music because I believe the universe works this way. Uncle Joe and Roberto Clemente and I, we were destined to interact with each other. It doesn't matter that Joe died last week and Clemente died over twenty-five years ago and I'm still around. That's how time works sometimes.

And, I am to find out, that's how writing is sometimes. I start out chasing one story and then another story starts to chase me. I want to write about Uncle Joe but Roberto Clemente jumps in. And then other forces become involved. You see how it is. Sometimes a writer has no choice.

Uncle Joe's story is still warm; Roberto Clemente's trail is cold. As I write about them both, as I turn and chase them both, I re-enter the past and play games with time. I tell you, it's the best part of writing sometimes, to play hide and seek this way with the past, to live things again, and to write about ragtime.

ENTER SCOTT JOPLIN

The year is 1896. The place is Sedalia, Missouri, a gathering spot for ragtime musicians, a town still part of the American frontier. It is night. The East Main Street that by day is a collection of feed and hardware stores and harness shops is now the "District."

Sundown fills the wooden sidewalks with gamblers, dance-hall girls, sports, pimps, and just regular men out on the town. Honky tonks like the Williams brothers' Maple Leaf Club are wide open in this tenderloin district. Bets are placed. Liaisons arranged. In the bordellos and clubs, black and white customers hang around the Victorian-style bars, pool and gaming tables. The hanging gas chandeliers do not give off light so much as haze but, even so, clearly visible through the smoke in a far corner is an upright piano and on its lushly-covered stool sits a black man. The piano player. He plays all night. His music both describes and accompanies the melee around him. He plays ragtime.

The man at the upright that night in Sedalia may even have been Scott Joplin himself. Joplin, who would become the Ragtime King, the greatest ragtime composer ever, had just arrived in Sedalia in 1896 and it wasn't long before he was at the center of Sedalia's ragtime community.

It's a mystery how the fabric called ragtime came to be. A rag was originally a simple black folk melody. Early ragtime composers, men like Joplin, collected these rags, these scraps of melody they heard in the air around them, and sewed them into extended musical compositions called piano rags. They built their rags around folk melodies and strong rhythmic variations called syncopation. Ragtime, while not exclusively black, blended the gaiety of freedom with the underlying sadness of slavery.

Yes, it's possible. Joplin's music might have been what the piano man played that night in the tenderloin of Sedalia: lilting, contagious, ironic, spirited but somehow melancholy, gentle music filled with repetition and melody and rhythm.

THE CROWD GATHERS

The year is 1999. The month is July. The day is 17. Jimmy's already grilling the memorial meat when I arrive at his collection of condos along the Fall River. Once Jimmy told me he would piss on Joe's grave but he apparently has reconsidered.

I walk into the convention center where Jimmy is hosting the barbecue and Uncle Joe is everywhere. A long table, draped with a bright red Indian blanket, is covered with photographs and personal articles that belonged to Joe. The decades I had shared with Uncle Joe spread out before me.

I take it all in, this majestically pitiful sweep of a life, decades compressed and expanded, recalled by this collection of Joe's things: The keys to his van. A road atlas held open by a magnifying glass. A travel journal. Two hand saws next to a dusty hand drill. Reading glasses and Civil War books. Joe's hockey skates. A bowler hat and a walking cane with a rattlesnake head. I study the photographs on the wall. There's Joe as a young sailor, Joe close up in his Navy uniform, Joe and Dorothy at the altar of St. David's Church, Joe with his first son Michael, Joe with Michael and Jimmy, Joe alone in his old house with his last dog, his blind Airedale Quincy. But Jimmy's memorial is about more than Joe. As I walk along the wall, past the ink sketches of the Homestead steel mill, I pass pictures of my dead parents, of other long-departed aunts and uncles.

Jimmy has been following me along the wall. "Everyone's here," he says, in his husky drawn-out way, his sly voice that could mean almost anything.

Everyone *was* here, gathered from only God knows where, come to Estes Park for the barbecue. In the photos, Dorothy ages along with Joe, but even as she ages, she dazzles. Dorothy and Michael, both smiling, sit side by side on the living room sofa, shortly before Michael died. We were all happy then. Dorothy's blonde hair is pulled back, her black dress low-cut and elegant. Michael wears what appears to be a cutaway jacket, white shirt open at the neck, his red hair thinning, his red beard impeccable.

A large greeting card sits in the middle of the table, next to Joe's ice skates. Dorothy had once sent this card to Joe. Joe had saved it and now the card belongs to Jimmy. The front of the card shows a rabbit and a donkey, apparently a married couple, sitting back to back, each one secretly fuming about the other. The donkey is thinking, "You dumb bunny." The rabbit is thinking, "You jackass." The sentiment inside the card captures Dorothy's wit and sarcasm and bitterness about her marriage: "It's so nice having these conversations with you." Yet, as if to show that one reality is never the whole story, in her flowing graceful script, my aunt had signed the card, "Love, Dot."

RAGTIME AGAIN

The year is still 1896. Ragtime music generates controversy when it first becomes popular in the 1890s. There is, first of all, the predictable moralizing about ragtime's low origins: prejudice, beer, and back rooms are undeniably linked to ragtime. Ragtime's syncopations, broken rhythms, and shifting accents also cause great uproar. "Who put the sin in syncopation?" critics want to know.

Syncopation, ragtime's most recognizable rhythmic characteristic, superimposes an irregular rhythm over a regular one and comes from the interrelationship of the right and left hands. The left hand on the piano plays the stride bass *or basso continuo*, keeping the pulse with the characteristic *oom pah* beat. The right hand plays the melodies and rhythmically works against the left hand, displacing the left hand's *oom pahs*, putting the beat on the off-beat.

Scott Joplin wants to make sure the ragtime players can take in all the rhythms, melodies, and counter melodies of a piano rag, and so his advice on tempo is categorical: "Play slowly until you catch the swing, and never play ragtime fast at any time." Play ragtime like a slow march, Joplin says. Joplin wants ragtime seen as a legitimate art form accepted by people of culture. Not that anyone calls ragtime illegitimate, but the implications are clear. It just isn't good enough for some folks.

COUSIN JIMMY PLAYS

The barbecue is underway and I hang on the fringes, watching Jimmy greet the arriving guests. He is gracious. A gracious host. I haven't seen Jimmy since last February when we had sat and talked, as we had many times before, over lunch at the Boulderado Hotel.

Jimmy, who in past years and for past lunches had sauntered into the Boulderado looking like Dirty Harry, rugged and sexy and slightly sinister in black leather jacket and orange sunglasses, this sunny day in February just looks weary. His thinning hair is no longer red, just dark blond and straggling, hanging to his shoulders, and his face has become his mother Dorothy's face: the same skin, the same dazzling teeth and crystal clear blue eyes.

I tell Jimmy he looks tired. He nods. Then I ask about Joe.

Jimmy tells me Joe is still drinking. Joe drinks in secret and thinks no one knows. Joe's knees are bad and he has a hard time walking but he still drives through Rocky Mountain National Park every day. Joe takes over Jimmy's kitchen each night, cooking food no one wants, ranting at Jimmy. Joe rants in the kitchen and Jimmy goes to Alcoholics Anonymous meetings. Sometimes Joe goes with him. Every day it's like this.

Jimmy grins his wide, almost demonic smile that is either very open or very closed, I'm never sure which, leans toward me across his plate, and says, "Christine, I don't need all this opportunity for personal growth."

We reminisce. "It's sad we're such a small family," I say. Cousin Jimmy smiles.

"We're small but we're getting bigger every day." He grins his grin.

"I have a daughter," he says.

"I know. Six-year-old Lila," I say.

"No, another daughter. Annie. She's twenty-one.

"Oh," I say.

Jimmy tells me about finding this daughter Annie. Since joining AA he's been trying to fix the broken places, smooth the ragged edges of his life. Jimmy's trying to make perfect time. Or make time perfect, I think. He answers my question before I ask.

"Annie's last name is Martinez," he tells me. His blue eyes are far away now. "That's why I couldn't marry her mother. I never could've taken a Mexican woman home to my dad. You know how it was back then, Christine. In Pittsburgh. Twenty years ago. You remember."

TIME TRAVELER

I used to think of time as something that flows like a river, a continuum that moved from the past, through the present, and into the future. "Roberto Clemente" has disrupted this linear view of time. How can I be floating down this time river, all nice and easy, and suddenly find myself upstream when I haven't walked along the bank to get there?

But it happened. Some tributary lost in time took me back to Pittsburgh that night I heard "Roberto Clemente" for the first time, back up the Ohio River, back to where the Ohio is formed from the waters of the Allegheny and the Monongehela Rivers, back to the placed called The Point where the Ohio is born and where my grandparents lived with the other immigrants a century ago and where one day Roberto Clemente would play baseball at Three Rivers Stadium.

"Roberto Clemente" makes my mind play tricks with time, scrolling through events backwards and forwards in strange ways. I tell you the brain can be a time machine and sometimes, like when you hear ragtime, you can become a time traveler. Like this.

It is 1955. Pittsburgh is a smoky city, a dirty, tough steel mill town, still deeply entrenched in its ethnic enclaves of Germans, Italians, Irish, Latvians, and Poles, and Roberto Clemente, a black man from Puerto Rico, is a rookie for the Pittsburgh Pirates. The Pirates still play at Forbes Field. When Clemente comes to Pittsburgh, the Pirates are spectacular losers. Clemente chooses 21 for his uniform number, it is said, because his full name, "Roberto Clemente Walker," has exactly twenty-one letters.

Clemente struggles to gain acceptance in his new home. Pittsburgh has fixed racial barriers. Clemente describes himself as a "double nigger," both black and Latin, unable to speak much English, isolated and subjected to racial slurs, even from his own teammates and especially from the press. It's hard to look back and see how we were and have to say this is true. Sports writers, none of whom can speak Spanish, use phonetics to make Clemente look stupid, quoting Clemente as saying be "heet the peeetch gut" and the weather was "veree hot." When his style seems flamboyant, Pittsburgh sports writers call him a "Puerto Rican hot dog." When he finishes eighth in the balloting for MVP in 1960, after the Pirates' dramatic World Series win over the Yankees, Clemente feels he was denied the award, or at least a higher ranking, because he is Latin American.

I tell some friends that an essay is hounding me that somehow has something to do with Roberto Clemente. They're skeptical. "You can't write about Clemente," one male friend, also a writer, says. "You don't know anything about baseball."

For a while, I agree with them but then I realize that I do know the most important thing about baseball: baseball is about running home. Here's what I mean.

No one but my grandfather ever took me to baseball games, and then only a few times, when I was in grade school, all the way out to Forbes Field near Schenley Park where we would sit on the bleachers in the hot afternoon sun and Grandpap would follow every play carefully and silently.

Grandpap loved the Pirates. He would sip from his silver flask and occasionally pass the program to me. He bought me Coke and hot dogs. I mostly remember how handsome Grandpap looked in his pearl gray suit trousers, his wide gray-and-white striped suspenders, and his starched white monogrammed shirt, his sleeves rolled up, his French cuffs disappearing for a few hours while we sat watching the Pirates play baseball.

I skim some biographies of Clemente. My interest picks back up. Clemente was wary of writers. He's a prickly, enigmatic character. Baseball transformed him. Some say he transformed baseball.

He also died on my birthday.

When I read that, or remember that, for I must have known it once, the headlines blared it so at the time, when I read again that Clemente died on my birthday, I know that, somewhere our paths have surely crossed. Roberto Clemente must be in this story about Uncle Joe's ashes.

Clemente Dies

The year is 1972. The month is December. The day is 31. Clemente boards a plane in San Juan, Puerto Rico, to personally accompany relief aid to earthquake victims in Nicaragua. Clemente believes that the military will not siphon off the donated food and clothing if he, El Magnifico, is there to supervise. He is tired. In his last game of what would prove to be his last season, he made hit number 3,000. He had felt the need to hurry and make this hit because, he tells reporters, he suspects he won't live to be old.

There are other premonitions that Clemente doesn't heed. His son sees the plane crashing. Clemente tells his wife "when your time comes, it comes." His father asks him not to go but Clemente boards the plane anyway. The plane crashes into the ocean about one mile off the coast of Puerto Rico, killing everyone aboard.

Thousands gather for days after the crash, standing at the ocean's edge at a place called Puente Maldonado outside of San Juan, watching the waves that stole Clemente's life. Clemente's body is never found. Clemente's sock, and later his briefcase, drift ashore. Everyone wants to know where Clemente is but the rescuers can find no trace of his body. When Pittsburgh catcher Manny Sanguillen hears about the crash, he runs to the beach and tries to jump into the water, but some of the waves that night are twelve feet tall. For the next five days, Sanguillen searches, making futile attempts to dive for Clemente's body. Thousands stand on the beach, just looking for some sign of Clemente.

More Baseball and More Ragtime

Ed Kaizer is the best pianist I know. We sit in his studio at Bradley University and talk about ragtime music and "Roberto Clemente." Ed understands both subjects. He is a classical pianist who also plays ragtime. He has played ragtime around the world. Ed also is from Pittsburgh and used to play semiprofessional baseball there in the late 1950s, but Ed never knew Clemente personally. Ed remembers once pitching a game in Forbes Field, though, when he was in high school. I guess you don't forget things like that.

Ed talks about piano rags and rhythm, reminding me how ragtime's distinctive syncopation comes when the left hand keeps the rhythm, the *oom pah* beat, while the right hand works out the melodies and plays the themes. Ed plays "Roberto Clemente" several times. When Ed's initial play-through doesn't sound like my CD, I realize how possessive I've become of the image I have in my head of Clemente. In Ed's hands, a different Clemente plays right field.

Ed hears what I hear in the piece. He goes with me back to Pittsburgh. "We can couch our memories in ragtime," he says. "It's nostalgic. It takes you wherever you want to go."

El Magnifico

Clemente was called "El Magnifico." The Magnificent One. A true Baseball Man. In the Caribbean there are a few who are called Baseball Men. For Baseball Men, baseball is a calling, a deep passion.

Dodger scout Al Campanis noticed the young Clemente when Clemente was seventeen and playing baseball in Puerto Rico. Campanis recognized his ferocious talent, called him "the greatest natural athlete I ever saw as a free agent," but did he know that Clemente would one day rise to the level of myth?

For eighteen seasons, 1955–72, Clemente was the mainstay of the Pittsburgh Pirate outfield. He won four National League batting crowns. His lifetime batting average was .317. in his career he scored 240 home runs and had 1,350 RBIs. He hit safety in all seven games of the 1960 and 1971 World Series and won the Most Valuable Player Award for the 1971 Series against Baltimore, where he batted .414 and hit two home runs. Clemente was a twelve-time All Star and twelve-time Gold Glove Award winner. He was the League's Most Valuable Player in 1966. He became only the eleventh player in major league history to record 3,000 hits. After his death in 1972, Clemente became the first Hispanic player elected to the National Baseball Hall of Frame. The Pirates then permanently retired Number 21.

Arriba! Arriba!

So skilled and alive and purposeful was Clemente when he played baseball that those who watched him have never forgotten. For Clemente, life was always about the right way to play the game, like when, in a game against the Astros, he ran flat-out into a wall, risking injury on a relatively meaningless play. "A catch for the ages," the *Houston Chronicle* called it, but some were dismayed.

Why did you *do* this? Why risk injury on a nothing play?

Genuinely puzzled because the answer was so obvious, Clemente answered simply. "I wanted to catch the ball."

Clemente put right field on the map. Throwing on the run from center field, Clemente let the ball loose at up to 110 miles per hour, it is said. He ran almost in desperation, as if chased by a beast, so furious was his speed. He slid with skill and at times hung suspended in air, parallel to the field, flat and fleeting as a shadow.

Clemente would swing at anything. He was a pitcher's nightmare. Someone once said he could hit .299 in an iron lung. And when Clemente hit, when his bat really connected with the ball, it would rise on a silent trajectory, kind of like time's arrow, flying away through space as if blasted from a shotgun. No wonder sports writer Roger Angell said Clemente played "a kind of baseball that none of us had ever seen before."

I'm surprised by how many people have a Clemente story. All this time there was a world of Clemente memories out there that I didn't know existed until now. Cousin Jimmy tells me this story about Roberto Clemente.

When he was in seventh grade, Jimmy and his friends liked to go to Forbes Field to watch the Pirates and they always sat in right field. He said they were drawn there. They tried to sit near Clemente. "He had a *baseball* look to him," Jimmy remembers. "Clemente was very proud and he would hold his head very high and move his neck." Jimmy calls this Clemente's "peacock thing."

In one game, Hank Aaron, who was playing for the Braves, hit a ball out of the infield and it rolled up toward second base. Jimmy says the ball lay on the ground about fifteen feet away from Clemente. Clemente never moved toward the ball. He dared Aaron to try for second. Aaron took off. Clemente ran so fast he scooped up the ball and threw Aaron out by a few inches. "It was the *Superman* move! Only Clemente could do that. We screamed '*Arriba! Arriba!*' We didn't know what that meant but we screamed '*Arriba!*' We couldn't believe it!"

As Jimmy is yelling "*Arriba!*" into the phone, jolting the lines between Illinois and Colorado, I notice that on my desk is a brochure for a new musical playing in Pittsburgh about Clemente that's called "*Arriba! Arriba!*" The Roberto Clemente Story."

No Simple Stories

I think it would be nice to write a simple story for once but there are no simple stories. Just simple ideas and little insights that take a long time in telling. All of this back and forth, the meshing of the pieces of this ragtime puzzle, is how I sort through the ideas that fill my head when I write.

So many lovely parts to this puzzle. I turn over all the little bits looking for the right fit: A rag, originally a black folk tune, grew to describe an instrumental syncopated march. To rag an existing melody is to shift the accents. "To rag" also means to tease, to incorporate surprises, to introduce an unexpected rhythm. The crowds cheer when a baseball player hits a home run. Ragtime or jazz musicians say the music is "coming home" when, in the last strain or next-to-last, the tempo changes and the rhythm increases.

There's more. Ragtime came to be a written music. That was important. And Joplin insisted that players play note-for-note from the written score. No one could change the parts he didn't like. "Play it as I wrote it." Joplin said. Joplin's first published work in 1899 is called "Original Rags" and the last, published after his death in 1917, is aptly titled "Reflection Rag—Syncopated Musings."

I told you before. We really don't choose our stories. When we're hot, our stories chase us until we catch them.

Coming Home

Intense syncopation produces music that ragtime lovers call "hot." Clemente was hot. So hot in the 1971 World Series that the organist at Three Rivers Stadium played "Jesus Christ Superstar" every time Clemente came to bat.

Although the initial racial tensions faded and Pittsburgh loved him long before 1971, Clemente had always wanted national recognition of his baseball ability. Clemente wanted to be seen at the best ballplayer in the world. "I play as good as anybody . . . but I am not loved," Clemente said once. "I don't need to be loved. I wish it would happen. Do you know what I mean?"

Clemente was loved in Puerto Rico and he loved his homeland in return. Clemente's wife returned to Puerto Rico for the birth of each of their children, at her husband's request, and Clemente spent his off seasons in Puerto Rico. Clemente was always going home.

There's lot of ways to go home. It's instinctive, this returning, this circling the bases. Like birds and turtles and salmon, like Uncle Joe in his van making his loops between Colorado and Pittsburgh and like Roberto Clemente playing baseball, and maybe even like dying, we find ways to make that trip back upstream. Show me someone who has no desire for a return ticket and I will show you someone who has never heard ragtime.

CLEMENTE: DREAMER AND POET

In the final analysis, I think, we matter for the qualities we embody in this life and for the depth of our dreams. Clemente's dream was a build *Ciudad Deportiva*, City of Sport, for the underprivileged children of Puerto Rico. Today Clemente's City of Sport sits on 240 acres, just a few miles from where El Magnifico died and where, since his death, over 100,000 children have learned about sports and about hope. My research turns up a poem that Clemente wrote one Father's Day during a game at Three Rivers Stadium. Here, I believe, I have tapped into Clemente's soul.

> Who am I?
> I am a small point in the light of the full moon.
> I only need one ray of the sun to warm my face.
> I only need one breeze from the Alisios to refresh my soul.
> What else can I ask if I know that my sons really love me?

I had never before thought of baseball players as wise men but Clemente is right. What do any of us need, after all, beyond the sun and the breeze and the love of our children?

LOVE AGAIN LOST

The year is 1999. The month is March. The day is 5. Joe sits in my kitchen and tells me about Annie.

"I have a new granddaughter. She's a nice girl. Her name is Annie Martinez." At eighty-one, with time running out, Joe doesn't seem bothered any more by the sound of last names and the boundaries of old ethnic neighborhoods.

"She's getting married in September and Jim is giving her away. I gave her $10,000 for a wedding present." He chews thoughtfully on a piece of Italian bread. I almost choke on my spaghetti. Joe has always been tight with his money.

Ten thousand, I repeat.

Joe pauses and his fork with the spaghetti dangling stops in mid-air.

"Dorothy would have loved to have had a granddaughter. She would have loved to buy her pretty clothes, Annie would have made Dorothy so happy. I wish I had known." His voice trails off and I figure he's thinking about Dorothy's sad life and her despair at the end. The fork continues on toward his mouth. And then Joe starts to talk about his airplane.

Joe always was a traveler. Sometimes in his car and sometimes in his plane, he would just disappear. One day Joe told Dorothy he was going to the store to get groceries and he didn't come back for a week. When he returned, he said he had driven to the Outer Banks of North Carolina, just to look at it. Joe did things like that all the time. He drove to the place where the roads end just so he could drive back home again.

When we live our lives in metaphor like this, we risk that people won't understand.

Joe often went along to the AA Fellowship meetings with Jimmy. Sometimes Joe had a few drinks before he went to the meeting and sometimes he left early so he could have a few more before he went home. Because Joe's knees were filled with arthritis, he needed a comfortable chair and Jimmy had Joe's old brown living room chair moved into the AA hall. The brown chair still sits in the meeting room. I guess some other old man sits in it now.

Jimmy says he initially took care of Joe because it was the right thing to do, not because he loved him. Perhaps Jimmy loved his dad and doesn't know it yet. I asked Jimmy why he didn't have a traditional funeral for Joe. He thought for a minute and then said, "There was nothing to say."

Maybe saying nothing is better than saying the wrong thing. Silence is easier to take back or to amend. Scott Joplin had asked his wife to have the Maple Leaf Rag, his most famous work, played at his funeral. When the time came, she said no.

"How many, many times since then, I've wished to my heart that I'd said yes."

THE FELLOWSHIP

Most of the guests at the barbecue are Jimmy's friends from the AA Fellowship Hall. A man with tattoos on his arms and a bear claw around his neck arrives on a big black Harley. A pudgy man in brown trousers and flowered sport shirt says hello. Ladies carry plates of deviled eggs and fruit salads and bags of potato chips. While Jimmy cooks sausages, Annie sets out platters for the meat. Everyone is eating the sausages as fast as Jimmy can grill them.

Jimmy's friends take brief note of the pictures on the table. They never really knew the Joe who is in all these photographs. They just remember him as Jimmy's dad who used to go to some of the AA meetings with Jim and finally stood up one night and said, "My name is Joe and I am an alcoholic."

I only have Joe's version of what took place, Joe said he had been going with Jimmy to the AA meetings for months. He liked to hear the stories and needed some place to spend time, he said. He was lonely in Estes Park. He missed Pittsburgh.

Joe said everyone was happy when he finally stood up and said that yes, he, too, was an alcoholic and he said he told some pretty hair-raising stories of his own. But it wasn't because he had a drinking problem that he went to the meetings, he told me. It was because they had really good food afterwards and he liked having a place to go for dinner.

The last time Joe visited me, he signed our guest book, my family's way of keeping track of all the people who pass through our house. "AA Hall—Keep coming back!! Joe R., Estes Park Colorado, 3–5–99."

I remember Joe laughing as he wrote. "That's what they keep saying after those damn AA meetings, Chris. 'Keep coming back. Keep coming back.' Hell, I just like the food."

HYPERTIME

Time, modern physicists say, is really an extra dimension. Einstein understood this. He said that the distinction between past, present, and future is only an illusion, even if a stubborn one. Einstein also believed that the road on which we travel through time can curve and go backwards; it doesn't have to be the straight-as-an-arrow trajectory Newton envisioned.

I scan back and forth over my ideas and stories like a composer scans back and forth over a musical score. A musical score gives a solid shape to time, allowing the composer to hold past, present, and future in his hands all at once. Perhaps then composers live outside of time in what physicists call "hypertime."

David Thomas Roberts is the composer of "Roberto Clemente." He lives not in hypertime but in Moss Point, Mississippi. Roberts is also a writer, artist, and poet. He studies metaphysics. He is as deeply immersed in his musical compositions as he is in the landscape. The American landscape is his passion. "American Landscape" is also the title of his CD that I carry with me everywhere so I can listen to "Roberto Clemente."

Our conversation takes a seemingly odd tack in the beginning. Roberts tells me that a good friend of his had died the night before. I tell him I first heard "Roberto Clemente" the night before my uncle's memorial. Is it a coincidence, I then ask, that I sit talking to you about your composition the night after your friend's death?

"Synchronicity," he replies, "is built into our reality, and there may be no such thing as coincidence."

WHAT THE MUSIC MEANS

Roberts was moved to write "Roberto Clemente" after seeing a film about Clemente during the 1979 World Series, and he describes the piece as a "folk elegy" and a "country funeral." After viewing the film, Clemente became for Roberts "a myth to be recalled with affection." I wonder, but do not ask, if Clemente has become for Roberts a part of the American landscape he loves so much, just as Uncle Joe has become a myth to me, a myth I recall with affection, a key figure in my personal landscape.

As a musical composition, "Roberto Clemente" has four musical themes or melodies. These themes vary and repeat, vary and repeat, returning with nuances and interpretations determined by the composer and the performer.

To me this sounds a lot like life.

"Roberto Clemente" is not, Roberts says, a retelling of Clemente's life and career as a sound poem might be, but the music evokes "the man as I had viewed him via the documentary." Roberts tells his concert audiences that he heard elements of the first phrase of the second theme in his head as he watched the Clemente film and that he associates this theme most implicitly with Clemente the man. Even so, he cautions. "Don't say 'that's what the music means.' . . . The symbolism is more elusive. More fragile. You can't reduce the irreducible."

Roberts then tells me something he has never told anyone. The Clemente documentary used footage of waves washing up on the shore in Puerto Rico and footage of Clemente circling the bases. Roberts can't recall if the pictures were actually superimposed in the film or if he just remembered them in conjuncture. But it was these two images, the waves on the shore and Clemente circling the bases, running home, that he wanted to communicate in his composition.

Roberts has written about the "plaintiveness" and "gentle anguish" that is associated with ragtime, and I tell him I feel this gentle pain when I listen to "Roberto Clemente" and think about Clemente's life.

"I was touched by the mingling of tragedy and hope that is all around us," Roberts tells me. "And I was asking myself this question: *What is so meaningful in this tough school which is what I believe the earth is?*"

"Do you think Clemente's death was unfair?" I ask Roberts.

"I think we choose our births and deaths," he tells me. "We are unconsciously fulfilling what we've mapped or assented to have mapped. I don't believe in tragedy in the conventional sense any longer."

Grace Notes

A grace note is a musical term for a quick note frequently used in ragtime that is usually attached to another note and is out of time with the rest of the piece. Roberts describes the grace notes in "Roberto Clemente" as *lagniappe*, a Creole term for "a little something extra" or "a show of appreciation," and points out how the grace notes in "Roberto Clemente" add to the Latin feel of the piece. Ed Kaizer calls these extra notes "embellishments" but I prefer to say "grace notes."

To me, grace notes, in music or in life, are those unexpected blessings that pass by so quickly we take them for granted unless we listen very carefully to the music. Grace notes, like synchronicities, are really little miracles.

The Hoax Revealed

Jimmy says there really is no Transcendental Explorers Club International. He tells me he made it up when, after talking to the undertaker, he felt Joe's obituary was lacking in accomplishments.

I think Jimmy is mistaken about there not being a club for transcendental explorers. Why else would we wonder where we are and where we're going and what exactly we have to do to get home? Why else would life go round and round us like ragtime, defining itself by the off-beat, dangling the hope ahead of the tragedy and offering us the occasional grace note? Why else would Roberto Clemente speak to me in a song?

I think *Jimmy* is really the elite member of this club, twice decorated, as he said of Joe. Otherwise he would have set lower sights for Joe when he added the grace note to his father's obituary. After all, he could have said Joe was the Grand Pooh-bah of the Shriners.

DOROTHY'S ASHES

The month is July. The day is 17. The year is 1999. There's no formal announcement. Those of us who really knew Joe just sense that it's time and we gravitate to the river. Jimmy and his wife and son climb across some boulders that reach out into the Fall River. River is really too big a word today for the water that flows by Jimmy's resort, just a fast-moving mountain stream it is, dashing among rocks and leaving trails of white foam at every turn. Joe's ashes are going to be scattered in this stream, but because Jimmy's condo construction had caused a fish kill in this same river last spring and the Environmental Protection Agency had levied a substantial fine against him, Jimmy hasn't talked much about his plan. The ashes have been kept under wraps.

I walk down close to the river's edge, so I can say goodbye to Uncle Joe as his ashes pass. Jimmy opens the container that holds Joe's ashes and removes the plastic bag. As he hands the bag to his son, I see another small brown cardboard box cut on the rock. Jimmy opens that box and removes another plastic bag that he holds close to his heart for a moment. Dorothy's ashes. Jimmy still has his mother's ashes.

The year was 1996. The month was February. The day was 21. Dorothy's funeral. Gentle anguish, Roberts would call it. As the priest talked about the pain that had lived in Dorothy's heart for too many years, I heard the ragtime piano player in the bawdy house back in Sedalia. His *basso continuo* pumped out the rhythm, the relentless *oom pah*, of her life. In the end, the priest had nothing more than words for comfort. After all, he's not a piano man.

But I hoped Joe was listening. Roberts understood the question: What is so meaningful in this tough school which is what I believe the earth is? Did Joe hear the repeats and the themes returning? As he buried Dorothy, I wanted Joe to hear the grace notes.

After mass, Joe and I sat in the pew. Joe turned to me and in a loud annoyed voice complained about the sermon. He said his hearing aid wasn't working right.

"Will someone please tell me what that damn priest was talking about? All I could hear was every now and then he said 'Dorothy.' I couldn't make out any other damn thing he was saying."

COMING HOME AGAIN

That was three years ago, the last time I saw Dorothy's ashes. Today Jimmy holds his mother close to his heart and then, as he dumps her into the Fall River, his son pours Uncle Joe into the river alongside Dorothy. The current rushes past me. I listen to the water. The voices are clear as the ashes pass by.

"Dumb bunny," the donkey says.

"Jackass," the rabbit answers.

Swirling from eddy to eddy, they're after each other again. Alive and sad and angry and hopeful. Playful, the tumbling ashes are. Rolling over large stones, like the stride bass of a piano rag. In a hurry. Defying Joplin's advice about never playing ragtime fast. The music is coming home now.

I wanted to catch the ball, Clemente said. *I don't need to be loved but I wish it would happen. What more can we ask if we know our children love us?* The piano shakes as the rags roll out. The left hand plays *oom pah, oom pah* and won't quit. The right hand spins and re-spins the melody. *Ragtime takes us anywhere we want to go.*

Keep coming back, Uncle Joe wrote in my book. *Never say that's what the music means,* Roberts told me.

The time of our lives. Time torn in pieces. Time sewn back together. Little bits of melody plucked from the air. Jagged time. Ragged time.

"Dumb bunny."

"Jackass."

I close my eyes and remember all the ragged times and wonder if this damn ragtime will ever stop. I don't want a life played out like a piano rag anymore and I'm tired of the tragedy even if it carries along a little hope. Then I remember the grace note. I remember that Dorothy had signed her bittersweet card to Joe with "Love."

"Love, Dot."

The music softens and the notes dance around silence. The crowds are waiting, hoping for another home run. A Superman move. Clemente jerks his neck, unwinds his bat, and seeks another meaningful connection.

"Arriba! Arriba!" we yell as the ball disappears over the stadium wall.

The Friendship Tarot

Nancy Willard

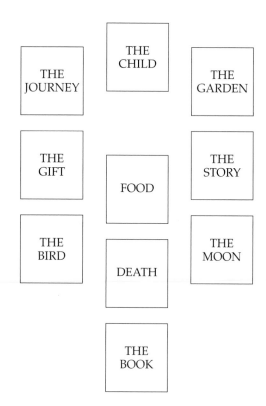

I lay out the cards of our friendship.

The Child

The card shows a child with chocolate on his face wandering through an art gallery in downtown Poughkeepsie devoted—for two weeks—to illustrations from children's books. Ilse Vogel and I have not met, but we both have work in this show. In one room stands the six-foot doll's house I made when I was writing *A Visit to William Blake's Inn*. In the next room hang Ilse's meticulous pen-and-ink drawings for her book *Dodo Every Day*.

What I saw: an elegant woman with white hair, a knitted cloche, and eyes that missed nothing.

What she saw: a woman with a seven-year-old boy whose face was smeared with chocolate.

What I thought: Who is this remarkable person?

What Ilse thought: Her child has a dirty face, but does she worry about it? No. And neither does the child.

The Garden

The card shows two married couples eating dinner in a garden: Eric and me, Howard and Ilse. Four artists: one painter (Howard), one photographer (Eric), one writer (me), and Ilse, who can't be pinned down to one category since she illustrates her own stories. The dinner Ilse has prepared is exquisite. Butter blooms in a little pot; Ilse has sculpted it into the face of a sunflower. Howard helps her carry dishes from the tiny kitchen into the Francesa, a shelter shingled in nasturtiums and morning glories. The front is entirely open to view; over the edge of the second story dangle the tails of four sleeping cats. Once it was a rickety outbuilding for storing tools. Now it is paved with round river stones chosen and put into place years ago by Ilse. Shortly after she'd laid the last stone, she felt chest pains. The day she came home from the hospital, Howard filled the house with anemones.

Ilse heaps seconds on our plates without asking us and tells us they bought this small yellow house in the country because they loved the apple tree blooming outside the kitchen window. The soil is rocky but the garden is full of flowers; Ilse has put out one hundred and four pots of flowers. When a large tabby springs from behind one of them, Ilse explains that they are down to ten cats.

"Ten cats!" exclaims Eric.

"We have only two," I add apologetically.

Is this the first step into friendship? Ilse knows right away she can discuss the excellence of cats without boring me: Velvet Paws, Parsley, Comedy Cat, Mr. Goldie, Chives. Summer and winter the ten cats that live with Howard and Ilse sleep in the garage at night.

Winter and summer the two cats that live with Eric and me sleep at the foot of our bed so they can watch over us.

The Journey

The card shows three people in a car headed for New York. Ilse wears the same knitted cloche she wore at the gallery, and Howard's hat is the identical shade of oatmeal. When I remark on this, Ilse explains that she knitted them both.

We three are traveling to New York to see *The Tin Drum.* On the way, Ilse explains that she lived in Berlin all during the war, so naturally she's curious to see this film.

Of the movie I remember only a few scenes, not because the film was forgettable but because of what happened on the trip back.

The Story

The card shows a woman talking and a woman listening.

I am riding in the back seat of the car and I lean forward and ask, "Ilse, was it really like that in Germany?"

Ilse answers by telling me about the day the Russians marched into Berlin.

"When the Russians came so close to the house, you could hear them talking and shouting. And all the inhabitants of the house were sitting in the bunkers except me, because I hated to be down there with the Nazis. I was in my apartment with a friend of mine. And then we heard shooting and voices, and then we heard a sound as if masses and masses of water would come rushing in, and then my friend said, 'Oh, something has hit the canister of gasoline,' and within seconds I saw the flames and the gasoline floating in under the doorway of my apartment, and everything was in flames. There was just one window where we could get out. We crossed the yard to the door of the bunker and went inside and then the house did burn with tremendous speed. Smoke came and people started to pray and to sing, and others cursed and screamed. I sat with my friend and we held hands and I said, 'This is the end, there's no way out.' And my friend had a little flute with him which he always carried. I'll show it to you tomorrow—I still have it. He pulled it out and played a little Bach sonata for us, to comfort us."

She tells me how she worked in the Resistance against Hitler, hiding Jews in her apartment and printing passports to smuggle them out of Germany. Two hours later we are back in Poughkeepsie.

"Ilse," I say, "have you written this down?"

"It's not a story for children," she says. "And I can't find the right voice to tell it."

"You must tell it," I say, "so people don't forget." Ilse asks to use the bathroom. When she emerges she says with a smile, "I'm so glad your house isn't neat all the time."

The Gift

The card shows a restaurant strung with red and green lights.

The week before Christmas, Ilse and Howard and Eric and I meet for lunch at Dickens. Ilse calls ahead so that we can have the same table we had last year—a table intended for six. She tells the waitress we are expecting another person, a man, and during the meal she laments his bad manners—why couldn't he have phoned? She brings the snapshots we took of each other last year. In the snapshots we are always opening presents. Here I am, opening the present Ilse made for me: a muff, to keep my hands warm. It is made of brown corduroy, lined with synthetic lamb's wool, and decorated in orange and turquoise and lavender: braid, felt hearts, pyramids, and silver beads, each bead no bigger than a mustard seed. It has a corduroy strap and a pocket, into which Ilse has tucked a bright red handkerchief.

Since I ride a bicycle to class and my arms are usually full of books, I seldom have the leisure to use a muff unless I decide to take a muff-walk: a walk with no other purpose than exercise and pleasure. Which is probably why Ilse gave it to me.

This year Howard gives Eric a book of Vuillard's paintings and Ilse gives me a Waring hand-held blender which, she assures me, will make cooking much easier.

Eric gives Howard a photograph he took inside the conservatory of the New York Botanical Gardens and I give Ilse a set of flannel sheets and pillowcases printed with cats.

Food

The card shows dinner tables, side by side.

When we eat dinner at their house, they serve hors d'oeuvres and drinks in the living room or the garden, just for the four of us. Ilse makes the salad dressing. The courses arrive in succession at the proper time.

When they eat dinner at ours, I am famished from having skipped lunch to meet with students, and I rush everything to the table at once. The salad dressing is Paul Newman's finest, the cake is the handiwork of the Aurora Café Bakery. The last time I baked a cake, it collapsed like an old hat and I filled in the holes and cracks with frosting, which made it astonishingly heavy but quite tasty. Howard warned Ilse not to eat it.

"All that chocolate is bad for your heart," he said softly.

She smiled and took another bite.

The Moon

The card shows four people perched on top of the world.

Ilse phones us in great excitement. Tonight, if we stand on a certain hill a mile from their house, we can watch the sun go down and the moon come up, all at the same time. She has checked the weather; the sky will be clear.

The road to the hill runs past stables and pastures broken by white fencing into parcels that give expensive horses enough room to run free by keeping them apart from each other. Howard regrets that the landscape feels so owned.

When we climb out of the car and look east and west from the crest of the windy hill, the valley sweeps broadly around us; could we see the Hudson if we knew where to find it?

As the sun slides into its nest of light behind the Catskills, the moon rises silently, secretly. She is so pale and thin that she might be the shed carapace of some large round animal. As darkness gathers, she grows solider, more golden.

"In German, the moon is masculine," says Ilse. "And the sun is feminine."

I can't think of another language in which those genders are assigned to my old friends in the sky.

Ilse says she is trying to write about those last days before the fall of Berlin, but she is not yet ready to read me what she has written.

The Bird

The card shows an empty cage in a garden.

Ilse phones us—can we come over and see the dove? It seems that the post-mistress in their little town of Bangall runs an animal adoption service on the side, and she has presented Ilse with a dove.

When we arrive, Ilse has put its cage on a pile of stones in the garden, like an altar to flight. The cage is made of the sticks that Ilse gathered in the yard, but it is very small, and when Eric and I approach, the dove beats her wings against the bars. All during dinner she makes endearing noises.

"You can't imagine how we enjoy hearing that wonderful sound," says Ilse. "And the cats don't seem to notice her."

We sit outside and watch the singular stars arrive, one by one, like notes in a music box winding down to silence.

The next day I telephone Joanne, a friend of mine who does excellent carpentry, and ask her to make a catproof cage for Ilse's dove. I tell her it should be made of sticks gathered in a forest and it should be huge. Ilse's birthday is two weeks away—could she possibly have it finished by then?

Two weeks later, Joanne drives up with a cage nearly as tall as herself on her truck. It is a gazebo, a minaret, a chapel, it is the mother of all birdcages. I phone Howard and tell him we want to deliver it as a surprise to Ilse, who likes surprises but does not like unexpected visitors. Howard can tell her whatever he likes; we will arrive with the cage at eleven o'clock on Thursday.

When we appear, the two of them are sitting in the garden, attended by Velvet Paws. Joanne and I carry the cage across the lawn. Ilse is speechless with astonishment. That is just the way I hoped she would be.

"You've given me exactly what I wanted!" she exclaims.

The dove takes to the cage at once. Soon it no longer feels like a cage; Ilse adds branches and leaves and nasturtiums and she removes the bottom so that the dove sits directly on the grass. How good the grass feels on her little coral feet! All night long she enjoys dewfall and moonrise and starshine. When the sun warms the dark world, Howard arrives with her breakfast.

One morning Howard goes to feed the dove and finds a dash of bloody feathers. There is a snake in Eden; nothing but a snake could insinuate itself into so stout a cage.

Ilse mourns her dove. All winter the cage is filled only with cream-colored twigs—and the curious seedpods that catch her eye in the garden. One day the postmistress telephones her. A relative of the slain dove has recently laid a clutch of eggs; two of them hatched. Would Ilse like two doves? Howard snakeproofs the cage. It is spring again and the voices of Ilse's doves are heard in the land.

Death

The card shows a shelf on which Ilse has arranged the skulls of their cats. After their deaths, she digs them up. The skulls are light and beautiful as parchment.

"Some people think it's a strange thing to do," she says, "but see how beautiful their bones are!"

When I cook chicken, I save not only the wishbone but the breastbone. Scrubbed clean and dried, the breastbone looks like a mask or a saddle intended for an animal unaccustomed to carrying passengers. On the apple tree in our back yard hang the shells of half a dozen horseshoe crabs I found on Cape Cod. Anyone passing the tree would take it for the site of a secret ceremony devoted to saving what holds us up but is never seen under the living flesh.

The Book

The card shows pages falling and gathering like snow. Ilse is now seriously at work on her stories about life in Germany under Hitler. Howard is typing them for her. The stories arrive in the mail, one by one, in white envelopes bordered with a green stripe.

Without telling her, I am sending them to my editor at Harcourt Brace.

Velvet Paws has had her kittens behind a canvas of Howard's which he imprudently left leaning against an upstairs wall. Ilse invites us to view the kittens. Eric and I sit in the living room of the little white house and wait for the great moment. We wait and wait. And suddenly here is Ilse, presenting them to us in a basket lined with violets and strawberry leaves, as if she had just picked them in the garden.

Later, as we are leafing through a box of old photographs, I pull out a picture of two blond girls standing side by side: Ilse and her twin sister, Erika, who died of diphtheria when they were nine.

"Which one is you?" I ask.

Ilse is not sure.

"Perhaps that one, with the knees bent a little. Erika was born first and she always was the more courageous one."

Eight years ago, when I published my first novel, *Things Invisible to See,* I dedicated it to Ilse and Howard.

Today I open the book of Ilse's stories, *Bad Times, Good Friends,* and find it is dedicated to Eric and me. Over the dedication is Ilse's pen-and-ink drawing of a dove turning into a woman. She is flying over a bed of pansies, carrying three tulips in one hand and pointing to our names with the other.

"They didn't want a dove-woman on the dedication page," says Ilse. "I had to fight for it."

Part 2

Talking about Creative Nonfiction

One reason we're so enthusiastic about this evolving genre is the role of writers and teachers of creative nonfiction in defining the terms of the conversation. As both teachers and writers we've benefited from that conversation ourselves, and so we believe that writers entering the genre can gain from hearing these writers talk about the making of their own work. After all, in the long tradition of the genre, essayist/critics from Montaigne through Addison, Steele, Lamb, and Hazlitt to E. B. White have not only written the most enduring examples of the essay but also provided the most valuable commentary on the form.

Therefore, in Part Two, Talking about Creative Nonfiction, we've chosen pieces—many of them written by authors in Part One—that reflect these writers' thoughts, opinions, speculations, theories, and critiques of creative nonfiction. They provide a multivoiced discussion of the genre on a wide range of topics related to writing creative nonfiction—from definitions of the form and overviews of some of the subgenres to informal histories of the genre, personal accounts of writing, and hints about strategies and practices. Some writers, such as Bret Lott and Steven Harvey, discuss their personal reasons for writing; others, including Sydney Lea, talk about their composing strategies. Still others offer us insight into the particular forms of creative nonfiction in which they work: Mary Clearman Blew, Annie Dillard, Patricia Foster, and Patricia Hampl give us different perspectives on the memoir, especially the ways imagination transforms and transposes memory; Phillip Lopate and Scott Russell Sanders talk about the history of the personal essay; Tracy Kidder discusses his views and his experiences in literary journalism.

Along with the writers whose work appears in Part One, others offer us insight into the issues surrounding creative nonfiction. Rebecca Blevins Faery and Robert Root explain and illustrate how and why they write disjunctive essays; Peter M. Ives and Mimi Schwartz address the issue of accuracy and honesty; Jocelyn Bartkevicius and Michael Pearson examine attempts to define and identify creative nonfiction; and Marianna Torgovnick discusses the reasons she practices and promotes experimental critical writing with its use of personal voice in academic discourse.

As we've mentioned earlier, many of these pieces can be paired with writings in Part One. Just a glance at the table of contents will show you which authors appear in both sections of the book. A cursory look at the titles will give you some sense of the specific concerns that are represented here. For example, if you were to look at Jocelyn Bartkevicius's Part One essay, "Out of the Garden," you'd discover an evocative story of her relationships with her grandmother and her parents told in terms of her connection to the earth. If you then read her Part Two essay, "The Landscape of Creative Nonfiction," you'd find a reference to the opening scene of "Out of the Garden" and a discussion of the accuracy of memory and the significance of the term "creative nonfiction" for the telling of the story.

Conversely, let's suppose that you want to read some of the Part Two essays to gain a sense of a particular writer's theory of creative nonfiction before you read his or her sample of it in Part One. For example, in his Part Two piece, "Whatever Happened to the Personal Essay?" Phillip Lopate discusses the history of the personal essay and reveals his own particular slant on the kinds of essays he writes. Given that context, Lopate's Part One essay, "Portrait of My Body," becomes a model for what he means by "interrogating the self." Similarly, if you first read Scott Russell Sanders' essay on essays in this section, you will then read his personal essay, "Cloud Crossing," with an awareness of what he hopes to accomplish in his writing.

Several of the writers whose works are presented in Part Two are also working teachers in whose courses students often study creative nonfiction. Some of them teach courses expressly focused on creative nonfiction as a subject in itself. As a result, their pieces are at least tangentially about the connections between writing and teaching writing, especially writing and teaching creative nonfiction. Like Donald Murray, who first modeled this sensibility in *A Writer Teaches Writing* thirty years ago, each teacher/writer, such as Robert Root, Lynne Sharon Schwartz, and Michael Steinberg, takes a writerly approach to this genre.

Although some of these selections involve critical analysis, they do not present a detached theoretical approach. All of these essays are designed to offer a writerly perspective on the evolving dialogue about creative nonfiction. As a result, the works selected for Part Two ground creative nonfiction in the behaviors and motives of working writers and teachers, reflecting back on the examples of the form in Part One and projecting ahead to essays on composing in Part Three.

The Landscape of Creative Nonfiction

Jocelyn Bartkevicius

[I]naccuracy is very often a superior form of truth.

—Virginia Woolf, "Incongruous Memories"

1. The Stranger

I was standing in a garden, tomato plants ripening, chickens dashing about, when I first learned I was a stranger. I was quite young, maybe six or seven, watching my grandmother pick tomatoes and tell stories about her life as a farm girl in Eastern Europe. She had just gotten to the part about hiding in the forest from waves of invading armies—Russians then Prussians then Russians again—when she stopped, stood up, looked me in the eye, and said: "But you are an American; you don't understand."

How can I convey the force of these words? Of course, as a school girl I was familiar with the idea of "being an American." I said the pledge of allegiance, hand on heart like all the other kids. I sang the "Star Spangled Banner" (except for those unreachable glaring red high notes). But this identity had never been pinned upon me so specifically, so singularly, or as an impediment. "Being an American" had never made me an outsider. Standing in my grandmother's garden, among plants and animals raised the old ways, I was the other.

In memory, when she speaks these words, my grandmother is looking me right in the eye. She was a small woman, possibly reaching five feet at her healthiest, before the osteoporosis formed a permanent stoop. And I was a gangly girl

275

who got all her height early. But now that I look at the memory, examine it instead of experiencing it, I must admit that a five-foot-tall six year old is an unlikely creature. Something is wrong with the memory. It is incongruous.

And then there are holes in the memory: I can't remember whether my grandmother continued her story after she stood up and spoke to me. Or whether she returned to her gardening. Or why she began the story at all. It was hard to get her to talk about Lithuania, especially about the years when, as a very young woman, she had to bury food in the forest to survive, had to prepare constantly to flee soldiers and their various hungers, had to watch city people (who could not grow their own food) sicken and die. Perhaps my father stood off to the side prompting her. But he is not in the memory. Maybe I—normally a very shy child and fearful of misunderstanding her difficult Lithuanian accent—had a rare fit of boldness and asked her a question about Europe.

The scene is one that I return to often, for her words fixed the moment as indelibly as a brand. I used to think that the memory drew me in spite of its incongruities and holes. But I am beginning to realize that this memory compels me *because* of the incongruities and holes. The pitted, nearly invisible landscape of the past is a mysterious, inviting place. Each exploration reveals a different topography.

Looking back, I find that my grandmother bequeathed layers of strangeness that day. Her words taught me that I was a stranger in her world. And they taught that, while there had been some unevenness in my life—near poverty, my parents' divorce, and so on—I was nevertheless a stranger to profound suffering and struggle. And now, looking not just at the moment but at the memory itself, at the moment as incongruous memory, I find that my grandmother's words taught me that there is a stranger within. That is, certain moments will not survive unravaged, that going back in time and memory I will discover losses, unreachable territories. Some of the territories remain, buried beneath the surface of daily life and ordinary reminiscence, inaccessible but for accident or imaginative self-interrogation.

In the case of my grandmother's garden, incongruities and obvious gaps drew me back to the memory, signaled its importance. Other moments may disappear without a trace, leaving no path, and the act of writing may be the only way to unearth them.

A few years after I stood with my grandmother in her garden, my father bought a farm—or what I called a farm before I moved from Connecticut to Iowa and saw working farms, counted among my friends actual farmers, and learned that in relation to Iowa farms, my father's place had been not a farm at all but an acreage. There on his land I built a miniature version of my grandmother's garden using compost from the manure pile, sprinkling lime from a stocking to discourage bugs. I followed my father around, riding barely trained horses, acting the cowboy, zipping through forests, sleeping under the stars. And this is how I remember those years, as a little grandma, a little immigrant, a peasant girl in a store-bought peasant blouse (it was the sixties), bringing home-grown organic carrots to high school for lunch. I remember a peaceful Eden punctuated by moments of playing the stereo in my father's hand-built log cabin, Joni Mitchell singing about getting back to the garden, Neil Young loving his country girl.

But recently, I found buried in an old trunk a black and white snapshot of my father and me, pitchfork and all like the pair in Grant Wood's *American Gothic*. Our pitchfork, though, is angled; we both stare at it, and impaled upon one of the tongs is a small bat. In my memory, I am a Romantic peasant girl, gardening as it has been handed down by my Eastern European ancestors, embracing Woodstock, barefoot to Joni and Neil. In the photograph I am a party to the slaughter of a benign and beneficial mammal. Writing about the photograph awakened darker memories from the farm: another child's pointing a loaded pistol at me, my aiming a loaded BB gun at a sleeping bat as it hung from the shed door, and leaving the cabin after an argument to disappear alone into the dark country night.

The self—at least *my* self—is composed of misremembered and unremembered scenes. The path back to that uneven landscape is the path of the mind. Students in my creative nonfiction workshops frequently ask me to define for them, concisely and with directions for construction, "the personal essay." Usually I try to do so by offering a variety of creative nonfiction pieces along with several writers' working definitions of the form. But at times I ask them to define for me, concisely (but without directions for construction), "a person." The definition of "personal essay" is as complicated and various as that of "person," and the personal essay is just one possible manifestation of creative nonfiction.

In writing creative nonfiction, in order to tell the truth, I must let the incongruities be. I was standing in the garden with my grandmother and we were eye to eye although we could not be the same height. I was six while also being ten— perhaps six with shyness and the language barrier and ten chronologically. Or ten in my boldness and six chronologically. Or I was somehow taller for being a stranger and my grandmother was somehow shorter for changing my world. And in order to tell the truth in creative nonfiction I must explore the gaps. I was an earth child on my father's farm and yet I was shooting bats. I focus on the unremembered photograph and dig for more. Memory, the mind's path, enacts wonders, and the creative nonfiction writer's work is not to reason those wonders away with mathematical formulae, but to embrace them, to recreate layer after layer of incongruity.

2. The Terms

The first time I heard the term "nonfiction," I was sitting with twenty other third graders at a veneered table in a grammar school library. I watched the librarian walk from wall to wall tapping books and signs with her pointer. Each book had a hand-typed Dewey decimal system number taped to its spine. Each section had a hand-printed sign fixed above it. She paused at the section labeled "fiction," tapped a row of spines, tapped the sign above, and said: "These books are fiction. They're made up; they aren't true." She stepped to the left, swung her pointer at the next section, labeled "nonfiction," tapped the sign, and said: "These books are not fiction. They aren't made up; they are fact." While the librarian went on with her presentation, my mind went elsewhere. Fiction was not true and nonfiction was not fiction; therefore nonfiction was *not* not true. She was using the forbidden double negative. I sat at the table wondering what made fiction, the not-true, so central that the term "nonfiction" was formed from it.

I probably would have forgotten that moment in the library if similar moments had not recurred throughout my life. The string of assumptions goes like this: Fiction is "made up," and thus crafted, invented, "made." Fiction is art because its creator draws upon imagination. Nonfiction is "not made up," and thus recorded, reported, "unmade." Nonfiction makes itself, the writer is a mere tape recorder or camera. Or, in cases where the material of nonfiction needs some shaping, the writer draws upon reason and logic alone.

Such assumptions are in part an issue of terminology. "Fiction," the root word, comes from "fingere," to form, mold, devise. "Non" simply means "not." Thus we get the implication that nonfiction is not formed, molded, or devised. Although this "non" negates the term "fiction," it is not the strongest available negative prefix. "Dis," which implies expulsion, as in "disfrock" or "disbar," would give us disfiction, a genre deprived of fiction, even, perhaps, expelled from it. "Un," which means "against" or "anti," would give us unfiction, a genre opposed to fiction. Nonfiction, looked at in this context, is not deprived of fiction or opposed to fiction, but simply, like the librarian said, not fiction.

There remains, however, an unsettling nuance to "non." While calling someone non-American does not brand them an enemy (as calling that person un-American would), it still suggests that they are other. A non-American is a foreigner, or, as my grandmother was sometimes called, an alien. Nonfiction is to fiction as non-American is to American. Thus, nonfiction is the stranger, the foreigner (or alien) in the land of fiction. What's more, in both cases, the root word is the point of reference. Many writers and editors add "creative" to "nonfiction" to mollify this sense of being strange and other, and to remind readers that creative nonfiction writers are more than recorders or appliers of reason and objectivity. Certainly many readers and writers of creative nonfiction recognize that the genre can share some elements of fiction; dialogue, place, characters, and plot, for example, might occur in both. When a piece of creative nonfiction resembles fiction, the "non" might suggest not so much "not," as something like "kicking off from." Why else insist that it is not fiction unless it is in danger of being mistaken for fiction?

If "nonfiction" might mean a work that is related to but different from fiction, perhaps works in the genre that are more akin to poetry—sharing with it lyric and image or a structure built on association and repetition rather than on narrative—would benefit from another name. I read some of Virginia Woolf's nonfiction (her lyrical, personal pieces like "Evening Over Sussex," and "The Death of the Moth," for example) for its poetry. Other writers come to mind: Terry Tempest Williams's *Desert Quartet*, for example, a lyrical, concentrated work with gaps and craters, a book written not only from reason, but also from imagination, dreams, and the body. Such works, while not poems per se, use poetry as their inspiration, their model, their "kicking off point." For them, I suggest the term "nonpoetry."

To play with terms and search for definitions can be more than an academic exercise. I'm interested in the genre's possibility, a possibility not just theoretical but practical—that is, involving practice. Rather than map out territory (and thus limit it) I mean to expand it. Rather than build fences, knock them down.

3. The Stars

A few months ago, a formerly estranged cousin gave me a copy of an old home movie. Over antipasto made the old way, we watched ourselves together, children moving in and out of a series of silent, disjointed scenes in black and white. My cousin and I sat together as his father's last birthday party unfolded before us; we watched ourselves celebrate just a few yards from the spot where an accident would later kill his father, shattering our family for decades. But on that night preserved on film, we all sit together on the pool deck of the hotel and nightclub his father and my stepfather ran together, happy beneath the stars. We sit at a long table, laughing and talking silently. Suddenly, my stepfather rises up, grabs a torch-like candle, and begins dancing around our table. While he circles the rest of us, we watch my uncle cut his Italian rum cake from Romano's.

My cousin broke the silence of that old flickering movie. "There must have been bugs," he said, "that's got to be a bug torch and he's spreading the fog around our table." But that's not what I saw. Though I didn't at first remember the scene, I knew my stepfather. He was dancing out his joy, his exuberance, the energy that pored from each cell of his body. "I'd rip the stars out of the sky for you," he used to tell my half sister, the child of his middle age, and there he was, ripping the stars out of the sky, lighting the night for one of our last happy moments together.

The camera recorded the scene for perpetuity. And yet my cousin and I, with similar family experiences, with memories of that moment, and with objective evidence before us, saw it differently. If put alone in separate rooms and interrogated or given blank sheets of paper and told to write that scene, we would come up with different stories. We both sat at the family table that night, and so the party is in our memories, embedded in the very matter of our brains. And we both watched the tape, separately and together, several times in recent months. Nevertheless we tell different stories. Which one is true? Which one imagined?

His story and mine, I believe, contain elements of fact and imagination. Both are true, for they are true to how we remember, how we see, they recreate the topographies of our minds. We can return to the film and we can return to our memories. Either way, each of us returns to a different place.

Recently, I attended another birthday party, for a friend who is a writer. After he blew out the candles, and everyone made the requisite jokes about aging, our conversation turned to writing and memory. "You could never write this scene as nonfiction," one friend, a fiction writer, said. "You couldn't remember the dialogue verbatim; you'd end up remembering words wrong and so you'd have to change them. You'd forget things and leave them out. That would make it fiction." Several others at the table agreed, assuming that without a tape recorder you'd be left with fallible memory and therefore be incapable of creating nonfiction. There were only two ways to write the scene with dialogue, they believed, to write it as fiction (and freely invent and recreate words), or to write it as nonfiction (and record, transcribe, and then report the words exactly as spoken).

One of the guests, a lawyer, objected. "You should read briefs," he said. "Recorded dialogue doesn't make any sense."

"You need the background," another friend, a nonfiction writer, added, "the color of the walls, the smell of the food. How can you understand the dialogue without the scene?"

"What if someone's words trigger a memory?" I asked. "Let's say that as you're speaking, I'm reminded of a scene from my past, like standing in my grandmother's garden. Even if we filmed and taped this party, that wouldn't show up, and yet it changes my experience of the party."

"I was wondering," the literary theorist said, "what I'd do with that moment when I became obsessed with the pattern on this plate, or when I concentrated on the taste of the red beans and rice."

If my birthday party companions read this dialogue, they would no doubt revise it according to their own memories and perceptions. In fact, that same night we suggested—as a joke or perhaps as a challenge—that each of us, two fiction writers, a poet, two creative nonfiction writers, a theorist, a lawyer, and a decorator—should go off immediately and write the scene. By the time we were well into the cake and coffee, we more or less agreed that if we were true to the events as we'd each experienced them, if we didn't write, for example, that the lawyer had stood up, reached across the table, and punched the guest of honor as he blew out his candles (since he had done nothing of the kind), we would be writing creative nonfiction.

We reached common ground in the end, I think, because we shifted both our working notion of genre and our view of "the person." When my friends claimed that nonfiction could work only with the aid of a tape recorder, their concept of the person was external, the person as captured by a machine. They had shared the assumption, arrived at by habit, that nonfiction was restricted to objectivity and reporting, that incongruity must be reasoned away. Fact, as Virginia Woolf points out, is not necessarily the same as truth, and as we talked that night, we explored what it means to be at a birthday party, what it means to participate in a conversation, how much more it is than the sounds we make, the words we speak. What we say and how we move—what machines can pick up—is only the surface of the scene. "Nonfiction" is not a synonym for "recorded surface." It has the range to sweep inward, follow the path of the mind, add layers of contemporaneous imagination, memory, and dream to the observable events of the present moment.

Patricia Hampl, who has said that memory is a place, has also said that the nonfiction writer is homeless.

One such occasion was an informal talk after her reading in the third floor lounge of a certain university's humanities' building. Graduate students used to joke about the symbolism of the building's design: Fiction and poetry were on the top floor. Freshman composition was in the basement. In the middle (just above philosophy) was nonfiction, tucked away in a corner of the literature department. Although Hampl's reading drew a large audience, only a small group of die-hard nonfictionists showed up for the talk.

In our small quarters, nearly invisible in a wing of the literature department, her discussion of the nonfiction writer's homelessness rang true. The department had just changed the name of our program from "expository writing" to "nonfiction writing" and would soon rename it "creative nonfiction." We could see that we were the new kids on the block, that to many, our genre was ill defined and invisible. But there we sat listening to a writer who had made a career of creative nonfiction, who had written two memoirs and many personal essays, and who spoke optimistically about the genre's range and possibility. Many of us felt at home for the first time—not in our lounge, but in her words.

The prospect of literary homelessness drives and limits certain writers to formulae, say, memoir in five parts (action scene followed by predictable summation followed by continuation of the action and so on, like a sitcom or a mini series). They find a "home" and hole up in the corner. And they pass along a favored formula to groups of beginner or intermediate writers, regardless of any particular student writer's emphasis, place of origin, gender, culture, aesthetic, or concept of the self. Handing over a prepackaged piece of creative nonfiction is, in essence, putting the writer into a cell. The bolder explorers, happy not to be enclosed, take advantage of the unsettled terrain of nonfiction, wandering and exploring, allowing themselves to be vulnerable, following the path of the mind even when they enter shadows, pressing on into the territory of the unknown, the mysterious, the incongruous.

Creative nonfiction is at once flourishing and invisible, set and contested. The genre that embraces the often paradoxical nature of the self is itself often paradoxical (in its position in the world of writing and letters). Patricia Hampl provides the metaphor of the creative nonfiction writer as homeless. And she also turns it around. We're lucky, she says, we get to be out under the stars.

The Art of Memoir

Mary Clearman Blew

One of the oldest and loveliest of quilt patterns is the Double Wedding Ring, in which bands of colors lock and interlock in endless circles. If you want to make a Double Wedding Ring quilt, be a saver of fabric. Treasure the smallest scraps, from the maternity dress you have just sewn for your oldest daughter or the Halloween costume you cobbled together for your youngest, from the unfaded inside hems of worn-out clothing or the cotton left over from other quilts. Keep a pair of sharp scissors on hand, and also a pattern, which I like to cut from fine sandpaper, and which will be about an inch wide by two inches long and slightly flared, like a flower petal that has been rounded off at both ends. Whenever you have a scrap of fabric, lay out your pattern on it and snip out a few more blocks.

Save your blocks in a three-pound coffee can. When the can is full, empty the blocks out on the floor and arrange them in the shape of rainbow arcs with a juxtaposition of colors and textures that pleases you. Seven pieces to an arc, seventy-two arcs to a quilt. You can sew the blocks together on a sewing machine, but I like the spell cast by hand sewing. I use a #11 needle, which is an inch-long sliver of steel with an eye so fine that it will barely take the quilter's thread, which measures time by growing infinitesimally shorter with each dip and draw of the needle, and I wear the hundred-year-old thimble of a woman named Amelia Bunn on my finger.

When you have pieced your seventy-two arcs, you must choose a fabric to join your arcs, in a process that is called "setting up" the quilt. Traditionally a Double Wedding Ring quilt is set up on white, but remember that you have all colors to choose from; and while choosing one color means forgoing others, remind yourself that your coffee can of pieces will fill again. There will be another quilt at the back of your mind while you are piecing, quilting, and binding this one, which perhaps you will give to one of your daughters, to trace her childhood through the pieces. Or perhaps you will give it to a friend, to speak the words the pattern spoke to you.

For years I thought of myself as a fiction writer, even during the years in northern Montana when I virtually stopped writing. But in 1987 I came to a divide. My father had died, and my husband was suffering a mental breakdown along with the progressive lung disease that eventually killed him. I was estranged from my older children. Then I lost my job. It was the job that mattered the most. I had a small child to support. And so I looked for another job and found one, teaching in a small college in Idaho, with the northern Rockies between me and the first half of my life.

Far from home and teaching again after years in higher-ed. administration, I felt a hollowness that writing fiction seemed to do nothing to fill. And so I started all over again, writing essays to retrieve the past—in my case, the Montana homestead frontier with its harsh ideals for men and women, its tests and its limitations. The conventions of fiction, its masks and metaphors, came to seem more and more boring to me, like an unnecessary barricade between me and the material I was writing about. But because fiction was what I knew about, I used the techniques of fiction in these essays: plot, characterization, dialogue. What I began to discover was a form that worked for my purpose.

I would select an event out of family legend and retell it in a voice that grew out of my own experience and perceptions. Often the events that beckoned to me the most urgently were the ones that had been preserved in the "secret stories" my grandmothers and my great-aunts told around their Sunday tables after the dishes had been washed, elliptical and pointless and mystifying, in hushed voices that dropped or stopped altogether at the approach of one of the men or an unwise question from an eavesdropping child. Eventually I was trusted with a few of the secret stories, myself. I remember how my aunt's voice fell and her sentences became sparing when she told me a story about her mother, my grandmother. The story was about a time when my grandmother had lived alone on the homestead north of Denton, Montana, for eighteen months without seeing another woman. She had two small children and another baby on the way—her husband was away for weeks on end, trying to sell life insurance to make ends meet—and she had to carry her water in a bucket from a spring a quarter of a mile from the homestead shack, which she did at twilight, when the heat of the sun was not so oppressive. She began to hallucinate. She saw the shapes of women on the other side of the spring, shapes that looked like her dead mother and her dead sister, beckoning to her. She decided she was going crazy. She had her little children to think about. They might not be found for weeks if she broke down. And so she began to go for her water in the heat of the day, when the sun scorched her trail and bleached the color out of the grass and rocks. She never saw the beckoning shapes again.

Unlike my grandmother, I have chosen to follow the beckoning shapes. I don't understand the significance of that story for my grandmother, or why she kept it a secret except for the one time she whispered it to her younger sister in, I presume, those same stark sentences in which her sister whispered it to her niece, my aunt, the same sentences in which my aunt whispered the story just one time to me. But then, I don't fully understand why I continue to wear Amelia Bunn's thimble—it is sterling silver and engraved AB in a fine script—any more than I know what my great-grandmother looked like in life or as she appeared in the dying heat waves of that long-ago Montana twilight.

But sometimes I think I can see the turning points in the lives of dead men and women. For example, my grandmother's decision to return to schoolteaching in 1922, even though it meant breaking up her family, boarding out her oldest daughter, taking the younger children to live with her in a teacherage, leaving her husband alone on the homestead. What did that decision mean to her? I know what it means to me. Or my aunt's mowing machine accident in June of 1942, when a runaway team of sorrel horses spilled her in the path of a sickle bar that nearly cut off her foot. The disaster forced her out of the path of teaching in rural schools that she had been following and into a new life on the Olympic Peninsula. Did she understand the opportunity in the teeth of the sickle bar?

I feel an uneasy balance between writing about my grandmother and my aunt as their lives "really" were and writing about them as a projection of my own experiences. I keep reminding myself that the times when they lived are not my times. Nor do the nuances of their stories necessarily reflect my assumptions about language. And yet I am who I am because of these women and the stories they told; and, as I write about them, they live and breathe again through the umbilical tangle between character and writer.

I've been fortunate in my family's being one of storytellers and private writers who have "documented" their past. Tales, diaries, notebooks, and letters—they saved every scrap. Of course their stories were fictions as much as mine are, told over and over again and given shape and significance. Their connection to literal truth is suspect.

For my part, I struggled for a long time with the conflicting claims of the exact truth of the story and its emotional truth as I perceived it. I restrict myself to what I "know" happened: the concrete details, the objects, the history. When I speculate, I say so.

But any story depends upon its shape. In arranging the scraps that have been passed down to me, which are to be selected, which discarded? The boundaries of creative nonfiction will always be as fluid as water.

Students often ask, what can you decently write about other people? Whose permission do you have to ask? What can you decently reveal about yourself?

I can only speak for myself. I own my past and my present. Only I can decide whether or how to write about it. Also, I know that once I write about the past, I will have changed the past, in a sense set it in concrete, and I will never remember it in quite the same way. The experience itself is lost; like the old Sunday storytellers who told and retold their stories until what they remembered was the tale itself, what I will remember is what I have written.

Certainly, something personal is being sacrificed, for when I write about myself, I transform myself just as I do the past. A side-effect is that while the writing process itself can be painful, I experience a detachment from the finished essay, because I have come to exist in it as a character as separate from myself as any fictional character. I find that I can read my essays to audiences with very little emotion, although once, reading Annick Smith's essay "Homestead" to a creative writing class, I began to cry and thought I would not be able to go on. Her nonfiction character moved me in a way my own could not.

Lately I have been reading my aunt's diaries, which she kept without fail for fifty years. I feel haunted by the parallels between her life and mine. She chose, perhaps with greater self-discipline, perhaps from being closer to the source of the old punishing pressures, to stay all her life on a straight and narrow path I had been perilously near to embarking on. Her diaries reveal her unhappiness, her gradual, unwilling resignation to her lot, and finally, in her old age, her reconciliation with the lone woman she had set out to be. Which has left me with an enormous determination to resist those pressures and to try a new direction: having written my past, I will write the present and transform myself, as she did, in the interstices between fragment and pattern, through the endless interlocking connections between storyteller and story.

We'll see, we'll see. Opportunity lies in the teeth of the sickle bar.

To Fashion a Text

Annie Dillard

I'm here because I'm writing a book called *An American Childhood*, which is a memoir—insofar as a memoir is any account, usually in the first person, of incidents that happened a while ago. It isn't an autobiography, and it isn't "memoirs." I wouldn't dream of writing my memoirs; I'm only forty years old. Or my autobiography; any chronology of my days would make very dull reading—I've spent about thirty years behind either a book or a desk. The book that I'm writing is an account of a childhood in Pittsburgh, Pennsylvania, where I grew up.

The best memoirs, I think, forge their own forms. The writer of any work, and particularly any nonfiction work, must decide two crucial points: what to put in and what to leave out.

So I thought, "What shall I put in?" Well, what is the book about? *An American Childhood* is about the passion of childhood. It's about a child's vigor, and originality, and eagerness, and mastery, and joy.

It's about waking up. A child wakes up over and over again, and notices that she's living. She dreams along, loving the exuberant life of the senses, in love with beauty and power, oblivious of herself—and then suddenly, bingo, she wakes up and feels herself alive. She notices her own awareness. And she notices that she is set down here, mysteriously, in a going world. The world is full of fascinating information that she can collect and enjoy. And the world is public; its issues are moral and historical ones.

So the book is about two things: a child's interior life—vivid, superstitious and timeless—and a child's growing awareness of the world. The structural motion of the book is from the interior landscape—one brain's own idiosyncratic topography—to the American landscape, the vast setting of our common history. The little child pinches the skin on the back of her hand and sees where God made Adam from spit and clay. The older child explores the city on foot and starts to work on her future as a detective, or an epidemiologist, or a painter. Older yet, she runs wild and restless over the city's bridges, and finds in Old Testament poetry and French symbolist poetry some language sounds she loves.

The interior life is in constant vertical motion; consciousness runs up and down the scales every hour like a slide trombone. It dreams down below; it notices up above; and it notices itself, too, and its own alertness. The vertical motion of consciousness, from inside to outside and back, interests me. I've written about it once before, in an essay about a solar eclipse, and I wanted to do more with it.

For a private interior life, I've picked—almost at random—my own. As an aside, this isn't as evident as it may seem. I simply like to write books. About twelve years ago, while I was walking in Acadia National Park in Maine, I decided to write a narrative—a prose narrative, because I wanted to write prose. After a week's thought I decided to write mostly about nature, because I thought I could make it do what I wanted, and I decided to set it all on the coast of Maine. I decided further to write it in the third person, about a man, a sort of metaphysician, in his fifties. A month or so later I decided reluctantly to set the whole shebang in Virginia, because I knew more about Virginia. Then I decided to write it in the first person, as a man. Not until I had written the first chapter and showed it around—this was *Pilgrim at Tinker Creek*—did I give up the pretext of writing in the first person as a man. I wasn't out to deceive people; I just didn't like the idea of writing about myself. I knew I wasn't the subject.

So in this book, for simplicity's sake, I've got my own interior life. It was a lively one. I put in what it was that had me so excited all the time—the sensation of time pelting me as if I were standing under a waterfall. I loved the power of the life in which I found myself. I loved to feel its many things in all their force. I put in what it feels like to play with the skin on your mother's knuckles. I put in what it feels like to throw a baseball—you aim your whole body at the target and watch the ball fly off as if it were your own head. I put in drawing pencil studies of my baseball mitt and collecting insects and fooling around with a microscope.

In my study on Cape Cod, where I write, I've stuck above my desk a big photograph of a little Amazonian boy whose face is sticking out of a waterfall or a rapids. White water is pounding all around his head, in a kind of wreath, but his face is absolutely still, looking up, and his black eyes are open dreamily on the distance. That little boy is completely alive; he's letting the mystery of existence beat on him. He's having his childhood, and I think he knows it. And I think he will come out of the water strong, and ready to do some good. I see this photograph whenever I look up from my computer screen.

So I put in that moment of waking up and noticing that you've been put down in a world that's already under way. The rushing of time wakes you: you play along mindless and eternal on the kitchen floor, and time streams in full flood beside you on the floor. It rages beside you, down its swollen banks, and when it wakes you you're so startled you fall in.

When you wake up, you notice that you're here.

"Here," in my case, was Pittsburgh. I put in the three rivers that meet here. The Allegheny from the north and the Monongahela from the south converge to form the Ohio, the major tributary of the Mississippi, which, in turn, drains the whole continent east of the divide via the Missouri River rising in the Rocky Mountains. The great chain of the Alleghenies kept pioneers out of Pittsburgh until the 1760s, one hundred and fifty years after Jamestown.

I put in those forested mountains and hills, and the way the three rivers lie flat and moving among them, and the way the low land lies wooded among them, and the way the blunt mountains rise in the darkness from the rivers' banks.

I put in Lake Erie, and summers along its mild shore. I put in New Orleans, the home of Dixieland jazz, where my father was heading when he jumped in his boat one day to go down the river like Huck Finn.

I put in the pioneers who "broke wilderness," and the romance of the French and Indian Wars that centered around Fort Duquesne and Fort Pitt. I put in the brawling rivermen—the flatboatmen and keelboatmen.

I put in the old Scotch-Irish families who dominate Pittsburgh and always have. The Mellons are Scotch-Irish, and so were Andrew Carnegie and Henry Clay Frick. They're all Presbyterians. I grew up in this world—at the lunatic fringe of it—and it fascinates me. I think it's important. I think it's peculiarly American—that mixture of piety and acquisitiveness, that love of work. They're Calvinists, of course—just like the Massachusetts Puritans—and I think I can make a case that their influence on American thought was greater than the Puritans'. There were far more Scotch-Irish Presbyterians, after all, and they settled all over the American colonies and carried their democracy and pragmatism with them.

In Pittsburgh the Scotch-Irish constitute a world of many families whose forebears knew each other, who respect each other's discretion and who admire each other for occupying their slots without fuss. The men are withdrawn, the women are ironic. They believe in their world; they all stay in Pittsburgh, and their children stay there. I alone am escaped to tell thee. I and David McCullough, who grew up a few houses away. And James Laughlin, the publisher. All of us Pittsburgh Scotch-Irish Presbyterians.

My sisters and I grew up in this world, and I put it in *An American Childhood.* I put in our private school and quiet club and hushed neighborhood where the houses were stone and their roofs were slate. I put in dancing with little boys at dancing school, and looking at the backs of their interesting necks at Presbyterian church.

Just to make trouble, I put in money. My grandmother used to tell me never to touch money with my bare hands.

I put in books, for that's where this book started, with an essay I wrote for the *New York Times Magazine* on reading books. Almost all of my many passionate interests, and my many changes of mind, came through books. Books prompted the many vows I made to myself. Nonfiction books lured me away from the world—as I dreamed about working for Scotland Yard, doing field work in freshwater streams, rock collecting in the salt desert, painting in Paris. And novels dragged me back into the world—because I would read whatever was handy, and what was handy in those years were novels about the Second World War. I read so many books about the Second World War that I knew how to man a minesweeper before I knew how to walk in high heels. You couldn't read much about the war without figuring out that the world was a moral arena that required your strength.

I had the notion back then that everything was interesting if you just learned enough about it. Now, writing about it, I have the pleasure of learning it all again and finding that it *is* interesting. I get to inform myself and any readers about such esoterica as rock collecting, which I hadn't thought about in almost thirty years.

When I was twelve a paperboy gave me two grocery bags full of rock and mineral chunks. It took me most of a year to identify them. At a museum shop I bought cards of what they called thumbnail specimens. And I read books about a fairly absurd batch of people who called themselves rockhounds; they spent their evenings in the basement sawing up slabs of travertine into wavy slices suitable, they said, for wall hangings.

Now, in this memoir, I get to recall where the romance of rock collecting had lain: the symbolic sense that underneath the dreary highways, underneath Pittsburgh, were canyons of crystals—that you could find treasure by prying open the landscape. In my reading I learned that people have cracked knobs of granite and laid bare clusters of red garnets and topaz crystals, chrysoberyl, spudomene and emerald. They held in their hands crystals that had hung in a hole in the dark for a billion years unseen. I liked the idea of that. I would lay about me right and left with a hammer and bash the landscape to bits. I would crack the earth's crust like a piñata and spread its vivid prizes in chunks to the light. That's what I wanted to do. So I put that in.

It's also a great pleasure to write about my parents, because they're both great storytellers—comedians, actually—which gives me a chance to tell their wonderful stories. We were all young, at our house, and we enjoyed ourselves.

My father was a dreamer; he lived differently from other men around him. One day he abruptly quit the family firm—when I was ten—and took off down the Ohio River in a boat by himself to search out the roots of jazz in New Orleans. He came back after several months and withdrew from corporate life forever. He knew the world well—all sort of things, which he taught us to take an interest in: how people build bridge pilings in the middle of a river, how jazz came up the river to be educated in Chicago, how the pioneers made their way westward from Pittsburgh, down the Ohio River, sitting on the tops of their barges and singing "Bang Away, My Lulu."

My mother was both a thinker and what one might call a card. If she lay on the beach with friends and found the conversation dull, she would give a little push with her heel and roll away. People were stunned. She rolled deadpan and apparently effortlessly, her arms and legs extended tidily, down the beach to the distant water's edge where she lay at ease just as she had been, but half in the surf, and well out of earshot. She was not only a card but a wild card, a force for disorder.

She regarded even tiny babies as straight men, and liked to step on the drawstring of a crawling baby's gown, so that the baby crawled and crawled and never got anywhere except into a little ball at the top of the gown.

She was interested in language. Once my father and I were in the kitchen listening to a ballgame—the Pirates playing the New York Giants. The Giants had a utility infielder named Wayne Terwilliger. Just as Mother walked through the kitchen, the announcer said, "Terwilliger bunts one." Mother stopped dead and said, "What was that? Was that English?" Father said, "The man's name is Terwilliger. He bunted." Mother thought that was terrific. For the next ten or twelve years she made this surprising string of syllables her own. If she was testing a microphone, or if she was pretending to whisper a secret in my ear, she said, "Terwilliger bunts one." If she had ever had an occasion to create a motto for a coat of arms, as Andrew Carnegie had, her motto would have been "Terwilliger bunts one." Carnegie's was "Death to privilege."

These fine parents taught my sisters and me moral courage, insofar as we have it, and tolerance, and how to dance all night without dragging your arms on your partner, and how to time the telling of a joke.

I've learned a lot by writing this book, not only about writing but about American history. Eastern woodland Indians killed many more settlers than plains Indians did. By the time settlers made it to Sioux and Apache country those Indians had been so weakened by disease and by battles with the army that they didn't have much fight left in them. It was the settlers in the Pennsylvania forests and in Maryland and Virginia who kept getting massacred and burned out and taken captive and tortured. During the four years the French held Pittsburgh at Fort Duquesne they armed the Indians and sent them out from there, raiding and killing English-speaking settlers. These were mostly Scotch-Irish, because the Penn family let them settle in Pennsylvania only if they would serve as a "buffer sect" between Quakers and Indians. When the English held Pittsburgh at Fort Pitt they gave the Indians unwashed blankets from the smallpox hospital.

I put in early industry, because it was unexpectedly interesting. Before there was steel, everything was made out of wrought iron—which I find just amazing. Railroad ties were made out of wrought iron, as if they were candle sconces. Men had to carry wrought iron railroad ties all up and down the country. Wrought iron is made by iron puddlers, who belong to the iron puddlers' union, the Sons of Vulcan. It's a very difficult process: you stir slag back into iron, and it requires skilled labor because carbon monoxide bubbles up. The language is also nice. To sinter, for instance, is to convert flu dust to clinker. And I finally learned what coke is. When I was a child I thought that Coca-Cola was a by-product of steelmaking.

I learned about the heyday of the big industrialists and the endless paradox of Andrew Carnegie, the only one of the great American moguls who not only read books but actually wrote them, including one with a very American title, *The Gospel of Wealth*. He sold U.S. Steel to J. P. Morgan for $492 million, and he said, "A man who dies rich dies disgraced." He gave away ninety percent of his fortune in the few years he had left. While he was giving away money, many people were moved, understandably, to write him letters. He got one such letter from his friend Mark Twain. It said:

> You seem to be in prosperity. Could you lend an admirer a dollar & a half to buy a hymn-book with? God will bless you. I feel it. I know it. P.S. Don't send the hymn-book, send the money.

Carnegie was only five feet three inches tall. He weighed 133 pounds. He built the workers free libraries and museums and an art gallery at the same time that he had them working sixteen hours a day, six days a week, at subhuman wages, and drinking water full of typhoid and cholera because he and the other business owners opposed municipal works like water filtration plants. By 1906 Pittsburgh had the highest death rate in the nation because of wretched living conditions, and yet it was the seat of "wealth beyond computation, wealth beyond imagination." People built stables for their horses with gold mirrors in the stalls. The old Scotch-Irish families were horrified at the new millionaires who popped up around this time because they liked things pretty quiet. One new millionaire went to a barber on Penn Avenue for his first shampoo and the barber reported that the washing brought out "two ounces of fine Mesabi ore and a scattering of slag and cinders."

And what to leave out?

Well, I'm not writing social history. This is not one of those books in which you may read the lyrics or even the titles of popular songs on the radio. Or the names of radio and TV programs, or advertising slogans or product names or clothing fashions. I don't like all that. I want to direct the reader's attention in equal parts to the text—as a formal object—and to the world, as an interesting place in which we find ourselves.

So another thing I left out, as far as I could, was myself. The personal pronoun can be the subject of the verb: "I see this, I did that." But not the object of the verb: "I analyze me, I discuss me, I describe me, I quote me."

In the course of writing this memoir I've learned all sorts of things, quite inadvertently, about myself and various relationships. But these things are not important to the book and I easily leave them out. Since the subject of the book is not me, other omissions naturally follow. I leave out many things that were important to my life but of no concern for the present book, like the summer I spent in Wyoming when I was fifteen. I keep the action in Pittsburgh; I see no reason to drag everybody off to Wyoming just because I want to tell them about my summer vacation. You have to take pains in a memoir not to hang on the reader's arm, like a drunk, and say, "And then I did this and it was so interesting." I don't write for that reason.

On the other hand, I dig deeply into the exuberant heart of a child and the restless, violent heart of an adolescent—and I was that child and I was that adolescent.

I leave out my private involvement with various young men. I didn't want to kiss and tell. I did put in several sections, however, about boys in general and the fascination they exerted. I ran around with one crowd of older boys so decadent, so accustomed to the most glittering of social lives, that one of them carried with him at all times, in his jacket pocket, a canister of dance wax so that he could be ready for anything. Other boys carry Swiss Army knives for those occasions which occur unexpectedly; this boy carried dance wax for the same reason. He could just sprinkle it on the dining room floor and take you in his arms and whirl you away. These were the sort of boys I knew; they had worn ties from the moment their mothers could locate their necks.

I tried to leave out anything that might trouble my family. My parents are quite young. My sisters are watching this book carefully. Everybody I'm writing about is alive and well, in full possession of his faculties, and possibly willing to sue. Things were simpler when I wrote about muskrats.

Writing in the first person can trap the writer into airing grievances. When I taught writing I spent a lot of time trying to convince young writers that, while literature is an art, it's not a martial art—that the pages of a short story or a novel are no place to defend yourself from an attack, real or imagined, and no place from which to launch an attack, particularly an attack against the very people who painstakingly reared you to your present omniscience.

I have no temptation to air grievances; in fact, I have no grievances left. Unfortunately, I seem to have written the story of my impassioned adolescence so convincingly that my parents (after reading that section of my book) think I still feel that way. It's a problem that I have to solve—one of many in this delicate area. My parents and my youngest sister still live in Pittsburgh; I have to handle it with tongs.

As a result of all of this, I've promised my family that each may pass on the book. I've promised to take out anything that anyone objects to—anything at all. When I was growing up I didn't really take to Pittsburgh society, and I was happy to throw myself into any other world I could find. But I guess I can't say so, because my family may think that I confuse them with conventional Pittsburgh society people in the '50s.

I know a writer who cruelly sticks his parents into all his short stories and still pleases them both, because his mother is pleased to see his father look bad and his father is pleased to see his mother look bad. I had, I thought, nothing but good to say about all named people, but I'll make all that better yet. I don't believe in a writer's kicking around people who don't have access to a printing press. They can't defend themselves.

My advice to memoir writers is to embark upon a memoir for the same reason that you would embark on any other book: to fashion a text. Don't hope in a memoir to preserve your memories. If you prize your memories as they are, by all means avoid—eschew—writing a memoir. Because it is a certain way to lose them. You can't put together a memoir without cannibalizing your own life for parts. The work battens on your memories. And it replaces them.

It's a matter of writing's vividness for the writer. If you spend a couple of days writing a tricky paragraph, and if you spend a week or two laying out a scene or describing an event, you've spent more time writing about it than you did living it. The writing time is also much more intense.

After you've written, you can no longer remember anything but the writing. However true you make that writing, you've created a monster. This has happened to me many, many times, because I'm willing to turn events into pieces of paper. After I've written about any experience, my memories—those elusive, fragmentary patches of color and feeling—are gone; they've been replaced by the work. The work is a sort of changeling on the doorstep—not your baby but someone else's baby rather like it, different in some way that you can't pinpoint, and yours has vanished.

Memory is insubstantial. Things keep replacing it. Your batch of snapshots will both fix and ruin your memory of your travels, or your childhood, or your children's childhood. You can't remember anything from your trip except this wretched collection of snapshots. The painting you did of the light on the water will forever alter the way you see the light on the water; so will looking at Flemish paintings. If you describe a dream you'll notice that at the end of the verbal description you've lost the dream but gained a verbal description. You have to like verbal descriptions a lot to keep up this sort of thing. I like verbal descriptions a lot.

Let me put in a word now for a misunderstood genre: literary nonfiction. It's interesting to me because I try to write it and because I respect the art of it very much.

I like to be aware of a book as a piece of writing, and aware of its structure as a product of mind, and yet I want to be able to see the represented world through it. I admire artists who succeed in dividing my attention more or less evenly between the world of their books and the art of their books. In fiction we might say that the masters are Henry James and Herman Melville. In nonfiction the writer usually just points to the world and says, "This is a biography of Abraham Lincoln. This is what Abraham Lincoln was about." But the writer may also make of his work an original object in its own right, so that a reader may study the work with pleasure as well as the world that it describes. That is, works of nonfiction can be coherent and crafted works of literature.

It's not simply that they're carefully written, or vivid and serious and pleasing, like Boswell's *Life of Johnson,* say, or St. Exupéry's wonderful memoir of early aviation, *Wind, Sand, and Stars.* It's not even that they may contain elements of fiction, that their action reveals itself in scenes that use visual descriptions and that often use dialogue. It's not just these things, although these things are important. It's that nonfiction accounts may be literary insofar as the parts of their structures cohere internally, insofar as the things are in them for the sake of the work itself, and insofar as the work itself exists in the service of idea. (It is especially helpful if the writer so fully expresses the idea in materials that only a trained technician can find it. Because the abstract structure of a given text, which is of great interest to the writer and serves to rouse him out of bed in the morning and impel him to the desk, is of little or no interest to the reader, and he'd better not forget it.)

Nonfiction accounts don't ordinarily meet these criteria, but they may. Walden Pond is the linchpin of a metaphysic. In repeated and self-conscious rewritings Thoreau hammered at its unremarkable and rather dreary acres until they fastened eternity in time and stood for the notion that the physical world itself expresses a metaphysical one. He picked up that pond and ran with it. He could just as readily have used something else—a friend, say, or a chestnut. You can do quite a bit with language.

Hemingway in *Green Hills of Africa* wrote a sober narrative account of killing a kudu, the whole of which functions as an elaborate metaphor for internal quests and conquests. Loren Eiseley lays in narrative symbols with a trowel, splashing mortar all over the place, but they hold. In his essay "The Star-Thrower," Eiseley's beachcomber who throws dying starfish back into the surf stands for any hope or mercy that flies in the face of harsh natural law. He stands finally for the extravagant spirit behind creation as a whole; he is a god hurling solar systems into the void.

I only want to remind my writing colleagues that a great deal can be done in nonfiction, especially in first-person accounts where the writer controls the materials absolutely. Because other literary genres are shrinking. Poetry has purified itself right out of the ballpark. Literary fiction is scarcely being published—it's getting to be like conceptual art. All that the unknown writer of fiction can do is to tell his friends about the book he has written, and all that his friends can say is "Good idea." The short story is to some extent going the way of poetry, limiting its subject matter to such narrow surfaces that it can't handle the things that most engage our hearts and minds. But literary nonfiction is all over the map and has been for three hundred years. There's nothing you can't do with it. No subject matter is forbidden, no structure is proscribed. You get to make up your own form every time.

When I gave up writing poetry I was very sad, for I had devoted fifteen years to the study of how the structures of poems carry meaning. But I was delighted to find that nonfiction prose can also carry meaning in its structures and, like poetry, can tolerate all sorts of figurative language, as well as alliteration and even rhyme. The range of rhythms in prose is larger and grander than it is in poetry, and it can handle discursive ideas and plain information as well as character and story. It can do everything. I felt as though I had switched from a single reed instrument to a full orchestra.

Let me close with a word about process. There's a common notion that self-discipline is a freakish peculiarity of writers—that writers differ from other people by possessing enormous and equal portions of talent and willpower. They grit their powerful teeth and go into their little rooms. I think that's a bad misunderstanding of what impels the writer. What impels the writer is a deep love for and respect for language, for literary forms, for books. It's a privilege to muck about in sentences all morning. It's a challenge to bring off a powerful effect, or to tell the truth about something. You don't do it from willpower; you do it from an abiding passion for the field. I'm sure it's the same in every other field.

Writing a book is like rearing children—willpower has very little to do with it. If you have a little baby crying in the middle of the night, and if you depend only on willpower to get you out of bed to feed the baby, that baby will starve. You do it out of love. Willpower is a weak idea; love is strong. You don't have to scourge yourself with a cat-o'-nine-tails to go to the baby. You go to the baby out of love for that particular baby. That's the same way you go to your desk. There's nothing freakish about it. Caring passionately about something isn't against nature, and it isn't against human nature. It's what we're here to do.

wandering
message richer
no immediate point
slow down
see the parts.
does talk about the points of an essay

Jamie
I don't
know what
to do with
myself

On the Possibilities of the Essay: A Meditation

Rebecca Blevins Faery

When one looks from inside at a lighted window, or looks from above at the lake, one sees the image of oneself in a lighted room, the image of oneself among trees and sky—the deception is obvious, but flattering all the same. When one looks from the darkness into the light, however, one sees all the difference between here and there, this and that. Perhaps all unsheltered people are angry in their hearts, and would like to break the roof, spine, and ribs, and smash the windows and flood the floor and spindle the curtains and bloat the couch.

Marilynne Robinson, Housekeeping

I

I had, it seemed, to my surprise, terror, and delight, bought a house.

It was high summer, July of 1988, the peak of a season of dazzling heat and soul-wrenching drought. As I drove between Iowa City and Dubuque, where I was teaching a seminar, I watched the corn in fields on either side of the two-lane highway shrivel relentlessly week by week under the baking sun until I heard, or thought I heard, as I drove, a very high-pitched keen or wail, coming from the corn, begging for rain.

Moving day arrived when the seminar ended, according to plan. During the weeks I was away teaching, assorted carpenters and dry-wall workers and plumbers and painters had executed my preliminary plans for turning the house into my own. It was—is—a grand house, old and possessed of great dignity, so I had a lot to work with: high ceilings, wide mahogany pocket doors at once dividing and connecting all the downstairs rooms, multiple tall windows looking out on a wide lawn with room for a terrace, a garden, a grape arbor, a bed of multi-hued lilies. A house full of promise, of possibilities.

The unpacking and settling-in were a strain in the dry heat, well over a hundred degrees day after sizzling day. Indulging a fantasy which my new identity as owner of this grand house allowed me, I adopted in interludes the persona and habits of a woman of leisure and splurged on a Yucatan hammock, which I hung between an old box-elder and a leaning cedar not far from the back porch. I took refuge in their shade when fatigue overtook me, swaying as I read. The novel in my hands, as I recall myself in those moments through the screen of memory, is Marilynne Robinson's *Housekeeping.*

Mornings I rose, made coffee, soothed the cat out of her nervousness at waking in a house whose unfamiliarity she had daily to confront anew, and set to work to establish the cleanliness and order I've been taught to believe is next to godliness. My domestic inclinations I gave full rein: this was my home, my haven, nest, stay against the confusion of impermanence, each room a stanza of the poem to fixity I was trying to make of the enterprise. I had married this house with enthusiasm, and I took up the familiar role and tasks of housewife with an energy made vigorous by commitment. "I was born to live in this house," I said to my friends in the romantic flush of love for my new home; "I intend to stay here forever."

It must be understood, for this tale to make any sense at all, that I have yearned all my adult life for permanence, for "home," for a long commitment to a place, a dwelling that would house me securely and comfortably in return for my love and attention, its walls my fortress against flux and fortune's whims. Yet every home I've had I've lived in only briefly; I've been, despite my longings, a woman forever on the move. Or, more precisely, several women, simultaneously and in succession, and all of them on the move.

In the heat of that summer, I was making another stab at it. I labored in splendid isolation toward splendid order in the arrangement of furniture, pictures on the walls, dishes in the cupboards. This finely articulated distribution of my possessions soothed me into pretending that I was indeed protected from the shifting boundaries of identity, from the fraying and unraveling that are the lot of us all.

The dissonances between my determined housekeeping and the interpolations of lazy late afternoon hours of suspended reading of *Housekeeping* did not escape me. The novel drew me away from my busyness to the still hours in the swaying hammock, drew me with its exquisite sentences, its elegiac tone, its visions that all efforts to stop the flow of time, change, displacement, discomposing are fruitless. It's a vision I share, indeed advocate; the old must be abandoned in pursuit of the new. The difference is that the women in the novel act on that knowledge. I, on the other hand, sometimes at least, act as if I *don't* believe it, though I do. In the novel, Sylvie knows that something means to undo a house, so she opens the doors and windows and lets the undoer in. She underscores the silly futility of housewifely saving and storing by collecting useless things—empty cans, old newspapers—and arranging them neatly against the walls of all the rooms. Sylvie refuses the bourgeois ideologies of "home" with all their attachments to class privilege, ideologies that confine women within the predictable roles and ordered spaces of domesticity; she embraces the road rather than the cottage beside it. I try to do these things too, in my own way. But I, on the other hand, dweller in contradictions, also batten down, hunker, and hope.

II

In their essay "Feminist Politics: What's Home Got to Do with It?" Biddy Martin and Chandra Talpade Mohanty use their reading of another essay, Minnie Bruce Pratt's "Identity: Skin Blood Heart," to consider the political ideologies of "home": house, family, kin, community in the immediate sense; personal identities grounded in race, class, gender, sexuality, convictions and claimed affinities in the wider sense. And while the following passage from Martin and Mohanty addresses Pratt's remarkable essay alone, I offer it as a perspective on the possibilities of the essay in general:

> [The essay] is a form of writing that not only anticipates and integrates diverse audiences or readers but also positions the narrator as reader. The perspective is multiple and shifting, and the shifts in perspective are enabled by the attempts to define self, home, and community that are at the heart of Pratt's enterprise. The historical grounding of shifts and changes allows for an emphasis on the pleasures and terrors of interminable boundary confusions, but insists, at the same time, on our responsibility for remapping boundaries and renegotiating connections. These are partial in at least two senses of the word: politically partial, and without claims to wholeness or finality.

The essay as a performance of reading. The essayist as reader. The reader of essays as reader. All readings contingent, partial, multiple, shifting. Nothing is fixed, and nobody has a corner on truth.

When Samuel Johnson in his famous *Dictionary* defines the essay as "a loose sally of the mind; an irregular, undigested piece," I at least suspect the privileging of reason over feeling, intellection over intuition. It is the article or treatise which earns from Johnson an implicit description as "a regular, orderly composition," the thing the essay, by his definition, is not. What makes for the difference? The meanderings, for one thing, of the essayist's persona, made precedent by Montaigne. A "composition" requires the writer's subjugation to a monumental discourse. The essay is written by somebody who sallies into a subject loosely, leaving—or making—holes that are not knitted up, carrying along and exploring the myriad possible specificities of the writer's experience and identity. The essay rests on perspective, on the position of the essayist within the web of culture. It allows the essayist to say, "This is how the world looks to *me*, from my particular place in it." The essay has, then, the potential for being at least an inroad, if not indeed an attack, on monumental discourse because as a form it negotiates the split

between public discourse—formal, ordered, impersonal, knowing, with preten-
sions to universality and fixity, and private utterance—tentative, personal, quest-
ing, provisional. If the "composition" is an edifice, the essay is a nomad's tent. It
moves around.

The essay, then, is and has been a form open to the articulation of estrange-
ments and contradictions, a place for expressing the strains, differences, rejections
as well as connections experienced by those who feel or have felt particularly
marginalized by the discourses which have composed the social text. I am thinking here of writers like James Baldwin, Nancy Mairs, Alice Walker, Audre Lorde,
Minnie Bruce Pratt, and many others who have recognized in the essay a potential site for the operations of contesting discourses and have used it to explore and
construct in language the multiple perspectives which variant experiences and
identities produce.

Virginia Woolf, for instance. Think of all those polite essays she wrote about
her reading and published in the *Times Literary Supplement.* Think of how comforting, how comfortable they are, spoken from the privileged position of a
woman of means, of well-placed family, of culture. And then think of others, *A
Room of One's Own* and *Three Guineas,* in which she speaks from a position as outsider, attempting to undo the cultural stories that have placed her there, on the
margins, because of her gender. Such writing from the margins is "guerrilla writing," a term I heard recently and have not been able to forget. In the terrain of
monumental discourse, such pieces are eruptions of personal presence based on
shifting experiences and identities, eruptions that aim to dis-compose the power
relations that reside in textuality. And such moments are accomplished not only
by particular essays within the field of more orderly forms of writing; they occur
also *within* essays, as in Woolf's "Professions for Women," when that-which-
cannot-be-said about a woman's experience of her body slips away like a fish escaping a line. Or in "The Moment: Summer's Night," when an imaged scene of
domestic violence—"He beats her"—intrudes upon and contrasts with the cultivated civility of the narrator and her companions. Or in "22 Hyde Park Gate,"
which closes with the astonishing revelation of the sexual abuse Woolf and her
sister were subjected to by their half-brother. Is Woolf in these texts violating her
own dictum that the purpose of the essay is "to give pleasure"? What sort of pleasure can we get from scenes of wife-beating and forced incest and the taboos
against expressing bodily experience? Perhaps the pleasures of heresy—the thing
Adorno calls "the law of the innermost form of the essay." And the pleasures of
heresy are not small. Carl Klaus has aptly termed the essay an "antigenre, a rogue
form of writing in the universe of discourse." I would elaborate only to observe
that the essay can be, has been, rogue or heretical not only in form but in effect. As
"antigenre," it has the capacity to work against, even to undo, the presumptions
that have structured western discourse.

Look, for another example, at what is happening in the realm of conventional academic writing. A couple of years ago, a friend gave me a copy of Jane
Tompkins' essay "Me and My Shadow" in an effort to help me out of a difficult
period of inability to write. I read about Tompkins' anger at the "straitjacket" of

the suppression of the personal voice and personal experience in academic writing, about the "two voices" she felt within her, one of which had been systematically silenced. I read her plea for redressing the damage done by the conventions of intellectual discourse, a plea based on the conviction that readers "want to know about each other":

> Sometimes, when a writer introduces some personal bit of story into an essay, I can hardly contain my pleasure. I love writers who write about their own experience. I feel I'm being nourished by them, that I'm being allowed to enter into a personal relationship with them, that I can match my own experience with theirs, feel cousin to them, and say, yes, that's how it is.

Yes, I said to myself as I read, a seemingly endless stream of tears rolling down my cheeks—whether tears of grief, or joy, or both, I'm still not clear—yes, that's how it is.

Sometimes, though, the voice relating personal perspective and experience in an essay draws me, excites me, because what I read challenges rather than confirms my own experience and thus opens up for me new perspectives on the world. Then my response is not "That's how it is," but "Is that how it is?" If I am to act in the world in a way that attempts to respect and accommodate differences, I need to know what the world is like not only for people who are in some way like me, but also for people who are in some way different. I must be taught as well as teach. Patricia Williams, a Black feminist legal scholar, begins an essay on commercial transactions by telling the story of the rape and impregnation at age twelve of her great-great-grandmother by the girl's white owner. The essay, "On Being the Object of Property," is a dazzling poetic display which inserts the continuing personal pain of such a heritage into the affectless tradition of legal scholarship and thereby unsettles that tradition. It links Williams' meditations on her personal and racial histories, her experiences of race and gender in a hierarchical culture, with legal issues like the "Baby M" case and the forced sterilization of women of color. The essay accommodates passages like this one:

> There are moments in my life when I feel as though a part of me is missing. There are days when I feel so invisible that I can't remember what day of the week it is, when I feel so manipulated that I can't remember my own name, when I feel so lost and angry that I can't speak a civil word to the people who love me best. Those are the times when I catch sight of my reflection in store windows and am surprised to see a whole person looking back. Those are the times when my skin becomes gummy as clay and my nose slides around on my face and my eyes drip down to my chin. I have to close my eyes at such times and remember myself, draw an internal picture that is smooth and whole; when all else fails, I reach for a mirror and stare myself down until the features reassemble themselves like lost sheep.

The passage is a metaphoric description of the dis-composing effect of monolithic racist and sexist discourses on Williams, and of the composing effect of her own writing, in which she reconstructs—*re-members*—a self, however momentary, however *partial* in both senses of the word: invested with self-interest and without claim to finality. Williams' writing simultaneously composes herself and discomposes conventional discourses which in a variety of ways deny her. She makes use of the literary qualities of language, whose task, in their origins in the oral traditions of poetry, was to make memorable the stories of the tribe or culture in order to assure they would be repeated and thus not forgotten. Williams' essay is a frontal attack on the master's house, a stream of words aimed at eroding the rock of oppression at the foundation of culture. Her essay insists that there is never just one story; rather, there are many stories which can and must be told, which must be heard. In this essay Williams, like Sylvie in *Housekeeping,* is an undoer. And that cannot be a futile effort because, as James Baldwin, filled with simultaneous despair and desperate hope, writes in his beautiful essay "Nothing Personal," "For nothing is fixed, forever and forever and forever, it is not fixed; the earth is always shifting, the light is always changing, the sea does not cease to grind down rock."

What the pedagogical implications might be of such a view of the essay I have considered here hardly at all, and then only indirectly. Certainly the form itself has been an outsider in the institution of literary studies, relegated mostly to the composition classroom where, too often, its essential qualities of perspective and personal voice have been masked or even banned. What could happen if we admit the "anti-genre" not only into our polite and scholarly forms of writing, but also into the rigidly generic classrooms and hallways of our educational institutions—what Nancy Mairs calls "the ivory phallus"—I can scarcely imagine. I know I'd like to be around to watch.

III

So. What did I leave out of my story of buying a house, of my attempts to shore up its walls against some imagined ruin? Some of the reasons. I belong, by race and by family tradition, to a propertied class, where owning a house stands in direct equation with respectability. It is my toehold. Also because I am a woman who came of age in an era when "home" was woman's sphere, even when she's also the "head of household." Also because I've been, most of my adult life, relatively rootless, following along after one man, one life plan, in flight from others. Now, my children grown and gone, I become paradoxically even more obsessive about a "nest."

If you wonder why I of all people proved so susceptible to the seductions of "home" with all its attendant ideologies, I can tell you only and simply that I am a woman partially constructed by such ideologies.

But perhaps I've painted an overly romantic picture of the house and my relation to it. It's been almost two years now, after all, since I moved in, two years of mild winters and early springs and one temperate summer. Like all love affairs, this one has lost some of its glow. The house is still grand, I admit; but water pipes burst, the roof leaks, the porches sag. The deep and dark waters of the lake at

Fingerbone reach all the way to Iowa and lap at my edges. The house is after all less comfortable, less comforting than I had hoped, and other yearnings have started to surface. I manage to muster, twice a year, the thousand dollars to pay the property tax. But I feed the squirrels that eat holes in the eaves to winter over in the attic, though my more prudent friends urge me to trap them humanely and move them out into the country west of town. And I think I forgot to mention that I share the house—and not just with my cat. In fact I live only in those hardly discrete rooms of the first floor, rooms that flow liquidly one into another. In the upstairs apartment are Karen and Wayne, their black cat and their books. Wayne writes novels, Karen makes poems, so on our good days, all of us are more preoccupied with meanings than with maintenance. In the spare parking place next to the alley, a huge and ancient Buick appears several days a week beside my tenants' Toyota. The Buick is ventilated with rusted-through holes the size of my fist. It belongs to Alex, broad-faced member of the Mesquakie tribe from the settlement over at Tama. He wears a long braid down his back, a feather in his black felt hat; he won a dance competition, he told me, at a pow-wow on the shores of Lake Michigan just a few months ago. Karen and Wayne mentioned casually once that he was "visiting"; instead, I think he lives there with them on the days he needs to be in Iowa City to go to school. They don't tell me that because, I suppose, they think the same impulse that led me to lay a brick terrace and plant lilies would make me exercise a white law and kick him out. But I say nothing. I'm learning to live with, live through contradictions, even learning to love them. I grow weary of defending territory to which I'm not sure I can lay just claim. And I want to be an undoer too, as well as one of the undone. I want this house to be open. Alex, when he sees me in the yard, greets me and calls me "the landlady." The term gives me a start, especially coming from him. Whose home is this, anyway?

I know, I know, it is in some sense mine. But I can give it up. And surely someday, some way or other, I will.

Note

The texts cited in this essay are: T.W. Adorno, "The Essay as Form," in *New German Critique*, 1984; James Baldwin, "Nothing Personal," in *The Price of the Ticket*, 1985; Carl Klaus, "Essayists on the Essay," in *Literary Nonfiction*, ed. Chris Anderson, 1989; Nancy Mairs, *Remembering the Bone House: An Erotics of Place and Space*, 1989; Biddy Martin and Chandra Talpade Mohanty, "Feminist Politics: What's Home Got to Do with It?" in *Feminist Studies/Critical Studies*, ed. Teresa de Lauretis, 1986; Minnie Bruce Pratt, "Identity: Skin Blood Heart," in Bulkin, Pratt, and Smith, *Yours in Struggle*, 1984; Marilynne Robinson, *Housekeeping*, 1981; Jane Tompkins, "Me and My Shadow," in *New Literary History*, 1987; Patricia Williams, "On Being the Object of Property," in *Signs*, 1988; Virginia Woolf, "Professions for Women," in *The Death of the Moth and Other Essays*, 1942; Woolf, "The Moment: Summer's Night," in *The Moment and Other Essays*, 1948; Woolf, "22 Hyde Park Gate," in *Moments of Being*, 1976.

The Intelligent Heart

Patricia Foster

What's at issue is that the personal essay is dead, the "I" evicted from the fashionable venues of literary nonfiction. Or so I've been told.

"The world is just *sick* of people writing about their lives," a colleague complains to me behind the closed door of my office. He is clever, wry, visionary, and I feel myself shrink as his eyes make a panoramic sweep of my desk where pages of a memoir lie stacked in a disheveled mess. I think of what I've written there, how my family hacked our way out of poverty and nailed ourselves to the middle class, the spikes digging deep into the marrow of our skills. I think of my mother who saves string, my father who prefers to eat in the kitchen, my aunt who says, "Ain't that right, honey?" when she wants to assert that the world is a rough and perilous place.

"Think about it," my colleague says. "All that narcissism, all that unresolved emotion."

When he leaves, I briefly worry that my writing is irrelevant, old-fashioned, tied too fervently to fury, to self-obsession, to the complicated issues of class. Perhaps I have no right to material so close to me, stories that fester and clot inside me like the beginnings of a chronic disease. Perhaps it is passé to write about the struggle between temperaments, the duel of consciousness within a family. Perhaps the old way of storytelling in the essay is dead. Now it's time to be experimental, sexy, to jump on the bandwagon of the new, new thing, those essays that intimidate and confuse, essays that defy the rest of us to see them with uncritical awe.

"It's better if it's a little more obscure," a student responds in class to an essay about a young man's relationship to his father. "If it has gaps, you know."

"Yeah, we need to unpack it," another student agrees. "That's what we're supposed to do . . . figure it out, you know, like unpacking a box, not being sure what we've got, not being sure what's really there, only what we *think* is there."

I see myself yanking out conflicts, tossing out reliable narrators, letting them wobble and shudder to a stop.

"The more fragmented, the better," the first student says. "Then it's one discourse pitted against another."

Well, maybe, I think to myself. But these are merely the buzzwords of academia, and such words—so easily misunderstood—often have little to do with the success of an essay, the clarity of the thinking, the hills and furrows of a meditative form, the ability of the writer to engage the intelligent heart.

But what is the intelligent heart and who gives a fig about that anymore?

Sometimes I think I sit alone in my room, in a solemn universe of me and like-minded friends to whom I can point and say frankly, "We care. We believe in the intelligent heart!" We believe that personal stories matter, that whether autobiographical or cultural, the story must act as a catalyst for thinking and feeling, that it is the congruence of both that elevates the essay to the status of art. The intelligent heart is the heart that seeks revelation in dreams, then turns dreams into insight, and insight into wisdom. The intelligent heart is the balance beam, the quivering tightrope we walk when we dip perilously into our psyches and gather up the stray bits and pieces we patch together and call art. Perhaps, more often, the intelligent heart is a masquerade, a carnival, a devilish trickster we wrestle with constantly, fighting shadows and phantoms in our attempt to find its true shape. Not that its true shape will give us any peace. Its true shape merely defines for us the oppositions we can work with, the strands of ambivalence we hold up to soft morning light. When functioning properly, the intelligent heart knocks at our door, awakens us from dreams, shudders from the drafty places in our apartments, and demands a quick audience. *Write this*, it says. *And this. And this. And this.* Faithfully we write it down, trying to quiet the alarm that it will be embarrassing, stupid, irrelevant, or that most insulting of faults: already done. We listen because it is urgent, because it sneaked up behind us and blithely tongued our ear. We listen because it seemed hungry and furious, as alive as thunder before a late summer rain. We listen because we know that stories come from the mystery of knowable places, the slime coating the muscle of an oyster, the brine of a shrimp, the tough, thready strands of a tangerine. We know that everything we receive—*even this, this summons*—must be untangled and distilled, worked like the unraveling of rope, piece by piece, thread by thread, then put back together with the embrace of two broken thumbs. The intelligent heart is no mere bud of ornamentation. The intelligent heart is the source, the goods, the first principle from which everything else is made.

But this is not to say that the intelligent heart is all. Should anyone demand this, I would rise up in protest and draw my sword. "All" is something that can't be defended, dictated, enlisted, tabulated, or decreed. In every piece of good writing there is something suspect, a shadow lurking in the corner, a stray hair fluttering across the page, a drift of wind, a low banked fog that obscures the promise of understanding. In every piece of good writing there is trouble, the quirks of personality and temperament, the dizzying gradations of self-love. No, the intelligent heart, in the end, is something elusive and longed for, the thing that can't quite be attained. The real problem for most of us is that the intelligent heart often remains buried for years, letting us grind out bare, quixotic but emotionless forms, forms that please our cerebral betters, that thrill grant committees, that delight bored academics. These are forms that grow hairy with stylish weight, but that live, we secretly know, because of lack. And there is safety in lack. Safety in style. There is even, I admit, a kind of awe.

But when all the huff and puff of fashion slips away, the safe, stylish essay cooked in the safe, stylish brain, is nothing but a husk, a fancy dress, a decorative facade covering an unknowable story, a secret life.

"Nobody wants any more of those personal stories," my colleague says. "Who cares about the I? Who cares about the woman in the storm? The family drowning? The mother clawing her way out of filth and dreary disease? Who cares?" he asks.

But I don't bow my head. "I do," I say, gathering up the pages of my story. I refuse to be dead.

Memory and Imagination

Patricia Hampl

When I was seven, my father, who played the violin on Sundays with a nicely tortured flair which we considered artistic, led me by the hand down a long, unlit corridor in St. Luke's School basement, a sort of tunnel that ended in a room full of pianos. There many little girls and a single sad boy were playing truly tortured scales and arpeggios in a mash of troubled sound. My father gave me over to Sister Olive Marie, who did look remarkably like an olive.

Her oily face gleamed as if it had just been rolled out of a can and laid on the white plate of her broad, spotless wimple. She was a small, plump woman; her body and the small window of her face seemed to interpret the entire alphabet of olive: her face was a sallow green olive placed upon the jumbo ripe olive of her black habit. I trusted her instantly and smiled, glad to have my hand placed in the hand of a woman who made sense, who provided the satisfaction of being what she was: an Olive who looked like an olive.

My father left me to discover the piano with Sister Olive Marie so that one day I would join him in mutually tortured piano-violin duets for the edification of my mother and brother who sat at the table meditatively spooning in the last of their pineapple sherbet until their part was called for: they put down their spoons and clapped while we bowed, while the sweet ice in their bowls melted, while the music melted, and we all melted a little into each other for a moment.

But first Sister Olive must do her work. I was shown middle C, which Sister seemed to think terribly important. I stared at middle C and then glanced away for a second. When my eye returned, middle C was gone, its slim finger lost in the complicated grasp of the keyboard. Sister Olive struck it again, finding it with laughable ease. She emphasized the importance of middle C, its central position, a sort of North Star of sound. I remember thinking, "Middle C is the belly button of the piano," an insight whose originality and accuracy stunned me with pride. For the first time in my life I was astonished by metaphor. I hesitated to tell the kindly

Olive for some reason; apparently I understood a true metaphor is a risky business, revealing of the self. In fact, I have never, until this moment of writing it down, told my first metaphor to anyone.

Sunlight flooded the room; the pianos, all black, gleamed. Sister Olive, dressed in the colors of the keyboard, gleamed; middle C shimmered with meaning and I resolved never—never—to forget its location: it was the center of the world.

Then Sister Olive, who had had to show me middle C twice but who seemed to have drawn no bad conclusions about me anyway, got up and went to the windows on the opposite wall. She pulled the shades down, one after the other. The sun was too bright, she said. She sneezed as she stood at the windows with the sun shedding its glare over her. She sneezed and sneezed, crazy little convulsive sneezes, one after another, as helpless as if she had the hiccups.

"The sun makes me sneeze," she said when the fit was over and she was back at the piano. This was odd, too odd to grasp in the mind. I associated sneezing with colds, and colds with rain, fog, snow and bad weather. The sun, however, had caused Sister Olive to sneeze in this wild way, Sister Olive who gleamed benignly and who was so certain of the location of the center of the world. The universe wobbled a bit and became unreliable. Things were not, after all, necessarily what they seemed. Appearance deceived: here was the sun acting totally out of character, hurling this woman into sneezes, a woman so mild that she was named, so it seemed, for a bland object on a relish tray.

I was given a red book, the first Thompson book, and told to play the first piece over and over at one of the black pianos where the other children were crashing away. This, I was told, was called practicing. It sounded alluringly adult, practicing. The piece itself consisted mainly of middle C, and I excelled, thrilled by my savvy at being able to locate that central note amidst the cunning camouflage of all the other white keys before me. Thrilled too by the shiny red book that gleamed, as the pianos did, as Sister Olive did, as my eager eyes probably did. I sat at the formidable machine of the piano and got to know middle C intimately, preparing to be as tortured as I could manage one day soon with my father's violin at my side.

But at the moment Mary Katherine Reilly was at my side, playing something at least two or three lessons more sophisticated than my piece. I believe she even struck a chord. I glanced at her from the peasantry of single notes, shy, ready to pay homage. She turned toward me, stopped playing, and sized me up.

Sized me up and found a person ready to be dominated. Without introduction she said, "My grandfather invented the collapsible opera hat."

I nodded, I acquiesced, I was hers. With that little stroke it was decided between us—that she should be the leader, and I the sidekick. My job was admiration. Even when she added, "But he didn't make a penny from it. He didn't have a patent"—even then, I knew and she knew that this was not an admission of powerlessness, but the easy candor of a master, of one who can afford a weakness or two.

With the clairvoyance of all fated relationships based on dominance and submission, it was decided in advance: that when the time came for us to play duets, I should always play second piano, that I should spend my allowance to buy her the Twinkies she craved but was not allowed to have, that finally, I should let her copy from my test paper, and when confronted by our teacher, confess with convincing hysteria that it was I, who had cheated, who had reached above myself to steal what clearly belonged to the rightful heir of the inventor of the collapsible opera hat. . . .

There must be a reason I remember that little story about my first piano lesson. In fact, it isn't a story, just a moment, the beginning of what could perhaps become a story. For the memoirist, more than for the fiction writer, the story seems already *there*, already accomplished and fully achieved in history ("in reality," as we naively say). For the memoirist, the writing of the story is a matter of transcription.

That, anyway, is the myth. But no memoirist writes for long without experiencing an unsettling disbelief about the reliability of memory, a hunch that memory is not, after all, *just* memory. I don't know why I remembered this fragment about my first piano lesson. I don't, for instance, have a single recollection of my first arithmetic lesson, the first time I studied Latin, the first time my grandmother tried to teach me to knit. Yet these things occurred too, and must have their stories.

It is the piano lesson that has trudged forward, clearing the haze of forgetfulness, showing itself bright with detail more than thirty years after the event. I did not choose to remember the piano lesson. It was simply there, like a book that has always been on the shelf, whether I ever read it or not, the binding and title showing as I skim across the contents of my life. On the day I wrote this fragment I happened to take that memory, not some other, from the shelf and paged through it. I found more detail, more event, perhaps a little more entertainment than I had expected, but the memory itself was there from the start. Waiting for me.

Or was it? When I reread what I had written just after I finished it, I realized that I had told a number of lies. I *think* it was my father who took me the first time for my piano lesson—but maybe he only took me to meet my teacher and there was no actual lesson that day. And did I even know then that he played the violin—didn't he take up his violin again much later, as a result of my piano playing, and not the reverse? And is it even remotely accurate to describe as "tortured" the musicianship of a man who began every day by belting out "Oh What a Beautiful Morning" as he shaved?

More: Sister Olive Marie did sneeze in the sun, but was her name Olive? As for her skin tone—I would have sworn it was olive-like; I would have been willing to spend the better part of an afternoon trying to write the exact description of imported Italian or Greek olive her face suggested: I wanted to get it right. But now, were I to write that passage over, it is her intense black eyebrows I would see, for suddenly they seem the central fact of that face, some indicative mark of her serious and patient nature. But the truth is, I don't remember the woman at all. She's a sneeze in the sun and a finger touching middle C. That, at least, is steady and clear.

Worse: I didn't have the Thompson book as my piano text. I'm sure of that because I remember envying children who did have this wonderful book with its pictures of children and animals printed on the pages of music.

As for Mary Katherine Reilly. She didn't even go to grade school with me (and her name isn't Mary Katherine Reilly—but I made that change on purpose). I met her in Girl Scouts and only went to school with her later, in high school. Our relationship was not really one of leader and follower; I played first piano most of the time in duets. She certainly never copied anything from a test paper of mine: she was a better student, and cheating just wasn't a possibility with her. Though her grandfather (or someone in her family) did invent the collapsible opera hat and I remember that she was proud of that fact, she didn't tell me this news as a deft move in a childish power play.

So, what was I doing in this brief memoir? Is it simply an example of the curious relation a fiction writer has to the material of her own life? Maybe. That may have some value in itself. But to tell the truth (if anyone still believes me capable of telling the truth), I wasn't writing fiction. I was writing memoir—or was trying to. My desire was to be accurate. I wished to embody the myth of memoir: to write as an act of dutiful transcription.

Yet clearly the work of writing narrative caused me to do something very different from transcription. I am forced to admit that memoir is not a matter of transcription, that memory itself is not a warehouse of finished stories, not a static gallery of framed pictures. I must admit that I invented. But why?

Two whys: why did I invent, and then, if a memoirist must inevitably invent rather than transcribe, why do I—why should anybody—write memoir at all?

I must respond to these impertinent questions because they, like the bumper sticker I saw the other day commanding all who read it to QUESTION AUTHORITY, challenge my authority as a memoirist and as a witness.

It still comes as a shock to realize that I don't write about what I know: I write in order to find out what I know. Is it possible to convey to a reader the enormous degree of blankness, confusion, hunch and uncertainty lurking in the act of writing? When I am the reader, not the writer, I too fall into the lovely illusion that the words before me (in a story by Mavis Gallant, an essay by Carol Bly, a memoir by M. F. K. Fisher), which *read* so inevitably, must also have been *written* exactly as they appear, rhythm and cadence, language and syntax, the powerful waves of the sentences laying themselves on the smooth beach of the page one after another faultlessly.

But here I sit before a yellow legal pad, and the long page of the preceding two paragraphs is a jumble of crossed-out lines, false starts, confused order. A mess. The mess of my mind trying to find out what it wants to say. This is a writer's frantic, grabby mind, not the poised mind of a reader ready to be edified or entertained.

I sometimes think of the reader as a cat, endlessly fastidious, capable, by turns, of mordant indifference and riveted attention, luxurious, recumbent, and ever poised. Whereas the writer is absolutely a dog, panting and moping, too eager for an affectionate scratch behind the ears, lunging frantically after any old stick thrown in the distance.

The blankness of a new page never fails to intrigue and terrify me. Sometimes, in fact, I think my habit of writing on long yellow sheets comes from an atavistic fear of the writer's stereotypic "blank white page." At least when I begin writing, my page isn't utterly blank; at least it has a wash of color on it, even if the absence of words must finally be faced on a yellow sheet as truly as on a blank white one. Well, we all have our ways of whistling in the dark.

If I approach writing from memory with the assumption that I know what I wish to say, I assume that intentionality is running the show. Things are not that simple. Or perhaps writing is even more profoundly simple, more telegraphic and immediate in its choices than the grating wheels and chugging engine of logic and rational intention. The heart, the guardian of intuition with its secret, often fearful intentions, is the boss, its commands are what a writer obeys—often without knowing it. Or, I do.

That's why I'm a strong adherent of the first draft. And why it's worth pausing for a moment to consider what a first draft really is. By my lights, the piano lesson memoir is a first draft. That doesn't mean it exists here exactly as I first wrote it. I like to think I've cleaned it up from the first time I put it down on paper. I've cut some adjectives here, toned down the hyperbole there, smoothed a transition, cut a repetition—that sort of housekeeperly tidying-up. But the piece remains a first draft because I haven't yet gotten to know it, haven't given it a chance to tell me anything. For me, writing a first draft is a little like meeting someone for the first time. I come away with a wary acquaintanceship, but the real friendship (if any) and genuine intimacy—that's all down the road. Intimacy with a piece of writing, as with a person, comes from paying attention to the revelations it is capable of giving, not by imposing my own preconceived notions, no matter how well-intentioned they might be.

I try to let pretty much anything happen in a first draft. A careful first draft is a failed first draft. That may be why there are so many inaccuracies in the piano lesson memoir: I didn't censor, I didn't judge. I kept moving. But I would not publish this piece as a memoir on its own in its present state. It isn't the "lies" in the piece that give me pause, though a reader has a right to expect a memoir to be as accurate as the writer's memory can make it. No, it isn't the lies themselves that makes the piano lesson memoir a first draft and therefore "unpublishable."

The real trouble: the piece hasn't yet found its subject; it isn't yet about what it wants to be about. Note: what *it* wants, not what I want. The difference has to do with the relation a memoirist—any writer, in fact—has to unconscious or half-known intentions and impulses in composition.

Now that I have the fragment down on paper, I can read this little piece as a mystery which drops clues to the riddle of my feelings, like a culprit who wishes to be apprehended. My narrative self (the culprit who has invented) wishes to be discovered by my reflective self, the self who wants to understand and make sense of a half-remembered story about a nun sneezing in the sun. . . .

We only store in memory images of value. The value may be lost over the passage of time (I was baffled about why I remembered that sneezing nun, for example), but that's the implacable judgment of feeling: *this,* we say somewhere deep within us, is something I'm hanging on to. And of course, often we cleave to things because they possess heavy negative charges. Pain likes to be vivid.

Over time, the value (the feeling) and the stored memory (the image) may become estranged. Memoir seeks a permanent home for feeling and image, a habitation where they can live together in harmony. Naturally, I've had a lot of experiences since I packed away that one from the basement of St. Luke's School; that piano lesson has been effaced by waves of feeling for other moments and episodes. I persist in believing the event has value—after all, I remember it—but in writing the memoir I did not simply relive the experience. Rather, I explored the mysterious relationship between all the images I could round up and the even more impacted feelings that caused me to store the images safely away in memory. Stalking the relationship, seeking the congruence between stored image and hidden emotion—that's the real job of memoir.

By writing about that first piano lesson, I've come to know things I could not know otherwise. But I only know these things as a result of reading this first draft. While I was writing, I was following the images, letting the details fill the room of the page and use the furniture as they wished. I was their dutiful servant—or thought I was. In fact, I was the faithful retainer of my hidden feelings which were giving the commands.

I really did feel, for instance, that Mary Katherine Reilly was far superior to me. She was smarter, funnier, more wonderful in every way—that's how I saw it. Our friendship (or she herself) did not require that I become her vassal, yet perhaps in my heart that was something I wanted; I wanted a way to express my feeling of admiration. I suppose I waited until this memoir to begin to find the way.

Just as, in the memoir, I finally possess that red Thompson book with the barking dogs and bleating lambs and winsome children. I couldn't (and still can't) remember what my own music book was, so I grabbed the name and image of the one book I could remember. It was only in reviewing the piece after writing it that I saw my inaccuracy. In pondering this "lie," I came to see what I was up to: I was getting what I wanted. At last.

The truth of many circumstances and episodes in the past emerges for the memoirist through details (the red music book, the fascination with a nun's name and gleaming face), but these details are not merely information, not flat facts. Such details are not allowed to lounge. They must work. Their work is the creation of symbol. But it's more accurate to call it the *recognition* of symbol. For meaning is not "attached" to the detail by the memoirist; meaning is revealed.

That's why a first draft is important. Just as the first meeting (good or bad) with someone who later becomes the beloved is important and is often reviewed for signals, meanings, omens, and indications.

Now I can look at that music book and see it not only as "a detail," but for what it is, how it *acts*. See it as the small red door leading straight into the dark room of my childhood longing and disappointment. That red book *becomes* the palpable evidence of that longing. In other words, it becomes symbol. There is no symbol, no life-of-the-spirit in the general or the abstract. Yet a writer wishes—indeed all of us wish—to speak about profound matters that are, like it or not, general and abstract. We wish to talk to each other about life and death, about love, despair, loss, and innocence. We sense that in order to live together we must learn to speak of peace, of history, of meaning and values. Those are a few.

We seek a means of exchange, a language which will renew these ancient concerns and make them wholly and pulsingly ours. Instinctively, we go to our store of private images and associations for our authority to speak of these weighty issues. We find, in our details and broken and obscured images, the language of symbol. Here memory impulsively reaches out its arms and embraces imagination. That is the resort to invention. It isn't a lie, but an act of necessity, as the innate urge to locate personal truth always is.

All right. Invention is inevitable. But why write memoir? Why not call it fiction and be done with all the hashing about, wondering where memory stops and imagination begins? And if memoir seeks to talk about "the big issues," about history and peace, death and love—why not leave these reflections to those with expert and scholarly knowledge? Why let the common or garden variety memoirist into the club? I'm thinking again of that bumper sticker: why Question Authority?

My answer, of course, is a memoirist's answer. Memoir must be written because each of us must have a created version of the past. Created: that is, real, tangible, made of the stuff of a life lived in place and in history. And the down side of any created thing as well: we must live with a version that attaches us to our limitations, to the inevitable subjectivity, of our points of view. We must acquiesce to our experience and our gift to transform experience into meaning and value. You tell me your story, I'll tell you my story.

If we refuse to do the work of creating this personal version of the past, someone else will do it for us. That is a scary political fact. "The struggle of man against power," a character in Milan Kundera's novel *The Book of Laughter and Forgetting* says, "is the struggle of memory against forgetting." He refers to willful political forgetting, the habit of nations and those in power (Question Authority!) to deny the truth of memory in order to disarm moral and ethical power. It's an efficient way of controlling masses of people. It doesn't even require much bloodshed, as long as people are entirely willing to give over their personal memories. Whole histories can be rewritten. As Czeslaw Milosz said in his 1980 Nobel Prize lecture, the number of books published that seek to deny the existence of the Nazi death camps now exceeds one hundred.

What is remembered is what *becomes* reality. If we "forget" Auschwitz, if we "forget" My Lai, what then do we remember? And what is the purpose of our remembering? If we think of memory naively, as a simple story, logged like a documentary in the archive of the mind, we miss its beauty but also its function. The beauty of memory rests in its talent for rendering detail, for paying homage to the senses, its capacity to love the particles of life, the richness and idiosyncrasy of our existence. The function of memory, on the other hand, is intensely personal and surprisingly political.

Our capacity to move forward as developing beings rests on a healthy relation with the past. Psychotherapy, that widespread method of mental health, relies heavily on memory and on the ability to retrieve and organize images and events from the personal past. We carry our wounds and perhaps even worse, our capacity to wound, forward with us. If we learn not only to tell our stories but to listen to what our stories tell us—to write the first draft and then return for the second draft—we are doing the work of memoir.

Memoir is the intersection of narration and reflection, of story-telling and essay-writing. It can present its story *and* reflect and consider the meaning of the story. It is a peculiarly open form, inviting broken and incomplete images, half-recollected fragments, all the mass (and mess) of detail. It offers to shape this confusion—and in shaping, of course it necessarily creates a work of art, not a legal document. But then, even legal documents are only valiant attempts to consign the truth, the whole truth and nothing but the truth to paper. Even they remain versions.

Locating touchstones—the red music book, the olive Olive, my father's violin playing—is deeply satisfying. Who knows why? Perhaps we all sense that we can't grasp the whole truth and nothing but the truth of our experience. Just can't be done. What can be achieved, however, is a version of its swirling, changing wholeness. A memoirist must acquiesce to selectivity, like any artist. The version we dare to write is the only truth, the only relationship we can have with the past. Refuse to write your life and you have no life. At least, that is the stern view of the memoirist.

Personal history, logged in memory, is a sort of slide projector flashing images on the wall of the mind. And there's precious little order to the slides in the rotating carousel. Beyond that confusion, who knows who is running the projector? A memoirist steps into this darkened room of flashing, unorganized images and stands blinking for a while. Maybe for a long while. But eventually, as with any attempt to tell a story, it is necessary to put something first, then something else. And so on, to the end. That's a first draft. Not necessarily the truth, not even *a* truth sometimes, but the first attempt to create a shape.

The first thing I usually notice at this stage of composition is the appalling inaccuracy of the piece. Witness my first piano lesson draft. Invention is screamingly evident in what I intended to be transcription. But here's the further truth: I feel no shame. In fact, it's only now that my interest in the piece truly quickens. For I can see what isn't there, what is shyly hugging the walls, hoping not to be seen. I see the filmy shape of the next draft. I see a more acute version of the episode or—this is more likely—an entirely new piece rising from the ashes of the first attempt.

The next draft of the piece would have to be a true re-vision, a new seeing of the materials of the first draft. Nothing merely cosmetic will do—no rouge buffing up the opening sentence, no glossy adjective to lift a sagging line, nothing to attempt covering a patch of gray writing. None of that. I can't say for sure, but my hunch is the revision would lead me to more writing about my father (why was I so impressed by that ancestral inventor of the collapsible opera hat? Did I feel I had nothing as remarkable in my own background? Did this make me feel inadequate?). I begin to think perhaps Sister Olive is less central to this business than she is in this draft. She is meant to be a moment, not a character.

And so I might proceed, if I were to undertake a new draft of the memoir. I begin to feel a relationship developing between a former self and me.

And, even more compelling, a relationship between an old world and me. Some people think of autobiographical writing as the precious occupation of a particularly self-absorbed person. Maybe, but I don't buy that. True memoir is written in an attempt to find not only a self but a world.

The self-absorption that seems to be the impetus and embarrassment of autobiography turns into (or perhaps always was) a hunger for the world. Actually, it begins as hunger for *a* world, one gone or lost, effaced by time or a more sudden brutality. But in the act of remembering, the personal environment expands, resonates beyond itself, beyond its "subject," into the endless and tragic recollection that is history.

We look at old family photographs in which we stand next to black, boxy Fords and are wearing period costumes, and we do not gaze fascinated because there we are young again, or there we are standing, as we never will again in life, next to our mother. We stare and drift because there we are . . . historical. It is the dress, the black car that dazzle us now and draw us beyond our mother's bright arms which once caught us. We reach into the attractive impersonality of something more significant than ourselves. We write memoir, in other words. We accept the humble position of writing a version rather than "the whole truth."

I suppose I write memoir because of the radiance of the past—it draws me back and back to it. Not that the past is beautiful. In our communal memoir, in history, the death camps *are* back there. In intimate life too, the record is usually pretty mixed. "I could tell you stories . . ." people say and drift off, meaning terrible things have happened to them.

But the past is radiant. It has the light of lived life. A memoirist wishes to touch it. No one owns the past, though typically the first act of new political regimes, whether of the left or the right, is to attempt to re-write history, to grab the past and make it over so the end comes out right. So their power looks inevitable.

No one owns the past, but it is a grave error (another age would have said a grave sin) not to inhabit memory. Sometimes I think it is all we really have. But that may be a trifle melodramatic. At any rate, memory possesses authority for the fearful self in a world where it is necessary to have authority in order to Question Authority.

There may be no more pressing intellectual need in our culture than for people to become sophisticated about the function of memory. The political implications of the loss of memory are obvious. The authority of memory is a personal confirmation of selfhood. To write one's life is to live it twice, and the second living is both spiritual and historical, for a memoir reaches deep within the personality as it seeks its narrative form and also grasps the life-of-the-times as no political treatise can.

Our most ancient metaphor says life is a journey. Memoir is travel writing, then, notes taken along the way, telling how things looked and what thoughts occurred. But I cannot think of the memoirist as a tourist. This is the traveller who goes on foot, living the journey, taking on mountains, enduring deserts, marveling at the lush green places. Moving through it all faithfully, not so much a survivor with a harrowing tale to tell as a pilgrim, seeking, wondering.

The Art of Translation

Steven Harvey

Writing essays is like realizing that you love your wife after all. We sing poems and dream fictions but speak in mere sentences. Sentences are our friends, taken for granted, until one day a few singers and dreamers let go of all that is far away and, watching the face across the kitchen table, see for the first time in years a smile that was there all along, the smile of the girl they married, and learn in lowly prose how to want what they have.

Close your eyes and you can picture a poem as it takes its sinewy shape in the mind. It is seductive and memorable. The personal essay has a shape, too, and a certain loveliness about it, but walk away and try to picture it or describe it to a friend, and you have little more than mousy-brown hair and cute freckles over the nose. Book stores don't even know where to put collections of essays, lumping our shy girls in plain wrappers with how-to books and biographies bearing the slim, the rich, the wild, and the glamorous on their glossy covers.

In the on-going battle to name the genre, I prefer the venerable "personal essay" over other contenders, primarily because it lowers expectations. With "Creative Nonfiction" we are tempted to capitalize and court the grandiose. "This is just not a fiction," the term announces. "It's real! This is not just nonfiction. It's creative!" You open a book of Creative Nonfiction ready for the best of all possible literary experiences—nothing ahead except disappointment. But with the lowly personal essay, the reader, expecting some dull tract, can be surprised.

The phrase "personal essay" is a pleasant mouthful. "Essay" is appropriately serious, coming from the Latin, "exagium," meaning to weigh, a reminder that essayists ponder and measure and take stock of the world by weighing their words carefully. It suggests thought, and without a modifier is, probably, a little too austere, conjuring up another word, "examination," with which it is too often linked, and bringing back memories of dreaded bluebooks. Putting the word "familiar" in front of "essay" is probably a little too cozy, giving a misleading suggestion of safety and shared assumptions, but adding the modifier, "personal," says that, behind these words, is a human being—a unique recombination of dirt and water and sky.

What they are called matters less than what they do. "Good for what?"—that is my aesthetic. Poetry, of course, is good for nothing, and proud of it, according to W. H. Auden. "Poetry changes nothing," he wrote, and whether he is right or wrong, we know what he means. The reaffirmation of mere beauty is enough. Personal essays, by contrast, are very busy, performing many jobs. They supply information, entertain, and provide flawless and therefore irksome models for millions of college students learning how to write decent prose, but their main business is the expression of the solitary soul in a changing world, a clear and valuable mission.

The personal essay is uniquely positioned for the task. Unlike the ceremonial and communal forms—poetry and drama—the essay came into its own recently, during the Renaissance, and functioned as a vehicle for the voice of the individual. The essay carries on this hard work into our century, which still gives lip service to individualism but no longer believes that any one of us makes much of a difference. The novel, born at the same time, bears this burden as well, but does so by placing the hero among the contending voices of other characters in defining social situations. The personal essay, by contrast, is the lone voice.

The novel—with its party atmosphere—has always been the more popular form, leading envious essayists to ransack the house of fiction. Dialogue, scene, verbal high jinks, narratives, character development, juxtapositions, even fictions are all in the essayist's repertoire of effects. Anything that is good in my essays is true, I like to tell people, and some of the best parts were invented.

And yet, an essay feels very different from a story. Fiction writers hunt for those details which seem striking and memorable. A novelist might describe a character who bolts machine parts and an electric fan to the hood of his car and drives through town. Such choices, whether they come from real life or not, seem made up precisely at the point that they achieve a memorable oddity. "I've got to put that in my next story!"—we suspect the author has said, glad to come upon a detail that we cannot overlook. "Give your character a scar," I once heard Alice Walker tell a group of fiction writers. Essayists, drawn to the mundane rather than the sensational, tend to be suspicious of such scars.

A friend of mine who is an expert on the Romantic poets once told me that when Wordsworth and Coleridge used to walk through the Lake District of England together, they had radically different experiences. Coleridge did not see much around him. Instead, he allowed the landscape to stir his imagination and encourage invention, the walk giving him freedom to look within and examine interior states. Wordsworth, on the other hand, knew the names of wild flowers and trees and noted subtle changes in the landscape and season as he walked, looking outside himself for inspiration. The essayist is more like Wordsworth than Coleridge and the difference can be felt by reading "Tintern Abbey" and "The Rime of the Ancient Mariner" back to back.

It helps to have a dull life. Novelists, dreaming up other lives, can forget the mess they are making of their own as they create strange new worlds to fulfill the yearnings of this one. But personal essayists are never off duty, which makes even simple acts like showering, driving, or sex difficult, if not dangerous. "Much is in little," Horace wrote, and essayists keep the job manageable by thinking for a long, long time about hardly anything at all, an uneventful life allowing the writer to care more about "what is" than "what happens." Desire is the subject of novels—not what I have, but what I want. Capable of glamour and often at odds with the world as God made it, the novel is the prince of prose and apt, at times, to do the devil's business. The essay is the lowly monk of literature quietly going about God's work.

This reverence for the way things usually are marks the essay, though it is not a requirement of the form, and explains the elegiac nature of these works that are recording a present that is continually slipping away, largely unnoticed. Perhaps that is why the form is congenial to the ends of civilizations—when an entire way of life is threatened—and offers a clue for why some of the earliest examples of the personal essay occurred in the Hellenistic period and later at the end of the Roman Empire.

"Getting it right" in fiction means something different than it does in an essay. Fiction tends to myth. It becomes real only as it represents lives on the reader's side of the page. One way to "get it right" in fiction, then, is to make the tale convincing, a plausible sequence of surprises.

Essays begin with something that exists and has meaning before it reaches the page, establishing a different contract between the reader and the writer, a different set of literary obligations. Essays are not arranged by plot, but by anxieties. They don't wonder, "What next?" Instead, like a worried parent, they ask, "Now what?" with a groan. The anxieties are relieved not so much by the telling, like confession, but by the arranging, the way some of us fix a problem at work by cleaning up the desk. "Getting it right" for an essayist means putting events and details into a revealing—a revelatory—relationship with one another. Strolling through the museum of love and change, the essayist rearranges for all to see the treasures we cannot keep.

These differences should not be pushed too hard. Essayists occasionally look up from the turtles and earthworms and moths of everyday life and bring the extraordinary into the lens of their prose, and essays do tell stories. Joan Didion, an exact and exacting essayist, reminded us of the tenacity of the narrative impulse. "We tell stories in order to live," she wrote. But stories and essays are different in one crucial and revealing way, an essential difference inherent in the forms. The Pandora's box of fiction, unavailable to the personal essayist, is dramatic irony.

The novelist can create a character who speaks in the first person but does not share all—or any—of the author's views. The character becomes that infamous thing, an unreliable narrator, a literary tool that allows the author, as Joyce suggests about Flaubert, to be everywhere in a work and nowhere present at the same time. Novelists—masters of bad faith—often hide behind this device, usually making fun of the character who tells the tale for them, sometimes letting the readers in on the joke, sometimes not. This ironic edge is always present in a first person novel—we are, after all, the last to know the truth about ourselves. Flaubert even perfected a strategy of indirect address, an aping of a character's voice and attitude, which allows the author to create the same effect in third person prose. "Madame Bovary, c'est moi," he wrote. Don't believe it.

So in one famous example the governess telling the tale may blame others for the demise of the children in her care, but we readers, upon whom nothing will be lost, catch the author's wink between the lines and suspect that the governess herself is, in fact, the guilty party. Is the author winking? On Monday, Wednesday and Friday the governess is guilty as sin and duping us. On Tuesday and Thursday she seems more crazy than sinister and therefore guilty without knowing it. And on Saturday we bemoan our tendency to intellectualize every damn thing, pick up a hard ball and glove, and declare the poor woman innocent. Who knows? The screw turns and turns and turns, endlessly. It's a tricky and sophisticated game, the subject of great debate, and a mountain of literary criticism.

Irony of this kind obviously enriches a text, rendering the simplest tale suddenly subtle and ambiguous, and the writers of personal essays, by the nature of their task, cannot use the technique. Essayists lie and mislead and invent—who doesn't? In all ways except one they remain incorrigibly human and therefore thoroughly unreliable. But there is a lie that they cannot tell with a straight face: They cannot get any aesthetic distance on the narrator. If the essay is personal (and here I leave out some excellent essays, by writers like Swift and Russell Baker, which are not personal in the way I mean), the distinction between author and narrator, by definition, collapses; they see the world eye-to-eye, so to speak. Who you read is what you get.

The personal essayist, by sacrificing the unreliable narrator, removes one tool for complexity from the literary arsenal but suffers no loss. Dramatic irony is the fictional tool that has turned literature in this century into a hall of mirrors. With the author everywhere absent—and God, as Joyce added, paring his fingernails—the reader is left alone in an era of great loneliness. Even when we read masters of these techniques—writers like Nabokov, for instance, in "Pale Fire"—we begin to suspect that literature has been reduced to a game. It may be animated by a great heart, but we sense mainly an absence behind it all—the human being who is speaking the words is so impeccably camouflaged that she or he might as well not be there at all.

In the personal essay, as Thoreau reminded us a century and a half ago in the opening page of Walden, we are stuck with the voice of the author, no intermediary. There are several ways for the writer to offer relief from the inevitable monotone.

A mixed diction helps: Aristotle first taught us that, encouraging us to use the whole range of vocabulary that is available to the author's voice. The vulgar requires vulgarity, damn it, and the divine demands all the verbal splendor that the dictionary has to give. Many essayists use quotations as a way of clearing their throats before going on. First-person accounts in novels are often restricted to the speaking voices of the characters, but the first-person voice of the personal essayist can be, without strain, the speaking voice liberated by the reading mind.

A last resort—often required by the essayist whose voice is sounding shrill—is the joke. Out on the limb of a ridiculous proposition or situation, the essayist hands himself a saw. Self-deprecation is the essayist's most convincing tool—the equivalent in writing of comforting others by saying, "You think that's bad?" Such humor is not an evasion or a case of false humility, but a way of making readers feel less alone with their own foibles. And, of course, once we have laughed together, it is easier to talk.

Essayists have an arsenal of techniques like these for modulating, without undermining, the narrator's solo voice, ways of engaging in the dialogue which is the path, Socrates taught us, to wisdom. But that does not mean that the essayist can be, like the novelist, everywhere and nowhere at once in his work. "Here I am," the personal essayist says, like the Old Testament prophets when they were called, trembling, before God, and like the prophets the writer often feels like adding, "Oh Lord." Personal essayists may not have a thesis, a clearly thought out position on the world's imponderables, but they are, at least, willing to stand, come what may, in the same verbal patch as the voice of the essay.

This limitation—the collapse of ironic distance—is chastening for any writer. "Say what you mean and mean what you say," my father used to caution in his firmly tautological way. "Discipline," according to Michel de Montaigne, the father of the personal essay, requires that "one is the same within, by his own volition, as he is outside for fear of the law and what people will say." It is true. In my own case, I have grown to distrust those who talk one way in public and another in private, their pieties in front of others followed by rib-poking obscenities over a beer in a back room. I have grown to distrust myself when I act that way.

The joy in all this is that the reader of the essay is allowed to hear this voice play occasionally with an idea. Ideas haven't fared well in our century, and the prospect for the next century does not seem much better. Poets have, in essence, followed William Carlos Williams in abandoning them. "Not in ideas, but in things," he wrote about poetry, contributing to the impoverishment of the form. Novelists put ideas on the lips of characters they don't trust and say to the reader, in essence, 'You decide, I can't." That is why essayists turn the ideas over and over, considering possibilities, allowing for contradictions, aware that the blame will, eventually, fall their way. It is a relief, in fact a privilege, in our age of images and ideologies to follow these solitary minds, these questioning voices willing to offer tentative assertions which they hold as true—at times even self-evident—in context, a context that the essay, itself, generously supplies.

There is, out there in the world of readers, a longing for a reality behind words. I see it manifested in the tendency to read fiction as biography. Readers study authors' pictures on flaps, looking for clues to the text, trying to invest novels with the authors' real lives. The personal essay goes a long way toward meeting this longing, not because it sticks to reality any more than the novel does—or the poem or the painting, for that matter. But the essayist is stuck with himself or herself, in sickness or health, for richer or poorer, till death—an indicator of the stakes. The essay may not be honest to God or the world, but it had better be honest to a voice.

Being at home in the world—that is the task. Essayists learn to live with what they have and who they are, poking fun at that yakking voice in the head, yes, but respecting it and attending to it as well. Something is always lost in translation, and it is easy to be ironic about what words can't catch. Learning to relax the irony requires an act of generosity, but we do it all the time. If we are generous and lucky when we hear an old tune, we can get past the sappy lyrics to a true emotion. Loving what we have, we find the girl in the wife, or, reversing the metaphor, see the fair-haired boy in the bald man snoring beside his glass of sherry in an easy chair across the room. Creating the possibility for such generosity on the part of readers is the unique work of the personal essay, the by-product of its art, and as it accomplishes this task, as it sets us up for loving all that we will lose, it helps us to be human.

The Whole Truth

Peter M. Ives

I

About a year ago, I gave my sister, Kitty, a draft of an essay I'd been working on. Up to that point, I had never shared any of my autobiographical writing with a family member. Part of the essay dealt with the day of our father's death, and I was sincerely interested to see if she could add any details or observations. I spent an anxiety-filled week, second-guessing my decision, before calling her. I was quite surprised by her reaction. It wasn't that she was offended or angry—I had prepared myself for that possibility. No, in fact she was quite generous in her comments about the piece. However, what caught me off guard was the degree to which her memories of that day—April 5, 1969—conflicted substantially with my own recollections.

She remembered the day as being sunny. I remembered a light drizzle with low gray clouds. She remembered being with me in the bedroom when I found my father's body. I remembered only my brother John being there. She remembered the coroner pronouncing my father dead before Father Ramsey came to perform the last rites. I remembered Father Ramsey arriving before the coroner. As we talked, it became clear to me that this event—indisputably the most central instance of my childhood—was subject to conflicting perspectives.

There were other details where our memories conflicted, but in the end it didn't matter whether or not it had been sunny or rainy or whether it was the priest or coroner who arrived first, because one thing has always remained certain: our father died that day, and both of us remembered watching the ambulance attendants carry his body out the front door.

II

Shortly after that revelatory conversation with my sister, I came across an essay written by Anna Quindlen for the *New York Times Book Review*. In her piece, "How Dark? How Stormy? I Can't Recall," Ms. Quindlen questioned the legitimate employment of specific details in memoir. It seems that because the author couldn't remember the name of her kindergarten teacher, she felt compelled to question how Frank McCourt—the author of *Angela's Ashes*—could remember "the raw, itching sore that erupted between his eyes when he was a boy, or the sight of himself in a mirror on his fourteenth birthday." In support of her incredulity, Ms. Quindlen continued: "I can't remember the spread on my parents' bed. If it was quilted satin, I can't remember running my hand over its smooth surface when I was seven or eight years old. If it was chenille, I can't recall feeling the bobbles beneath my palm as I sat and watched in the mirror as my mother braided my long hair." To be fair, Ms. Quindlen reminds readers that she spent most of her life as a reporter, and that the "strictures of her trade run deep." In this regard, it is completely understandable that Ms. Quindlen is, by nature, suspicious of anything as unverifiable as memoir.

As for me, I know very little about quilted satin, and—to the best of my knowledge—my mother never braided my hair. But I do remember the oil stains on my father's callused hands, how his finger nails were bitten down almost to the cuticles; I remember how he used to wear an oversized, fluorescent, orange raincoat to my JV football games—rain or shine—so I could see him as he pranced up and down the sidelines shouting instructions; I remember the doilies my grandmother used to keep on the mahogany dresser in her bedroom, the Jell-O-like flesh that drooped below her upper arms; I remember my mother singing in the kitchen on school mornings; I remember the first time I had the wind knocked out of me; I remember my grandfather on his death bed, rolling imaginary Bull Durham cigarettes and offering them to my grandmother (who'd been dead for eight years); I remember how my mom used to take her boys out to the back fence, line us up, and give crew cuts, washing us off with the hose afterwards so we wouldn't scatter loose hair in the house; I remember faking a stomachache when I was six and winding up having my appendix taken out; I remember playing in a sand pile and almost being eaten by a pig.

These are vivid, honest memories. But I would never swear to them as facts. They are honest and true only in that this is how I remember them, verifying where I can, letting the reader know whenever I step over the line into uncertainty or even imaginative re-recreation. But within each of these memories is a story loaded with details, dialogue, and imagery. And I've told these stories hundreds of times.

III

"The blurring of reality" is a catchy new phrase proclaimed by a self-appointed few out to rescue a gullible reading public from an ontological meltdown. It reminds me of the old "Twilight Zone" episode where a browbeaten author permanently dispatches his wife by burning the tape recording on which he described (dictated) her into being: she feels woozy, puts the back of her hand to her forehead and slowly dissipates into oblivion. Who are these critics? For the most part, I suspect that they are talented writers, columnists, and intellectuals who regard the imminent collapse of the wall separating fiction and nonfiction as having ominous reverberations for literature and for society as a whole. In many ways, I think their concerns are justified. But are they justified in singling out memoir as the prime component of a world slipping into virtual reality?

Turn on the TV and you'll get John Wayne pitching beer commercials or Humphrey Bogart drinking Diet Coke or Fred Astaire dancing with an Electrolux. Watch any broadcast of the national political news then pick up a video of *Wag the Dog* or *Primary Colors.* An article in a recent issue of *Harper's* describes how digital technology calls into question the legitimacy of still photography. Our ability to manipulate images has become so sophisticated that it is now nearly impossible to tell whether an image is a representation of the real world or the product of a hard drive. We are now told that Ansel Adams, the patron saint of nature photography, played around in his dark room "Making little circles with [a] wand over the area he wanted lightened," laughing in "crazy, nasal, Mephistophelean" glee.

Nevertheless, critics continue to blame memoir for a disproportionate share of this blurring of reality. No less a writer than Joyce Carol Oates has jumped into the fray. In a recent article for the *New York Times*, Ms. Oates suggested that "Memoir testifies, perhaps, to our desperate wish that some truth of the spirit be presented to us, though we know it's probably invented. We want to believe! We are a species who clamors to be lied to." I am not going to address, at least directly, what I consider to be the depressingly elitist, cynical, and patronizing tone of Ms. Oates' observations. Rather, I would like to suggest that what people desperately want, what they've always wanted, is not to be lied to, but to be told a story. And if nonfiction is burning up the best seller lists, it's not because memoirists have learned to become better liars than fiction writers; maybe it's because they're just telling a better story.

In a 1997 interview, fiction writer and essayist Bob Shacochis commented upon the underlying hostility within the literary community over the "appropriation" of traditional fiction techniques—dialogue, scene construction, vividly recollected detail—into today's nonfiction. The real issue, he says, is the quality of storytelling, not whether it's invented or remembered, and "beyond that the arguments become uninteresting, and they get precious. If someone tells you that the memoir or essay is this certain thing, they're really not telling you what they know so much as they're telling you what they've read. It doesn't address the magnitude and diversity of what's been done, or being done out there. They try to tell you that 'objectivity' is the rule in nonfiction, where I regard subjectivity as the greater witness."

For all I know, all of my memories could be inaccurate. But as I write, I am not consciously dissembling, creating instances and scenes to fit the awkward angles of a story line. My past is not inhabited by a cast of stick figures awkwardly dramatizing a plodding, unimaginative plot line. And just because I can't remember everything doesn't—or shouldn't—mean I have to let my past evaporate, or say that it wasn't real. I am not ready to surrender my past, my life, to fiction. The world is a strange enough place as it is.

I don't remember what my father wore under his orange raincoat during my JV football games. But if I wrote about it, I'd tell the reader he had on an open collared, red plaid shirt, with black suspenders fastened to dark green cotton trousers—the kind school janitors used to wear. Oh yes! He'd also have on an old, frayed T-shirt, his thick, dark, chest hair curling over the neckband. I'd write all this because it was a standard outfit for my father, because his wearing it beneath his raincoat was both probable and possible. In my mind, when he opens his raincoat, he's not naked. I'm not being "flashed" while my imagination rummages around in wardrobe.

Mary McCarthy, in her memoir *Memories of a Catholic Girlhood*, directly confronted the difficulty of writing from memory. In her foreword, "To the Reader," she wrote: "Many a time, in the course of doing these memoirs, I have wished I were writing fiction. The temptation to invent has been very strong, particularly where recollection is hazy . . . Sometimes I have yielded, as in the case of conversations. My memory is good, but I cannot obviously recall whole passages of dialogue that took place years ago." McCarthy's discussion of the difference between memory and technical reproduction applies not only to dialogue, but to all the other facets of storytelling. A writer must deal honestly with whatever facts he or she has at hand, limited as the facts may be. This requires enormous storytelling skill, because the past is a moving image, requiring almost constant readjustment of the viewing lens. And the images we retrieve arrive in different ways. What transports me back to the past varies greatly: sometimes it's the way my son drops his head when I'm angry; sometimes it's an old Beatles song, a photo album, or a receipt I found in the pocket of a coat I haven't worn in years.

IV

So I would like to challenge the nature of memory, to question the notion that all must be known before an event can be rendered truthfully as story. Indeed, because a large part of our lives can never be retrieved, it is a storyteller's duty to use whatever tools are at hand.

In *How Proust Can Change Your Life*, Alain De Botton discusses Proust's concept of *voluntary* and *involuntary* memory. Voluntary memory is the memory of multiplication tables, bus schedules, and daily agendas—memories that we intellectually attempt to provoke. Involuntary memory, on the other hand, occurs when a recollection is stirred by "a long forgotten smell or an old glove." Something that has remained dormant since childhood and "therefore remains uncorrupted by later associations." These instances of almost epiphanic intensity are also known as *Proustian moments*.

In a letter, the essayist and critic Sven Birkerts elaborates on just such a distinction when he writes: "What we outwardly regard as important—the big events, the key moves, the prominent characters—may have nothing to do with the story that needs to be written. We can banish the idea of telling the story of our life and concentrate on evoking its mystery." He suggests following the patterns of memory, even if that means you "devote six pages to writing about a grandfather's cigar box, then jump to the memory of burning ants with a magnifying glass, and then recall the braid of a girl you sat behind in third grade." Birkerts suggests letting the force of memory, not public concerns, be the measure of an event's importance. As he puts it: "You may leave out entirely—or consign to the margins—the fact that your house was burned down or that your grandfather was George Bush. . . . [W]hat makes this kind of writing stick is the level of absorption. And if in your writer's soul you remember the smell of wool mittens more than you remember climbing Everest with your father, you may have to write the wool mittens." Involuntary memory—what is called up from deep emotional experience and of its own accord—is immensely valuable to writers of any genre. It is far more complicated than fact—the bus schedules of voluntary memory. It is where the heart and soul of our past resides.

V

To Virginia Woolf, the present was a platform for viewing the past, the string of experiences we drag behind us like a bedraggled train. We are not imagined. Our past is real, but it is not static. Like the cosmos, it moves unceasingly away from us, and what a memoirist captures is but a glimpse of its receding illumination, a recollective red shift that can only be adjusted through re-creation. Can we change the past? No. But we can change how it is remembered because we grow, change, and (hopefully) learn from our experiences. Or, as Tomás Eloy Martínez writes in his novel *Santa Evita*: "Every story is by definition, unfaithful. Reality, as I've said, can't be told or repeated. The only thing that can be done with reality is to invent it all over again."

So it comes back to what is real—the rightness of a memory or experience—because in order to make a claim on legitimacy, any story, with the possible exception of parable and allegory, must have a basis in reality. That is, what we read—whether fiction or nonfiction—must in some way correlate to our experience, to our sense of what is real. How many times have you put down a novel or story because the plot or characterizations or details seemed implausible? As Aristotle wrote in his *Poetics*: "It is not the poet's function to describe what actually happened, but the kind of things that might happen, that is, that could happen because they are, in the circumstances, either probable or necessary . . . Even if the poet writes about things that have actually happened, that does not make him any less a poet, for there is nothing to prevent some of the things that have happened from being in accordance with the laws of possibility and probability, and thus he will be a poet in writing about them."

Or, as author Sherwood Anderson put it: "While art is distinct from real life, the imagination must constantly feed upon reality or starve." But sometimes, in order that the real story may be told, the ineluctable passage of time is a necessity. In his magisterial short story "A Death in the Woods," Anderson describes the death of an old woman during a violent Midwestern snowstorm, a story based on an actual event in his childhood. In the following passage, Anderson's narrator, now an adult, reflects: "The whole thing, the story of the old woman's death, was to me, as I grew older, like music heard from far off. The notes had to be picked up slowly one at a time. Something had to be understood. . . ." What is essential, the narrator realizes, is the perspective of distance and age. As children, he and his brother were too young to understand the point of the story. "A thing so complete has its own beauty . . . I shall not try to emphasize the point. I am only explaining why I was dissatisfied then and have been ever since. I speak of that only that you may understand why I have been impelled to try to tell the simple story over again."

This same act of remembering and telling in order to arrive at an understanding is the basic premise of memoir: thinking out loud, retelling a story over and over again, using imagination to understand and reconcile a past where reality served as the background music. We recall it only with the greatest difficulty, following the tune as best we can, using our imaginations to improvise notes where the score goes blank. How many truths are there to an event? How much music have we failed to hear? And when the melody finally comes—a sense of longing, a sudden unexplained feeling of joy or sadness—the best we can do is whistle along, staying as close to the original melody as we can.

William Maxwell's *So Long, See You Tomorrow*, an almost perfect novel, is written in the form of a memoir in which an aging narrator reflects upon his Midwestern childhood. It is an evocative elegy to youth, centered on a fictional murder in a small Illinois farming town around World War I. Like his Midwestern literary predecessor, Sherwood Anderson, Maxwell uses simple and unadorned language that masks an uncompromisingly complex and richly detailed narrative. The genesis for this novel, published in 1980, can be found in another book he wrote nine years earlier: *Ancestors*, a memoir.

It is generally not wise to read a piece of fiction as though it were autobiography. But for anyone who has read both books, the comparisons cannot be avoided: each narrator had an older and younger brother; each lost a mother to the 1919 influenza epidemic; each had a businessman father who ultimately relocated the family to Chicago and remarried a much younger woman. Even some of the scenes are the same: the fictional and nonfictional boy with his arm wrapped around the father's waist as they paced the floor in the days after the mother's death, and the father blowing pipe smoke into the fictional and nonfictional boy's ear to cure an earache. Both books examine the ways in which memory can best interrogate the past. But on this last point they differ. In *Ancestors*, the earlier book, Maxwell writes: "I have to get out an imaginary lens and fiddle with the lens until I see something that interests me, preferably something small and unimportant." But in *So Long, See You Tomorrow*, Maxwell's approach to memory is more circumspect as he repeatedly and directly confronts the complexity and unverifiability of memory: "What we, or at any rate what I, refer to as memory—meaning a moment, a scene, a fact that has been subjected to a fixative and thereby rescued from oblivion—is really a form of storytelling that goes on continually in the mind and often changes with the telling. Too many conflicting emotional interests are involved for life ever to be wholly acceptable, and possibly it is the work of a storyteller to arrange things so that they conform to this end. In any case, in talking about the past, we lie with every breath we draw."

Is Maxwell suggesting that we are incapable of truth? That is not my reading of the passage. Rather, I believe he is speaking in phenomenological terms, suggesting that because of "conflicting emotions" and shifting circumstances everything we witness is but an illusion, representative of a deeper, underlying reality. In this way of thinking, fiction is a play upon illusion, and memoir is the illusion itself. So, in the end, neither is real. Or, put another way, both are equally real.

VI

It has been my experience that we do not perceive or write about things as they are, but, rather, we perceive or write about them as *we* are. What a memoirist describes is often confined to the perspective of an immediate and unfinished circumstance. But between what we remember and what really happened are the shadows from which the truth will ultimately reassert itself.

Vladimir Nabokov, in his memoir *Speak Memory*, addresses one of the most luminous aspects of memory: the conflict that arises when a child's experience is at odds with empirical reality. In one of the early chapters, Nabokov describes a scene in which his aristocratic father is pitched into the air by a group of celebratory villagers. Nabokov writes: "From my place at table I would suddenly see through one of the west windows a marvelous case of levitation. There, for an instant, the figure of my father in his windrippled white summer suit would be displayed, gloriously sprawling in midair, his limbs in a curiously casual attitude, his handsome, imperturbable features turned to the sky . . . and then there he would be, on his last and loftiest night, reclining, as if for good, against the cobalt blue of the summer noon. . . ." The final sentence of this recollection runs for 127 words, during which the child's vision evolves into an extended metaphysical presentiment of his father's death. Could a child have perceived all this? Probably not. But the pristine truth of Nabokov's numinous image serves as the framework for an extended, mature meditation. It is a vision of first things.

VII

There is a story about my father I'd like to write: My father. Forty-five years ago. I have yet to be born. He's flying a single-engine plane above the old house on Franklin Street. My mother is in the back yard hanging out laundry. There are only two children—Holley and John—whom Mom sends in the house when she looks up to see my father swooping low over the neighborhood. It's a beautiful summer evening—a Friday, so she knows that he's already made a quick tour of the city's gin mills.

He's done these fly-bys before, screaming down from above the tree tops in the plane he borrows from Jimmy Durr, a childhood pal. They both earned their wings eight years earlier, flying sub reconnaissance in the South Pacific. But tonight my father has decided to push his fly-by game to the limit. My mother tries to wave him off, but my father thinks she's calling him in closer, and he obliges her, eventually buzzing the whole block. It doesn't take long for Chief of Police Leo LeBeau and the fire trucks to come barreling in, sirens blaring, lights flashing. From the air it looks like a carnival.

Taking the hint, my father gently rolls the plane and heads north, crossing the mile-wide Saint Lawrence River in order to follow the Ontario shoreline. Every now and then he sweeps down to dip his wings to the ocean freighters, their giant hulls lumbering down the Seaway. The ships flash their running lights in salute as he rolls south, heading back, descending to just above the water as he comes into the mouth of the Oswegatchie, the last light of the day shooting like flames along the fuselage as he hot dogs it home under the Lafayette Street bridge.

I write about my father because there is no one else to write about him. Because he was real and vital and flawed. Because I loved him. Because I want to imagine him as a man close to my own age now. I no longer seek my father's understanding, I seek, through re-creation, to understand him. And so I return to the beginning—April 5, 1969—where, I suppose, the only accurate written history about my father's death can be found in a copy of his obituary. But my hometown newspaper got a couple of the facts wrong. It printed his date of birth as October 25, 1916 when, according to his birth certificate, he was actually born in 1915. The obituary also misrepresented his military service and the ages of two of my siblings. But these are only details.

So much for the first rough draft of history.

Courting the Approval of the Dead

Tracy Kidder

I have never written much about myself, but, like most writers I know, I am interested in the subject. We live in an era surfeited with memoirs. This is my contribution to the excess.

My writing career began at Harvard College about thirty-two years ago, shortly after I enrolled as an undergraduate. I planned to fix the world by becoming a diplomat. I began by studying political science. Thinking I should have a hobby, I also took a course in creative writing. I didn't invest a lot of ego in the enterprise and maybe for that reason the first short stories that I wrote were rather sprightly. I think they contained some dialogue that human beings might have uttered. Anyway, the teacher liked them and, more important, so did some of the young women in the class. My first strong impulse to become a writer sprang from this realization: that writing could be a means of meeting and impressing girls.

The next year I got into a class taught by the poet and great translator Robert Fitzgerald. He admitted only about a dozen students from among dozens of applicants, and I seem to remember that I was the youngest of the anointed group. This mattered to me. In high school I had been addicted to competitive sports, and I conceived of writing in sporting terms. I figured I had won part of the competition already, by being the youngest student admitted to the class. The yearning for distinction is common among writers, and in that sense I had begun to become a writer.

I want to try to summon Mr. Fitzgerald back from the dead. I remember him as a small, elegant man, then in his sixties, I believe. Occasionally during office hours he smoked a cigarette, and did so with great deliberation, making every puff count—I think he'd been warned off tobacco, and had put himself on short rations. He would enter the classroom with a green bookbag slung over his shoulder, and would greet us with a smile and a sigh as he heaved the bag onto the long seminar table. Mr. Fitzgerald's green bag contained our work, *my* work, with his comments upon it. I could not have been more interested in that object if Mr. Fitzgerald had been our adult provider, returning with food he'd found out in the world. But the way he sighed, as he heaved that sack onto the table, insinuated that what lay inside wasn't as valuable as food. Certainly it looked like a heavy load for one professor to carry.

I have always talked too much and listened too little. What is it about certain people that has made me pay attention to everything they say? Their confidence and wit, I guess, but most of all their interest in *me.* Mr. Fitzgerald paid his students the great compliment of taking us seriously. He flattered us, dauntingly. I remember the first day of that class. From his place at the head of the table Mr. Fitzgerald eyed us all. He had a pair of reading glasses, half-glasses, which he often used to great effect. He lowered them and looking at us over the top of them, said something like, "The only reason for writing is to produce something *classic.* And I expect that you will produce *classic* work during this term."

I recall thinking, "You do?"

Of course, none of us did, with the possible exception of one young woman who wrote a poem entitled "The Splendor and the Terror of the Universe as Revealed to Me on Brattle Street." I don't recall the poem, but I still like the title.

Having told us of his expectations, Mr. Fitzgerald offered his first advice for meeting them. He jabbed an index finger at the wastebasket beside him and said, "The greatest repository I know of for writers. And I do hope that it will *precede* me."

After a few weeks of Mr. Fitzgerald, I gave up on political science. I quit right in the middle of a lecture by the then-not-very-famous professor Henry Kissinger. The lecture bored me. Professor Kissinger was only partly to blame. I now described myself as a writer, and I thought a writer shouldn't be interested in politics. I had not yet realized that a writer ought to know about something besides writing, so as to have something to write about. When I left that lecture I went right to the English department office and signed up. I'd already begun to do a lot of reading on my own, mostly fiction, which I was consuming at a rate I've never equaled since. At the same time, I had suddenly acquired an assigned-reading disability and a sleep disorder. I had trouble reading books that appeared on formal course lists, and I often worked all night on stories for Mr. Fitzgerald, then went to sleep around the time when my other classes began.

During the first part of Mr. Fitzgerald's class, he would talk about writing and read aloud to us, very occasionally stuff that a student had written, and more often works by wonderful, famous writers he had known, such as his old friend Flannery O'Connor. He read us one of her stories, and when he finished, he said, "That story unwinds like a Rolex watch." Listening to him read such estimable work made me want to try my hand. I think he aimed for that effect, because in the second half of every class he had us write. He warmed us up, and then made us exercise. It is a testament to those warmups of his that I can't recall ever being unable to write *something* in that room for him. In his presence, even poetry seemed possible. Mr. Fitzgerald insisted I try my hand at a poem now and then. I struggled but complied. Finally, I got one off that he seemed to like. It came back from him with this comment at the bottom: "This is very like a poem."

I prefer other memories, especially this one: I had written a short story, which an undergraduate, literary friend of mine had read and disliked. This was the first and at the time the only literary friend I'd acquired, and I thought him very wise and perspicacious, because he had encouraged me. I guessed that my friend must be right about my story. Once he'd pointed out its flaws, I saw them clearly, too. But I decided to show the thing to Mr. Fitzgerald, just so he'd know that I was working. He opened the next class by saying that he was going to read a student's story, a story that he particularly liked, and I remember sitting there wishing that he would some day single out a story of mine in that way and I recall vividly the moment when I realized that it was my story he was reading. The mellifluous voice that had read to us from the likes of James Agee and Wallace Stevens and Flannery O'Connor was reading something of mine! I felt frightened. Then I felt confused. I don't think it had ever occurred to me that intelligent people could disagree about the quality of a piece of writing. If my literary friend thought the story was lousy, Mr. Fitzgerald surely would, too. I see myself sitting at that table with my mouth hanging open—and closing it fast when I remembered the young women in the room. At first I wanted to ask Mr. Fitzgerald to stop, and then I hoped he never would.

I hoped, indeed expected, to have that experience again. I remember that I had given Mr. Fitzgerald a story I knew to be marvelous, a story I knew he'd want to single out in class. When I came into his office for the private visit all of us periodically received, I said to him, in a voice already exulting at his answer, "How'd you like that story, Mr. Fitzgerald?"

He performed his ritual of the reading glasses, pulling them an inch down his nose and looking at me over the top of them. "Not much," he said.

And then, of course, he told me what was wrong with the story, and I saw at once that he was right. I still have this problem. My judgment of my own work sometimes seems so malleable as not to rate as judgment at all. Any critic, no matter how stupid in praise or transparently spiteful in blame, convinces me—at least for awhile. Generally, harsh criticism tends to make me fear that the critic has an intelligence far superior to mine, and has found out things about my writing that I've been too blind to see myself. A person as easily confused by criticism as I am might well have quit writing after a few rejection slips came in for stories that my girlfriend and my mother thought were really good. Perhaps inadvertently, Mr. Fitzgerald taught me the value of trusting the judgment of just one person above all others—and of getting that judgment as the work is in progress, and a lot of help besides. Which is the role I've inflicted on a single editor, Richard Todd, for more than two decades.

I took Mr. Fitzgerald's course again and again, right up until I graduated. After my first semester with him, I didn't perform very well. It wasn't for lack of trying or, God knows, desire. I had become self-conscious about writing. At one point I started a novel. I wrote twenty pages or so, but the most interesting parts were the comments and little drawings I made in the margins—and created with greater care than anything in the actual text—imagining, as I created these notes in the margins, my biographer's delight in finding them. During this period, almost all of the stories I wrote in my room late at night, and the pastiches I committed in class, came back with such brief comments as "O.K., but no flash," all written in an elegantly penned script, which I can still see in my mind's eye, my heart sinking all over again. Mr. Fitzgerald used to talk about something he called "the luck of the conception," an idea I still believe in, but no longer dream about. I used to have a dream in which I had come upon the perfect story. The dream did not contain the story itself, just the fact that I possessed it. It was a dream suffused with joy, and I'd awake from it with a kind of sorrow that I haven't felt since adolescence. As a reader I felt then as I feel now, that any number of faults in a piece of writing are forgivable if there is life on the page. And there was no life in anything I wrote. Oddly, as the small natural talent I'd had for making up stories began to wane, my ambitions grew immense. Or maybe it was the other way around, and ambition stood in my way.

I can't blame Mr. Fitzgerald. He had only suggested that writing could be a high calling. I alone invented my desire to write for posterity. I am embarrassed to admit to this, but what I really had in mind was immortality. Once as a very young boy at a lecture at the Hayden Planetarium in New York, I learned that the earth would be destroyed in some two and a half billion years, and in spite of all my mother said, I was inconsolable for weeks. Maybe I was born especially susceptible to the fears that attend the fact of human mortality. Maybe I was influenced by certain of the English poets, those whose poems declare that their poems will make them immortal. Or it may be, as my wife suggests, that once a young man has solved the problem of how to meet and impress girls, it just naturally occurs to him that his next job is to figure out how to become immortal.

After college I went to Vietnam as a soldier—not the most likely way of gaining immortality, though I was never in much danger there. I came home with my body and my vaunting literary ambitions still intact and wrote a whole novel about experiences I didn't have in Vietnam. I designed that book for immortality. I borrowed heavily from Conrad, Melville, and Dostoyevsky. About thirty-five editors refused to publish it, thank God. I went to the Iowa Writers Workshop, where it began to seem to me that the well from which I drew for fiction had gone completely dry. (I have written fiction since then, all of it published, but the sum total is three short stories.) I decided to try my hand at nonfiction. That term covers a lot of territory, of course, from weighty treatises on the great problems of the world to diet books—some diet books qualify as nonfiction don't they? I dove into something then labeled The New Journalism. As many people have pointed out, only the term was new. I believe that the form already had a distinguished lineage, which included work by George Orwell and Joseph Mitchell and Mark Twain and Lillian Ross and Edmund Wilson and, my particular favorite, A. J. Liebling. This kind of nonfiction writing, whatever it's called, relies on narrative. Some people describe it by saying that it borrows techniques of fiction, but the fact is that it employs techniques of storytelling that never did belong exclusively to fiction. It is an honorable literary form, not always honorably used, but one can certainly say the same about fiction.

When I first started trying to write in this genre, there was an idea in the air, which for me had the force of a revelation: that all journalism is inevitably subjective. I was in my mid-twenties then, and although my behavior was somewhat worse than it has been recently, I was quite a moralist. I decided that writers of nonfiction had a moral obligation to write in the first person—really write in the first person, making themselves characters on the page. In this way, I would disclose my biases. I would not hide the truth from the reader. I would proclaim that what I wrote was just my own subjective version of events. In retrospect, it seems clear that this prescription for honesty often served instead as a license for self-absorption on the page. But I was still very young, too young and self-absorbed to realize what now seems obvious—that I was less likely to write honestly about myself than about anyone else on earth.

I wrote a book about a murder case, in a swashbuckling first person. It *was* published, I'm sorry to say. On the other hand, it disappeared without a trace; that is, it never got reviewed in the *New York Times*. And I began writing nonfiction articles for the *Atlantic Monthly*, under the tutelage of Richard Todd, then a young editor there. For about five years, during which I didn't dare attempt another book, I worked on creating what many writer friends of mine call "voice." I didn't do this consciously. If I had, I probably wouldn't have gotten anywhere. But gradually, I think, I cultivated a writing voice, the voice of a person who was well-informed, fair-minded, and temperate—the voice, not of the person I was, but of a person I sometimes wanted to be. Then I went back to writing books, and discovered other points of view besides the first person.

Choosing a point of view is a matter of finding the best place to stand from which to tell a story. It shouldn't be determined by theory, but by immersion in the material itself. The choice of point of view, I've come to think, has nothing to do with morality. It's a choice among tools. I think it's true, however, that the wrong choice can lead to dishonesty. Point of view is primary; it affects everything else, including voice. Writing my last four books, I made my choices by instinct sometimes and sometimes by experiment. Most of my memories of time spent writing have merged together in a blur, but I remember vividly my first attempts to find a way to write *Among Schoolchildren*, a book about an inner-city schoolteacher. I had spent a year inside her classroom. I intended, vaguely, to fold into my account of events I'd witnessed in that little place a great deal about the lives of particular schoolchildren and about the problems of education in America. I tried out every point of view that I'd used in previous books, and every page I wrote felt lifeless. Finally, I hit on a restricted third-person narration.

The approach seemed to work. The world of that classroom seemed to come alive when the view of it was restricted mainly to observations of the teacher and to accounts of what the teacher saw and heard and smelled and felt. This choice narrowed my options. I ended up writing something less comprehensive than I'd planned. The book became essentially an account of a year in the emotional life of a schoolteacher. My choice of the restricted third person also obliged me to write parts of the book as if from within the teacher's mind. I felt entitled to describe her thoughts and feelings because she had described them to me, both during class and afterward, and because her descriptions rarely seemed self-serving. Believing in them myself, I thought that I could make them believable on the page.

Belief is an offering that a reader makes to an author, what Coleridge famously called "That willing suspension of disbelief for the moment, which constitutes poetic faith." It is up to the writer to entertain and inform without disappointing the reader into a loss of that faith. In fiction or poetry, of course, believability may have nothing to do with realism or even plausibility. It has everything to do with those things in nonfiction, in my opinion. I think that the nonfiction writer's fundamental job is to make what is true believable. I'm not sure that everyone agrees. Lately the job seems to have been defined differently. Here are some of the ways that some people now seem to define the nonfiction writer's job: to make believable what the writer thinks is true, if the writer wants to be scrupulous; to make believable what the writer wishes were true, if the writer isn't interested in scrupulosity; or to make believable what the writer thinks might be true, if the writer couldn't get the story and had to make it up.

I figure that if I call a piece of my own writing nonfiction it ought to be about real people, with their real names attached whenever possible, who say and do in print nothing that they didn't actually say and do. On the cover page of my last book I put a note that reads, "This is a work of nonfiction," and listed the several names that I was obliged to change in the text. I thought a longer note would be intrusive. I was afraid that it would stand between the reader and the spell that I wanted to create, inviting the reader into the world of a nursing home. But the definition of "nonfiction" has become so slippery that I wonder if I shouldn't have written more. So now I'll take this opportunity to explain that for my last book I spent a year doing research, that the name of the place I wrote about is its real name, that I didn't change the names of any of the major characters, and that I didn't invent dialogue or put any thoughts in characters' minds that the characters themselves didn't confess to.

I no longer care what rules other writers set for themselves. If I don't like what someone has written, I can stop reading, which is, after all, the worst punishment a writer can suffer. (It ought to be the worst punishment. Some critics seem to feel that the creation of a book that displeases them amounts to a felony.) But the expanded definitions of nonfiction have created problems for those writers who define the term narrowly. Many readers now view with suspicion every narrative that claims to be nonfiction, and yet scores of very good nonfiction writers do not make up their stories or the details in them—writers such as John McPhee, Jane Kramer, J. Anthony Lucas. There are also special cases that confound categories and all attempts to lay down rules for writers of narrative. I have in mind Norman Mailer and in particular his *Executioner's Song,* a hybrid of fact and fiction, carefully labeled as such—a book I admire.

Most writers lack Mailer's powers of invention. Some nonfiction writers do not lack his willingness to invent, but the candor to admit it. Some writers proceed by trying to discover the truth about a situation, and then invent or distort the facts as necessary. Even in these suspicious times, writers can get away with this. Often no one will know, and the subjects of the story may not care. They may not notice. But the writer always knows. I believe in immersion in the events of a story. I take it on faith that the truth lies in the events somewhere, and that immersion in those real events will yield glimpses of that truth. I try to hew to what has begun to seem like a narrow definition of nonfiction partly in that faith, and partly out of fear. I'm afraid that if I started making up things in a story that purported to be about real events and people, I'd stop believing it myself. And I imagine that such a loss of conviction would infect every sentence and make each one unbelievable.

I don't mean to imply that all a person has to do to write good narrative nonfiction is to take accurate notes and reproduce them. The kind of nonfiction I like to read is at bottom storytelling, as gracefully accomplished as good fiction. I don't think any technique should be ruled out to achieve it well. For myself, I rule out only invention. But I don't think that honesty and artifice are contradictory. They work together in good writing of every sort. Artfulness and an author's justified belief in a story often combine to produce the most believable nonfiction.

If you write a nonfiction story in the third person and show your face in public afterward, someone is bound to ask, "How did your presence in the scenes you relate affect the people you were observing?" Some readers seem to feel that third-person narration, all by itself, makes a narrative incomplete. The other day I came upon a book about the writing of ethnography. It interested me initially because its bibliography cited a couple of my books and one of its footnotes mentioned me. The author spelled my first name wrong and gave one of my books a slightly different title from the one I chose. I swear I don't hold a grudge on account of that. My first name is a little weird, and the title in question is a long one. But those little mistakes did make me vigilant as I read the following passage:

> Writers of literary tales seldom remark on the significance of their presence on the scenes they represent, and this is in some instances a bothersome problem to field workers in addition to the common concerns for reactivity in any situation. It is, for example, very difficult to imagine that as famous and dandy a writer as Tom Wolfe was merely a fashionable but unobtrusive fly on the wall in the classic uptown parlor scene of *Radical Chic* (1970), or that Tracey [sic] Kidder did not in any way influence the raising of the Souweines' roofbeams in *House* (1985). Since writers of ethnographic tales have begun to break their silence on these matters, it is seemingly time for writers of literary tales to do so too—especially when their accounts so clearly rest on intimacy.

I believe it's possible to learn something from anyone, including ethnographers who have begun to break their silence. But I can't work out the mechanics for calculating the *reactivity* that occurs during *field work.* As I imagine it, field work that is mindful of reactivity would have to proceed in this way: I'd open my notebook in front of a person I planned to write about, and I'd ask, "How did you feel when I opened my notebook just now?" Then I would probably be bound to ask, "How did you feel when I asked you that question about opening my notebook?"

I don't know for sure how my presence has influenced the behavior of any of the people I've written about. I don't believe that I can know, because I wasn't there when I wasn't there. To do the research for a book, I usually hang around with my subjects for a year or more. After a while, most seem to take my presence for granted. Not all do. It worked the other way with one of the carpenters I wrote about in *House.* I remember his saying at one point that he and the other builders ought to put a bell around my neck, so they'd know where I was at all times.

Obviously some readers expect to hear about the story behind the story. But all writing is selective. I think that a narrative should be judged mainly on its own terms, not according to a reader's preexisting expectations. As a reader, I know that I won't always sit still for the story behind the story. As a writer, I have often decided that it isn't worth telling.

I wrote my most recent book, *Old Friends,* which is about some of the residents of a nursing home, in the third person. I hope that I put my own voice in it, but I chose not to write about how I did my research and how I was affected by what I encountered inside the nursing home—never mind how my presence might, arguably, possibly, have affected the inmates' behavior—mainly because what I did—asking questions, listening, taking notes—was much less interesting than what I observed. It is true, however, that my solution to the problem that the book presented did have something to do with my own experience of life inside that place. After writing for a while, I realized that I wanted to reproduce, in a limited sense, the most important part of my experience there.

I entered the nursing home in the late fall of 1990. The place, which is situated in western Massachusetts, is called the Linda Manor Extended Care Facility. I went there with a notebook—I filled ninety notebooks eventually—and prowled around inside almost every day, and many nights, for about a year. And then for another year or so I spent about three days a week there. I chose a decent nursing home, not one of the very best but a clean, well-lighted place where residents weren't tied up and were allowed some of the trappings of their former lives.

I had visited a nursing home only once before in my life, and since then had averted both my eyes and thoughts as I passed by. That was part of the attraction; nursing homes seemed to me like secret places in the landscape. I went to Linda Manor tentatively, though. I was afraid that I might find it dull. I thought I might find myself in a kind of waiting room, a vestibule to eternity, where everything had been resolved or set aside and residents simply lay waiting to die. But waiting was the least of what went on in many of those clean, motel-like rooms. Nearly everyone, it seemed, was working on a project. Some were absurd—one resident kept hounding the office of a U.S. senator to complain about his breakfast eggs. Some were poignant—many of the demented residents roamed the halls searching for exits, asking everyone for directions home. A lot of projects were Quixotic. There was, for instance, one indomitable, wheelchair-bound woman who had set herself the task of raising about $30,000 to buy the nursing home its own chairlift van. She intended to do so through raffles and teacup auctions and by getting other residents to remember the van in their wills. There was also an elderly actress who kept herself and the place somewhat invigorated by putting on plays. Staging those productions took great determination, because Linda Manor had no stage and most of the actors and actresses were confined to wheelchairs and walkers. In between plays, when things got dull, the old actress livened things up by starting fights. There were many residents working doggedly to come to terms with the remorse they felt for past mistakes and offenses. There was also a man in his nineties named Lou Freed who summoned up memories with what seemed like the force of necessity, re-inhabiting his former life with something that resembled joy. And there were, of course, a number who knew their deaths were imminent and struggled to find ways to live in the face of that knowledge.

Even in a decent nursing home, the old often get treated like children. And yet many of the residents refused to become like children. The roommates Lou and Joe, for instance. Let me try to prove this point with a short passage from my book.

> Joe and Lou could not control most of the substance of their life in here, but they had imposed a style on it. The way for instance that Joe and Lou had come, in the past months, to deal with matters of the bathroom. Joe had to go there what seemed to him like a ridiculous number of times each day and night. He and Lou referred to the bathroom as "the library." The mock-daintiness of the term amused Joe. The point was to make a joke out of anything you could around here. Up in the room after breakfast, Joe would say to Lou, "I gotta go to the library. I have to do my, uh, uh, prune evacuation."
>
> This room was now their home. As in any household, people entering were expected to follow local rules. The nursing staff was overwhelmingly female. Lou and Joe referred to all of them as girls, and indeed, next to them, even the middleaged did look like girls. The staff had all, of course, been quite willing to talk frankly about matters of Lou and Joe's biology. Too frankly for Lou. Too frankly for Joe, once Lou had made the point. The aides, "the girls," used to come to the doorway, cradling opened in their arms the large, ledger-like Forest View "BM Book," and they'd call loudly in, "Did either of you gentlemen have a bowel movement today?" It was Lou, some months ago now, who responded to this question by inviting in the girls who asked it, and then telling them gently, "All you have to say is, 'Did you or didn't you.'" The way Lou did that job impressed Joe, Lou did it so diplomatically, so much more diplomatically than Joe would have. Lou, as he liked to say, had trained all the girls by now. Joe took care of reinforcement.
>
> It was a morning in December. Joe had the television news on. He and Lou were listening to the dispatches from the Middle East. Joe wasn't waiting

for the aide with the BM Book, but he had a question ready for her. When the aide came to the door, she asked, "For my book. Did you?"

"Yes." Joe tilted his head toward Lou. "And so did he." Then, a little smile blossoming, Joe looked at the aide and asked, "And what about you?"

"None of your business!" The aide looked embarrassed. She laughed.

"Well, you ask me," Joe said.

"But I get paid for it."

"*Good*bye," Joe said pleasantly, and went back to watching the news.

Many residents insisted on preserving their dignity, in spite of the indignities imposed by failing health and institutional confinement. Many people in there were attempting in one way or another to invent new lives for themselves. In the context of that place and of debilitating illnesses, their quests seemed important.

So when I began to write *Old Friends*, I didn't lack for interesting characters or stories. I felt I had an overabundance. I told myself before I started writing that I couldn't fit in everything, and then for about a year I tried to do just that. In the end I had to jettison a lot of portraits and stories that I had written many times and polished up. Among other things, I wrote four or five times and finally discarded what in all modesty I believe to have been the most riveting account of a session of Bingo ever composed. But the plain fact was that about half of what I wrote and rewrote got in the way of the main story that I wanted to tell.

Hundreds of articles and books deal with the big issues that surround aging in late-twentieth-century America. I read some of them. But I didn't want to approach this subject in a general way. It is useful, maybe even necessary, to imagine that a definable group called "the elderly" exists. But all such conceptions inevitably fail. It is accurate only to say that there are many individuals who have lived longer than most of the rest of the population, and that they differ widely among themselves. For various reasons, some can no longer manage what are called the activities of daily living at home, and, for lack of a better solution, some of those people end up living in nursing homes. I chose to write about a few of those people partly because so much well-meaning commentary on old age depicts white-haired folks in tennis clothes—a tendency, it seems to me, that inadvertently denigrates the lives of the many people who haven't been as lucky.

About five percent of Americans over sixty-five—about 1.5 million people—live in nursing homes and, according to one estimate, nearly half of all the people who live past sixty-five will spend some time inside a nursing home. Obviously, they are important places, but nursing homes weren't really the subject I wanted to address. There were already plenty of published exposés of bad nursing homes. I decided to do my research inside a good nursing home on the theory that a good one would be bad enough, inevitably a house of grief and pain, and also because I didn't want to write about the kinds of policy and management issues that would have assumed primary importance in a story set in an evil place. I wanted to write from the inside about the experience of being old and sick and confined to an institution. I wanted to come at the subject of aging, not through statistics, but through elderly people themselves. I wanted to write an interesting, engaging book. The residents of even a decent nursing home are people in a difficult situation, and I think that stories about people in difficult situations are almost always interesting, and often dramatic.

In some ways, research in that place was easy work. In the course of every story I'd done before, I had run into people who hadn't wanted to talk to me. But people in a nursing home never have enough willing listeners. A nursing home like Linda Manor may be the only place on earth where a person with a notebook can hope to receive a universal welcome.

Various sights, smells, and sounds distressed me at first. But gradually, I got used to the externals of the place and people. Almost everyone who has spent some time inside a nursing home begins to look beyond the bodies of the residents. It just happens. But around the time when that happened to me, another problem arose. I remember leaving the room of a dying, despondent resident and stopping in my tracks in a Linda Manor corridor, and hearing myself say to myself, "This is amazing! *Everybody* dies." And, of course, my next thought was, "Including me." I know that sounds silly. One is supposed to have figured that out before pushing fifty. But I hadn't believed it, I think.

I arranged some other troubling moments for myself, during my research. At one point, I decided that I ought to check into Linda Manor for a couple of days and nights, as if I were myself a resident. I hate the kind of story in which a perfectly healthy person decides to ride around in a wheelchair for a day and then proclaims himself an expert in what being wheelchair-bound is like. But I believe in the possibility of imaginatively experiencing what others experience, and I thought I might learn something. With vast amusement, a nurse ushered me into a little room. My roommate, an ancient man who couldn't speak much, terrified me as soon as I climbed into bed. He kept clicking his light on and off. At one point I saw his hand through the filmy, so-called "privacy curtain." His hand reached toward the curtain, grasping at it. He was trying to pull the curtain back, so that he could get a better look at me, and I had to stifle the impulse to yell at him to stop. Then, a little later, I heard a couple of the nurses in the hall outside, saying loudly, speaking of me, "Shall we give him an enema?" An old source of amusement among nurses, the enema.

I didn't learn much that I could use in my book, from my two-night stand at Linda Manor. Except for the fact that a few minutes can seem like eternity in a nursing-home bed and the fact that, from such a perspective, cheerful, attractive, average-sized nurses and nurse's aides can look huge and menacing. Those two nights I kept getting up and looking out the window, to make sure my car was still in the parking lot. I had planned to stay longer, but went home early the third morning in order to get some sleep.

At Linda Manor I got to know a nurse's aide who, when one of her residents had died, insisted on opening up the windows of the room. Asked why she did this, she said she felt she had to let the spirit out. All but a few of the staff were religious, at least in the sense that most believed in an afterlife. I think belief was a great comfort to them. At least I imagined it would be for me. But I possessed only a vague agnosticism. And I couldn't simply manufacture something stronger for the situation.

What troubled me most during my time at Linda Manor wasn't unpleasant sights or smells or even the reawakening of my fears about mortality. It was the problem of apparent meaninglessness. I watched people dying long before life had lost its savor for them or they their usefulness to others. I couldn't imagine any purpose behind the torments that many residents suffered in their last days. Sometimes I'd leave a resident's room feeling that everything, really everything in every life, was pointless. I remember thinking that we all just live awhile and end up dying painfully, or, even worse, bored and inert. What meaning could life have, I'd find myself wondering, if the best of the last things people get to do on earth is to play Bingo? At such times, I'd usually find my way upstairs to the room of the two old men named Lou and Joe. Gradually, I began to notice that a number of the staff did the same thing, even giving up their coffee breaks to go and chat with Lou and Joe. I didn't usually plan to go to their room at these moments of vicarious despair. I'd just find myself wanting to go there. After about ten minutes in their room, I usually felt much better. Lou and Joe had been placed together in one of Linda Manor's little rooms, in what for both would likely be their last place on earth, and they had become great friends. Other residents had formed friendships inside Linda Manor, but none was durable or seemed to run very deep. Out in the wider, youthful world, this accomplishment of Lou and Joe's would have seemed unremarkable but in that place it was profound.

The main thing I wanted to portray was that friendship, surrounded by the nursing home and all its varying forms of claustrophobia. I wanted to infuse the story of that friendship with sentiment, but not in a sentimental way. The difference, as I see it, is the difference between portraying emotion and merely asserting its existence, between capturing the reflection of something real on the page and merely providing handy cues designed to elicit an emotional response. It is, I realize, harder to depict manifestations of human goodness than manifestations of venality and evil. I don't know why that is. I do know that some people think that kindness, for example, is always superficial. That view is the logical equivalent of sentimentality. It's an easy way to feel and it gives some people a lot of pleasure. It has nothing to do with a tragic vision of life. It has about as much to do with an accurate vision of life as a Hallmark card. Anyway, that's how it seems to me. The world seems various to me, and depicting some of the virtue in it seems like a project worth attempting. I do not say that I pulled it off, but that's part of what I had in mind.

After my book was published, I continued to visit Linda Manor about once a week. I went partly because doing so made me feel like a good guy. But I had other reasons. Growing old with dignity calls for many acts of routine heroism, and some of the people I knew at Linda Manor were inspiring, admirable characters. All of them have died now, except for Lou, who has achieved the ripe old age of ninety-six. Joe died last winter. I visit only Lou now, but I used to go mainly in order to visit the two men. I *liked* visiting them. Their room was one place where I knew I was always welcome. They gave me good advice, on such subjects as child-rearing. They were funny, both intentionally and otherwise. Most important, their room was one place in the world where I could count on finding that amity prevailed. That was unusual, in my experience of the world. The crucial thing about Lou and Joe was that they remained *very good* friends, better friends every time I visited. They presented an antidote to despair, which is connectedness, and for me, I learned, it is only the connectedness of the human tribe that can hold despair at bay. Connectedness can, of course, take many different forms. One can find it in religion, or in family, or, as in the case of Lou and Joe, in friendship. Or perhaps in work, maybe even in the act of writing.

Harold Brodkey, who recently died of AIDS, wrote in an essay a couple of years ago, "I think anyone who spends his life working to become eligible for literary immortality is a fool." I agree. But I also think that only a fool would write merely for money or contemporary fame. I imagine that most writers—good, bad and mediocre—write partly for the sake of the private act of writing and partly in order to throw themselves out into the world. Most, I imagine, *endeavor* for connectedness, to create the kind of work that touches other lives and, in that sense at least, leaves something behind. I don't dream of immortality or plant marginalia for my biographers anymore. But I do wonder what Mr. Fitzgerald would think of what I've written and, especially, of what I'm going to write.

A few days after I got back from Vietnam, in June 1969, I traveled to Cambridge and called Mr. Fitzgerald from a pay phone. He invited me to lunch at his house the next afternoon. Of course, I didn't tell him this, but I wanted something from him, something ineffable, like hope. He had prepared sandwiches. I'm not sure that he made them himself, but I like to think that he did, and that he was responsible for cutting the crusts off the bread. I'm not sure why I remember that. It seemed a sweet gesture, a way of making me feel that I was important to him. It also made him seem old, older than I'd remembered him.

I saw Mr. Fitzgerald a few times more over the next year or two, and then he moved away and I moved out west for a while. I fell under other influences. My dreams of writing something classic gave way to my little dreams of writing something publishable, of making a living as a writer, which seemed hard enough. But those early dreams were dormant, not dead. When, almost ten years later, a book of mine, *The Soul of a New Machine,* was awarded the Pulitzer Prize and the American Book Award, my megalomaniacal dreams of literary glory came out of storage. I could tell myself at moments that I'd achieved them all. But I hesitated for a while before sending my book to Mr. Fitzgerald. I was afraid. When I finally worked up the nerve, I wrote an inscription to the effect that I hoped this piece of writing began to approach his expectations. I soon received a letter from him, in which he thanked me, remarked upon the "modesty" of my inscription—no doubt he saw right through that—and apologized for his inability to read the book just now. I wrote right back, proposing that I visit him. He did not reply. I never heard from him again. I don't remember exactly when he died. I think it was a few years later.

His silence has bothered me for a long time, not immoderately but in the way of those embarrassing memories that suddenly appear when you're checking the oil in your car or putting a key in a door. Two summers ago I met one of Mr. Fitzgerald's sons and told him the story. He insisted that his father would never have failed to answer my last letter, if he'd been able to read and write by then. I believed him. And I believe that if Mr. Fitzgerald had been able to read my book, he would have told me what he really thought. It's probably just as well that he never did. I've written other and, I think, better books since then. I'd rather know what he thought of *them*. I've been courting his approval ever since my first day in his class, and I continue to court his approval now, when he's certain to withhold it. That makes me sad sometimes, but not in my better moments. I'll never know if he'd approve of what I've written and am going to write. But I'll never know if he'd disapprove either. He's left me room to go on trying.

What We Didn't Know We Knew

Sydney Lea

If I begin by stating my unenthusiasm for the designation "creative nonfiction," it's because I lack enthusiasm for the term "creative" as applied to any writing. Is there not more of creativity in the making of a good soup, say, or of a salmon fly than of novel, story, poem or essay? None of these genres brings things into existence, thus "creating" them, so much as it assembles pre-existing things, both public and private. And however free-associative, such assembly of course depends on another pre-existent entity: language.

I admit, though, that "our" kind of essayizing is one I can name only vaguely. And variously: the personal essay, the familiar essay, the impressionistic essay, the informal essay, or—as I've come most often to describe it—the lyrical essay. Be our terms as they may, moreover, reasonable people could argue at length about what actually *characterizes* the work that Annie Dillard or Edward Abbey or Joan Didion or Edward Hoagland or Rick Bass or Terry Tempest Williams or W.D. Wetherell or Geoffrey Wolff or Kathleen Norris have been doing.

Where for example does their sort of essay begin and another leave off? Each of us might make such a division in idiosyncratic fashion. Still, we'd likely agree not only that our sort of essay exists but also that certain generalities apply to it: other kinds of essay veer closer to journalism; in those other kinds, presentation is more dependent on consecutive reasoning and empirical fact than "creative nonfiction's"; thesis is more insistent for Them than for Us, in whose work thesis, properly so called, may not even show.

I am less interested in defining categories than in learning how to do whatever we do with greater energy, greater facility, greater claim on readers' attentions. And yet I'll have to sneak up on such issues of strategy: anarchistic by nature, skeptical of the whole How-To frame of mind, I shy away from precepts, let alone rules, when I discuss writing of whatever variety. After all, whenever I hear precept or rule, no matter how attractive or acceptable to me; whenever I'm given a guideline about How To Do It, I seem automatically to think of literature that contradicts the same stipulation . . . and that wows me anyway.

So let me distinguish the lyrical essay—too simply, too reductively—from the more thesis-bound by asserting that the lyrical makes its point or points in a more indirect way than the reporter, reviewer, speechwriter or scholar makes hers or his.

I think for example of Norman Mailer's booklength essay on the moon landing. Rarely a fan of this author's work, still I recall how taken I was on first reading *Of a Fire on the Moon*. As usual, Mailer's protagonist is himself, but himself in the persona of "Aquarius." Rightfully or otherwise, he mounts his inquiry as a representative of the Love Generation, the Make-Love-Not-War party encountering NASA, whose military ties are historically evident.

Mailer, in short, gives himself an angle, but it is not so much an argumentative angle, a means to thesis, as a quirky point of view which will be important in and of itself. Such distinctive perspective will enable Aquarius to talk about his own sensibility at least as volubly as about the astronauts and their mission. I'll be making much of that aim, not so much in connection with Mailer as with the whole genre under discussion.

In *Of a Fire on the Moon*, Aquarius also finds himself moved, unpremeditatedly (or so the book would suggest), to rely very heavily on his sense of smell in talking about his nominal subject. Once again, the object is specifically not to provide conventional consideration of a highly scientific enterprise but to get at that enterprise in a way that no one, including the author, might have predicted. As it turns out, the sense of smell (or frequently smell-lessness) offers a path to real eloquence, at the same time offering a motif that structurally binds his account. It relieves Mailer/Aquarius, sometimes also called The Nose, of offering coherence by way of dialectical argument.

Of a Fire on the Moon comes to my mind principally as instance of the oblique and peculiar perception that typifies so-called creative nonfiction. Information about the space program's crowning moment does get imparted, but is not primary. And with Mailer as my first exhibit, I'll suggest that the lyrical essay, brief or book-sized, has at its core the way in which the essayist him- or herself, whether as persona or as someone named "I," considers his or her own sensibility.

Or if need be invents that sensibility. For the authorial psyche is as much at the heart of our lyrical essay as it is, say, in a lyrical poem. Both sorts of writer explore the appropriateness or inappropriateness of a personal intellectual-emotional apparatus to a given context or event(s). And each wins either way: if that apparatus is serviceable, then the author has the luxury of a more or less seamless presentation; if it is not, then the clash may become the very subject.

Now in putting the writer's sensibility at the center of the lyrical essay's intentions, I don't mean simply to champion the sort of self-advertisement found in so much of Norman Mailer's work. Though that posture can and often does issue in splendid results, ranging from the book I've just mentioned to the better specimens in Ralph Waldo Emerson's canon, those less inclined to egoism should know there are writers of quite another cast who write brilliantly. I think for example of Ivan Doig, the memoirist of Montana, or of Louise Erdrich, an author of sufficient modesty as at times almost to disappear from her own meditations.

Almost, but never quite entirely. And that is what, I am arguing, constitutes the creative element, to label it so, in our sort of nonfiction.

A few broad statements will govern what follows. To select someone named "I" as the provider of a narrative or a series of impressions (or to select a persona for that I) is simultaneously to select thematic material. If critics sometimes distinguish between technique and content, form and idea, and so on, we writers must not. For us, the choice of first-person delivery, say, cannot be simply a technical one. And more to the point here, we must understand why virtually every lyrical essay makes that very choice: it's again that such an essay's energy is so connected to the identity and the emotional/intellectual makeup of its first person. To begin a narrative by saying even something so simple as "I feel" is automatically to indicate that "I" is an eminent subject in the narrative to come.

In these respects, the protagonist of the so-called American nature essay—from a Thoreau to a Gretel Ehrlich—has far more in common with the prototypical hero of American fiction or poetry than with the conventional magazine essayist, more in common with Melville's Ishmael, Twain's Huck, Whitman's "I" or even the "I" of Emily Dickinson's poetry than with a speaker who means simply to give us the goods, in the directest way possible, on a predetermined subject. We are more poets than journalists, and we must take advantage of our own nature . . . and of *not* having predetermined subjects.

All this is scarcely to say that our essays must begin in a complete vacuum; such a prospect seems impossible on the face of it anyhow. Mailer does mean to write "about" the NASA moon landing, just as Joan Didion, in *Slouching Toward Bethlehem*, means to write about late 20th-century Los Angeles and the great Ryszard Kapucinski means to write about pre-revolutionary Iran in his *Shah of Shahs*. It's just that the treatment of each of these outward subjects is overwhelmingly dependent for its success on presenting, as Wallace Stevens famously said of modern poetry, the mind in the act of finding what will suffice.

I acknowledge that such a presentation may and almost inevitably will be reconsidered, pondered, even much altered in revision. But this will be revision in the originative sense of the term, a "seeing again," an imaginative entry into the world we mean to render.

Instead of erecting an agenda to govern the lyrical essay, therefore, in all my discussion here—including discussion of choosing a subject—I do little more than throw out some suggestions as to how creative nonfiction can become what it wants to become. And in that regard I want right away to stress that we often begin better if we're in doubt, sometimes very considerable doubt, about where we are headed; to stress how important it is to resist any impulse to pre-program our observations; to stress that those observations need the feel of spontaneity, even if that be the result of endless rewriting.

I want in short to emphasize that the very concept of agenda is inimical to our efforts.

Let me turn for example to a writer who's drawn, precisely, to the nature essay, even though I think the gist of my argument (and his, if only implicitly) can apply to all modes of the genre under discussion. The following passage is from Rick Bass's *The Ninemile Wolves*. At the very start, in a marvelously evocative page or so, Bass imagines those Montana wolves pulling down a quarry; and then come some telling afterthoughts:

> They don't have thumbs. All they've got is teeth, long legs, and—I have to say this—great hearts.
>
> I can say what I want to say. I gave up my science badge a long time ago. I've interviewed maybe a hundred people for or against wolves. The ones who are "for" wolves, they have an agenda: wilderness, and freedom for predators, for prey, for everything. The ones who are "against" wolves have an agenda: they've got vested financial interests. It's about money—more and more money—for them. They perceive the wolves to be an obstacle to frictionless cash flow.
>
> The story's so rich. I can begin anywhere.
>
> I can start with prey, which is what controls wolf numbers (not the other way around), or with history, which is rich in sin, cruelty, sensationalism (poisonings, maimings, torture). You can start with biology, or politics, or you can start with family, with loyalty, and even with the mystic-tinged edges of fate, which is where I choose to begin. It's all going to come together anyway. It has to. We're all following the wolf.

Though I scarcely believe good writing in any genre is necessarily, or ever, antirational, in ours there is at least a great deal of *non*-rational energy . . . or, as the quotation above signals, there ought to be. Lest I myself tend too far toward mystic-tinged edges, however, too far toward abstraction, I'll need to root my observations in personal experience.

I've already hinted at one reason that I'm fonder of the term *lyrical essay* than of many other possible names for this sort of writing: namely that my own essays are born and develop much in the manner of my poems. Nor am I speaking here so much of aesthetics or technique as of far more literal matters, like my inclination to hike long distances in the woods alone, seeking not to think up "subjects" but to let my mind float free until, over time, perhaps over a dozen hikes or even years, I find that certain things have lodged themselves in my consciousness and now demand meditation—that *they* have subjected *me*. I surely hadn't imagined myself to be doing "research," but so it seems I was:

> Early June of 1992, below Stonehouse Mountain, Grafton County, New Hampshire—a place and time in which snowsqualls, routine enough just weeks ago, will at last deserve the name freakish. In freshet beds where waters flared and vanished, frail shoots of jewelweed declare themselves; grass bursts the voles'

winter tunnels; geese trail the Connecticut northward; the buck deer's antlers are in velvet; the woodchuck's busy to double in weight; trout sip the ponds' ephemerids; everywhere, the lovesick insistence of birds.

Our family has lived ten years on this foothill's flank, but soon after dawn this morning—beckoned by the full day ahead—I hiked down from its mild summit for perhaps the last time. The ramble, especially under such circumstances, brought back the many I'd made there, in company or alone, one recollection summoning another, and that one still another, till outward prospects opened onto vaster, more labyrinthine inward views.

This is the opening paragraph of "On the Bubble." But in truth it's a paragraph composed late in the construction of that piece, composed well after I happened on what it was "about." The essay actually began in my somehow remembering a brown-phase fisher, who almost stepped across my toes one fall while I was deer-hunting; that, and the fact that, at the time I began feeling an itch to write this chapter of *Hunting the Whole Way Home*, my family was on the point of moving from Stonehouse Mountain, which a so-called developer meant to ruin; that, and the memory of my son blowing bubbles one spring morning at the summit of the same mountain.

These several things were chronologically quite removed from one another; yet they had lodged themselves in my consciousness. My essay was, and is, about *what they all had to do with one another*.

In short, I began in the spirit of Rick Bass: "It's all going to come together anyway. It has to." As I have been arguing, the lyrical essay chiefly concerns the essayist's perception of his or her surroundings, whether natural or otherwise. And since it's concerned with perception, it is ultimately concerned with the essayist's own mind in action.

Perception in the lyrical essay, however, cannot remain static, or so my experience would indicate; it must unfold in the very act of writing, and writing should itself be an act (or acts) of unanticipated discovery. My aim as I sat down to indite "On the Bubble" was simply to see if I could write my way to a connection among a few things, however seemingly disconnected, that had stopped me in my tracks.

The appropriateness of the fragile bubbles my son blew, for example, to the theme of natural fragility that so exercised me when the bulldozers started to chew up the mountain I loved—that appropriateness was something that crept upon me, surprised me, and, however sad the circumstances reflected in my chapter, delighted me as a writer.

What I'm getting at is this: the death knell for any creative writing sounds whenever it knows too accurately where it is going. A novel whose plot has been predetermined will almost inevitably fail to surprise us, say, on the level of characterization, the characters having little to do but walk through their scripts. A poem whose theme has been fore-decided will clank along mechanically, each line illustrating a dominating "idea."

The same hazards can attend the lyrical essay. Indeed, these dangers may apply even more ruinously to such an essay than to the other genres I've referred to, since so often—or so we believe—our plot and setting and characters seem, exactly, to exist in their entirety before we write a word. We know how everything comes out, and who's involved, and where we are: it's simply a matter of recording all that, right?

Wrong. Or wrong, I believe, if you're in the business of writing creative nonfiction, in which, as I've suggested, the creative part must if anything be more important than the nonfiction part. We may too easily be misled by the very concept of nonfictionality; we may be inclined simply to chronicle the facts of a given matter, and to do so is to offer an account, not an essay of the kind most of us want. Ours is, after all, an art form, to which imagination is utterly crucial.

With all this in mind, I'll make some practical observations. At the outset, in grumbling about the word "creative," I pointed out the obvious fact that as writers we work with something that pre-exists, namely language—which I now want to suggest can help us to our "subjects," since language and subject are all but indistinguishably identified, each bound as it is to perception.

The *way* in which we phrase our responses, then, is as much what we are writing about as anything else, and with that in mind, I'll urge that in order to begin we ought to speak with as much particularity as we can. This doesn't mean that we can't muse, reminisce, worry, argue, preach, or even pontificate in our essays. We can. Lord knows, I do. It's only that such rhetorical gestures will always be more effective if they have grounds.

In "On the Bubble," the word "grounds" has a happy double meaning, so much of the essay's concerns having to do, exactly, with grounds, or with their loss. And thus it began with very specific renderings of vivid occurrences upon those grounds, with my effort to recapture the particulars of an encounter with a fisher. I wrote the memory as clearly and accurately as I knew how, and in doing so I was somehow led to other specific experiences in the same locale, notably the time when I took my son to the height of Stonehouse Mountain and watched him blow bubbles.

In the very process of writing out these experiences, in language that was as precise as I could make it, I came gradually to recognize what these two components might have in common: the wonder I felt at beholding that normally elusive weasel at such close distance seemed at least remotely akin to the wonder my five-year-old experienced as he watched his soap bubbles take flight above the granite moraine of Stonehouse Mountain. Each version of wonder was a bit childlike, and each, like childhood itself, was extremely fragile, indeed doomed.

Without setting out to do so, I had hit on the motif of wonder, and on plain facts to serve as its metaphors: weasel and bubble. Soon enough another metaphor presented itself—this one for doom—that seemed so obvious I was puzzled I'd ever missed it: the very sound of the bulldozers and chainsaws on the hillside. Very rapidly now, I came to see the connections among seemingly disparate snatches of memory and present experience.

I had written my way to awareness of those connections. I had written my way not to creativity but to what I prefer to call imagination, as the great poet and theorist Samuel Taylor Coleridge understood the term; he called it "an esemplastic power," which means, roughly, a power that forges unity out of diversity.

My point is that I foisted no metaphors or themes upon my perceptions. Rather, by beginning in particularity, without great regard for what my essay would be "about," I found organic metaphors and thematics coming to *me*. It would have been all too easy just to rant and rave out loud about the developer's greed and the despoliation of wildness; indeed, I had been doing so—eloquently, I hope—for some time. But I had done so in letters to my local paper, which were not by my understanding creative in the way that each of us wants to be in a lyrical essay.

Those letters had a thesis, and I argued it as persuasively and logically as I could. Yet the terms of my letters were for the most part abstract: terms, exactly, like "greed" and "wildness" and "despoliation." In my essay, I'd use the same terms, but now they would be . . . grounded. They'd be grounded in personal observation and unexpected discovery of the kind I've briefly catalogued above.

I was proud of the letters, but they didn't have the same value for me as a writer that the final essay had, and has. "Wildness" became associated with a particular animal, the fisher; the fisher's habitat appeared to be threatened by "despoliation," by a ruinous force associated with the developer's machinery; that machinery perfectly epitomized the brutal effects of "greed." And so the fisher's future, like my son's, perhaps, became as tenuous as the existences of those bubbles I remember my boy making.

With a bunch of specifics in my quiver, I could shoot as many arrows of rhetorical indignation as I wanted, without fear of lapsing from "our" sort of essay into that other sort I spoke of early on. But I repeat: I did not know what my outward subject or my rhetoric would be until I started writing, and I am glad I didn't know, for otherwise I'd merely have written one more letter to the editor. The only agenda I had was that vague poetic one: I sought to connect a number of moments that had stuck in my consciousness, and my only means of doing so was particularized language.

Language led me on, in the most fulfilling way. It permitted me both to learn what was on my mind and to learn how much I had to say about it. The composition of "On the Bubble," then, like the successful composition of any poem, resulted in a better self-understanding. Speaking for myself, this is among the happiest results that an author can experience.

In the famous formulation of a far greater poet than I, Robert Frost, by writing we discover what we didn't know we knew.

Note

See Peter Fritzell's illuminating *Nature Writing and America* (Iowa State University Press: Ames, 1990), whose commentary on the protagonist of American natural-historical literature, along with other keen insights, informs portions of this discussion.

What Happened to the Personal Essay?

Phillip Lopate

The personal or familiar essay is a wonderfully tolerant form, able to accommodate rumination, memoir, anecdote, diatribe, scholarship, fantasy, and moral philosophy. It can follow a rigorously elegant design, or—held together by little more than the author's voice—assume an amoebic shapelessness. Working in it liberates a writer from the structure of the well-made, epiphanous short story and allows one to ramble in a way that more truly reflects the mind at work. At this historical moment the essayist has an added freedom: no one is looking over his or her shoulder. No one much cares. Commercially, essay volumes rank even lower than poetry.

I know; when my first essay collection, *Bachelorhood*, came out, booksellers had trouble figuring out where to stock it. Autobiography? Self-help? Short stories? I felt like saying, "Hey, this category has been around for a long time; what's the big deal?" Yet, realistically, they were right: what had once been a thriving popular tradition had ceased being so. Readers who enjoyed the book often told me so with some surprise, because they hadn't thought they would like "essays." For them, the word conjured up those dreaded weekly compositions they were forced to write on the gasoline tax or the draft.

Essays are usually taught all wrong: they are harnessed to rhetoric and composition, in a two-birds-with-one-stone approach designed to sharpen freshman students' skills at argumentation. While it is true that historically the essay is related to rhetoric, it in fact seeks to persuade more by the delights of literary style than anything else. Elizabeth Hardwick, one of our best essayists, makes this point tellingly when she says: "The mastery of expository prose, the rhythm of sentences, the pacing, the sudden flash of unexpected vocabulary, redeem polemic. . . . The essay . . . is a great meadow of style and personal manner, freed

351

from the need for defense except that provided by an individual intelligence and sparkle. We consent to watch a mind at work, without agreement often, but only for pleasure."

Equally questionable in teaching essays is the anthology approach, which assigns an essay apiece by a dozen writers according to our latest notions of a demographically representative and content-relevant sampling. It would be more instructive to read six pieces each by two writers, since the essay (particularly the familiar essay) is so rich a vehicle for displaying personality in all its willfully changing aspects.

Essays go back at least to classical Greece and Rome, but it was Michel de Montaigne, generally considered the "father of the essay," who first matched the word to the form around 1580. Reading this contemporary of Shakespeare (thought to have influenced the Bard himself), we are reminded of the original, pristine meaning of the word, from the French verb *essayer*: to attempt, to try, to leap experimentally into the unknown. Montaigne understood that, in an essay, the track of a person's thoughts struggling to achieve some understanding of a problem *is* the plot. The essayist must be willing to contradict himself (for which reason an essay is not a legal brief), to digress, even to risk ending up in a terrain very different from the one he embarked on. Particularly in Montaigne's magnificent late essays, free-falls that sometimes go on for a hundred pages or more, it is possible for the reader to lose all contact with the ostensible subject, bearings, top, bottom, until there is nothing to do but surrender to this companionable voice, thinking alone in the dark. Eventually, one begins to share Montaigne's confidence that "all subjects are linked to one another," which makes any topic, however small or far from the center, equally fertile.

It was Montaigne's peculiar project, which he claimed rightly or wrongly was original, to write about the one subject he knew best: himself. As with all succeeding literary self-portraits—or all succeeding stream-of-consciousness, for that matter—success depended on having an interesting consciousness, and Montaigne was blessed with an undulatingly supple, learned, skeptical, deep, sane, and candid one. In point of fact, he frequently strayed to worldly subjects, giving his opinion on everything from cannibals to coaches, but we do learn a large number of intimate and odd details about the man, down to his bowels and kidney stones. "Sometimes there comes to me a feeling that I should not betray the story of my life," he writes. On the other hand: "No pleasure has any meaning for me without communication."

A modern reader may come away thinking that the old fox still kept a good deal of himself to himself. This is partly because we have upped the ante on autobiographical revelation, but also because Montaigne was writing essays, not confessional memoirs, and in an essay it is as permissible, as honest, to chase down a reflection to its source as to admit some past shame. In any case, having decided that "the most barbarous of our maladies is to despise our being," Montaigne did succeed, via the protopsychoanalytic method of the *Essais*, in making friends with his mind.

Having taken the essay form to its very limits at the outset, Montaigne's dauntingly generous example was followed by an inevitable specialization, which included the un-Montaignean split between formal and informal essays. The formal essay derived from Francis Bacon; it is said to be "dogmatic, impersonal, systematic, and expository," written in a "stately" language, while the informal essay is "personal, intimate, relaxed, conversational, and frequently humorous" (*New Columbia Encyclopedia*). Never mind that most of the great essayists were adept at both modes, including Bacon (see, for example, his wonderful "Of Friendship"); it remains a helpful distinction.

Informal, familiar essays tend to seize on the parade and minutiae of daily life: vanities, fashions, oddballs, seasonal rituals, love and disappointment, the pleasures of solitude, reading, going to plays, walking in the street. It is a very urban form, enjoying a spectacular vogue in eighteenth- and early nineteenth-century London, when it enlisted the talents of such stylists as Swift, Dr. Johnson, Addison and Steele, Charles Lamb, William Hazlitt, and a visiting American, Washington Irving. The familiar essay was given a boost by the phenomenal growth of newspapers and magazines, all of which needed smart copy (such as that found in the *Spectator*) to help instruct their largely middle-class, *parvenu* readership on the manners of the class to which it aspired.

Although most of the *feuilletonistes* of this period were cynical hacks, the journalistic situation was still fluid enough to allow original thinkers a platform. The British tolerance for eccentricity seemed to encourage commentators to develop idiosyncratic voices. No one was as cantankerously marginal in his way, or as willing to write against the grain of community feeling, as William Hazlitt. His energetic prose style registered a temperament that passionately, moodily swung between sympathy and scorn. Anyone capable of writing so bracingly frank an essay as "The Pleasures of Hating" could not—as W.C. Fields would say—be all bad. At the same time, Hazlitt's enthusiasms could transform the humblest topic, such as going on a country walk or seeing a prizefight, into a description of visionary wholeness.

What many of the best essayists have had—what Hazlitt had in abundance—was quick access to their blood reactions, so that the merest flash of a prejudice or opinion might be dragged into the open and defended. Hazlitt's readiness to entertain opinions, coupled with his openness to new impressions, made him a fine critic of painting and the theater, but in his contrariness he ended by antagonizing all of his friends, even the benign, forgiving Charles Lamb. Not that Lamb did not have *his* contrary side. He, too, was singled out for a "perverse habit of contradiction," which helped give his "Elia" essays, among the quirkiest and most charming in the English language, their peculiar bite.

How I envy readers of *London* magazine, who might have picked up an issue in 1820 and encountered a new, high-spirited essay by Hazlitt, Lamb, or both! After their deaths, the familiar essay continued to attract brilliant practitioners such as Stevenson, DeQuincey, and Emerson. But subsequently, a little of the vitality seeped out of it. "Though we are mighty fine fellows nowadays, we cannot write like Hazlitt," Stevenson confessed. And by the turn of the century, it seemed rather played out and toothless.

The modernist aesthetic was also not particularly kind to this type of writing, relegating it to a genteel, antiquated nook, *belles lettres*—a phrase increasingly spoken with a sneer, as though implying a sauce without the meat. If "meat" is taken to mean the atrocities of life, it is true that the familiar essay has something obstinately non-apocalyptic about it. The very act of composing such an essay seems to implicate the writer in humanist-individualist assumptions that have come to appear suspect under the modernist critique.

Still, it would be unfair to pin the rap on modernism, which Lord knows gets blamed for everything else. One might as well "blame" the decline of the conversational style of writing. Familiar essays were fundamentally, even self-consciously, conversational: it is no surprise that Swift wrote one of his best short pieces on "Hints Toward an Essay on Conversation"; that Montaigne tackled "Of the Art of Discussion"; that Addison and Steele extensively analyzed true and false wit; that Hazlitt titled his books *Table Talk*, *Plain Speaker*, and *The Round Table*, or that Oliver Wendell Holmes actually cast his familiar essays in the form of mealtime dialogues. Why would a book like Holmes's *The Autocrat of the Breakfast Table*, a celebration of good talk that was so popular in its time, be so unlikely today? I cannot go along with those who say "The art of conversation has died, television killed it," since conversation grows and changes as inevitably as language. No, what has departed is not conversation but conversation-flavored writing, which implies a speaking relationship between writer and reader. How many readers today would sit still for a direct address by the author? To be called "gentle reader" or "*hypocrite lecteur*," to have one's arm pinched while dozing off, to be called to attention, flattered, kidded like a real person instead of a privileged fly on the wall—wouldn't most readers today find such devices archaic, intrusive, even impudent? Oh, you wouldn't? Good, we can go back to the old style, which I much prefer.

Maybe what has collapsed is the very fiction of "the educated reader," whom the old essayists seemed to be addressing in their conversational remarks. From Montaigne onward, essayists until this century have invoked a shared literary culture: the Greek and Latin authors and the best of their national poetry. The whole modern essay tradition sprang from quotation. Montaigne's *Essais* and Burton's *Anatomy of Melancholy* were essentially outgrowths of the "commonplace book," a personal journal in which quotable passages, literary excerpts, and comments were written. Though the early essayists' habit of quotation may seem excessive to a modern taste, it was this display of learning that linked them to their educated reading public and ultimately gave them the authority to speak so personally about themselves. Such a universal literary culture no longer exists; we have only popular culture to fall back on. While it is true that the old high culture was never really "universal"—excluding as it did a good deal of humanity—it is also true that without it, personal discourse has become more hard-pressed. What many modern essayists have tried to do is to replace that shared literary culture with more and more personal experience. It is a brave effort and an intriguing supposition, this notion that individual experience alone can constitute the universal text that all may dip into with enlightenment. But there are pitfalls: on the one hand, it may lead to cannibalizing oneself and one's privacy; on the other hand, much more common (and to my mind, worse) is the assertion of an earnestly honest or "vulnerable" manner without really candid chunks of experience to back it up.

As for popular culture, the essayist's chronic invocation of its latest bandwagon fads, however satirically framed, comes off frequently as a pandering to the audience's short attention span—a kind of literary ambulance chasing. Take the "life-style" pages in today's periodicals, which carry commentaries that are a distant nephew of the familiar essay: there is something so depressing about this desperate mining of things in the air, such a fevered search for a generational *Zeitgeist*, such an unctuously smarmy tone of "we," which assumes that everyone shares the same consumerist-boutique sensibility, that one longs for a Hazlittean shadow of misanthropic mistrust to fall between reader and writer. One longs for any evidence of a distinct human voice—anything but this ubiquitous Everyman/woman pizzazzy drone, listing tips for how to get the most from your dry cleaner's, take care of your butcher block, or bounce back from an unhappy love affair.

The familiar essay has naturally suffered from its parasitic economic dependency on magazines and newspapers. The streamlined telegraphic syntax and homogenized-perky prose that contemporary periodicals have evolved make it all the more difficult for thoughtful, thorny voices to be tolerated within the house style. The average reader of periodicals becomes conditioned to digest pure information, up-to-date, with its ideological viewpoint disguised as objectivity, and is thus ill-equipped to follow the rambling, cat-and-mouse game of perverse contrariety played by the great essayists of the past.

In any event, very few American periodicals today support house essayists to the tune of letting them write regularly and at comfortable length on the topics of their choice. The nearest thing we have are talented columnists like Russell Baker, Ellen Goodman, Leon Hale, and Mike Royko, who are in a sense carrying on the Addison and Steele tradition; they are so good at their professional task of hit-and-run wisdom that I only wish they were sometimes given the space to try out their essayistic wings. The problem with the column format is that it becomes too tight and pat: one idea per piece. Fran Lebowitz, for instance, is a very clever writer, and not afraid of adopting a cranky persona; but her one-liners have a cumulative sameness of affect that inhibits a true essayistic movement. What most column writing does not seem to allow for is self-surprise, the sudden deepening or darkening of tone, so that the writer might say, with Lamb: "I do not know how, upon a subject which I began treating half-seriously, I should have fallen upon a recital so eminently painful. . . ."

From time to time I see hopeful panel discussions offered on "The Resurgence of the Essay." Yes, it would be very nice, and it may come about yet. The fact is, however, that very few American writers today are essayists primarily. Many of the essay collections issued each year are essentially random compilations of book reviews, speeches, journalism, and prefaces by authors who have made a name for themselves in other genres. The existence of these collections attests more to the celebrated authors' desires to see all their words between hardcovers than it does to any real devotion to the essay form. A tired air of grudgingly gracious civic duty hovers over many of these performances.

One recent American writer who did devote himself passionately to the essay was E. B. White. No one has written more consistently graceful, thoughtful essays in twentieth-century American language than White; on the other hand, I can't quite forgive his sedating influence on the form. White's Yankee gentleman-farmer persona is a complex balancing act between Whitmanian democratic and patrician values, best suited for the expression of mildness and tenderness with a resolute tug of elegiac depression underneath. Perhaps this is an unfair comparison, but there is not a single E.B. White essay that compares with the gamy, pungent, dangerous Orwell of "Such, Such Were the Joys . . ." or "Shooting an Elephant." When White does speak out on major issues of the day, his man-in-the-street, folksy humility and studiously plain-Joe air ring false, at least to me. And you would never know that the cute little wife he describes listening to baseball games on the radio was the powerful *New Yorker* editor Katharine White. The suppression or muting of ego as something ungentlemanly has left its mark on *The New Yorker* since, with the result that this magazine, which rightly prides itself on its freedom to publish extended prose, has not been a particularly supportive milieu for the gravelly voice of the personal essayist. The preferred model seems to be the scrupulously fair, sporting, impersonal, fact-gathering style of a John McPhee, which reminds me of nothing so much as a colony of industrious termites capable of patiently reducing any subject matter to a sawdust of detail.

The personal, familiar essay lives on in America today in an interestingly fragmented proliferation of specialized subgenres. The form is very much with us, particularly if you count the many popular nonfiction books that are in fact nothing but groups of personal essays strung together, and whose compelling subject matter makes the reading public overlook its ordinary indifference to this type of writing. Personal essays have also appeared for years under the protective umbrella of New Journalism (Joan Didion being the most substantial and quirky practitioner to emerge from that subsidized training ground, now largely defunct); of autobiographical-political meditations (Richard Rodriguez, Adrienne Rich, Vivian Gornick, Marcelle Clements, Wilfrid Sheed, Alice Walker, Nancy Mairs, Norman Mailer); nature and ecological-regional writing (Wendell Berry, Noel Perrin, John Graves, Edward Hoagland, Gretel Ehrlich, Edward Abbey, Carol Bly, Barry Lopez, Annie Dillard); literary criticism (Susan Sontag, Elizabeth Hardwick, Seymour Krim, Cynthia Ozick, Leslie Fiedler, Joyce Carol Oates); travel writing and mores (Mary McCarthy, V. S. Naipaul, Joseph Epstein, Eleanor Clark, Paul Theroux); humorous pieces (Max Apple, Roy Blount, Jr., Calvin Trillin); food (M. F. K. Fisher). I include this random and unfairly incomplete list merely to indicate the diversity and persistence of the form in American letters to-day. Against all odds, it continues to attract newcomers.

In Europe, the essay stayed alive largely by taking a turn toward the speculative and philosophical, as practiced by writers like Walter Benjamin, Theodor Adorno, Simone Weil, E. M. Cioran, Albert Camus, Roland Barthes, Czeslaw Milosz, and Nicola Chiaromonte. All, in a sense, are offspring of the epigrammatic style of Nietzsche. This fragmented, aphoristic, critical type of essay-writing became used as a subversive tool of skeptical probing, a critique of ideology in a time when large, synthesizing theories and systems of philosophy are no longer trusted. Adorno saw the essay, in fact, as a valuable countermethod: "The essay does not strive for closed, deductive or inductive construction. It revolts above all against the doctrine—deeply rooted since Plato—that the changing and ephemeral is unworthy of philosophy; against that ancient injustice toward the transitory, by which it is once more anathematized, conceptually. The essay shies away from the violence of dogma. . . . The essay gently defies the ideals of [Descartes'] *clara et distincta perceptio* and of absolute certainty. . . . Discontinuity is essential to the essay . . . as characteristic of the form's groping intention. . . . The slightly yielding quality of the essayist's thought forces him to greater intensity than discursive thought can offer; for the essay, unlike discursive thought, does not proceed blindly, automatically, but at every moment it must reflect on itself. . . . Therefore the law of the innermost form of the essay is heresy. By transgressing the orthodoxy of thought, something becomes visible in the object which it is orthodoxy's secret purpose to keep invisible."

This continental tradition of the self-reflexive, aphoristically subversive essay is only now beginning to have an influence on contemporary American writers. One saw it first, curiously, cropping up in ironic experimental fiction—in Renata Adler, William Gass, Donald Barthelme, John Barth. Their fictive discourse, like Kundera's, often resembles a broken essay, a personal/philosophical essay intermixed with narrative elements. The tendency of many postmodernist storytellers to parody the pedantry of the essay voice speaks both to their intellectual reliance on it and to their uneasiness about adopting the patriarchal stance of the Knower. That difficulty with assumption of authority is one reason why the essay remains "broken" for the time being.

In a penetrating discussion of the essay form, Georg Lukács put it this way: "The essay is a judgment, but the essential, the value-determining thing about it is not the verdict (as is the case with the system), but the process of judging." Uncomfortable words for an age when "judgmental" is a pejorative term. The familiar essayists of the past may have been nonspecialists—indeed, this was part of their attraction—but they knew how to speak with a generalist's easy authority. That is precisely what contemporary essayists have a hard time doing: in our technical age we are too aware of the advantage specialists hold over us. (This may explain the current confidence the public has in the physician-scientist school of essayists like Lewis Thomas, Richard Selzer, Stephen Jay Gould, F. Gonzalez-Crussi, Oliver Sacks: their meditations are embedded in a body of technical information, so that readers are reassured they are "learning" something, not just wasting their time on *belles lettres*.) The last of the old-fashioned generalists, men of letters who seemed able to write comfortably, knowledgeably, opinionatedly on everything under the sun, were Edmund Wilson and Paul Goodman; we may not soon see their like again.

In *The Last Intellectuals*, Russell Jacoby has pointed out the reticence of writers of the so-called generation of the sixties—my generation—to play the role of the public intellectual, as did Lionel Trilling, Harold Rosenberg, C. Wright Mills, Irving Howe, Alfred Kazin, Daniel Bell, Dwight Macdonald, Lionel Abel, etc., who judged cultural and political matters for a large general readership, often diving into the melee with both arms swinging. While Jacoby blames academia for absorbing the energies of my contemporaries, and while others have cited the drying up of print outlets for formal polemical essays, my own feeling is that it is not such a terrible thing to want to be excused from the job of pontificating to the public. Ours was not so much a failure to become our elders as it was a conscious swerving to a different path. The Vietnam War, the central experience of my generation, had a great deal to do with that deflection. As a veteran of the sixties, fooled many times about world politics because I had no firsthand knowledge of circumstances thousands of miles away (the most shameful example that comes to mind was defending, at first, the Khmer Rouge regime in Cambodia), I have grown skeptical of taking righteous public positions based on nothing but simpatico media reports and party feeling. As for matters that I've definitely made up my mind about, it would embarrass me, frankly, to pen an opinion piece deploring the clearly deplorable, like apartheid or invading Central America, without being able to add any new insights to the discussion. One does not want to be reduced to scolding, or to abstract progressive platitudes, well founded as these may be. It isn't that my generation doesn't think politics are important, but our earlier experiences in that storm may have made us a little hesitant about mouthing off in print. We—or I should say I—have not yet been able to develop the proper voice to deal with these large social and political issues, which will at the same time remain true to personal experience and hard-earned doubt.

All this is a way of saying that the present moment offers a remarkable opportunity for emerging essayists who can somehow locate the moral authority, within or outside themselves, to speak to these issues in the grand manner. But there is also room, as ever, for the informal essayist to wrestle with intellectual confusion, to offer feelings, to set down ideas in a particularly direct and exposed format—more so than in fiction, say, where the author's opinions can always be disguised as belonging to characters. The increasing willingness of contemporary writers to try the form, if not necessarily commit themselves to it, augurs well for the survival of the personal essay. And if we do offend, we can always fall back on Papa Montaigne's *"Que sçay-je?"*: What do I know?

Toward a Definition of Creative Nonfiction

Bret Lott

The Reverend Francis Kilvert, an English curate in the Welsh Border region, kept a journal of his life—where he went, what he did, what he dreamt, who he knew, and what he thought—from 1870 to 1879. In the journal he wrote, "Why do I keep this voluminous journal! I can hardly tell. Partly because life appears to me such a curious and wonderful thing that it almost seems a pity that even such a humble and uneventful life as mine should pass altogether away without some record such as this." *Kilvert's Diary*, published in 1941 and reprinted in 1960, serves as a beautiful, moving, and genuine glimpse into country life of that time nonetheless. All well and good, but how does it help define what creative nonfiction is?

That passage serves, I hold, to illuminate as best as any passage from any piece of literature I can find the longing each of us carries, or ought to carry, in our hearts as human beings first, and as writers second. Creative nonfiction is, in one form or another, for better and worse, in triumph and failure, the attempt to keep from passing altogether away the lives we have lived.

And though that may sound like a definitive pronouncement on what creative nonfiction is, I mean what I say in giving this essay the title it has: *Toward* a Definition of Creative Nonfiction. We aren't going to arrive anywhere here. We can no more understand what creative nonfiction is by trying to define it than we can learn how to ride a bike by looking at a bicycle tire, a set of handlebars, the bicycle chain itself. Sure, we'll have something of an idea, maybe a glimpse into the importance of finding your balance when we look at how narrow those tires are. But until we get on that thing and try to steer it with this weirdly twisted metal tube and actually try to synchronize pushing down on the pedals and pushing forward at the same time, we won't have a clue.

Any definition of true worth to you as a writer will and must come to you experientially. What creative nonfiction is will reveal itself to you only at the back end of things, once you have written it. Kilvert wrote his journal in the midst of his life, looking back at what had happened that day, trying to piece together the meaning of his life from the shards of it, however exquisitely beautiful or sharply painful they were. It was the piecing together of it that mattered, and that matters to us here, today.

And because we are human beings, as such we are pattern makers, a species desirous of order, no matter how much we as "artists" may masquerade otherwise. Yet looking back at our lives to find that order—and here is the sticky part— must *not* be an effort to reorder our lives as we want them to be seen; rather, we are after, in creative nonfiction, an understanding of what it is that has happened, and in that way to see order, however chaotic it may be.

Frank O'Connor, arguably the most important and influential short story writer of this century, wrote in a letter to a friend, " . . . there are occasions when we all feel guilt and remorse; we all want to turn back time. But even if we were able, things would go in precisely the same way, because the mistakes we make are not in our judgments but in our natures. It is only when we do violence to our natures that we are justified in our regrets . . . We are what we are, and within our limitations we have made our own efforts. They seem puny in the light of eternity, but they didn't at the time, and they weren't."

It is in creative nonfiction we try to divine from what we have done, who we have known, what we have dreamt and how we have failed, an order to our lives. "The test of a first-rate intelligence," F. Scott Fitzgerald wrote in his landmark essay "The Crack-Up," "is the ability to hold two opposed ideas in the mind at the same time, and still retain the ability to function." The two opposed ideas of creative nonfiction are finding order in chaos without reforming chaos into order; retaining the ability to function is the act of writing all this down for someone else to understand.

So let's begin with just that much: a desire not to let slip altogether away our lives as we have known them, and to put an order—again, for better and worse— to our days.

Creative nonfiction can take any form, from the letter to the list, from the biography to the memoir, from the journal to the obituary. When I say we are trying to find order in what has happened, I do *not* mean creative nonfiction is simply writing about what happened to me. Rather, it is writing about oneself *in relation to* the subject at hand. A book review is creative nonfiction in that it is a written record of the reviewer *in relation to* the book in question; John Krakauer's fantastic book *Into the Wild* is a biography of an idealistic young man, Chris McCandless, who upon graduation from college disappeared into the wild, his decomposed body found four months later in an abandoned bus in the Alaskan wilderness. The biography becomes creative nonfiction as the author increasingly identifies himself with the young man, increasingly recognizing in the stupidity of the boy's folly his own reckless self—Krakauer sees himself *in relation to* the subject at hand: the death of Chris McCandless. This essay itself is a form of creative nonfiction in that it is my attempt at defining an abstract through the smallest of apertures: my own experience *in relation to* creative nonfiction. So creative nonfiction is not solely, What happened to me today, and why is it important?

Creative nonfiction can be and often is a euphemism for the personal essay, and my earlier assertion that creative nonfiction's being understood only through its being written is borne out rather handily in the meaning of the word *essay* itself.

The French word *essai* means to attempt something, to give something a trial run, to test. Michel de Montaigne, considered the writer who identified if not invented the form, was the first to use the word *essai* to describe his writings, the first collection of which was entitled strangely enough *Essais,* and which was written between 1572 and 1574. This notion of the attempt, of testing one's words lined up in an order one deems close enough to reveal a personal understanding so that all may have that same understanding is, and will always be, only an attempt. The essay as trial run is inherent to any definition of creative nonfiction; you will only come to know this form by running your own tests.

Montaigne, a landowner and lawyer from a nominally wealthy family in the Perigord region of France, wrote out of his own interests, but wrote convinced that it was his own interest as a human being in a matter or topic at hand that made his attempts universal: "Each man bears the entire form of man's estate," he wrote, and therefore, he reasoned, what he was attempting to render in words might make his attempts of interest to all. Philip Lopate, in his indispensable anthology *The Art of the Personal Essay,* writes, "What Montaigne tells us about himself is peculiarly, charmingly specific and daily: he is on the short side, has a loud, abrasive voice, suffers from painful kidney stones, scratches his ears a lot (the insides itch), loves sauces, is not sure radishes agree with him, does his best thinking on horseback, prefers glass to metal cups, moves his bowels regularly in the morning, and so on. It is as if the self were a new continent, and Montaigne its first explorer."

The self as continent, and you its first explorer: another definition of creative nonfiction. For self, however at the center of what you are writing or however tangential, must inform the heart of the tale you are telling. It is indeed *self* that is the *creative* element of creative nonfiction. Without you and who you are, a piece of writing that tells what happened is simply nonfiction: a police report. But when I begin to incorporate the sad and glorious fact that the way I see it shapes and forms what it is to be seen, I end up with creative nonfiction.

As a kind of sidebar, I'd like to interject here the fact that one doesn't have to have had a bizarre life before that life becomes worthy of writing about. Contrary to popular belief, that belief borne out by even the most cursory look at the lineup of victim-authors on afternoon and morning TV talk shows and evening newsmagazines, one's life needn't have been wracked by incest or murder or poorly executed plastic surgery to be worthy of examination. Which is, of course, not to say that those lives are not worth writing about. They most certainly are. But E. B. White's words from the introduction to his *Letters of E. B. White* speak as eloquently as I have seen to this matter of whether or not one's life has been miserable enough to record: "If an unhappy childhood is indispensable for a writer, I am ill-equipped: I missed out on all that and was neither deprived nor unloved. It would be inaccurate, however, to say that my childhood was untroubled. The normal fears and worries of every child were in me developed to a high degree; every day was an awesome prospect. I was uneasy about practically everything: the uncertainty of the future, the dark of the attic, the panoply and discipline of school, the transitoriness of life, the mystery of the church and of God, the frailty of the body, the sadness of afternoon, the shadow of sex, the distant challenge of love and marriage, the far-off problem of a livelihood."

These normal fears, if we have been paying the least bit of attention to our lives, inform us all; and if E. B. White, who is the greatest American essayist of this century, found in that uneasiness the material for a lifetime, we too have all we need.

But *how* do we look at ourselves in order best to inform our readers that who we are matters, and is worthy of their attention? In the Tyndale commentary on the Book of Proverbs, Derek Kidner writes that the sayings and aphorisms of King Solomon, and to a lesser degree Lemuel and Agur, constitute "not a portrait album of a book of manners: [the Book of Proverbs] offers a key to life. The samples of behavior which it holds up to view are all assessed by one criterion, which could be summed up in the question, 'Is this wisdom, or is this folly?'" I believe that this same criterion is one that helps define creative nonfiction as well. In examining the self as continent, in seeing the way self shades and informs the meaning of what has happened, the writer must be inquiring of himself, Is this wisdom, or is this folly? The self as inquisitor of self is integral to an examination of one's life; it calls for a kind of ruthlessness about seeing oneself in relation to others: Why did I do that? What was I thinking? Who was I trying to kid? What did I hope to achieve? These questions must be asked, and asked with all the candor and courage and objectivity one can muster, though objectivity is an abstract to be hoped for, and not to be achieved; it is, after all, *you* who is writing about you.

Which brings me to another major point on our way toward a definition: creative nonfiction cannot at any time be self-serving. There is no room here for grandstanding of oneself. To my way of thinking—and this is me speaking as a follower of Christ, and therefore one well aware of my transgressions, my iniquities, my falling short of the glory of God—ninety-nine times out of a hundred the answer to the question, Is this wisdom, or is this folly? is, Folly. Hands down.

Phillip Lopate writes, "The enemy of the personal essay is self-righteousness, not just because it is tiresome and ugly in itself, but because it slows down the dialectic of self-questioning . . . The essayist is someone who lives with the guilty knowledge that he is 'prejudiced' (Mencken called his essay collections *Prejudices*) and has a strong predisposition for or against certain everyday phenomena. It then becomes his business to attend to these inner signals, these stomach growls, these seemingly indefensible intuitions, and try to analyze what lies underneath them, the better to judge them."

So, our definition thus far: a desire not to let slip altogether away our lives as we have known them; to put an order, for better and worse, to our days; this is only a test; the self as continent, you its first explorer; is this wisdom, or is this folly?; no self-righteousness.

This last point, however, seems at odds with the entire notion of the personal essay, all this business about me: isn't talk about myself in relation to others by definition egotistical? Wasn't I taught in seventh grade never to include 'I' in an essay? Who cares about what I think in the first place?

Thoreau, in answer to this assertion we have had pounded into our heads most of our lives, wrote in the opening of *Walden*, "In most books the I, or first person, is omitted; in this it will be retained; that, in respect to egotism, is the main difference. We commonly do not remember that it is, after all, always the first person that is speaking." And if one is honestly seeking to understand, circling with a cold eye one's relation to events, places, people—whatever the subject of the essay—then that search's chances of being construed as egotistical will be dismissed. Seventeenth-century English writer Alexander Smith wrote, "The speaking about one self is not necessarily offensive. A modest, truthful man speaks better about himself than about anything else, and on that subject his speech is likely to be most profitable to his hearers . . . If he be without taint of boastfulness, of self-sufficiency, of hungry vanity, the world will not press the charge home."

Another element of any definition of creative nonfiction must include the form's circling bent, its way of looking again and again at itself from all angles in order to see itself most fully. The result is literary triangulation, a finding of the subject in a three-dimensional grid through digression, full-frontal assault, guerrilla tactics and humble servitude, all in an effort, simply, to see. The creative nonfiction form attempts in whatever way it can to grab hold hard and sure its subject in any manner possible. Eudora Welty writes in *One Writer's Beginnings*, "In writing, as in life, the connections of all sorts of relationships and kinds lie in wait of discovery, and give out their signals to the Geiger counter of the charged imagination, once it is drawn into the right field . . . What I do make my stories out of is the whole fund of my feelings, my responses to the real experiences of my own life, to the relationships that formed and changed it, that I have given most of myself to, and so learned my way toward a dramatic counterpart." The dramatic counterpart of which she here writes is, of course, her stories—fiction—but I maintain that this "whole fund" of feelings, the complete range of our responses to our own real experiences, must inform creative nonfiction as well. Only when we use our "whole fund" can we circle our subjects in the most complete way, wringing from our stores of knowledge and wisdom and the attendant recognition of how little we have of both—*the essence of who we are*—then coupling those recognitions with what in fact we do not know altogether, will we find what we have come looking for: ourselves and, by grace and by luck, the larger world perhaps we hadn't seen before.

Lopate writes, "The personal essay is the reverse of that set of Chinese boxes that you keep opening, only to find a smaller one within. Here you start with the small—the package of flaws and limits—and suddenly find a slightly larger container, insulated by the essay's successful articulation and the writer's self-knowledge."

I agree with Lopate in how the essay reveals larger and larger selves in itself, but rather than the Chinese box, the image that comes to my mind is that of the Russian nesting dolls, one person inside another inside another. But instead of finding smaller selves inside the self, the opposite occurs, as with Lopate's boxes: we find nested inside that smallest of selves a larger self, and a larger inside that, until we come to the whole of humanity within our own hearts.

Now back to our definition: a desire not to let slip altogether away our life as we have known it; to put an order, for better and worse, to our days; this is only a test; the self as continent, you its first explorer; is this wisdom, or is this folly?; no self-righteousness, though it is always the first person talking; circle the subject to see it most whole.

I'm saving perhaps the most conundrum-like element for nearly last. What role, we have to ask once all these prior elements are taken into account, does *truth* have here? If you look at the pieces of our definition thus far, each one contains within it the angle of perception: the fact that it is only me who is seeing. That is, I don't want to let slip away my life as I have seen it, but who is to say I am telling the truth? In my attempt to put order to my days, am I deluding myself, inflicting an order that was and is now nowhere to be seen? If this is only a test, who is to say I pass? If I am the explorer of my self as continent, what does my discovery matter—didn't Leif Erikson set up shop in North America 500 years before Columbus discovered the place? Isn't one man's wisdom another man's folly? How do I know if I'm not being self-righteous unless there's somebody outside myself to cut me down to size? In circling my subject, isn't it me who determines my course, my longitude and latitude, and therefore am I, by definition, being the most subjective of anyone on planet earth when it comes to my subject?

The answer to each and every one of these questions is: continue to question. Only through rigorous and ruthless questioning of the self can we hope to arrive at any kind of truth.

If you wish to understand creative nonfiction, hope to find a definition, then it is up to you to embrace the fact that, as Montaigne saw, "Each man bears the entire form of man's estate." Inherent to that form are the eccentricities, egotism, foolishness, and fraud of all mankind; inherent as well are the wisdom and self-recognition, the worth and value and merit available to mankind, once enough scouring of what we know and do not know has taken place. V. S. Pritchett, in his memoir *Midnight Oil*, wrote, "The true autobiography of this egotist is exposed in all its intimate foliage in his work. But there is a period when a writer has not yet become one, or, just having become one, is struggling to form his talent, and it is from this period that I have selected most of the scenes and people in this book. It *is* a selection, and it is neither a confession nor a volume of literary reminiscences, but as far as I am able I have put in my 'truth.'"

Pritchett puts the word *truth* in quotation marks; he predicates it with the possessive pronoun *my*. We must recognize that this is the deepest truth we can hope to attain on our own: quotation marks, calling it our own. Only when we have scoured as clean as possible by self-inquiry, even interrogation, what we *perceive*, can we approach calling it *truth*; and even then that crutch of the quotation marks and the assignation of who it belongs to—me—must be acknowledged.

Finally, we have to try and further illuminate *why* we write creative nonfiction. Certainly that first element—a desire not to let slip altogether away our lives as we have known them—is a beginning point, but simply trying to capture our lives before they slip away seems more *reactive* than *proactive*. Writing is, I believe, both, and so any definition must encompass both the reactive and the proactive.

Karen Blixen, AKA Isak Dinesen, in a dinner meeting speech she gave in 1959 at the National Institute of Arts and Letters in New York, addressed the subject, "On Mottoes of My Life." In it she said, "The family of Finch Hatton, of England, have on their crest the device *Je responderay*, 'I will answer.' . . . I liked it so much I asked Denys . . . if I might have it for my own. He generously made me a present of it and even had a seal cut for me, with the words carved on it. The device was meaningful and dear to me for many reasons, two in particular. The first . . . was its high evaluation of the idea of the answer in itself. For an answer is a rarer thing than is generally imagined. There are many highly intelligent people who have no answer at all in them. . . . Secondly, I liked the Finch Hatton device for its ethical content. I will answer *for* what I say or do; I will answer *to* the impression I make. I will be responsible."

This is the proactive element of creative nonfiction, and the final element of my *essai* to define creative writing: *our responsibility as human beings to answer for and to our lives.* It is a responsibility that must encompass all the elements laid out in all this talk about definitions; it is a responsibility that must be woven through the recognition of the fleeting nature of this span of days we have been given, woven through our attempt to see order in chaos, through our understanding that we are only attempting this test and through our being the first explorers of the continent of ourselves. This responsibility to answer for and to ourselves must be woven through the interrogation of self as to whether this is folly or wisdom, through the pledge to humility and to avoiding the abyss of self-righteousness, through the recognition that it is always and only me—the first person—talking, and through the relentless circling of the subject to see it most completely. And this responsibility to answer for and to ourselves must be woven through our recognition that the only truth I can hope to approach will finally and always and only be *my truth.*

But if we are rigorous enough, fearless enough, and humble enough to attempt this responsibility, this way of seeing—for creative nonfiction, like fiction, like poetry, is simply and complexly a way of seeing—the rewards we will reap will be great: we will *understand.* To understand, and nothing more, and that is everything.

The Other Creative Writing

Michael Pearson

Creative writing is the art of storytelling, an art as elemental as fire and the circle of civilization. Poetry goes back to our farthest dreams of the past, joining language to our very heartbeat. Writing fiction, or telling lies to find the truth, is as old as Scheherazade and Odysseus, and playwriting is an ancient and respected activity. Our most sacrosanct anthologies include poetry, fiction, and drama, but rarely, and only very recently, do any include nonfiction as literature. If we see a mention of Edward Gibbon or James Boswell, it is most often as historian and biographer, not as literary artists. The Norton anthologies appropriately include modern fiction writers like John Cheever, Joyce Carol Oates, and Ralph Ellison, but where are E. B. White, John Hersey, or Joseph Mitchell? Where are we to place Joseph Mitchell's *The Bottom of the Harbor*, Truman Capote's *In Cold Blood*, Tom Wolfe's *The Electric Kool-Aid Acid Test*, John McPhee's *Coming into the Country*, Joan Didion's *Slouching Toward Bethlehem*, Edward Abbey's *Desert Solitaire*, or Frank McCourt's recent bestseller *Angela's Ashes*? Where do we include *this* literature made not of imagined reality but of verifiable fact, this literature that holds fast to historical truth even as it pursues a truth beyond the facts. Where do we place this "other" creative writing?

The first question to ask might be: does it make a difference if we make our stories out of facts or fictions any more than it matters if a sculptor makes a statue out of marble or clay? One material is more malleable than the other, but either can be used to create a work of art. In the end, everyone who aspires to be a writer makes stories out of the same source—words, the best ones in the best possible order. The essence of language is metaphor, and all metaphor—as Walker Percy said—is a wonderful, illuminating mistake. It's the sort of mistake that lifts the curtain of cliché and dull habit that blinds us, and it permits us to see, to really see ourselves and the world for a moment. That's where language and stories lead us—fiction and nonfiction writers and readers—toward some re-creation of experience, actual or imagined, toward some making of art out of marble or clay. All creative writers work with language, with metaphor, crafting dialogue and description, building character and symbol, using narration and drama. Usually, the progress is crab-like, the writer slowly suggesting, allowing one thing to lead to another, word shaping word until a new world is created. In this respect, all writers—poets, novelists, and nonfiction artists—face the same challenge: how to build something memorable out of something as insubstantial and strangely enduring as language. Nonfiction writers engage in the same activity that all writers are engaged in, attempting to conjure images for the purblind wayfarer, to make stories that by their very nature are ethereal and fundamental, there and not there at the same time.

The best nonfiction bestows a range of pleasures: it offers both information and stories, the specific site and shape of experience and a glimpse of its mysterious soul. In certain circles, actual pleasure in reading is tantamount to an intellectual sin. As David Denby recently wrote, "In some quarters, pleasure in reading has itself become a political error, rather like sex in Orwell's *1984*." Over 30 years ago, Barbara Tuchman objected to the narrowing of the word literature, saying, "I see no reason why the word should always be confined to writers of fiction and poetry while the rest of us are lumped together under the despicable term 'Nonfiction'—as if we were some sort of remainder."

Literature, and that means fiction or nonfiction, is a dreamworld, containing, as Northrop Frye says, both the nightmare and the wish-fulfillment. Similar to dreams, literature has an hallucinatory vividness, a reality that is somehow unreal, what Frye calls a vertical perspective that puts us, alternately, into the darkness and the light. The uniqueness of nonfiction literature is that it also affords a horizontal perspective. It compels our attention outward, toward the Life that it swears to represent accurately. Of course, the obligation to adhere to the known, the reported, the verifiable fact, often limits the depths a piece of nonfiction can discover or the heights it can reach. But, despite the limitations of the form, nonfiction must honor the facts and attempt to get beyond them. Nonfiction writers can use words with the force of poets, they can shape characters syllable by syllable until we feel that we know them better than we know ourselves, they can carve landscapes out of blank space: artistic nonfiction can reach into us as deeply as any literature. And it has the added power of being about actual people and real events.

Literary nonfiction carries a genuine obligation to factual truths. It is a form that has one sacred principle: you can't make it up. Imaginative speculation, based upon the gathered information, is fine as long as the writer tells the reader what he is doing and why. Richard Preston, *The New Yorker* writer, did it fairly and to good effect in *The Hot Zone*; John Demos, the historian, did it in his narrative of early American life *The Unredeemed Captive*. But the nonfiction writer can't just imagine the color of a character's eyes or change the street names to suit the music of the sentence. The dialogue must be accurate, the dates exact, the events real. During the past few years some scholars and writers have put their minds to the task of defining this genre, although there is not yet even consensus on what to call it (creative nonfiction, literary nonfiction, new journalism, personal journalism . . .), and these critics and artists have described many of the characteristics of the form.

Tom Wolfe called it the "new journalism" and with his typical magnification said that it would oust the novel from importance. He felt that it was possible "to write journalism that would . . . read like a novel." It would require, he said, scenic telling, full dialogue, the use of symbolic details, and a point of view that allowed the reader inside characters' minds. Gay Talese talked about the necessity of immersion reporting, of going so deep into the observation of people and scene that the writer attained a semblance of omniscience. The scholar Norman Sims extended the ideas about immersion and accuracy and added to the discussion about the necessary complexity and contradiction that readers should find in such nonfiction narratives. He also focused on the unique voice and the double responsibility of the writer to subject and to truth. Susan Orlean referred to what she called the heart of this kind of nonfiction: a type of writing that chronicles "the dignity of ordinariness," a phrase that reminds me of James Joyce's definition of *epiphany*, "the moment in which the soul of the commonest object . . . seems to us radiant." Although most readers might not see a clear kinship between Joyce and modern writers of nonfiction literature, the relationship exists. Joyce's belief that the artist is charged to find epiphanal moments not among the gods but in the lives of men and women in ordinary, even unpleasant, circumstances could as well be a description of Joseph Mitchell's philosophy in his nonfiction stories about New York.

Classics in the genre like James Agee's *Let Us Now Praise Famous Men* or John Hersey's *Hiroshima* depict the experiences and emotions of common people, not movie stars or politicians or generals. In this respect, as Mark Kramer said, there is something inherently democratic about literary nonfiction. It is "pluralistic, pro-individual, anti-cant, and anti-elite." Such nonfiction achieves creativity not by imagining people or events but by discovering a vision of character or situation, by finding a structure in the facts that will permit the writer to find "truth in the details of real lives." Ultimately, writers of literary nonfiction look to create a story that will endure. "The point," Tracy Kidder once said, "is to write as well as George Eliot in *Middlemarch* and to find a way to do that in nonfiction." The nonfiction writer might be wise to remember Flannery O'Connor's admonition—"to be humble in the face of what-is." Writers, as she suggested, transcend their limitations by staying within them. And probably the surest path to "perdition and melancholy," as Walker Percy reminded us, is to go after the BIG TRUTH. It's always smarter to get all the small details right, and the larger ones will take care of themselves.

Writers of literary nonfiction have been tending to the details for a number of years now. Although many people believe that the genre sprang full grown onto the scene in 1965 with Capote's *In Cold Blood*, the roots of nonfiction literature reach far deeper and were entangled with fiction from the very beginning.

Aphra Behn's 17th-century novella *Oronooko* might be considered a highly stylized work of nonfiction, a work of observation and research. Daniel Defoe's *A Journal of a Plague Year*, which appeared in 1722, is a precise description of the Black Plague from the point of view of a person who experienced it. But the relationship between what is imagined and what is observed or reported is not always clear in either of these books. In 19th-century works by Melville or Twain such as *Typee* or *Roughing It*, the reader is left with the same questions about what is made up and what is verifiably accurate. Writers like Stephen Crane and Ernest Hemingway played with the possibilities of literary nonfiction, but it wasn't until the 1930s that Joseph Mitchell began to write a nonfiction that had the echoes and resonances of literature while at the same time demanding an adherence to the verifiable or observed fact. Mitchell wrote a brand of nonfiction that seemed vital and new. He wrote about the denizens of the Bowery, those who gathered in McSorley's Saloon, the people who spent their days along the wharves and in the fish markets of lower Manhattan. He wrote with great care and patience, a symbolist who looked more to James Joyce than to his fellow journalists for ways to develop his characters and themes. When Mitchell writes about the rats in New York City, their claws rasping on the sidewalks, he is Kafka in nonfiction, and as readers we are haunted by the story, an eerie vision of the facts. There were other writers during the 1930s and '40s who demonstrated the elasticity and power of nonfiction—George Orwell, A. J. Liebling, E.B. White, John Hersey, Lillian Ross—and they opened the doors to the explosion of nonfiction writers in the last 30 years—from Capote's poetic vision of horror to Annie Dillard's clear-eyed view of Tinker Creek. Writers like Bruce Chatwin, Ian Frazier, and William Least Heat-Moon followed paths marked for them by diarists and travel writers in the 16th- and 17th-centuries. Gay Talese and Tracy Kidder must have learned something about immersion reporting from James Boswell's 18th-century account of Samuel Johnson's life. John McPhee could be kin to both Henry David Thoreau and Joseph Mitchell, both artist and reporter.

Most of these writers find a way of making memorable, in stories, the ordinary lives that they encounter. McPhee's description of the inhabitants of New Jersey's Pine Barrens or Didion's depiction of the suburban malaise in the land of golden dreams lingers in our imaginations as all true literature does. Nonfiction literature can appear in many forms: a "comic strip" about the Holocaust by Art Spiegelman or a piece of surrealistic reporting about the Vietnam War by Michael Herr. It can be a memoir by Tobias Wolff or Mary Karr or a satire by Hunter S. Thompson or Terry Southern. It can be seen in the courtroom play and human drama of Jonathan Harr's *A Civil Action*. It can stay with us in the alliterative imagery of Truman Capote's last sentence in *In Cold Blood*: "Then, starting home, he walked toward the trees, and under them, leaving behind him the big sky, the whisper of wind voices in the wind-bent wheat." Or it can reverberate with the power of Joan Didion's opening line to "Slouching Towards Bethlehem"—"The center was not holding"—and her unforgettable chronicling of the drug scene in Haight-Ashbury during the late '60s.

This brings me back to my original question: where do we place this "other" creative writing? For me, the answer is in the work itself: we enjoy it as literature, we place it alongside any other literature, any writing that has found what George Orwell described as a language charged with meaning to the utmost possible degree, whether it is poetry or nonfiction or drama. In his monumental nonfiction narrative about the Civil War, Shelby Foote said that before he began writing about any campaign he had to learn everything he could from all the available sources and then digest it until it was clear in his own mind. Once he had done that he had to try to reproduce it with even more sharpness and clarity than he had seen it before. He described the finished product as "a great wide sea of words with a redoubled necessity for precision." Finally, this may be the best definition of literary nonfiction that we have, a form of writing that Mark Twain might have said sounds like poetry even though it's the petrified truth.

Collage, Montage, Mosaic, Vignette, Episode, Segment

Robert L. Root, Jr.

It's a common problem among student writers, starting too far back in the narrative or trying to encompass too much time or too much activity in a single chronology. A paper about high school begins at the moment the writer entered the building for the first time in ninth grade and moves inexorably toward the moment of graduation, growing more perfunctory year by year; a paper about making the team or the cheerleading squad presents a minute by minute account of decision, preparation, and competition that loses more and more energy the longer it goes on.

But it isn't just a novice writer's problem alone. Any writer runs up against the insidious demands of linear presentation of material whenever he or she selects chronology—from the beginning to the end, from the first step through each individual step to the final step, from the inception through the planning and execution to the result—as the organizing principle of an essay or article. Linear schemes of organization come easily to us. We all tell stories and chronology is the simplest system of organization ("We began by . . ., then we . . ., and finally . . ."); process is the most accessible scheme of exposition ("First you . . ., next you . . ., and you conclude by . . ."); linear movement structures description the most directly ("Her hair was the color . . . her feet spilling out of tattered sandals"; "On the east side of the building . . . in the middle was . . . on the west side we saw"). But linear schemes don't automatically help with issues of compression and focus, particularly in an age of increasingly shorter attention spans and little patience for leisurely development of plot and character and theme.

The more complex the story is, the more interwoven with other subjects, ideas, incidents, experiences, the harder it is to make it all connect in a linear way that doesn't extend the narrative or the development beyond the patience of writer and reader alike. Moreover, the connections and associations that come so readily in the memory and in the imagination often defy simple linearity, easy transition from one subtopic to the next, when the writer has to force them into words on a page.

Mike, now past fifty, has been cleaning his mental attic for the past several years, rummaging through his souvenirs and writing essays about a lifetime playing sports—the high school pitching, the conflicts with coaches, the visits to historic ballparks. Now he begins an essay about how he came to give up his annual summer stint as manager and player for a fastpitch softball team.

He starts an early draft with a brief scene set in the present which serves as the trigger for a flashback that gives him the opportunity to review his long career with the team. "It's a lazy summer evening and I'm driving home from campus," he begins, and then tells how his weariness momentarily vanishes when he notices a game in progress at the ball park where he used to play: "for a moment I want to jump out of the car, climb into my softball uniform, and trot out to my old position in left field." He describes gazing at the field and continuing home. After these two brief paragraphs of introduction, he introduces the past in the third paragraph: "That night while reading my mind wanders, and for a suspended moment it is 1969 again. That summer, I was . . ." From here he relies on the act of composing itself to help him rediscover the subject matter. Chronology decides the order. He traces the arc of his involvement from the moment he decided to join the team, and one memory provokes another until he reaches his last game and the end of the draft.

By then he has covered a lot of ground. His draft surfaces deep-seated feelings about playing ball, about giving it up, about the satisfactions of moving on to new places in his life and expending his energies elsewhere. But it takes a long time to get to the place where these important and powerful feelings get voiced, because so much detail has emerged in his review of the chronology—early days on the team, the change from player to manager, road trips, destinations, the interaction with players, the near-misses for spots in regional and state tournaments, the interests that distracted him from the game, the aging processes that slowed him down. In the associative links of memory every detail makes sense, makes connections, but on the page the slow linear march of the chronology dissipates all the emphatic force of the narrative—there's a reason no one is proposing to cash in on the natural disaster film genre ("Twister," "Volcano") with a movie called "Glacier!" These narrative elements establish not only theme but also tone and voice, and many of them need to stay in the next draft, but he knows that he needs to lift scenes out of this linear history and highlight them as well as give more emphasis to the final summer.

His revision starts almost at the end of the previous draft, placing him on the road to the final tournament. "It's three A.M. Friday Labor Day weekend 1985. I left Sutton's Bay at ten P.M. headed for Houghton, which is about as far as driving to Nashville. I'm wearing my softball uniform and my wife Carole is asleep in the back seat, cotton balls stuffed in each ear while the tape deck blasts out a medley of

Beach Boys and Beatles tunes—my favorite road music." But the present-tense narrative of that summer experience has barely begun before Mike inserts a paragraph break, white space on the page signaling a shift of scene or time, and in the past tense recounts his initial involvement with the softball team years before. A page later he inserts another break and shifts back to the present tense and the immediate circumstance to establish that he and his wife have plane tickets for Paris that conflict with the tournament dates (a point of information barely mentioned in the earlier draft's conclusion) and that they have put off foreign travel in the past to be available for championships that never materialized. The dramatic tension in this conflict makes the reader wonder from the beginning which option they will take in the end. Telling this part of the essay in present tense heightens that tension and establishes a sense of immediacy about the experience, as if the outcome had not been decided long ago.

Throughout the remainder of the essay past tense vignettes of a softball life alternate with present tense scenes from the decisive summer. Paragraph breaks allow Mike to crosscut between the past and the present and to ignore connections and transitions in either chronology. When he has finished his revisions, he has avoided the linear chronology that bogged down his earlier draft and achieved a tight, dense essay with more dramatic and pointed individual segments. The overall effect of the essay is the same he had hoped to achieve in the earlier draft, but it is more focused and consequently more powerful.

The white spaces on the page—the page breaks or paragraph breaks—are part of the composition. They serve as fade outs/fade ins do in films, as visual cues that we have ended one sequence and gone on to another. Often, somewhere in the early part of each segment, a word or phrase serves as a marker indicating the change of time or place, very much as a superimposed title on a movie scene might inform the viewer: "Twelve years later. Northern Michigan," to suggest that a lot has happened since the screen went dark and a new image began to emerge.

In almost any contemporary collection of creative nonfiction, many selections are segmented, sectioned off by white spaces or rows of asterisks or subheadings in italics or boldface. A thematic issue of the travel narrative journal *Grand Tour* has no unsegmented essays. In a recent essay issue of *Ploughshares*, fourteen of the twenty-three essays are segmented by paragraph breaks or, occasionally, some more pronounced method of subdividing. In a similar issue of *American Literary Review*, fifteen out of nineteen essays are segmented, their segments separated by rows of diamonds or white spaces, divided by subheadings, or numbered; only four essays are completely unsegmented.

In some of the *ALR* essays the segmenting in the fifteen is barely noticeable, almost a printer's convention rather than an actual break in the flow of thought or language; in most, however, the segmenting is emphatic, crucial. William Holtz numbers his thirteen segments in "Brother's Keeper: An Elegy" and begins eleven of them with the same sentence, "My brother now is dead," usually as the main clause in sentences with varying subordinate or coordinate elements. The repetitions give the segments the power of incantation or prayer. Lynne Sharon

Schwartz, writing about translating the book *Smoke Over Birkenau*, begins her essay with a series of English words she listed in an Italian edition of the book—the opening line reads: "Strenuous. Grim. Resolute. Blithe. Alluring. Cringe. Recoil. Admonish." Occasional excerpts from the list interrupt the essay from time to time in place of asterisks or numbers or subheadings between segments ("Haggard. Cantankerous. Imploring. Dreary. Plucky. Banter. Superb. Vivacious. Snarling. Prattled.") Frederick Smock's "Anonymous: A Brief Memoir" opens with a section of Gwendolyn Brooks's poem, "Jane Addams," and is divided into segments subtitled by locations in his anonymous subject's home: "The Great-Room," "The Landing," "The Dining Room," "The Grotto," and so on. Paul Gruchow's "Eight Variations on the Idea of Failure" has eight numbered sections with self-contained vignettes of varying length that thematically explore the subject of failure. These are essays that call attention to their segmentation; they announce very early on to the reader that progress through them will not be linear, although it may be sequential, and that the force of the segments will come from their juxtaposition with one another and the effect of their accumulation by the end.

These are not traditional essays, the kind that composition textbooks usually teach you to write, the kind that begin with some sort of thesis statement, then march through a linked, linear series of supporting, illustrative paragraphs to a predictable, forceful conclusion. Textbooks tend to teach either the unattainable and ideal or the undesirable but teachable. The segmented essay has been with us for quite some time and may well be the dominant mode of the contemporary essay, but we are only just beginning to recognize it and try to teach it.

Shaken by her son's death in the crash of his Air Force jet, Carol sets out to retrace the path of his life. She and her husband drive from Michigan across the country to California, and then come back by way of the southeastern United States, all the while trying to connect to the life he led in scattered places. Throughout the trip she keeps a journal of her travels and eventually decides to write an essay about the journey.

As she begins writing, she finds herself hampered by the amount of detail she has accumulated about the trip, about her son's life, about her reactions to each location. So much information seems relevant and interrelated that it is difficult for her to be inclusive and yet get to the end of both the essay and the trip, where the real significance of her pilgrimage comes home to her. It is a trip of several weeks and thousands of miles and, unless she is to make it booklength, which she doesn't want to do, she needs to find another way to come at this mass of strongly felt material.

Eventually she discovers the key to the composing in the materials on which she bases the essay: the narrative of the trip, the reflections in her private journal, the references to her son's life. Alternating among episodes of narration, reflection, and reference, she uses the separate strands of her materials to comment on one another and to justify her breaking off one segment to move to another. The essay begins with a passage of narration and description about the onset of the journey ("We need this trip like the desert needs rain. For months the dining area has looked like a war games planning room with maps everywhere."); it is followed by an excerpt from her journal remarking on how she feels a few days later, set in italics to identify it immediately as separate from the narrative (*"June 7. Badlands. Last night when we walked back to our campsite in true dark, stars in the sky notwithstanding, we became disoriented."*); this is followed by description of another location, further down the road ("In Wyoming, as we drive north toward Sheridan, we watch antelope standing far off . . ."); then another excerpt from the journal; then a section reflecting her son's experiences ("Kirk loved Wyoming. In 1976 his father and I took him and his brother and sister to Yellowstone . . ."), and so on throughout the essay. Paragraph breaks between segments and changes in font make it easy for the reader to follow the shifts and jumpcuts. It becomes a travel montage with "voiceover" commentary and an alternating strand of personal history. The juxtaposition of landscape, biography, and commentary move us more quickly through the essay than full linear chronology could do, and yet the chronology is there, a beginning, a middle, and an end, given an almost cinematic force by the accumulation of a series of concentrated segments.

The recognition of the segmented form, if not the form itself, is so new that we have not yet settled on a name for it. At present it is most often called a "collage" essay, a term coined by Peter Elbow, referring to the technique in visual art of assembling disparate images into an integrated whole which expresses a specific theme (like the "American Dream" collage) through the interrelationships of the parts. Some use the filmmaking term "montage," the editing technique that arranges a series of shots and images into an expressive sequence. Carl Klaus, who has mulled over the terminology and objected to both collage and montage, has suggested "disjunctive" (as opposed to the more unified and "conjunctive" linear form), which he admits may have negative connotations, or "paratactic" (a grammatical term for "segments of discourse" arranged without connections or transitions), which may be too obscure. Rebecca Blevins Faery has described the form as "fragmented" and "polyphonic." At times all these terms seem applicable to some essays and not to others, perhaps because segmented essays tend to invent their own forms, not merely imitate established forms.

Take, for example, "The Ideal Particle and the Great Unconformity" by Reg Saner. In this complex essay, Saner connects two terms from geology which identify two different concepts of scale. The ideal particle is the term for a grain of sand one tenth of a millimeter, "the size most easily airborne in wind, thus the likeliest to begin a surface effect known as saltation," where one grain strikes other grains with enough force to make them capable of becoming airborne (163); the Great Unconformity is a gigantic gap in the geological record, a place where, following the Grand Canyon walls down the deposits of millennia, you encounter a layer so much older than the layer above it that 1,200 million years of deposits must have been erased before the layers you have been following were laid down. The Great Unconformity was created by the erosive power of the ideal particle and the enormity of the span of time in the life of the planet.

But Saner is not simply explaining these two concepts as a geology textbook might readily do in a paragraph or two. Rather, he is attempting to give the reader some sense of the scale involved here as well as what it is like to experience the scale. Thus, while the essay discusses the history of geological studies and major markers for dating the planet, it also has a personal narrative running through it. Saner recounts a hike into the Grand Canyon, alternating speculations and observations about geological theory and evidence with vignettes of encounters with other hikers. In order to understand the subject of the essay as Saner understands it, the reader has to experience it with him, not simply have it explained to him.

> Slowly we accepted the curve of the earth. It dawned on us like a great change of mind, after which, earth's size came easy. Not its age. Evidence was everywhere underfoot, unmistakable. We chose not to see it. (154)

This opening segment is a brief verbal fanfare that sounds the theme of the essay. The segments that follow alternate exposition and argument with narration and description, taking the reader deeper and deeper into both the subject matter and the experience. We dig down through the segments, like layers of sedimentary deposits, the white spaces between segments marking them like layers of geologic time. Perhaps this is a geologic essay, then, or a tectonic essay, where the segments are like plates moving and colliding and rearranging themselves on the crust of the essay.

The ability to arrange and rearrange segments frees writers to generate unique forms. Mark Rudman has created a series of essays he refers to as "mosaics," such as his "Mosaic on Walking." The mosaic metaphor suggests an essay composed of little sections, like mosaic tiles, which create a larger picture by the way they are cumulatively arranged. For example, the opening tiles are these segments separated from one another by the grouting of white space:

> In this season I am often sulky, sullen, restless, withdrawn. I feel transparent, as if inhabited by the weather.
>
> Only while walking am I relieved from distress, only then, released from the burden of self, am I free to think. I wanted to say walking brings relief from tension without sadness and then I think it is not so—these walks bring their own form of *tristesse*. There is discomfort when movement stops.
>
> Though not exceptionally tall (a shade under six feet), I am a rangy, rambly walker. I take up a lot of space! (138)

In "Mosaic on Walking" the sequentiality of the arrangement is difficult to perceive; it might well have been written simply by composing a random number of segments which in some way relate to the theme of walking and then either haphazardly or systematically arranging them in a disjunctive or non-sequential order on the page—the way you might copy a list of sentences about walking in the order you discovered them in *Bartlett's Familiar Quotations*. The mosaic, at least as Rudman uses it, seems lacking in design, capable of being read in any order, virtually devoid of transition or sequence; it uses an accumulation of associative segments to create mood or attitude. Maybe we should use the term "cumulative essays" or "associative essays."

But Nancy Willard, in "The Friendship Tarot," begins with the image of a tarot card arrangement on the page ("I lay out the cards of our friendship"). Each section of the essay which follows is named for a specific tarot card in that arrangement—The Child, The Journey, The Garden, The Book—and opens with a description of the picture on the card ("The card shows a child with chocolate on his face wandering through an art gallery in downtown Poughkeepsie devoted— for two weeks—to illustrations from children's books."). The segments lead us through the sequence of the tarot reading to get at issues of change and growth in a particular friendship. Perhaps it is a "tarot essay" but I don't know if the term applies to all segmented essays or, in all the history of essays, to her essay alone.

It isn't that collaging or segmenting abandons structure—it's that it builds essay structure in ways that may be organic with the subject, ways that may not be immediately recognizable but which incrementally explain themselves as the reader progresses through the essay. In the models of structure that composition textbooks traditionally provide, the ancient and venerable rhetorical topic of arrangement is handled by providing molds into which to pour the molten thought and language of the essay: comparison/contrast, thesis/support, process—all prefabricated shapes to be selected off the rack to fit the body of the topic—or the five-paragraph theme, the one-size-fits-all product of the rhetorical department store. The segmented essay, on the other hand, attempts a tailor-made design, a structure that may be appropriate only to itself.

I am at a writer's workshop in Montana, happy to be among a talented group of writers who have brought manuscripts on the outdoors and thrilled by my first experience in the Western mountains. In the mornings we workshop one another's manuscripts under Gretel Ehrlich's directions; in the afternoon we hike the foothills of the Bitterroot Range or raft the Bitterroot River or ramble the valley floor. Late at night or early in the morning I write in my journal about the workshop sessions and the hiking, particularly where I have gone and what I have seen. In the end I have records of three hiking expeditions, one that takes me only a little way up Blodgett Canyon, one that takes me to a falls a few miles up the Mill Creek Trail, and a third that brings me to the awesome Bear Creek overlook on the shoulder of a mountain. When I try to analyze my frustrations and satisfactions about those hikes, I begin to see the possibility of an essay coming out of the experience.

Back in Michigan after the workshop, tinkering sullenly with the critiqued manuscript, I drop everything and instead begin writing about my Montana hiking. I give the essay the working title "Bitterroot" but eventually call it "Knowing Where You've Been," a title inspired by a Normal Maclean story about Blodgett Canyon which had helped me set a hiking destination in the first place. Perhaps because the other essays in the workshop have so often been segmented, divided into brief episodes or scenes or vignettes, I don't consider for a moment constructing an argumentative essay built around conclusions reached and made up of rationales for reaching them. At once I understand that I have come to the conclusions I have by taking three separate hikes, each of which went successively further into the wilderness, all of which culminated at the end of the final hike with a blissful moment of triumph and contentment, with a sense of arrival I hadn't had in the earlier hikes. I wonder if I can come at this by taking my reader through the three hikes with me, taking her deeper on each hike, leading her to the same moment and the same site of discovery that I reached. In brief, I wonder if I can somehow get the reader to reach my conclusions for herself by experiencing through my prose the same things I experienced.

This is risky, I know. Gretel Ehrlich's off-hand crack about the "plodding mid-western prose" of my workshop manuscript still chafes my ego like a fresh wound I can't stop picking at long enough to let heal. If I am to make my readers hike, the hiking better be brisk, lively, and limited, and each hike better be distinctive, so that it becomes clear why they've had to do three of them. I write the hikes in present tense, to make them feel more immediate, and I start them off the same way: I chip away at narrative that fills in the gaps of time between the hikes and tighten the prose for strength and speed. I also insert reflective interludes between the hikes, past tense segments responding to the hike just completed and pointing towards the next hike.

In the end the essay has five tight segments: hike ("The first afternoon. We walk the Blodgett Creek Trail"); interlude ("'When you look back at where you've been,' Norman Maclean writes, 'it often seems as if you have never been there or even as if there were no such place.'"); hike ("The second afternoon. We mill around after the morning workshop, plans shifting, destinations uncertain, finally resolving to go back into the mountains, to another trail."); interlude ("When I asked my friend from Montana about places to hike in the Bitterroot Valley, he looked thoughtful for a moment, shook his head, and said, 'Well, as early as you're going, there'll be too much snow to bag a peak.'"); hike ("The final afternoon. The morning workshop over, the group disperses for various tours and activities."). Each hike takes the narrator (and the reader) deeper into wilderness; each interlude raises issues that only an additional hike can resolve; the physical experiences of moving deeper and higher are echoed by intellectual and spiritual experiences, so that the physical moment of final achievement coincides with the spiritual moment of arrival. The successive drafts make me better understand exactly what it is I was feeling at the end of that hiking and push me to prepare the reader for that epiphany on the mountain ("It isn't how far at all but how deep. I need to go as deeply into wilderness as it takes before the wilderness comes into me.") in a way that makes it unnecessary for me to explain it afterward or add an epilogue of explication that breaks the reader down both physically and emotionally. The essay has to end on the mountain and the segmented format invites me to end it there.

The segmented essay makes demands not only on the writer but on the reader as well. Carl Klaus has noted how segments can be read both as isolated units and as reverberating links to other segments; it is "a strange reading experience, unlike that produced by any other kind of prose" which produces in him "an irresolvable tension between two different ways of reading and responding." From reading each segment "as a discrete entity as well as . . . in connection with its immediate neighbor," he finds that his "accumulating sense of recurrent or contrastive words, phrases, images, metaphors, ideas, topics, or themes" forces him to "intuitively mak[e] connections or distinctions between and among the segments, almost as if I were experiencing some of the very same associative leaps that might have provoked the essayist to write a piece in disjunctive form" (48). These "associative leaps" may replicate the fragmentary nature of "recollection and reflection" but they also suggest a willingness to accept unresolved or undefined associations.

Such writing demands that the reader learn to read the structure of the essay as well as its thought. That is a task for which the twentieth century reader is well prepared, because the episodic or segmented or disjunctive sequence is a familiar design in many other genres:

- the interrelated collection of short stories, for example, a concept suggested by Hemingway with the interludes between stories in *In Our Time* or carried out in Ray Bradbury's *The Martian Chronicles*;
- the playing with chronology and the episodic structure of novels like Milan Kundera's *The Unbearable Lightness of Being* and Kurt Vonnegut's *Slaughterhouse-Five*;
- cycles of thematically linked poems, each poem separate and independent but enriched by juxtaposition with poems on similar subjects or with similar perspectives;
- the "concept" album of interlinked songs—the Beatles' *Sgt. Pepper's Lonely Hearts Club Band* or the "suite" on half of *Abbey Road*, Pink Floyd's *The Wall*, or the more loosely thematic *Nebraska* and *Born In the USA* albums of Bruce Springsteen;
- sequences of brief scenes in motion pictures—Quentin Tarantino's *Pulp Fiction*, Gus Van Sant's *To Die For*, the recent critical favorites *The English Patient* and *Shine* all present their stories out of chronological sequence. In none of these is it hard to reconstruct the chronology, but telling the story in strict chronological order would have changed the emphases of these films. But even in strictly chronological films, the film progresses by sequences of shots or scenes, each separated from one another by visual cues as definite as chapter headings or theatrical intermissions.

Examples abound. It might be argued that the modern reader/viewer is more accustomed to disjunctiveness than to strict continuity.

I write this essay in segments. How can I explain what the segmented essay is like, or how it comes about, in an unsegmented essay?

I get up early in the morning to write, a common writer's habit. I am following a vague outline in my head of alternating segments—a more or less narrative example of someone composing a segmented essay alternating with a more or less expository section discussing the form. Practice alternates with theory. I have a lot of examples in mind that I think I might be able to use, and sometimes I type a section break or white space and insert a line of reference to spur my memory when I get to that segment ("Sandra's essay is giving her lots of trouble"; "I write this essay in segments"). Sometimes, by the time I reach that line, I have decided not to use it or have already used the example and I delete the line.

Some days I complete the draft of a segment in a single session, partly because I know I will have to revise it—go back to Mike's drafts to compare them again and to dig out more material for illustration, reread Carol's essay to refresh my memory about specific references, ask somebody about tarot readings, work on the concreteness of the language and clarity of the explanations. At first I am interested chiefly in having a structure to work in, and I have already cut and pasted segments in this draft to juxtapose them in different sequences.

Other days I only get through a portion of a segment. Some are harder than others to write, some have more detail, more development, quotes to look up and copy. I don't mind leaving them undone, because I think that when I return to them the next day my subconscious will have worked on them a little bit and it will be easier to launch into the drafting again. Even in an essay that isn't segmented we still work from section to section; it really isn't much different here.

And finally one morning when I feel I've said enough and need to worry less about finding something more to say than about finding ways to say what I've said better, I run off the full draft and try to work with what I have. Sometimes whole segments disappear or merge with others, sometimes new segments announce their necessity and have to be drafted and revised, sometimes the order of the segments changes again and again. I work harder on the language now, when I'm certain the ideas will stay. I am always reassured by a quote whose source may or may not have been Oscar Wilde: "I always revise everything eleven times, ten times to get the words right, and the eleventh time to put in that touch of spontaneity that everyone likes about my writing."

I teach creative nonfiction and composition classes, talk to friends about their essays, work on essays of my own. Sometimes I bring work in progress to my students, like a draft on men's rooms I photocopied, cut up, and distributed in pieces to see how different people would reassemble them and why. Often I advise other writers stuck in linearity and chronology, "Why don't you try collaging this?" I like making a verb of the noun, outraging any grammarians who overhear me.

I insist that my nonfiction students write at least one segmented essay during the term and provide such ways into the segmented essay as these:

- *definitions:* Simply explaining the segmented essay form calls up a range of alternatives: collage, montage, mosaic, vignette, episode, segment—all ways of approaching the form that suggest alternatives at that same time that they define distinctive forms.
- *models:* Readers respond to a handful of segmented essays with immediate understanding—Nancy Willard's "The Friendship Tarot," Annie Dillard's "Living Like Weasels," Susan Allen Toth's "Going to Movies," William Holtz's "Brother's Keeper," Naomi Shihab Nye's "Three Pokes of a Thistle," Reg Saner's "The Ideal Particle and the Great Unconformity."

- *strategies:* Segmented essays tend to go together in several different ways—

  - by juxtaposition, arranging one item alongside another item so that they comment back and forth on one another (Toth's "Going to Movies" is four vignettes, three dates with different men, the fourth a solitary trip to the theater);
  - by parallelism, alternating or intertwining one continuous strand with another (a present tense strand with a past tense strand, a domestic strand with a foreign strand, the alternate strands of a piece like "The Ideal Particle and the Great Unconformity");
  - by patterning, choosing an extra-literary design and arranging literary segments accordingly (as Willard does with tarot cards in "The Friendship Tarot" or Frederick Smock does with rooms in "Anonymous: A Brief Memoir");
  - by accumulation, arranging a series of segments or scenes or episodes so that they add or enrich or alter meaning with each addition, perhaps reinterpreting earlier segments in later ones, up to a final segment (as Holtz does in "Brother's Keeper");
  - by journaling, actually writing in episodes or reconstructing the journal experience in drafts (Sydney Lea asks students to write lyrical essays trying to connect disparate items in their journals; Gretel Ehrlich uses the journal form as a narrative device in many of her works, such as the recent "Cold Comfort").

In the classroom I make students cluster and list and map ideas, all of which encourage segmentation, separate items to work from. They produce partial or full rough drafts in whatever format they choose and then they help each other find ways of collaging or segmenting appropriate to the pieces they're working on. Once they're open to the possibility of the segmented essay, there's virtually no limit to the variations a roomful of imaginative young writers can bring to the form.

Collage, montage, mosaic, vignette, episode, segment—I've never found a descriptive term for anything that, if I pressed on it, wasn't somehow incapable of bearing the weight of definitive definition. I don't worry about the most accurate term for this kind of essay, because when one writer suggests to another, "Why don't you collage this?" the result may as much define the form as conform to it.

Works Cited

Best American Essays 1991. Ed. Joyce Carol Oates. Series Editor: Robert Atwan. Boston: Ticknor and Fields, 1991.

Dillard, Annie. "Living Like Weasels." *Teaching a Stone to Talk: Expeditions and Encounters.* New York: Harper, 1982. 29–34.

Ehrlich, Gretel. "Cold Comfort." *Harper's* 294:1762 (March 1997): 34–44.

Elbow, Peter. *Writing With Power.* New York: Oxford University Press, 1981.

Faery, Rebecca Blevins. "Text and Context: The Essay and the Politics of Disjunctive Form." *What Do I Know? Reading, Writing, and Teaching the Essay*. Ed. Janis Forman. Portsmouth, NH: Boynton/Cook, 1996. 55–68.

Grand Tour, "Virtues & Vices" 1:4 (Fall 1996).

Gruchow, Paul. "Eight Variations on the Idea of Failure." *Old Friends, New Neighbors: A Celebration of the American Essay, American Literary Review*. Ed. W. Scott Olsen. 5:2 (Fall 1994): 31–38.

Holtz, William. "Brother's Keeper: an Elegy." *Old Friends, New Neighbors: A Celebration of the American Essay, American Literary Review*. Ed. W. Scott Olsen. 5:2 (Fall 1994): 147–63.

Klaus, Carl H. "Excursions of the Mind: Toward a Poetics of Uncertainty in the Disjunctive Essay." *What Do I Know? Reading, Writing, and Teaching the Essay*. Ed. Janis Forman. Portsmouth, NH: Boynton/Cook, 1996. 39–53.

Nye, Naomi Shihab. "Three Pokes of a Thistle." *Never in a Hurry: Essay on People and Places*. Columbia: University of South Carolina Press, 1996. 26–31.

Old Friends, New Neighbors: A Celebration of the American Essay, American Literary Review. Ed. W. Scott Olsen. 5:2 (Fall 1994).

Ploughshares. Ed. Rosellen Brown. 20: 2–3 (Fall 1994).

Rudman, Mark. "Mosaic on Walking." *The Best American Essays 1991*. Ed. Joyce Carol Oates. Boston: Ticknor and Fields, 1991: 138–153.

Sanford, Carol. Unpublished essay ["Always Looking"].

Schwartz, Lynne Sharon. "Time Off to Translate." *Old Friends, New Neighbors: A Celebration of the American Essay, American Literary Review*. Ed. W. Scott Olsen. 5:2 (Fall 1994): 15–30.

Smock, Frederick. "Anonymous: A Brief Memoir." *Old Friends, New Neighbors: A Celebration of the American Essay, American Literary Review*. Ed. W. Scott Olsen. 5:2 (Fall 1994): 68–72.

Steinberg, Michael. Unpublished essay ["'I've Got It, No, You 'Take It': An Aging Ballplayer's Dilemma" and "On the Road Again: A Softball Gypsy's Last Go-Round"].

Toth, Susan Allen. "Going to the Movies." *How to Prepare for Your High-School Reunion and Other Midlife Musings*. New York: Ballantine Books, 1990. 108–112.

Willard, Nancy. "The Friendship Tarot." *Between Friends*. Ed. Mickey Pearlman. Boston: Houghton Mifflin, 1994. 195–203.

The Singular First Person

Scott Russell Sanders

The first soapbox orator I ever saw was haranguing a crowd beside the Grey-hound Station in Providence, Rhode Island, about the evils of fluoridated water. What the man stood on was actually an upturned milk crate, all the genuine soap-boxes presumably having been snapped up by antique dealers. He wore an orange plaid sports coat and matching bow tie and held aloft a bottle filled with mossy green liquid. I don't remember the details of his spiel, except his warning that fluoride was an invention of the Communists designed to weaken our bones and thereby make us pushovers for a Red invasion. What amazed me, as a tongue-tied kid of seventeen newly arrived in the city from the boondocks, was not his message but his courage in delivering it to a mob of strangers. I figured it would have been easier for me to jump straight over the Greyhound Station than to stand there on that milk crate and utter my thoughts.

To this day, when I read or when I compose one of those curious mono-logues we call the personal essay, I often think of that soapbox orator. Nobody had asked him for his two cents' worth, but there he was declaring it with all the eloquence he could muster. The essay, although enacted in private, is no less arro-gant a performance. Unlike novelists and playwrights, who lurk behind the scenes while distracting our attention with the puppet show of imaginary charac-ters, unlike scholars and journalists, who quote the opinions of others and shelter behind the hedges of neutrality, the essayist has nowhere to hide. While the poet can lean back on a several-thousand-year-old legacy of ecstatic speech, the essay-ist inherits a much briefer and skimpier tradition. The poet is allowed to quit after a few lines, but the essayist must hold our attention over pages and pages. It is a brash and foolhardy form, this one-man or one-woman circus, which relies on the tricks of anecdote, conjecture, memory, and wit to enthrall us.

Addressing a monologue to the world seems all the more brazen or preposterous an act when you consider what a tiny fraction of the human chorus any single

383

voice is. At the Boston Museum of Science an electronic meter records with flashing lights the population of the United States. Figuring in the rate of births, deaths, emigrants leaving the country and immigrants arriving, the meter calculates that we add one fellow citizen every twenty-one seconds. When I looked at it recently, the count stood at 249,958,483. As I wrote that figure in my notebook, the final number jumped from three to four. Another mouth, another set of ears and eyes, another brain. A counter for the earth's population would stand somewhere past five billion at the moment, and would be rising in a blur of digits. Amid this avalanche of selves, it is a wonder that anyone finds the gumption to sit down and write one of those naked, lonely, quixotic letters-to-the-world.

A surprising number do find the gumption. In fact, I have the impression there are more essayists at work in America today, and more gifted ones, than at any time in recent decades. Whom do I have in mind? Here is a sampler: Wendell Berry, Carol Bly, Joan Didion, Annie Dillard, Stephen Jay Gould, Elizabeth Hardwick, Edward Hoagland, Phillip Lopate, Barry Lopez, Peter Matthiessen, John McPhee, Cynthia Ozick, Paul Theroux, Lewis Thomas, Tom Wolfe. No doubt you could make up a list of your own—with a greater ethnic range, perhaps, or fewer nature enthusiasts—a list that would provide equally convincing support for the view that we are blessed right now with an abundance of essayists. We do not have anyone to rival Emerson or Thoreau, but in sheer quantity of first-rate work our time stands comparison with any period since the heyday of the form in the mid-nineteenth century.

Why are so many writers taking up this risky form, and why are so many readers—to judge by the statistics of book and magazine publication—seeking it out? In this era of prepackaged thought, the essay is the closest thing we have, on paper, to a record of the individual mind at work and play. It is an amateur's raid in a world of specialists. Feeling overwhelmed by data, random information, the flotsam and jetsam of mass culture, we relish the spectacle of a single consciousness making sense of a portion of the chaos. We are grateful to Lewis Thomas for shining his light into the dark corners of biology, to John McPhee for laying bare the geology beneath our landscape, to Annie Dillard for showing us the universal fire blazing in the branches of a cedar, to Peter Matthiessen for chasing after snow leopards and mystical insights in the Himalayas. No matter if they are sketchy, these maps of meaning are still welcome. As Joan Didion observes in her own collection of essays, *The White Album*, "We live entirely, especially if we are writers, by the imposition of a narrative line upon disparate images, by the 'ideas' with which we have learned to freeze the shifting phantasmagoria which is our actual experience." Dizzy from a dance that seems to accelerate hour by hour, we cling to the narrative line, even though it may be as pure an invention as the shapes drawn by Greeks to identify the constellations.

The essay is a haven for the private, idiosyncratic voice in an era of anonymous babble. Like the bland-burgers served in their millions along our highways, most language served up in public these days is textureless, tasteless mush. On television, over the phone, in the newspaper, wherever humans bandy words about, we encounter more and more abstractions, more empty formulas. Think of the pablum ladled out by politicians. Think of the fluffy white bread of advertising. Think, lord help us, of committee reports. By contrast, the essay remains stubbornly concrete and particular: it confronts you with an oil-smeared toilet at the Sunoco station, a red vinyl purse shaped like a valentine heart, a bowlegged dentist hunting deer with an elephant gun. As Orwell forcefully argued, and as dictators seem to agree, such a bypassing of abstractions, such an insistence on the concrete, is a politically subversive act. Clinging to this door, that child, this grief, following the zigzag motions of an inquisitive mind, the essay renews language and clears trash from the springs of thought. A century and a half ago, in the rousing manifesto entitled *Nature*, Emerson called on a new generation of writers to cast off the hand-me-down rhetoric of the day, to "pierce this rotten diction and fasten words again to visible things." The essayist aspires to do just that.

As if all these virtues were not enough to account for a renaissance of this protean genre, the essay has also taken over some of the territory abdicated by contemporary fiction. Whittled down to the bare bones of plot, camouflaged with irony, muttering in brief sentences and grade-school vocabulary, peopled with characters who stumble like sleepwalkers through numb lives, today's fashionable fiction avoids disclosing where the author stands on anything. In the essay, you had better speak from a region pretty close to the heart or the reader will detect the wind of phoniness whistling through your hollow phrases. In the essay you may be caught with your pants down, your ignorance and sentimentality showing, while you trot recklessly about on one of your hobbyhorses. You cannot stand back from the action, as Joyce instructed us to do, and pare your fingernails. You cannot palm off your cockamamie notions on some hapless character.

To our list of the essay's contemporary attractions we should add the perennial ones of verbal play, mental adventure, and sheer anarchic high spirits. To see how the capricious mind can be led astray, consider the foregoing paragraph, which drags in metaphors from the realms of toys, clothing, weather, and biology, among others. That is bad enough; but it could have been worse. For example, I began to draft a sentence in that paragraph with the following words: "More than once, in sitting down to beaver away at a narrative, felling trees of memory and hauling brush to build a dam that might slow down the waters of time. . . ." I had set out to make some innocent remark, and here I was gnawing down trees and building dams, all because I had let that *beaver* slip in. On this occasion I had the good sense to throw out the unruly word. I don't always, as no doubt you will have noticed. Whatever its more visible subject, an essay is also about the way a mind moves, the links and leaps and jigs of thought. I might as well drag in another metaphor—and another unoffending animal—by saying that each doggy sentence, as it noses forward into the underbrush of thought, scatters a bunch of rabbits that go bounding off in all directions. The essayist can afford to chase more of those rabbits than the fiction writer can, but fewer than the poet. If you refuse to chase any of them, and keep plodding along in a straight line, you and your reader will have a dull outing. If you chase too many, you will soon wind up lost in a thicket of confusion with your tongue hanging out.

The pursuit of mental rabbits was strictly forbidden by the teachers who instructed me in English composition. For that matter, nearly all the qualities of the personal essay, as I have been sketching them, violate the rules that many of us were taught in school. You recall we were supposed to begin with an outline and stick by it faithfully, like a train riding its rails, avoiding sidetracks. Each paragraph was to have a topic sentence pasted near the front, and these orderly paragraphs were to be coupled end-to-end like so many boxcars. Every item in those boxcars was to bear the stamp of some external authority, preferably a footnote referring to a thick book, although appeals to magazines and newspapers would do in a pinch. Our diction was to be formal, dignified, shunning the vernacular. Polysyllabic words derived from Latin were preferable to the blunt lingo of the streets. Metaphors were to be used only in emergencies, and no two of them were to be mixed. And even in emergencies we could not speak in the first person singular.

Already as a schoolboy, I chafed against those rules. Now I break them shamelessly, in particular the taboo against using the lonely capital *I*. Just look at what I'm doing right now. My speculations about the state of the essay arise, needless to say, from my own practice as reader and writer, and they reflect my own tastes, no matter how I may pretend to gaze dispassionately down on the question from a hot-air balloon. As Thoreau declares in his cocky manner on the opening page of *Walden*: "In most books the *I*, or first person, is omitted; in this it will be retained; that, in respect to egotism, is the main difference. We commonly do not remember that it is, after all, always the first person that is speaking. I should not talk so much about myself if there were anybody else whom I knew as well." True for the personal essay, it is doubly true for an essay about the essay: one speaks always and inescapably in the first person singular.

We could sort out essays along a spectrum according to the degree to which the writer's ego is on display—with John McPhee, perhaps, at the extreme of self-effacement, and Norman Mailer at the opposite extreme of self-dramatization. Brassy or shy, center stage or hanging back in the wings, the author's persona commands our attention. For the length of an essay, or a book of essays, we respond to that persona as we would to a friend caught up in a rapturous monologue. When the monologue is finished, we may not be able to say precisely what it was about, any more than we can draw conclusions from a piece of music. "Essays don't usually boil down to a summary, as articles do," notes Edward Hoagland, one of the least summarizable of companions, "and the style of the writer has a 'nap' to it, a combination of personality and originality and energetic loose ends that stand up like the nap of a piece of wool and can't be brushed flat" ("What I Think, What I Am"). We make assumptions about that speaking voice, assumptions we cannot validly make about the narrators in fiction. Only a sophomore is permitted to ask if Huckleberry Finn ever had any children; but even literary sophisticates wonder in print about Thoreau's love life, Montaigne's domestic arrangements, De Quincey's opium habit, Virginia Woolf's depression.

Montaigne, who not only invented the form but nearly perfected it as well, announced from the start that his true subject was himself. In his note "To the Reader" at the beginning of the *Essays*, he slyly proclaimed:

> I want to be seen here in my simple, natural, ordinary fashion, without straining or artifice; for it is myself that I portray. My defects will here be read to the life, and also my natural form, as far as respect for the public has allowed. Had I been placed among those nations which are said to live still in the sweet freedom of nature's first laws, I assure you I should very gladly have portrayed myself here entire and wholly naked.

A few pages after this disarming introduction, we are told of the Emperor Maximilian, who was so prudish about exposing his private parts that he would not let a servant dress him or see him in the bath. The Emperor went so far as to give orders that he be buried in his underdrawers. Having let us in on this intimacy about Maximilian, Montaigne then confessed that he himself, although "bold-mouthed," was equally prudish, and that "except under great stress of necessity or voluptuousness," he never allowed anyone to see him naked. Such modesty, he feared, was unbecoming in a soldier. But such honesty is quite becoming in an essayist. The very confession of his prudery is a far more revealing gesture than any doffing of clothes.

A curious reader will soon find out that the word *essay*, as adapted by Montaigne, means a trial or attempt. The Latin root carries the more vivid sense of a weighing out. In the days when that root was alive and green, merchants discovered the value of goods and alchemists discovered the composition of unknown metals by the use of scales. Just so the essay, as Montaigne was the first to show, is a weighing out, an inquiry into the value, meaning, and true nature of experience; it is a private experiment carried out in public. In each of three successive editions, Montaigne inserted new material into his essays without revising the old material. Often the new statements contradicted the original ones, but Montaigne let them stand, since he believed that the only consistent fact about human beings is their inconsistency. In a celebration called "Why Montaigne Is Not a Bore," Lewis Thomas has remarked of him that "He [was] fond of his mind, and affectionately entertained by everything in his head." Whatever Montaigne wrote about—and he wrote about everything under the sun: fears, smells, growing old, the pleasures of scratching—he weighed on the scales of his own character.

It is the *singularity* of the first person—its warts and crotchets and turn of voice—that lures many of us into reading essays, and that lingers with us after we finish. Consider the lonely, melancholy persona of Loren Eiseley, forever wandering, forever brooding on our dim and bestial past, his lips frosty with the chill of the Ice Age. Consider the volatile, Dionysian persona of D. H. Lawrence, with his incandescent gaze, his habit of turning peasants into gods and trees into flames, his quick hatred and quicker love. Consider that philosophical farmer, Wendell Berry, who speaks with a countryman's knowledge and a deacon's severity. Consider E. B. White, with his cheery affection for brown eggs and dachshunds, his unflappable way of herding geese while the radio warns of an approaching hurricane.

E. B. White, that engaging master of the genre, a champion of idiosyncrasy, introduced his own volume of *Essays* by admitting the danger of narcissism:

> I think some people find the essay the last resort of the egoist, a much too self-conscious and self-serving form for their taste; they feel that it is presumptuous of a writer to assume that his little excursions or his small observations will interest the reader. There is some justice in their complaint. I have always been aware that I am by nature self-absorbed and egoistical; to write of myself to the extent I have done indicates a too great attention to my own life, not enough to the lives of others.

Yet the self-absorbed Mr. White was in fact a delighted observer of the world, and shared that delight with us. Thus, after describing memorably how a circus girl practiced her bareback riding in the leisure moments between shows ("The Ring of Time"), he confessed: "As a writing man, or secretary, I have always felt charged with the safekeeping of all unexpected items of worldly or unworldly enchantment, as though I might be held personally responsible if even a small one were to be lost." That may still be presumptuous, but it is a presumption turned outward on the creation.

This looking outward helps distinguish the essay from pure autobiography, which dwells more complacently on the self. Mass murderers, movie stars, sports heroes, Wall Street crooks, and defrocked politicians may blather on about whatever high jinks or low jinks made them temporarily famous, may chronicle their exploits, their diets, their hobbies, in perfect confidence that the public is eager to gobble up every least gossipy scrap. And the public, according to sales figures, generally is. On the other hand, I assume the public does not give a hoot about my private life. If I write of hiking up a mountain with my one-year-old boy riding like a papoose on my back, and of what he babbled to me while we gazed down from the summit onto the scudding clouds, it is not because I am deluded into believing that my baby, like the offspring of Prince Charles, matters to the great world. It is because I know the great world produces babies of its own and watches them change cloudfast before its doting eyes. To make that climb up the mountain vividly present for readers is harder work than the climb itself. I choose to write about my experience not because it is mine, but because it seems to me a door through which others might pass.

On that cocky first page of *Walden*, Thoreau justified his own seeming self-absorption by saying that he wrote the book for the sake of his fellow citizens, who kept asking him to account for his peculiar experiment by the pond. There is at least a sliver of truth to this, since Thoreau, a town character, had been invited more than once to speak his mind at the public lectern. Most of us, however, cannot honestly say the townspeople have been clamoring for our words. I suspect that all writers of the essay, even Norman Mailer and Gore Vidal, must occasionally wonder if they are egomaniacs. For the essayist, in other words, the problem of authority is inescapable. By what right does one speak? Why should anyone listen? The traditional sources of authority no longer serve. You cannot justify your words by appealing to the Bible or some other holy text, you cannot merely stitch together a patchwork of quotations from classical authors, you cannot lean on a podium at the Atheneum and deliver your wisdom to a rapt audience.

In searching for your own soapbox, a sturdy platform from which to deliver your opinionated monologues, it helps if you have already distinguished yourself at some other, less fishy form. When Yeats describes his longing for Maud Gonne or muses on Ireland's misty lore, everything he says is charged with the prior strength of his poetry. When Virginia Woolf, in *A Room of One's Own*, reflects on the status of women and the conditions necessary for making art, she speaks as the author of *Mrs. Dalloway* and *To the Lighthouse*. The essayist may also lay claim to our attention by having lived through events or traveled through terrains that already bear a richness of meaning. When James Baldwin writes his *Notes of a Native Son*, he does not have to convince us that racism is a troubling reality. When Barry Lopez takes us on a meditative tour of the far north in *Arctic Dreams*, he can rely on our curiosity about that fabled and forbidding place. When Paul Theroux climbs aboard a train and invites us on a journey to some exotic destination, he can count on the romance of railroads and the allure of remote cities to bear us along.

Most essayists, however, cannot draw on any source of authority from beyond the page to lend force to the page itself. They can only use language to put themselves on display and to gesture at the world. When Annie Dillard tells us in the opening lines of *Pilgrim at Tinker Creek* about the tomcat with bloody paws who jumps through the window onto her chest, why should we listen? Well, because of the voice that goes on to say: "And some mornings I'd wake in daylight to find my body covered with paw prints in blood; I looked as though I'd been painted with roses." Listen to her explaining a few pages later what she is up to in this book, this broody, zestful record of her stay in the Roanoke Valley: "I propose to keep here what Thoreau called 'a meteorological journal of the mind,' telling some tales and describing some of the sights of this rather tamed valley, and exploring, in fear and trembling, some of the unmapped dim reaches and unholy fastnesses to which those tales and sights so dizzyingly lead." The sentence not only describes the method of her literary search, but also exhibits the breathless, often giddy, always eloquent and spiritually hungry soul who will do the searching. If you enjoy her company, you will relish Annie Dillard's essays; if you don't, you won't.

Listen to another voice which readers tend to find either captivating or insufferable:

> That summer I began to see, however dimly, that one of my ambitions, perhaps my governing ambition, was to belong fully to this place, to belong as the thrushes and the herons and the muskrats belonged, to be altogether at home

here. That is still my ambition. But now I have come to see that it proposes an enormous labor. It is a spiritual ambition, like goodness. The wild creatures belong to the place by nature, but as a man I can belong to it only by understanding and by virtue. It is an ambition I cannot hope to succeed in wholly, but I have come to believe that it is the most worthy of all.

That is Wendell Berry in "The Long-Legged House" writing about his patch of Kentucky. Once you have heard that stately, moralizing, cherishing voice, laced through with references to the land, you will not mistake it for anyone else's. Berry's themes are profound and arresting ones. But it is his voice, more than anything he speaks about, that either seizes us or drives us away.

Even so distinct a persona as Wendell Berry's or Annie Dillard's is still only a literary fabrication, of course. The first person singular is too narrow a gate for the whole writer to squeeze through. What we meet on the page is not the flesh-and-blood author, but a simulacrum, a character who wears the label *I*. Introducing the lectures that became *A Room of One's Own*, Virginia Woolf reminded her listeners that "'I' is only a convenient term for somebody who has no real being. Lies will flow from my lips, but there may perhaps be some truth mixed up with them; it is for you to seek out this truth and to decide whether any part of it is worth keeping." Here is a part I consider worth keeping: "Women have served all these centuries as looking-glasses possessing the magic and delicious power of reflecting the figure of man at twice its natural size." It is from such elegant, revelatory sentences that we build up our notion of the "I" who speaks to us under the name of Virginia Woolf.

What the essay tells us may not be true in any sense that would satisfy a court of law. As an example, think of Orwell's brief narrative, "A Hanging," which describes an execution in Burma. Anyone who has read it remembers how the condemned man as he walked to the gallows stepped aside to avoid a puddle. That is the sort of haunting detail only an eyewitness should be able to report. Alas, biographers, those zealous debunkers, have recently claimed that Orwell never saw such a hanging, that he reconstructed it from hearsay. What then do we make of his essay? Or has it become the sort of barefaced lie we prefer to call a story?

Frankly, I don't much care what label we put on "A Hanging"—fiction or nonfiction, it is a powerful statement either way—but Orwell might have cared a great deal. I say this because not long ago I was bemused and then vexed to find one of my own essays treated in a scholarly article as a work of fiction. Here was my earnest report about growing up on a military base, my heartfelt rendering of indelible memories, being confused with the airy figments of novelists! To be sure, in writing the piece I had used dialogue, scenes, settings, character descriptions, the whole fictional bag of tricks; sure, I picked and chose among a thousand beckoning details; sure, I downplayed some facts and highlighted others; but I was writing about the actual, not the invented. I shaped the matter, but I did not make it up.

To explain my vexation, I must break another taboo, which is to speak of the author's intent. My teachers warned me strenuously to avoid the intentional fallacy. They told me to regard poems and plays and stories as objects washed up on the page from some unknown and unknowable shores. Now that I am on the other side of the page, so to speak, I think quite recklessly of intention all the time. I believe that if we allow the question of intent in the case of murder, we should allow it in literature. The essay is distinguished from the short story, not by the presence or absence of literary devices, not by tone or theme or subject, but by the writer's stance toward the material. In composing an essay about what it was like to grow up on that military base, I *meant* something quite different from what I mean when concocting a story. I meant to preserve and record and help give voice to a reality that existed independently of me. I meant to pay my respects to a minor passage of history in an out-of-the-way place. I felt responsible to the truth as known by other people. I wanted to speak directly out of my own life into the lives of others.

You can see I am teetering on the brink of metaphysics. One step farther and I will plunge into the void, wondering as I fall how to prove there is any external truth for the essayist to pay homage to. I draw back from the brink and simply declare that I believe one writes, in essays, with a regard for the actual world, with a respect for the shared substance of history, the autonomy of other lives, the being of nature, the mystery and majesty of a creation we have not made.

When it comes to speculating about the creation, I feel more at ease with physics than with metaphysics. According to certain bold and lyrical cosmologists, there is at the center of black holes a geometrical point, the tiniest conceivable speck, where all the matter of a collapsed star has been concentrated, and where everyday notions of time, space, and force break down. That point is called a singularity. The boldest and most poetic theories suggest that anything sucked into a singularity might be flung back out again, utterly changed, somewhere else in the universe. The lonely first person, the essayist's microcosmic "I," may be thought of as a verbal singularity at the center of the mind's black hole. The raw matter of experience, torn away from the axes of time and space, falls in constantly from all sides, undergoes the mind's inscrutable alchemy, and reemerges in the quirky, unprecedented shape of an essay.

Now it is time for me to step down, before another metaphor seizes hold of me, before you notice that I am standing, not on a soapbox, but on the purest air.

Full Disclosure

Lynne Sharon Schwartz

It was a warm June day, maybe four o'clock, four-thirty. I was wearing a navy blue and white striped sleeveless mini dress, more like a long tank top actually, and in my right hand I held a vegetable spoon, and in a small room off the hall was my eighteen-month-old baby standing up and rattling the bars of her crib the way they do at that age. I was stirring chicken and chunks of pineapple in the electric frying pan—sweet and sour chicken, which I didn't particularly like but it seemed festive—when I heard footsteps. I went to look. Approaching from the end of the long ball was a thin, sallow kid in droopy jeans and a windbreaker and a porkpie hat. My first thought was what a long reach it was from the fire escape to the bedroom window, and what a long drop. He had taken quite a risk. Next I thought he would rape me because of the mini dress, or kill me, or maybe both, and if not for the baby in the crib I would have preferred, at that moment, just to be killed.

I was preparing the sweet and sour chicken for the parents of a Barnard student from Cleveland for whom I was acting as a big sister. They were visiting their daughter in the big city for the first time; I was not much older than the student myself and I wanted to do everything just right. Months earlier, before I met the student who was to be my little sister, a friend in the alumnae office had called to say, I just want to let you know your sister is black, so when she appears at your door you don't look surprised. Her warning was unsettling, even offensive, to me as well as to the student. But things were in such turmoil then, thirty-odd years ago, that people of good will often behaved with astounding clumsiness. No doubt my friend was trying to protect the student from my possible surprise. That was unnecessary, I thought; I wouldn't have shown any surprise, or so I hoped. I would never know for sure. Anyway, I was determined to make the evening go smoothly.

I said to the kid. What do you want? and he said, I came to tell you your house is on fire, the hall is full of smoke. I didn't believe him but I had to be sure, so I walked toward him with the vegetable spoon raised like a weapon, and past his skinny tense body, to open the door and see. Those two seconds when I passed him, when we were inches apart, I thought, Goodbye, life. He didn't touch me, but now he was closer than I was to the room with the baby. The hall was not full of smoke. I stood at the open door, and if I'd been alone I would have run out, but I couldn't leave the baby. He came toward me, a shuffling, arrogant walk; again we would be inches apart but I could see he wanted to get out now. Once he was past me and out the door he started to run. Up the stairs to the roof.

I knocked on the doors of two of my neighbors for help. The first was the anthropology professor next door, the flirt, to put it politely; his field was Mayan culture and he and his wife were always going to Mexico. I knew he owned a machete, something to do with his archeological digs among the ruins, and he had once said to me jokingly, If you ever need help just bang on the door and I'll come with my machete. Many of his remarks had a double entendre, but at this moment I literally wanted him with his machete and said so, and he rose to the occasion, wearing his usual plaid bathrobe and carrying the machete as promised.

The other neighbor was an actor who would later appear on *Sesame Street*, the father of four children. My own children—the one now standing up in her crib and the one not yet born—would watch him on *Sesame Street* and be thrilled to see him in the halls and to play in his apartment with his children, who by that time would number five, but the thrill would quickly wear off. He too came with alacrity, and the two men chased the intruder over the roof while I went back to see to the baby in the crib—I was afraid to leave her alone—but they didn't catch him. I thought, well, anyway, my neighbor the professor is more than just a flirt— he made good on his word.

I thanked them and went back and finished cooking the sweet and sour chicken; it seemed the logical thing to do: nothing was really changed except in my mind, and why shouldn't the festive dinner still take place? The parents had come all the way from Cleveland. My husband came home from work and my little sister and her family arrived; the sweet and sour chicken was appreciated and it was a pleasant evening, all in all. I told my story and my audience was duly shocked. Out-of-towners love to hear New York crime stories; they enjoy having their worst fears confirmed, and while that usually irritates me, this time it was extremely gratifying.

After that incident in the hall I couldn't sit still at the front end of the apartment for more than fifteen minutes at a stretch for fear that someone was climbing in the back window. I had to keep walking down the hall to check the window. Every little noise, I thought was another intruder. At night, if my husband was working late and I was home alone with the baby, I imagined a boy just like the boy in the porkpie hat walking down the hall. I couldn't concentrate on reading in the living room because my ears were on the alert for his footsteps; sometimes I couldn't stay in the living room at all but had to take my book to the bedroom so I could keep an eye on the window. But out of pride I refused to keep the window closed all that hot summer. I refused to give in to my fear. I wouldn't give the boy—or my fear—the satisfaction of my discomfort in a stuffy apartment. I thought of going to a psychiatrist—it was that bad—but, knowing little about therapy at the time, I reasoned that it would do no good since my fear was based on a real incident, not a fantasy or neurotic exaggeration. Things improved slightly when the weather got cold and I had a legitimate reason to close the window, but still that was a dark and terrible year. I thought I would never get over my fright. Then gradually I did.

Later, my sister married a Columbia student and they had a baby named Chad after the lake in Africa; the name also had other ethnic significance which they must have explained but I no longer remember. They invited my husband and me over for an African dinner, a very good stew in which peanuts were a key ingredient. Later they got divorced.

Many years later, soon after the game professor next door unexpectedly died, there was a fire in the building and the hall truly was full of smoke, but as it happened I wasn't there to see it because I had a temporary job out of town. I was living alone in a large house in a small city and always kept the door unlocked and was never afraid. The children were big then and I left them with my husband for several months—they had long since stopped watching *Sesame Street* and the actor and his wife were divorced too; she took the five children and moved to the suburbs and he shortly remarried and had two more children. No one was hurt in the fire, but our apartment and the apartment of the actor and of the professor's widow were pretty much ruined. I never made sweet and sour chicken again—I had never made it before that night—and I never wore that dress again either.

That part was easy to write. More or less. Nothing is truly easy to write, but I mean it didn't present any excruciating difficulties or demands. What follows will be harder. In the interests of full disclosure—not my usual mode—I will say that the above is the result of an exercise I assigned to a group of students. I told them to write about an incident from their past, giving as many tangible details as they could manage but omitting all interpretation or subjectivity. Just the facts. It's an exercise that diverts students, at least briefly, from their seductive and endless and often fruitless soul-searching and forces them to concentrate on things and words. They resist, but in the end they're always amazed, as I am, at how much better their writing is when the goal ceases to be self-expression.

I did the exercise with them. That always feels so democratic: see, I'm the same as you, we all have to start from scratch each time. There's not much else to do, anyway, for those fifteen or twenty minutes that they're scribbling. And I thought I might get something useful out of it, the germ of something. When we read the pieces aloud (the students trading papers and reading anonymously so they wouldn't be inhibited by the disclosure of intimate secrets, not that they'd be too inhibited in any case, privacy being very nearly an obsolete value), I liked the way mine sounded and decided to work it up into something. In the process, as is obvious, I broke my own rules here and there, but outside the classroom rules are of no importance.

Maybe it was too easy. When I showed it to someone, she said, But what's the point? There was something missing, she said, something maybe I was trying to avoid. She suspected it had to do with race. Was the intruder black, and was there some unexamined connection between that and the student's being black? Also, why didn't I close the window? she asked. I thought I had explained that adequately: a reader has to accept a writer's perversities—they are an essential part of the story.

But I thought long and hard about the issue of race. Actually I didn't know what race the intruder was; he had the kind of olive-skinned face that at first glance might have been anything, and I was too terrified to study him closely. His race didn't, and doesn't, seem a crucial matter. I searched my soul the way the students do and found nothing. Only his clothes remain vivid—the droopy jeans, the dark windbreaker, much too hot for the weather, and the ridiculous hat. His race especially didn't seem to have anything to do with my sister and her family, who viewed the boy as our common enemy; the divisiveness of class is intricately tangled with that of race and possibly even more powerful, and my sister's parents were archetypally middle-class and genteel, so genteel and well-dressed, I recall, that I was slightly abashed at the artsy-craftsy, eclectic surroundings in which I was entertaining them. I hoped they wouldn't think I was *outré*, a bad influence. Of course the presence of a husband and a clearly well-cared-for baby was a mitigating factor. But at the time none of this felt very important; it only sounds important now because I was compelled by my reader to think about it. In fact the more I think about that reader's response the more it appears analogous to the warning of my friend in the alumnae office that my sister was black: making an issue out of what should be a non-issue. Then again, race is always an issue, which I suppose is why I included it in the first place. The story wouldn't have seemed complete or true to its moment without it, unfortunately.

That warning, though, was definitely an issue. In time I got to be good friends with my little sister, especially after she graduated from college and grew up. But the fact that my friend in the alumnae office had alerted me that she was black always remained as a faint shadow on our friendship, something about its genesis that I could never tell her, and this something was not of my making nor of hers: it too intruded, unwelcome, from outside.

I was fond of that friend in the alumnae office; she was a remarkably kind and bouncy person who had overcome great obstacles, and yet somehow we lost touch. Thinking over this incident, I wonder if her well-meant remark had anything to do with our losing touch. Hard to say; I've lost touch with many people for no special reason. Only writing this makes me think about it and regret it. I could look her up. I've lost touch with my sister too: she moved back to Cleveland with her child shortly after her divorce and I never heard from her again. I wouldn't know where to begin finding her. Through the alumnae office, I suppose.

But to return: I considered carefully what I might be avoiding in the essay and what the point was, although the latter is not a question I usually worry over—it seems more suited to geometry than to prose. I worry more over what a piece of prose is about, which is not quite the same thing as what is the point. This is such an old-fashioned worry, almost as obsolete as privacy, that students tend to laugh, in a friendly way, when I inquire yet again what their stories are about. I don't mind their laughing and I remain convinced despite it that a piece of prose needs to be about something, even if students today can't be convinced of this.

I went back and examined each of the elements of my story to see where I might be hedging. The first thing that stopped me was those pineapple chunks I was stirring in the electric frying pan. I would never cook anything involving pineapple chunks today. I noted in the piece that I didn't like pineapple, or to be precise, that I didn't like sweet and sour chicken; today I wouldn't cook anything I didn't like, even to please guests. But beyond that, pineapple chunks are so out of fashion, I wouldn't be caught dead serving them. Also, on the subject of food, I found it curious that I went right on cooking the dinner even though I was so upset. If a similar incident were to occur today—God forbid!—I'd probably drop everything, have a fit, pour a stiff drink, and when the guests came, call out for Chinese or Indian food; I wouldn't worry about proving my stoicism or resilience or culinary skills, which by now have been amply proven: with the passage of time one has so much less to prove. I'm older now than the Cleveland parents were then, and I know they would have understood. (On the other hand, decent take-out food was far less available back then.)

I felt some nostalgia over that mini dress, which I probably wouldn't wear today any more than I would serve pineapple chunks, but for different reasons. Also, on the subject of the mini dress, my phrase "I thought he would rape me because of the mini dress . . ." is questionable. We all know now, better than we did then, that rape is not primarily motivated by sexual attraction, and thank goodness the "she was asking for it" defense has been discredited, at least publicly if not in some hearts and minds. (But surely I couldn't be accused of asking for it in my own home; even the most prehistoric legal minds, I hope, wouldn't go that far.) The fact is, though, that I'd probably think the same thing today, even if I know better.

In the end, food and clothing weren't really germane to my quest: even if my attitudes have proved subject to revision, the transcription of them is not evasive. (It would have been evasive to try to sneak my current revisions into my account, making my younger self sound more sophisticated, which is always a temptation.)

The hall is full of smoke: those were the words the boy spoke to me. And as I say toward the end, years later the hall indeed was full of smoke since there was a fire in the building. Volumes could be written about that, and as a matter of fact I did write one, so I feel no need to reiterate it here—it wouldn't improve or enhance the story—and I feel safe from the charge of avoiding anything on that score.

I thought about the minimal mention of my husband. Was I being cagey there? I think not. He wasn't home for the incident and I didn't get a chance to discuss it with him in private until late that night when the guests had left and we were cleaning up. We did talk about it at length, and he was suitably concerned and even put bars on the window (much as they seemed impregnable, they did little to ease my terror, so I guess a psychiatrist might have been in order); he did all that could be expected, but none of that seemed part of the story.

I thought about the tactic of ramification, which I used, I think, to good effect. Here's where I might be most open to a charge of avoiding something, or rather to being arbitrarily selective, choosing certain details to elaborate rather than others. I chose those instinctively, I suppose through a sense of what would be dramatic or piquant or obliquely connected to the subject. (I find it lethal to analyze such choices, so I won't go any further.) Other details did occur to me but I passed over them—for instance a couple of items in the lives of my little sister or my neighbors—because however piquant, such items would violate their privacy and to no particular purpose: the only essentials in this story are the intrusion itself and its aftermath; the details are deliberately arbitrary and reflect the peculiarities of memory and association at times of crisis. I might have said, with no danger to anyone's privacy, that I once offered my sister a piece of a very hard, sweet Italian concoction called *panforte* and quipped, Don't break a tooth on it, and then she did just that, and I felt very bad and arranged an appointment for her with my dentist. Or that my next-door neighbor, the professor, died very suddenly and tragically of toxemia: thereby hangs a tale, as they say. Or that the seventh child of my other neighbor, the actor who later appeared on *Sesame Street* and divorced and remarried, grew up to be a famous rock star. But none of that is necessary. And why, anyway, should I mention his child who became a rock star rather than one of the six others, say, who became an engineer? (I don't know if any did become an engineer, I'm just plucking that out of the air as an example.) Because a rock star is the kind of profession one would note if one noted anything at all in that vein; this is not democratic, alas, but true. As a famous writer once remarked, Literature is not an equal opportunity employer (to be quite honest, she was referring to writers, not details). Anyway, that piquant detail didn't figure in this case.

My conscience is clear now. I have nothing to hide: I wrote the piece in order to write about my fear. The point, if there must be one, was to articulate the fear that once gripped me, have it out in the world, shaped and visible, rather than unseen, in me. Even before the actual writing, while I was watching the students scribble away and casting about for a subject of my own, the reason this incident and not some other came to mind is that the fear is always available, always on tap. I don't mean I'm still afraid of intruders; I'm not. I rarely think about intruders. Anyway, since the fire we've lived in another apartment with a different layout; I couldn't feel the same fear without the same long hall and the same window. I mean that the shape and texture of that particular fear—not the momentary fear of the boy but the long fear afterwards of someone like the boy climbing in that window, so that for a year I couldn't sit still unless I had my eye on it—has lodged in me for good; now and then I visit it, say hello. I might even miss it were I to forget it, but there's no danger of that. And I don't marvel at it as a strange thing of the past, now outgrown, the way I marvel that I ever cooked pineapple chunks or calmly prepared and served a whole dinner in a state of suppressed terror; the fear strikes me as entirely natural and comprehensible. It's part of me, like a scar you grow attached to. Precious, if not exactly beloved. I don't wish it gone, though of course I would have preferred the intruder never to have intruded. But since he did, the fear he caused is mine now, preserved in amber, the insect's delicate wing forever caught mid-tremor.

I told my older daughter I had written a few pages about this incident but that a reader had found it wanting. While I didn't wholly accept her comments, I said, I felt they had a grain of truth. My daughter is grown now: she was the eighteen-month-old baby standing in the crib and rattling its bars when the intruder entered, the baby I was afraid to leave alone when my instinct was to flee the scene. She said maybe I should write more, write about my unease and the ambiguities surrounding the piece. She knows me well and I take her advice seriously; this time I felt specially prone to do so, for she was there at the time, exposed to the same peril as I was, and that gives her some rights in the matter. So I've done what she advised, although doing so defies all my writerly instincts, which run opposite to the aesthetic of full disclosure; I prefer concealment, cunning, and artifice. But somehow I felt honor bound to her suggestion. And why not, I thought, it might be good for me, like the exercises I give students and consider good for them.

I think I didn't do justice, in the story, to my fear. I didn't do it justice because, for one thing, my own feelings and experiences—recounted in a straightforward way, that is—rarely entice me as raw material. That's not writing, in my view, at least not my kind of writing. Terrible and frightening things happen every day. They're not enough. What entices is not what happened but transforming it. So what I wrote is unsatisfying because it's merely true. It's not even cathartic—not that that would justify its existence—since the fear remains, in amber, as vivid and gleaming as the day it was born. I'm mildly glad to have shaped it into words after so long, to have played around with it and made it a thing that stands in the world like a piece of granite rather than a delicate, hidden insect in amber. And in some strange way, having shaped it for public disclosure makes it all the more mine. Still, I don't know that fear, even when standing in the world, set in a context of class, race, and young urban married life, means anything beyond itself. It's not porous or malleable, but rather solid and intransigent. And that's not enough either.

It would be enough only if I had transformed all the details—the pineapple chunks, the mini dress, the neighbors, the family from Cleveland—disguised them like guests at a masked ball so that only the fear kept its true face, standing out in the masked crowd, that face alone stark and bare, grimacing, leering, potent beyond measure, the image of every fear that ever was and will be.

Memoir? Fiction? Where's the Line?

Mimi Schwartz

> *"It was very cold the night my mother died . . ."*
>
> Anna Quindlen

I don't remember what my second grade teacher wore! How can I recall the dialogue when my Dad left 10 years ago? All my summers in Maine blur together. That's what my students will say tomorrow when I return their first efforts at turning memories into memoir. They are mostly 21- and 22-year-old college seniors, plus a few retirees and second careerists, all eager to explore their lives on paper for themselves, friends and the world. No one is famous, although one woman said she won the lottery.

The memory worries will come mainly from marine biologists, psychology and history majors who deal in term papers and lab reports, rarely from poets and fiction writers who have taken enough creative writing workshops to understand, as V.S. Pritchett once wrote about memoir, "It's all in the art. You get no credit for living."

Some of these "creative" writers assume such advice excludes their boring lives, and so I have written "Great detail!" in many margins of first essays only to find out that the date rape or house burning down didn't happen. No, no, you can't do that, I say. That's fiction, not memoir. You have to play by the rules; there's a line you can't cross. And where is that? they ask. I don't know, only that if you make up too much, you've crossed it. The murkiness makes writer Anna Quindlen choose fiction over memoir. In "How Dark? How

Stormy? I Can't Recall!" (*New York Times Book Review*), she says that the newspaper reporter in her made her check old weather charts before she could publish the line, "It was very cold the night my mother died." Like my fact-conscious students, she worries: "Was it very cold or was that just the trick memory played on a girl who was sick and shivering, at least metaphorically?" and this worry, combined with a lousy memory, makes Quindlen avoid memoir, "a terrain too murky for me to tread." She says she can't, like Frank McCourt in *Angela's Ashes*, "remember half a century later the raw, itching sore that erupted between his eyebrows when he was a boy." So she writes fiction, preferring to create a world "from the ground up, the imagined minutiae of the lives of characters I invent from my knowledge of characters."

"But what about your *true* stories?" I would ask, if Anna were in my class. Don't you tell your friends, family, especially your children, about who you were, who your family was once upon a time? And do you want those stories to last more than one minute? If we stick only to facts, our past is as skeletal as black-and-white line drawings in a coloring book. We must color it in.

I tell the Annas in my class what I tell myself as memoir writer: Go for the emotional truth, that's what matters. Yes, gather the facts by all means. Look at old photos, return to old places, ask family members what they remember, look up time-line books for the correct songs and fashion styles, read old newspapers, encyclopedias, whatever—and then use the imagination to fill in the remembered experience. You don't need a tape recording of what your parents said to "remember" what they said that day. You don't need a photo of your kindergarten teacher to describe her; the clothes you imagine will match your feeling about her. Maybe you see a red, mini-suited girl; maybe you see a woman in a thick, long black dress with white cuffs. Either way, we see the teacher as you saw her. And who knows? She might even have worn those white cuffs! The subconscious is remembering.

That's also what I told my mother last week when she called to tell me that an essay I'd sent her about my love affair with horses was wrong. "I picked you up that day you fell off that horse, Sultan."

"You did not. I still remember everyone staring because my pants were ripped, my knee all bloody on the bus ride home."

"You were crying in the Pontiac."

"I was not."

It was her memory against mine with no one else to ask, so I wasn't changing my story. It was true for me—the humiliation following my glory riding Sultan—and she could tell her version, I said. That's what Rosemary Wolff threatened when her two sons, Geoffrey and Tobias, wrote separate and conflicting memoirs of their youth. (Or so Geoffrey Wolff said once in a workshop I took in Aspen.)

How subjective can you be in memoir, accidentally or on purpose? That is a central question, and different writers have different solutions. I teach the possibilities. You might start with a disclaimer the way John Irving did in "Trying to Save Piggy Sneed." He warns readers up front to "Please remember that all memoir is fiction," and then tells a wonderful story about how a retarded garbage man started him on his career as a writer. You might hint a disclaimer in your title, as

Mary Carr does in *The Liar's Club*, and leave the reader wondering. You might tip off the reader with phrases such as "I imagine her . . . " or "Perhaps he said . . . ", the way Jane Bernstein does in her retelling of her sister's murder 2,000 miles away and 20 years before. You might use exaggeration as Russell Baker does in *Growing Up*, so that the dialogue of his interview to become a paperboy sounds as if he were being interviewed to head up IBM.

You might even give a lament that you don't remember, as Bret Lott does in his book, *Fathers, Sons, and Brothers*, before he gives a rich description of the morning that his son stopped calling him Mommy:

> The sad thing, though, is that I can't recall the first day he called me Daddy when I went into his room. I could make up a story about it, here and now; I could tell you how it was on a Tuesday—Melanie's morning—and how there seemed something different in his voice as I came up from sleep. . . .

Whatever else, there's always Joan Didion's wonderful permission in "On Reading a Notebook"—that if you remember it, it's true. I use it often.

> Perhaps it never did snow that August in Vermont; perhaps there never were flurries in the night wind, and maybe no one else felt the ground hardening and summer already dead even as we pretended to bask in it, but that was how it felt to me, and it might as well have snowed, could have snowed, did snow.

How it felt to me! What a relief to memoir writers who want to explore the emotional truth of memory. It may be "murky terrain," you may cross the line into fiction and have to step back reluctantly into what really happened—the struggle creates the tension that makes memoir either powerfully true or hopelessly phony. The challenge of this genre is that it hands you characters, plot and setting, and says, "Go figure them out!"—using fact, memory and imagination to recreate the complexity of real moments, big and small, with no invented rapes or houses burning down. If the challenge intrigues you, imaginatively and emotionally, and you find the right voice—one savvy and appealing enough to make the reader say, "Yes. I've been there. I know what you mean!"—you have something good. But if the voice you adopt annoys, embarrasses or bores because of lack of insight, then beware. The reader will say, "So what? I don't care about you!" often in anger.[1]

It's that personal, the judgment. It's YOU, not some anonymous character they are talking about. Like a smile at a cocktail party, the voice of memoir—far more than in fiction—can evoke a quick response. Phony or real. I like this person. I hate this person. Nothing lukewarm or impersonal about it.

---

[1] James Woolcott's recent article, "Me, Myself and I," in *Vanity Fair* is a good example of that anger. He attacks Anne Roiphe as "the true queen of the daytime soaps," Creative Nonfiction as "civic journalism for the soul," and others like Laurie Stone as "navel gazers"—as if the person, genre and subject ("no detail is too mundane to share") and not the art sinks the "I" of true stories.

That vulnerability—more than a bad memory, I suspect—makes many agree with writer Pam Houston: "I write fiction to tell the truth." The seeming anonymity of fiction, even autobiographical fiction, can be creatively freeing, as Jamaica Kincaid shows in *Annie John*. She makes her real-life, older brothers disappear so that the emotional focus is on a girl and her mother, and she calls the story fiction—even though other basics are true. (Kincaid, like the main character, Annie, grew up on the island of Antigua and left at 17.) But if your story is really about Mom in Iowa, why turn her into a half-sister in New York—unless in the transformation, you, like Kincaid, tap into the real story you need to tell?

One essay, out of the 25 I just finished reading, does hook me with its savvy. This young woman of 22, Nicole Ross, already knows what it has taken me years to figure out: that the ambiguity of memoir, its shifting planes of truth and memory, can take you somewhere important:

> I want to remember a childhood brimming with sunlight, with just enough suffering to make it seem real. Each Christmas becomes bleaker than the last; it always seems as if there are fewer presents under the tree, and less laughter as my grandparents grow older. Ironically, the Christmases of my childhood have become lavish feasts of endless caroling because I don't remember them any more. I think that my collection of memories is nothing more than a soothing deception; many details have been supplied by a fertile imagination. It can't be all bad, though, because my parents still smile at me the way they do in my memories of those early Christmases.

Unlike Anna, Nicole is comfortable with how memory, fact and imagination mix up her Christmases; she trusts the process. I wrote "Great!" in every margin of her six pages. I believed every word, heard the caroling, saw her parents smile.

There *is* one reason not to write memoir, aside from worries about memory and the restraints on creative freedom: Mom may not speak to you again if you write her story, and you care. Frank McCourt waited to publish his memoir until after his mother died because he didn't want to hurt her. Others don't wait and call their story fiction, so they can tell Mom, family, friends, anyone real who appears on the page: "Of course that isn't you. I made that part up." No one is fooled, but you save face, maybe a lawsuit.

A writer does have some fictive leeway even in memoir, I believe—*if* you are cautious (and not too famous). Tomorrow I will tell the student who wrote about her bulimic roommate that her profile could be just as powerful and less hurtful if she moved the girl next door, changed her hair color and did not call her Kimmie.[2] I will tell the class that in a memoir about six months in my marriage, I made a few composite characters of minor characters and wrote this disclaimer in

---

[2]This anonymity is essential if, like me, you have students share their work in progress in class. Why should the roommate's problems become public knowledge?

my introduction: "The story is 90 percent factual; the rest is made up to protect those who didn't ask to be in this book." The problem was not my husband and my children (I was willing to take my chances with them); it was my friends, like the one who was leaving her husband just as I was deciding to stay with mine. In fact, I had three friends who were thinking about divorce, so in the book, I made a composite character and we met for cappuccino.

Depending on the story's focus, you sometimes collapse time and characters as well, I will tell my students, and still are "true" on my truth scale. Writer Jack Connor, in a personal essay about a weekend of watching eagles, collapsed three days into one morning and mentioned only two of the four students who accompanied him on that trip. He wanted to capture how young people reawakened in him the simple pleasure of birding even in a mid-January freeze, and the number of days, the number of people, didn't matter—although in a scientific field report they would. I will show my students how his original journal entry of facts and private observations evolved many drafts later into a published story ("A Lesson from Mott's Creek") with a voice and a point of view.

Journal Entry:

1/11/94   —eagle weekend—
one of the best birding experiences of the last year this weekend—the eagle survey with Jerry Liguori, Brian Sullivan, two folks from Ocean City (mcdermotts?), and on Sunday with Joe Mangion and Bil Seng.

. . . both days cold—and windy. temp in teens, with wind chill, probably below 10, maybe even bordering on zero. but blue sky, growing cloudy on saturday around one and then mostly cloudy. Sunday, blue until 2 or so and only partly cloudy after that. . . .

Essay Opening:

"Binoculars in my fingers, tears in my eyes from the January glare, face stiff from the hard wind, I am standing between Brian Sullivan and Jerry Liguori and wonder, "Why don't I come out here every single day?"

I will also tell my students about a friend who is writing about her aunt who had a lobotomy 50 years ago. My friend visited the mental institution where it happened, looked up records, talked to a nurse and doctor who remembered her aunt and tried writing what her aunt's life was like. But those "facts" weren't enough to recreate the story. She must take an imaginative leap, our writing group told her, imagine herself as her aunt and what would it feel like, maybe write in first person. Draft in hand, my friend can then check with a psychiatrist— "Does this ring true?"—and with relatives, before revising for more accuracy.

The Joan Didions and John Irvings in tomorrow's class will nod their heads in agreement. The Anna Quindlens will not. They want clear-cut boundaries and would side with my writer friend, Andrea Herrmann, who warns me: "If the writer can make a composite character, what prevents her from making up scenes, blending parts of places together, switching historical time frames?" Making up anything, for them, is crossing the line into fiction and should be called that. But I disagree. If the main plot, characters, and setting are true, if the intent is to make honest sense of "how it felt to me" and tell that true story well (with disclaimers as needed), it's memoir to me.

In "Why Memoir Now?" Vivian Gornick writes, "What happened to the writer is not what matters; what matters is the larger sense that the writer is able to make of what happened. For that the power of a writing imagination is required." Use that imagination in memoir, I tell myself and my students, to find the language and complexity of real lives, not imagined ones. It's OK to trust yourself (with a bit of Quindlen's and Herrmann's wariness)—even if you can't remember the temperature on the night Mom died.

Finding the Inner Story in Memoirs and Personal Essays

Michael Steinberg

The comment I find myself making most frequently to my students and to many of the writers who submit personal narratives to *Fourth Genre* is, "The main thing that's missing in this piece is *your story*." You're probably thinking, here comes another endorsement of those confessional narratives—the ones that give creative nonfiction a bad name. Actually, one of the reasons why I think we're seeing too many of those pieces is because a lot of nonfiction writers are narrating *only* the literal story of their experience, and leaving out the "inner story"; that is, the story of their thinking.

Let me give you a personal example. A while ago, I wrote a memoir called "Trading Off." It was about a four-year struggle I had with a high school coach who might or might not have been anti-Semitic. While I was writing it, I was trying to recall the shame I felt and the humiliation I allowed myself to put up with—both of which, I discovered, were the price I paid for wanting to play baseball for this punitive coach. At readings, whenever I introduce the piece as a baseball memoir, I watch the expressions on the faces of several of the women in the audience. Some roll their eyes, some cross their arms, some even grimace. To them, it's another a baseball story, about some poor kid's bad experience with a mean-spirited coach—the kind of jock story their boyfriends or husbands may have told them over and over again.

It doesn't always happen that way, but often enough by the time I've finished reading the piece, the audience's body language has changed. Some people, men and women alike, have figured out that the memoir isn't really about

405

baseball. Baseball is the setting, the stage for the conflict between the young boy and the coach. The coach is the gatekeeper and the narrator wants more than anything else at 13 to pitch for the high school baseball team. But the more interesting and important story is what goes on in the mind of the narrator as he agonizes over how badly he wants this, at the same time as he's questioning his decision to put up with this coach's tactics.

What he repeatedly asks himself throughout the memoir is "Why am I doing this?" Indeed, why *is* he doing it? What makes him so determined, and so desperate? And how much humiliation is he is willing to put up with in order to make the team? Quite a bit, it seems. That's why I titled the memoir "Trading Off."

Often, during the question-and-answer period, or after the reading, some of the same people who initially resisted the piece will tell me their own stories about humiliating experiences they've had with similar kinds of gatekeepers: punitive teachers, abusive parents, cruel childhood friends, and so on. A woman once volunteered that the memoir reminded her of her own teenage struggle with a harsh and demanding ballet teacher.

That's exactly the kind of response I hope for. I don't want the reader to come away from the memoir thinking that it's another "poor, poor, pitiful me" story. I want the reader to feel the humiliation and shame that I did, as well as to understand that I willingly chose to make this tradeoff in order to prove myself to this hard-nosed coach.

But, I doubt that readers—especially the skeptical ones—would have been able to make those personal connections had I written only the literal "here's what happened to me" story.

In her book *The Situation and the Story: The Art of Personal Narrative,* Vivian Gornick makes this same point when she writes, "Every work [of literature] has both a situation and a story. The situation is the context or circumstance, sometimes the plot; the story is the emotional experience that preoccupies the writer: the insight, the wisdom, the thing one has come to say" (13).

When I teach workshops in personal narrative, most students bring memoirs. At *Fourth Genre,* over 75 percent of our submissions are memoirs. There are as many different reasons or impulses for writing a memoir as there are memoirists; some write to tell their story; some write to preserve a family history; some simply want to reminisce.

When I teach the form, I'm always urging my students to go beyond or probe beneath the literal story. My own editor for the memoir I'm currently writing is always challenging me to "dig deeper," to write, as she describes it, "more vertically."

I nudge my students, as well as myself, to examine why they're telling this particular story, and why it matters enough to write about it. How, I ask them, did this experience shape you? How did it change you? What were the costs? What was at stake? What, in other words, is compelling you to write the piece? Hopefully, these will all be discovered in the process of writing.

I also advise writers to think about memoir as having two stories: the story of the actual experience—the surface subject, the facts, the sequence of remembered events (what Gornick calls "the situation"), and the story of their thinking—that is, what do those facts and events mean? What are you thinking and feeling as you write the specific scenes? What I'm really asking the writer is: How do *you* interpret the story of your own experience?

A memoir, then, can have more than one voice. Sometimes it must. There's the voice that tells the surface story, and another, more reflective voice that comments, digresses, analyzes, and speculates about the story's events—in other words, a voice or narrative persona that looks to find a human connection or larger meaning in his/her personal experience.

Everything I've said about finding the inner story in memoir comes from reading, writing, and reading about personal essays. Since one of the hallmarks of the personal essay is its intimacy, most personal essays are inner explorations that open a window to the writer's inner life.

Scott Russell Sanders says that the "essay is the closest thing we have, on paper, to a record of the individual mind at work and play . . . the spectacle of a single consciousness making sense of part of the chaos' of experience." (189–90). The essay works by "following the zigzag motions of the inquisitive mind. . . . The writing of an essay is like finding one's way through a forest, without being quite sure what game you are chasing, what landmark you are seeking."

Working in the essay form, according to Phillip Lopate, "allows you to ramble in a way that reflects the mind at work . . . [I]n an essay, the track of a person's thoughts struggling to achieve some kind of understanding of a problem is the plot, the adventure. The essayist must be willing to contradict himself . . . to digress, and even to end up in an opposite place from where he started. . . . The essay offers the chance to wrestle with one's own intellectual confusion" (qtd. in Heilker 93).

The late critic and memoirist Alfred Kazin says, "The genuine essayist . . . [i]s the writer who thinks his way through the essay—and so comes out where perhaps he did not wish to. . . . He uses the essay as an open form—as a way of thinking things out for himself, as a way of discovering what he thinks. . . . [A]n essay is not meant to be the 'whole truth'. . . . [I]t is an expression of the self thinking" (qtd. in Heilker 90). In an essay, it is not the thought that counts but the experience we get of the writer's thought; not the self, but the self thinking."

In "The End," an essay by Judith Kitchen, she suggests that Kazin's point is the purpose of writing creative nonfiction. "The building of a process of thought," Kitchen says, "is what interests the reader. In essays, we participate by paying attention to the attention that is paid. The intimacy of the essay is a sharing of thought. We look as much for how an author approaches a subject as for the subject itself" (228). Kitchen closes the essay with some useful teaching advice. She writes,

Here are five things my students deny themselves as their stories draw to a close:

1. Retrospection—a looking back, an assessment
2. Intrusion—a stepping in, a commentary
3. Meditation—a thinking through and around, finding a perspective

4. Introspection—a self-examination, honest appraisal and discovery
5. Imagination (as distinct from invention)—which allows for alternatives, projections, juxtapositions, whatever could provide a larger frame (228)

I agree with Kitchen when she says that these are things her students "deny themselves." It's a generous and, I think, accurate way to phrase it. I'll add these others:

- reflection: thinking things out, searching for meaning
- speculation: playing "what if"
- self-interrogation: asking the hard questions, the ones you don't always want to know the answers to
- digression: allowing the mind to wander away from the subject
- projection: trying to predict what might happen.

There are many other touchstones we could all add. But the point is that in any human situation or encounter, we can't get through 30 seconds without utilizing most or all of these things. We're *always* reacting internally.

The mind never stops searching for connections and asking questions. And that's the thinking/feeling self I'd like to see more of in the personal narratives I read, both as a teacher and as an editor.

Works Cited

Gornick, Vivian. *The Situation and the Story: The Art of Personal Narrative.* New York: Farrar, Straus and Giroux, 2001.

Heilker, Paul. *The Essay: Theory and Pedagogy for an Active Form.* Urbana: NCTE, 1996: 90.

Kitchen, Judith. "The End." *Fourth Genre.* 3:2 (Fall 2001): 228–234.

Sanders, Scott Russell. "The Singular First Person," *Secrets of the Universe: Scenes from the Journey Home.* Boston: Beacon, 1991. 187–204.

Experimental Critical Writing

Marianna Torgovnick

At the 1988 MLA Convention I gave a paper called "Malinowski's Body." Since I was afraid to give this paper, I had announced it in the program by the deliberately neutral title "Looking at Anthropologists" so that I could change my mind up to the last minute and substitute something else instead. I was afraid because "Malinowski's Body" does not resemble the usual MLA paper in style or content. I knew that the audience would listen to it and respond to it, and I knew that some members of the audience would not like it and might even walk out—and not because there was another talk they wanted to hear at the same hour.

"Malinowski's Body" did not begin its life in any of the ways I have been taught to consider legitimate. In fact, I wrote it, almost as a dare, after my writing group found the first material I wrote on Malinowski dull. To prove I could do better I went home and wrote several pages that begin this way:

> Malinowski's body looks like Lord Jim's. It's cased rigidly in white or beige trousers and shirt that sometimes becomes stained a muddy brown. When this happens, Malinowski summons his servants and has the clothes washed, immediately. For his clothes somehow seem to him an important part of his body, not just a covering for it.
>
> It's a small body, well fed but not kindly disposed enough toward itself to put on flesh. It has a narrow chest—pale, with just a few hairs and no nipples to speak of. It has thin legs yearning for massive thighs; in fact, if this man does put on weight in later life (and he may) it will show in his thighs first. The buttocks lie flat, unwelcoming, with maybe a stray pimple. The penis is a center of anxiety for him but is in fact no smaller—and no bigger—than anyone else's. It's one of the few points of identification he can settle on between his body and theirs.
>
> Their bodies—almost naked—unnerve him. His body needs its clothes; his head, its hat. He rarely looks at his body—except when washing it. But he has to look at theirs. The dislike he sometimes feels for the natives comes over

him especially when in the presence of their bodies. "Come in and bathe," the natives say from their ponds and rivers. "No, thanks," says Malinowski, retrieving the pith helmet and camera he momentarily laid aside on the grass. He looks at their bodies and takes notes about size, ornamentation, haircuts, and other ethnographic data. He takes photographs. He talks to them about customs, trade, housing, sex. He feels okay about the customs, trade, and housing, but the sex makes him uneasy.

The pages are based on an intuition and a hunch about what Malinowski looked like that were formed before I had found any pictures of him. They begin with an image rather than with the kind of concise generalization that had been my customary opening. And they were designed to loosen my prose by giving my imagination free play. Inevitably, I used what I had read by and about Malinowski—but in an almost unrecognizable way. My premise was that I would undress the ethnographer for study as Malinowski himself undresses subjects in his ethnographies and undresses, in his diary, the women he meets in daily life. When I wrote "Malinowski's Body" I did not intend to use it in the book I was writing. My goals were simply to limber up my style and to get in touch with what I wanted to say. But "Malinowski's Body" makes so many points about the ethnographer's scripting of himself according to conventional ideas of what is moral and manly that I decided to include it in my book. It is a creative piece, risky for the MLA. And yet my audience, or at least most of its members, seemed delighted. They asked questions about my "intentions" and "effects" that made me feel like a writer, not just a critic—a heady moment for me and a reception that gave David Laurence reason to invite me to present my thoughts on experimental critical writing. And it was a moment that had not come easily.

When I began to write my newest book—called *Gone Primitive* and published in the spring of 1990—I knew that I wanted to write something significantly different in tone and style from my first two books. I had recently been tenured and then promoted to full professor, and I felt that I was no longer writing for any committees—I was writing for myself. It was not that I would rewrite the books I had written; I am in fact proud of them. What I wanted was to reach a larger audience and to go somewhere new. What I discovered was that at first I did not know how.

The turning point came when I showed an early chapter to the members of my newly formed writing group. I was writing on an untraditional, uncanonical topic—Edgar Rice Burroughs' Tarzan novels—but my approach was conventional and scholarly. I began by surveying the critical literature on Tarzan and protesting (a little uneasily) that earlier critics either had overidentified with Burroughs or had not taken Tarzan seriously with regard to race and gender relations. I tried to pack lots of statistics and facts in the opening paragraphs to prove that Tarzan was important. In my eagerness to meet accepted standards of academic seriousness, I had succeeded (to borrow a phrase Wayne Booth once used to describe the freshman essay) in being "boring from within."

The members of my group, from whom I had asked no mercy that day, showed none. The chapter was sluggish, they said; the prose was lifeless and cold. It had no momentum, no narrative. Instinctively, I defended myself; I talked about all the interesting things that happened as I was researching and writing the chapter, telling them how I often found articles on the rebirth of the Tarzan phenomenon in issues of magazines that report the assassination of President Kennedy and reproduce those astonishing pictures we all remember of Jackie and little John-John and of Oswald. I had tried in the chapter to place the Tarzan series in the contexts of the twenties (the decade of its first great popularity) and the sixties (the decade of its rebirth). But I had used a style that censored my own experiences and visceral responses and that hid my writing's source of energy. One member of the group said, cannily, "You know, none of what you've just said comes out in this chapter. And there's a huge difference between the things you say and the things you write. You never write anything funny. You often say funny things." She was right. The other members of the group asked me to say more about La, a barbarian priestess in the Tarzan novels whom I had mentioned in passing. As I warmed to my description of La's importance and La's wrongs, my friend said, "When you start to get dull, pretend you are La—because you *are* La." And she was also right.

For me, "writing like La" became a metaphor for getting to a place where I was not afraid to write in a voice that had passion as well as information—a voice that wanted to be heard. "Writing like La" meant letting myself out of the protective cage of the style I had mastered—a style I now call the thus-and-therefore style because it naturally tends to include distancing words like those. Before I could change my thus-and-therefore style, I had to defamiliarize it; I had to know my cage so that I could open it at will. A fifteen-minute exercise I did with my writing group was a significant breakthrough. In this exercise, I parodied my own dullest style in a description of grocery stores in Durham, North Carolina. I began the description with just the kind of generalization that was one of my primary tics as a writer: "In Durham, one can shop at Food Lion for bargains, or Kroger's for selection. The most interesting shopping of all, however, is done at Harris Teeter." This exercise made me laugh at my own habits and made it impossible for me afterward to write unknowingly in my usual way. But there were still many low points, when I found myself unable to do anything *but* write in my dullest style. In fact, I wrote my excruciatingly bad beginning on Malinowski— the material I replaced with "Malinowski's Body"—roughly eighteen months after I vowed to leave my old style behind.

In preparing this presentation, I discovered in my files my first draft on Malinowski. I would like to share part of its beginning with you as an example of one sort of standard academic prose:

> Implicitly, I have been suggesting that "objectivity" is a delusory principle undergirding both important strands of social scientific and ethnographic thought and aesthetic and artistic-literary theories and methods. Rereading Malinowski, I think I've found a direct and interesting analogy.

Malinowski founded what is called functionalism in anthropology, the theory (and derived method) that explains all elements of a culture in terms of interlocking functions: the ethnographer explicitly "constructs" a model in which all the parts are presumed to contribute to a whole that is organic and unified (though quirkier than a machine). To make his construction, the ethnographer lives inside the culture, inhabits it as a text. He tries to replicate the native's point of view, which is the ground and touchstone of meaning and "accuracy." Functionalism leads, in anthropology, to what is called structural functionalism and then, later, to structuralism.

A point-by-point analogy with New Criticism and other formal approaches exists. Here too the "student" (critic) inhabits the text, assuming the unity of the parts as a whole and constructing an account of that whole in terms of the interlocking functions of its parts. The original ground of meaning is the author's intentions.

What I was doing in these paragraphs was the writerly equivalent of scratching at a scab. I had to say what was closest to the surface of my mind in order to get rid of that content, in order to discover whether it was useful or not, interesting or not. Sometimes, what I write first as a throwaway turns out to contain the intellectual core of my argument; sometimes, as in this real throwaway, it does not. The difference is usually whether I begin with material that I really care about or with material that I think I should care about. In this instance, I began with critical categories and genealogies of influence that I knew, by training, were considered important—and I trotted them out dutifully. Other critics had scratched these scabs; now it was my turn. The paragraphs include a lot of qualifications and distinctions, often inserted in parenthetical remarks, that would be unlikely to interest anyone but me. Sticky academic language coats the whole—"implicitly," "explicitly," "strand of thought." And I explain things in more detail than most people would want to read.

I would be too embarrassed to reproduce this rejected passage if I did not realize that it's representative of the prose that I—and I suspect many of you—habitually write. For this style typifies a great deal of academic writing. How did it come to be a norm? Largely, I think by establishing itself in an era when less criticism was published and the circle of critics was small enough to allow its members to believe they were contributing to the building of a common edifice. In this construction project all the names could and should be named, like those of contributors on a memorial plaque; Professor Z would build on what Professors X and Y had said in their essays; years later, Professors A and B would come along and add some decorative touches or do major renovations.

All of us who write criticism today wrote dissertations yesterday. And our teachers often tried, and succeeded in handing on what they perceived as the correct—that is, the careful, the judicious, the fair—way to write. But the styles we were taught can't work now in the same way as they worked fifty or even fifteen years ago. No one who gets around to writing a book, or even an essay, ever reads everything that has been written about its subject. Yet we cling to the fiction of completeness and coverage that the academic style preserves. This style protects us, we fondly believe, from being careless or subjective or unfair. It prescribes certain moves to ensure that the writer will stay within the boundaries that the academy has drawn.

Like many people who choose an academic life, I have a fundamental need for approval. I needed approval from my graduate advisers, tenure and promotion committees, and reviewers; I need it from my students and colleagues. It has been crucial for me in the last few years to have a writing group that approved of my new writing style: the group provided a different audience from the one I once imagined as my academic superiors, who judged the material I wrote according to more traditional standards. But I have also become aware that I am now not just someone in need of approval but also someone (like many of you) who gives or withholds approval. When we pass on the academic style to our graduate students or newest colleague, we train them to stay within the boundaries, both stylistically and conceptually. When we encourage experimental critical writing, we do not always know what we will get, but we stimulate the profession to grow and to change. We don't control the future of the profession only when we give grades or make hiring or tenure decisions; we control it at the level of the sentence.

At this point I need to back up a bit. It seems pretty clear to me that if all we want to do is to write for professional advancement, to write for a fairly narrow circle of critics who exist within the same disciplinary boundaries as we do, there is nothing really wrong with the traditional academic style. In fact, it's the right style, the inevitable style, because it says, in every superfluous detail and in every familiar move, You don't need to read me except to write your own project; I am the kind of writing that does not want to be heard.

But when critics want to be read, and especially when they want to be read by a large audience, they have to court their readers. And the courtship begins when the critic begins to think of himself or herself as a writer as well, a process that for me, as for some other critics of my generation, means writing as a person with feelings, histories, and desires—as well as information and knowledge. When writers want to be read they have to be more flexible and take more chances than the standard scholarly style allows: often, they have to be more direct and more personal. In a very real way (although my writing includes precious few autobiographical revelations), I could not think of myself as a writer until I risked exposing myself in my writing.

I am not talking here, necessarily, about full-scale autobiographical writing—though I am not ruling it out either. But I am saying that writerly writing is personal writing, whether or not it is autobiographical. Even if it offers no facts from the writer's life, or offers just a hint of them here and there, it makes the reader know some things about the writer—a fundamental condition, it seems to me, of any real act of communication. And real communication is exciting. For me, at any rate, the experience of this new kind of writing—which not only recognizes the pitfalls of the standard academic style but goes out of its way to avoid them—has been exhilarating.

Part 3

Composing Creative Nonfiction

In the earlier sections of the book you've had the chance to pair up what people write when they write creative nonfiction with what people talk about when they talk about creative nonfiction. Many of the writers whose work appears in Part One also talk about the genre in which they work in Part Two. They often also talk about the ways they typically create the work they do in creative nonfiction. In Part Three we take the discussion a little farther by pairing four pieces that could have gone in the first part of the book with four pieces in which their authors describe how they wrote them.

Writers' descriptions of what they did and what they went through as they wrote a particular essay or article often suggest strategies that other writers can use. Even the most experienced writers occasionally find themselves stymied by a project they've been working on, but because they are experienced they have strategies to fall back on which help them to begin writing again. Often their strategies arise not from their own problem solving but by the example of another writer. For example, many writers in many different forms have subscribed to Horace's advice, "Never a day without a line." They try to write every day, even if only for a limited time, because they find there is a creative equivalent of the law of inertia—"A mind in motion tends to stay in motion; a pen at rest tends to stay at rest." To that perhaps they add Hemingway's advice to quit writing for the day before you've exhausted your energy and your ideas and to return to writing the next day knowing where you're going to start up again. There are many sound principles and practices in the creative life, and writers often have to rummage among them for the ones that work for them. They also have to be prepared to discard them if they aren't working or if they don't seem to be very useful for a different project. Writers have to be flexible and adaptable in order to be productive, and the best place to find useful strategies and techniques other than those you discover for yourself is in the discoveries that other writers have made for themselves.

Even when writers have been successful in the past and would appear to know a number of moves they might make in their writing, they sometimes need to be reminded of the things they already know about writing. Sometimes the press of a work-in-progress makes it difficult to step back from it and apply alternative approaches, until the writer stumbles on something someone else did and re-members that he or she knew about that approach before. Some writers collect quotes about writing and, to help them remember, tape them to the wall or the word processor—some writers have *a lot* of stuff sticking to their wall, because there's *a lot* of relevant advice out there.

Consider this section, then, as a way to see what other writers have done as they wrote the kind of writing you've been reading in this book. Taken as a whole, the Composing Creative Nonfiction section presents four pairs of essays, arranged alphabetically by author. The first piece in each pair is the work that serves as the focus of the second piece, which explains the writer's composing processes on that particular work. Reading all eight pieces together is like sitting in on a writing group where each member reads something she's written and then explains what she went through to get the final draft. The writing is different enough that the responses of the writers and the shifting demands of purpose and form offer a range of strategies and creative decisions. Emily D. Chase's "Warp-ing Time with Montaigne" is a personal critical essay linking the practices of Mon-taigne, the original essayist, with those of contemporary writer Richard Rodriguez in his essay "Late Victorians"; her "Notes from a Journey toward 'Warping Time'" explains how this piece of what Marianna Torgovnick calls "experimental critical writing" came about. Simone Poirier-Bures writes a travel memoir in "That Shining Place: Crete, 1966"; her "Afterword: Writing 'The Greece Piece'" traces the course of her attempts to write about the experience more than twenty years later. Mary Elizabeth Pope's "Teacher Training" is an essay running in two paral-lel strands, one about her first teaching experience, the other about her fourth-grade teacher; "Composing 'Teacher Training'" follows the development of the essay from inception to publication, including changes after the piece was ac-cepted. Maureen Stanton writes a very personal memoir of her fiance's illness in "Zion" and recounts how she composed the essay in "On Writing 'Zion'." Four very different essays, four very different composing processes.

The selections here also connect to pieces in other parts of the book, and they can be be read separately, in conjunction with other examples and discussions. Emily D. Chase's work is related to other pieces demonstrating or discussing per-sonal voice in academic writing, such as those by Jane Tompkins in Part One and Marianna Torgovnick in Part Two. Simone Poirier-Bures's pairing connects to the other writing about time and place in the book, whether in memoir, essay, or liter-ary journalism, including the writing by Mary Clearman Blew, Patricia Hampl, Pico Iyer, and Mimi Schwartz. Mary Beth Pope's writing can handily supplement the segmented essays in the book, especially those that leap lightly across time and space, like that of Mary Clearman Blew, Naomi Shihab Nye, and Nancy Willard. Maureen Stanton's memoir is appropriate to read along with any of the other memory pieces in the book as well as the essay dwelling on the human body by Phillip Lopate. Already in trying to cite a few relevant examples we've begun to repeat references, but that's because the writing in Part Three reverberates in so many other readings throughout the book.

The other connection these selections make is, of course, to your writing. The process pieces here, where the writers describe composing their essays, don't prescribe failsafe procedures to which you should conform—quite the contrary. As these examples show, writers don't follow a rigid set of universal rules for composing; instead, they rely on general approaches and alternative strategies that they can alter to fit the shape of their individual works-in-progress. The experiences of these writers suggest strategies that you might be able to adapt to your own projects. They would be valuable to consult when you find yourself beginning or developing similar writing projects.

Finally, as you compose your own essays and assignments, you might consider keeping a journal on your own composing processes, to get a handle on what you generally do when you write and what you've done especially for certain projects. Think of Composing Creative Nonfiction as sitting in on a writing group in session, and feel free to enter the conversation with your own writing about your own composing.

Warping Time with Montaigne

Emily D. Chase

I sit bent over the breast beam of my 38 inch LeClerc floor loom pulling individual threads of brilliant, durable yarn through the metal heddles of its six harnesses. The heddles that have already been threaded hang in orderly lines waiting for the command to raise and lower those threads of yarn in the process of creating fabric; the unthreaded heddles hang in unorganized clusters patiently waiting for their turn to take part. This threading process is called "warping the loom" because the yarn that is being threaded onto the loom will become the "warp"—or lengthwise threads—in the fabric that will be woven. This process of reaching through the heddle with the threading hook, catching a strand of yarn, and pulling it back through the heddle does not require a lot of thought, other than that required to make sure the right piece of yarn gets threaded through the right heddle. My mind is free to wander as it will while I prepare my loom. "My style and my mind alike go roaming," Montaigne said (761). Of course I think of Montaigne; I have just spent two weeks reading essays by Montaigne, about Montaigne, and about essayists who have written essays on Montaigne. I have Montaigne on the brain: What sort of essays would Montaigne write if he were still alive? What would he say about the essays being written today? In particular, what would he say about Richard Rodriguez's essay "Late Victorians"? I pull a strand of yarn through a heddle and think of Montaigne and Rodriguez.

Rodriguez's essay uses many of the elements of the genre that Montaigne created. If Montaigne had not spun the first ideas of the essay into a new genre of literature, Rodriguez would not have been able to write "Late Victorians" without first spinning the thread of the genre on his own. I see that Montaigne's thoughts and ideas have been pulled through time to be used as the warp of essays since Montaigne's book *Essais* was first published in 1580. Now I am the one sitting at the loom of time, pulling the thoughts and ideas of Montaigne through the heddles. The full body of Montaigne's essays lies rolled up upon itself on the warp beam of the loom, waiting to be used by anyone with the knowledge and patience to thread it through time and secure it to this side of the past.

I reach through the eyelet of a heddle for a piece of Montaigne and imagine Rodriguez doing the same thing as he created "Late Victorians." For, certainly, he pulled Montaigne's motto through time—"Que scais-je?" (What do I know?). Rodriguez explores this question in "Late Victorians" as he asks himself how he should live his life and how he should *have lived* his life. These are the central questions and themes of his essay. He asks himself if he should have pursued "an earthly paradise charming," like the gay men he has known who have since died of AIDS (131). He considers the possibility of having pursued a career in office buildings which "were hives where money was made, and damn all" (128). At the end of "Late Victorians," he questions his future: Should he remain shifting his "tailbone upon the cold, hard pew," or should he rise to join the volunteers of the local AIDS Support Group (134)?

The genre of the essay offers Rodriguez an opportunity to explore these issues by using Montaigne's question, "What do I know?" Montaigne says:

> This . . . happens to me: that I do not find myself in the place where I look; and I find myself more by chance encounter than by searching my judgment. I will have tossed off some subtle remark as I write. Later I have lost the point so thoroughly that I do not know what I meant; and sometimes a stranger has discovered it before I do. If I erased every passage where this happens to me, there would be nothing left of myself. (26–27)

The form of the essay as Montaigne conceived it allows Rodriguez the freedom to seek answers, or to appear to seek answers, *while* he writes rather than exclusively *before* he writes. For Montaigne, writing was an *essai*, a trial or attempt. The presence of self and the absence of conclusion create a sense of freedom within Montaigne's essays. As he says: "The surest thing, in my opinion, would be to trace our actions to the neighboring circumstances, without getting into any further research and without drawing from them any other conclusions" (241). Like Montaigne, Rodriguez comes to no irrefutable conclusions in "Late Victorians." Instead, his thoughts wander through memories and observations as he seeks an understanding of the world by examining the things which touch his life directly.

As I consider the themes of "Late Victorians," I think of the title of one of Montaigne's essays, "By diverse means we arrive at the same end" (3). It occurs to me that this title describes the realm in which Rodriguez's thoughts wander. For what is Rodriguez writing about but diverse lifestyles and inevitable death? Running across his essay are the threads of gay life and death from AIDS. The texture of the weave is enhanced by Rodriguez's use of details from his own experience; these details form the weft of his essay, the crosswise threads. This weft is beaten into the fabric of "Late Victorians," as the "beater" on a loom locks the warp and weft tightly together by pushing each strand of weft snugly against the preceding strand, creating a cohesive, durable piece of fabric. Rodriguez weaves the fourteen sections of "Late Victorians" in this way, choosing different yarns for the weft of each section to create different textures and density of prose.

The first section is brief and is composed of two conflicting quotes. The first, by St. Augustine, hints at our discontent on earth in our mortal form due to our intuition that we are destined for a better life after death. Life is something to be restlessly passed through. The second quote, by Elizabeth Taylor, speaks of "cerulean" days in this life being undermined by sadness in the knowledge that these days and this life must end. These quotes show that, like Proteus, we are able to change our shape (the shape of our thoughts) as we try to avoid being bound by life. We are free to choose which way we will view life, whether we will suffer life and rejoice the end or embrace life and mourn the end. In "Late Victorians," Rodriguez tries to decide which view is the better view. He weaves these two quotes into his text to prepare us for the creation which is to follow. What is life? What is death? Which one wears the mask covering reality?

Throughout the essay, Rodriguez portrays the paradox of homosexual life in San Francisco. He uses the image of the Victorian house to help him accomplish this. By noting that the "three- or four-story Victorian house, like the Victorian novel, was built to contain several generations and several classes under one roof, behind a single oaken door" (123), he reveals the irony of the housing market whereby "gay men found themselves living with the architectural metaphor for family" (122). From this image, Rodriguez goes exploring through the homosexual landscape of his life and discovers multiple conflicting images. Rodriguez says, "The age-old description of homosexuality is of a sin against nature," yet he observes that as the peaceful, domestic, homosexual community of the Castro district thrived, the perverted "assortment of leather bars . . . outlaw sexuality . . . eroticism of the dark" on heterosexual Folsom street also thrived (124–25). In the Castro district, thanks to gays, "where recently there had been loudmouthed kids, hole-in-the-wall bars, [and] pimps," there were now "tweeds and perambulators, matrons and nannies" (125). The gay men, who have chosen to embrace "the complacencies of the barren house," have made the streets safe once again for the family (127).

This depiction of peaceful homosexual life is strikingly linked to another paradox of gay life as Rodriguez describes two parades in which gay men with AIDS march for gay rights. Rodriguez depicts gay men in one Gay Freedom Day parade as "the blessed in Renaissance paintings," martyrs who cherish "the apparatus of [their] martyrdom" (119). This passage is followed immediately by a description of a parade five years later, which includes "plum-spotted young men." The juxtaposition of the two passages creates the disturbing impression that these people are fighting to choose the way they wish to die rather than the way they wish to live.

How is Rodriguez going to reconcile all of these conflicting images? I pull another strand of Montaigne through time and see that the essay, as a form, allows Rodriguez to go exploring without *having* to reconcile these images. Montaigne says in his essay "Of repentance":

> This is a record of various and changeable occurrences, and of irresolute and, when it so befalls, contradictory ideas: whether I am different myself, or whether I take hold of my subjects in different circumstances and aspects. So, all in all, I may indeed contradict myself now and then; but truth, as Demades said, I do not contradict. If my mind could gain a firm footing, I would not make essays; I would make decisions; but it is always in apprenticeship and on trial. (611)

Montaigne is speaking of his contradictory thoughts and ideas, and yet the passage is equally applicable to Rodriguez's treatment of the paradox of gay life.

Montaigne's passage makes me wonder, as I slowly and steadily thread my way across the loom, if ALL of Montaigne is present in the warp of Rodriguez's essay. Would all of Montaigne's writings have to be threaded through time as an inseparable skein of thought, in order to remain true as a body of writing? Or could a person be selective when choosing which parts she pulled through time? I think of the warp on my loom, and I know that it is not possible to thread just part of a warp through the heddles. ALL of the strands of warp must be threaded, or the warp becomes tangled and knotted on the loom. For this reason, I have to think that all of Montaigne's thoughts are present in the warp of an essay, even when an essay presents an opposing view of that held by Montaigne.

I ponder this question because of the way I have linked Montaigne's quote from his essay "Of repentance" to the image of the AIDS victims in the Gay Freedom Day parades. The quote is pertinent as it applies to the issue of contradictions and paradox, yet Montaigne and Rodriguez do not agree completely on the actual subject of repentance. Both Montaigne and Rodriguez recognize the value of youth and of what is often deemed youth's foolishness. Rodriguez says:

> Though I am alive now, I do not believe that an old man's pessimism is truer than a young man's optimism simply because it comes after. There are things a young man knows that are true and are not yet in the old man's power to recollect. (120)

This is similar to a passage of Montaigne's, in his essay "Of repentance" in which he says:

> I should be ashamed and resentful if the misery and misfortune of my decrepitude were to be thought better than my good, healthy, lively, vigorous years, and if people were to esteem me not for what I have been, but for ceasing to be that. (619)

On the issue of repentance itself, however, Montaigne and Rodriguez differ. While Montaigne declares, "If I had to live over again, I would live as I have lived" (620), Rodriguez says, "It was then I saw that the greater sin against heaven was my unwillingness to embrace life" (132). There is an edge of repentance in Rodriguez's text, which does not exist in Montaigne's writings.

We are never sure, however, of what it is that Rodriguez feels the need to repent. In boldly talking about the gay community in San Francisco, Rodriguez appears to be revealing himself as a gay man, yet Phillip Lopate says, "Richard Rodriguez, for instance, is a master of the confessional tone, yet he tells us that his family calls him 'Mr. Secrets,' and he plays a hide-and-seek game of revealing himself" (xxvii). This is the case in "Late Victorians." Rodriguez describes the gay community of San Francisco from the perspective of a person who has been a part of that community. He has marched in a Gay Freedom Day parade; he has many male friends who are gay; he lives in a Victorian house which has been reclaimed and redecorated by gay men and now contains "four apartments; four single men"; he says, "To grow up homosexual is to live with secrets and within secrets" (122). And yet, on his deathbed, a friend of Rodriguez's, Cesar, says with irony that Rodriguez "would be the only one spared," that he was "too circumspect" (131). Rodriguez never actually says that he is gay. What are we to think?

I continue the process of pulling strands of yarn and thought through the loom: Does it matter if Rodriguez is gay? Does it matter if he tells us he is or isn't gay? What do I, as a reader, think of the authority of voice in the piece if this information appears to be purposefully concealed? Essayist E. B. White declared, "There is one thing the essayist cannot do—he cannot indulge himself in deceit or in concealment, for he will be found out in no time" (xxvi). And yet Alexander Smith wrote of Montaigne, "If you wish to preserve your secret, wrap it up in frankness" (Lopate xxvii). Montaigne said, "We must remove the mask," but he also said that he has "painted [his] inward self with colors clearer than [his] original ones" (504). Clearly, the act of making one's private thoughts public is not as simple as just recording the observations of one's life or even of simply attempting to capture one's mind in the act of thinking, as Montaigne set out to do.

I look back across the loom at the threads I have pulled through the heddles and am reminded that essays consist of explorations, questions, and contradictions. In his essay "Late Victorians," Rodriguez questions his life and lifestyle. Should he embrace life and mourn death, as his gay friends do, or should he withhold himself from life and look forward to death, as he does in his role as a skeptic? "Skepticism became my demeanor toward them—I was the dinner-party skeptic, a firm believer in Original Sin and in the limits of possibility" (Rodriguez 131). Rodriguez does not find the answer to his question in "Late Victorians." In the essay, he remains shifting his "tailbone on the cold, hard pew" while he tries to decide which role to play—which mask to put on or, perhaps, which mask to take off.

It is the *quest* for answers rather than the answers themselves that distinguishes the Montaignian essay. In this respect, "Late Victorians" is a good example of a contemporary essay that has been woven on a warp of Montaigne. In other respects, such as the inclusion of quotations, the essay differs from those of Montaigne. (Montaigne's essays include numerous quotations, Rodriguez's few.) However, when I gaze across the warp threaded through my loom, I am reminded that even this difference is a tribute to Montaigne, for I see Montaigne's strand of thought that advocates rebellion against accepted forms of discourse, including his own.

It is likely that Montaigne's thoughts go warping through most literary nonfiction essays. This is very different from what Montaigne envisioned when he wrote the preface, "To the Reader," for his book *Essais:*

> I have had no thought of serving either you or my own glory. My powers are inadequate for such a purpose. I have dedicated it to the private convenience of my relatives and friends, so that when they have lost me (as soon they must), they may recover here some features of my habits and temperament, and by this means keep the knowledge they have had of me more complete and alive. (2)

I think of this quote as I pull the last strand of warp through its heddle and secure it to the cloth beam on my side of the loom. My loom is now ready to be used to create a piece of individuality. I wonder what I will create. Shall I weave in some of the texture of Rodriguez or of Reg Saner? Emerson or Ehrlich? The possibilities are endless. I step on a treddle to open the warp, throw my shuttle of weft across the threads, and allow "my style and my mind alike" to go roaming. I have warped my loom with Montaigne.

Works Cited

Lopate, Phillip, ed. *The Art of the Personal Essay.* New York: Anchor Books, 1994.

Montaigne, Michel de. *The Complete Works of Montaigne.* Trans. Donald M. Frame. Stanford: Stanford UP, 1957.

Rodriguez, Richard. "Late Victorians." *The Best American Essays 1991.* Ed. Joyce Carol Oates. New York: Ticknor & Fields, 1991. 119–34.

White, E.B. *Essays of E.B. White.* New York: HarperCollins, 1977.

Notes from a Journey toward "Warping Time"

Emily D. Chase

The path that I took to create the essay "Warping Time with Montaigne" was not a direct path through the writing process. I meandered through personal experiences and through unfamiliar research before I found a thread to connect the two and to help me reach some sort of meaningful understanding of Montaigne and of myself. Since writing that essay, I have noticed that my path through the writing process is almost always indirect and that quite often the meandering path is the most direct way for me to get to insight and understanding. What follows here is essentially a travelogue of my journey toward "Warping Time with Montaigne."

The first time that I heard of Michel de Montaigne was in a course in Graduate Composition. Before that time, the term "essay," to me, was a generic term used by English teachers to refer to short pieces of nonfiction writing. I had no sense of the history of the term or the genre; however, I immediately became interested in Montaigne's writings and therefore decided to write about him for the required research paper in the class. The research paper was written immediately prior to "Warping Time with Montaigne" (the essay included here) and provided me with enough background information to pique my interest and to make me want to have some fun with the information in another piece of writing.

As part of the in-class prewriting for the research paper, I did a cluster/web off of the central term "literary nonfiction." The freewriting that followed the cluster exercise reveals the general direction in which I was drawn:

> Having to research an area of, or a figure in, literary nonfiction, I might like to compare and contrast the original essays everyone quotes—Montaigne, Newman, Emerson, Thoreau—with the modern essayists (especially the nature writers)—Dillard, Ehrlich, Selzer, White—to see if the originals have affected

the moderns. I'd like to find the ties, if any, between personal interaction with nature, religion . . . and the desire to write LNF essays. Part of this study would be taking a look at how each essayist recorded his thoughts (i.e. Thoreau and his journals). Is each day a personal scrutiny of life? an appreciation of being alive? Part of LNF is taking a real daily event and personalizing it by recording your interaction w/it.

But where is this going in terms of research?—Study the masters, study the moderns, draw conclusions. What are people already saying about this link? Has anyone already taken this tack? Is this productive? Is this worthwhile?

I see in this freewrite the idea of not just the original research paper I did on Montaigne but perhaps also the germ of the idea behind "Warping." I never let go of this interest in the correlation between the early essayists and the current essayists.

In just ten days, I discovered a topic and pulled together a reasonable essay about Montaigne and his influence; I used the metaphor of building construction as I discussed the construction of the genre of literary nonfiction upon the foundation of Montaigne's writings. I think better and have more fun writing when I use metaphors to organize and present my thoughts. This fact, no doubt, played a major role in the process that I went through to create the "Warping" essay.

As I was finishing the research paper on Montaigne and just before I began the "Warping" essay, I read Gerald Early's essay "Life with Daughters: Watching the Miss America Pageant" and Jane Tompkins' essay "At the Buffalo Bill Museum." I was overwhelmed by the power of Early's piece, and my original reaction to this essay in my journal reflects this:

> Wow! What an essay! . . . Like a freight train, the fully loaded essay started slowly, exerting effort to overcome inertia, then slowly accumulated speed until it rushed, unstoppably, toward its destination. With Early's final sentence, "My knees had begun to hurt and I realized, painfully, that I was much too old, much too at peace with stiffness and inflexibility, for children's games," the train rushed off the end of the track into the great unknown void of the future. Wow!

By contrast, I did not like Tompkins' essay—or rather I did not understand her essay. My journal reaction to her essay is one long attempt to understand her point; I never do reach that understanding but come to the conclusion that "this is a disturbing piece because I can't see where the author is coming from. I'm not sure a rereading would help." It may seem irrelevant that I read these two essays between writing my two Montaigne essays, yet I think it was crucial that I read as powerful a creative commentary essay as Early's and that I read (and struggled with) Tompkins' essay just as I was directed to write an analysis paper of current literary nonfiction in which I would "explore an individual essay, a series of essays, or a particular author or authors." Both Early and Tompkins use objects and events that they see in their surroundings to launch themselves into realms of contemplation. I must have subconsciously hung onto this technique such that it resurfaced later as I tried to figure out what to do with the analysis assignment.

My initial plans for the analysis paper returned to my interest in the link between Montaigne and the essayists that are writing today. I was still too interested in Montaigne and too convinced of his importance as a crucial element in the genre of literary nonfiction to let go of him. However, we were instructed to comment upon (interpret/analyze) a more current essay. I began to play with possible ways to link Montaigne with current essayists.

On the day that we began working on the analysis paper, I wrote the following prewrite in class:

> Having the chance to write on one element or author in nonfiction, I think I'd like to pursue the elements of Montaigne's essays which can be found in the works of other essayists. Perhaps I could tackle Emerson's essay, "Montaigne," and show how that essay uses Montaignian practices in the process of praising Montaigne. This is a possibility. However, I'd also like to look at Montaigne versus Bacon in terms of voice in the essay and then apply that comparison to critical articles today—(i.e. tackle the 4-woman writers' group who are trying to write "readable" literary criticism [Tompkins, Kaplan, Torgovnik, Davidson]). I'd need to find out if there is much out there in terms of articles/essays on this debate. If *College English* is including these articles now but labeling them as opinion, is anyone reacting to this practice? Is Tompkins? Is Sommers? I think that this could be a much more interesting topic/issue than the piece on Emerson. It would also get me involved in a current intellectual discussion. Having had "Critical Theory" I feel that I have a fairly good base to stand on. Where would Dillard's book, *Living by Fiction,* fit in? or would it? Robert Coles? Who is arguing for Baconian essays in academia? Does Montaigne ever get mentioned in support of personal criticism?—Probably not. But a discussion of Montaigne vs Bacon could be fairly enlightening. I have lots of articles discussing this. I have the background material. I'd just have to dig into the contemporary information. Back to the MLA Bibliography. . . .

I find it interesting as I reread this entry and as I dig through various drafts of the "Warping" essay that one comment I received during a peer editing session of the paper says, "Personally, I think this is better than a lot of the jargon-filled stuff I've read in academic journals." Again, I must have internalized the idea of "readable" criticism such that it resurfaced on its own later in the process.

On the same day that I wrote the above journal entry, as I was beginning work on this final paper, I kept trying to find a way to bring Montaigne into a criticism of a current essay. Because I have watched innumerable episodes of "Star Trek," it did not seem inconceivable to me that one of those hypothetical warps in the space-time continuum could allow Montaigne to suddenly appear in person to comment on the essays being written today. In the preceding research paper, I had already looked at how essayists since Montaigne had used his ideas and examples to help them create their own essays, so it seemed only fair that Montaigne should now have his say about the current essays that are being written.

The word "warp" turned out to be the necessary spark that ignited an inspirational firestorm.

I remember the excitement that I felt when it struck me that the word warp carries a number of different meanings. I had been thinking of the term with a Star Trekian mentality of traveling through time and dimensions of reality, but I am also a weaver, and so as I thought of "warping time," I automatically thought of "warping a loom"—threading a warp onto a loom. After writing the journal entry about Montaigne and Bacon, I jotted down the following notes to myself:

exciting	
Some ^ thoughts-	"Warping Time: Montaigne on _____"
& ideas	sitting at loom, threading warp, thinking about
	assignments/readings
	critique article in my head by remembering
	what Montaigne & critics of M.
this	have said.
could	get up to pursue details for more specifics
be	tie in with images of: thread
really	warp/weaving
fun!	distorted/warped time
	structure & patterns & variations of woven cloth
	lay warp on loom, like laying _____ on M.
	or like laying M on _____.

In one moment of inspiration, I made the connection between the elements and process of threading a loom and the elements and process of writing an essay. I couldn't wait to start writing; all I needed was a modern essay to interpret in order to fulfill the requirements of the paper assignment.

It is probably important to note here that I had only one week in which to select and interpret a current essay. The title of Richard Rodriguez's "Late Victorians" drew me to his essay, and then his mix of dry humor and deadly seriousness fascinated me. As I read his essay with the warping idea in mind, I began to see Rodriguez as a weaver of essays and the fourteen sections of "Late Victorians" as variations of weft on the same warp. His essay seemed to be the perfect one for me to work with, and I could barely contain myself as I told my editing group about the ideas for my paper. I can still picture my teacher leaning forward on his chair with keen interest as I explained what I envisioned for my paper.

The writing of both my Montaigne papers was aided in large part by exercises and peer editing that were conducted as part of coursework in the Graduate Composition class. The drafting of each paper was preceded by a number of prewriting exercises to generate and organize ideas, and then once the drafting had begun, several different drafts of each paper were shared with a group of fellow students. I was a part of a four person editing group that provided valuable feedback and suggestions for revisions at every step of the drafting and revising process. The interaction of the editing group also tended to nurture creativity and spontaneity that proved to be crucial in the creation of "Warping Time with Montaigne."

Once I had shared my ideas for the paper with my group and with just two days left before my paper was due in class, I wrote the following journal entries as a way of organizing my thoughts and figuring out what I wanted to do with them in my paper:

> "Warping time" has the potential to be a really interesting essay. I need to list everything I want to be sure to say about Rodriguez's essay, those quotes of Montaigne's which directly apply to the points I want to make, and, then, the precise affiliations I want to assign to each metaphor of time and the loom. I wish I had more time to work on this.
>
> What are the parts to my metaphor? If the loom = time, the warp = Montaigne, and the weft = Rodriguez, then what is the process of "warping the loom"? Is the threading of Montaigne through the hettles of time, the same as Montaigne's transcendence of time? His thoughts have to be durable enough to stand the strain put on the warp by the tension of the loom as well as the wear of the opening and closing of the shed and the friction of the beater as it swings along Montaigne and locks the weft of Rodriguez's ideas into the grasp of Montaigne's warp, while at the same time the interlocking of Rodriguez into Montaigne creates a brand new unique object formed by the interaction of the inter-working parts of time with the materials of Montaigne and Rodriguez.
>
> The ideas of original thinkers get spun into yarn for warp. Rodriguez's end product is a piece of cloth which is available to the reader to use to make other things such as clothing, blankets, or?.
>
> If Montaigne is the warp, what do the 2 ends signify? The first end is the full body of Montaigne wound around itself in its full potential. The end I am threading is his ideas being taken through time to be used in the creation of new essays. 2 steps to trip through time—hettles and dent. What are they? hettles = individual thoughts and quotes (arranged to create potential of a pattern). dent = combining and spacing of ideas to assure a solid, even weave of the new fabric—literature vs nonliterature? Final step is to tie off Montaigne in the present on the cloth beam in order to hang onto his thoughts in the present to enable the creation of new essays.
>
> My thoughts as I thread the loom consider the process Rodriguez went through in the creation of "Late Victorians." As I tie off the warp on my loom, I have secured Montaigne for use in my own creation and I have examined the creation of an accomplished weaver to glean ideas and techniques. I am ready to write—conceivably the result is essay in the reader's hands. How to do that?
>
> Ending—my thoughts pull Montaigne into the present, now I am ready to weave my thoughts into an essay, I step on the treadles to raise the shed, throw the first pass of the shuttle and create, "I sit bent over the breast beam of my 38 inch LeClerc floor loom . . . "

This last journal entry was written after I had begun drafting my paper but before I had figured out how to conclude the essay. I have quoted the first line of the paper, yet my ideas are still just beginning to take form. I had originally planned to create a circular essay in which the ending leads back to the beginning in a never-ending retelling of this process; however, that idea got too confusing to be adequately devel-oped in the limited amount of time that I had and therefore was changed in favor of the current ending.

I had a number of issues that needed to be sorted out as I tried to create a complete draft of the paper; therefore, as a way of figuring out what ideas I wanted to weave into the paper, I entered in my journal the following lists of what I believed were critical points to be dealt with in my paper:

Individual thoughts of Montaigne:

- Que scais-je?
- I want to be seen in simple, natural . . . it is myself I portray
- essai = trial or attempt
- self-portrait vs autobiography
- to be known not remembered
- to follow wanderings of his mind in process of thinking
- my mind & my thoughts . . .
- find self through writing
- loose disconnected structure—mirrors spontaneous thought
- portrait as friendly gesture
- familiar tone
- rebellion against rigid styles, formal language
- absence of dispositio
- sense of honesty

Points from Rodriguez:

- we choose our lifestyles
- sometimes we choose our deaths
- we all die
- wisdom in youth's foolishness
- R. focused on tragedy   Cesar—you cannot forbid tragedy
- R. full-time skeptic (131)(121)
- jealousy of responsible of irresponsible
- Victorian house as symbol of family—gay reclaim neighborhood
- new residents, new vision of family (Yuppies—birth control)
- masks (123)(131)
- caustic language (124–5) shock value, coarse cloth
- flipping of normal perspectives
- gays vs feminists
- nakedness (129)
- self-questioning in text (129)
- flowing thoughts (131)
- regret, repentance? (132)(134)

I spent successive late nights in the final week of the class working on this paper, as well as on revisions of other papers from that class. On the day before the final draft of the warping essay was due, my eyes felt unnaturally wide open from too much coffee and too little sleep, and yet still every time I thought about my paper, I felt excited about its possibilities. Not only did I not want to sleep, I knew that I couldn't sleep as long as I had the potentials of the warping metaphor at play in my head. It was with enthusiasm and playfulness, not with fatigue or despair, that I wrote the following journal entry:

> I am making progress on my "Warping" essay, but I have so far to go in the 24 hours I have left before I have to hand in the paper. I realize that I cannot get it into a polished state of existence in that time, but I would like to at least have the skeleton of the complete essay put together with some of the shaping musculature before I hand it in to be graded. I can drape it with the appropriate clothing after that. At this point I have 8 1/2 pages written and I feel as if I am 3/4 of the way through the essay. The essay still seems extremely muddy to me, so I am unable to see clearly the points I am trying to make. I need to sort out *exactly* what I want to say about Rodriguez's essay in order to clarify my essay. From there I need to weave my metaphor of the loom more thoroughly and securely into the piece. The entire piece has the substance of gauze, when I want the density of linsey-woolsey. It is also patched together with scraps of yarn, when I want high quality materials. And so I work on it. It is still fun and exciting to play with this essay. The metaphor of the loom and the warp has *many* possibilities. Time. I need a bigger loom for this project.

The final push through those twenty-four hours produced the tenth draft of the essay "Warping Time with Montaigne."

As with the first Montaigne paper, the beginning of this paper appeared in the first draft and remained largely unchanged throughout the remaining drafts. The rest of the essay changed drastically from draft to draft, and it was not until the eighth draft that I found the conclusion to the paper. The middle of the essay continued to grow and take shape, but the ending remained loose and unfinished. I had a loose collection of quotes and comments at the end of the early drafts that I knew I wanted to fit into the paper somewhere. I tend to do this when I write: I cultivate a garden patch of interesting and related thoughts at the end of whatever I am working on as a way of feeding life into my essay (and as a way of keeping me from forgetting insights I may have along the way). There are wonderful passages in that collection that never made it to the final draft. If I were to revise this paper again, I might try harder to fit them into the essay. At the time I was drafting this paper, though, I didn't have time to fit them in, and so after the essay became complete in the eighth draft, I used the ninth and tenth drafts to polish the language and the metaphor. I was forced to be done polishing when the due date arrived and I needed to submit the paper for a grade.

Looking back upon the process I went through to create "Warping Time with Montaigne" makes me realize that I almost always contain a heightened sense of excitement when I am in the process of learning something new or when

I am playing with language. I love every stage of the writing process because I am at play throughout all of it. Even when I am struggling with a concept or with an adequate way to present a concept, I am excited by the infinite possibilities that present themselves to me. I may procrastinate before I start to write, but once I sit down to write, the rest of the world disappears, or becomes a resource at my beck and call. In this sense, the process I went through when I wrote "Warping Time with Montaigne" is not unlike my normal writing process. It was simply heightened by a metaphor that possessed particularly great potential. As part of my response to a journal prompt that was given at the end of the class asking me to "compare the Research and Analysis papers with the earlier papers in the course (my experience)," I wrote the following passage:

> It was very difficult to make the transition from personal essay to academic paper. I felt like I had just gotten the hang of the personal essay and was enjoying the freedom of the collage essay, when suddenly, I had to juggle references, documentation, and other people's arguments. It was not that the research paper was particularly difficult, as the *switch* was difficult. However, having made the switch, I then felt like I was on excellent footing for writing the analysis paper. I had felt the freedom of the personal essay and had plumbed my depths to discover the wealth of details I have within me to use for my writing; I had then felt the rigid demands of the research paper with all of its formality and tradition. Having gone through these two exercises, I was better able to appreciate what literary nonfiction essayists are trying to accomplish. I was able to appreciate Tompkins' "Buffalo Bill" essay in a way that I was incapable of at the beginning of the course. As a result, I felt tremendous excitement about writing the analysis paper. I understood the requirements expected of me in terms of scholasticism, yet I felt the freedom to assert my own voice and technique. What fun!

THIS is the process that led me to "Warping Time with Montaigne." It was a journey of discovery: first of myself and my knowledge, then of different forms of writing available for my use, and finally of the power of freedom, innovation, and inspiration. Fortunately for me, I am now able to start from here as I prepare future journeys through the writing process.

That Shining Place: Crete, 1966

Simone Poirier-Bures

In the photo I remember, Maria looks straight at the camera. A smile flutters at the corners of her mouth, as if she is hesitant to show her ferocious pride, as if she dares not enjoy this moment, surrounded by her children, lest some jealous god yank it away. She rests her hands on the shoulders of Ireni, who barely comes up to her waist. Somber Ireni, whose eyes are large and unsmiling. Smaragdi and Katina stand at their mother's right, their heads reaching just to and just below her shoulders; Katina, distracted by something, looks off to the side. Yannis, at the left, is barely as tall as Smaragdi, though he is older than his sisters. He stands a little apart from the others, as if, as the only male, he feels a need to disassociate himself from the women.

There is something hopeful in their expressions, in the way they are poised there, their faces curious, expectant, as if they are used to standing on the sidelines watching, waiting for things to happen.

Behind them, the stuccoed wall is yellowish brown and peeling. It's the wall of my house, the one I occupied for four months, 31 years ago. Theirs, very much like mine, stands directly across the street. I remember also in this picture the hindquarters of a donkey, a brown shaggy one who carried things for the old man who delivered goods to the small store a few doors down, but perhaps I am confusing this photo with another.

Maria's husband Giorgos is missing from this family portrait, but that is usual. Every morning he would leave his house at dawn, return for the noon meal and a few hours rest, then leave again. He would spend his evenings in one of several *tavernas* along the waterfront. I seldom saw him at home, though I waved to him whenever I saw him along the old harbor, bringing in his catch. And he would wave back, in front of the other fishermen, giving a surprised but pleased smile to this young foreign woman. A friend of his wife's.

The *Yaya*, too, is absent. Maria's mother, all in black, would sit at her chair by the front window watching the goings on. Like all *Yayas*, she knew how to stay in the background, to help when there was work to be done, but otherwise, to remain invisible. I feel her hovering behind the photo, silently moving her toothless mouth.

They are all frozen in that moment—yet as I think of the picture, time softens, moves. Maria stands below my window, yelling "See-moan-ay! See-moanay!" It is 10:15 AM, far too late for decent people still to be sleeping, and anyway, she has something to tell me, or she is lonesome and wants some company, or it is the day for making some Greek delicacy, and I must come and watch so I can learn how.

It is 1966 and I am 21. I am in Chania, on the island of Crete, searching for something. Some truth that keeps eluding me. Some peace I long for. I am fleeing old griefs, trying to lose myself, find myself.

I am not completely alone; I am part of a small group of temporary expatriates—Canadians, Americans, Brits. We all live in the old quarter, in ancient three-story houses built by the Venetians in the 14th and 15th centuries. We live there, instead of in the newer parts of the city where there are flush toilets and running water, because the streets in the old quarter are narrow and picturesque, because the rent is cheap, and because none of us cares about flush toilets and running water. We are all there for our own reasons—we do not ask each other such questions—and together we form a community of sorts. We go to the *tavernas* at night, dance with the sailors, drink too much, help each other find the way home.

Much of my day, however, is with Maria. She has "claimed" me. When we walk through the neighborhood she holds my arm and tells the people we meet: "Apo tin Ameriki." I correct her gently: from Canada. She shrugs and laughs. Wherever I am from, it does not matter. She was the first to have me in her house, so now I am known as "Maria's friend."

Come to my house for some *raki*, a woman down the street calls out to me. No, Maria says to her fiercely, she cannot. She is with me. Later, Maria tells me: That woman is not a good woman. But Athena, as she is called, will not give up so easily. When she sees me coming down the street without Maria, she rushes out to speak. She is thirtyish, a few years younger than Maria, but unmarried. She lives with her sister (also unmarried), and with her mother; occasionally she goes out with men from the nearby NATO base, and this makes her vaguely disreputable. I am curious about Athena, this loud, persistent woman who dyes her hair red, who hovers on the edge of respectability, but I do not wish to offend Maria, so I decline her invitations.

In the evenings, when I slip out to dance with the sailors on the waterfront, to drink, to behave in a way that is totally unacceptable for Greek women, I wonder what Maria thinks, at home, alone with her children. The rules are different for me; this is part of my appeal. Come with us, I say to her one Saturday evening when the winds are warm and we can smell spring coming. Giorgos never stays home—why should you? She clicks her tongue and throws her head back. I have proposed something preposterous, impossible. I might as well have proposed that we fly to the moon. She laughs, chides me for being so silly, but she puts on lipstick, and I know she is tempted.

At first I thought I was merely her trophy—something to show off in this city of few westerners. But Maria remained my friend long after it was expedient or prudent.

"See-moan-ay! See-moan-ay!" she yells through the front window. It is unshuttered and open because it is a lovely warm day, even in mid-January. Behind her stands Yannis, ready to supply the appropriate English if I do not understand what his mother tells me. He is 11, small and sturdy, with a curious, intelligent face. He is learning English in school, and eager to try out his new words. When his friends invite him to play kickball down the street, he demurs, telling them he can't right now, that his mother needs his help. I understand enough Greek to catch this, and to know that we could manage without him. He looks at me shyly—I am not like Greek young women—I tease him, and he hides his smiles.

Maria's friend Varvara has invited us for coffee. I must come now. Varvara is one of the band of gypsies who winter over every year in Chania. I know this because I have seen her pull her small cart laden with colorful woven blankets and rugs through the narrow streets of the old quarter. She is short and compact like Maria, with dark fierce eyes like hers. But Varvara has a shrewdness about her. I do not trust her. A few weeks ago, I bought a blanket from her; later I discovered I had paid far too much.

I am surprised to learn that Varvara is Maria's "friend," as the gypsies are not well-liked here. Faces tighten, mouths curl as the gypsies pass. But I do not question this odd alliance. I, too, am an outsider, and I, too, am Maria's friend.

The gypsies are encamped behind the old city wall, a few minutes walk from our street. Yannis may not come, it is only for the women, Maria tells him. Yannis turns away in disappointment. The *Yaya*'s face appears in Maria's front window. She will watch the children. It is a beautiful afternoon and as we walk, I tell Maria about the blanket. She throws her head back and laughs. In Greece, anything is fair in business.

The path to the encampment takes us along the top of the old wall, now crowded with tiny, whitewashed shacks. In the 500 years since the wall was built, the inner face has totally disappeared; the town has sloped up to meet it. Only when you stand at the edge and look down, do you realize that you are on a wall, and how high you are. Maria and I stand there for a moment, looking down. In the clearing below, about two dozen tents form a tiny village, complete with rickety-looking wooden wagons, a motley group of horses and donkeys, a few old cars. A trash fire burns on one side, upwind from the tents. A dog barks. It is eerie to see this scene, like something out of time, something from the Middle Ages. I want to express this observation to Maria, but it is too complicated for my simple Greek vocabulary, so I smile and squeeze her arm, and we follow the path down.

As we approach the camp, we become the focus of attention. I am suddenly aware of my long yellow hair hanging loosely to my waist, my blue eyes. The dark eyes of the men follow me, openly, aggressively. They resemble Greek men in their darkness, in their luxurious mustaches, but their faces are narrower, their cheekbones more pronounced. I hold Maria's arm more tightly. One of them asks us what we want there. Maria tells him in a loud voice that we are looking for Varvara's tent. He points the way. I realize, then, with a sudden twinge of fear, that Maria has never been here before. Is this all some elaborate trap? Has Varvara tricked Maria into bringing me here so that I can be stolen, then sold as a white slave? The youth hostels in Europe were full of such stories.

A man approaches us with a proprietary air. He jerks his head to the right, indicating that we follow him. He spreads his arms out and around us, as if to shield us from the curious eyes of the others. I feel Maria relax a little. Varvara's husband, she tells me.

Their canvas tent, like all the others, is a grayish, stained tan.

Through the partly open front flap we see Varvara, who rises to greet us. We take off our shoes before we enter, leaving them with the others in a neat row outside. The inside is both roomy and cozy. Layers of blankets and rugs in patterns of bright blue, green and red pad the floor. Varvara and her husband exchange a few words in their own language; the husband darts a last look at me, then leaves, pulling the door flap down behind him.

Varvara invites us to sit down on the carpets and we do, forming a circle around a square slab that holds a small stove and a few cooking utensils. I am not sure what to expect from all this, but I suddenly realize that being invited here is a great honor. Maria seems to understand this too, and nods at me solemnly. Varvara lights the stove, a tiny one-burner, fueled by gas. She takes a handful of coffee beans from a burlap bag, puts them in a flat, long-handled copper pan, and shakes them over the fire for a few minutes. The tent fills with a wonderful burnt-brown smell. While the beans cool, she opens a long brass cylinder and begins to assemble what I see now is a coffee grinder. It's a beautiful thing, obviously very old, the elaborate engraving well worn. I wonder for a moment, how many generations of gypsy women have owned this grinder, how many continents it has traveled.

As Varvara grinds the beans, the tent smells more and more aromatic. I wave my hand in front of my nose and say "orea," beautiful, beautiful. Varvara nods at me gravely, but says nothing. She places a few spoonfuls of the powdered coffee with water into a small brass pot, then adds a few large spoonfuls of sugar. When the coffee froths up, she fills three small white cups, paper thin, and hands one each to Maria and me.

Now Varvara smiles. Welcome, my friends, she says. We sip our coffee slowly. Varvara inquires about Maria's family; Maria inquires back. She asks me about my health; I ask back. We are formal, ceremonial. Here, in her own element, Varvara is beautiful. She has loosened her hair and it hangs over her back in a thick mantle of glossy black. She looks softer than before, yet at the same time more powerful. I let the strong, sweet liquid linger on my tongue. Though I have had Greek coffee before, this is the best I have ever tasted. I am in a gypsy camp, I say to myself. A gypsy has called me "friend." I forgive Varvara for the blanket.

You come down through one of the narrow, twisting streets, barely wide enough for a small car, and you come upon it: the old harbor, opening before you like a flower.

A wide paved area separates the buildings from the water, very much like an Italian piazza, which is appropriate, given that this part of Chania was built by the Venetians. At the edge of the piazza, the water is deep, and small fishing boats pull right up to the edge to unload their catches. Mid morning they bring in the octopus. Glossy and silvery gray, raw octopus look like the internal organs of extraterrestrials. There is something vaguely obscene about those thick, slimy appendages; cooked up, however, they are an amazing delicacy. The fishermen throw the octopus by the handfuls on to the pavement, then pick them up and throw them down again, beating them like this to release the dark blue inky substance, and to tenderize them. The octopus are then hung on makeshift racks and lines to dry, and the fishermen wash down the pavement with buckets of sea water.

Sometimes it's sea urchins they bring in, one or two buckets of them, their greenish gray shells bristling with needle-sharp spines. Inside, flesh the color of smoked salmon. I have never tried them—they are food for the wealthy—though I am told they are wonderful. Mostly though, the boats are full of fish and octopus, and all morning the air is briny and aromatic. By noon, all trace of the fishermen is gone.

Everything around the old harbor is a bit shabby. The facades of some of the buildings have begun to crumble. Old paint peels from walls and woodwork like outgrown skin. Some of the buildings are whitewashed, but most are not, unlike the picture postcards one sees of sparkling white Greek villages. Here the buildings are mostly a drab gold—the color of limestone—or light ocher, or the grayish tan of unpainted cement.

Still, there is something enormously pleasing about it all. The crowded buildings face the water like flowers facing the sun. Roofs of red tile and wide doors painted a glossy blue flash patches of color. Old oil cans grow huge red geraniums. The rounded domes of an ancient mosque, a legacy of the Turkish occupation, shimmer in the sun like white hills. A bright green fishing boat moors on the water. Everything seems harmonious, comforting. On fine days, the restaurants spill out into the piazza. Tables and chairs appear on the pavement, inviting. On weekends, the aroma of roasting meat fills the air.

On my way home from the *Instituto*, I stop at one of the sweet shops for a *galato-buriko*, or a bowl of rice custard, or a piece of *baklava*, and look out at the harbor water. Sometimes blue, sometimes black, the water riffles lightly or bristles with foam, depending on its mood. Though the ancient sea wall contains it—a small opening permits the comings and goings of small boats—the harbor water is never totally placid, more like some wild thing, barely domesticated. And it seems emblematic somehow, of all of Crete: Hungers surge up, then subside, waiting for their own good time. A thin layer of order overlays roiling chaos—Apollo and Dionysious held in delicate balance.

At the *Instituto Amerikaniko-Helleniki* I taught three classes: a group of 12- and 13-year-old boys, a co-ed class of about a dozen high school seniors preparing to take the Cambridge proficiency exams, and a group of seven or eight local merchants.

While the other shopkeepers take their meals at home, sleep with their wives, or do whatever they all do between one and four in the afternoon when the shops are closed, these men spend an hour, three afternoons a week, practicing their English with me. They range in age from their late twenties to late forties, and their manner toward me is formal. They call me "Miss," and hold doors open for me, bowing slightly, as if I were a visiting dignitary. I acknowledge their deference with a smile, wondering what their wives would think—their husbands treating a woman this way, while they are expected to obey and please.

We spend about half of our time in general conversation; I gently correct their grammar and pronunciation and supply words when I can guess the intent. We converse mostly about "Amerika"; they are passionately interested in "Amerika." They have heard there is a sexual revolution going on there, and they are eager to learn how it works. "In America, is it true that a girl can go alone at night with a boy who is not her brother, and her parents do not know his parents?" I am careful with my reply, aware of my position, a single woman about whom there is already too much speculation. And in Chania, the old codes still prevail: a boy who dishonors someone's sister is likely to feel a knife in his back.

"It's very different there," I tell them. "Being alone together does not necessarily mean that something shameful will happen." They wrinkle their faces in puzzlement. They would never believe that a man sleeping alone on the third floor of a house would not sometimes wander at night to the bed of a woman, sleeping alone on the second. They would never believe that a woman who dances the *hassapico* with sailors and sometimes sits on their laps, and drinks with them, and sometimes walks home alone with one and lets him kiss her, does not allow him other things as well. But all that is part of my other life, my life in the old quarter. These men never go to the old quarter.

These men live in the better part of the city, in houses with water heaters, small refrigerators, stoves. Their wives do not carry the Sunday roast to the bakery down the street to be cooked in the public oven for a few *drachma* like Maria does. Their wives wear wool and rayon instead of cotton, their coats have fur collars. And at night, when the *tavernas* crackle with music and the scent of grilled *brisoles* wafts through the air—when *retsina, metaxa,* and *ouzo* flow, when feet fly in dance, plates crash on the floor amid cries of "oopa!"—these men are at home with their wives and children.

I know this because I regularly visit such a home. On Saturday mornings I privately tutor the younger sister of one of my 13-year-old boys. There are no English classes for 10-year-old girls, and to send her with the boys would not be proper. The father is not among my businessmen, but he could be; he and they are the same. My pupil's house is relatively new. The surfaces are smooth, the corners of the rooms sharp and well-defined, unlike the rooms of the houses in the old quarter. There are plenty of windows, covered with lace curtains and hung with heavy drapes of velvet and brocade. The chairs and sofas are heavy and ornate.

Solid looking. In this part of town, you never see bedding flung out over the balcony to air like you do in the old quarter.

The mother is attractive in a plump, soft sort of way. She smiles sweetly and greets me graciously in spite of the cheap cotton skirts and shabby tops I wear. She, too, calls me "Miss." I call her *Kyria*—Mrs. Like Maria, she speaks no English and relies on her son to translate. Unlike Maria, she shows no curiosity toward me. Each time I come, she offers me tea in a flowered china cup, then leaves the money for each lesson discreetly on the side-board, near my coat.

One Friday, the boy says to me after class: "My mother, she say no come tomorrow. Come Sunday, for to go on picnic. Three o'clock. We go to country. You come?"

When I arrive, slightly before three, they are all waiting. The children are happy to see me and the mother looks both pleased and relieved, as if she had feared that I wouldn't show. The *Kyrios,* her husband, acknowledges me with a slight nod. This is only the second time I have seen him. On the day of my first lesson with his daughter, he nodded at me on his way out. I suspect he had stayed behind to catch a glimpse of me, to make sure I was "safe," and to give his approval. A *Yaya* appears from one of the back rooms. I have not seen her before and wonder whose widowed mother she is—his or hers. It's impossible to tell. She is dressed all in black with a black wool kerchief pulled over her head like the *Yayas* in the old quarter. She is the one link between these two worlds. She is not introduced.

A big black Mercedes waits out front. The *Yaya* sits in the front with the man and woman, near the door. I sit in the back between the two children. The girl, who is still very much a beginner in English, holds my hand and looks at me adoringly. The boy keeps smiling, as if he can't believe I am really there, his English teacher, on an outing with his family. The adults sit stiffly, silently, in the front. I wonder briefly whose idea it was to invite me. The children's? The mother's?

Kyria says something in Greek to the boy, gesticulating with her head that he should tell me. "My mother she say to tell you that the orchards will be beautiful today." I smile at her: "I'm looking forward to seeing them. I am very happy that you invited me to come." She nods as I speak. She understands more English than she lets on. She translates my words to her husband and returns her eyes to the road. He glances at me through the rearview mirror. He seems aware of me, but not aware; I am part of the women's world with which he need not concern himself.

His wife, however, pulses with awareness. Throughout the ride I feel her controlled attention. Though she speaks mostly to her husband or looks out at the countryside, she is acutely aware of what is going on in the back seat. If we all do not have a wonderful time, she will blame herself. This is my first encounter with upper middle-class Greek life, and I am carefully taking it all in, noting how different this woman is from Maria, how different they all are from the villagers I have met, and from the people in the old quarter. Maria and I would be singing by now. Laughing out loud. Exclaiming over the beauty of the hills. She would be teaching me the Greek names of things.

The girl beside me squeezes my hand. "Is good day, yes?"

There is a tacit understanding that I speak only English, so that makes it difficult to communicate with the adults. The school is total immersion, and we teachers are discouraged from admitting to any knowledge of Greek. I suspect I have been invited along to give the children a chance to practice their English. Why else? *Kyrios* and *Kyria* do not ask me about life in "Amerika," or my life here or what I think about things. And yet I feel they are studying me, discreetly.

The country house is utterly charming—whitewashed stucco and surrounded by a low stone wall. It is grander than any of the houses I saw in my wanderings around the island, though it is still relatively simple. *Kyria* points to the small outhouse, apologizing profusely for the lack of an indoor toilet. This strikes me as very funny, given my own living conditions, but I suppress my smile. Wide windows look out over row upon row of orange trees.

Huge baskets are unloaded from the trunk of the Mercedes and there is a flutter of activity. The women will not let me help and shoo me out of the kitchen. The children hover around me like bees.

"My father say to come and see the orchard," the boy says.

Kyrios stands at the door fingering his worry beads. The children and I follow him out. The day is glorious, the air dazzling in its sweetness, and I want to jump into the air and shout with joy. But I control myself, as seems to be required, and smile demurely. Two donkeys, tied to a stake by a shed, stare at us with comic faces. I have a particular fondness for donkeys, and rush over to stroke their necks and ears. *Kyrios* gestures for me to get on one of them. It's the first time he has addressed me directly. The children shriek with glee when I swing my leg up over the donkey's back. They quickly climb onto the other one.

Their father takes the reins of my donkey and leads us down the rows of the orange grove. The trees are much smaller than I ever imagined they could be, with enormous bright fruit hanging heavily from the branches. *Kyrios* pulls down an orange the size of a cannonball and slices it open with a knife he pulls from his waist. Then he presents it to me with a little bow. I am reminded again how everything in Greece seems fuller, riper, bursting with life. Even the oranges are unrestrained, glorious in their hugeness, their sweetness, their intense color. By now I have lost all reserve and exclaim aloud at the beauty of everything. "It's all so lovely! Lovely!" I tell them. "I feel like a queen!" The children find everything I say and do amusing, and laugh and laugh.

When we get back to the house we find a beautiful meal laid out on a long rectangular table in a shaded area outside—feta cheese, black olives, bread, *dolmathes, taramasalata,* two kinds of beans, several plates of things I don't recognize, and a huge bottle of retsina. We are all more relaxed now, more comfortable with each other. Even the *Yaya* nods and smiles. The sun beats down, waves of fragrance waft in from the orange grove. After a few glasses of retsina, *Kyrios* raises his glass and sings a few lines of a song: "Ego tha kopso to krassi, ya sena agapi mou chrisi . . ." His wife throws him a disapproving glance and mutters something, but too late. I clap my hands, delighted. A drinking song! This is the first sign of passion I've seen in these upper middle-class Greeks.

I insist on learning the song, and sing it over and over, a bit tipsy myself by this time. My pupils and their father sing it with me. *Kyria* sings a few lines herself, though she looks uncomfortable, as if she is doing something vaguely improper.

After the meal, the children and I take a last stroll through the orchard. It's a wonderful afternoon, and I am sorry when it ends.

On the way home we are again subdued, polite. My hosts ask where I live so that they can deliver me to my house. I protest that the streets are too narrow for their car, and ask to be let out by the old harbor, saying that I will walk the rest of the way. I do not want them to see where I live. I do not want them anywhere near my life there.

My class of 12- and 13-year olds was my favorite. A teasing, affectionate relationship existed between us. They found me endlessly amusing, and I was charmed by their small compact bodies, their dark curious eyes. Once when I came into the classroom and turned on the light switch, nothing happened. I flipped it off and on several times while the boys watched me. Nothing. Things often didn't work in Greece, so I shrugged and said, "I guess we'll just have to have class in the dark today." They all burst out laughing. One of the boys climbed up on his desk and turned the light bulb; another flicked on the switch and the room filled with light. We all laughed together. I had enjoyed this trick as much as they had, so when I walked into the classroom the day after my visit to the orange groves and felt an expectant tension in the air, I figured something was up.

One of the boys had just finished writing something in Greek on the blackboard and was hurrying back to his seat. All 16 of them were watching me, suppressing grins.

"Aha," I say, going along with it. "Someone left me a message. Help me translate it." Titters all over the room. "It's nothing," the boy whose sister I tutor says. "I'll erase it for you." He gets up and approaches the board. But something in his face makes me want to know what the words say.

"No, let's figure it out. It'll be good practice. Let's see, the first word is . . ." I squint at the Greek letters and sound out "Ego . . ." Someone from the back row calls out boldly: "Ego tha kopso to krassi."

General laughter. I glance quickly at my friend in the front row who hangs his head sheepishly. Obviously, he has told his friends about our excursion, and they have seized on the part they found most interesting.

"Oh yes, the song I learned yesterday," I say, feeling a little chilled, the private made a bit too public. "I like Greek songs. I'd like to learn a lot of them." The boys are restless, whispering things to each other, their eyes flashing a kind of wildness. One of them calls out something in Greek that I don't understand, and they all laugh again. The laughter has a new, aggressive edge.

"What did you say?" I ask him. He is silent. "Someone tell me what he said." No one answers, and a thick tension hangs in the air. Finally, I look at my friend in the front row. He, after all, started this whole thing. I ask him evenly, "Please tell me what he said."

He swallows hard and says, "He said that perhaps you would like to learn, um . . . *Krevata murmura*."

"And what, exactly, is that?"

He looks exceedingly uncomfortable, as does the rest of the class. But I persist.

"I don't know how to say in English, but it means the things a man and woman say to each other when they are in bed."

The boys are absolutely still, studying my reaction. The air crackles with danger.

"I see," I say. "Thank you for your translation." Then I turn to the rest of the class. "Take out your homework now, and let's see how well you've done on the exercises for today." I go on with the class as usual, though I smile less and make no joking asides as I usually do. Something between us has changed.

On my way home, I try to figure it out. A single woman drinking wine and singing—did this somehow mean sexual availability in the minds of these 12- and 13-year-old boys? The harbor water is greenish black today; two small boats, moored in the protected area, rock gently in the lapping tongues of water. Beyond the seawall, the water is deep blue; whitecaps surge and break. It's the same water; only the seawall separates it, only the seawall tames it. How easily things can turn, I think, how easily things can career out of control.

Afterword: Writing "The Greece Piece"

Simone Poirier-Bures

It began, I suppose, in 1982. I was auditing a writing course taught by Ursule Molinaro; she had no car, so after class I drove her home. I was only just beginning to write seriously then, and Ursule was a real writer; alone with her on those rides, I hoped some of her talent would rub off, or I'd learn some secret about how words work.

One afternoon I told her about my backpacking in Europe and the Middle East years before, my stay on the island of Crete. I described a brave young woman traipsing through exotic lands, only half aware of the disturbances her long blond hair created. I spoke of my younger self as I would a colourful ancestor—so removed from my present self did she seem. "That was my life's big adventure," I told Ursule, realizing at that moment that it was.

"You should write about it," Ursule said simply.

I had never thought of this. It had all happened so long ago, back in 1965–66, and my experiences were episodic, they had no centre around which to build a plot. Moreover, I sensed that the real story lay beneath the surface adventures; the real story had to do with friendship, loneliness, the making of a self. I was not quite ready to deal with all that.

Years later, in 1988, after I had finished several writing projects and was looking for another, I remembered Ursule's words and decided to try writing a novel about the four months I had spent in Greece. I would make up a heroine, myself in disguise, and embellish my experiences to make them neater, more story-like. I still occasionally dreamed about my house in Chania, the crumbling cement walls, the dark rooms that became, in those dreams, a labyrinth. Something important had happened there. Something left unfinished.

443

I was having a hard time getting started, so I began getting up at 5:30 AM and freewriting for an hour. Someone had given me Dorothea Brande's little book, *Becoming a Writer,* and she had suggested this exercise. It wasn't easy. Awakening memory, trying to shape and select its messages, dealing with my own feelings about my younger self—and doing this all at once. I would sit there watching the sky lighten against the window over my desk, my stomach tight, my brow throbbing, an urge to run out of the room rippling through my arms and legs.

Over a period of several weeks, I wrote twenty pages. In the opening scene, a North American woman negotiates with a Greek merchant over the price of a silver and turquoise bracelet. After a good deal of haggling, they settle on a price. Then suddenly they become good friends, in the way this happens in Greece. On the way home, with her new bracelet on her arm, Joanna berates herself: you didn't *need* it. In this way I introduce the theme of material things and Joanna's (my) ambivalence toward them. The day is overcast, damp and chilly, corresponding to Joanna's mood, but also to many days I actually remember in Crete.

Joanna goes home to her Venetian house in the old quarter and is met by her housemate, a bearded British artist (Jack), who is drying his socks by the charcoal brazier, the only source of heat. Relentlessly cheerful, Jack provides a sharp contrast to Joanna's gloominess. Joanna wishes she were in love with him. How much nicer life would be if she loved someone and someone loved her. It rains all night.

The next morning, after a chill, dreary night huddled in her sleeping-bag, Joanna wakes to the sound of her neighbour, Maria, calling her name. When she throws open the shutters, sunlight and warm air rush in. Joanna looks at the brilliant sky, at Maria's short square body, at the long narrow street bustling with activity, and is overtaken with joy.

This is as far as I got. How to develop all the threads? How to tell what happened and make it dramatic without doing injustice to the static-like quality of much of my life there?

I put the twenty pages away and forgot about them.

In 1991 my husband had a sabbatical and between his research trips, we decided to make a quick trip to Greece and Turkey. My husband had spent two years in Turkey in the late sixties helping to set up a land-grant style university, so we each had important memories associated with the two countries.

From the moment we decided on the trip, images of Maria and Chania began trickling steadily up from the past. One afternoon I hunted through an old trunk and found Maria's thin blue airmail letters with the spidery black handwriting. As I read them, I heard Maria's voice, saw her large sad eyes, and was seized with a deep need to see her again. I couldn't remember her last name, and because it was written in Greek script that I could not decipher, I tore off the small piece of envelope with her name and address in case I would have to inquire about her. I remembered that our street was named after El Greco—his Greek name—and though I could still see every detail of the houses and shops, the name eluded me. Fortunately, it was there on the envelope, under Maria's name.

What happened during our visit to Crete is described in the memoir.

After Crete, my husband and I went on to Turkey. In Istanbul, the sister of an old friend, a woman we barely knew, gave us a present—an old brass coffee grinder, almost exactly like the one Varvara had used 25 years before. Such an odd coincidence, I remember thinking. So many wonderful coincidences on this trip. We were busy with visiting and buying gifts, so I forgot about the grinder.

When we returned home, I was once again struck by the need to write about my time in Greece. But how? Months passed. At Christmas, I sent cards and letters to both Maria and Ireni, telling them how much our reunion had meant to me. In mid-January, a Christmas card and letter arrived from Ireni. "You must know," she said, "that always, since I've met you, I've been thinking about you." Her words reminded me piercingly of Maria's letters years ago. As I sat at the kitchen table reading and rereading Ireni's letter, my body felt as if it were literally bursting with memory, with the need *to tell*. The faces of Maria and the children as they had been long ago swam before me. I went up to my study and began writing: "In the photo, Maria looks straight at the camera . . . "

I wrote as far as the dancing scene. Exhilarated and a bit dazed, I went downstairs to make some tea. As I waited for the water to boil, I thought of the day Maria took me to the gypsy camp. I pulled out the coffee grinder the woman in Istanbul had given us and examined it. There was still a little coffee in it, powdered to make Turkish coffee, which is what Greek and gypsy coffee actually is. Suddenly the coffee grinder became like Proust's madeleine: I found myself walking the narrow path down to the gypsy camp; the thin high yelp of camp dogs rang in my ears, the faces of men with high cheekbones and fierce eyes surrounded me, the smell of roasting coffee beans filled the room. I was drowning in memory. The dark lustre of Varvara's hair, the feel of the thick rugs on the floor of the tent—details I had not thought about in decades roiled around me. I rushed upstairs and wrote about Varvara and the coffee.

I was thrilled with what I had written and went over it several times in the next few weeks, polishing the prose. But where to go from there? What was this thing, anyway? It had come from the need to tell; it wasn't trying to *be* anything.

I remembered my old attempt at writing a novel set in Greece, found my old computer file and printed it out. But it was not where I wanted to go anymore. I was fascinated, now, with memory.

I had kept no journal during that year of travel—something I berated myself for now. I hadn't even taken pictures. This had been deliberate. I wanted everything to be *in* me, not *outside*. I wanted memory to be part of my flesh.

I did, however, write letters. Lots of them. To my mother, my sister, and to a whole collection of girlfriends and boyfriends in Canada and the United States. I wrote, now, to my mother and sister and to the few friends from that era I am still close to: "Send my old letters," I begged, "if you still have them."

In the meantime, I wrote another section or two of text, and then stopped. I was stuck, just as I had been with the novel.

After a few months of despair and silence, I began writing down fragments. Whatever I remembered from that time, however small. I had to get it out. I could shape it into something later, I told myself. Often, I found, what started as a tiny memory bloomed into an entire scene. From the memory of stains on the ancient wood floor came the night of the party, the faces of the girls in the protection of their brothers, the near-fight, the persistent rain. It was like yanking at a small string and having a huge fish come up.

Finally, six letters came from my mother. I remember staring at them, the pale-blue airmail envelopes, the tissue paper, the Greek stamps, my handwriting. I was awed by them, and a little afraid. They were like apparitions—my own voice, my own thoughts from the past, a direct line to the person I had been 25 years before. What I remembered of that younger self sometimes embarrassed me, her naïveté, her awkwardness. But her idealism drew me, even as it reproached me. The girl who wanted nothing and the middle-aged woman secure in her comforts—how could they be the same person? With the letters, I would have to confront that old self, uncover her truth, measure the width of my betrayal.

I put the letters in chronological order and read the first one. I was struck by the tone of voice. It was cheerful, happy-go-lucky. A girl on a lark, having a blast, eager to share her adventures. There was none of the sadness, the loneliness, the groping searches I remembered. How could this be? As I read on, I concluded that the person writing was really a persona—one I had consciously developed for my mother and my friends. I was giving them surface. But what a surface it was—full of details and impressions, sights and sounds.

When I read that first letter, I had just finished writing about my arrival in Chania. I hadn't remembered that the youth hostel was a boys' school and that only a shower curtain separated our sleeping quarters from the classroom. I'd remembered being stared at by bunches of schoolboys, but couldn't quite place the circumstances. Reading my younger self telling it made it all come back—and more. I remembered, then, the middle-aged schoolmaster with his patient, wide brow and questioning eyes. But the elderly woman described in the letter, a friend of the schoolmaster, who had written six books of philosophy—who was she? No face emerged.

I went back to my manuscript and added the shower curtain, the staring boys. I did not mention the woman.

I read the letters one at a time, carefully, reverently. Sometimes weeks passed between reading one letter and another. They were rich, heady stuff, and I took them into my present slowly, cautiously. Besides memory, there was that carefree persona to deal with. How reconcile them to each other? How reconcile them to my present, middle-aged self? So many fragments that had to be integrated. Who and what was the real self?

Generally, I tried to write whatever I remembered of a particular period *before* reading the letter I wrote during that period. It was like tuning a guitar string before sounding the pitch pipe. While I was amazed at how much I actually remembered, I was also struck by what I could not recall even with the help of my own words, leaping up from the page. The most important thing that I do not remember has to do with my leave-taking. To my mother I wrote, "We had quite a send-off when we left . . . we had one last dinner with all the 'arty' colony of English-speaking people, and one last wild night at a 'joint' we all go to . . ." I remember nothing of this. I remember only the fear, the sadness. So which is real? Those parties must have occurred, and I am sure I made the most of them, singing and dancing. The persona again.

I have no doubt that if a needle were to be inserted into a part of my brain all those forgotten things would pop to the surface. But they are too far buried, now, ever to call back.

So what does this mean? That those forgotten things are not important? Without the direct link of memory, I cannot know. I chose to leave them out.

In June, 1992, I spent two weeks at the Virginia Centre for the Creative Arts, an artist's colony, where I was determined to finish "My Greece Piece," as I had come to call it. I wrote and wrote, overwhelmed by memory. Even when I lay down to rest on the cot in my studio, waves of images floated over me. Bryan—whose name I hadn't thought of in decades—appearing giddily at my door arm-in-arm with the dark-eyed young sailors. The smell of roasting meat drifting out over the harbour. The way the sea urchins looked in their spiky shells. I was swimming in a deep, rich river, grabbing hold of whatever I could. Sometimes I forgot where I was.

About half of the manuscript was written at VCCA. In those two weeks I wrote as much as I had written in the previous five months. But it was still all fragments. Pieces that had to be fit together into some coherent whole. During my last few days at VCCA I contemplated this. One entire wall of my studio was made out of bulletin board-type white tiles, and a previous occupant had left an assortment of colourful thumbtacks. This gave me an idea. I printed out the whole manuscript and pinned all the pieces up on the wall. Then I began arranging and rearranging. I'd read through the whole thing, then push this piece over here, that piece over there. It seemed as if the pieces could go anywhere—or nowhere. I didn't want a straight chronology; I wanted memory to overtake the present, like it had for me. But the manuscript still needed some kind of order, and that order seemed to escape me. A visual artist friend came by one day to take pictures. On an impulse, I got up and stood against my wall of manuscript, arms outstretched.

I was making a manuscript, but I was also making a self.

My "Greece Piece" still had no real title. Sometimes I called it "Maria" but that didn't seem to be the true focus. One evening I read from the manuscript, including the part about Katzanzakis's grave. A young poet came up to me after and we talked about its lack of a title. "Why don't you use the Katzanzakis quote?" he said. "'I want nothing, I fear nothing, I am free.' That seems to be what the whole thing is about." I went back to my studio and thought about this. He was right. My younger self was looking for freedom, trying to make herself want nothing and fear nothing, in order to find it. The fact that Katzanzakis had found his freedom in death added an additional irony, one that had escaped the notice of my younger self. The title stuck for a while, though I later changed it again.

When my residency at VCCA ended, I found re-entry into normal life extremely difficult. I was still living in Chania in 1966, and memory was more real than anything around me. For days I was unable even to make up a decent grocery list. I'd be on my way to the store and find that I had passed it. I'd have been thinking about the market in Chania, how the olives looked, shining out from huge glass jars. Gradually, painfully, the present asserted itself again.

I spent the rest of the summer shuffling parts, trying to find that elusive order. One afternoon I went looking for the old photos my mother had taken when she visited Maria in Crete. They were not at all as I had remembered them. Yannis was tall, the children were laughing. Their skirts were *short.* How could that be? After I thought about this for a while I realized that my mother's visit was four whole years after I had left. 1970. By then the hemlines had shot up, even in Crete. But why did I remember sombre expressions where the photos clearly showed them all smiling happily? Had I imagined the sadness in their lives? I pulled out Maria's letters again and reread them. No, I had not imagined it. My mother's experience of the family, the one caught by the camera, was not *my* experience of them. And memory had conveniently replaced the celluloid image with its own. I went back to the beginning of my text and changed it: "In a photo I *remember* . . ."

By the end of January the piece was finished, almost exactly a year after I had begun it. In March, I received a package and letter from my sister in Halifax. "I was cleaning out my basement and found these. Do you still want them?" More letters, with postmarks from Greece, Egypt, Lebanon. I was afraid to look at them. What if they were full of things I had not talked about in my memoir? Would I have to open the thing up all over again and integrate yet another layer of truth? I approached them cautiously. To my surprise, the tone of those letters was different from the tone in the letters to my mother. It was more natural, more authentic.

My sister had married at eighteen and was the mother of three by the time I embarked on my adventures. She had married a Lebanese man eleven years older than herself. There was a poignancy about her life that struck me. While I was off galivanting, she kept house, kept children, kept a husband. She was only a year and a half older than I, and her hands were cracked from too many dishes, too many washloads of diapers. I was travelling for her, too, as well as for my mother.

From Greece, I went on, eventually, to Lebanon, to the small village in the mountains where my sister's husband's sisters and their families lived, as well as the whole extended family of cousins and uncles. My sister had never met them. I went there because she couldn't, and described everything in great detail. That was my job.

The letters to my sister from Greece contained no new revelations, but they made me consider the whole matter of personas again. The persona who wrote to my mother was a small part of myself—pushed forward because that's what my mother wanted, that's what would reassure her, please her. The persona who wrote to my sister represented a larger part of myself—more level-headed, less breathy—but still only a part. The real self, I have come to believe, is memory. And that is what I put in my memoir.

Teacher Training

Mary Elizabeth Pope

I stand at the drinking fountain in the hallway outside my classroom. It is the first day of classes, and it is my first day as a graduate teaching assistant. I have no teaching certification to prepare me for this position, and as my qualifications are limited to the grades I earned as an undergraduate in English, I have no idea how I will meet the challenge of teaching Freshman Composition. Earlier, as I passed the classroom, I glanced in to see a number of students sitting in their desks, waiting. I think of all those students now, and wonder about all their different needs—how can I address them collectively, and still address them as individuals? How can I know what they need from me when I have no training or experience with teaching? My watch reads 7:59 am, so I move reluctantly toward the door behind which my students sit. My hands are shaking, and the knot in my stomach is threatening to snap me in half. My heels click on the tiled floor as I enter the classroom and make my way to the podium.

I sat in the new desk on the first day of fifth grade, watching my new teacher pass out textbooks. It was all I could do to sit still for so long; I had been waiting for this day all summer. The new pencils and paper and folders I'd saved my fifty cent allowance for were already arranged in my tray, and I placed each new textbook that Mrs. Crane handed out beside them, feeling very mature. The first day of school was like a clean slate for me; all of the mistakes from fourth grade left safely behind me in Mr. Smith's room and in Mr. Smith's mind. I watched my new teacher as she handed out books; she was a woman of about fifty, and very pretty in a hard sort of pancake makeup way. She walked more purposefully than any woman I had ever known, her posture perfect as she slowly, deliberately put one high-heeled shoe out and placed it carefully in front of her before shifting her weight directly onto it. Her careful, composed walk would be something I would never forget—the way her shoulders moved as she walked, the way her hair didn't, the angle at which she held her chin. I knew instantly that I wanted her to like me, that I wanted to do well in her class, to please this woman whose authority radiated from her every gesture, rang clear in her every word. I rode the bus home that afternoon, bursting with excitement, anxious to tell my mother all about my new teacher.

My students stare at me the first day. Some of them look at me directly; others avert their gaze in case my eyes meet theirs. They are sizing me up. That's okay; I am sizing them up, too. I pass out the syllabus, and discuss classroom policy and course requirements with them. I tell them they must have a C in order to pass my class. They say nothing until I ask them to introduce themselves to the class and say where they are from. After much shifting in their seats, and mumbling out their introduction sentence, they gratefully return their eyes to me. I try hard not to smile too much on the first day, although it is hard. I try to encourage them to understand how my class will help them with all of their classes; I try hard to make them understand that they all have something important to say, that they are all unique and no single other person has the perspective they do. They look at me. I look back at them. I don't know if they believe me or not when it is time to dismiss them, but I watch them file out, and feel hopeful.

I stood in the dime store for maybe thirty minutes, wondering what Mrs. Crane's favorite color was. The folders were there on the shelf—pink, yellow, green, blue, red. On another shelf sat the folders I wished for: clear, plastic binders with front picture slots on the cover. I could just see a collage of Abraham Lincoln underneath those picture slots—Mrs. Crane would like that for sure. But I had only fifty cents, and the clear plastic binders were ninety-nine cents, while the colored cardboard folders were thirty-nine cents. Mrs. Crane wore a lot of blue—navy blue—but since the dime store only carried a cornflower color of blue—and because it seemed the only color suitable for Abraham Lincoln of the colors available, I took one blue folder to the counter, and watched the lady ring it up. I was sad. What could I do with a plain blue folder that would make Mrs. Crane notice it? I wanted her to know how hard I'd worked on my report, and how much I wanted to do everything right for her. I wanted her to like me.

Holly comes to my office at least once a week. She worries all the time; so much so, that she is terrified to commit anything to paper. She is careful to meet all of the requirements in an assignment, yet she is so careful that it stifles all of the creativity in her expression. She always asks me what I want her to write. Today, her curly brown hair is pulled back in a bun, and above her ruddy cheeks, her eyes are tired and bloodshot, no doubt from staying up all night working, or worrying that she should be working. She is a perfectionist to the point of self-destruction, and although I am pleased with her work, I know she could be more expressive if she were not so afraid of making mistakes.

The assignment I give today is to freewrite about what they want to say in their coming papers. I tell them I won't be grading these and that the only thing that matters is what they discover about their topic. I give them thirty minutes, and I watch Holly hunch over her desk and begin writing. After class, I ask her to stay behind a moment so I can look at her writing. It is thoughtful and original, and much better than what she has been turning in to me on a regular basis. I tell her I want to see her this week, knowing I will anyway. I am hopeful that we can make some progress.

Mrs. Crane stood regally before the class, holding a stack of reports in her hand. I could hardly wait to get mine back and read what she had written. I had worked so hard, and had so carefully and creatively constructed the cover, that I was sure that she would love it. "Class," she began, "why don't we take a look at some of the reports you handed in to me?" I was even more excited—I just knew she would pick mine as a good example for a creative cover, and I could hardly wait to see what she said about it when she held it up. "This is James' report—see how he pasted a mapped picture of Michigan on the cover of his folder for his Michigan report? Very nice. . . .". Next, she held up a crumpled sheet of paper which was half written on in pencil. "This . . ." she paused and her voice fell, as she extended the paper away from her body and pinched it between two fingers, as if it were dirty, or smelled bad, ". . . is Kevin's report." She quickly put Kevin's report on the bottom of the pile, and picked up the next one, commenting favorably on the reports she liked, and giving the same disdainful look and treatment as Kevin's report got to those she did not appreciate. I waited excitedly. I could see the blue edge of my folder sticking out of the pile . . . closer and closer it came to the top . . . and then it was in her hand. "This is Mary Beth's report," she said quickly, and made no comment on it at all, quickly replacing it on the bottom of the pile. I was crushed. My blue folder, with the pennies glued on to form the letters A and L, looked pitiful in the light of Mrs. Crane's disinterest in it. I had been so proud of it, had so carefully selected the shiniest pennies in my father's penny jar to use for the lettering, had handed it in with such confidence; now it seemed a pathetic idea, and I felt embarrassed as my cheeks glowed hotly, wondering how many students were looking at my flushed face, my burning ears.

Jonathan demands a lot of attention. He sits in the front row of my 9:00 class, and has assumed the role and voice of ringleader for the class. He is very entertaining, and I enjoy having him in class most of the time. His constant need to prove that he is the "best" or the most intelligent student in my class, however, is frustrating, because when the class gets into a debate over a particular issue, he cannot let a subject go until he feels he has won. I try to remain a neutral facilitator, although I have at times had to interrupt when Jonathan gets out of hand. I can tell this frustrates him, and I struggle to understand this unfulfilled need he has to be in the spotlight at all times.

Today, I hand back all of the papers except for one that I have saved to read to the class. It is well written, funny, and it meets the assignment's requirements. I choose it because it is a good example, but I have another motive. "I have a paper I'd like to read to you," I tell them. "I enjoyed it and I think all of you will, too." As I read, the class laughs appreciatively, and I do, too. When I am finished, I launch into a description of the next assignment. The students bend over their notes and begin writing, and I casually set Jonathan's paper on his desk. He is smiling, and beads of sweat have formed on his forehead. He is happy, and I am glad. For the rest of the period, things go well.

When Mrs. Crane handed back the folders, I had a second flash of hope: maybe she had only disliked the cover—maybe she had liked the report itself. I watched the other students read her comments, and when my folder was finally in my hands, I flipped through the pages, anxiously looking for her scrawling red script. I couldn't find anything, except for a check mark to signify that she had read it. I looked again, more frantically, and then realized that she had written nothing at all.

Nicole sits in the fifth row, hidden behind Drew, who is tall, and Thomas, who is large. I can just see the top of her blonde head peering at me occasionally as I teach; she is tentative, curious, nervous. Sometimes when class is over and she is on her way out the door, she will glance at me shyly and smile, a blush travelling from her ears to her nose. Nicole works very hard at my assignments; all of her in-class writing is printed, perfectly neat and straight. She is always the last to finish writing. Her papers are very well done, and she is meticulous about meeting every requirement I ask for in each paper. Her writing also reflects the deep thought she puts into the ideas we discuss in class. In Freshman Composition, I could not ask for a better student.

I like to watch her when I hand back papers. On this particular day, what little of her face I can see is lit up, and I am glad for what I have written on the bottom of her paper. "Nicole—this is excellent. Again, I commend you. You meet all of the requirements for this paper, and express your depth of thought on these issues very well. This is the highest grade I have given on this paper, so you should feel proud." I can see all the way from the front of the room that she does.

My name was on the blackboard. Mrs. Crane posted the names of students who had misspelled words in their weekly assignments there until those students could find the correct spelling for the words they had missed. On Monday, my name stood out among the other names simply because it was my name and it had never been on that list before. Then, as the names were gradually erased, those spelling ex-convicts were allowed to join the ranks of the anonymous students who had spelled perfectly that week. Slowly, the list dwindled, and by Thursday, my name was the only one left. I was frustrated. The word was "no one" and it was not one word, as I later learned, but two. I had written "noone," and Mrs. Crane had circled it. I had stared at it for a long time, and then fetched a dictionary from the back shelf of the room. I knew that "someone" and "anyone" and "somebody" and "anybody" and "nobody" were all words. Where was "noone"? I tried "noon," thinking it could be used two ways. Still, it came back marked wrong. I tried "nowan," and again it was marked wrong. On Thursday, I showed Mrs. Crane that it was not in the dictionary. "Well," she had replied frostily, "I can't do anything about that, Mary Beth. The ways you have tried are all wrong." She then dismissed me. I walked back to my desk with heavy heart and burning cheeks, staring at my name on the board. All of the other names were gone, and now everyone knew that I was the stupid girl who couldn't spell. For two long weeks, I stared at my name on the board, the chalky white letters seeming to jump off the blackboard and proclaim to the class my ignorance. Every night, I would hope that some diligent custodian would erase my name by accident. Every morning, my mark of shame would still be there. And every day, Mrs. Crane told me, "It's still wrong."

Darrin sits in the second row of my 9:00 class. I have just returned his paper, and I can see the disappointment that registers on his face. Most mornings, Darrin hides beneath a baseball cap, watching me furtively from beneath it, retreating turtle-like under the visor if my gaze lands momentarily on him. He is a hard worker, and shows up regularly to my office hours to ask for help. I am sorry when I receive his work to have to give it a C+ because of his errors. Darrin has difficulty with spelling and commas, but his work in general is often entertaining and interesting. On the bottom of this particular paper, I have written, "Darrin— this is very funny—I enjoyed reading it. I can see that you are improving the organization and maintenance of focus in your writing. Keep it up (smiley face)! I am still concerned about your use of commas and number of spelling errors that have appeared here. Come see me and we'll talk about it. Good work overall." I know that Darrin will come to my office hours after class. I know what I will say to him. I know how he will respond. And regardless of whether or not he uses the dictionary or spellcheck, regardless of whether the exercises with commas that I will cover with him improve his writing, I know that he will leave my office feeling that he is a good writer who needs a little brushing up, rather than feeling he is a bad writer who is hopeless. He will leave knowing he is capable of doing better, and hopefully this will drive him to improve on his next paper.

On the day before Christmas vacation, we'd made ornaments in Mrs. Crane's class. My ornaments did not look like everyone else's. I had taken the pastry dough and twisted strips together to form candy canes, like the cookies my mother sometimes made at home. I loved art lessons, and I was happy with my ornaments. Mrs. Crane strolled up and down the aisle and paused to compliment those ornaments that she liked. She paused at my desk, and I waited, hopeful that she liked mine. She looked confused for a moment, and then walked quickly up to the front of the room and said, "Now class, let me show you again how to use the cookie cutters. Remember, these ornaments are going to hang on the tree in the big hallway, so we want them to look nice and neat." She searched for a particular cutter. "See," she said with false brightness, as she showed us how to cut the starchy dough, leaving a row of perfectly straight Gingerbread Men in her wake, "they all come out exactly the same if you use a cookie cutter."

Eric is angry. Ever since the first day he walked into my class, it has radiated from him, the aura of anger that surrounds him reminding me of the cloud of dust that follows the *Peanuts* character Pigpen everywhere he goes. With his long, red ponytail and goatee, he sits, withdrawn from the rest of the class, in the back corner, hiding behind his black leather jacket. Eric is brilliant; his forcefully written, anti-establishment, rebellious papers are testimony to this. He is by far the most openly creative student I have, and I handle him carefully because I know he is volatile. However, when he misses several classes in a row, I decide to take action. I stop him on his way out the door and ask him if he will make an appointment with me. He says yes, and we agree on a time. I don't know what I will say to him yet, or whether he will even show up. I only know that I do not want to lose this incredibly bright student, to let him slip through the cracks and disappear, never to return to my class. I am hoping that all he needs is some encouragement.

On the last day of fifth grade, we were allowed to take our brown bag lunches out-side and sit on the lawn in front of the school. I sat with my class and watched Mrs. Crane talk to the students who sat around her. I sat far on the outside of the circle with another girl, and we traded Lifesavers and halves of our sandwiches. When the buses pulled up to take us home that day, Mrs. Crane stood by the door, and hugged each of us. I waited, dreading the hug, but knowing I couldn't get past her. She made a big show out of it, telling the students how much she would miss all of them. When my turn came, she put her mushy arms around me and my cheek burned where it touched her neck. When she fin-ished hugging me, she put her hands on my shoulders and shook me a little. "I'm expect-ing big things from you, Mary Beth." My eyes filled up with tears. I managed good-bye and followed the other students on to the bus. I hated her even more for lying like that in front of all of my friends. As I stood behind the other students in line for my bus, I won-dered why she would say such a thing. The way she had treated me all year told me every-thing I ever wanted to know about what she expected from me.

Mark sits in the back row of my classroom with Walter and Jonathan. All three are football players, and while Walter and Jonathan often doze or talk dis-ruptively, Mark tries to listen closely to what I have to say. He asks questions in class and comes to my office regularly. He is creative and earnest, and usually manages to separate himself, if only in attention span, from his teammates.

I hand his paper back without a grade. While his writing is nearly error free, and might have been an "A" for another assignment, he has not met any of the re-quirements for this paper. Were I to grade it, it would have failed. I know he is a good writer and I do not want to discourage him, so I write on the bottom of his paper, "Mark—your writing, in terms of mechanics and style, is excellent. As a creative piece, this would have received an "A." However, for this assignment, you haven't met the requirements I needed to see. I know you are busy, but I'd like to meet with you and discuss what you need to change here. This is very good writing, Mark, but it doesn't meet the criteria I spelled out in class. You can take your time with it. See me first and we'll talk." Mark reads my comments and looks confused for a moment, but he nods slowly, and I know he understands. I know I haven't crushed him, and I know he will come see me and do better the next time.

Composing "Teacher Training"

Mary Elizabeth Pope

The idea for the "Teacher Training" piece came out of a journal activity assigned in a graduate nonfiction class asking each of us to make a list of all of the topics we would never write about and why. I wrote down "Mrs. Crane" [not her real name] among other things, because even though I was in fifth grade when I had her for a teacher, she was still affecting me in a negative way as a graduate student. The reason, though, that she had made it on the list of things I would never write about was because several months after I'd had her for a teacher, she'd been killed in a car accident. Although I'd never admitted it to anyone but my mother, I had gone home every day in fifth grade praying she would die somehow. I was still harboring a lot of guilt over that, because for years after she was killed, I had nightmares about her; I was convinced that God had answered my prayers and that I was responsible for her death. I still won't ever write about that aspect of my relationship with her, but the exercise got me thinking.

The third paper was to be a personal, non-fiction essay and we were all encouraged to experiment with a format we hadn't used very often. I wasn't sure what to write about, so I went back to my list of things I would never write about, took her name, put it in the middle of a blank page and did some clustering, just to see what would happen. As I clustered, I realized that I had a lot to say about this woman; from the clustering page, I started to freewrite and couldn't believe how angry I was getting just thinking about the things she used to do to me in class. She was the kind of teacher who used humiliation tactics to teach her students, and she really disliked me, even though I tried hard to be a good, hard-working, well-behaved student. I wasn't sure of what aspect of her teaching I wanted to focus on, or if I really wanted to focus more on my reaction to her techniques, but I knew I had a lot to say because I couldn't stop writing.

Another circumstance enters into this topic and my choosing to write about it—at the time I began to write this piece, I was in my second semester teaching freshman composition as a graduate assistant. The whole time I was scribbling about the things she used to do me in class, I was thinking about myself as a teacher and couldn't imagine ever treating my students the way she treated me. My own teaching position had given me a new perspective on the whole Mrs. Crane issue, and it was one I could never have had before then, because I'd never taught. So as I "freewrote," I kept thinking about that aspect of it, although it didn't enter into any of my initial writing.

It actually took me a long time to determine what I wanted to do with this piece, because I knew I had a lot to say about it, and it felt really good getting it on paper. I'd been carrying it around for about thirteen years and had never really discussed it in detail with anyone, except for my mother at the time Mrs. Crane was killed. She had had a profound effect on my confidence as a student. Before I had her for a teacher, my other teachers always made me feel like I was really bright and put me in advanced reading groups and had given me higher level workbooks; I'd always assumed that I was one of the "smart kids," I guess. Before I had her as a teacher, I'd never questioned my abilities or my intelligence; after I had her, I always questioned it, even into graduate school. Getting it out on paper gave me a sense of relief, but at the same time, there was this urgency to do something with it because I needed to make sense of it.

I started with a segmented essay. Although I knew I wanted to use specific episodes from my year in her classroom—I had most of those written—I wasn't sure what to juxtapose with them. I thought of, and actually played around with, a speech I'd been forced to give about her at a tree dedication ceremony. The circumstances were odd—no other student was available to give the speech, and so my sixth grade teacher asked me to do it and gave me about two weeks to prepare. So I had to think about what I could say. No matter what I said about her, if it was nice, it would be a lie. My mother and I worked out a way where I could give the speech without actually saying that I had liked her or that I missed her. And so I played around with juxtaposing the day I gave that speech and the episodes in her classroom. One of the segments went like this:

> "My name is Mary Beth Pope," I began hesitantly, and swallowed out of fear involuntarily. "I was a student in Mrs. Crane's class last year." I paused, thinking of the things I was about to say, and looked at my first notecard. "Mrs. Crane taught us to sing The Grand Old Flag," I said, thinking that all she really taught us was to doubt ourselves, to be afraid, to never put yourself into anything you did lest it be rejected utterly and completely. "She . . . she, uh, liked us to push our . . . uh, chairs in . . ." She also liked to push us until we cried. I looked out at the crowd, and the principal, and at her husband and sisters who sat directly below me. I did not belong here, giving this speech. The wind blew my dress and made me shiver. My voice broke and I began, "She also . . ." I stopped.

It worked okay, but it wasn't really saying what I needed it to say.

After I had done that first freewriting, I prepared for this piece further by visiting the school and classroom where I'd had her for a teacher. The building wasn't being used as an elementary school at the time; it was part of an adult education site, and so there were big desks and bulletin boards with announcements instead of seasonal decorations. But the green shag carpet was still there, and the low chalkboards, and the same heaters where we used to dry our mittens under the window ledges. And the smell was exactly the same. I just stood there and looked. I couldn't breathe very well and the whole thing felt very claustrophobic. I couldn't believe how nothing had changed in terms of my reaction to the room; I instantly felt stupid and ashamed and on guard just by walking through that door at the age of 23, as intensely as I had felt it every morning when I would get off the bus and head for the room when I was ten. It was wild—it really triggered a lot of memories that helped me to remember more specific details in the segments from fifth grade.

After I made that visit to the classroom I talked to my mom about it. We talked about different days that I had come home crying because of something she'd done to me, and Mom even remembered things I had forgotten. The combination of the visit to the classroom and the discussion with Mom helped me to gel some of the ideas that had been brewing or seemed disconnected, and really got me going on the Mrs. Crane segments, although I still was playing around with the "speech" contrast idea and not feeling like it was going in the right direction.

What ultimately happened was that in a peer workshop session, I brought up my concerns about it, and a fellow graduate assistant and I talked about how awful some of our teachers were, and how, now that we were teachers, we couldn't imagine treating our students the way we'd been treated. This was very much an issue for me as I'd been working on the piece, and my friend suggested that maybe I should focus on that aspect of it and drop the whole "speech" thing. Everything fell into place when she said that, and I went home that night after class and just wrote it all out, using different students to compare my teaching style with Mrs. Crane's. I started with a clustering exercise using a few students who struggled with things similar to the issues I struggled with in Mrs. Crane's class, and tried to line up my fifth grade issues with their issues in my class. Then I did a journal entry on how to put it together in the essay, which went like this:

> What I need to do with this paper is show how having been through Mrs. Crane's class, I am much more sensitive to their feelings—I see the defenses, I see the fear, I see the need for approval in them. What I need to do is match one incident from fifth grade with one I've had with my students. For instance, match Darrin with my spelling, Nicole with my need for Mrs. Crane to like me, Mark with the math problems, Jonathan with my need to be admired, Brian with my frustration level, Eric with my need to be understood and accepted, Jason with my need for freedom and creativity within an assignment.
>
> I need to show the little fight I have every day trying to build their confidence while improve their writing skills.
>
> A final paragraph might be me, hunched over a stack of papers late at night. My comments are long—I write at the very least a half a page per student. I am tired. It would be easier to pick out the wrong things and scribble all over their pages, but I cannot.

I still wasn't sure about the exact structure the paper would take—like what student or incident in Mrs. Crane's class to use first, second, etc., but I knew what direction I wanted to go with it, and started writing and rearranging.

Once I had that figured out, the major problem I ran into was how to introduce the piece and how to conclude. I wasn't even sure what exactly I was trying to say, except that having a teacher who made me feel badly about myself helped me to be more sensitive to my own students—I remembered how it felt when she would ignore me or downplay my efforts or tell me I was stupid or wrong. I figured that a logical way to begin would be with the beginning of my first semester teaching, or at the end, looking back on how I had felt at the beginning. I had worried a lot about having had no training in teaching, only in English, and it had bothered me that whole first semester. Over the course of the semester I realized that I had plenty of experience with teaching because I'd been a student my whole life, watching teachers teach. I would think about my favorite English teachers (which was easy because all of my favorite teachers in high school and college taught English) and how they did things, and I'd try and be like them. It never occurred to me that I might have learned the most about how to teach from the worst teacher I'd ever had.

Also, I wanted to conclude by saying that having Mrs. Crane for a teacher made *me* a better teacher—that I had a better understanding of student needs because I'd had experience with my own needs not being met. The problem was how to get it across without making it sound like, "Mrs. Crane was a terrible teacher and I'm a great teacher because I don't do things the way she did," as that wasn't the point. The point was to show that I was able to turn that negative experience into something positive for both my students and myself. I also was hoping that it would be the kind of thing that other teachers could read which would make them think about teachers *they'd* had who'd hurt *them*, and get in touch with their own perspectives as former students. It's kind of a universal experience—I mean, we've all had bad teachers—and I was banking on that so I wouldn't have to do so much explaining.

Actually, I did a lot of explaining anyway in the first draft of the paper—the first paragraph began at the end of the semester of teaching, looking back, and sort of telling what I had learned. This is what it looked like:

> For weeks before my first semester of teaching began, I suffered from severe nausea. My main concern was that I had no experience with teaching—no classes, no training, no nothing. I walked into class on the first day, opened my mouth to speak, and before I knew it the semester was over. I wondered where I had learned to teach, and it was only after that first semester was over, and I had time to think about it, that I realized that I had been a student my whole life. I realized that my real training began in the fifth grade with Mrs. Crane. I have come to believe that only so much of teaching is curriculum; the rest is instinct. For most of my life I have hated this woman who destroyed my self-esteem and all the confidence I'd ever had in myself as a student at the age of eleven. Now, I thank her. Perhaps because of her—or maybe in spite of her—I am too sensitive to my students' needs, and at times I worry that I am too gentle with them. But I am not sorry; in fact, I prefer to be that way, because I

know now that my experiences in her classroom that year have made me a better teacher.

It's awful, when I look at it now, because I manage to sound exactly the way I didn't want to. I concluded the same way, with the teaching evaluations the students wrote at the end of the semester, and I used examples of what they said about me to confirm what I "said" in the body of the paper, comparing my experience with Mrs. Crane to my experience as a teacher. The truth is that when I got back the evaluation she`ets that the students had written at the end of that first semester, I sat on the floor of my kitchen and was terrified to open them. When I finally did, and I read the nice things that the students had said about my teaching, I realized that maybe I was a good teacher and that I hadn't done the horrible job that I thought I had. I cried for about two hours that day because the whole semester I'd been afraid I wasn't a good teacher and that my inexperience showed. A lot of them said that they felt like I really cared about them, and that made me think about Mrs. Crane, and how she hadn't cared at all. So when I wrote the conclusion, all that went into it because it was exactly what I was experiencing at the time.

I didn't recognize immediately that both the introduction and conclusion were too self-conscious, and told more than they showed. I didn't really need either—I'd made my point by virtue of the contrast—but I felt obligated to set up some kind of a chronology and demonstrate what I'd learned about my teaching. When my composition instructor handed back the first draft, he said that he liked all of it except the introduction paragraph, which he felt "covered too much ground," and so I took that out and changed it to a scene of me waiting outside my classroom on the first day of class, worried about how I would manage to teach fifty students when I had no experience with teaching at all. Once I did that, I was really happy with it—it gave it the feeling that the reader was going to be there with me, walking into the classroom, scared to death like I was, and it removed that filter of my self-consciousness. I also did some major revisions on what my students said to me in the evaluations—because although I'd taken the quotes right off the evaluations, they were so unbelievably positive and sweet that it made me sound like I was bragging which, again, wasn't the point. What I was trying to do with the evaluations was to give the reader the same sense of "wow" and relief that I'd felt when I read them myself on the floor of the kitchen that day.

That was the point the paper was at when I handed it in for a final grade at the end of the semester, and that was close to the form it was in when I submitted it to the *Language Arts Journal of Michigan*. I did feel at one point that the sections on Mrs. Crane were too wordy, too self-pitying, and that the segments about my teaching were too self-righteous; however, when I was writing it, it felt good to discover something positive had come from that terrible year, and I got really excited about it. Before I submitted it to *LAJM*, I tried to tone it down a little, although after I went back and read it again, I realized I didn't need to make as many changes as I thought.

The draft I sent out ended with the following segments (I had chosen to distinguish past and present by putting the experiences with Mrs. Crane in past tense and italics and my experiences as a teaching assistant in present tense and plain text):

The tears in my eyes blurred the long division problems together until I couldn't see anymore. This was the best day of the month—free morning—and all of the other kids were down in the gym playing games and having fun. Three times I had redone the missed problems, eight of the forty she had given us, and run excitedly down the three flights of stairs to the gym, anxious to join my friends. Three times I had trudged back up the stairs, and been made to sit and rework the problems. I was so frustrated that I couldn't even see the paper, which had been erased so many times that I could see the pattern on my desk through what was left of the paper. Added to this were the tears that now made the page not only wet, but the answers I had gotten right, blurry. I couldn't bring myself to face her again, and I just knew that I could never do it right for her. I hated long division. Mrs. Crane hated me. And I had no idea what to do about it. I couldn't understand why she had singled me out to rework my missed problems—after all, I had worked as hard as all of the other students. And how was it that they all had answered their questions right? Was I the only one who couldn't get the problems right? Maybe it had nothing to do with the work, I thought. Maybe I wasn't pretty enough. She liked Erin and Laurie, who were both pretty. That had to be it—I worked as hard as both of them, but she still didn't like me. Or maybe it really was that I was the only one who didn't know how to do long division exactly right every time. I gave up wondering, and forgot about the gym. It hurt too much to hope that she would let me be like everyone else, so I abandoned my problems and went to look out the window instead.

Mark sits in the back row of my classroom with Walter and Jonathan. All three are football players, and while Walter and Jonathan often doze or talk disruptively, Mark tries to listen closely to what I have to say. He asks questions in class and comes to my office regularly. He is creative and earnest, and usually manages to separate himself, if only in attention span, from his teammates.

I hand his paper back without a grade. While his writing is nearly error free, and might have been an "A" for another assignment, he has not met any of the requirements for this paper. Were I to grade it, it would have failed. I know he is a good writer and I do not want to discourage him, so I write on the bottom of his paper, "Mark—your writing, in terms of mechanics and style, is excellent. As a creative piece, this would have received an "A". However, for this assignment, you haven't met the requirements I needed to see. I know you are busy, but I'd like to meet with you and discuss what you need to change here. This is very good writing, Mark, but it doesn't meet the criteria I spelled out in class. You can take your time with it. See me first and we'll talk." Mark reads my comments and looks confused for a moment, but he nods slowly, and I know he understands. I know I haven't crushed him, and I know he will come see me and do better the next time.

On the last day of fifth grade, we were allowed to take our brown bag lunches outside and sit on the lawn in front of the school. I sat with my class and watched Mrs. Crane talk to the students who sat around her. I sat far on the outside of the circle with another girl, and we traded lifesavers and halves of our sandwiches. When the buses pulled up to take us home that day, Mrs. Crane stood by the door, and hugged each of us. I waited, dreading the hug, but knowing I couldn't get past her. She made a big show out of it, telling the students how much she would miss all of them. When my turn came, she put her mushy arms around me and my cheek burned where it touched her neck. When she finished hugging me, she put her hands on my shoulders and shook me a little. "I'm expecting big things from you, Mary Beth." My eyes filled up with tears. I managed good-bye and followed the other students on to the bus. I hated her even more for lying like that in front of all of my friends. As I stood behind the other students in line for my bus, I wondered why she would say such a thing. The way she had treated me all year told me everything I ever wanted to know about what she expected from me.

I sit on the floor of the living room on the day I receive my student evaluations back. I have no idea what they have said, and I wonder if after reading them I will feel better or worse about my performance this past semester. I open them slowly, afraid of what they could say. I can remember really giving it to some of my teachers; I wonder if anyone has done that to me. I pick up the first one and read what it says: "I really liked this class and teacher. She was always so chipper in the morning." I smile, wondering who wrote it. I pick up the next one: "Miss Pope was a very good teacher. This was a great class, even though it was at 8:00 in the morning. The journals were fun—maybe you could do more of those in your next class." The next one reads: "This is the only class I didn't drop." I laugh, flattered by this student who chose to stick with me, and read another one. "Miss Pope really cares about her students and always has something positive to say about our work, even when we get a low grade." I pick up the next one, and the next. I smile until I come to the one that reads: "Miss Pope's class was my favorite class of all—and the only reason I got up for any of my classes." I don't recognize the writing, but I don't care. It is then that I realize my face is wet from my tears. I think about Mrs. Crane. And I thank her.

When the editors at *LAJM* wrote to me and told me they wanted to publish it, they asked that I make a few changes—essentially, take out two segments: one about the math exercise Mrs. Crane had made me rework instead of letting me play with the other kids in the gym, and the conclusion. I felt kind of funny chopping out the math segment part because I was so angry at her for that—and I think it showed, too, because it was long (probably why they wanted it out). Taking out the conclusion was fine with me, though, because once I realized that it was going to be published and other people besides my composition instructor and classmates would read it, it occurred to me that the conclusion could seem exaggerated or too slanted toward glorifying my teaching success that semester.

The editors also asked me to make the last day of school the final segment for fifth grade, and finish with a segment about my student, Mark. In the passage above, then, I was dropping the first and last segments and reversing the order of the middle two. I was actually really happy with that revision because it gave the piece a nice feeling of continuity, instead of closure, which made it seem as if there had been an end to what I'd learned. And for the purposes of the journal, I could see why they wanted it that way.

When the journal came out, and I saw it in print, and read it again, I realized that I was really happy with the way that it was written. The whole experience of writing it and revising it and then seeing it in print was important for me for a couple of reasons. The first was that I felt like it was okay for me to have really disliked Mrs. Crane as much as I had—I'd never wanted to admit that after she died because it seemed like such an awful thing to say about someone who was dead (especially since I'd wished her that way so often before it happened). Also, it helped me to see that I had left that year in her class with something important—that she really did teach me something significant by not giving me the things that I needed, and that though it was difficult to endure at the ages of ten and eleven, it had become a really significant learning experience for me.

There has been some carryover from writing this piece into the writing I am doing now indirectly. I learned that when I am writing, I need to watch myself think, and not try so hard to make everything go in a particular direction right away. For instance, if I had paid attention to the fact that I kept thinking "I would never treat a student that way" as I was writing the segments about Mrs. Crane, maybe it wouldn't have taken me so long to recognize that *that* was the direction the writing really wanted to go. A lot of times, I will sit down with what seems like a great idea, but then I can't figure out where to go with it. If I just pay attention to what I am thinking, and trust it, and not dismiss it as just an external observation about the work I'm doing, I can get a better perspective on how I really feel about what I am writing. It's hard to do, but I've been trying.

Zion

Maureen Stanton

Sometimes I wake up in the middle of the night and I don't know where I am. My bed is a flying carpet. Flat on my back, I am looking up at the stars, whizzing around in blackness. Then I slow down, the carpet lands. I figure out which direction I am facing and get a map of the room in my head. I recognize the window and the streetlight. The bed, the door, the lamp. I remember where I am, the longitude and latitude of my life. Fixed to locale, nailed to a place, I can begin to make order.

I am dozing in the hospital bed with Steve when he pulls me.

"Mo, something is happening to me. My head is shrinking."

"What do you mean? What does it feel like?"

"It feels like it's the size of a grapefruit." He starts to cry, the first time since all this started. I run to the nurses' station. "Help. Something weird is happening to Steve." Fay and Dora come and give Steve a shot, but this causes his tongue to swell and his eyes to roll back in their sockets. Fay holds his mouth open, while Dora gets a doctor who injects something into Steve's bicep, and after a few seconds he breathes normally.

"It was just a reaction to the new pain medicine," Fay tells us, like it was nothing more than a bee sting. I stand near Steve's head and try not to touch him too much. The feeling that his head is small stays with him the whole night.

We are at the hospital of last resort, a small brick building in Zion, Illinois, an hour north of Chicago. It's a hospital where the bedspreads are worn thin and have holes. A hospital that serves carrot and celery juice, and offers alternative treatments for cancer. One week a month we come here. Steve gets his poison. I bleed.

The doctors here are different than at the hospital Steve checked out of back in Michigan. For one thing, most of them are Filipino. It unnerves Steve's parents who discourage our decision (false hopes, grasping at straws). But here the doctors don't give up as easily. Steve's first oncologist wrote a note on his chart which we read during our flight to Chicago. *It is very sad to see that the patient cannot accept the poor prognosis.* Two months, she predicted for a twenty-nine-year-old man with three small children, then patted his hand and walked out of the room, dry as a desert, tearless, leaving us in the starkness of Steve's future.

Dr. Sanchez and Dr. Melijor give us information, allow us to see Steve's nuclear scans. Married to gray film, Steve's skeleton glows. Small black dots are sprayed from his skull to his kneecaps as if someone plugged him with bird shot. Cranium, sternum, ribs, vertebrae, pelvis, femur. It is a frightening lesson in anatomy. I try not to act shocked, but the black dots are more numerous than I had envisioned when the previous doctors spoke of "widespread metastases" and "multiple tumors." "Multiple" meant six or seven, a six-pack, a touchdown, a number we could beat. I count more than two dozen specks on the little x-ray man that is Steve—malignancies humming inside his flesh. Not to mention his liver, marbleized like a high priced cut of beef, with cancer cells. Now it is real.

I arrive at the hospital at nine in the morning and climb in bed with Steve as if I am joining him in his body, unzipping his skin like it's a space suit, and snuggling in. His roommates, Greg and Chuck, don't seem to mind. Greg is an insect exterminator from South Carolina with testicular cancer. He sleeps most of the time, or reads his Bible. The only noises he makes are vomiting, or buzzing for the nurses. Hand him his urine jug, fix his pillow, bring him a drink. He thinks he is at a resort.

Chuck is in the other bed. He has a clear tube taped inside his nose that pumps oxygen from tanks on the side of his bed into his drowning, malignant lungs. He is an earthbound scuba diver. Chuck breathes loud and heavy, and coughs wet, phlegmy coughs which temporarily paralyze his wife's kinetic fingers as she sits in a chair by his bed and knits violently, like she is weaving Chuck a new set of lungs.

Days pass by slowly. Flowers arrive for Steve from his parents. *When God closes a door, he opens a window.* I put the card on the nightstand, open the curtains and watch activity below, cars and people. Fat, slow winter flies buzz against the sealed glass. They appear out of nowhere, it seems, these retarded creatures, and now they are desperate to get out, as if they know they are trapped, as if they have some power of cognition. That's what I learn when I accompany Steve to the hospital. Empty hours. Time to think.

We walk around the hallways, Steve holding onto his pole like a staff. Bottles are suspended from the pole, clear liquids that feed the catheter in Steve's chest and flow into the big subclavian vein direct to his heart, like a fast underground train. Nitrogen mustard, 5-FU, methotrexate. The names remind me of the defoliants that were dropped on Vietnamese jungles. They cause hair to fall out of Steve's head, off his chest. His underarms and legs are bare. His eyebrows are missing. His pubic hair is gone. He looks like a fetus, a tall, skinny fetus. Still, he is handsome with his heavy eyelashes and soupy blue eyes, purple hollows below them, like watercolor. His eyes look bigger with his face so thin and his skin wrapped so tightly over his bones. Delicate bones.

Visitation ends at eight, but the nurses understand that hours matter and allow me to stay until midnight. Then I walk to the room I have rented from a notice I saw posted in the hospital cafeteria. Three blocks away and ten dollars a night. The couple who own the house are up when I arrive.

"Wipe down the shower before you get out. Don't use too much toilet paper. And use the towel more than once." Noma scolds me before I have transgressed. She is a tiny woman with messy gray hair and one sharp, pointy tooth, like an egg tooth a baby bird uses to peck its way out of a shell.

"Who've ya got in the hospital?" she asks.

"My boyfriend."

"Isn't that a shame." She asks me where I am from, and then says, "Emil's got a cousin in Detroit."

Emil has filmy blue eyes and hair that is sugar white with bangs cut straight across his forehead. He looks like an old angel.

"They come from all over to go to that hospital. We've had people from Florida, Kentucky . . . New Zealand! Staying right in your room," he says, as if I am privileged.

"We're blessed with good health, thank the Lord," Noma cuts in. "Emil broke his ankle forty years ago. It was healed by a miracle at our church and it never bothered him since, right, Em?"

"Still march with the Brothers of Zion band sixty years now. I'm the oldest clarinet player." Emil opens a closet and pulls out a red, wooly coat and matching pants with gold braiding up the seams.

"It's no coincidence you're in Zion," he says. "This is a holy town. Miracles take place all the time."

"That's very nice," I say, and manage to excuse myself. Behind the bedroom door, I flop onto the lumpy single bed and cry. I do every night. It's part of my sleep.

Later I am poked awake by noises in the kitchen: a spoon clinking against a dish, footsteps, cupboards opening and shutting, a toilet flushing. Then the sequence repeats. I can hear snoring from Noma and Emil's room. They would have had to pass me to get to the kitchen, but I didn't hear anyone in the hall. I become convinced there is a ghost just outside my door, making that last meal over and over again, unable to let go. I pull my blankets up around my chin. My heart is pounding, pushing my tired blood, echoing in the small room. I pray. *Please, God, don't let it come in here.* I lie in stiff fear until gray light when spirits are banished, then wake up at eleven, groggy. Emil's white toupee is on a styrofoam head on the kitchen table and his teeth in a jar of water on the bathroom sink. I ask Noma if she heard noises in the night.

"Just me eating my cereal," she says. "I get up about three every morning and have some cereal."

"What about the flushing?"

"Oh, that's the pump clearing water out of the basement."

In the daytime, I can get along. There are objects, events, people to hold on to, give texture to time, divide up space. But at night, I lose my way, lose my mind. It's easy.

The next month I find a room for $75 a week at the Harbor Hotel. The office is the living room of a small house that smells like curry. A boy is playing on the rug in the fuzzy penumbra of the television. A woman with a red dot on her forehead gives me a key and says there are no refunds, then directs me to their other hotel down the street.

The rooms are in the basement of a small, brick apartment building. There is no front desk, only a broken pay phone, and leaves blowing around the hallway. A disheveled man is loitering near the telephone. As far as I can tell, I am the only guest.

Ramona and Sue and Estherine and Georgia are on the same chemotherapy schedule as Steve, so we see them every month. Steve flirts with them, bald and in their bathrobes. They laugh when he tells them he is going to wear his camouflage hunting shirt and fatigues for his upper G. I. test. He likes the audience, but I don't care to share him much. Of what little he has left, I want it all. I am with him most of the time, in the bathroom even, keeping him company. He sits on the toilet and rests his head on the back of a fold-up chair. I sit on the chair and touch his back lightly. His skin is hot all the time now and I like to put my cold hands on it. We sit there in silence waiting for him to pee.

Steve naps and I read. Mysteries. Cheap little stories that completely absorb me, simple words I can eat, pages I can bend and fold. Perry Mason novels are the main staple of my diet. Perry always finds the killer, always wins his cases. I like the surety of that. There isn't anything in the stories to disturb me, or throw me off balance. They ask nothing of me.

At night I read to Steve, poems, clips about U.F.O.'s from *Omni* magazine, and stories from supermarket tabloids. GIANT FLYING CATS TERRIFY TOWN. WOMAN ABDUCTED BY ALIENS CAN NOW TALK TO ANIMALS. CANCER MAN'S LAST REQUEST: A JAGUAR CAR PARTS CATALOGUE. I envision a man in a leotard and cape with a big "C" on his chest, an action hero defying death. Cancer Man.

This month Cancer Man is undergoing an experimental treatment—whole body hyperthermia. His body temperature will be raised to 108 degrees Fahrenheit. The theory is that abnormal, mutant cancer cells slough off at 107 degrees, while healthy cells, skin, organs, muscle, brain tissue, begin to die at temperatures just above 108. It is a precarious balancing act to reach the right temperature, sustain it long enough to do specific damage, then lower it again. Steve has signed a liability waiver, a disclaimer of some kind that contains the words "result in possible death."

Dr. Kim, the anesthesiologist, brings me into the treatment room to see Steve. He has been stripped naked and wrapped head to toe in gauze like a mummy. To raise his temperature, he is wrapped in a heated plastic blanket filled with water and alcohol. A thermometer in his mouth, one in his rectum, and two others will monitor his fever for the next eight hours.

I spend the day wandering along Lake Michigan, the Illinois side which is not as sandy and beautiful as the Michigan side. Blame it on the wind, I think, noticing this habit I have of searching for culprits. I go to the library and draft a letter to Steve's insurance company pleading with them to pay for the hyperthermia. In the park, a large bird boldly garbed in a blood red hood and black and white tuxedo clings to the bark of a tree, a red-headed woodpecker. It stands out among the muted browns and greens and feels like a gift, blatant beauty. When I return Steve is knocked out, in intensive care, sleeping it off. He wakes later delirious, mumbling like a drunk, lashing out with his hands, yanking at the tubes and bandages. Wild. For two days Steve sleeps fitfully. Finally, he recognizes me. I say, "Tell yourself each day you are going to get better and better." He says, "I'm going to get better and better. I'll be the best."

These treatments—chemicals, radiation, hyperthermia—attempt to murder Steve each time; push him to the brink, lull him back, give him time to fortify then zonk him again. It's a tease, an oxymoron, Orwellian doublespeak. We must kill you to cure you, make you sick to make you better. It's a lie, a trick with fun house mirrors. We don't trust anyone.

The Harbor Hotel is quiet all week. Then late Friday night I hear people yelling and kicking the doors to the rooms, moving towards mine. I click off my lamp so they won't see a sliver of light leaching under my door into the hallway. I'm afraid that if they find me they will kill me. It is my nighttime logic. I practice saying "Who's there?" in a deep, male voice. After a while, they manage to break into a room a couple of doors down and party all night. I make myself small and quiet like the tiny baby cockroaches that scatter whenever I turn on the fluorescent light in the bathroom. I plan my escape out the small casement window above the television, level with the ground. Finally I sleep hard and wake up to the sounds of Big Wheels on pavement.

Outside, I blink at the sunlight. Mothers sit on the brick steps smoking cigarettes. They stare at me like I am an alien, out of my country, away from my land. Timeless, placeless, bodiless.

When I get to the hospital Chuck's bed is empty. He died during the night after a long coughing fit. His wife, Carol, is gone without a trace, not one thread left behind. Steve has gotten scorched from the hyperthermia. Bad wrapping job. The soles of his feet and his scrotum are tender. He's pissed off about this, but when Jane, a volunteer, comes around he forgets for a while. Steve and I stare at her round and bouncy firm flesh encased in stretchy nylon like she is wearing beach balls, at her unruly white hair and huge blurry eyes behind thick glasses. She hands out newspapers and carnations, and speaks in a flat, nasally voice, yogic, like a Sufi chant. "I have five dogs, two cats, a mallard (now in my freezer waiting for the Guinness Book of World Records to verify it as the oldest albino duck—seventeen years, as old as my niece), and a pet starling that barks like a dog and shouts 'thief' every time a stranger comes in my house."

Jane invites me to eat with her in the hospital cafeteria. She talks while she chews, projecting bullets of deviled ham and masticated bread bits. One lands on my cheek and it is all I can focus on, don't know what words she is saying. I avoid her after that. I give Steve enemas, put my fingers in his rectum, mop up his vomit, swab the raw, pink flesh around his catheter site, but none of that fazes me the way having to eat with Jane seems an insurmountable task. Everything seems odd. Off.

This life develops a rhythm: three weeks home, one in Zion. Months go by this way. I dial a number pinned to the hospital bulletin board and a woman named Martha says she has an extra room in her apartment. When I get there Martha is gone and her son, Jeff, is playing chess on a small hand-held computer, smoking a cigarette with a puddle of gray cat on his lap. He explains that Martha was called to take care of someone for the week. She is a home-care aide.

"Bummer," he says, after he asks why I am there. He is in his early twenties with long hair parted in the middle and scruffy sideburns zigging down his jaw line.

"I'm trying to quit drinking," he says. "I haven't had a drink in over two weeks."

"Good." I feel my head bobbing up and down like one of those spring-necked ceramic cats you see on dashboards. I've noticed this: when you tell people your boyfriend has cancer they feel they must ante up their own pain and lay it on the table. At first, I thought it was nice, a kind of offering, but now it just makes me mad. Nobody's pain is equal to ours. I feel self-righteous and chosen. Anointed and doomed at the same time.

When I get up the next day, Jeff is mixing a glass of lemonade, smoking a cigarette and playing chess.

"I guess you like to play chess." I feel obliged to address this man in whose living room I am a stranger.

"Keeps me out of trouble," he replies. "I'm on probation for dealing drugs."

"Good luck," I say. Fucking wingnut, I think. Who cares? It feels good to be mean.

Put your troubles in the hands of the Lord and he will help you. Steve flings this month's card from his parents across the room. I pick it up and set it on the nightstand. I can't stomach the tension of a thing being where it doesn't belong, throwing off order, tempting chaos. I fill a plastic urine jug with water for the flowers and arrange them. I check selections on Steve's menu card, cut his toenails, get ice from the machine down the hall for his pitcher, try to keep busy before succumbing, inevitably, to watching television. Nothing airs in the morning except for talk shows, game shows, and odd sports, like curling, a bizarre contest involving a puck and a broom, a tight little silly game. Lunch arrives. Steve looks at it and puts the metal lid back on. I walk across the street and pick up some Kentucky Fried Chicken.

Later Steve unhooks himself from the tubes and we escape from the hospital. Outside it is cold and gray. We walk around holding hands. I like Steve's hands, his long, slender fingers, nails brittle and yellowed, his palms still rough and callused though he has not worked in over a year. He has two warts on his left hand, stubborn, rubbery bumps that I like to bite. They're large, these hands, but deft as he glues a part on a model car with his son, or takes an eyelash out of my eye. Steve used to stand behind me and press my nipples between his fingers while I stirred spaghetti sauce, and when we slept, his leg draped over mine, clinging like sweaty children, he cupped my breast in his palm like it was a dove. Now touching hurts him, so the only kisses I give are little brush strokes.

Steve makes it one block to a park near the hospital before he tires. We sit on a bench and watch a mother absentmindedly hand bread to her daughter. The little girl stuffs fistfuls of the bread into her mouth, every now and then flinging a crust at the ducks. Steve laughs, and I kiss his knuckles as the girl fills her cheeks and her mother stares at something else across the pond.

Friday night Jeff is playing chess with the television shouting in the background. I crawl into bed and stare at squares of light on the wall. Street lights, window panes, simple inanimate objects make me feel sad.

Hours later I am awakened by a cat screeching, then Jeff laughing loudly. The sound is distorted, like in a tunnel. Too loud for laughing alone, I think. My eyes are wide open, sucking in the dim light. I hear Jeff's maniacal laugh again and the cat yelps painfully. I envision Jeff screwed up on hallucinogens, torturing the cat. Greenish street light burnishes the door knob, which I expect to rotate at any moment, Jeff entering my room to rape me and carve me up with a knife, laughing that wild, enormous laugh the whole time. I stuff the corner of the pillow in my mouth to muffle sobs.

Nights can be like this—scenes from frightening horror films. Disaster is no longer an abstract concept. Anything is possible and danger is everywhere. I have a hard time differentiating the real from the imagined. Steve used to scare me, curling his index finger and growling, "redrum redrum redrum" like the little boy in *The Shining,* amused by how I had to skulk from light switch to light switch to pee in the middle of the night. I have asked him not to come back and haunt me, even if it is just a joke. He has asked me not to write about him, wants to disappear. I am terrified of his leaving, waking up next to a stiff corpse. I think about it every night when I lie down beside him, of being left alone, abandoned.

I wake up at seven stiff-necked, and for a second surprised to be alive and okay. Lines pressed into my face from the wrinkled sheets make a map, look like a place. I gather my stuff, don't stop to wash. Downstairs, Jeff is gone. I leave the key on the table and walk to the hospital. The nurses break the rules and let me sleep in Chuck's old bed for one night. In the morning, the long black hospital limousine delivers Steve and me to the airport. People in cars pass us on the highway and stare into our opaque windows like we are celebrities. We can see them, but they can't see us, as if we are ghosts. We exist in a parallel life: we can see our peers (getting married, having babies, buying houses), but we can't touch them anymore. We are headed somewhere else.

On Writing "Zion"

Maureen Stanton

"Zion" began as journal entries made in 1986 when the events in the essay were taking place. I wasn't thinking then that in the future this might be a story or an essay, but was writing for the same reason I record anything in my journal—to understand what is happening in my life. (This isn't always the case. There are other experiences that I know I will want to turn into an essay, so I keep specific notes, though they are mostly facts, ideas, and observations rather than the "talking to myself" of journal writing.)

I didn't look at the journal until probably two years after the experience. Grief over the death of Steve, the subject of this essay, consumed me, and I was busy trying to figure out how to fill up my life, which had revolved around Steve's cancer for eighteen months. Also, Steve had asked me not to write about him and I was struggling with this issue. When I started to write Zion as a "piece," I talked with a counselor who had helped me through this period about whether I could write about Steve. She was blunt and logical. Steve was dead, and this was my story too so I had a right to tell it.

After the fogginess of grief started to lift I began to remember interesting details of the experience, interactions and events I couldn't seem to recall when I was engulfed by emotions. The lifting of the veil of grief brought a flurry of raw material forward and I jotted notes everywhere, often waking up at night to write down a sentence that would later trigger a whole episode.

This has become my modus operandi for writing. I get very excited about an idea and become preoccupied with it. My mind is constantly tugged back to that subject whenever it is not engaged (usually when I am trying to sleep, but I will always sacrifice sleep for inspiration, even when it means arriving at work the next day a bit exhausted).

These scribbled thoughts, observations, words, and memories are stashed in a file because they seem somehow related. The file thickens and at some point reaches a critical mass. Visually, I think of it as a bunch of free-floating atoms and molecules ranging around in their own individual orbits, then something like the Big Bang happens, a tiny pop perhaps, and these particles react to one another and begin to attract and repel, combine and multiply to create a cluster of raw material. This is accompanied by an almost physical restlessness to write the piece, and suddenly (it often seems) I begin to work on it in earnest (leaving other pieces I am working on half-finished).

For this piece, which at various times was titled, "Cancer Man," "The Rooms I Stayed In" (thankfully that one didn't last long), then "Dreaming in Zion," the critical mass occurred about three years after Steve died. I pulled the piece together and brought it to a fiction workshop at the Iowa Summer Writing Program. I had been writing short stories exclusively, largely because that is what I focused on in creative writing classes in college. No one ever mentioned anything about essays. In fact, in four undergraduate and one graduate creative writing classes, I never heard the word essay mentioned, nor was it offered as a course on its own. Even in the writing groups I joined everyone seemed to be writing fiction.

The version of "Zion" I took to the workshop was only slightly different than this final version, yet I was naively trying to pass it off as a short story. That version was straight narrative, factual recitation with detailed description but little reflection. The workshop attendants wanted to see more of "me" in the piece, and they thought that, although it was moving, it was not complete and was not a successful short story. As with nearly all of my writing at that time, I didn't know what it was or what to do with it. I wasn't really writing short stories but I kept trying to squash my pieces into that mold.

I tried to put more "me" into the story but what came out, I see now, was not poignant reflection but raw emotion, untempered anger and resentment mostly. The piece took on a maudlin and self-pitying tone. I did not know what to do with Zion at this point, so I did nothing. It sat for a while before I decided to bring it to a living room writing group I participated in (after removing the added "me"). Two of the members of the writing group were professors of English and accomplished writers, and the others were professionals of all ages, all good writers and critics. This group felt the piece was flat, and although the writing was good, it lacked something. I still did not know what to do with the piece, so it landed back in hibernation, this time for about three years. But it was in that living room group that I first heard the term creative nonfiction from Mike Steinberg. I didn't grasp immediately what he was talking about, but as I slowly began to open up to this genre, I felt like I was finding my way home. This was the type of writing I naturally tended to and I was excited about it, but I still didn't know what made good creative nonfiction.

Having been somewhat liberated from my fixation with short stories and the constraints of trying to fit my personal experiences into that format (and feeling like a liar and a fraud doing so), I began to write about whatever stirred me without trying to set up dialogue, point of view and develop characters. (Although I think what I learned in fiction workshops helped me with pacing, tone, freshness of language, and precision.) I wrote two more essays, both about

Steve, who managed to work himself into nearly everything I was writing regardless of how remotely related he seemed to be to the subject at hand. Both of these essays were published, but I felt that it was dumb luck, that I had stumbled into something that I couldn't sustain or duplicate as I was unaware of how I did it or why people liked the essays.

At this time, I began to get increasingly frustrated with my demanding job, which was eclipsing my free time and energy to write. (Writing had always been my umbilical cord to a meaningful existence.) I saved money for over a year, quit my job, and moved to the homes of friends and family members where I could live inexpensively. (Although this was frightening financially, as soon as I did this part-time and consulting opportunities began to fall into my lap. It was uncanny.) This is significant because if I had not done this, I feel strongly that "Zion" and many other pieces would never have been resurrected at all. (More importantly, continuing to live an artless, passionless existence and working a thankless, dull job would have caused my soul to wither on the vine, the marrow in my bones to dry up.) With the luxury of time I could put my heart and soul into creating more finished works that gave me a greater sense of satisfaction.

Having bought myself time to write (I envisioned a big parking meter into which I deposited my hard-won savings that now registered one year of time, ticking, ticking . . .), I began to work on my essays and to read other essayists in literary journals, collections, and magazines. It was this reading that helped to bring me along. Who knows how long it would have taken for me to discover truths about writing creative nonfiction on my own? Although I did not retrieve "Zion" to work on right away, in this incubation period I was beginning to get a sense of what makes a good essay, and why people bother to write essays after all. (I do think that it was good, though, to write creative nonfiction without formally studying it at first. There was a terrific freedom about not knowing what I was trying to do, to let the writing range freely. I think it allowed my voice to emerge.)

I attended a creative nonfiction workshop at the Stonecoast Writers' Conference in 1996, encouraged by Mike Steinberg, the man who had first introduced me to the term "creative nonfiction." This was the first time I had ever taken a workshop in this genre. The workshop was excellent. It reminded me of a trip I took to Brazil where I was immersed in the Portuguese language, yet could only pick up a word or two from each exchange. Then, after three weeks there, something happened, some leap of understanding, where I began to be able to interpret whole sentences and chunks of conversation. I liken that experience to Stonecoast because afterwards, instead of moving towards the writing blindfolded, occasionally glimpsing into some secret chamber of knowledge, I began to comprehend holistically the concept of creative nonfiction so that I could now purposefully sculpt the subconscious or "blind" part of my writing.

After the workshop, I pulled "Zion" from its entombment. It had been one of my favorite subjects, the surrealness of the experience, and I wanted to perfect it as much as I could. I didn't want it to sit in my file drawer forever. I wanted people to read it, like most anything I write. I wanted to create a thing of beauty, a story that intrigued and moved people. A decade had passed since the actual experiences in Zion, but writing it in the present tense returned me to the scene, placed me squarely back in the hospital and those seedy rooms where I slept. I cried every time I read each revision. It was biologically ordained, this weeping, from a deep, forgotten place inside me.

My process is to work on a computer draft, then to rearrange paragraphs, edit, and mark up the text by hand, then back to the computer, only to repeat the process. I revised the manuscript probably two dozen times over the course of a month or so, sometimes setting the piece aside for a day or two and working on something else, or gardening, which is my form of meditation. I originally intended to change the piece from present to past tense after getting it all down. I was only using the present to make the experience come alive for me again, to sharpen details, but as the writing progressed, I began to grow attached to the piece the way it was. I liked the immediacy of the story, the sense of being transported into the hospital or hotel room. And I had a strong desire to preserve the authenticity of that section of my life, to keep it intact, like a clipping from a film reel. I wanted to keep the memory pure, not to muddy the events with thoughts that represent how I feel now rather than how I felt then.

I can become obsessed with a piece, and lately I am fortunate enough to have time for obsessions. With Zion, the prose seemed sparse, pared down (compared to all that happened in real life and compared to earlier drafts). Every word mattered so I often spent a half-hour on one word, going back and forth, changing my mind then changing it back to the way it was originally. I realized I needed to be exact about Steve's chemotherapy instead of relying on my memory. Staring at the names of cancer drugs in the library released waves of memories about this experience. Sometimes I would go in search of metaphors, once sitting in the library all afternoon reading the Biblical references to Zion (which I didn't import into the essay after all since they felt forced). Sometimes I think I was trying too hard to create a "thing" instead of letting the "thing" create itself, but I usually recognized the artificial passages after a few days time and removed them (no matter how fond I was of the phrase or image I wanted to push into the piece).

I dug back into my original journals of a decade before, reread my old letters from Steve and listened to a tape of his voice. In the end, I added little to the factual bulk of the piece. I reviewed earlier drafts with comments made by my peers at the Iowa Workshop and in my writers' group. My typed out questions to the living room group at the bottom of the essay demonstrate my confusion about what I was attempting. These "questions for the group" were: what tense should the story be told in? Should this be a short story or an essay? Is there such a thing as true fiction? It seems I was still leaning towards writing fiction.

I found the copy of the manuscript from Mike Steinberg. His comments, thoughtfully offered four years prior to this rewrite, were exactly what the piece needed. He liked a lot of the external description, but said, "I'd like to see you get more reflective about the experience . . . and yes, we'll talk about your questions regarding autobiographical essay/fiction." He pointed out places where the piece could be "opened up." It appears I wasn't ready for his comments when he gave them to me years ago, but after the Stonecoast workshop, I finally understood what he was getting at. (I have saved all the manuscripts from workshop reviewers over the years because I value their comments, but interestingly, Mike Steinberg was the only one who referred to Zion as an "essay" and treated it as such when critiquing it.)

When it was obvious that I was doing nothing more than fiddling with prepositions and articles, the tiniest bits of text, I decided the piece was done. In any event, I simply didn't know where else to go with it and called it done. I may someday rewrite this piece in past tense, as I have been encouraged to do, and maybe this will strengthen the story and give it more weight and relevance. But more time will have to pass. When I work on something as intensely as I did this, I get weary of it. I start to feel ridiculous about the amount of time I am spending on it (which feels disproportionate to things taking place in the larger world around me). This happens often with my writing. I tire of pieces (they wear me out), so I put them away, which usually turns out to be a good thing. When I return to them later, what is missing, what is false or contrived, what is sloppy or sophomoric becomes more obvious. And I, for the distance passed (often years), am wiser in my approach to the piece. Unfortunately, this does not make me a prolific writer, only a careful one.

Overall "Zion" has not changed dramatically since its original incarnation nearly a decade ago and many, many hours of labor later. The format turned out to be the same, and the opening and ending paragraphs are similar. Some passages are verbatim from the original draft. But the difference lies in telling phrases, observations, and reflections, which give the narrative facts a luminescence that only distance and learning can yield. It seems that finally, after a decade, I could look with relative detachment at this experience and see it for what it really was, and in subtle ways, infuse these small epiphanies into the essay.

In looking back, I see four stages that this, and most of my other essays, passed through. The first is the molecular stage, that early collection of bits of information, what I find fascinating, unusual, funny or poignant at the time it occurs, whether I retain it in memory or in a physical form on pieces of paper. The critical mass stage is next. The particles are vibrating on their own in proximity to one another until they reach a critical mass and a reaction occurs. The writing begins in a fury, raw data, raw memory, stream of consciousness writing.

Incubation happens throughout the writing when I walk away from the piece and it sits inside me, silently arranging itself, so that when I next visit it, I have made important connections. Then I edit and rewrite. The placement of events and observations creates irony, mood, pathos, humor. Events are taken out of the chronological or random order and purposefully placed, refined, commented on. With Zion, incubation occurred over ten years as I intermittently resuscitated the piece, but also during the active writing periods, each night when I turned off my computer and went to bed with the essay on my mind. This seems important, that the essay was written only partially at the desk. Much of it was written while I gardened or walked or lay in bed mulling it over.

Insight is the last thing to come, what the story is really about. I often don't know until very late in the process, and the story is frequently about something other than I intended, if I let the piece take the path it wants (which I did not do when I was forcing it to be a short story). The sensation I get when taking a train from Grand Central station, sitting in a seat facing where you just came from (not being able to see where you are headed) is the same one I feel when I read Zion. Distance. Perspective. It took me ten years to learn how that experience sculpted me, to tell the story, to locate its pulsing heart.

Alternative Contents

Approaches to Writing and Discussing Creative Nonfiction

Memoir

Writers on Their Work

Further Discussion of the Form

Personal Literary and Cultural Criticism

Writers on Their Work

Further Examples of the Form

Further Discussion of the Form

Literary Journalism

Writers on Their Work

Examples of the Form

On Composing Processes

On Form and Genre in Nonfiction

Notes on Authors

André Aciman, the author of *Out of Egypt: A Memoir* and *False Papers*, an essay collection, teaches at Bard College.

Angela M. Balcita is enrolled in the University of Iowa's MFA in Nonfiction Writing Program.

Jocelyn Bartkevicius, an award-winning essayist, teaches at the University of Central Florida.

Jo Ann Beard is the author of the essay collection *The Boys of My Youth*.

Mary Clearman Blew wrote *All but the Waltz, Balsamroot: A Memoir,* and *Bone Deep in Landscape.*

Emily D. Chase is a ferrier in Michigan.

Lisa D. Chavez has published essays in *Fourth Genre* and *The Clackamas Literary Review.*

Judith Ortiz Cofer is the author of *Silent Dancing* and *Woman in Front of the Sun: On Becoming a Writer.*

Frank Conroy is the author of *Stop-Time* and *Dogs Bark but the Caravan Moves on.*

Meghan Daum is the author of the essay collection *My Misspent Youth.*

Annie Dillard's work includes *Pilgrim at Tinker Creek, An American Childhood,* and *Teaching a Stone to Talk.*

Gretel Ehrlich wrote *The Solace of Open Spaces, Questions of Heaven, A Match to the Heart,* and *This Cold Heaven.*

Rebecca Blevins Faery is co-editor of *In Depth: Essays for Our Time* and teaches at MIT.

Patricia Foster, University of Iowa, is the author of *All the Lost Girls: Confessions of a Southern Daughter.*

Dagoberto Gilb is the author of the essay collection *Gritos.*

Adam Gopnik writes for *The New Yorker,* where he published essays collected in *Paris to the Moon.*

Patricia Hampl is the author of *A Romantic Education, Spillville, Virgin Time,* and *I Could Tell You Stories.*

Steven Harvey's essays are collected in *A Geometry of Lilies, Lost in Translation,* and *Bound for Glory.*

Linda Hogan is the author of *The Woman Who Watches Over the World: A Native Memoir* and *Dwellings.*

Peter M. Ives teaches at Trinity Prep in Orlando, Florida, and writes essays and reviews.

Pico Iyer's books include *The Lady and the Monk, Global Soul, Falling Off the Map,* and *Tropical Classical.*

Tracy Kidder's book include *The Soul of a New Machine, Among Schoolchildren, Old Friends,* and *Hometown.*

Nicole Lamy is the former managing editor of the *Boston Book Review* and a freelance writer.

Sydney Lea, the founding editor of *New England Review,* collected his essays in *Hunting the Whole Way Home.*

Phillip Lopate is the author of *Bachelorhood*, *Against Joie de Vivre*, *Portrait of My Body*, and *Getting Personal.*

Bret Lott is the author of *Fathers, Sons, and Brothers: The Men in My Family* and co-editor of *A Year in Place.*

Rebecca McClanahan is the author of the essay collection *The Riddle Song and Other Rememberings.*

John McPhee has published twenty-five books, including the Pulitzer Prize-winning *Annals of the Former World.*

Michele Morano, DePaul University, has published essays in *The Missouri Review* and *Fourth Genre.*

Naomi Shihab Nye is the author of the essay collection *Never in a Hurry: Essays on People and Places.*

Chris Offutt is the author of the memoirs *The Same River Twice* and *No Heroes: A Memoir of Coming Home.*

Michael Pearson, director of the Creative Writing Program at Old Dominion, is the author of *A Place That's Known.*

Brenda Peterson is the author of *Living by Water* and *Singing to the Sound.*

Simone Poirier-Bures,Virginia Tech, wrote the Evelyn Richardson Award-winning memoir *This Shining Place.*

Mary Elizabeth Pope teaches at the College of Notre Dame of Maryland in Baltimore.

Wendy Rawlings teaches creative writing at the University of Alabama and is a widely published essayist.

Chet Raymo's nonfiction includes *Honey from Stone, The Soul of Night, Natural Prayers,* and *The Path.*

Robert L. Root, Jr. has written *Recovering Ruth, Wordsmithery,* and two studies of nonfiction writers.

Arthur Saltzman, author of *Objects and Empathy,* teaches at Missouri Southern State College.

Scott Russell Sanders' books include *Writing from the Center, Hunting for Hope,* and *The Force of Spirit.*

Reg Saner's essays have been collected in *The Four-Cornered Falcon* and *Reaching Keet Seel.*

Lynne Sharon Schwartz is the author of *Ruined by Reading* and the essay collection *Face to Face.*

Mimi Schwartz is the author of *Thoughts from a Queen-Sized Bed* and the editor of *Writing in Many Roles.*

Maureen Stanton, winner of the Mary Robert Rinehart Award in nonfiction, is a widely published essayist.

Michael Steinberg, author of *Still Pitching,* is the founding editor of *Fourth Genre: Explorations in Nonfiction.*

Jane Tompkins wrote *A Life in School* and *West of Everything: The Inner Life of Westerns.*

Marianna Torgovnick's essays are in *Crossing Ocean Parkway: Readings by an Italian-American Daughter.*

Susan Allen Toth is the author of *Blooming: A Small Town Girlhood* and *Ivy Days: Making My Way Out East.*

Christine White, a essayist studying Creative Nonfiction at Goucher College, died in a plane crash in June 2001.

Nancy Willard, award-winning children's author, collected her essays in *Telling Time: Angels, Ancestors, and Stories.*

Credits

Index